Photoshop® CS3
Layers Bible

Photoshop® CS3 Layers Bible

Matt Doyle and Simon Meek

Wiley Publishing, Inc.

Photoshop® CS3 Layers Bible

Published by
Wiley Publishing, Inc.
10475 Crosspoint Boulevard
Indianapolis, IN 46256
www.wiley.com

Copyright © 2008 by Wiley Publishing, Inc., Indianapolis, Indiana

Published by Wiley Publishing, Inc., Indianapolis, Indiana

Published simultaneously in Canada

ISBN: 978-0-470-08211-9

Manufactured in the United States of America

10 9 8 7 6 5 4 3 2 1

For general information on our other products and services or to obtain technical support, please contact our Customer Care Department within the U.S. at (800) 762-2974, outside the U.S. at (317) 572-3993 or fax (317) 572-4002.

Library of Congress Control Number: 2007936465

About the Authors

Matt Doyle. Born and bred in England, Matt discovered the joys of computing from an early age, thanks to his mom's prudent decision to invest in a rusty old build-it-yourself computer with a whopping 4K of RAM. Since then, he's never looked back, gaining a B.Sc. in Computer Science and moving into the IT industry.

After working at various companies in such disparate roles as IT manager, C programmer, software tester, Web designer, and Web developer, Matt decided it was time to start his own business. In 1997 he teamed up with Simon to form ELATED, a company dedicated to building better websites for people, while also helping them build better websites for themselves.

Although ostensibly a developer for much of his career, Matt finds playing with software to be much more fun than writing it, and he loves exploring the innermost depths of any application he can get his mitts on. As such, he has slyly been expanding his Photoshop knowledge over the years to near-encyclopedic levels.

In 2002, deciding he'd had enough of the freezing English weather, he retreated to the sunny shores of Sydney's Northern Beaches in Australia with his wife, Cat, where they now live with their baby son, Isaac.

Simon Meek. Simon was raised in a tiny village in Bedfordshire, England. Having emerged from the depths of the countryside, he completed a degree in Agricultural Economics (Matt Doyle typed his thesis), and then played guitar for most of his early twenties. Obviously this is fertile ground for a career in the design industry.

In search of an actual income, Simon moved into design work in preference to getting a proper job, and has been a professional designer since 1996. Mostly specializing in online work, he has been using Photoshop since version 2.5, and fondly remembers such advances as editable type and, of course, layers.

He also dabbles in music, photography, and scriptwriting. For the record, he still feels playing guitar is more fun than Photoshop, though it's a pretty close thing.

He now lives in Brighton, on the south coast of England, with his wife, Mo, two cats (who often crop up in this book), and his beautiful wee boy, Jack.

Credits

Senior Acquisitions Editor
Kim Spilker

Project Editor
Beth Taylor

Technical Editor
Rob Barnes

Copy Editor
Kim Heusel

Editorial Manager
Robyn Siesky

Business Manager
Amy Knies

Senior Marketing Manager
Sandy Smith

Vice President and Executive Group Publisher
Richard Swadley

Vice President and Executive Publisher
Bob Ipsen

Vice President and Publisher
Barry Pruett

Project Coordinator
Adrienne Martinez

Graphics and Production Specialists
Brooke Graczyk
Joyce Haughey
Jennifer Mayberry
Ronald Terry

Quality Control Technicians
Laura Albert
John Greenough
Todd Lothery

Media Development Project Manager I
Laura Moss-Hollister

Media Development Assistant Producer
Josh Frank

Proofreading and Indexing
C.M. Jones
Infodex Indexing Services Inc.

Preface

Welcome to the Photoshop CS3 Layers Bible. Since its inception in 1988, Photoshop has evolved in leaps and bounds to become the king of photo editing applications that it is today. Each new release has brought with it tons of useful new features, from vector paths in version 2 through to the wonderful Spot Healing Brush tool and Vanishing Point filter in CS2.

Arguably one of the most important milestones in Photoshop's history was the addition of layers in version 3, way back in 1994. For the first time, designers could create and manipulate graphic elements independently within the same image, opening up a world of creative possibilities.

Since version 3, the reign of Photoshop's Layers palette has been consolidated through the addition of a powerful range of layer features. For example, we now have adjustment layers, for applying re-editable photo adjustments; fill layers, for creating powerful fill effects; layer styles, for adding dynamic effects to layers; type layers, for adding re-editable text to images; and shape layers, for creating filled vector shapes. CS3 adds even more layer-based fun in the form of Smart Filters that let you apply "live" Photoshop filters to your images. In fact, it's probably safe to say that most of your work in Photoshop these days revolves around the Layers palette, one way or another.

In this book we're going to take you on an adventure through the world of Photoshop layers, with the aim of giving you a thorough grounding in all of Photoshop's layer features. We'll also introduce you to a wealth of useful layer-based tips and techniques that we've picked up over the years. Our aim is to make this book useful to you, whether you're a Photoshop novice or a seasoned veteran of this powerful program.

Layers are a big topic, as you can probably tell just from the weight of this book. To make the book a little more digestible, and your reading experience more enjoyable, we've carved it up into four distinct parts.

Part I deals with the fundamentals of layers — what they are, how they work, and how you can work with them. Part II delves into the more specialized layer types that we touched on above; we take an in-depth look at type layers, shape layers, adjustment layers, and fill layers. Part III looks at the wonderful features Adobe has embellished layers with over the years, including blending modes, Smart Objects, masks, layer styles, and layer comps.

Finally, Part IV takes a more practical, hands-on approach to Photoshop layers. In this part, we look at some useful strategies for working with layered Photoshop documents, and we explore how Photoshop layers interact with other applications such as the CS3 suite, Lightroom, and QuarkXpress. We then share a range of useful techniques and workflows for using Photoshop in a wide range of contexts, from Web designing and making a montage through to photo manipulation and creating posters and flyers.

Acknowledgments

This book wouldn't have been possible without the help and support of many people at Wiley Publishing. We'd like to thank Kim Spilker for her help in getting the book off the ground and for putting her faith in us.

We'd also like to thank Beth Taylor, the project editor, as well as Kim Heusel, the copy editor, and Rob Barnes, the technical editor, for working so hard to improve the book and keep it on track.

Contents at a Glance

Contents

Contents

Contents

Contents

Contents

Introduction

Hopefully you'll find that this book is pretty much self-explanatory. However, just to avoid any potential confusion, we'll list a few of the conventions that we've used throughout the text.

Icons used in the book

You'll find the following icons peppered throughout the book. We've used them to highlight points that you may find particularly interesting, noteworthy or helpful.

CAUTION When you see a Caution icon, it's warning you of potential pitfalls that you might encounter with a particular technique or feature. While there's a limit to how much damage you can do with Photoshop — unless you're writing a nuclear power plant instruction manual with it — it's probably worth reading these pieces of text to avoid tearing your hair out further down the line.

CROSS-REF Photoshop is a big application with a zillion features, so inevitably there's some crossover between topics. We use this icon to highlight other sections or chapters in the book that are relevant to the topic at hand.

NEW FEATURE Whenever we introduce a feature that's new, or significantly changed, in Photoshop CS3, we'll highlight it with a New Feature icon and explain a bit about the feature. If you've just moved up from a previous version of Photoshop, these icons are a great way to explore new CS3 features at a glance.

 When we want to explain some small, relatively unimportant, point related to the current topic, we'll highlight the explanation with a Note icon. You'll find these icons useful for gaining extra insight into the workings of Photoshop.

 A Tip icon provides you with a handy trick or shortcut that you can use to work faster or more effectively with Photoshop. If you want to impress your friends and colleagues with your super-human Photoshop skills, these are the icons to read.

 This icon indicates that the CD-ROM contains a related file.

Terms and phrases

Photoshop isn't rocket science, and most of the terms associated with the program are fairly easy to understand, particularly if you've used the program a bit already. For example, phrases such as the Layers palette, the Move tool, and layer groups probably won't give you too much trouble.

Generally, when we introduce a new term that you may not be familiar with, such as *kerning,* we write it in italics — like we just did, in fact — and then explain the term.

Interface items

As a rule, when we describe parts of Photoshop's user interface, such as menus, palettes, and tools, we capitalize the first letter of each word: the File menu; the Layers palette; the Type tool; and so on. (We don't capitalize articles or prepositions though, such as "an" and "for".)

We write menu options using an arrow (⇨) to separate a menu option or submenu from its parent menu. For example, "choose File ⇨ Open" means "choose the Open option from the File menu", while "choose Layer ⇨ Layer Style ⇨ Drop Shadow" means "choose Layer Style from the Layer menu, then choose Drop Shadow from the Layer Style submenu".

Keystrokes

We indicate keys on the keyboard by capitalizing their initial letter, so "Shift" means the Shift key, while 'N' means the letter N (without pressing Shift as well). If you need to press more than one key at once, we indicate the key combination with + (plus) symbols, as in "Press Control+Shift+E".

Some keys are different on Windows and Mac OS platforms. For example, Command (⌘) on the Mac is generally used in place of Control on Windows, while Windows' Alt key usually maps to the Mac's Option key. For key combinations that differ between Windows and Mac OS, we generally introduce the Windows key combination first, followed by the Mac combination in brackets.

While PCs tend to use the word "Backspace" for the big delete key and "Delete" for the little one, Macs tend to use "Delete" for both (or "Forward Delete" for the little Delete key). Generally, when we use the word "Delete" for the Mac, we're talking about the big (backward) delete key. Similarly, whereas the big carriage return key on a PC is usually called "Enter", on a Mac it's called "Return".

Finally, many Photoshop menus and features are accessed by right-clicking. Whenever we suggest right-clicking in the book, you can Control+click on the Mac if you're using a one-button mouse. If you use a two (or more) button mouse with your Mac, you can Control+click or you can right-click — whichever you prefer.

The CD-ROM

As you've no doubt noticed by now, this book comes complete with an accompanying CD-ROM. While not essential for reading and understanding the book, it's well worth checking out. It features full, layered Photoshop files for pretty much every example and figure used in the book, letting you play with the examples directly in Photoshop.

We've also included source photos and other images used in the examples, where relevant, as well as a batch of our own stock photos that you're welcome to use when trying out the techniques in the book.

A last word

As you're no doubt aware, Photoshop is a vast application with a prodigious array of features, but that doesn't mean it has to be hard to use. We hope that this book helps you really get to grips with the ins and outs of Photoshop's layer features, as well as helping you to expand your repertoire of Photoshop tricks and techniques.

Most importantly, though, we hope that you thoroughly enjoy reading this book, and that it makes using Photoshop layers that much more fun and rewarding for you.

Have fun!

Part I

Layer Basics

Introducing Layers

If you've used Photoshop for any length of time, you've no doubt used layers; they're such a key feature of the software. In fact, if you're doing anything other than simple photo retouching, layers are pretty much essential.

The beauty of layers is that you can work on different parts of your image independently; if you draw on one layer, the other layers in your image remain untouched. This means you can easily try out different ideas (and easily scrap them if you don't like them!).

Layers offer you a great deal of flexibility when it comes to creating your images. If you don't like the position of a logo, for example, simply drag it to a new position — if it's on its own layer, then it'll move on its own, without disturbing the rest of the image.

You can also use layers artistically. For example, layer blending modes give you a wealth of composition tricks that you can use to really make your images come to life, while adjustment layers allow you to make tonal adjustments to your images without altering the underlying pixels.

CROSS-REF Learn more about layer blending modes in Chapter 7.

In this chapter, you look at the history of layers in Photoshop and explore key concepts such as the Layers palette and transparency. Each of the basic layer types is explained, and some of the uses and applications of layers are discussed. Finally, we finish off with a simple example to help cement the concepts that are introduced.

IN THIS CHAPTER

Getting to know layers

Learning the Layers palette

Understanding transparency

Exploring layer types

Discovering layer tricks and techniques

Touching on the new layer features in CS3

Applying layers to real-world situations

Understanding the Layers Concept

A good way to understand the concept of layers is to think of them as physical sheets of acetate laid on top of each other (see Figure 1.1). You can add, copy, and delete layers; you can hide them, and move them around horizontally and vertically in the image; and you can also move layers up and down the stack to change their order. When you change something on one layer, you only affect that layer.

FIGURE 1.1

Layers are like sheets of acetate — each layer is independent of the others.

Layers and Photoshop

Before layers were introduced in version 3 of Photoshop, every change you made to your image was effectively applied to a single layer. You can imagine how difficult this made things for Photoshop designers! All changes were pretty much permanent. Photoshop didn't even have a History palette then, so you only had one undo level. Understandably, folks using Photoshop 2 and earlier used to make a lot of backup copies of their Photoshop files!

Now you have a variety of layer types to choose from and a range of powerful layer editing features. It's hard to imagine working in Photoshop without using layers; they really have become a central part of the software.

Most of the time, when you work on an image in Photoshop you're working on a single layer at a time. For example, most of the filters, the image adjustment functions under Image ⇨ Adjustments, and the standard cut and copy commands (Edit ⇨ Cut and Edit ⇨ Copy) all work on the current layer only.

NOTE Some tools, such as the Type tools and the Shape tools (by default at least), also create new layers when you use them.

Introducing the Layers Palette

Most of the layer-based action in Photoshop hinges around the Layers palette, as shown in Figure 1.2, so take a quick look at its features. If this palette is not currently visible, you can enable it by choosing Window ⇨ Layers or pressing F7.

FIGURE 1.2

The Layers palette in Photoshop

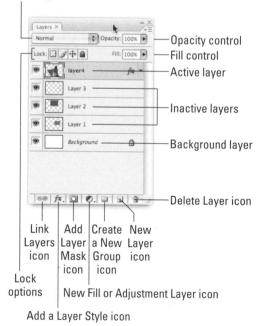

Blending Mode

Opacity control

Fill control

Active layer

Inactive layers

Background layer

Delete Layer icon

Link Layers icon

Add Layer Mask icon

Create a New Group icon

New Layer icon

Lock options

New Fill or Adjustment Layer icon

Add a Layer Style icon

The Layers palette usually shows at least one currently selected layer (called the *active layer*). Photoshop also gives each layer a name to help you identify it more easily. The name of the active layer is always shown in bold text in the Layers palette, and the layer itself is shaded a different color to the other layers in the palette. The active layer's name is also shown in the title bar of the document window, which is handy for those times when your Layers palette is buried under ten document windows and seven other palettes.

The Layers palette includes the following controls to help you work with layers:

- **Blending Mode:** This pop-up menu lets you control how the active layer blends with the layers below it. For more information, refer to Chapter 7.

- **Lock options:** These four buttons allow you to lock various aspects of a layer — its transparency pixels, its image pixels, its position, or all three. For more information, see Chapter 2.

- **Opacity and Fill controls:** These options let you specify how much of the image underneath the active layer shows through. For more on these controls, see Chapter 2.

- **Link Layers icon:** Use this icon to link two or more layers together so that they can be manipulated as one layer. See Chapter 2 for more details.

- **Add a Layer Style icon:** As its name suggests, this icon lets you add styles to layers. Layer styles allow you to add effects such as drop shadows and beveling. Layer styles are covered in detail in Chapter 10.

- **Add Layer Mask icon:** Use this icon to create a layer mask for the current layer. See Chapter 9 for more on layer masks.

- **Create New Fill or Adjustment Layer icon:** You can use this icon to quickly create either a fill layer (for adding a solid color, gradient or pattern fill effect to your image) or an adjustment layer (for applying adjustments to other layers in your document). Chapter 6 explores these layer types.

- **Create a New Group icon:** This icon allows you to group your layers together. For more on this topic, see Chapter 2.

- **Create a New Layer icon:** This is for creating a new, empty layer in your document. Learn about the different ways you can make new layers in Chapter 2.

- **Delete Layer icon:** Use this icon to remove unwanted layers from your document. This and other ways to delete layers are covered in Chapter 2.

> **TIP**   You can resize the Layers palette (like all palettes in Photoshop) by clicking and dragging the resize box in the bottom right-hand corner of the palette. A small palette is great if you lack screen real estate, and a big palette is handy when you need to look at a lot of layers at once. If the palette really gets in the way, you can minimize it by double-clicking the Layers tab at the top of the palette, or by clicking the little minimize icon to the left of the Close button at the top right of the palette. Double-click the tab again, or click the icon again, to reopen the palette.

Layers in the document window

The contents of all visible layers in a document are displayed in the document window. Each layer in your document appears in the palette in the order in which it is stacked in the document, so the foremost layer is always at the top of the list and the background layer is at the bottom. Figure 1.3 shows how layers in the Layers palette relate to their contents in the document window.

The Layers palette shows the layers for the currently selected document. If you have several documents open at once, you see the Layers palette change as you flip between the document windows.

How layers appear in the Layers palette and in the document window

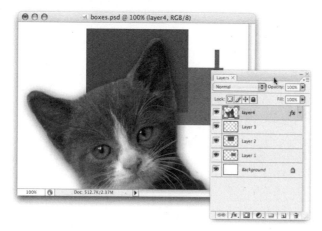

The anatomy of a layer

Although there are many different types of layers in Photoshop, all layers share the following features (see Figure 1.4):

- **Eye icon:** This indicates whether the layer is visible in the document or not. Click the eye icon to hide the layer; click it again to show the layer.

- **Thumbnail:** The thumbnail image shows you a small preview of the layer. It also shows you which parts of the layer are transparent, indicated by a grid of white and gray (by default) squares.

- **Layer name:** This helps you identify the layer. You can easily change a layer's name by double-clicking it, then typing the new name. (By the way, if you double-click the layer outside the layer name, the Layer Style dialog box appears, allowing you to create layer styles such as drop shadows. Layer styles are covered in Chapter 10.)

- **Lock icon:** This icon shows you whether the layer is unlocked (no icon), partially locked (light lock icon), or fully locked (dark lock icon).

FIGURE 1.4

Each layer always has an eye icon (hidden if the layer is invisible), a thumbnail, a name, and, potentially, a lock icon.

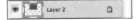

> **TIP**   You can customize the look of the layer thumbnails by clicking the triangle in the top-right corner of the Layers palette and then choosing Palette Options from the pop-up menu. You can choose from three thumbnail sizes (or no thumbnails at all) and also specify whether you'd like each thumbnail to show just the contents of the layer (Layer Bounds) or show the position of the layer in the whole document (Entire Document). You can also reach these options by right-clicking any layer thumbnail in the Layers palette.

Understanding Layer Transparency

Just like sheets of acetate, layers in Photoshop are inherently transparent. This means that the parts of a layer that haven't been painted on allow the pixels from the layers underneath to show through. You can also make a whole layer semitransparent by adjusting its Opacity slider (see Chapter 2 for more on layer opacity).

> **NOTE**   The exception to the transparency rule (there's always an exception) is the special Background layer, which can't be made transparent at all. As the name implies, it's always at the back of the document—nothing can get behind it—so it has no need of transparency. More on this maverick layer in the section "The Background layer."

Each pixel in a layer can be completely transparent, completely filled with color, or translucent (somewhere in between). This is all controlled by a *transparency mask* associated with each layer. The transparency mask determines how transparent or opaque each pixel in the layer is.

> **TIP**   You can load a layer's transparency mask as a selection by Ctrl+clicking (⌘+clicking on the Mac) the layer's thumbnail in the Layers palette, or by right-clicking the thumbnail and choosing Select Pixels from the pop-up menu.

You can see the transparent areas of a layer by looking at its thumbnail image in the Layers palette—the transparent parts are shown as a gray and white checkerboard pattern. Also, try Alt+clicking (Option+clicking on the Mac) the eye icon of a layer in the Layers palette to hide all other layers; if your layer has any transparent parts you see them as a checkerboard pattern in the document window, as shown in Figure 1.5. (Alt/Option+click the layer's eye icon again to return to normal.)

FIGURE 1.5

A layer on its own in the document window, showing the transparency grid behind

TIP If you find the default checkerboard pattern hard to see in a particular situation — working with a photo of a chess board springs to mind — you can change its color and size. To do this, choose Edit ➪ Preferences ➪ Transparency & Gamut (Photoshop ➪ Preferences ➪ Transparency & Gamut on the Mac) or, more quickly, press Ctrl+K then Ctrl+6 (⌘+K then ⌘+6 on the Mac). You can then choose a grid size (or turn the grid off altogether) and choose from a predefined list of grid colors (or roll your own).

Many functions in Photoshop just work on the nontransparent areas of a layer and leave the transparent areas intact. Other tools, such as the painting tools for example, will, of course, paint over the transparent areas (unless you have the layer transparency locked). If you want to make part of your layer transparent again, paint on it with the Eraser tool, or select the part you want to make transparent and press Backspace (Delete on the Mac).

TIP To fill a layer entirely with the foreground color, press Alt+Backspace (Option+Delete on the Mac). Want to fill with the background color instead? Just press Ctrl+Backspace (⌘+Delete on the Mac). To fill just the opaque and translucent areas, leaving the transparent areas intact, either lock the layer's transparency first, or use the previous keyboard shortcuts with the Shift key as well. This is a super-quick way to recolor an object on a layer.

Types of Layers

Photoshop features a few different types of layers and, although all the layer types share common ground, there are important differences among them. Let's take a brief look at the different members of Photoshop's layers family.

The Background layer

Images created with a white or colored background are created with a special layer called Background (see Figure 1.6). There cannot be more than one Background layer in a document. The Background layer is always at the back of the document (and therefore the bottom of the Layers palette), and it never has any transparent areas. You can't move this layer up and down the Layers palette, nor can you move its contents around with the Move tool, or change its blending mode or opacity, which are permanently locked.

However, you can delete the Background layer, which makes your document transparent. Likewise, you can create a new transparent document, which has no Background layer. You can also hide the Background layer to make your document temporarily transparent.

CROSS-REF   See Chapter 2 for more on showing and hiding layers and groups.

By now you're probably wondering what the point of the Background layer is, as it just seems to be a normal layer with its hands tied behind its back. In fact, its limitations are really its strengths: Because it's always at the back of your document and can't be made transparent, you can always rely on it as a canvas or backstop, if you will. Without a Background layer you can never be totally sure that some bits of your document aren't transparent (although you'd find out soon enough if you later tried overlaying your image on top of something else).

NOTE   If you choose File ➪ Open to open an image that's in a format that doesn't support layers — for example a JPEG photo — then Photoshop automatically assigns the image to the Background layer in the opened document.

FIGURE 1.6

The Background layer. As its name implies, this special layer always sits in the background of your image document.

Generally, you want a Background layer in your document unless you need the document to be transparent — for example, if you print it out onto transparencies, or you're saving out a transparent GIF for use on the Web.

CROSS-REF   You can convert between the Background layer and a normal layer (and vice versa). Find out how to do this in Chapter 2.

Normal layers

The most common layers you encounter in Photoshop are normal layers (see Figure 1.7). The basic job of these layers is to hold the various bitmapped images that make up your document. The Background layer described previously is essentially a normal layer that's locked down to the back of the document.

FIGURE 1.7

A normal layer. To create a new normal layer, simply click the New Layer icon.

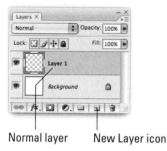

Normal layer   New Layer icon

To create a new normal layer, click the New Layer icon at the bottom of the Layers palette, as shown in Figure 1.7.

Type layers

As you might imagine, type layers (see Figure 1.8) are used specifically for storing type — otherwise known as text. They were a godsend when first introduced in Photoshop 5, as they allow you to edit, scale, rotate, and generally muck about with your type after you create the layer. The reason they can do this is that they store the type as vector information rather than as bitmapped images. (Versions of Photoshop before version 5 allowed you to create type, but the type was stored as a bitmapped image, making transforming or editing after the fact practically impossible.)

FIGURE 1.8

A type layer. To make a new type layer, use the Type tool.

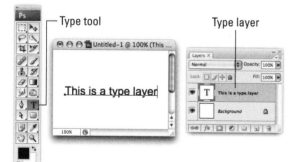

Type tool   Type layer

Comparing Bitmaps and Vectors

A bitmapped (or raster) image is an image made up of pixels — for example, a JPEG photo from a digital camera or a GIF image in a Web page. Bitmapped images are great for storing real-world images, such as photos, that can't easily be mathematically defined. The main disadvantages of bitmapped images are their large file size and the fact that they can't be scaled well — if you enlarge a bitmapped image you quickly start seeing *aliasing* or, to use a technical term, "jaggy bits."

In contrast, a vector image is defined mathematically using lines and curves. It's not made up of pixels like a bitmapped image is. This means that vector images are resolution-independent; it doesn't matter how big or small you scale a vector image, it never loses detail. Vectors are great for storing images that are easily described using lines and curves and that need to stay pin sharp at any resolution — for example, type, logos, geometric shapes, and charts.

To create a new type layer, select the Type tool in the Toolbox as shown in Figure 1.8, click in your document window, and start typing. Press Ctrl+Enter (⌘+Return on the Mac) when you finish typing.

CROSS-REF Type layers and the Type tool are given a thorough treatment in Chapter 4.

Shape layers

You can create shape layers (see Figure 1.9) using the Pen and Shape tools by enabling the Shape Layers option in the tool's options bar. Although they're described as a distinct type of layer in Photoshop, a shape layer is really just a fill layer in disguise (see the next section) with a linked vector mask. The fill layer gives the shape its color, gradient, or pattern, and the vector mask gives the shape its, well, shape. Because vectors are used to describe the shape, shape layers can be scaled, rotated, and otherwise manipulated with no loss of detail.

To create a new shape layer, select a pen tool or a shape tool, as shown in Figure 1.9, make sure Shape Layers is selected in the tool's options bar; then draw in the document window.

CROSS-REF For more on shape layers see Chapter 5.

FIGURE 1.9

A shape layer. Create new shape layers using the Pen or Shape tools.

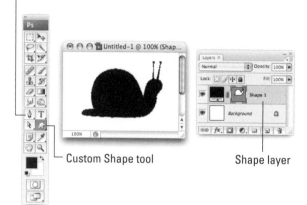

Pen tool

Custom Shape tool

Shape layer

Fill layers

Fill layers (shown in Figure 1.10) hold a solid color, a gradient, or a pattern. The basic fill always fills the whole canvas area, so fill layers really come into their own when you use them with a linked layer mask. By drawing on the mask with, for example, the Brush or Pen tool, you can define which areas of your document are filled and which are masked off from the fill.

In fact, when you first create a fill layer it comes complete with its own linked (bitmap) layer mask that you can use to define the shape of your fill. Similarly, when you create a new shape layer (see the section on shape layers) the created fill layer ships with a linked vector mask defining the shape.

FIGURE 1.10

A fill layer. Click the New Fill or Adjustment Layer icon to create new fill layers.

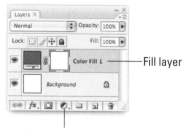

Fill layer

New Fill or Adjustment Layer icon

To create a new fill layer, click the New Fill or Adjustment Layer icon at the bottom of the Layers palette (see Figure 1.10) and choose Solid Color, Gradient, or Pattern.

CROSS-REF Learn about fill layers in Chapter 6.

Adjustment layers

Adjustment layers (shown in Figure 1.11) are fairly unique in that they work by affecting the layers below them, rather than holding image information themselves. (If you add an adjustment layer to a document containing no other layers, you won't see anything happen in the document.)

The wonderful thing about adjustment layers is that you can happily adjust aspects of your image such as levels, color balance, brightness, and contrast without permanently affecting the actual pixels of the image. This is often called *nondestructive* editing.

For example, if you really turn up the brightness of your photo by choosing Image ➪ Adjustments ➪ Brightness/Contrast, then try lowering the brightness later, you'll see that your image has lost a lot of contrast — the Brightness/Contrast adjustment has permanently altered the pixels and some of the image information has been lost. However, if you create a new Brightness/Contrast adjustment layer, you can happily change the brightness as much as you want at any time without affecting the underlying image.

This makes adjustment layers great for trying out adjustments that you might want to tweak later on.

FIGURE 1.11

An adjustment layer. Create new adjustment layers with the New Fill or Adjustment Layer icon.

Adjustment layer

New Fill or Adjustment Layer icon

To create a new adjustment layer, first click the New Fill or Adjustment Layer icon at the bottom of the Layers palette, as shown in Figure 1.11, and then choose any option apart from Solid Color, Gradient, or Pattern.

Figure 1.12 shows all the previous layer types in action in a document, with a cute kitten thrown in for good measure. See if you can guess what the job of each layer is in the document.

FIGURE 1.12

Different types of layers in action. Notice how the layers stack together and interact with each other to produce the finished image.

Using Layers in Photoshop

As you might have gathered by now, layers are an extremely handy feature in Photoshop. Here are just some of the feats you can achieve with layers:

- You can create as many new layers as you want in your document. The number of layers in your document is limited only by the memory available to Photoshop. Be careful though, because each layer adds to the file size of your Photoshop document; if you're not careful you can end up with very large files. (For more on creating new layers, see Chapter 2.)

- Select one or more layers in your document, and you can work on just the selected layer or layers. You can select layers using the Layers palette or directly in the document window. (To find out more about selecting layers, see Chapter 2.)

- You can make copies of layers, both in the same document and between documents. You can move the contents of a layer around the document window, either independently or in tandem with other layers, and you can align or distribute different layers in your documents. You can change the stacking order of layers in your document; you can lock aspects of layers to prevent them being accidentally altered; and, of course, you can delete layers that you no longer need. (To learn any of these techniques, see Chapter 2.)

- If you want, you can link layers together so that they can be manipulated as a single layer. You can also group layers together to help organize documents with lots of layers; hide selected layers and groups to try out different designs; and color-code layers and groups for easy access — great if you have several layers or groups related to a particular part of your document. (All of these features are described in Chapter 2.)

- Using blending modes, you can control how a layer blends with the layers below it to create all sorts of interesting effects and enhancements. (For more information on blending modes, see Chapter 7.)

- You can mask off areas of your layer so that only some areas are visible. You can also use masks with adjustment layers to apply the adjustments to selected parts of your image. (For more information on masks, see Chapter 9. Adjustment layers are covered in Chapter 6.)

- A layer can be used to mask the contents of another layer or layers above it, allowing you to achieve all sorts of creative effects. (For more on this, see Chapter 9.)

- You can add many artistic effects to a layer using layer styles. Even better, you can go back and tweak these effects at any time without touching the contents of the layer itself. (For more on layer styles, see Chapter 10.)

- As mentioned previously, adding text to your documents is easy with Photoshop's Type tool. This tool creates special type layers that can be edited, transformed, and generally mucked about with long after they are created. (The Type tool is covered in depth in Chapter 4.)

- Photoshop lets you take several snapshots of your document's layers, including their visibility, position and appearance, and flip between them instantly, great for trying out different designs and arrangements of layers. (For more information, see Chapter 11.)

New Layer Features in Photoshop CS3

With the launch of Photoshop CS3, Adobe has added a wealth of useful new features to the mix, making it a worthy successor to CS2. This section concentrates on the new, flexible user interface in CS3, as well as the new layer-related features that Adobe has included in CS3.

The new interface

One of the major changes in CS3 is the introduction of a new user interface. Not only does it give Photoshop a new, revamped look, but it also changes the way you work with the software, thanks to its new workspace features. Maximized Screen Mode, for example, creates a workspace where your document window automatically resizes, depending on the layout of the palettes, to fill the maximum space possible. You can choose this option from the Toolbox using the Change Screen Mode button at the bottom. Figure 1.13 shows Maximized Screen Mode in action.

As well as grouping palettes together in palette groups, as you could in CS2, you can now also group palettes and palette groups into bigger docks. These docks can be contracted when they're not in use, with the palettes and palette groups inside turning into cute icons, as you can see in Figure 1.13. It's a handy feature that helps you to maximize your screen real estate.

FIGURE 1.13

The new interface in Maximized Screen Mode, with the palette docks expanded (top) and collapsed to icons (bottom). Note that the document window you're working on resizes with the palettes, so that it always fills the available space.

There are also changes to the Toolbox, which can now be presented as a single-column view. This may give seasoned Photoshop users a twinge of fear, because the new layout can feel a little odd in comparison to the old style two-column version. Don't panic, though; with a single click on the small arrows at the top of the Toolbox you can bring back the familiar two-column view. In fact, if you find you really can't get along with the new interface at all, you can flip over to a legacy version that mimics the old CS2 interface, by choosing Window ➪ Workspace ➪ Legacy.

Smart Filters

Photoshop CS2 introduced the concept of Smart Objects — special layers that allow you to resize, rotate, and warp bitmap images nondestructively. In CS3, this functionality is expanded with the addition of Smart Filters. This feature allows you to add "live" filters to a Smart Object nondestructively. The Smart Filters also have their own mask, so that you can apply the filters selectively to the Smart Object.

In practice this means that you can apply a Radial Blur filter to a Smart Object, for example, and then reedit or remove that blur later on in the process if you change your mind. Figure 1.14 shows a Smart Object with such a Smart Filter applied. This is a major leap forward for Photoshop and brings it more into line with the nondestructive tendencies of many major applications in the graphics world, as well as the audio/visual world. New photo-editing applications such as Adobe's Lightroom and Apple's Aperture, for example, allow for nondestructive editing.

NOTE This nondestructive feature of Smart Objects is great for normal bitmap layers: Simply add your normal layer to a Smart Object, and you can transform the Smart Object over and over again without progressively degrading the image. However, any transform you make still results in some loss of quality; for example, scaling a bitmap by 1000 percent is likely to produce a fairly blocky result, even if it's within a Smart Object. This is a fundamental issue with bitmaps and is one reason why vector type and shape layers are an attractive alternative.

CROSS-REF Smart Objects and Smart Filters are covered in detail in Chapter 8.

FIGURE 1.14

Applying a nondestructive Radial Blur to a Smart Object, using the new Smart Filters feature of Photoshop CS3

New adjustment layers

In Photoshop CS3, there are two very welcome new adjustment layers, both aimed squarely at photographers: Black and White, and Exposure.

The Black and White adjustment layer provides a new way to convert color photos to black and white. Traditionally this has been a somewhat fraught task involving much voodoo using the Channel Mixer, or through Lab color conversions. With this adjustment layer, you can also add a tint to the image at the same time, which is great for those images requiring a sepia tint, for example. You can see this adjustment layer in action in Figure 1.15. Note that this adjustment is also available in destructive form under Image ⇨ Adjustments.

CROSS-REF In Chapter 15, you see how many of the traditional black-and-white conversion techniques stack up against this great new feature.

FIGURE 1.15

Converting an image to black and white using the new Black and White adjustment layer

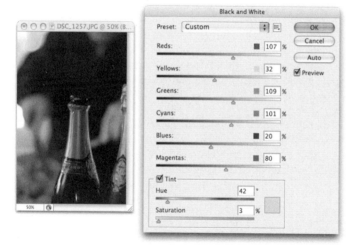

The Exposure adjustment layer, shown in Figure 1.16, allows you to mimic the effect of increasing the exposure setting in-camera. If you have a woefully underexposed image, there's a good chance you can save it using this feature. It really is great for enhancing those slightly lackluster photos. And of course, because adjustment layers have their own masks, you can choose to increase the exposure just on selected areas of the image.

NEW FEATURE While the destructive Exposure adjustment — found under the Image ⇨ Adjustments menu — has existed in previous versions of Photoshop, this is the first time that you've been able to apply Exposure nondestructively as an adjustment layer.

FIGURE 1.16

Increasing the exposure of a photo with the new Exposure adjustment layer

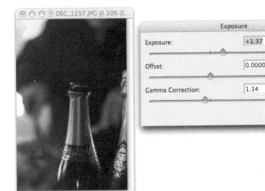

Auto-Align Layers and Auto-Blend Layers

Imagine you have two or more images that you want to merge into one. This might be a double exposure of a landscape, a panorama, or a photo of the same environment with different people in it, for example. Photoshop CS3 introduces two great new commands — Auto-Align Layers and Auto-Blend Layers — that can help you enormously with this merging process. These two commands are both available from the Edit menu.

The Auto-Align Layers command, whose dialog box is shown in Figure 1.17, automatically aligns images on separate layers by subtly distorting each image so that they line up as precisely as possible. You can then use masks to reveal the elements from each layer that make up the final image. Because Photoshop is doing the alignment work, a small movement in perspective when taking the original photos is less important. In other words, if you're stuck without a tripod, it's no longer necessarily the end of the world!

The Auto-Blend Layers command works in conjunction with Auto-Align Layers when creating panoramic shots. When you apply it to a newly aligned set of layers in a panoramic format, this feature creates a new layer mask for each layer and applies its best guess for blending the photos to each mask, softening sharp edges created by auto-aligning the layers. It also compensates for any exposure differences when the individual photos were shot by changing the colors within each layer, smoothing out the differences between warmer and cooler images.

FIGURE 1.17

The Auto-Align Layers dialog box. This command automatically aligns two or more layers by subtly distorting each layer.

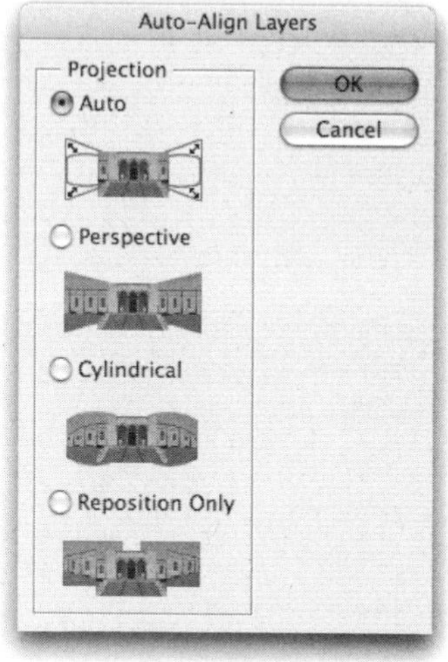

The results for the Auto-align and Auto-blend combination are very good, and are also now integrated into the Photomerge feature used for stitching panoramic shots. In CS2, the results of the Photomerge feature created layers with no masks, but in CS3 the feature creates individual layers with masks, resulting in a much faster workflow and more control over the end result.

CROSS-REF Both of these new features are explored in depth in Chapter 15.

Putting Theory into Practice

Now that the basics of layers in Photoshop have been covered, we can begin with a practical example. In this short tutorial, it is assumed that you're lucky enough to own a yacht and that you want to invite some friends to sail it with you. You're going to produce a simple invitation, with a photo of your boat and some text with relevant information.

NOTE Obviously, you won't have this yacht photo yourself. No problem; for the sake of this tutorial, any photo will do. Ideally it should be in portrait format and at least A6 size (4 x 6 inches) at 300 dpi. A photo taken with a modern digital camera should be fine.

Creating a new document

The first step to designing your invitation is to create a new Photoshop document. Choose File ➪ New or press Ctrl+N (⌘+N on the Mac). The New dialog box appears. You want to create an A6 invitation, which is 105 x 148 mm, at 300 dpi. To do this, choose International Paper for the Preset option; then choose A6 for the Size option. Make sure Resolution is set to 300 pixels/inch. Stick with the default RGB color mode for this example. Choose a white background, give the document a name, and click OK to create the document, as shown in Figure 1.18.

FIGURE 1.18

Creating the new invitation document

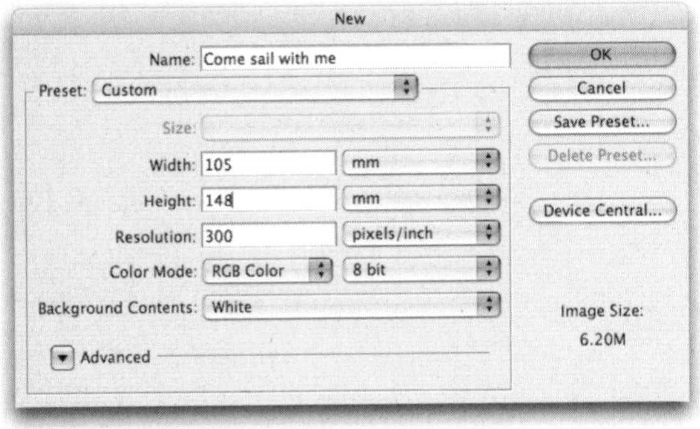

A document window appears for your new document — it's the right size and it has a white Background layer, ready for you to start adding your layers.

Adding the photo

The next step is to open the photo and add it to your invitation. Choose File ➪ Open, or press Ctrl+O (⌘+O on the Mac) and choose a suitable photo from your photo library. Your photo opens in a new document window.

Now, add the photo to the invitation. Make sure the document window containing the photo is selected and look at the Layers palette (choose Window ➪ Layers or press F7 if you can't see the palette). You should see a single layer, called Background, with a little thumbnail image of your photo (see Figure 1.19). This is the layer that contains the photo you just opened.

FIGURE 1.19

The photo layer in the Layers palette

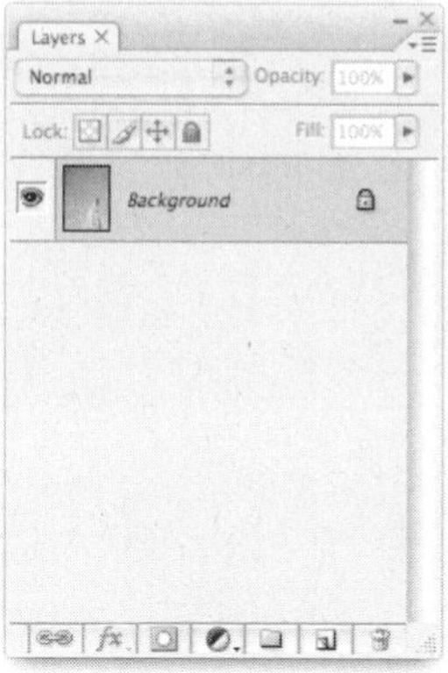

You're now going to copy this layer into your invitation document. To do this, click the layer in the Layers palette, and while holding down the Shift key, drag the layer to the invitation document as shown in Figure 1.20, and release the mouse button. After a short pause your photo appears in the invitation document.

NOTE Holding down Shift while dragging the layer automatically centers the photo in the invitation document.

FIGURE 1.20

Dragging the photo layer across to the invitation document

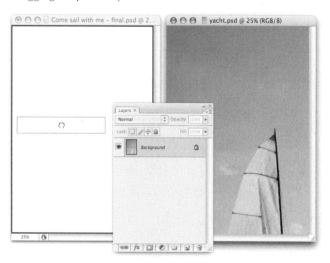

Look at the Layers palette for the invitation document (if the invitation document isn't selected, select it first), and you see that the photo has been added to the document as a new layer, as shown in Figure 1.21. You now have two layers in your invitation: the original white Background layer, and the new photo layer.

Give your photo layer a name so it's easier to identify. Double-click the name of the layer — this is probably Layer 1 — and type **Yacht** (or whatever you want to call your photo); then press Enter (Return on the Mac).

FIGURE 1.21

The photo in the invitation document and its layer in the Layers palette

Creating a box for the text

Add a white box to the invitation that you can place the text in. To do this, follow these steps:

1. **Select the Yacht layer by clicking it in the Layers palette.** This step ensures that your new box layer is created above the Yacht layer.

2. **Click the Shape Tool icon and hold down the mouse button.** (The Shape tool icon sits below the Type Tool icon in the Toolbox.) After a second, a pop-up menu appears, with a list of different shape tools.

3. **Click the Rectangle Tool icon.** The Shape tool icon changes to a rectangle.

4. **Click the Default Foreground and Background Colors icon in the Toolbox (or press D).** This resets your foreground and background colors to their defaults of black and white respectively.

5. **Now click the Switch Foreground and Background Colors icon (or press X).** You should now have a foreground color of white and a background color of black showing in the Toolbox. The Rectangle tool uses the foreground color as the fill color of the box, so your box is created with a white fill.

6. **Make sure the Shape Layers option is selected in the Options bar.**

7. **Create the box.** Click somewhere near the top-left corner of the invitation document, and drag down and to the right, then release the mouse button to create the box (see Figure 1.22).

FIGURE 1.22

Creating the white box shape

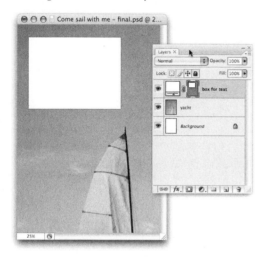

Notice that you've created a new shape layer in the document. Click the shape layer's name in the Layers palette to edit it, type **Box**, and press Enter (Return on the Mac).

Adding the text

Now, add some text in the white box. Use a text color taken from the photo. Click the Eyedropper tool in the Toolbox (or press I); then click an area of your photo that you want to use for your text color (see Figure 1.23). In the figure, a blue color is selected from the sky in the photo. The color of the pixel that you click becomes the new foreground color.

Next, make sure the Box layer is selected by clicking it in the Layers palette. This ensures that the type layer is created above the Box layer.

FIGURE 1.23

Picking a color from the photo

CAUTION Ensure that the Box layer's vector mask is not active, or the type will be anchored to the vector mask. To do this, look at the vector mask thumbnail for the Box layer (the little rectangle just to the left of the layer name). If the thumbnail has a highlight border around it, click in the thumbnail to remove the highlight and deselect the mask.

Click the Type Tool icon in the Toolbox and hold the mouse button down. From the pop-up menu, select the Horizontal Type Tool option.

Choose an appropriate font and style for your text. In the Type tool's options bar (see Figure 1.24) choose a simple sans serif font such as Arial or Helvetica, select a Regular font style, and choose an appropriate size for the type (18 points or 72 pixels should do it).

TIP When creating type, you can choose between points and pixels (and millimeters, too) by choosing Edit ⇨ Preferences ⇨ Units & Rulers (Photoshop ⇨ Preferences ⇨ Units and Rulers on the Mac) and picking a unit from the Type pop-up menu.

FIGURE 1.24

Choosing type options

Click in the document window near the top-left corner of your white box and type **Come sail with me!**. Press Enter (Return on the Mac) a couple of times to move the cursor down toward the bottom of the box. Choose a smaller type size in the options bar (for example, 10 points or 48 pixels). Type the next line, **23rd April**, and press Enter (Return). Repeat for the last two lines, **9am at The Marina** and **Bring a coat!**.

When you've typed all your text, press Ctrl+Enter (⌘+Return on the Mac) to exit the text entry mode.

You now have a fourth layer in your document: a type layer. Photoshop uses the text you typed as the name of the layer; however, you can change this if you want by double-clicking the layer name, typing a new name and pressing Enter (Return on the Mac).

Congratulations — you've created your invitation! It probably looks something like Figure 1.25.

FIGURE 1.25

The finished invitation

Playing with the layers

Your invitation design is made up of four separate layers. From bottom to top in the Layers palette, they are:

- The white Background layer
- A normal layer containing your photo
- A shape layer containing your white box
- A type layer containing the text inside the white box

Try playing with the different layers. For example, click the Move tool in the Toolbox (or press V), select one of the layers, then click in the document window and drag with the mouse. Notice how the layer moves around independently of the other three layers. Notice also how you can't move the content of the Background layer.

CROSS-REF   If you do ever need to move the content of the Background layer, convert it to a normal layer first. Find out how to do this in Chapter 2.

Click a layer in the Layers palette and drag it up or down to a different position in the palette. Notice how changing the stacking order of the layers in the Layers palette affects how the layers appear in the document window. For example, if you drag the type layer below the Box layer in the Layers palette, the type is then obscured by the white box.

Ctrl+click (⌘+click on the Mac) the type and Box layers to select both of them, then click the Link Layers icon at the bottom of the Layers palette. The two layers are now linked. Try moving one of the layers using the Move tool. Notice how the other layer moves with it. To unlink the layers, select one of the layers in the Layers palette and click the Link Layers icon again.

CROSS-REF   Learn all about linking layers in Chapter 2.

Maybe that white box is a bit too big or small? No problem — it's a shape layer so you can resize is as much as you want without losing any quality. Select the Box layer in the Layers palette then choose Edit ➪ Transform, or press Ctrl+T (⌘+T on the Mac). Click a transform handle at a corner or edge of the white box in the document window; then drag with the mouse to resize the box. Press Enter (Return on the Mac) when you're happy with the new size.

CROSS-REF   For more on the wonders of shape layers, see Chapter 5.

This example project gives you a small taste of layers in Photoshop. You've looked at creating normal layers, shape layers and type layers, learned how layers work together to form the finished document, and seen how layers can be manipulated independently of each other.

Summary

This chapter introduced you to layers in Photoshop: what they are and why they're such useful beasts. You learned how to get around in the Layers palette, and you also learned what layer transparency is and how it works.

The different types of layers available in Photoshop have been touched on, from normal layers through to type layers, shape layers, adjustment layers, and fill layers, as well as the special Background layer. You've looked at just a few of the things you can do with layers, and finished with a simple example to help you get to grips with the concepts that were introduced.

The remaining chapters of this book cover the finer points of working with layers in Photoshop.

Chapter 2

Managing and Organizing Layers

In this chapter, you look at the nuts and bolts of layers in more depth. We cover the nitty-gritty of creating new layers and then look at different methods of selecting layers in your document. We show you how to duplicate layers, both within the current document and across documents. After that, we look at moving layer content — manually by using the Move tool, and automatically through the use of Photoshop's functions to align and distribute layer content.

We look at some different ways that Photoshop lets you change the order of layers in a document, then cover renaming layers and changing their color. We show how to lock various aspects of your layers to prevent them being changed accidentally, and we also look at the different ways of deleting unwanted layers.

Finally, we look at ways to organize your layers, including linking layers, creating layer groups, and color-coding layers and groups for easy access.

As discussed in Chapter 1, there are a few different types of layers in Photoshop: normal bitmap layers, type layers, shape layers, fill layers, and adjustment layers. Although each of these layer types has its own particular features, uses, advantages, and disadvantages, you can generally manage them all in the same way. Pretty much everything in this chapter applies equally to all these types of layers.

Creating Layers

Chapter 1 showed you the quickest and easiest way to create a new normal layer: Simply click the New Layer icon in the Layers palette. This creates a new layer above the active layer.

TIP Hold down Ctrl (⌘ on the Mac) while clicking the icon to create the new layer below the active layer.

You can also Alt+click (Option+click on the Mac) the New Layer icon, choose Layer ➪ New ➪ Layer, or press Shift+Ctrl+N (Shift+Option+N on the Mac). If you do any of these things, the New Layer dialog box appears, allowing you to give your new layer a name, as well as set some initial options for the layer, as shown in Figure 2.1. Choosing New Layer from the Layers palette menu has the same effect.

FIGURE 2.1

The New Layer dialog box lets you choose options for newly created layers.

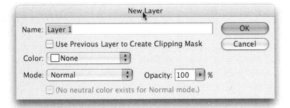

The options in the New Layer dialog box work as follows:

- **Name:** This is, of course, the name of your new layer. It's always a good idea to name your layers rather than just going with the default Layer 1, Layer 2, and so on. You'll thank yourself later when you're working with 100-layer documents.

- **Use Previous Layer to Create Clipping Mask:** Select this option to use the active layer as the clipping mask layer for your new layer. The current layer is then linked with the new layer as a clipping mask, controlling which parts of the new layer are visible.

CROSS-REF For more information on clipping masks, see Chapter 9.

- **Color:** This assigns a color to the new layer, helping you identify it and group it with similarly colored layers in the Layers palette. (For more on color-coding layers, see the section "Renaming layers and changing their color.") If you don't want to assign a color to your new layer, leave Color set to None.

- **Mode:** This pop-up menu lets you choose a blending mode for the new layer. The default of Normal does what you'd expect — the new layer's pixels sit on top of the previous layers, with no blending between the pixels of each layer. The remaining blending modes can produce a range of interesting (and sometimes surprising) effects, with the pixels of the new layer interacting with the layer or layers below it.

CROSS-REF Blending modes are covered in detail in Chapter 7.

- **Opacity:** Use this option to specify how opaque or transparent your new layer will be. A value of 100 percent prevents anything under the layer's pixels from showing through, while a value of 0 percent makes the layer completely transparent. Set a value by clicking in the box and typing, or click and drag the slider to get the value you're after. For more on layer opacity see the section "Setting a layer's opacity and fill."

- **Fill With Neutral Color:** This option is only available for certain blending modes. Select this check box to fill the new layer with a color that has no blending effect on the layers below. For example, if you choose a blending mode of Lighten then this option fills the layer with black because black pixels have no lightening effect on the underlying layers. This option is useful if you want to create a blank canvas layer to paint your blending mode effect onto.

When you're satisfied with your options, click OK or press Enter (Return on the Mac) to create your new layer.

TIP To create a new layer quickly using the keyboard, without the New Layer dialog popping up, press Shift+Ctrl+Alt+N (Shift+⌘+Option+N on the Mac).

Creating a layer from a selection

Rather than starting with a new empty layer, you can create a new layer based on your current selection. To do this, make your selection using one of the selection tools (or load a saved selection), then choose either Layer ➪ New ➪ Layer via Copy or Layer ➪ New ➪ Layer via Cut:

- Layer via Copy copies the contents of your selection to the new layer (see the top illustration in Figure 2.2). You can also press Ctrl+J to achieve the same effect.

- Layer via Cut removes the contents of your selection and pastes them into the new layer (see the bottom illustration in Figure 2.2). Press Shift+Ctrl+J to achieve the same effect.

In each case, a new layer is created above the current layer, with the pixels of the selection pasted into the new layer. Photoshop keeps the layer contents in alignment; in other words, the new layer contents sit directly on top of the previously selected area.

FIGURE 2.2

Creating a layer from a selection with Layer via Copy (left) and Layer via Cut (right)

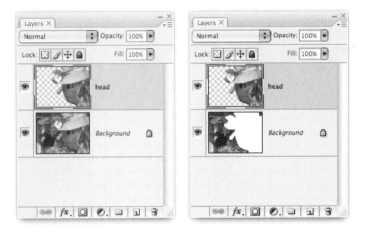

> **TIP** You can also create a new layer from a selection by choosing Edit ➪ Cut or Edit ➪ Copy followed by Edit ➪ Paste; however, Photoshop pastes the contents into the middle of the new layer, rather than keeping them aligned with the previously selected area. So if you need to keep your layers in alignment, make sure you choose Layer ➪ New ➪ Layer via Copy or Layer ➪ New ➪ Layer via Cut.

Other ways to create layers

You can duplicate an existing layer to create a new layer. For more information, see the section "Duplicating layers" later in this chapter.

In addition, some tools automatically create new layers when you use them. For example, the Type tool creates a new type layer when you click in your document. In a similar way, the Custom Shape tool, by default, creates a new fill layer with a vector layer mask (also known as a shape layer) once you start dragging out the shape in your document.

> **CROSS-REF** For more on creating different types of layers, see Chapter 1.

Selecting Layers

Most of the time, you'll want to work on at least one of the layers in your document. To do this, you first need to select your layer or layers. Selected layers are highlighted in the Layers palette, as shown in Figure 2.3.

FIGURE 2.3

Selected layers in the Layers palette

Selecting a single layer

Many layer-based operations are carried out on a single layer — painting with the Brush tool, or applying a filter under the Filter menu, for example. To select a single layer to work on (called the *active layer*), you can do one of the following:

- Click the layer in the Layers palette.
- Select the Move tool, enable the Auto-Select option in the options bar, choose Layer from the menu to the right of Auto-Select, and click the layer's content in the document window.
- From within any tool except the Hand tool, Ctrl+Alt+right-click (⌘+Option+right-click on the Mac) the layer's content in the document window (this works regardless of the Move tool's Auto-Select setting).
- From within another tool, first ensure that the Move tool's Auto-Select option is enabled, with Layer chosen from the menu to the right of Auto-Select; then Ctrl+click (⌘+click on the Mac) the layer's content in the document window.

 The last technique only works from within tools that support Ctrl+clicking (⌘+clicking on the Mac) to temporarily switch to the Move tool. For more information on this, see the section "Accessing the Move tool temporarily" later in this chapter.

CROSS-REF To learn more about using the Move tool to select layers, see the section "Selecting layers with the Move tool."

Selecting multiple layers

You can also select multiple layers. Do the following:

- To select a range of contiguous layers (layers that are next to each other in the Layers palette), click the first layer then Shift+click the last layer.

- To select multiple, noncontiguous layers — layers that are scattered throughout the Layers palette — Ctrl+click (⌘+click on the Mac) each layer that you want to select. To deselect a layer, Ctrl+click (⌘+click) it again. Figure 2.3 shows a Layers palette with three non-contiguous layers selected.

- To select all the layers in your document (except the Background layer), choose Select ⇨ All Layers, or press Ctrl+Alt+A (⌘+Option+A on the Mac).

To deselect all layers, click in the space below the layers in the Layers palette or, if there's no space because you have too many layers, you can select a single layer then Ctrl+click (⌘+click on the Mac) it in the Layers palette to deselect. Alternatively, choose Select ⇨ Deselect Layers.

You can also select layers of a similar type in your document; for example, all fill layers or all type layers. To do this, select one of the layers then choose Select ⇨ Similar Layers, or right-click the layer in the Layers palette and choose Select Similar Layers from the pop-up menu.

Finally, if you link some layers together, you can select all those linked layers by clicking one of them then choosing Layer ⇨ Select Linked Layers, or choosing Select Linked Layers from the Layers palette menu.

Selecting layers with the Move tool

If you have many layers in your document, you may be struggling to find the layer you want in the Layers palette, which isn't good when you're trying to hit that deadline. Luckily, there's a quick way to select the layer directly in the document window without having to find it in the Layers palette.

Simply select the Move tool, enable the Auto-Select option in the Move tool's options bar, and choose Layer from the menu to the right of Auto-Select. You can now click directly on a layer's pixels in the document window to select that layer. (If several layers are stacked on top of each other, the topmost layer is selected.) Figure 2.4 shows this in action.

To select more than one layer at once using the Move tool, enable Auto-Select and choose Layer, then Shift+click the layers you want to select.

The Group option in the menu next to Auto-Select works in a similar way — when you click the content of a layer that's in a layer group, Photoshop also selects all other layers in the same group. This is great for selecting the entire contents of a layer group at once.

Selecting a layer with the Move tool. Enable Auto-Select, choose Layer from the menu next to Auto-Select; then click the layer's pixels in the document window to select that layer.

CROSS-REF For more on layer groups, see the section "Organizing layers into layer groups" later in this chapter.

Provided the Auto-Select option is enabled in the Move tool's options bar, you can use this feature even when you're not using the Move tool. To do this, simply Ctrl+click (⌘+click on the Mac) the layer contents in the document window.

CROSS-REF In general, holding down Ctrl/⌘ temporarily accesses the Move tool. For more on this handy feature, see the section "Accessing the Move tool temporarily" later in this chapter.

Even better, you can select a layer in the document window from any tool except the Hand tool by Ctrl+Alt+right-clicking (⌘+Option+right-clicking on the Mac) the layer content. This works even if the Move tool's Auto-Select option is disabled. (Hold down Shift as well if you want to select multiple layers.) If you're already within the Move tool, you can save yourself an extra keypress and just Alt+right-click (Option+right-click on the Mac) the content.

Another great way to select multiple layers with the Move tool is by dragging a selection rectangle in the document window. First, select the Move tool, and make sure the Auto-Select option is turned off in the options bar. Now Ctrl+click (⌘+click on the Mac) a blank area of the document window, such as the Background layer; then drag out a marquee. As you drag, any layer whose content falls inside the marquee gets added to the list of selected layers. You can use this technique to select any layer except the Background layer. It's really handy for those times where you want to select a bunch of layers that are clustered together in the document window — a group of stars, for example.

If you want to select a layer or group that's underneath one or more layers in the document window, right-click the topmost layer in the window while using the Move tool, or Ctrl+right-click

(⌘+right-click on the Mac) the layer if using a different tool. You'll see a pop-up menu appear, listing all the layers and groups under the point where you clicked. Pick a layer or group from the menu to select it. To select more than one layer or group in this way, hold down Shift as you right-click, then pick a layer or group to add to, or remove from, the selection. (These tricks work regardless of the Auto-Select setting.)

Managing Layers

In this section, you learn how you can manage your layers in Photoshop. We cover duplicating and merging layers; converting to and from the Background layer; moving layers in the image; aligning and distributing layer content; reordering layers in the Layers palette; renaming and color-coding layers; controlling opacity and fill opacity; locking layers; and, of course, deleting layers.

Duplicating layers

Photoshop provides you with several ways to duplicate an existing layer or layers. To start, you can simply drag the layer in the Layers palette down to the New Layer icon at the bottom of the palette. This creates a duplicate of the layer above the current layer and gives the new layer a default name (for example, Layer 2). If you want to duplicate more than one layer, select all the layers you want to duplicate, then drag them to the New Layer icon.

Duplicating layers interactively

If you prefer to name your duplicate layer at the same time, or choose which document to put the duplicate layer in, hold down Alt (Option on the Mac) as you drag the layer to the New Layer icon. A dialog box appears (see Figure 2.5). This dialog box allows you to name the layer (only available if duplicating a single layer), and also to choose the document that the new layer is placed in (the default is always the current document). If you choose to place the layer in a different document, Photoshop adds it above the active layer in that document. You can also choose New from the Document drop-down list, which creates a new document with the same dimensions as the existing document, and places the duplicate layer in that. Enter a name for the new document in the Name box below the Document option.

You can also duplicate the active layer, or a bunch of selected layers, by choosing Layer ➪ Duplicate Layer(s) to display the Duplicate Layer dialog box just described.

> **TIP** If you're running Windows and want to duplicate the layer or layers using the keyboard without displaying the Duplicate Layer dialog box, press and hold Alt, press L followed by D, then release Alt. Sadly, this tip is Windows-dependent; there's no equivalent keyboard shortcut for this on the Mac.

FIGURE 2.5

The Duplicate Layer dialog box

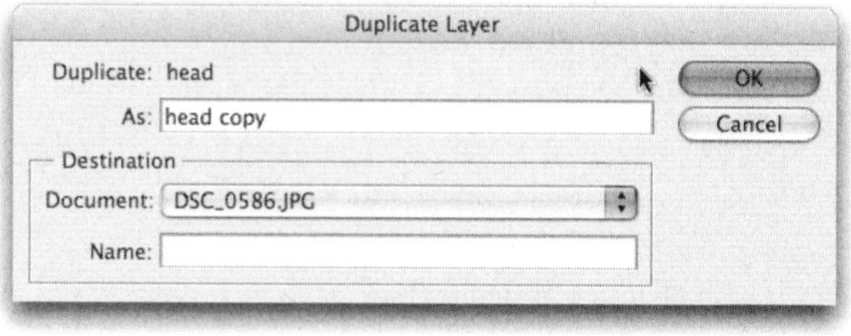

```
                        Duplicate Layer
  Duplicate:  head                            (   OK   )
        As: head copy                         ( Cancel )
  ┌ Destination ─────────────────────────────
  Document:  DSC_0586.JPG              ▲▼
     Name:
```

Another way to duplicate layers is to display the Layers palette menu (click the little arrow icon in the top-right corner of the palette) and choose Duplicate Layer(s). Alternatively, right-click a layer or a bunch of selected layers in the Layers palette and choose Duplicate Layer(s) from the pop-up menu.

Duplicating layers with the Move tool

The Move tool provides a really quick way to duplicate a layer and position the duplicate in the document window at the same time. Select the Move tool, select the layer, and then Alt+click (Option+click on the Mac) the layer's pixels in the document window and drag. A copy of that layer is instantly created and you can position the new layer in the document window with the mouse. Figure 2.6 shows a layer being duplicated in this way. You can also duplicate a group by selecting the group and then Alt+dragging (Option+dragging on the Mac) the group's contents in the document window with the Move tool.

FIGURE 2.6

Duplicating a layer with the Move tool

To duplicate multiple layers with the Move tool, select the layers you want to duplicate (see the section "Selecting multiple layers" earlier in the chapter), and then Alt+click (Option+click on the Mac) one of the layers in the document window and drag to create the duplicates and position them.

Other ways to copy layers between documents

As well as using the Duplicate Layer dialog box (see the section "Duplicating layers interactively" earlier in the chapter), you can simply drag the selected layer — or layers, if you selected more than one — from the Layers palette to the other document window, as shown in Figure 2.7.

Alternatively, select the Move tool (see the section "Moving the content of layers"), and drag the contents of the layer from one document window to the other. After positioning the layer, release the mouse button, and the duplicate layer is dropped into the new document at that position.

TIP To put the layer contents in the same position as they were in the original document, hold down the Shift key as you drop the layer(s) in the new document. This only works if the two documents are of the same dimensions; if they're different, the layer or layers are placed at the center of the new document or, if the new document has an active selection, at the center of the selection.

FIGURE 2.7

Duplicating a layer by dragging it from the Layers palette to another document

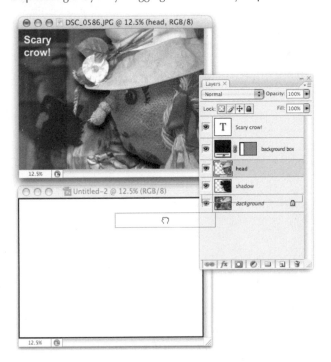

Merging layers together

Great though layers are, there are a few small drawbacks to having tens or hundreds of layers in a document. These include the following:

- Layers take up RAM. This means that if you keep adding layers to your document Photoshop eventually slows to a crawl, or even (if it's having a really bad day) starts protesting about not having enough memory.

- Layers increase file size. This may not be such a big issue if you have terabytes of storage, but if you don't, or you occasionally need to e-mail Photoshop files around, then it's nice to keep those file sizes down if you can.

- It can be tricky to find the layer you want in a document with a hundred layers, although being able to select layers with the Move tool really helps here, as does grouping layers.

> **CROSS-REF**   Selecting with the Move tool and grouping layers are covered in the sections "Selecting layers with the Move tool" and "Organizing layers into layer groups."

Luckily, Photoshop makes it easy to merge several layers together to form one single layer, thereby reducing RAM usage, file size, and the number of layers you have to deal with, all in one fell swoop.

> **CAUTION**   After you merge a bunch of layers you can't then edit them individually, so it's best to merge layers only when you finish working on them.

Merging a layer with the layer below it

You can quickly merge the active layer with the layer sitting underneath it, provided the underlying layer is a normal layer. To do this, select the layer and choose Layer ➪ Merge Down, or simply press Ctrl+E (⌘+E on the Mac). The new merged layer is given the name of the lower of the two layers.

> **TIP**   You can also access Merge Down, as well as the other Merge functions described later, from the Layers palette menu, or by right-clicking the layer in the Layers palette and choosing the option from the pop-up menu.

Merging several layers together

To merge a bunch of layers together, select them (see "Selecting multiple layers" earlier in this chapter), then choose Layer ➪ Merge Layers or press Ctrl+E (⌘+E on the Mac). You can merge any types of layers together this way.

> **NOTE**   The new merged layer is given the same name as the topmost of the selected layers.

>    If you want to merge the active layer with the layer below it, and the underlying layer
>   isn't a normal layer, you can't press Ctrl/⌘+E to Merge Down. However, you can
> Ctrl/⌘+click both layers to select them, and then press Ctrl/⌘+E or choose Layer ➪ Merge Layers.

Merging all visible layers

This is a useful way to choose layers to merge. Hide the layers you don't want to merge by clicking their eye icons, so you're left with just the layers you want to merge visible in the document window. (This means you can preview what you're about to merge in the document window, which is pretty handy.) Merge the layers by choosing Layer ⇨ Merge Visible or press Ctrl+Shift+E (⌘+Shift+E on the Mac).

CAUTION   Merge Visible also merges the layers with the Background layer if it's visible. If you don't want this to happen, hide the Background layer first by clicking its eye icon.

Stamping layers

If you want to hedge your bets and keep the original layers after the merge, you can stamp the layers instead. Stamping creates a new layer containing all your selected layers merged together, but also preserves the originals.

To stamp two or more layers together, select them then hold down Alt (Option on the Mac) before choosing Layer ⇨ Merge Layers. You can also press Ctrl+Alt+E (⌘+Option+E on the Mac) to do the same thing. This creates a new layer above your selected layers, and that new layer contains the merged contents of those layers. You're then free to continue working on those original layers (or trash them if you're happy with the merge).

You can also stamp the visible layers to a new layer in a similar way. Hold down Alt (Option on the Mac), then choose Layer ⇨ Merge Visible, or simply press Ctrl+Alt+Shift+E (⌘+Option+Shift+E on the Mac). The contents of all the visible layers are copied to a new layer above the active layer.

CAUTION   You can also stamp the active layer on top of the layer below (known as stamping down), provided the underlying layer is a normal layer. To do this, hold down Alt (Option on the Mac) while choosing Layer ⇨ Merge Down, or press Ctrl+Alt+E (⌘+Option+E on the Mac). Be careful with this method, though; it won't create a new merged layer as you might expect! Instead, it stamps the active layer onto the layer below, permanently altering the lower layer.

Merging and stamping groups

If you've selected a group in the Layers palette, the Merge Down option in the Layer menu changes to Merge Group. Choose this option, or press Ctrl+E (⌘+E on the Mac), and Photoshop merges all the layers (and any groups) inside the group into a single, flattened layer.

To stamp the group instead, hold down Alt (Option on the Mac) while choosing Layer ⇨ Merge Group, or press Ctrl+Alt+E (⌘+Option+E on the Mac). This creates a new layer above the group, containing the merged contents of the group.

TIP   You can also merge more than one group together by selecting all the groups, and then choosing Layer ⇨ Merge Layers. The contents of the groups then get converted to a single layer. As always, hold down Alt (Option on the Mac) to stamp the group contents to a new layer instead.

Making a merged copy

Copy Merged is a handy command that you can use to copy the merged contents of all visible layers within a selection. To use it, make a selection with one of the selection tools (you can also choose Select ⇨ All if you want to make a merged copy of the whole document), and then choose Edit ⇨ Copy Merged or press Shift+Ctrl+C (Shift+⌘+C on the Mac). Photoshop makes a flattened copy of all visible layers within your selection area. Choose Edit ⇨ Paste to paste the merged copy into a new layer.

Copy Merged is a great way to take a flattened "snapshot" of a multilayered document, without having to mess around with merging layers. For example, it's handy for exporting slices of a document for Web use: Make your selection, choose Edit ⇨ Copy Merged, create a new document and choose Edit ⇨ Paste to paste the flattened slice into that document. You can then export via File ⇨ Save for Web.

Flattening an image

You can *flatten* an image, which means turning all the visible layers in the document into a single Background layer. Because this is a drastic move, it's best used with caution — you'll usually only want to do this when you finish working on an image and you no longer need the individual layers. To flatten the image, choose Layer ⇨ Flatten Image (or choose Flatten Image from the Layers palette menu, or right-click in the Layers palette and choose Flatten Image).

> **TIP** You can also save a flattened copy of the current document without touching the original. To do this, choose File ⇨ Save As or press Ctrl+Shift+S (⌘+Shift+S on the Mac), and then deselect the Layers option in the Save As dialog box.

Converting the Background layer

The Background layer is introduced briefly in Chapter 1. This layer has some unique properties that make it suitable for some situations, but not so useful in others. Fortunately, it's easy to convert the Background layer to a regular layer, and vice versa.

Converting the Background layer to a regular layer

Sometimes it's handy to be able to convert the Background layer to a regular layer so you can move it around, change its blending mode, and so on. To change the Background layer to a regular layer, double-click the Background layer in the Layers palette, or choose Layer ⇨ New ⇨ Layer From Background. This displays the New Layer dialog box, where you can name the converted layer and set its options.

Converting a regular layer to the Background layer

You can also go the other way and turn a regular layer into the Background layer. To do this, simply select the layer you want to convert in the Layers palette; then choose Layer ➪ New ➪ Background From Layer. The layer is instantly converted into the Background layer. If the layer is a vector layer, such as a type or shape layer, it is rasterized first (the Background layer is always a bitmap layer).

Moving the content of layers

Thanks to each layer being independent of the others, you can move a layer's content around the document window without affecting the content on any other layer. Photoshop lets you move layer content in a number of ways.

Moving layers with the Move tool

The Move tool provides you with the most options for moving your layer content. Select the layer whose content you want to move around; then select the Move tool by clicking the Toolbox icon shown in Figure 2.8, or by pressing V. The mouse pointer changes to the Move tool icon. You can now drag your layer content around with the mouse.

> **TIP** If you have enabled the Auto-Select option in the Move tool's options bar, you can also select a layer or group to move by clicking directly on the layer or group's pixels in the document window. For more information, see the section "Selecting layers with the Move tool" earlier in the chapter.

The Move tool allows you to move and transform a layer at the same time. Select the Show Transform Controls option in the Move tool's options palette; then select a layer. The transform controls appear on the layer in the document window. You can still drag the layer around as usual, but if you click or drag the transform controls, the Free Transform command is enabled, allowing you to transform your layer as well as move it. Figure 2.8 shows this in action. You can also click the Switch Between Free Transform And Warp Modes button in the options bar to flip over to Warp mode. When you're happy with the results of the transformation, press Enter (Return on the Mac) to exit the Free Transform command.

> **CROSS-REF** You explore the Free Transform command in depth, as well as other ways to transform layers, in Chapter 3.

> **TIP** You can also use the Move tool to duplicate a layer and move the duplicate in one go, and also to copy a layer into another document. See the section "Duplicating layers" earlier in this chapter for more information.

FIGURE 2.8

Using the Move tool to move and transform a layer at the same time

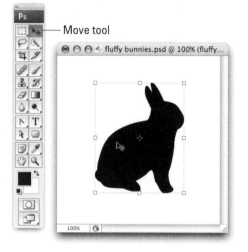

— Move tool

Moving with the keyboard

Rather than dragging the contents of a layer around with the mouse, you can use the keyboard to nudge the contents. This is often quicker for small movements, and it gives you more precise control.

To move the contents of a layer one pixel at a time, select the Move tool, select the layer or layers; then use the arrow keys to nudge the contents around. You can also move the contents 10 pixels at a time by holding down the Shift key while using the arrow keys.

Accessing the Move tool temporarily

The Move tool is an essential tool that you probably use quite a bit. Having to select it by clicking its icon or pressing V each time can be a bit of a pain, especially as you then have to reselect the tool you were using before you switched to the Move tool.

Luckily, there's a useful shortcut to the Move tool, available from most other tools. Hold down Ctrl (⌘ on the Mac) and the mouse pointer changes to the Move tool. You can then use the Move tool as if you'd selected it from the Toolbox. Releasing Ctrl or ⌘ instantly returns you to the tool you were using. Very handy!

> **TIP** To duplicate layers at the same time as moving them, hold down Alt (Option on the Mac) as well. For more information on this feature, see the section "Duplicating layers" earlier in the chapter.

NOTE This Ctrl/⌘ key shortcut obeys the settings of the Auto-Select option in the Move tool's options bar, so if you have this option enabled it also applies when using Ctrl or ⌘ to access the Move tool. Assuming Auto-Select is enabled, you can also hold down Shift along with Ctrl/⌘ to select multiple layers or groups. However, you can't transform and move at the same time with this shortcut, so the Show Transform Controls option has no effect.

When using this shortcut you can also nudge the layer content in 1-pixel steps. Simply hold down Ctrl (⌘ on the Mac) and press the arrow keys to nudge the content around. To nudge in 10-pixel steps, also hold down Shift.

You can use this shortcut from within all tools except the following:

- The Pen and Freeform Pen tools
- The Path Selection and Direct Selection tools
- The Hand tool
- The Slice Select tool
- The Add/Delete Anchor Point and Convert Point tools

This is because the Ctrl/⌘ key is reserved for other uses when these tools are active.

Aligning layer content

Photoshop allows you to align two or more layers with each other, or align one or more layers with a selection. This is great for quickly lining up content along margins and edges.

Aligning layers with each other

To align two or more layers with each other, first select the layers, either in the Layers palette or by using the Move tool techniques described earlier. You can then align the layers in various ways by choosing from the menu options under Layer ⇨ Align. Alternatively, if you're already using the Move tool you can click the corresponding icons in the tool's options bar, as shown in Figure 2.9. The available options are:

- **Top Edges:** This moves the selected layers so that their top edges are aligned with the topmost pixel among all the selected layers.
- **Vertical Centers:** This moves the selected layers so that their center points are vertically aligned with the average center point of the selected layers.
- **Bottom Edges:** This moves the selected layers so that their bottom edges are aligned with the bottommost pixel among all the selected layers.
- **Left Edges:** This moves the selected layers so that their left edges are aligned with the leftmost pixel among all the selected layers.
- **Horizontal Centers:** This moves the selected layers so that their center points are horizontally aligned with the average center point of the selected layers.

- **Right Edges:** This moves the selected layers so that their right edges are aligned with the rightmost pixel among all the selected layers.

FIGURE 2.9

Use these icons in the Move tool's options bar to align your layers.

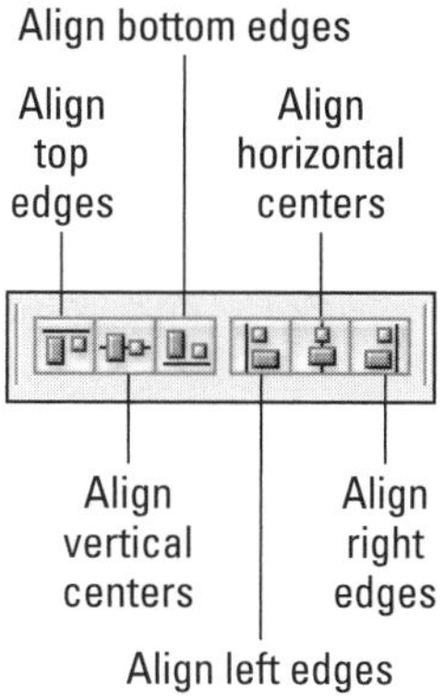

Align bottom edges

Align top edges

Align horizontal centers

Align vertical centers

Align right edges

Align left edges

Aligning layers with a selection

To align one or more layers with a selection, make your selection using one of the selection tools, then select the layers, either in the Layers palette or using the Move tool. (If you prefer, you can select the layers first, then make your selection with a selection tool.) You can then align the layers to your selection using the same menu options or icons described earlier. Rather than aligning the layers with each other, the layers are aligned with the selection instead:

- **Top Edges:** This moves the selected layers so that their top edges are aligned with the topmost pixel of the selection border.

- **Vertical Centers:** This moves the selected layers so that their center points are vertically aligned with the center point of the selection.

- **Bottom Edges:** This moves the selected layers so that their bottom edges are aligned with the bottommost pixel of the selection border.

- **Left Edges:** This moves the selected layers so that their left edges are aligned with the leftmost pixel of the selection border.

- **Horizontal Centers:** This moves the selected layers so that their center points are horizontally aligned with the center point of the selection.

- **Right Edges:** This moves the selected layers so that their right edges are aligned with the rightmost pixel of the selection border.

NEW FEATURE Photoshop CS3 features a handy new command called Auto-align Layers. Despite the similar sounding name, this command is actually quite different to the commands under Layer ➪ Align. Auto-Align Layers lets you line up photos in two or more layers by distorting one layer so it matches the other. This is covered in detail in Chapter 15.

Evenly distributing layer content

In addition to aligning layers, you can distribute the content of three or more layers evenly across the document. To do this, select at least three layers; then distribute the layers by choosing from one of the menu options under Layer ➪ Distribute. If you already happen to be using the Move tool, you can click the distribute icons in the tool's options bar, as shown in Figure 2.10. The available options are:

- **Top Edges:** This distributes the selected layers so that the topmost points of the layers are vertically spaced evenly apart.

- **Vertical Centers:** This distributes the selected layers so that the center points of the layers are vertically spaced evenly apart.

- **Bottom Edges:** This distributes the selected layers so that the bottommost points of the layers are vertically spaced evenly apart.

- **Left Edges:** This distributes the selected layers so that the leftmost points of the layers are horizontally spaced evenly apart.

- **Horizontal Centers:** This distributes the selected layers so that the center points of the layers are horizontally spaced evenly apart.

- **Right Edges:** This distributes the selected layers so that the rightmost points of the layers are horizontally spaced evenly apart.

FIGURE 2.10

Distribute your layer content evenly by using these icons in the Move tool's options bar.

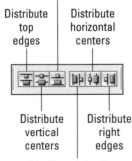

Distribute bottom edges

Distribute top edges

Distribute horizontal centers

Distribute vertical centers

Distribute right edges

Distribute left edges

Changing the order of layers

If you have at least two non-Background layers in your document, you can change their stacking order. To do this, click a layer in the Layers palette, then drag the layer to the new position. As you drag your layer, a thick highlighted line appears in the Layers palette, indicating where the new layer will be placed. When you're satisfied with the position, release the mouse button and the layer is moved there.

You can also change the layer order by selecting a layer then choosing an option from the submenu under Layer ➪ Arrange. Choose from the following options:

- **Bring to Front:** This moves the selected layer to the front of the document; that is, the top of the stack in the Layers palette. This option is dimmed if your selected layer is already at the front of the document. Keyboard shortcut: Shift+Ctrl+] (Shift+⌘+] on the Mac).

- **Bring Forward:** Moves the selected layer one position forward in the document; that is, one position up the stack in the Layers palette. This option is dimmed if your selected layer is already at the front of the document. Keyboard shortcut: Ctrl+] (⌘+] on the Mac).

- **Send Backward:** Moves the selected layer one position backward in the document; that is, one position down the stack in the Layers palette. This option is dimmed if your selected layer is already at the back of the document (above the Background layer, if it exists). Keyboard shortcut: Ctrl+[(⌘+[on the Mac).

- **Send to Back:** Moves the selected layer to the back of the document; that is, the bottom of the stack in the Layers palette (but not below the Background layer). This option is dimmed if your selected layer is already at the back of the document (above the Background layer, if it exists). Keyboard shortcut: Shift+Ctrl+[(Shift+⌘+[on the Mac).

- **Reverse:** This reverses the order of the selected layers in the document, so that the bottommost layer becomes the topmost of the selected layers, and vice versa. This option is only available if you selected at least two layers (for obvious reasons).

> **TIP** You can reorder more than one layer at once. Select your layers (see the section "Selecting multiple layers" earlier in the chapter), then drag your layers in the Layers palette or use an option under Layer ➪ Arrange, as described earlier.

Renaming layers and changing their color

It's a good idea to name each layer you create, as the contents of a layer are not always obvious from the layer thumbnail.

The quickest way to rename a layer is to double-click the layer's name in the Layers palette. The layer name then becomes editable; type your new layer name and press Enter (Return on the Mac).

You can also rename the active layer, as well as choose a color for it, through the Layer Properties dialog box, as shown in Figure 2.11. Color-coding layers can be a useful way to group layers visually; for example, when creating a Web layout you can give all your menu option layers the same color.

FIGURE 2.11

The Layer Properties dialog box

To display the Layer Properties dialog box, you can:

- Hold down Alt (Option on the Mac) and double-click the layer in the Layers palette. (Make sure you don't click the layer's name or you'll rename the layer instead.)
- Choose Layer ➪ Layer Properties from the main menu.
- Choose Layer Properties from the Layers palette menu.
- Right-click the layer and choose Layer Properties from the pop-up menu.

Type a new name for your layer, choose a new color for it if you want, and then click OK or press Enter (Return on the Mac).

Setting a layer's opacity and fill

Although by default a layer's opaque portions obscure anything below the layer, it doesn't have to be an all-or-nothing proposition. Using the layer's Opacity setting, you can control how much of the underlying layers shows through to create some cool semitransparent effects, such as the example in Figure 2.12.

You can give each layer an Opacity setting on a scale of 0 percent to 100 percent, where 0 percent is completely transparent (the layer is invisible) and 100 percent is completely opaque (opaque pixels in the layer completely block out anything below them). The default opacity setting for a layer is 100 percent.

NOTE Even a layer with an Opacity setting of 100 percent may have semitransparent pixels. Each pixel in the layer has its own opacity level ranging from 0 (fully transparent) to 255 (fully opaque). This is known as the layer's *transparency mask*. For example, if you paint on a layer using the Brush tool with its Opacity set to 50 percent in the options bar, you paint semitransparent pixels onto the layer. Even with the layer's Opacity set to 100 percent, these pixels are only 50 percent opaque. With the layer's Opacity at 50 percent, the pixels are 25 percent opaque, and so on.

The Fill setting is similar to Opacity, but Fill ignores any effects that you add to the layer. In other words, it just affects the opacity of the layer's pixels, but doesn't touch the opacity of the layer effects. You can see this in Figure 2.13, where an Outer Glow style is applied to the layer. The Fill value of the layer on the right is reduced to zero, but the opacity of the Outer Glow is unaffected.

FIGURE 2.12

A layer with the default Opacity setting of 100 percent (left), and the same layer with an Opacity of 50 percent (right)

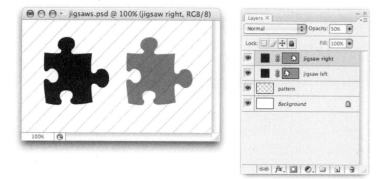

FIGURE 2.13

A layer with an Outer Glow effect applied. In the left example the layer's Fill value is 100 percent; in the right example it's 0 percent. The Outer Glow around the jigsaw piece remains unaffected by the Fill setting.

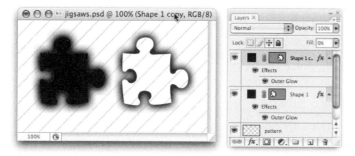

To change a layer's Opacity or Fill setting, select the layer, then double-click in the Opacity or Fill box at the top of the Layers palette and type a new value. The opacity of the layer changes instantly in the document window. You can also click the arrow on the right-hand side of the Opacity or Fill box to display a slider, which you can then click and drag, or nudge up and down in 1 percent increments with the arrow keys (hold the Shift key to nudge in increments of 10 percent).

TIP You can also change the active layer's Opacity setting very quickly using the keyboard — press 1 for 10 percent, 2 for 20 percent, and so on. Or if you want to specify 15 percent, press 1 and 5 in quick succession. You can change the Fill setting in the same way by holding down the Shift key at the same time. This trick works from within pretty much any tool except the painting tools, where pressing a number changes a setting within the tool itself (for example, Exposure for the Dodge tool).

NOTE   You can't change the Opacity or Fill of a fully locked layer or the Background layer. If you want to change these settings for a fully locked layer, unlock it first by clicking the Lock All icon at the top of the Layers palette. For the Background layer, you need to convert it into a normal layer first (see the section "Converting the Background layer to a regular layer" earlier in the chapter).

Locking layers

Photoshop gives you the ability to lock various aspects of a layer to prevent you (or others) from accidentally changing them. You can view and set the locks on a layer with the Lock icons at the top of the Layers palette, as shown in Figure 2.14.

The available locks are:

- **Transparent Pixels:** This prevents the transparent areas of the layer from being changed. For example, if you try to use the Brush tool to paint on a layer with this lock enabled, you find that you can only paint over the already nontransparent areas of the layer. This is great for painting inside a shape in your image, as it stops you from accidentally painting outside the edges.

- **Image pixels:** This prevents any of the pixels on the layer from being changed (including transparent pixels). If you try to paint on a layer with the image pixels locked, you get an error about the layer being locked.

- **Position:** Locking the layer's position prevents you from using the Move tool or any other method to move the layer's pixels around (you get an error about the layer being locked if you try). However, you can still draw on the layer or otherwise change its content, provided the image pixels are unlocked. This is handy for those times when you've painstakingly aligned 20 layers so they look just right, and you don't want to accidentally knock them out of whack.

- **All:** As you might imagine, this locks both the transparent and image pixels and also the layer's position, preventing any modification of the layer's content at all. However, you can still carry out actions that don't change the layer's content, such as changing the layer's stacking order in the Layers palette or renaming the layer.

FIGURE 2.14

The Lock icons in the Layers palette

A layer that has one or more of the first three locks applied is said to be *partially locked*, while a layer that has the All lock applied is known as a *fully locked* layer. You can tell the difference by looking at the little lock icon on the right-hand side of the layer in the Layers palette. If the lock is a light color then the layer is partially locked, whereas a dark color indicates a fully locked layer.

You can also lock and unlock a bunch of layers at once. To do this, select the layers; then choose Layer ⇨ Lock Layers, or choose Lock Layers from the Layers palette menu. A dialog box appears that allows you to set or unset lock options for all the selected layers. When you're satisfied with your choices, click OK to apply them to the layers.

Deleting layers

As you add new layers and duplicate existing ones, you can quickly end up with tens if not hundreds of layers in your document, so you'll probably want to delete layers fairly often. Photoshop provides a number of different ways to delete layers.

The easiest way to delete the active layer is to click the Delete icon in the Layers palette. If you don't want Photoshop to ask for confirmation, hold down Alt (Option on the Mac) when you click the icon. You can also delete multiple layers at once by selecting them then clicking or Alt+clicking (Option+clicking on the Mac) the Delete icon.

Another way to delete a layer or layers is to drag the selected layer(s) to the Delete icon. This deletes without asking for confirmation.

TIP   If you find the confirmation dialog gets in the way and you never click No, select the **Don't show again** check box in the dialog box, and Photoshop will never ask you for confirmation again. You can always choose Edit ⇨ Undo Delete Layer if you ever delete a layer by mistake. If at a later point you want to reenable Photoshop's confirmation dialog boxes, choose Edit ⇨ Preferences ⇨ General (Photoshop ⇨ Preferences ⇨ General on the Mac), or press Ctrl+K (⌘+K on the Mac) and click Reset All Warning Dialogs.

Of course, if you're a menu junkie you can also delete layers by choosing Layer ⇨ Delete ⇨ Layer(s), or choosing Delete Layer(s) from the Layers palette menu. Finally, you can delete a layer or layers by right-clicking the layer(s) and choosing Delete Layer(s) from the pop-up menu.

TIP   If you happen to be using the Move tool at the time, you can also delete a layer by pressing Backspace (Delete on the Mac).

Deleting hidden layers

You can delete all the hidden layers in your document — that is, layers with no eye icon next to them in the Layers palette — by choosing Layer ⇨ Delete ⇨ Hidden Layers. You can also choose Delete Hidden Layers from the Layers palette menu.

TIP   This is a great way to purge your unwanted layers at the end of a project. After you have your document looking the way you want it, you'll probably have some hidden layers containing versions that you tried out but didn't like. Simply choose Layer ⇨ Delete ⇨ Hidden Layers to remove all those old layers from your document.

Deleting linked layers

If you have a bunch of layers linked together, you can delete them easily in one fell swoop by choosing Layer ⇨ Select Linked Layers, then deleting the selected layers using one of the previous techniques.

TIP Older versions of Photoshop only allowed you to select one layer at a time. If you're used to an older version, you may be familiar with this trick to delete lots of layers: Link the layers together, merge them together by choosing Layer ⇨ Merge Linked, and delete the single merged layer. Now that Photoshop lets you select multiple layers, this old kludge is no longer necessary — simply select all the layers you want to delete; then click that Delete icon!

Controlling Layer Positioning

In the last section you looked at using the Move tool to shift the content of layers around the document window. You also looked at aligning and distributing your layers automatically using Layer ⇨ Align and Layer ⇨ Distribute. In fact, Photoshop provides you with many other useful tools to help you get your layers pixel-perfect: rulers, guides, Smart Guides, the grid, snapping, and the Ruler tool.

Working with rulers

Just as physical rulers let you measure the positions of real-world objects, you can use Photoshop's rulers to track exactly where the contents of your layers sit in the document. There are two rulers in Photoshop: a horizontal ruler, running across the top of your document window, and a vertical ruler down the left-hand side, as shown in Figure 2.15.

To toggle the display of rulers within a document window, choose View ⇨ Rulers, or press Ctrl+R (⌘+R on the Mac). Rulers can be toggled for each document window, so you can turn on rulers just for the windows where you need them, and save screen space by hiding them in other windows. In addition, whenever you create a new document window — by choosing File ⇨ New or Window ⇨ Arrange ⇨ New Window — Photoshop uses the rulers setting of the current window for the new window.

You'll see full-width tick marks on each ruler, with a number next to the mark representing how far away that mark is from the ruler's origin (in the current ruler units). Depending on your zoom level, you'll probably also see smaller tick marks, subdividing the units as appropriate; for example, centimeters get divided up into millimeter subdivisions, while inches are divided into quarters, eighths and so on.

As you move your mouse around the document window, you'll notice that little markers move along the rulers tracking the mouse cursor position, helping you to place the cursor precisely. This can be a great help when drawing shapes with the shape tools, or when making selections using one of the marquee tools.

FIGURE 2.15

Photoshop's horizontal and vertical rulers help you measure and position layers in the document window.

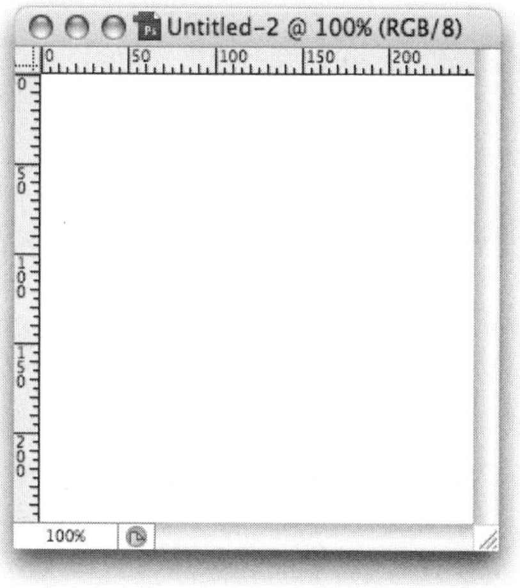

You can also change the measurement units used by the rulers. To do this, choose Edit ➪ Preferences ➪ Units & Rulers (Win) or Photoshop ➪ Preferences ➪ Units & Rulers (Mac). You can now choose a unit — pixels, inches, centimeters, millimeters, points, picas or percent — from the Rulers menu in the Preferences dialog box. You can also quickly access these preferences by double-clicking a ruler in the document window. An even quicker way to change units is to right-click either ruler, or click the little + (plus) symbol in the bottom-left corner of the Info palette, and pick new units from the pop-up menu that appears.

NOTE Most of these ruler units will no doubt be familiar, but a few of them could do with a bit of an introduction. The *point* is a measurement frequently used in typography and, these days, commonly represents 1/72 of an inch. (Handily, at the common screen resolution of 72 pixels per inch, 1 point = 1 pixel.) Its close cousin, the *pica*, is also a common typographic unit; there are 72 picas to the foot, and therefore 6 picas to the inch, and 12 points to the pica. Finally, *percent*, in the context of ruler units, represents a percentage of the document width — in the case of the horizontal ruler — or height, for the vertical ruler. Percent units are great for measuring out areas of the document proportionally - for example, when creating design grids.

NOTE The ruler units are always the same across all visible rulers in Photoshop; you can't mix and match ruler units between document windows.

By default, the rulers measure from the top left corner of your document, but you can position the rulers' origin — the (0,0) point — anywhere you like. To change the origin, click the origin icon that sits between the horizontal and vertical rulers in the top-left corner of the document window and drag down and to the right, as shown in Figure 2.16. As you drag you'll see the cursor change to a crosshair. Release the mouse when you've positioned the origin where you want it. To reset the origin back to the top-left corner of the document, double-click the origin icon.

FIGURE 2.16

To change the (0,0) position of the rulers, click the origin icon and drag down and to the right.

Origin icon

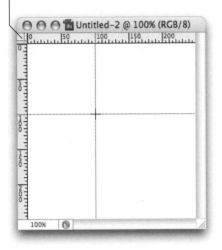

> **TIP**   To make sure you're accurately positioning the origin, you might first want to enable snapping to guides, the grid, or slices by choosing an option under View ➪ Snap To. (We cover snapping in detail later in this chapter.) You can also snap to the tick marks on the rulers by holding down Shift as you drag.

> **TIP**   Changing the origin is handy if you want to measure the position of one object relative to another. Drag the origin to a point on the first object, such as the top left corner. You can then position the second object precisely, relative to the first.

Creating and using guides

Rulers are handy for measuring the positions of objects in the document window, but Photoshop offers a really good visual way to position and align objects, in the form of guides. These are horizontal and vertical guidelines that you create yourself, and that float over your document in the document window. They're not printed or exported; they're purely used to help you position elements in your document.

> **NOTE**   Guides are preserved in your document, provided you save it in one of the following file formats: PSD, PSB, TIFF, JPEG, EPS, or PDF. If you save your document in another format in Windows, your guides are gone forever. If you use a Mac, however, Photoshop saves the guides in a Mac resource fork along with the document. This means that guides are saved with all types of images on the Mac, provided the resource fork remains intact. To play it safe, though, save your image using one of the formats listed above if you want to preserve your guides.

Adding and manipulating guides

To create a guide, first make sure your rulers are visible (press Ctrl+R (⌘+R on the Mac) if they're not). Then click in either ruler and drag from the ruler into the document window. Drag from the horizontal ruler downwards to create a horizontal guide; drag rightwards from the vertical ruler to create a vertical guide. Figure 2.17 shows this in action.

 To create a vertical guide by dragging from the horizontal ruler, or a horizontal guide while dragging from the vertical ruler, hold down Alt (Option on the Mac) as you drag.

FIGURE 2.17

Creating a new guide by dragging from the horizontal ruler

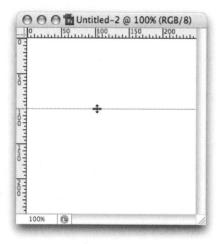

If you know exactly where you'd like to place a guide (for example, 3 inches from the top edge of the document) choose View ➪ New Guide, and select either Horizontal or Vertical in the New Guide dialog box to specify the type of guide. You can now enter a value in the Position box to place the guide that distance from the ruler origin. For example, select Horizontal and enter 3 inch in the Position box to place a horizontal guide 3 inches below the origin. Or select Vertical and enter -1 cm to position a vertical guide 1 centimeter to the left of the origin (which, unless you've moved the origin, puts it outside the document boundary). By default, the units in the Position box match the current ruler units, but you can enter a guide position using any units you like.

To move an existing guide, select the Move tool and drag the guide. You can also Ctrl+drag (⌘+drag on the Mac) the guide while using any other tool except the Hand and Slice tools. Hold down Shift as you drag to snap the guide to the ticks on the appropriate ruler. There's nothing to stop you positioning a guide outside the document boundaries, either; simply make the document window larger than the document to reveal the gray area outside the document (the rulers still extend to the width and height of the window) and drag your guide or guides into the gray area. This is great if you need to position an element that lies partially outside the document bounds.

You can also lock your guides to prevent them being accidentally moved as you drag other elements of your design around. To do this, choose View ⇨ Lock Guides, or press Ctrl+Alt+; (⌘+Option+; on the Mac). To unlock the guides again, choose the same menu option, or press the same key combination.

To delete a guide, drag it outside the document window with the Move tool (or Ctrl/⌘+drag it if you're not using the Move tool). To delete all guides in the document, choose View ⇨ Clear Guides.

You can convert a horizontal guide to a vertical guide (and vice-versa) by Alt+clicking (Option+clicking on the Mac) the guide using the Move tool. To convert a guide while using another tool, Ctrl+Alt+click (⌘+Option+click on the Mac) the guide.

If you find your guides are getting in the way of your work, you can toggle them on and off by choosing View ⇨ Show ⇨ Guides, or pressing Ctrl+; (⌘+; on the Mac). Whenever you add a new guide, Photoshop redisplays any existing guides if they were previously hidden.

You can also change the color of the guides from the default cyan, which is handy if the cyan clashes with the colors in your design. To do this, choose Edit ⇨ Preferences ⇨ Guides, Grid & Slices (Photoshop ⇨ Preferences ⇨ Guides, Grid & Slices on the Mac), and pick a new color from the Color option in the Guides section. Click the Custom option, or click the color box to the right, to specify your own, custom color. You can also pick a custom color from your image by clicking in the document window. Finally, you can change the style of the guides from the default solid line to a dashed line using the Style option. This can help to make the guides stand out against your design.

TIP You can also quickly access the Guides, Grid & Slices preferences by double-clicking a guide when using the Move tool, or Ctrl+double-clicking (⌘+double-clicking on the Mac) a guide when using another tool.

Aligning layers with the help of guides

Once you've added guides to your document, you can use them to visually align elements within the document window. You can also enlist the help of Photoshop's snap features to snap your layer contents to guides as you move them. To toggle snapping to guides, choose View ⇨ Snap To ⇨ Guides. With snapping enabled, drag your layer contents around using the Move tool. The edges and center point of the contents snap to the guides as they get close to them.

CROSS-REF We talk about snapping to guides, as well as to other features, in "Snapping," later in this section.

In Figure 2.18 we used guides to create a box, then added more guides to help us line up a type layer within the box.

FIGURE 2.18

After creating some outer guides for our box, we created the box as a shape layer, snapping the box to the guides as we dragged it out. We then added inner guides for the left and right margins of the type layer, and a horizontal guide to position the type's baseline. We created the type layer, scaled it to fit between the left and right guides, and then snapped the type layer's baseline onto the horizontal guide.

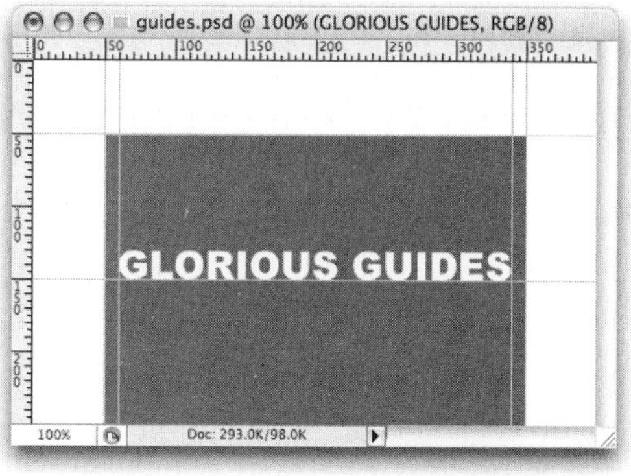

Using Smart Guides

Smart Guides are thin horizontal and vertical guidelines that appear automatically when you move an edge or center point of a layer or path directly into alignment with an edge or center point of another layer, or directly onto an edge of the document. So when you see a Smart Guide appear, you know that your two elements are in perfect alignment along those particular edges or center points.

To toggle Smart Guides on and off, choose View ➪ Show ➪ Smart Guides.

Smart Guides offer a quick visual cue when you're positioning one element relative to another. Because they only appear while you're moving things, they don't clutter up your workspace like guides can. This is especially appealing when working with a detailed Web page design, for example. Here, you might have guides in place for the basic design grid, but you also need to line up individual elements as you create them within that grid. Smart Guides allow you to position elements relative to each other without having to create further distracting guides.

In Figure 2.19, you can see Smart Guides in action. We've dragged our top type layer so its baseline is aligned with the top of the left rectangle, and its left hand edge is aligned with the type below it, causing the two Smart Guides to appear. All we have to do now is release the mouse button, and the layers are in perfect alignment.

FIGURE 2.19

Using Smart Guides, we can ensure that the layers in our business card are perfectly aligned without having to manually create a single guide.

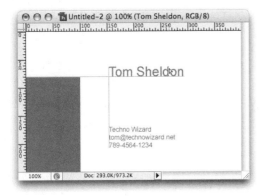

NOTE Smart Guides appear when you bring a type layer's baseline into alignment with another layer's center or edge, or another type layer's baseline. Perfect for lining up text precisely.

If you find the default magenta color of Smart Guides somewhat unappealing, you can change the color to suit. Choose Edit ➪ Preferences ➪ Guides, Grid & Slices (Photoshop ➪ Preferences ➪ Guides, Grid & Slices on the Mac) and pick a new color from the Color menu in the Smart Guides section. You can also create a custom color for the Smart Guides by choosing the Custom option from the Color menu, or by clicking the color box to the right.

Positioning using the grid

Photoshop's grid is — unsurprisingly enough — a grid of equally-spaced lines that you can use to help position your design elements. Like guides and Smart Guides, the grid merely floats on top of the document window while you're editing your image; it doesn't print. If you need to space a lot of layers equally, or position many elements at precise, measured points in your document, you'll find that Photoshop's grid comes into its own.

To show and hide the grid, choose View ➪ Show ➪ Grid, or press Ctrl+' (⌘+' on the Mac). Figure 2.20 shows a grid overlaid onto a document. A grid is made up of gridlines (the solid lines) and subdivisions (the dotted lines in between the gridlines).

FIGURE 2.20

A grid is a series of nonprinting horizontal and vertical guidelines floating above the document.

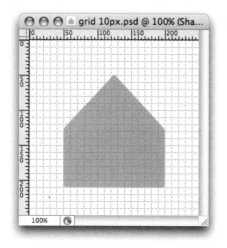

Photoshop lets you adjust the color of the gridlines, as well as choose between different styles of grid. You can also choose the scale of the gridlines, and the number of subdivisions between each gridline. To set all these properties, choose Edit ➪ Preferences ➪ Guides, Grid & Slices (Photoshop ➪ Preferences ➪ Guides, Grid & Slices on the Mac). The Grid options work as follows:

- **Color:** Pick a preset color for the gridlines from the Color menu, or roll your own color by choosing the Custom option (or by clicking the color box on the right). To pick a color from the image, Alt+click (Option+click on the Mac) in the document window.

- **Style:** This changes the way that the gridlines are displayed. Choose Lines to use solid gridlines with dotted subdivisions. Dashed Lines draws both the gridlines and the subdivisions as dotted lines, which, of course, means you can't tell one from the other (though it does give the grid a "cleaner" appearance). Finally, choose Dots to render the grid using single points for each intersection in the grid. This is a good choice if you don't want the grid to get in the way of your work, although it can be hard to spot those dots unless you pick a contrasty color.

- **Gridline Every:** This option lets you choose the scale of your grid. Enter a value in the box, and use the menu to the right to pick the units. For example, enter 10 in the box and choose Pixels from the menu to place a gridline every 10 pixels. You can enter fractional numbers in the box too — for example, 2.5.

TIP The Percent units are particularly handy when it comes to setting up design grids. For example, enter 33.3 and choose Percent, and you'll get a grid that neatly divides your image up into thirds.

NOTE As with the ruler ticks, the visible spacing between the gridlines is somewhat influenced by your zoom level. For example, if you're viewing a 5-megapixel photo at 100% and you set gridlines every 4 pixels, you'll probably see gridlines placed every 8 pixels instead. Otherwise the grid would just be a solid mass of pixels.

- **Subdivisions:** Enter the number of subdivisions that you'd like to appear between each gridline, from 1 to 100. If you'd rather not have any subdivisions, enter 1.

Snapping

We've covered snapping briefly when talking about rulers and guides. Snapping is a handy feature that lets you accurately position elements of your design without having to mess about with zooming in and nudging.

Snapping occurs when you move one element (such as a layer's contents or a guide) towards another element, until the elements are 8 screen pixels or closer to being in alignment, either horizontally or vertically. When you do this, the moved element jumps, or snaps, into alignment with the static element, saving you having to align the elements precisely yourself. If you use the Move tool to snap layer contents to a snappable feature, such as a guide or the document bounds, the Move tool cursor turns from black to white when the snapping kicks in, as shown in Figure 2.21.

FIGURE 2.21

Snapping in action. Here we're dragging a shape towards the intersection of two guides using the Move tool (left). As the shape gets within 8 pixels of the guides, the shape jumps into alignment with the guides, and the Move tool cursor changes from black to white, indicating that snapping has taken place (right).

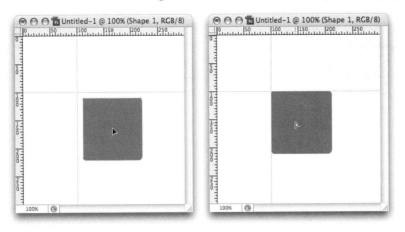

Snapping to some features, such as guides and the grid, also happens when drawing or dragging out new elements (for example, when creating shapes with the shape tools, drawing with the Pencil tool, or creating selections using the marquee or lasso tools). In these cases, the edges of the drawn or dragged-out element snap to the nearest guide or gridline.

However, snapping has its disadvantages. It's obviously a hindrance if you want to position elements three pixels apart, for example, as the snapping will just force the elements into exact alignment. In addition, Photoshop sometimes gets it wrong; hey, nobody's perfect — and misses by a pixel here and there.

Fortunately, you can toggle snapping on and off, both globally, and to specific elements such as guides and the grid. To toggle snapping in general, choose View ➪ Snap, or press Ctrl+Shift+; (⌘+Shift+; on the Mac). To turn snapping to particular elements on and off, choose from the options under View ➪ Snap To, as follows:

- **Guides:** Choose this option to snap drawn, dragged-out or moved elements to the guides in your document.

- **Grid:** This option snaps drawn, dragged-out or moved elements, including guides, to the grid.

- **Layers:** With this option enabled, moved elements, including guides, snap to the edges and center points of the contents of visible layers in the document.

- **Slices:** Enable this option to snap drawn, dragged-out or moved elements, including guides, to the horizontal and vertical boundaries of any slices in your document. (This includes user slices, auto slices and layer-based slices.)

- **Document Bounds:** Choose this option to snap guides, slices, and elements moved with the Move tool, to the horizontal and vertical edges of your document.

A check mark next to an option indicates that snapping is enabled for that option. A minus sign indicated that snapping would be enabled for that option, if you didn't have snapping turned off in general.

You can also turn on snapping to all the above elements at once by choosing View ➪ Snap To ➪ All, or turn them all off with View ➪ Snap To ➪ None.

NOTE As you might expect, snapping only works if the thing being snapped to is visible. For example, if you hide the guides then View ➪ Snap To ➪ Guides has no effect. Similarly, you can't snap to a hidden layer, even when View ➪ Snap To ➪ Layers is enabled.

TIP To snap to just one element, such as the guides only, first turn off snapping, if necessary, by choosing View ➪ Snap, then choose your option under View ➪ Snap To. Photoshop automatically enables snapping for that option only, deselecting the other options in the submenu.

A couple more things to note about snapping:

- If you move a type layer near a snappable horizontal element, such as a horizontal guide, a horizontal document edge, or another type layer, you'll find that, in addition to the top edge, bottom edge and center point snapping to the element, the baselines of each line of text in the type layer also snap. This is handy for making sure different type layers are properly aligned.

- If you move a shape layer or path using the Path Selection tool, the anchor points within the path snap, rather than the edges and center point of the shape.

Measuring distances and angles with the Ruler tool

The final tool that you can use to help position your image elements exactly is the Ruler tool (called the Measure tool in previous versions of Photoshop). The Ruler tool behaves like a real-world ruler and protractor combined, allowing you to accurately measure the distance between two points, as well as the angle between an edge and the horizontal and vertical. You can also add a third point and measure the angle created between the two connecting lines, as well as the length of each line. Figure 2.22 shows the Ruler tool in action, helping to measure the length and angle of one side of a roof cross-section.

FIGURE 2.22

Here we're using the Ruler tool to measure the length of a roof edge, as well as the angle it makes with the horizontal. You can see in the options bar that the angle of our roof isn't quite 45 degrees!

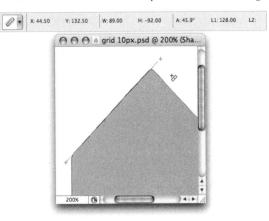

To start using this wondrous instrument, click its icon in the toolbox; unsurprisingly, it looks like a little ruler. It's grouped with the Eyedropper and Color Sampler Tools, so hold down the mouse button over the icon until a menu pops up, then choose the ruler icon. As with other grouped tools in the toolbox, you can also repeatedly Alt+click (Option+click on the Mac) the icon, or keep pressing Shift+I, until it cycles round to the Ruler tool.

Now you can measure the distance between two points in your document by clicking one point, holding down the mouse button, and dragging the measurement line to the second point. If you want to measure the angle between two lines, you can create a second measurement line by Alt+clicking (Option+clicking on the Mac) one of the points at either end of the first line, and dragging.

NOTE Like guides and the grid, measurement lines appear onscreen only; they don't print with your document.

Once you've created your measurement line or lines, the figures in the options bar tell you all sorts of useful measurements, as follows:

- **X and Y:** These values are the X and Y coordinates of the start point (the point you dragged from). They're measured in the current ruler units, with (0,0) being the ruler origin (which, by default, is the top left corner of the document).

CROSS-REF Find out how to change the ruler origin in "Working with rulers," earlier in this chapter.

- **W and H:** These figures only appear if you've created just one measurement line. They represent the width and height of an imaginary box in which your measurement line is the diagonal. Again, they're measured in the current ruler units.

- **A:** If you've drawn just one measurement line, this is the angle that the measurement line makes with the horizontal. It's measured in degrees. A horizontal line traveling left to right has an angle of 0 degrees, while a line traveling right to left makes an angle of 180 degrees. 90 degrees represents a line running from bottom to top, while -90 degrees represents a line traveling from top to bottom. If, on the other hand, you've drawn two measurement lines, this figure is the angle between the two lines, in degrees.

- **L1:** This is the length of your measurement line in the current ruler units. If you've drawn two measurement lines, then this is the length of the first line.

- **L2:** If you've drawn two measurement lines, this figure shows you the length of the second line.

NOTE You can also view the measurement figures in the Info palette (Window ⇨ Info, or F8).

TIP By default, the start point of each measurement line you draw is the point you dragged from, while the end point is the point you dragged to. However, you can swap these over by clicking the start point. The two points then flip over: the start point becomes the end point, and the end point becomes the start point. You'll see the measurements in the options bar change accordingly.

You can reposition your measurement line after you've created it by dragging it in the document window. As you do, the X and Y values in the options bar update to reflect the new position. You can also drag a point at either end of a line to change the line's length and angle.

NOTE   The measurement line snaps to guides, the grid, or slices in your document if you've enabled these options under View ⇨ Snap To.

Your measurement line remains as long as the current window is open. Switch to another tool and the line vanishes, but when you switch back to the Ruler tool, it returns. You can even create different measurement lines in different windows (created by choosing Window ⇨ Arrange ⇨ New Window For). However, once you close a document window, the measurement lines are gone forever.

To start again with a new measurement line, click and drag somewhere else in the window. You can also remove a measurement line entirely by dragging it out of the document window, or clicking the Clear button in the options bar.

TIP   The Ruler tool is fantastic for straightening crooked photos. Select the Ruler tool, and drag out a measurement line along a part of your photo that should be dead horizontal or vertical. Now choose Image ⇨ Rotate Canvas ⇨ Arbitrary. Photoshop pre-fills the Rotate Canvas dialog box with the exact angle needed to straighten the image. Simply click OK, and you're done.

Organizing Layers

After you start to have a lot of layers in your documents, having each layer sitting independently in the Layers palette becomes a bit unwieldy. You'll probably want to organize them more effectively, which is what this section is all about. Here you look at how to link layers together, how to organize your document by grouping layers, and how to show and hide layers and layer groups in the document.

Linking layers together

Often it's handy to associate two or more layers with each other so that you can manipulate them in unison. While you can do this by selecting all the layers at once, sometimes you want to associate the layers on a more long-term basis. You can do this in Photoshop by linking layers.

To link two or more layers together, first select the layers; then click the Link Layers icon in the Layers palette. Your selected layers now have little link icons on their right-hand sides in the Layers palette, as shown in Figure 2.23.

The layers are now linked together. Try selecting one of the layers, then moving its content around the document window with the Move tool. The linked layers also move.

You can also apply transformations to one of the linked layers using the Transform and Free Transform commands, and the transformations also apply to the other linked layers.

FIGURE 2.23

Linked layers in the Layers palette

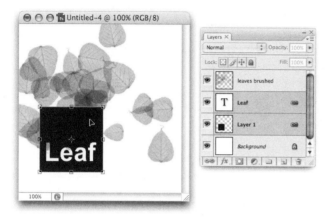

As is often the way with Photoshop, there's more than one way to do the job. You can also link layers by selecting them, then doing one of the following:

- Choosing Layer ➪ Link Layers
- Choosing Link Layers from the Layers palette menu
- Right-clicking your selected layers and choosing Link Layers from the pop-up menu

Unlinking layers

To unlink layers that you previously linked, select the layer or layers that you want to unlink and click the Link Layers icon in the Layers palette. Also, provided you selected at least two layers, you can do one of the following:

- Choose Layer ➪ Unlink Layers
- Choose Unlink Layers from the Layers palette menu
- Right-click your selected layers and choose Unlink Layers from the pop-up menu

You can also temporarily unlink a layer by Shift+clicking the link icon on the right-hand side of the layer in the Layers palette. This is handy if you want to keep one linked layer still while you move the others. Shift+click the layer's link icon again to relink it.

 To quickly unlink a bunch of linked layers, select one of the layers, choose Layer ➪ Select Linked Layers; then click the Link Layers icon in the Layers palette.

Organizing layers into layer groups

Photoshop lets you organize your layers into layer groups to make them easier to access and manipulate. Figure 2.24 shows how layer groups look in the Layers palette. You can also nest layer groups, which is handy if your document contains a large number of layers.

A layer group in the Layers palette has a little folder icon instead of a thumbnail image. In fact, you can think of layer groups as being a bit like folders in Windows Explorer or the Mac Finder, with layers themselves being the equivalent of files.

All of the layers and groups within a group are indented slightly, which makes it easy to spot which layers and groups are grouped and which are not.

FIGURE 2.24

Layer groups in the Layers palette

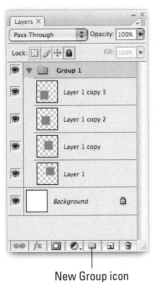

New Group icon

NOTE   In older versions of Photoshop, layer groups were called *layer sets*.

Creating layer groups

Creating a new layer group is very much like creating a new layer, although there are a few subtle differences. The quickest way to create a new layer group is to click the New Group icon at the bottom of the Layers palette, as shown in Figure 2.24. This quickly creates a new group above the active layer or group.

You can also Alt+click (Option+click on the Mac) the New Group icon, or choose Layer ➪ New ➪ Group. This displays the New Group dialog box, shown in Figure 2.25, where you can give your new group a name as well as set some initial options for the group. Choosing New Group from the Layers palette pop-up menu has the same effect.

FIGURE 2.25

The New Group dialog box

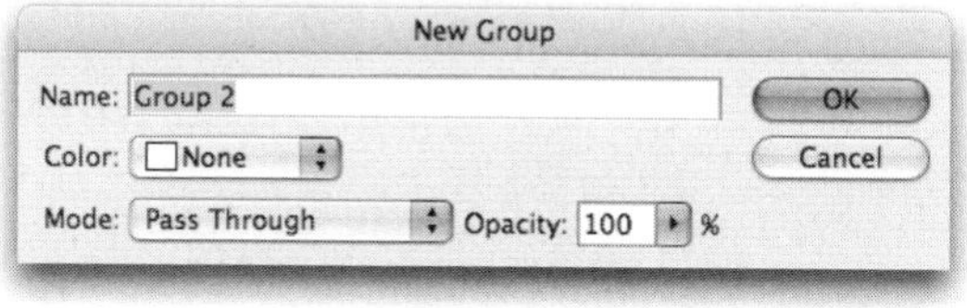

The options in the New Group dialog box work as follows:

- **Name:** This is the name to give the new group. It usually makes sense to name the group after a specific element in your document — for example, Headline or Menu.

- **Color:** This option assigns a color to the group, much like color-coding layers. It's a good way to associate several groups together without having to have too many nested groups. If you don't want to assign a color to your new group, leave Color set to None. (For more on color-coding, see the section "Renaming layers and changing their color" earlier in this chapter.)

- **Mode:** This pop-up menu specifies the blending mode for the group. The options are similar to those available for individual layers; however, blending modes behave slightly differently for groups. The default option, Pass Through, means that the group has no blending mode of its own; the individual blending modes of layers within the group behave as normal, blending with any underlying layers, both within and below the group. However, if you select any other blending mode for the group, all the layers within the group are merged together using their individual blending modes, then the resulting image is blended with the other layers and groups in the document using the group's blending mode.

CROSS-REF Blending modes are covered in more detail in Chapter 7.

- **Opacity:** The Opacity value allows you to specify the opacity of the group. A value of 100 percent makes the group completely opaque, while a value of 0 percent makes the group completely transparent. Enter a value by clicking in the box and typing, or click and drag the slider to get the value you want.

NOTE The Opacity value of a layer group interacts with the opacities of any layers within the group by multiplying the two opacities together. For example, a layer with an opacity of 50 percent inside a group with an opacity of 50 percent is equivalent to a stand-alone layer with an opacity of 25 percent.

When you're satisfied with your options, click OK, or press Enter (Return on the Mac), to create your new layer group.

Placing the new group

By default, Photoshop adds the new group above the active layer or group. If you prefer, you can Ctrl+click (⌘+click on the Mac) the New Group icon to create the new group below the active layer or group.

NOTE If the active group is open (with its triangle pointing down), the new group is created inside the active group when you Ctrl/⌘+click the New Group icon.

Creating a group from existing layers

To create a new group quickly from an existing layer or layers, select the layer(s) then choose Layer ➪ Group Layers or simply press Ctrl+G (⌘+G on the Mac). Alternatively you can drag the selected layers to the New Group icon at the bottom of the Layers palette.

If you want to name your group at the same time, select your layers and choose Layer ➪ New ➪ Group From Layers, or choose New Group From Layers from the Layers palette menu. You can then give your group a name and choose other options for the group. For more information on these options, see the section "Creating layer groups" earlier in this chapter.

Opening and closing groups

Each layer group has a small triangle to the left of its folder icon in the Layers palette. A triangle pointing to the right means that the group is closed (its contents are hidden in the Layers palette); a triangle pointing down indicates an opened group (its contents are visible). Figure 2.26 shows an opened and a closed group in the Layers palette.

NOTE Closing a group merely hides the group contents in the Layers palette — the contents are still visible in the document window. To hide a layer or group in the document window, click its eye icon. For more on this topic, see the section "Showing and hiding layers and groups" later in the chapter.

To open or close a group, click its triangle or, if you fancy exercising your clicking finger a bit more, right-click its triangle and choose Open/Close This Group from the pop-up menu. You can also choose Open Other Groups from the same pop-up menu to open all the other groups in the Layers palette (the active group remains unaffected).

TIP Alt+click (Option+click on the Mac) a closed group's triangle to open the group and any nested groups inside that group. Similarly, Alt/Option+click an opened group's triangle to close the group and any nested groups inside it.

FIGURE 2.26

An opened and a closed group in the Layers palette. Click the triangle to the left of a group's folder icon to open or close the group.

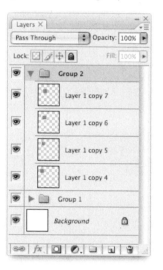

Adding layers to an existing group

To add a layer to a group, click and drag the layer onto the group in the Layers palette. Photoshop places the layer at the end of the group.

To add the layer to a particular position within the group, make sure the group is open (click the group's open/close triangle if necessary); then drag the layer to the desired position within the group.

 You can add multiple layers to a group. Select all the layers you want to add; then drag the layers onto the group as described previously.

To add a new layer to a group, make sure the group is opened, click the group to select it, and then click the New Layer icon in the Layers palette. The layer is placed at the top of the group. Alternatively, you can click a layer within the group to select it; then click the New Layer icon. Photoshop adds the new layer above the selected layer in the group.

 You can use any of the methods for creating a new layer to also create layers inside groups. For a full list of these methods, refer to the section "Creating Layers" near the start of this chapter.

Nesting groups

You can place groups within groups, and place those groups inside other groups, and so on (up to five levels of nesting, or the limit of your own sanity, whichever kicks in first).

To place a group or groups inside another group, click and drag the groups(s) onto the target group in the Layers palette. The group or groups that you dragged are moved to the end of the target group.

To place the group in a particular position within the target group, make sure the target group is open (click the group's open/close triangle if necessary), then drag the group to the desired position within the target group.

To add a new group to an existing group, make sure the existing group is open, click the group to select it, and then click the New Group icon in the Layers palette. Photoshop adds the new group at the top of the selected group. Alternatively, click a layer or group within the group to select it, and then click the New Group icon. The group is then placed above the selected layer or group.

> **TIP** You can use any of the methods for creating a new group to add new groups inside groups. See the section "Creating layer groups" earlier in this chapter for more info on creating groups.

Deleting groups

Deleting groups is similar to deleting layers. You can delete a group by first selecting the group, then doing one of the following:

- Click the Delete (trash can) icon in the Layers palette.
- Choose Layer ➪ Delete ➪ Group.
- Right-click the group and select Delete Group.
- Choose Delete Group from the Layers palette menu.

Each of these methods displays a confirmation dialog box, as shown in Figure 2.27, which asks you what to do about any layers or groups inside the group you're about to delete.

FIGURE 2.27

When deleting a group, this dialog box lets you choose what to do about any layers or groups inside the group you're deleting.

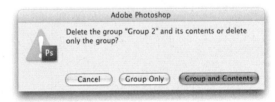

If you want to delete any layers or groups inside the group, as well as the group itself, click Group and Contents. If you just want to delete the group and move the group's contents outside the group, click Group Only. To cancel the delete operation altogether, click Cancel.

NOTE You can also delete multiple groups by selecting them then using one of the methods just described. If you do this, the menu options are called Delete Layers rather than Delete Groups, and you don't get the confirmation dialog box; Photoshop deletes the groups immediately.

Deleting the group and contents without confirmation

If you're sure you don't want to keep the group or any of its contents, you can do one of the following:

- Click and drag the group to the Delete icon in the Layers palette.
- Select the group, then Alt+click (Option+click on the Mac) the Delete icon in the Layers palette.

Both of these actions skip the confirmation dialog box.

Deleting the group without confirmation but keeping its contents

If you want to delete a group quickly but preserve its contents, select the group and choose Layer ➪ Ungroup Layers, or right-click the group and choose Ungroup Layers from the pop-up menu. You can also press Ctrl+Shift+G (⌘+Shift+G on the Mac). The group is deleted and its contents moved outside the group.

Working with groups

Many of the layer techniques described in this chapter can also be applied to groups. Each technique is briefly touched on here, as well as how to use the technique on a group.

Selecting and duplicating groups

You can select a single group by clicking it in the Layers palette. Many operations, such as moving with the Move tool or transforming with the Transform and Free Transform commands, then apply to all the layers in that group.

You can select multiple groups in the same way as multiple layers, by Shift+clicking and Ctrl+clicking (⌘+clicking on the Mac). For more information on multiple layer selections, see the section "Selecting multiple layers" earlier in this chapter.

You can select groups with the Move tool just as you can select layers. To do this, enable the Auto-Select option in the Move tool's options bar, and choose Group from the menu to the right of Auto-Select. For more information on selecting with the Move tool, see the section "Selecting layers with the Move tool" earlier in the chapter.

Duplicating groups works in exactly the same way as duplicating layers. For more information, see the section "Duplicating layers" earlier in the chapter.

Moving the content of groups

When you select a group, using the Move tool moves the content of all the layers in the group at the same time. To move just one layer within the group, select that layer in the Layers palette rather than the group. For more information on moving layer content, see the section "Moving the content of layers" earlier in this chapter.

You can align the content of groups much like you can align layers. Select two or more groups, then choose Layer ⇨ Align. For more information on aligning layers, see the section "Aligning layer content" earlier in this chapter.

You can also distribute groups in same way as layers: Select three or more groups; then choose an option from Layer ⇨ Distribute. For more on distributing layers, see the section "Evenly distributing layer content" earlier in the chapter.

 When aligning and distributing groups, the layers in each group are treated as if they were merged together as a single layer, so they all move by the same amount.

 You can't align or distribute a group with a group that's nested inside it.

Reordering groups

You can change the order of groups as you do with layers: Drag the group from one position in the Layers palette to another. You can also choose options from Layer ⇨ Arrange to change the order of groups. For more information on this, see the section "Changing the order of layers" earlier in this chapter.

 You can't reverse the order of groups via Layer ⇨ Arrange ⇨ Reverse. This function works on layers only.

Reordering layers within groups

You can also change the order of layers within groups, either by clicking and dragging the layers, or by selecting a layer (or layers) and choosing an option from Layer ⇨ Arrange:

- **Bring to Front:** This moves the selected layer to the front of the group. If the layer is already at the front of the group, it is taken out of the group and moved to the front of the document (that is, the top of the Layers palette).

- **Bring Forward:** Using Bring Forward moves the selected layer forward one position within the group. If the layer is at the front of the group, it's taken out of the group and moved to the next position in front of the group.

- **Send Backward:** This moves the selected layer back one position within the group. If the layer is at the back of the group, it is taken out of the group and moved to the next position behind the group.

- **Send to Back:** Select this option to move the selected layer to the back of the group. If the layer is already at the back of the group, it is removed from the group and moved to the back of the document (in front of the Background layer, if it exists).

Renaming groups and setting group properties

Just as with layers, the default names of Group 1, Group 2, and so on aren't very helpful, so it's worth renaming your groups to something more meaningful. The quickest way to do this is to double-click the group's name in the Layers palette, type the new name, and press Enter (Return on the Mac).

You can also rename the active group and set its properties through the Group Properties dialog box, as shown in Figure 2.28, which you can access in one of the following ways:

- Hold down the Alt key (Option on the Mac) and double-click the group (but not on the group's name) in the Layers palette.
- Choose Layer ➪ Group Properties from the main menu.
- Choose Group Properties from the Layers palette menu.
- Right-click the group and choose Group Properties from the pop-up menu.

FIGURE 2.28

The Group Properties dialog box lets you rename a group, color-code it, and show or hide its color channels.

In this dialog box, you can type a new name for your group and choose a color for it. You can also turn each of the group's color channels (red, green or blue) on or off using the Channels check boxes. When you're done, click OK to apply the changes to the group.

A Channels Primer

An image in Photoshop is made up of one or more *channels*. A channel is a grayscale version of the image, with the value of each pixel ranging from black (0) to white (255) when working with 8-bit images. A grayscale image contains only one channel (gray). An RGB image contains three channels — one for red, one for green, and one for blue. A CMYK image contains four channels for cyan, magenta, yellow, and black. These color channels are combined together to get the *composite* image, which is the color image you normally see.

You can also create additional channels in your image, called *alpha channels*. These are useful for masking and selecting parts of your image. For more on alpha channels, see Chapter 9.

Locking groups

You can lock groups in similar way to locking layers; the main difference is that you can apply only a full lock to a group. When you apply a lock to a group, the lock is applied to all layers in the group. To fully lock a group, select the group in the Layers palette, and click the Lock All icon in the Layers palette. Click the icon again to unlock the group.

To partially lock all the layers in a group, apply the locks on the layers themselves. You can do this by selecting the group, then choosing Layer ➪ Lock All Layers in Group, or choosing Lock All Layers in Group from the Layers palette menu. A dialog box appears (see Figure 2.29) that allows you to choose which lock or locks to apply: Transparency, Image, Position, or All. Make your selection and click OK to apply the locks. You can also remove locks in the same way.

FIGURE 2.29

Applying partial locks to the layers in a group

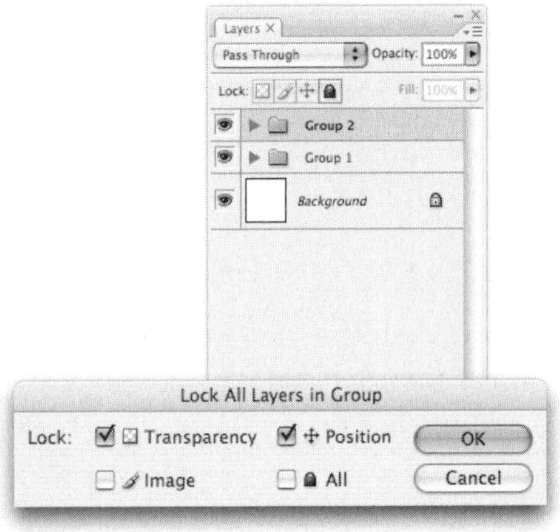

NOTE   When a group is locked, each layer in the group has a dimmed lock icon.

Linking groups

You can link groups together, just as you can link layers. Simply select two or more groups, then click the Link Layers icon to link them. Link icons appear next to each group in the Layers palette, indicating they are linked, and light-gray link icons appear next to each layer within the linked groups when the groups are selected, showing you that these layers are implicitly linked together.

You can also link a layer with a group. To do this, select the layer and the group, then click the Link Layers icon. Link icons appear next to both layer and group in the Layers palette and, when a layer or group is selected, light-gray link icons appear next to each layer in the linked group. So now the layer, and all the layers in the linked group, can be moved in unison. (You can even link a layer with its parent group, although you might as well just select the group and move that. The effect is the same, and it's a lot less confusing.)

Photoshop also lets you link layers across groups; the fact that they're in different groups doesn't bother it at all. Simply open the groups, select the layers you want to link together, and click the Link Layers icon. This is handy if you want to move some layers around together regardless of how they happen to be grouped.

Showing and hiding layers and groups

Photoshop lets you selectively show and hide the layers and groups in your document. This is great for trying out ideas and alternative designs; you can flip among different layers and groups by showing and hiding them. It's also handy to be able to hide distracting layers and groups so that you can concentrate on a particular aspect of your design.

NOTE   Any layers or groups that you hide aren't printed when you print the document.

To hide a layer or group, click its eye icon in the Layers palette. The eye icon disappears, and that layer or group is then hidden in the document window. To show the layer or group again, click the eye icon once more.

You can also hide everything except a particular layer or group by Alt+clicking (Option+clicking on the Mac) the eye icon for that layer or group. Provided you don't then click the eye icons of the hidden layers and groups, you can Alt+click (Option+click on the Mac) the original layer or group's eye icon again to redisplay the hidden layers and groups.

TIP   This feature is handy for those times when you need to work on a particular layer or group in isolation, or you just want to see what a certain layer or group looks like on its own.

There's also a really quick way to show or hide lots of consecutive layers and groups at once. Click the eye icon for one of the layers or groups; then drag through the other eye icons (either up or down) until you hide all the layers or groups that you want to hide. Figure 2.30 shows this in action. Similarly, if you click the eye icon (or rather the box that contained the eye icon) for a hidden layer or group, you can then redisplay consecutive layers and groups by dragging through their eye icons.

FIGURE 2.30

Dragging through eye icons to show or hide multiple layers

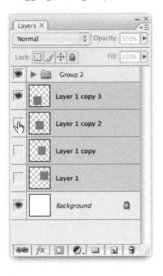

| TIP | You can also show and hide layer effects by clicking or dragging through the eye icons for the effects. For more information on layer effects and styles, see Chapter 10. |

Summary

In this chapter, you learned all the nitty-gritty of working with layers. You looked at creating layers, different ways to select them, how to duplicate them and merge them together, and how to convert to and from the Background layer.

This chapter also showed how to move layer content around the document window, both manually and also automatically through the use of Photoshop's Align and Distribute menu options. You also looked at how to change the stacking order of layers, how to rename them and color-code them for easy identification, how to adjust their opacity levels, how to lock them to prevent them being accidentally altered and, of course, how to delete them.

You also learned how to use rulers, guides, Smart Guides, the grid, snapping, and the Ruler tool to easily and accurately position layer contents in your document. Finally, in "Organizing Layers," you learned how to link layers together, how to group them and work with groups, and how to show and hide layers and groups in your document.

Resizing and Transforming Layers

Photoshop gives you a multitude of useful ways to transform layers. When talking about "transforming" in Photoshop, we're referring to stretching, squeezing, flipping, rotating, and generally altering the shape of objects in your images. We're not talking about robots transforming into aircraft or anything like that.

All of Photoshop's layer transform commands are available in the submenu under Edit ➪ Transform. As an alternative, you can use the all-in-one transform command, Edit ➪ Free Transform, which is also available by pressing Ctrl+T (⌘+T on the Mac). Free Transform gives you quick access to most of the functions under Edit ➪ Transform, allowing you to scale, rotate, skew, distort, and apply perspective, all in one handy command. You can even use Free Transform to apply more than one of these transformations at once on the same layer.

Another excellent transformation feature is Warp, which really lets you cut loose with your layers. Use Warp to twist and bend your layers into all sorts of interesting shapes. Warp gives you a few useful presets to work with, or you can freely warp your layers to your heart's content.

Finally, if you need to transform layers with a greater level of precision, you can transform numerically by typing values into the transform command's options bar.

This chapter discusses transforming layers in general. Each of the transform commands is explored in turn, and you look at a practical example that shows off some of these handy Photoshop features.

Bitmaps versus Vectors

Chapter 1 discussed the difference between bitmap layers and vector layers. Transforming vector layers generally produces better results than transforming bitmap layers. The reason for this is that vector layers don't lose information when they're transformed, but bitmap layers do. You may not notice this degradation the first time you transform a bitmap layer (unless you stretch it a lot), but if you do a couple more transforms on the same bitmap layer, then the drop in quality really starts to show. You can see this in Figure 3.1.

FIGURE 3.1

Applying several transformations on a vector layer (left) and a bitmap layer (right). Notice how the bitmap layer is starting to lose detail, whereas the vector layer is as good as new.

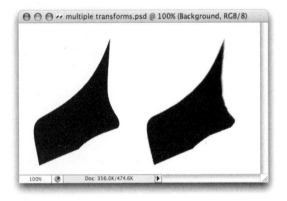

This is one reason why type layers are so great — they're vectors, so you can stretch and squeeze your text as many times as you want without any loss in quality. Compare the blown-up vector type layer against the blown-up bitmap type layer in Figure 3.2.

We don't want to put you off using bitmap layers, as they're essential when you need them — for example, only bitmap layers can hold photographic images. Just be aware that they lose quality each time you transform them, even though Photoshop does a pretty good job of preserving as much quality as possible.

TIP It's possible to transform a bitmap layer repeatedly without continuously losing detail if you use Smart Objects. Simply turn the bitmap layer into a Smart Object, and transform the Smart Object instead. However, you always lose a bit of detail in the transform; it's the nature of bitmaps. For more on Smart Objects, see Chapter 8.

FIGURE 3.2

A scaled-up vector type layer (left) compared to the same scaling on a leading brand of bitmap type layer (right). The results speak for themselves!

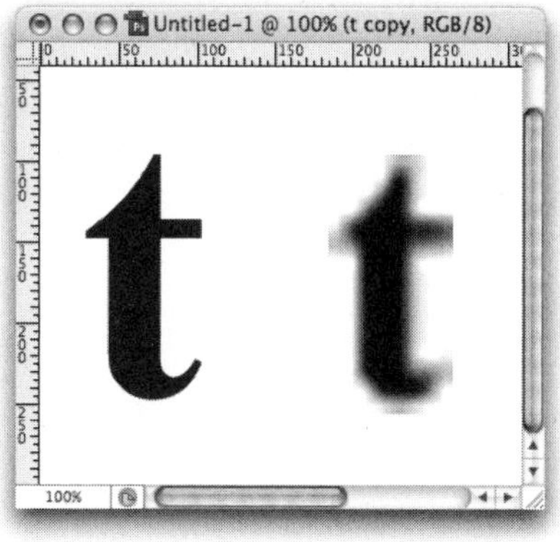

The Transform Commands

Photoshop's transform commands are all under the Edit ⇨ Transform menu option. You can transform the contents of a layer or layers, the contents of a selection, even the contents of a type layer as you're creating it. You can also transform layer masks, paths, shapes, and alpha channels. (For info on transforming things other than layers, see the section "Transforming Other Content" near the end of this chapter.)

To transform a layer, select the layer; then choose a transform command from under Edit ⇨ Transform. You can also transform multiple layers by selecting all the layers you want to transform, or linking or grouping them together, then choosing a transform command. The transformation effect will apply to all the layers at once. You can even transform different types of layers — for example, a text layer and a bitmap layer — at the same time.

You can also move a layer as you transform it. Move the cursor inside the bounding box, and you see it change to an arrow cursor. You can then click and drag to move the layer contents around the canvas.

> **TIP** Hold down Alt (Option on the Mac) while selecting a command from under Edit ⇨ Transform to automatically create a duplicate of the layer and transform the duplicate, leaving the original untouched.

> **CAUTION** You cannot transform a layer that has its position locked or that is fully locked. Unlock the layer first before applying the transform. For the same reason, you cannot transform the Background layer, as it is permanently locked. Turn the Background layer into a normal layer first. Find out more about locking layers and converting the Background layer in Chapter 2.

Moving the reference point

Every transform command features a *reference point* about which the transformation occurs. For example, when you rotate a layer, the layer rotates around its reference point, as you can see in Figure 3.3. The reference point is shown by a circle with crosshairs. By default the reference point is in the center of the object or selection you're transforming, but you can move it to anywhere you want — even outside the object.

FIGURE 3.3

Rotating a layer around its reference point

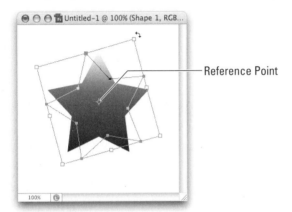

To move the reference point, simply click it with the mouse and drag, as shown in Figure 3.4. You can also use the reference point locator in the transform command's options bar, also shown in Figure 3.4, to move the reference point to a preset point on the object — a corner, the center of an edge, or back to the center of the object. Click one of the little squares in the reference point locator to move the point. The black square indicates the current location of the point.

TIP You can also drag the reference point to the center of the bounding box, a corner of the box, or the center of an edge on the box. The reference point will snap to one of these points when you move it close enough.

FIGURE 3.4

Moving the reference point. Click the reference point and drag it, or use the reference point locator to snap the point to a preset position.

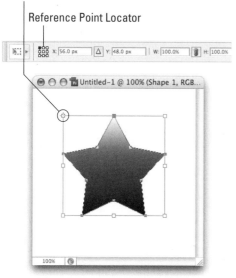

Committing or canceling a transformation

While you're using a transform command and the bounding box is visible, you are in "transform mode" and most of Photoshop's menu options are disabled. To exit the transform mode, you need to either commit (confirm) your transformation or cancel it.

> **TIP** Although many menu options are disabled, you can still navigate around your document using the Navigator palette (to view this palette choose Window ➪ Navigator) and use the corresponding keyboard shortcuts (for example, hold the Spacebar and drag in the document window to move around). You can also zoom in and out. This is worth knowing if you happen to be transforming a layer that's too big to fit in the current window.

 To commit your transformation, press Enter (Return on the Mac) or click the check mark button in the transform command's options bar. You can also double-click the transformed object to commit your changes.

 To cancel your transformation and return your layer to its previous state, press Esc or click the Cancel Transform button next to the check mark button in the options bar.

TIP While transforming a layer, you can undo the last change you made from within the transform command by choosing Edit ➪ Undo, or pressing Ctrl+Z (⌘+Z on the Mac).

By the way, Photoshop lets you flip between any of the transform commands before you commit your transform. So you can choose Edit ➪ Transform ➪ Scale to do a bit of scaling, then add some rotation by choosing Edit ➪ Transform ➪ Rotate. When you're satisfied, press Enter (Return on the Mac) to commit the transform. This is particularly useful when working with bitmap layers, because you're effectively applying multiple transformations in just one step, and therefore minimizing the degradation in quality.

Repeating a transformation

Need to apply the exact same transformation more than once? Simply choose Edit ➪ Transform ➪ Again or press Shift+Ctrl+T (Shift+⌘+T on the Mac). This shortcut is handy for applying the same transformation to different things such as a layer and a path, as shown in Figure 3.5. First, select the layer and apply the transformation to it; then select the path in the Paths palette and repeat the transformation.

FIGURE 3.5

Applying the same transformation to a layer (left) and to a path (right)

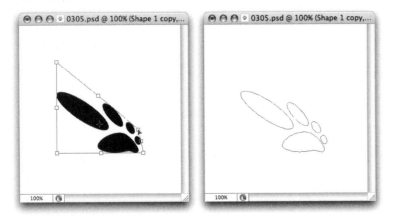

Scaling

The first transform command you're going to look at is the Scale command. This command lets you stretch or shrink a layer horizontally or vertically, or both at the same time. The Scale command works as follows:

- To scale a layer, select the layer then choose Edit ➪ Transform ➪ Scale. A bounding box with resize handles appears around the contents of the layer, as shown in Figure 3.6.

- To scale the layer horizontally, click and drag a resize handle on the left or right edge of the bounding box. Likewise, to scale vertically, drag a handle on the top or bottom edge of the bounding box.

- To scale horizontally and vertically at the same time, click one of the resize handles on the corners of the bounding box and drag. To preserve the proportions, or aspect ratio, of the layer as you resize it, hold down the Shift key while dragging a corner handle.

When you scale by dragging the resize handles like this, the reference point is ignored by default. To scale around the reference point, hold down Alt (Option on the Mac) while dragging. You can also combine this with the Shift key to scale proportionally around the reference point.

FIGURE 3.6

Scaling a layer vertically (left), proportionally (middle), and proportionally around its reference point (right)

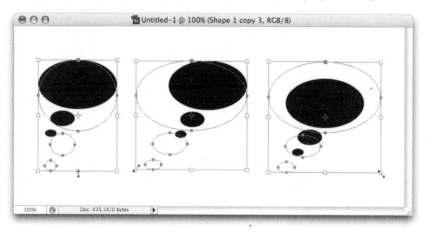

> **TIP** You can drag a resize handle past its opposite handle to flip the layer. For example, to flip horizontally, drag the resize handle on the right-hand edge left past the handle on the left-hand edge. You can also flip while preserving the layer's width and height by using the Flip commands (see the section "Flipping horizontally and vertically" later in the chapter).

Rotating

Photoshop lets you rotate a layer around its reference point (which is, of course, in the center by default). To do this, select the layer then choose Edit ➪ Transform ➪ Rotate. A bounding box appears around the contents of the layer, as shown in Figure 3.7.

FIGURE 3.7

Rotating a layer with the reference point in the middle (left) and with the reference point in the top-left corner (right)

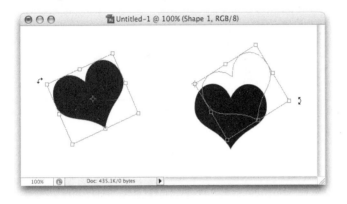

Move the cursor outside the bounding box and you see it change to a curved, double-headed arrow. You can now click and drag to rotate the layer about its reference point. Hold down the Shift key as you drag to constrain the rotation to 15-degree steps (handy if you want to rotate something by exactly 45 degrees, for example).

CROSS-REF Don't forget that you can rotate about any point (even a point outside the bounding box) by moving the reference point. See the section "Moving the reference point" earlier in this chapter.

Skewing

You can skew a layer, which means slanting it either vertically or horizontally. To skew, select the layer and choose Edit ➪ Transform ➪ Skew. The usual bounding box appears, with transform handles on the edges and corners of the box, as shown in Figure 3.8.

To skew the layer horizontally, click and drag the handle on either the top or bottom edge of the box. To skew vertically, drag the handle on the left or right edge of the box.

When skewing by dragging the edge handles like this, Photoshop ignores the reference point by default. To skew around the reference point instead, hold down Alt (Option on the Mac) while dragging.

TIP You can also distort a layer from within the Skew command (see the next section). Simply drag a corner handle rather than an edge handle to distort instead of skew. As with the Distort command proper, you can also hold down Alt (Win) or Option (Mac) while clicking a corner to pull the opposite corner symmetrically as well.

FIGURE 3.8

Skewing a layer horizontally (left) and horizontally around the reference point (right)

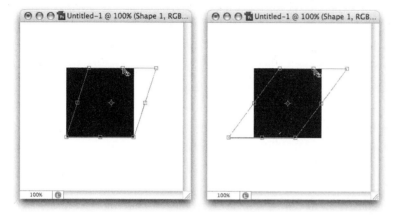

Distorting

The Distort command allows you to distort the shape of a layer by moving the corner points of the bounding box. To distort a layer, select it; then choose Edit ➪ Transform ➪ Distort to get the bounding box, as shown in Figure 3.9.

FIGURE 3.9

Distorting a layer

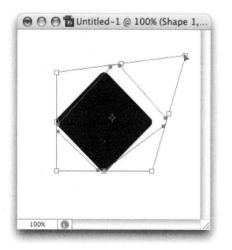

Click a corner handle of the bounding box and drag it to distort the layer. You can also hold down Alt (Win) or Option (Mac) while dragging a corner to pull the opposite corner symmetrically the other way. Alternatively, hold down Shift to constrain the distortion to one of the two edges adjacent to the dragged corner.

The position of the reference point is always ignored when using the Distort command.

You can do a Perspective transformation (which is really just a symmetrical distortion) by holding down Alt and Shift (Option and Shift on the Mac) while dragging a corner point. The adjacent corner point in the direction that you drag is then moved the opposite way, creating the perspective effect. You can see this in action in Figure 3.10.

FIGURE 3.10

Applying a Perspective transformation using the Distort command. Hold down Alt and Shift (Option and Shift on the Mac) and drag a corner.

You can also skew from within the Distort command (see the section "Skewing") by dragging an edge handle rather than a corner handle. Hold down Alt (Option on the Mac) to skew freely around the reference point, as shown in Figure 3.11. You can also hold down the Shift key to constrain the skewing to the line of the bounding box, which is, in fact, how the standard Skew command works.

Skewing via the Distort command. Drag an edge handle to skew freely, or Shift+drag an edge handle to constrain the skew.

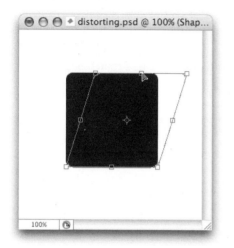

Applying perspective

You can apply a perspective effect to a layer using the Perspective transform command. Select the layer; then choose Edit ➪ Transform ➪ Perspective. Your familiar friend the bounding box appears, as shown in Figure 3.12.

Click a corner point and drag to apply the perspective effect. The adjacent corner point in the direction that you drag gets moved in the opposite direction, creating a narrowing or widening effect along that edge.

This transformation command is very handy if you've taken a photo at a steep angle and you want to correct the perspective to make the object of the photo look like it was shot straight on; see Figure 3.12 for an example.

FIGURE 3.12

Correcting perspective in a photograph with the Perspective command

 **TIP** You can also skew from within the Perspective command by dragging an edge handle rather than a corner handle. Hold down Alt (Option on the Mac) to skew around the reference point. The skewing is constrained to the line of the bounding box, much like the standard Skew command (see the "Skewing" section for more on Skew).

Warping

While the Distort command gives you some ability to distort the shape of your layer by dragging the corner points, the Warp command takes distortion to a new level. You can choose from a range of preset shapes to warp the layer into, or simply drag the control handles around to create your own unique warp effect.

To warp a layer, select it then choose Edit ➪ Transform ➪ Warp. Unlike the other transform commands, which give you a simple bounding box, the Warp command's bounding box contains a mesh of lines and has control points on each corner.

NOTE The reference point has no effect with the Warp command, and in fact is invisible when using it.

Warping with a preset shape

The easiest way to work with the Warp command is to choose a preset shape from the Warp Style pop-up menu in the options bar. This gives you a simplified version of the mesh, shown in Figure 3.13, with a single control point that you can drag to increase or decrease the amount of warping.

You can also control the amount of warping by typing a positive or negative percentage value into the Bend box in the options bar (negative values bend the shape in the opposite direction). The other boxes in the options bar, H and V, control how much horizontal and vertical distortion to apply at the same time. Positive H values make the right side of the grid taller than the left side; negative H values have the opposite effect. Similarly, positive V values make the bottom of the grid wider than the top; negative V values make the top wider than the bottom. The default values of 0 remove any distortion effect.

FIGURE 3.13

Warping a layer using the Arc shape from the Warp Style menu

To change the orientation of the preset warp shape, click the Change the Warp Orientation button in the Warp command's options bar. This flips the shape through 90 degrees. If you want to change the orientation by 180 degrees, simply drag the control point the other way, or type a negative value in the Bend box.

TIP If you like one of the preset shapes but want to tweak it more fully, select it from the Warp Style menu then select the Custom option from the same menu. This preserves the preset shape but gives you those lovely corner and control points, allowing you to really mess about with the shape, as the following section explains.

Custom warping

For finer control over the warp effect, choose Custom from the Warp Style pop-up menu in the options bar. The bounding box appears with the mesh and control points on each corner, as shown in Figure 3.14.

FIGURE 3.14

Custom-warping a layer using the Custom option from the Warp Style menu

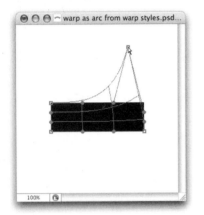

To warp the layer, you can do any or all of the following:

- Click anywhere in the mesh inside the bounding box and drag.
- Click a point on an edge of the bounding box, then drag to bend the edge around that point.
- Drag a corner point of the bounding box to move that corner.
- Click and drag the control points to change the shape of the bounding box edges. (These work in much the same way as the curve control points used with the Pen tool.)

NOTE The Bend, H, and V boxes in the options bar are unavailable when using the Custom option.

CAUTION For some reason, you can't warp a type layer that has any Faux Bold characters in it; the Edit ➪ Transform ➪ Warp menu option is disabled in this case. (However, you can warp Faux Italic characters.) In addition, Photoshop won't let you warp a type layer that contains fonts without outline data, such as bitmap fonts.

NOTE Warping a type layer with the Warp command is the same as using the Warp Text dialog within the Type tool. With both the Warp command and the Warp Text dialog, you can go back and reedit your warp effect at any time, with no loss in quality. Note that you can only warp type layers using the preset warp shapes; Custom is not available for type layers. For more on Warp Text, see Chapter 4.

Rotating by fixed amounts

If you just need to rotate a layer quickly through 90 or 180 degrees, you can choose Rotate 180°, Rotate 90° CW (clockwise), or Rotate 90° CCW (counterclockwise) from the submenu under Edit ⇨ Transform. These commands are also very handy when you know that you need to rotate precisely 90 or 180 degrees.

Flipping horizontally and vertically

You can flip a layer horizontally or vertically by choosing Edit ⇨ Transform ⇨ Flip Horizontal or Edit ⇨ Transform ⇨ Flip Vertical. This is great when you need to flip a photo to better fit a layout, as shown in Figure 3.15.

FIGURE 3.15

Flipping a photo to fit into the layout. The original photo (left) is flipped to fit the design (right) using the Flip Horizontal command.

NOTE Rotating by 180 degrees is not the same thing as flipping horizontally or vertically.

The Free Transform command

If you plan to perform more than one transformation on a layer at once — for example, scaling and rotating at the same time — you'll find Photoshop's Free Transform command very useful. This command also has its own keyboard shortcut of Ctrl+T (⌘+T on the Mac), making it quicker to access than the regular transform commands.

Free Transform lets you carry out scaling, rotation, skewing, distortion, and perspective transformations all in the one command. You can also flip quickly between Free Transform and Warp, so you have access to pretty much all of the transform commands at the same time.

To access this command, select the layer you want to transform then choose Edit ➪ Free Transform, or press Ctrl+T (⌘+T on the Mac). The familiar bounding box appears around the layer's contents, as shown in Figure 3.16.

CROSS-REF You can also access the Free Transform command from within the Move tool by enabling the Show Transform Controls option in the Move tool's options bar. For more on this feature, see Chapter 2.

FIGURE 3.16

Transforming with the Free Transform command

TIP Press Ctrl+Alt+T (⌘+Alt+T on the Mac) to create a duplicate of the layer and transform the duplicate, leaving the original untouched.

- **Scaling:** Resizing a layer works in exactly the same way as the Scale command. Click a resize handle on an edge or corner and drag to resize. Hold down the Shift key to resize proportionally. Hold down Alt (Option on the Mac) to resize about the reference point.

- **Rotating:** Again, rotation works exactly like the Rotate command. Move the mouse cursor outside the bounding box until the cursor changes to a double-headed arrow, then click and drag to rotate. Hold down Alt (Option on the Mac) to rotate in 15-degree steps.

- **Skewing:** To skew from within the Free Transform command, hold down Ctrl (⌘ on the Mac), then click an edge handle and drag.

TIP Skewing this way allows you to skew freely, which means that you can drag the edge handle up, down, left, and right. To constrain the skewing to the line of the bounding box so that it behaves exactly like the Skew tool, hold down the Shift key as well.

- **Distorting:** To distort a layer when using Free Transform, hold down Ctrl (⌘ on the Mac) and then click and drag a corner handle. Ctrl+Alt+drag (Win) or ⌘+Option+drag (Mac) a corner to pull the opposite corner symmetrically in the other direction. Or

Ctrl+Shift+drag (⌘+Shift+drag on the Mac) a corner to constrain the distortion to one of the two edges adjacent to that corner.

- **Perspective:** To apply perspective, hold down Ctrl+Alt+Shift (⌘+Option+Shift on the Mac) and then click and drag a corner handle. The adjacent corner handle in the direction that you drag moves in the opposite direction to create the perspective effect.

- **Warping:** To warp a layer from within the Free Transform command, click the Switch Between Free Transform and Warp Modes button in the Transform command's options bar. The bounding box switches to a bounding box and mesh, and the Warp command options appear in the options bar. After you finish warping your layer, you can switch back to the Free Transform command by clicking the button again.

Measuring Transformations

While you're using a transform command, you can view the changes that you're making numerically in the Info palette. To access this palette, choose Window ⇨ Info or press F8. While you're doing a transformation, this palette changes to show you the numeric values of your transformation, as shown in Figure 3.17.

FIGURE 3.17

Viewing a transform numerically with the Info palette

Top W and H values

Show the current width
and height as a percentage
of the original.

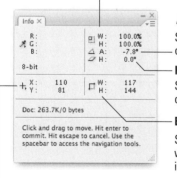

A.

Shows the amount
of rotation in degrees.

H/V.

Shows the amount
of skew in degrees.

Bottom W and H values.

Show the current
width and height
in absolute units.

X and Y values

Show the coordinates
of the top left corner
of the transformed layer.

The values include the following:

- **Top W and H:** These show you the current width and height of your transformed layer as a percentage of the original width and height.

- **A:** This figure shows you, in degrees, how much your layer has been rotated. A positive value indicates a clockwise rotation, while a negative value indicates a counterclockwise rotation.

- **H/V:** This shows you the degree of skew of your layer, either horizontally or vertically.

- **Bottom W and H:** These values show you the actual width and height of your transformed layer in the current Rulers unit of measurement.

- **X and Y:** These figures, to the left of the bottom W and H values, display the coordinates of the top-left corner of the layer you're transforming. Zero values for both X and Y represent the ruler origin which, by default, is the top-left corner of the document window.

TIP   To change the Ruler's measurement unit, choose Edit ➪ Preferences ➪ Units & Rulers (Photoshop ➪ Preferences ➪ Units & Rulers on the Mac) then pick a value from the Rulers pop-up menu. Alternatively, choose Palette Options from the Info palette menu then pick a value from Ruler Units in the dialog box that appears.

CROSS-REF   Find out how to change the ruler origin in Chapter 2.

Transforming by Numbers

With Photoshop, you're not limited just to viewing your transforms numerically — you can alter them numerically, too. You may have noticed lots of numeric boxes in each transform command's options bar, as shown in Figure 3.18. These options allow you to have precise, numeric control over your transformations. If you need to transform your layer by small, precise amounts then typing numbers is often easier than dragging by hand with the mouse.

FIGURE 3.18

The numeric transform options in the options bar

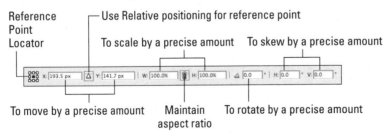

Reference Point Locator

Use Relative positioning for reference point

To scale by a precise amount   To skew by a precise amount

To move by a precise amount   Maintain aspect ratio   To rotate by a precise amount

To change these values, click in one of the boxes and edit the value. You can also double-click in a box to select it, then type a new value.

In addition, like pretty much all numeric fields in Photoshop, you can adjust the field values by fixed amounts using the mouse. Move the mouse over the field label to the left of the box until the mouse cursor changes to a pointing finger with a double-headed arrow. Click and hold the mouse button and move the mouse to the right to increase the value, or to the left to decrease it. For the boxes that use length and percentage units, the values change in steps of 1; for the boxes that use angle units (rotation and skew), the values change in steps of 0.1 degrees.

TIP   Hold down Alt (Option on the Mac) to change the values in steps of 0.1 (for length and percentage units) or to change the values more slowly (for angle units). You can also hold down Shift to change the values in steps of 10 (for length and percentage units) or 1 (angle units).

Moving by a precise amount

You can move the layer you're transforming by a precise amount horizontally, vertically, or both at the same time.

First, make sure the reference point is in the center of the bounding box, or on an edge or corner. You'll know this is the case if one of the tiny squares in the reference point locator is black. If none of the squares is black, click one of them to make it black.

Now click in either the X or the Y box and edit the value in the box to move your layer. The value you're editing is the absolute position of the reference point, relative to the ruler origin (the top left-hand corner of the document by default).

CROSS-REF   Chapter 2 explains how to reposition the ruler origin.

It's often easier to move by a relative amount rather than having to deal with absolute values. To do this, click the Use Relative Positioning for Reference Point button between the X and Y boxes. Type positive values to move the layer to the right of or below its original position; use negative values to move it to the left of or above its original position.

TIP   By default, the X and Y values are in pixels, but you can use any unit you want by typing the unit symbol after the value. For example, to move the layer 3 inches to the right, select the Use Relative Positioning option and type 3in in the X box.

Moving the reference point precisely

The previous technique moves both the reference point and the layer at the same time. What you're really doing is locking the reference point to a specified point in the layer (for example, the center or the top-left corner). As you move the reference point, the layer moves by the same amount.

However, you can also precisely move the reference point independently of the layer. First, make sure that the reference point isn't locked to the layer; none of the little squares in the reference point locator should be black. To do this, click the reference point in the document window and drag it slightly so that it's no longer locked onto one of the nine points of the reference point locator. You should then see that all the little squares in the locator are white.

You can now type horizontal and vertical position values in the X and Y boxes to move the reference point independently of the layer, as shown in Figure 3.19.

FIGURE 3.19

Moving the reference point by typing values in the X and Y boxes

> **NOTE**   When moving the reference point independently in this way, the values are always relative to the ruler origin, which, by default, is the top left corner of the document.

Scaling by numbers

To adjust the size of the layer you're transforming, you can type values in the W (width) and H (height) boxes in the options bar. As with the X and Y boxes, the default units are pixels, but you can type other units into the boxes, too — for example, type **4cm** in the W box to make the layer contents 4 centimeters wide.

> **CROSS-REF**   If you want to see the current width and height in your chosen ruler units, rather than in pixels, look at the bottom W and H values in the Info palette. For more on this, see the section "Measuring Transformations" later in the chapter.

 By default, you can adjust the values in the W and H boxes independently. Alternatively, you can lock them together so that the layer's width and height scale proportionally. To do this, click the Maintain Aspect Ratio button between the W and H boxes. You can then type a value in one box, and the other value adjusts itself accordingly to maintain the layer's aspect ratio.

Rotating by numbers

△ 2d0 · You can control the rotation of your layer right down to steps of 0.1 degrees. To do this, type a rotation value (in degrees) in the Set Rotation box in the options bar.

NOTE   **Positive values rotate the layer clockwise; negative values rotate counterclockwise.**

This feature is very useful for those times when your layer is slightly out of whack and you just need to nudge it around by a couple of tenths of a degree. It's hard to make such small adjustments with the mouse.

Skewing by numbers

You can also adjust the amount of horizontal or vertical skewing of your layer, although skewing is often easier to do by eye and mouse.

Type a positive angle value (in degrees) in the H box to skew the top edge of the layer to the left and the bottom edge to the right. Type a negative value to skew the opposite way.

Typing a positive value in the V box skews the left-hand edge of the layer up and the right-hand edge down; negative values skew the other way.

NOTE   **The angle values that you type are the angle between the left and right edges and the vertical (H) and the top and bottom edges and the horizontal (V). For this reason, you can't type a value of 90 degrees, as this makes the layer infinitely long and thin. (Try typing a value of 89 degrees and notice the effect.)**

You can type values in both the H and V boxes to skew the layer horizontally and vertically at the same time, as shown in Figure 3.20.

FIGURE 3.20

Skewing a layer horizontally and vertically with the H and V boxes

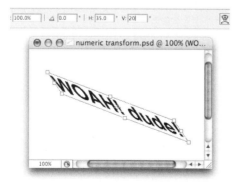

NOTE
You can also skew horizontally and vertically at the same time using the Skew command and the mouse. If you do this, Photoshop, rather than changing the values in both the H and V boxes, instead prefers to change just the H value and adjust the X, Y, W, H, and Rotation values (using some pretty scary math) to compensate. The end result is the same though.

Transforming Other Content

This book is about layers, so that's what this chapter concentrates on. However, the transform commands are so useful throughout Photoshop that we thought it best to touch on transforming stuff other than layers. Here's how to transform other things:

- To transform a selection, make your selection using one of the selection tools, then choose a transform command from Edit ⇨ Transform (or choose Edit ⇨ Free Transform). The selection is transformed along with the contents — for example if you stretch a selection, both the contents and the selection border (the "marching ants") stretch in unison.

TIP
To transform just the shape of the selection border without transforming the pixels inside the selection, choose Select ⇨ Transform Selection. This allows you to transform the selection using the Free Transform command (see the section "The Free Transform Command" earlier in the chapter). This is a great way to fine-tune the shape of a selection before you use it.

- To transform text while you're editing it, hold down Ctrl (⌘ on the Mac) to enter the Free Transform command. Click and drag to transform your text as desired, then release Ctrl (⌘) to return to text editing mode.

NOTE
You can only scale, rotate, and skew when using the Free Transform command in this way. You can't distort, apply perspective, or switch to the Warp command. If you need to warp text while remaining in text editing mode, click the Create Warped Text icon in the Type tool's options bar. (You can also choose Edit ⇨ Transform ⇨ Warp if you prefer warping with the mouse, but this takes you out of text editing mode.) If you want to distort a type layer or apply perspective to it, you need to rasterize the layer first.

- To transform a layer mask or vector mask, make sure the mask is unlinked from the layer (otherwise the layer contents will also be transformed), click the mask thumbnail in the Layers palette to select it, then choose your transform command.
- To transform a path or a shape, select the path or shape with the Path Selection tool, or select the appropriate path in the Paths palette, then choose a transform command.

TIP
You can also transform part of a path or shape. Use the Direct Selection tool to select just the part you want to transform (either by Shift+clicking anchor points or dragging over the anchor points you want to select), then choose your transform command.

- To transform an alpha channel, select the channel in the Channels palette then choose a transform command. (Make sure you have an active layer, and that the layer isn't hidden in the Layers palette, or Photoshop won't let you transform the selected alpha channel. It's a funny beast sometimes.)

Tutorial: Transforming Type Layers

The following example project showcases many of the transform commands in Photoshop. In this project, you create a flyer for a gallery invitation, and you're going to use the various transform commands to alter the typography in the flyer to get a nice end result.

The brief for this invitation to a new gallery is to keep the final artwork monochrome. The clients want "stark but exciting," using abstracts of the work on show, which are supplied. The clients want to use the Helvetica Neue Bold Compressed font for the type, as it's the font used for their other promotional materials. The clients also have a logo of a simple leaf shape they want to feature somewhere on the flyer, but there's no name for the gallery. That's the art world for you!

ON the CD-ROM As with all the examples in the book, you'll find the Photoshop files and image files for this tutorial on the accompanying CD-ROM.

Start by creating the basic invitation. To do this, follow these steps:

1. **Create a canvas and import the background image.** Choose File ➪ New, and create a new document in portrait format. Now import and position the dandelion image. Positioning the image off-center, as shown in Figure 3.21, allows the composition to use the classic "rule of thirds" and also to make space for your copy to come.

FIGURE 3.21

Start off with a nice silhouette of a dandelion, positioned off-center to make room for your flyer text to come.

2. **Add the text using the required font.** Add each line of text on a separate layer, so that you can transform them individually later on. The result looks OK, as you can see in Figure 3.22, but it's not very exciting. It doesn't have the drama that the clients are looking for.

Adding your basic text. Each line of text is on its own type layer, so you can manipulate the lines of text individually.

3. **Rework your type layers into a nice, justified block of text, as shown in Figure 3.23.** To do this, select each type layer in turn, and choose Edit ➪ Transform ➪ Scale to stretch the text out to the right width. Hold down the Shift key as you drag, so that the letters retain the correct proportions.

4. **Group your type layers.** Now that you have your block of text looking good, group the type layers together so that you can easily transform them as one object. To do this, select all the type layers, then choose Layer ➪ Group Layers, or press Control+G (⌘+G on the Mac) to group them into a new layer group. Photoshop gives the group a name such as Group 1, but you might like to rename it to something like Text so you can refer to it more easily.

By using the Scale command on each line of text, you get a nice, justified block of text that looks a tad more exciting.

Once your type layers are in a group, you can try resizing the block of text as a whole. Select the group in the Layers palette; then choose either Edit ➪ Transform ➪ Scale or Edit ➪ Free Transform. Free Transform's generally a better bet, as it's more versatile; plus you can select it quickly by pressing Ctrl+T (⌘+T on the Mac). Experiment with making the text bigger and smaller, and try dragging the text around the document window to position it around the imagery. Again, if you want to retain the text's proportions, hold down Shift as you resize. You can see some examples in Figure 3.24. The small text is cute and elegant, and the big text, positioned off the bottom of the invitation, is quite brave.

Here you've experimented with different sizes of text by transforming the group of type layers with the Scale command.

Your invitation is looking better, but that text still needs some drama added to it. Cue the remaining transform commands. To try these out, select the group, then choose a command under Edit ➪ Transform. If you don't like an effect, you can always choose Edit ➪ Undo or skip back in the History palette. Here's a take on the various commands:

- The Skew command (shown in Figure 3.25) gives the type a nice pop art feel, but that's not the tone you're after here. Combining an alternative skew and a rotation — which you can do all from within the Free Transform command — provides an interesting alternative effect.

- The Distort command (see Figure 3.26) is nice, but it doesn't work here from a composition point of view. (It would be great for adding text to a photo of a shop front taken from one side, though, for an interesting play on signage.)

- The Perspective command gives you the hilarious *Star Wars* effect shown in Figure 3.26, but unfortunately the client's not looking for comedy.

- The Warp command is great fun, as you can see in Figure 3.26, and provides a quirky alternative to the other more conservative effects.

FIGURE 3.25

Using the Skew command (left) and skewing and rotating with Free Transform (right) gives you a bit of a pop art look.

FIGURE 3.26

Here you've done some more experimenting on the text, using the Distort command (left), the Perspective command (right), and the Warp command (bottom).

Looking back at these examples, the Distort command produced the most promising result, but the composition was all wrong. Try selecting the dandelion layer, then using Edit ➪ Transform ➪ Flip Horizontal to flip the image over. That looks better. A quick nudge of the type layers group and you have a good result, as shown in Figure 3.27. The flyer has drama, and the branding element is used subtly in the top-left corner. This is the one to show the client.

 Layer comps can be invaluable when doing this kind of experimentation. See Chapter 11 for more on this topic.

FIGURE 3.27

Flipping the image over and nudging the text a bit gives you a pretty good end result.

Summary

In this chapter, you learned how to transform the contents of your layers using Photoshop's many transform commands. You've taken a brief look at transforming bitmap layers versus transforming vector shapes, and discussed some of the basics of layer transformations, including the reference point and how to commit and cancel transformations.

You explored each transform command in turn, including Scale, Rotate, Skew, Distort, Perspective, Warp, the fixed-amount rotation commands, and the Flip Horizontal and Vertical Commands. You also looked at Free Transform, which lets you apply many of these different transformations in the one command.

You learned how to measure transformations, as well as how to apply transforms numerically for greater precision. You also looked at transforming other content apart from layers, including selections, text, masks, paths, shapes, and channels. Finally, Photoshop's transform commands were demonstrated with a simple, practical example.

Part II

Exploring Special Layer Types

Chapter 4

Creating Text with Type Layers

In many areas, Photoshop has improved in leaps and bounds from one version to the next, and its Type tool is a prime example. In fact, the Type tool in CS3 is so smooth, powerful, and easy to use that it's almost a different animal compared to its ancestors. In version 4, for example, once you created your type layer, that was it — you were stuck with it. If you spelled something wrong, forgot to capitalize a letter, or used the wrong font, you had to start over.

Thankfully, those days are long gone, and with CS3 you have a Type tool to rival even a word processor or publishing package, with features such as:

- **In-place editing:** In the early days, you had to type your text into a separate dialog box, which was a drag. Now you can type and edit text directly on the canvas — what you see is 100 percent what you get.

- **Totally re-editable type:** You can go back and change the wording of your text as many times as you want. Even if you add effects and warp the text out of all recognition, it's still editable!

- **Vector type layers:** By default, the Type tool stores text as vectors in special type layers, which means you can scale, rotate, or skew your type layer as much as you want without losing any quality.

- **A range of advanced character formatting features:** These include a plethora of kerning options, control over leading, a choice of anti-aliasing methods, and a range of faux (simulated) styles such as bold, italic, superscript and subscript — great if the font you're using doesn't have these by default. Best of all, you can change all this formatting on a per-character basis.

- **Full paragraph formatting controls:** You can adjust alignment, justification, indenting, and hyphenation.

- **Type can follow the curves and lines of a path:** You can even make text flow inside a closed path or shape.

- **Conversion of type to shapes or paths:** Take your type layer and convert the letters to individual shapes that you can then bend and twist to your heart's content.

- **Rasterizing of type:** Convert a type layer to an old-school bitmap layer so you can edit its pixels individually.

- **Spell check:** Adobe throws in a spell checker and a search-and-replace feature. Can't say fairer than that!

What is a Type Layer?

Type layers are covered briefly in Chapter 1, but this chapter goes into a little more detail. A type layer is a special kind of layer designed specifically for storing type. You can't put anything else on a type layer, but that's rarely a problem — just group the type layer with your nontype layers and you can then treat them as a single layer if you need to.

 If you really want to put other stuff on a type layer, convert it to a normal layer first by choosing Layer ⇨ Rasterize ⇨ Type.

The big leap from fixed to editable type in version 5 was made possible because these special type layers are vector layers. Normal layers are made up of pixels; it's hard to go back and reedit a normal layer if you want to change any text on it. In contrast, the characters in a type layer are made up of vectors — lines and curves — that are much easier to modify after they've been created.

Apart from these important differences, type layers behave much like normal layers: You can duplicate them, drag them around with the Move tool, change their order in the Layers palette, change their opacity, use layer masks on them, and so on.

You can easily spot a type layer in the Layers palette by its big letter "T" in its thumbnail, as shown in Figure 4.1.

 A really quick way to select all the type in a type layer is to double-click the "T" in the layer's thumbnail. Photoshop even helpfully switches to the Type tool if you're not already using it.

FIGURE 4.1

A type layer in the Layers palette

| T | A Type Layer |

Adding a Type Layer

In this section, we take a look at how to add a type layer to your document. We don't go into massive detail here; the steps are covered in more detail and other features of the type tools are discussed later in the chapter.

To create a new type layer, follow these steps:

1. **Select the Type tool.** To do this, click the Type Tool icon (the letter "T") in the Toolbox, or press T. There are, in fact, four different variants of the Type tool; to choose a tools, hold down the mouse button over the Type Tool icon and choose from the pop-up menu, or press Shift+T to cycle through the tools. The available tools are:

   - **Horizontal Type tool:** This is the one you'll probably use most often if you're typing Western text. It creates a new type layer with the text flowing left to right and working down the page, in the traditional Western fashion.

   - **Vertical Type tool:** This tool creates a new type layer with text flowing top to bottom and working right to left. This makes it perfect for writing text in East Asian languages such as Chinese, Japanese, and Korean. You can also use it with Western type to create interesting stylistic effects.

   - **Horizontal Type Mask tool:** This writes in the same direction as the Horizontal Type tool, but rather than creating a new type layer it creates a mask, or selection, from the text. In all other respects it behaves like the Horizontal Type tool. After you create your type mask you can use it to mask off other layers, fill it with color, and so on. However, you can't reedit your text later as you're not creating a vector type layer, which limits this tool's usefulness.

   - **Vertical Type Mask tool:** As you might have guessed, this tool behaves like the Vertical Type tool but produces a type mask instead of a type layer. Both Type Mask tools are covered in the section "Creating Type as a Mask" later in this chapter.

TIP You can also create a mask from a type layer at any point by Ctrl+clicking (⌘+clicking on the Mac) the type layer's thumbnail (letter "T") in the Layers palette. In fact, this is generally a better idea than using the Horizontal and Vertical Type Mask tools, because you can always reedit your type layer in the future and create a new mask from it if necessary. You can't go back and edit the type in a type mask.

NOTE As the Horizontal Type tool is probably the type tool you use most, it is assumed you're using this tool in the rest of this chapter unless otherwise specified. By the way, you can flip a type layer between horizontal and vertical type at any time by choosing Change Text Orientation from the Character palette menu, or clicking the Change Text Orientation button in the Type tool's options bar.

2. **Choose a font, style, and size.** Pick a font family from the Font Family menu in the options bar — this menu shows all the fonts that are currently installed on your computer — and choose a style (for example, Bold or Italic) using the Font Style option. Finally, set your type size using the Font Size option. This option controls the height of the characters in your text. Type a value in the box, or pick a value from the list. Figure 4.2 shows these three options. You'll learn about them in detail later in the chapter.

FIGURE 4.2

Choosing a font, style and size in the Type tool's options bar

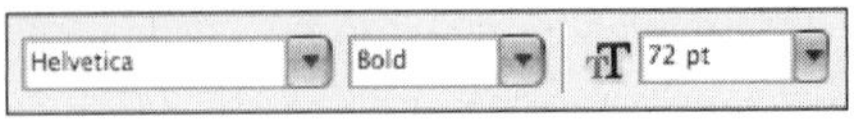

| Helvetica | ▼ | Bold | ▼ | 𝐓 | 72 pt | ▼ |

3. **Place the type.** Next, decide where you want to place the text in your document window, and click that point with the mouse. You can start typing straight away, or you can hold the mouse button and drag to create a box in the window, then type in the box. Each method produces a different flavor of type, as follows:

   - If you just click, you're creating *point type*, so called because you're typing text at a specific point in your document. Point type is best for short pieces of text, such as a title. Although you can press Enter (Return) to spread the text over more than one line, each line behaves independently of the others; Photoshop doesn't treat them as belonging to one paragraph.

   - If you click and drag a bounding box before typing, you're creating *paragraph type*. This form of type is better suited to longer paragraphs of text, such as the body text of a brochure. The bounding box defines the shape that the text should take, and Photoshop flows the text as paragraphs within that box.

CROSS-REF Find out more about point type versus paragraph type, including how to convert between the two, in the section "Point type and paragraph type" later in this chapter. You can also create type on a path, which is super cool. Learn more about this in the section "Type on a Path" toward the end of the chapter.

TIP If you click or drag on an existing type layer in the document window, Photoshop assumes you want to edit that type layer, rather than create a new layer. If you want to create a new type layer on top of an existing type layer, Shift+click or Shift+drag in the document window instead.

NOTE As soon as you click or drag in the document window, a new type layer appears in the Layers palette. For now, it will be called something boring like Layer 1, but after you finish typing Photoshop changes its name to the first 30 characters of the text that you entered.

4. **Enter your type.** A flashing cursor, called the *insertion point*, appears at the point where you clicked or started dragging. Type away or, if you prefer, you can copy text from another application and paste it at the insertion point by choosing Edit ➪ Paste or pressing Ctrl+V (⌘+V on the Mac). You can also cut or copy text from what you've already typed. Of course, you can erase any mistake you make as you're typing by pressing Backspace (Delete on the Mac) to delete the character to the left of the insertion point, or Delete (Forward Delete on the Mac) to delete to the right of the insertion point.

CAUTION Most of the options in the main menu are dimmed while you're entering type. Either commit or cancel your edits (see the section "Committing your edits") to access the menu options again.

TIP You can move your type layer around the document window even while you type your text. Simply hold down Ctrl (⌘ on the Mac) to switch to the Move tool, then drag your text around with the mouse. Release the Ctrl/⌘ key to continue typing.

5. **Commit your edits.** When you're satisfied with what you've typed, you're ready to *commit* the type, which simply means telling Photoshop that you've finished typing and you want to keep it. As usual, Photoshop gives you a myriad of ways to commit your type — use whichever of the following methods feels right for you:

   - You can click the check mark button in the options bar.

   - You can press Enter on your number keypad.

   - If the number keypad is a bit too far away right now, you can press Ctrl+Enter (⌘+Return on the Mac) instead.

   - Finally, you can commit your type simply by selecting another tool in the Toolbox, choosing a menu option, or clicking anywhere in the Layers, Channels, Paths, Actions, History, or Styles palette.

You might decide that your text isn't worth keeping. In that case, you can cancel your edits by doing one of the following:

- Clicking the Cancel button to the left of the check mark button in the options bar.

- Pressing Esc on your keyboard.

Selecting Type

The joy of Photoshop's type layers, of course, is that you can go back and edit the type after you create the layer. This section looks at how you can select existing type for editing.

Photoshop's pretty versatile when it comes to letting you select type. You can select anything from a single letter all the way up to all the type layers in your document at once.

You can edit any type layer by selecting one of the type tools (it doesn't matter which one) then clicking with the I-beam cursor on the type in the document window. This takes you into edit mode; the flashing insertion point appears where you clicked in the type. To exit edit mode, commit or cancel your edits (see the section "Adding a Type Layer").

While you're in edit mode, you can select a bunch of text by clicking and dragging with the mouse, or by using one of the keyboard selection methods.

 Appendix B includes all of the Photoshop keyboard shortcuts for selecting and editing text. If you use type layers a lot it's worth learning these shortcuts as they can save you a bundle of time.

To select all the text in a type layer while in edit mode, choose Select ➪ All or press Ctrl+A (⌘+A on the Mac). If you're not in edit mode, double-click the type layer's thumbnail in the Layers palette to enter edit mode and select all the text at the same time.

Most of the formatting options in the Character and Paragraph palettes (see the sections "Formatting Characters" and "Formatting Paragraphs") can be applied to whole type layers or even multiple type layers. To select more than one type layer, Ctrl+click (⌘+click on the Mac) each layer. You can then apply your formatting options, and they are applied across all your selected layers at once. This is great for making sweeping changes, such as font face and size, across your whole document.

TIP If you want to change some formatting across all type in your document, select one of your type layers, choose Select ➪ Similar Layers, and then choose your formatting options.

Working with Point Type and Paragraph Type

Photoshop features two distinct ways that you can enter type into your document: point type and paragraph type.

Creating point type

Point type is best suited to short pieces of text, ideally on a single line — for example, headings, titles, labels, and, if you're building Web pages, menu options.

To create a new layer of point type, select the Type tool and click the point in your document window where you want your type to appear. (You can always move it around later.) Then start typing, as shown in Figure 4.3.

FIGURE 4.3

Creating point type. Each line of text in point type behaves independently.

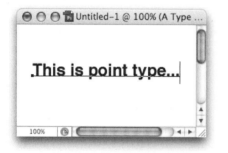

As you type, notice that the type always stays on the same line. In fact you can continue typing past the edge of your document and it just keeps on going — the type is still being entered, even if you can't see it all. If you want the type to go across more than one line, press Enter (Return on the Mac) at the end of each line as you type.

You may also notice a small square next to the type you entered, at the point where you clicked on the canvas, and a line extending from that point across the page. This line is the *baseline* of your text. As you can see in Figure 4.4, the baseline is the horizontal line on which the characters of the type are placed. Each font also has a *waistline*, also known as its *midline* or *x-height*, which is usually a line drawn through the top of the letter "x" in that font. Some characters in a font have an *ascender*, which is the bit that rises above the midline, and some, such as the letters "j" and "y", have a *descender*, which is the bit below the baseline.

After you finish entering your point type, commit or cancel your edits (see the section "Adding a Type Layer" earlier in the chapter).

TIP If you later decide that the type layer you create should be formatted as paragraph type instead, select the layer, then choose Layer ⇨ Type ⇨ Convert to Paragraph Text. Note that this option is unavailable if you're already in Edit mode — you need to commit or cancel your edits first.

FIGURE 4.4

The anatomy of a typeface. Each font generally has a baseline and a waistline, and letters in the font often have an ascender (which rises above the waistline) or a descender (which falls below the baseline).

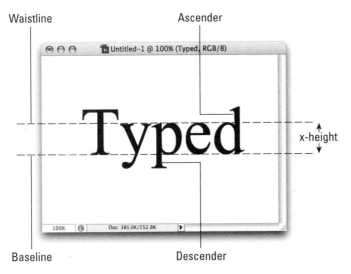

Creating paragraph type

The alternative to point type is the more powerful paragraph type. As you've probably guessed, it's better suited to paragraphs of text, such as brochure copy and body text.

To create paragraph type, choose the type tool that you want to use from the Toolbox, click in the document window where you want the type to start; then drag out a box with the mouse. This box is the *bounding box*, and it defines the margins of your paragraphs of type. When you're happy with the size and shape of the box, release the mouse button and start typing, as shown in Figure 4.5.

TIP You can also create paragraph type by Alt+clicking (Option+clicking on the Mac) in the document window. This displays a Paragraph Text Size dialog, allowing you to enter the width and height of the bounding box numerically, using any units you like (for example, you can type 10cm or 5 picas). This feature is great if your type layer needs to fit into a predefined area.

Creating paragraph type is similar to entering text in a word processor. As you type, you'll notice that the text wraps automatically once it reaches the edge of the bounding box. If you want to start a new paragraph, simply press Enter (Return on the Mac) a couple of times and continue typing.

You can change the size and shape of the bounding box at any time while typing your text. To do this, click one of the eight resize handles at the corners and edges of the box, and drag. Any text that you've already typed automatically reflows to fill the new dimensions of the box.

FIGURE 4.5

Creating paragraph type. Text flows in paragraphs when in paragraph type mode, controlled by the bounding box around the text.

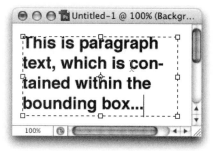

CROSS-REF In keeping with the word processor analogy, you can control various paragraph formatting settings, such as alignment, justification, and hyphenation, using the Paragraph palette. These options are covered in detail in the section "Formatting Paragraphs."

TIP You can convert paragraph type to point type at any time by selecting the type layer then choosing Layer ⇨ Type ⇨ Convert to Point Text. This splits your paragraphs into individual lines of point type. (This only works if you're not currently editing your text.)

Formatting Characters

Photoshop gives you a wide range of options for tweaking the look of the letters in your type, including:

- Font, style, and size
- Leading (the vertical gap between lines of text) and kerning (the horizontal gap between individual letters)
- Tracking (the horizontal gap between letters in entire blocks of text)
- Horizontal and vertical scaling of the type
- Baseline shift (the distance of letters from their baseline)
- Color of the type
- The type of anti-aliasing (smoothing) to use on the letters

NOTE The words "letter" and "character" are often used interchangeably in this book. Strictly speaking, a *letter* is a character in the alphabet that you're using, while a *character* is anything that you can type (numbers, hyphens, the copyright symbol, and so on).

You can control all these formatting options through the Character palette, as shown in Figure 4.6. To access this palette (and the Paragraph palette, which is covered later), click the Toggle Palettes button in the Type tool's options bar (shown in Figure 4.6). You can also choose Window ⇨ Character. Many of the options are also available through the Type tool's options bar, which is often quicker and easier to access.

If you're editing some type and want to access the Character palette quickly, press Ctrl+T (⌘+T on the Mac). Be careful though, as this only works if you're in Edit mode; if you're not, then you'll end up doing a Free Transform — probably not what you expected!

FIGURE 4.6

The options bar for the Type tool (top) and the Character palette, containing a wealth of character-formatting options (bottom)

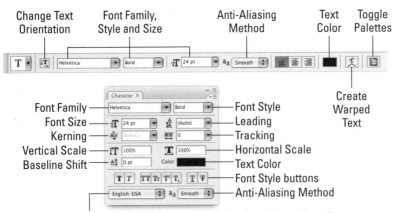

> **TIP**   You can access and use the Character palette from anywhere, not just from within the Type tool. For example, you can change the font used in a type layer by selecting the layer then choosing a font from the Character palette. This works even if you happen to be using the Brush tool at the time, for example.

> **TIP**   If you've just applied some particularly wacky formatting to a piece of text, you can quickly return the Character palette to its default values to save having to go through all the options and returning them to normal. To do this, choose Reset Character from the Character palette menu. (Make sure you haven't selected any type, or it resets the type, too.)

You can apply any of the character formatting options in the Character palette to individual characters, words, lines, whole paragraphs, or the entire type layer. Simply select the text that you want to apply the formatting to; then choose an option from the palette. If you have nothing selected, the option you choose applies to any text that you type from that point onward.

The remainder of this section looks at each of the options in the Character palette.

Choosing a font

The Font Family option, shown in Figure 4.6, is available in both the options bar and in the Character palette, and lets you choose a font from all the fonts installed on your system. By the way, a *font family* is a group of fonts that all share the same typeface (for example, Times New Roman) but with different sizes and styles. The terms *font* and *font family* are often used interchangeably.

To the right of each font name in the list is the word "Sample" written in that font, so you can see what it looks like. To the left of the name is a small icon that tells you whether the font is an OpenType font, a Type 1 font, or a TrueType font. Most of the time you probably don't need to know (or care) which type of font you're using, but if you want the gory details see the section "Font formats."

If you know the name of the font you want, simply click inside the Font Family control and type the first few letters of the font name. Photoshop auto-completes the font name, at which point you can just press Enter (Return on the Mac) to select the font.

TIP You can change the size of the "Sample" text next to each font name in the list. To do this, choose Edit ➪ Preferences ➪ Type (Photoshop ➪ Preferences ➪ Type on the Mac) and select Small, Medium, or Large for the Font Preview Size option (the default is Medium). You can also turn off the "Sample" text completely by deselecting the check box to the left of this pop-up menu.

TIP To find out how to install new fonts on your system, consult your system's user manual or online help.

Using smart quotes

By default, Photoshop uses *smart quotes* (also known as typographer's quotes) when you type text. These are the opening and closing curly quotes and the curly apostrophe, and they're generally nicer to read than straight quotes and apostrophes.

If you prefer the straight versions, however, you can turn off smart quotes. To do this, choose Edit ➪ Preferences ➪ Type (Photoshop ➪ Preferences ➪ Type on the Mac), and deselect the Use Smart Quotes option.

NOTE This setting only applies to text that you type from then onward; it doesn't change existing text.

Missing a font?

If you don't have a font installed that's needed for a document at the time you open it, Photoshop lets you know with the alert box shown in Figure 4.7. You then find that all type layers with missing fonts have a warning triangle symbol next to the "T" in their thumbnails.

Houston, we have a font problem.

You can leave the layers as they are, but they're basically bitmap layers at that point, with all the associated drawbacks (noneditable type, blockiness when scaling, and so on). If you need to turn them back into type layers, you have two choices:

■ Find the missing font (shown in the Type tool's options bar when you select the type layer) and install it. After it's installed, restart Photoshop, open the document again, and all will be well.

■ If you don't have the missing font, you need to use a suitable replacement. Double-click the type layer's thumbnail to switch to Edit mode and select all of the text; a dialog box appears warning you about font substitution. Click OK, and Photoshop replaces the missing font with its best-guess replacement (which will probably look nothing like the original). You can then select the relevant text and select a different font for it from the Font Family option in the options bar.

Font formats

At the time of writing there are three major formats of fonts in common usage: Type 1, TrueType, and OpenType. You can spot the format of a font by looking at the symbol to the left of the font name in the Font pop-up menu. Following is a brief look at each of these three formats.

Type 1

Type 1 fonts (also known as Adobe Type 1 and PostScript Type 1) are the oldest format of the three. The format was created as part of Adobe's PostScript page description language in the early 1980s. Adobe charged a lot of money to license the Type 1 technology in those days, which gave rise to the development of TrueType as an alternative (see the next section). Until the release of Windows 2000 and Mac OS X, you had to install a program called Adobe Type Manager if you wanted your Type 1 fonts to look decent on the screen. Support for Type 1 is now built into both of these operating systems.

Although Type 1 fonts are still often used, the Type 1 format isn't nearly as popular as it used to be due to the inroads made by TrueType and OpenType in the last ten years.

TrueType

Apple developed the TrueType font technology in the late 1980s, primarily as an alternative to Adobe's Type 1 format. Apple then licensed TrueType to Microsoft, and with Microsoft building TrueType support into Windows 3.1 it rapidly became the most common format used on PCs and Macs in the 1990s.

TrueType allows for more flexible hinting than Type 1, but it's also generally regarded as being harder to work with when creating fonts. In addition, many of the TrueType fonts available today are simply automatic conversions of Type 1 fonts, which means they can look a bit rough round the edges (literally) and don't take advantage of TrueType's advanced hinting capabilities.

NOTE *Hinting* (in font-speak) means adding instructions, or hints, to a font so that it looks good when displayed on low-resolution bitmap devices (such as a computer screen).

CAUTION If you ask a room of typographers which is the better format — Type 1 or TrueType — be prepared for a lively debate, and make sure you know where the nearest exit is in case things turn nasty.

OpenType

Billed as the successor to both Type 1 and TrueType, OpenType began life at Microsoft in the early 1990s. It was originally known as TrueType Open. Adobe joined forces with Microsoft on the project in early 1996, renaming the technology OpenType in the process.

Since then, OpenType has evolved continuously, and is currently in the process of becoming an open ISO standard (known as the Open Font Format).

OpenType fonts offer a number of significant advantages over Type 1 and TrueType fonts, including:

- **Platform-independent:** The same font file will work across Windows, Mac OS, and some UNIX-based systems.
- **Unicode encoding:** This means there is support for a wider range of languages and character sets.
- **Support for proper treatment of unusual typographic features:** Features such as ligatures (special characters used for certain pairs of letters) and swashes (flourishes used on certain letters) are supported.
- **Smaller size:** An OpenType font file is generally smaller than its equivalent Type 1 file.

OpenType looks to be the font format of the future, and both Windows and Mac OS X already ship with a wide variety of OpenType fonts preinstalled. Both operating systems support OpenType out of the box.

NOTE Fonts without icons next to their names are usually bitmap fonts (fonts without outlines) or fonts in some other format.

Font styles

The Font Style option in the options bar and Character palette — shown in Figure 4.6 — allows you to pick from the available styles for your selected font. Usually, you are able to choose from Regular, Italic, Bold, or Bold Italic. However, some fonts have only one or two styles, and many have no available styles at all.

Faux font styles

If your chosen font doesn't ship with bold or italic styles, no problem — Photoshop can simulate these styles for you. The results aren't as good as built-in font styles, but they're good enough for most uses. These simulated styles are known as *faux* styles (French for "fake", in case you were wondering).

 To apply a faux bold style, click the Faux Bold button at the bottom of the Character palette, or choose Faux Bold from the Character palette menu. You can also press Ctrl+Shift+B (⌘+Shift+B on the Mac) while editing text.

To apply faux italic, click the Faux Italic button at the bottom of the Character palette, or choose Faux Italic from the Character palette menu. Alternatively, press Ctrl+Shift+I (⌘+Shift+I on the Mac) while editing text.

NOTE If you use one of the previous keyboard shortcuts to apply faux bold or italic and the current font has a built-in bold or italic style, Photoshop applies the built-in style instead.

All Caps and Small Caps

You can format your text as All Caps or Small Caps. All Caps formats the entire text as uppercase characters, while Small Caps formats the text by replacing uppercase letters with big capital letters, and lowercase letters with small capital letters.

 To apply All Caps formatting to your text, click the All Caps button at the bottom of the Character palette, or choose All Caps from the Character palette menu. You can also press Ctrl+Shift+K (⌘+Shift+K on the Mac) while editing text.

 To apply Small Caps formatting instead, click the Small Caps button at the bottom of the Character palette, choose Small Caps from the Character palette menu, or press Ctrl+Shift+H (⌘+Shift+H on the Mac) while you're editing text.

NOTE When formatting text as Small Caps, Photoshop uses the font's built-in Small Caps style, if available; otherwise it creates a faux Small Caps style out of the font's capital letters and uses that instead.

Superscript and subscript

Superscript and subscript text is small text placed above or below the baseline, commonly used in chemical formulae and mathematical equations.

To apply a superscript style, click the Superscript button at the bottom of the Character palette, or choose Superscript from the Character palette menu. You can also press Ctrl+Shift and the + key (⌘+Shift and the + key on the Mac) while in text editing mode.

 To apply a subscript style, click the Subscript button at the bottom of the Character palette, or choose Subscript from the Character palette menu. Alternatively, press Ctrl+Alt+Shift and the + key (⌘+Option+Shift and the + key on the Mac) while editing text.

NOTE When formatting superscript and subscript text, Photoshop uses the font's built-in superscript and subscript characters, if it has any. If they're not available, Photoshop generates faux superscript and subscript letters.

TIP If you're not happy with the position of a superscript or subscript character, you can always adjust it by tweaking the baseline shift value. See the section "Shifting the Baseline" later in the chapter for more information. Of course, you can also create the superscript or subscript character on its own type layer to give you total control over the positioning; you can then link it with the original type layer so they move around together.

Underlined and strikethrough text

You can underline some text, or strike a line through the middle of the text, via the Underline and Strikethrough styles.

 To underline text, click the Underline button at the bottom of the Character palette, or choose Underline from the Character palette menu. Alternatively you can press Ctrl+Shift+U (⌘+Shift+U on the Mac) while editing text.

NOTE If you're formatting vertical text, the Underline option in the Character palette menu is replaced with two options — Underline Left and Underline Right — that allow you to choose which side of the text to place the underline.

To strike through text, click the Strikethrough button at the bottom of the Character palette, or choose Strikethrough from the Character palette menu. You can also press Ctrl+Shift+/ (slash) (⌘+Shift+/ on the Mac) while you're in text editing mode.

TIP You can mix and match many of these styles at the same time — for example, you can apply faux bold, faux italic, small caps, and superscript all at once.

OpenType features

As mentioned in the section "Font formats," many OpenType fonts support advanced typography features such as ligatures and swashes. If you use an OpenType font that supports one or more of these features, you can turn the features on and off by selecting an option under OpenType in the Character palette menu:

- **Standard and Discretionary Ligatures:** These are single-character replacements for certain letter combinations such as "fl" and "ct" (the exact combinations that are replaced depend on the font). An example of type with discretionary ligatures is shown in Figure 4.8. Standard ligatures are generally designed to enhance readability, while discretionary ligatures are more for ornamental purposes.

FIGURE 4.8

Type in an OpenType font with discretionary ligatures disabled (top) and enabled (bottom)

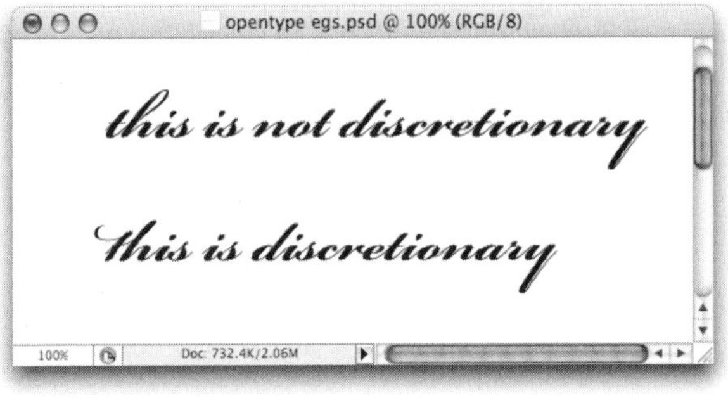

> **NOTE** Although the two letters may appear to be one character when using ligatures, they are still treated internally as separate characters in Photoshop for the purposes of spell-checking and so on.

- **Contextual Alternates:** These are often used in script (handwriting) typefaces to join letters together where appropriate. They produce a really nice flowing effect when enabled, and usually enhance legibility.

- **Swashes:** A swash is a stylized letter with big swirling flourishes. You can see an example of a swash in Figure 4.9.

FIGURE 4.9

Swashes in action. The top example has the Swashes option disabled; in the bottom example, it's enabled.

- **Oldstyle:** This option enables alternative old-school numerals, which are usually shorter and drop below the baseline.

■ **Stylistic Alternates:** These provide alternative characters to the defaults, usually for purely aesthetic reasons. Figure 4.10 shows a type example with stylistic alternates enabled.

FIGURE 4.10

This example shows off the stylistic alternates available in this OpenType font. The top example shows the standard font; the bottom example shows the same font with the Stylistic Alternates option enabled.

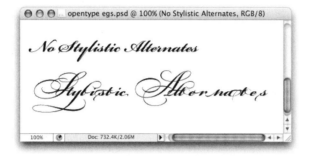

■ **Titling Alternates:** These are characters designed for use in titles; they are usually capitals and are often lighter in weight than the standard capitals.

■ **Ornaments:** Ornaments include features such as decorative borders and dividers.

■ **Ordinals:** This option converts the letters after ordinal numbers (such as the "st" after "1st") to proper superscripted characters.

■ **Fractions:** This converts typed fractions (such as "1/2" and "1/3") into proper fraction symbols.

■ **Asian OpenType options:** These are only displayed in the menu if you have enabled the Show Asian Text Options preference (see the following tip). The options — Japanese 78, Expert and Traditional; Proportional Metrics; Kana; and Roman Italics — are mainly concerned with choosing alternate Japanese glyphs and with tweaking text layout when using Asian fonts.

 If you work with Chinese, Japanese, or Korean type, Photoshop provides you with a few extra options in the Character and Paragraph palettes, including tsume for controlling the spacing around glyphs, tate-chu-yoko for rotating glyphs within vertical type, and the OpenType options just described. These options are hidden by default; to enable them, choose Edit ⇨ Preferences ⇨ Type (Photoshop ⇨ Preferences ⇨ Type on the Mac) and select the Show Asian Text Options check box.

NOTE If an OpenType font doesn't support any of the previous OpenType features, the OpenType option in the Character palette menu is grayed out.

Although you probably won't use these advanced OpenType features most of the time, they're a lovely way to add a really snazzy look to any type that you produce in Photoshop — handy if you're producing brochures and the like.

Setting font sizes

The Font Size option in the options bar — also available in the Character palette, shown in Figure 4.6 — controls the height of the characters in your text. Font size is measured from the top of the highest ascender in the font to the bottom of the lowest descender. You can pick a preset value from the list or double-click in the Font Size box and type a value yourself.

TIP You can also increase the current font size by 2 pixels, 2 points, or 1mm (depending on the type unit you're using) by pressing Ctrl+Shift+. (period) (⌘+Shift+. on the Mac), and decrease by 2 pixels, 2 points, or 1 mm with Ctrl+Shift+, (comma) (⌘+Shift+, on the Mac). Hold down the Alt key (Option on the Mac) as well to change the font size by 10-pixel, 10-point, or 5mm increments.

Font sizes are measured in pixels (px), points (pt), or millimeters (mm), depending on the default type unit. To change this unit, choose Edit ➪ Preferences ➪ Units & Rulers (Photoshop ➪ Preferences ➪ Units & Rulers on the Mac), or press Ctrl+K followed by Ctrl+7 (⌘+K then ⌘+7 on the Mac). You can pick your new value from the Type pop-up menu.

If you want to enter a font size in a different unit from the default, just type **px**, **pt**, or **mm** after the font size value and the size is automatically converted into the correct unit. For example, if your default type unit is pixels, type **12pt** in the Font Size box and it is converted to the correct font size in pixels (depending on the resolution setting of the current document).

NOTE There are 72 points in an inch, so if you work at a document resolution of 72 pixels per inch (the default) then 1 point = 1 pixel.

TIP There's another way to change the font size — in fact, this works for any numerical value in Photoshop. Simply click in the box; then use the up-arrow and down-arrow keys to change the value in steps of 1. Hold down the Shift key at the same time to change the value in steps of 10.

Setting line spacing (leading)

The Leading option controls the amount of vertical space, or leading, between each line of text, as shown in Figure 4.11. This space is measured from the baseline of a line of text to the baseline of the line of text above it.

NOTE The term *leading* (rhymes with "wedding") harks back to the days of nondigital printing presses. In order to space the type out vertically so that it didn't look cramped, strips of lead were inserted between each line of type.

Pick a leading value from the Leading pop-up menu, or double-click in the Leading box and type the value you want to use. The values are always measured in the default type unit (see the section "Setting font sizes").

FIGURE 4.11

Examples of type with different leading values

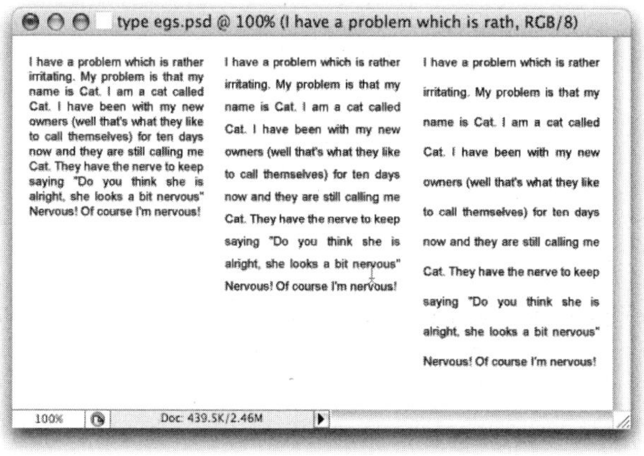

You can also select Auto, which automatically sets the leading in proportion to the current font size. The default value is 120 percent of the font size, which is good for most situations. If you need to change this, first switch to the Paragraph palette by clicking its tab or choosing Window ⇨ Paragraph, then select Justification from the Paragraph palette menu. You can then type a new percentage value in the Auto Leading box.

NOTE The Auto Leading setting only affects the currently selected type (or future type that you enter). So, for example, you can have two bits of text both using the Auto leading option, but with different Auto Leading values, resulting in different actual spacing.

When adjusting leading, remember that it's the gap between the current line of type and the line above. So if you want to adjust the leading between two lines, you need to select all the characters on the lower line and then adjust the leading value. Of course, if you want to adjust the leading for an entire type layer, simply select all the type on the layer then set the leading value.

NOTE If you specify several different leading values for different letters on a single line of type, Photoshop uses the largest of the leading values to determine the overall leading for that line, which is what you'd expect really.

TIP You can also adjust leading while editing text by pressing Alt+up-arrow and Alt+down-arrow (Option+up-arrow and Option+down-arrow on the Mac). This adjusts leading up and down in 2-pixel, 2-point, or 1mm increments.

Adjusting the kerning between letters

When you work with a proportionally spaced font (which most fonts are), you probably noticed that certain letter pairs don't look good together. For example, the "A" and "W" in the word "AWE" often have too much space between them (see Figure 4.12).

The reason for this is that the characters in proportionally spaced fonts have fixed left and right boundaries, known as *sidebearings*, that are used to separate one letter from the next. This generally results in an even spacing, but with certain pairs of letters, such as the "A" and "W" in this example, you really want the top of the "W" to sit over the foot of the "A" — in other words, you need the two letters to overlap slightly.

FIGURE 4.12

Examples of the word "AWE" in Times New Roman with no kerning (top), Metrics kerning (middle), and Optical kerning (bottom)

This is where kerning comes in. By adjusting the kerning, or horizontal spacing, between pairs of letters, you can make sure that the gap between each letter looks pleasing, no matter what combinations of letters you use.

NOTE   Another history lesson: *Kerning* originally referred to small corners cut out of letter blocks in the traditional printing press. The corners were cut in such a way that would allow, for example, the letters "A" and "W" to overlap slightly. The word "kern" probably comes from the old French word "carne," which means corner.

Automatic kerning

Although you can adjust the kerning manually between each pair of letters (see the section "Manual kerning"), this is a pain if you try to kern entire paragraphs of text. Much better to use one of Photoshop's automatic kerning features:

- **Metrics:** This is the best option if it's available. It uses kerning information built into the font itself to determine which letter pairs need kerning, and by how much.

- **Optical:** This adjusts the kerning by looking at the shapes of the letters to try to guess how much they should overlap. It doesn't always get it right, but it's your best bet when the Metrics option isn't available — for example, the font doesn't contain kerning information, or you're mixing and matching two fonts in the same word.

To get an existing block of text to use Metrics or Optical kerning, select the block of text then choose Metrics or Optical from the Kerning option in the Character palette, shown in Figure 4.6. If you don't select anything, the kerning option you choose is applied to text you type from that moment on.

Manual kerning

If neither of the automatic options works for you, you can always adjust your kerning manually. To do this, click between the two characters you want to kern then choose a numeric value from the Kerning option. You can also click in the Kerning box and type a value manually if you prefer. Positive values add more spacing between the letters, while negative values make the letters overlap. A value of 0 means no kerning is applied.

> **TIP** You can also adjust manual kerning while editing text by pressing Alt+left-arrow and Alt+right-arrow (Option+left-arrow and Option+right-arrow on the Mac). This adjusts the kerning value for the pair of letters on either side of the insertion point up and down in increments of 20. Hold down the Shift key at the same time to adjust the value in increments of 100.

Setting horizontal spacing (tracking)

Whereas kerning looks at the spacing between each pair of letters, tracking evenly adjusts the spacing between all letters in the text. It's the horizontal equivalent of leading.

Tracking is handy if you want to create spaced-out letters for artistic reasons, or make a line of text stretch out to fill a set width, as shown in Figure 4.13.

Setting the tracking is similar to setting kerning or leading. Type a value in the Tracking box, or select a value from the pop-up menu. If you select some type first, the tracking value applies to all the letters in your selection; otherwise, it applies to any type you enter from that point on.

FIGURE 4.13

Type with the default tracking value of 0 (top) and with a tracking value of 300 (bottom)

> **TIP** You can adjust the tracking of a block of selected text by pressing Alt+left-arrow and Alt+right-arrow (Option+left-arrow and Option+right-arrow on the Mac). This adjusts the tracking value for the selected text up and down in increments of 20. Hold down Shift at the same time to adjust the value in increments of 100.

> **NOTE** In case you're wondering what the values in the Kerning and Tracking boxes represent, they're measured in thousands of an em space. An *em space* is a unit of measurement that's proportional to the current font size: 1 em in a 12-point font equals 12 points, 1 em in a 14-point font is 14 points, and so on. This means that the values are always proportional to the font size that you're currently using, which is what you want for consistency.

Stretching and squeezing type

You can stretch and squeeze characters in your type to make them appear thinner or fatter. This can create some eye-catching effects, as shown in Figure 4.14.

To do this, change the values in the Vertically Scale and Horizontally Scale boxes in the Character palette (shown in Figure 4.6). A value of 100 percent means no scaling; 200 percent makes the characters twice as tall (vertical scaling) or wide (horizontal scaling); 50 percent makes the characters half as tall or wide, and so on.

You can tweak either the horizontal scaling or the vertical scaling, or both at the same time. To quickly return the horizontal scaling back to 100 percent press Ctrl+Shift+X (⌘+Shift+X on the Mac). Likewise, to reset the vertical scaling to 100 percent press Ctrl+Alt+Shift+X (⌘+Option+Shift+X on the Mac). These keyboard shortcuts only work while you're editing text.

> **CROSS-REF** If you just want to make characters bigger or smaller and keep their normal proportions, change the font size for those characters. See the section "Setting font sizes" earlier in this chapter for more details.

> **CROSS-REF** You can also scale the entire type layer horizontally or vertically (and do a lot more besides) using the Free Transform command. See Chapter 3 for the full picture.

Creating interesting type effects with scaling

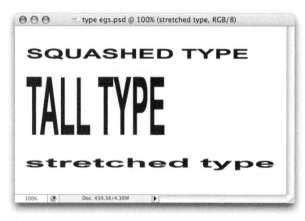

Shifting the baseline

The Baseline Shift option in the Character palette — shown in Figure 4.6 — lets you control the vertical position of individual characters. This is great for fine-tuning superscript and subscript characters, and also for lining up characters in picture fonts such as the Webdings font. Figure 4.15 shows some examples of baseline shifting.

Characters with varying baseline shift values

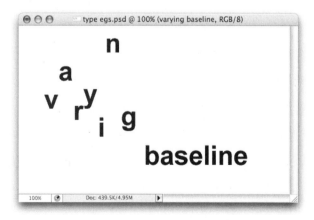

To adjust the baseline shift, type a value in the Baseline Shift box in the Character palette. As with the Font Size box, the default type unit is used, or you can type **px**, **pt**, or **mm** after your value to specify a different unit. To remove the baseline shift and return the type to its normal position, type a value of 0.

> **TIP** You can also adjust baseline shift while editing text by pressing Alt+Shift+up-arrow and Alt+Shift+down-arrow (Option+Shift+up-arrow and Option+Shift+down-arrow on the Mac). This adjusts the baseline shift up and down in 2-pixel, 2-point, or 1mm increments. Hold down Ctrl (⌘ on the Mac) at the same time to adjust the value in increments of 10 pixels, 10 points, or 5mm.

Choosing a type color

You can select a color for your type by clicking the Text Color box in the options bar or in the Character palette, as shown in Figure 4.6. The standard Photoshop Color Picker dialog box appears, allowing you to choose the color you want to use.

You can also choose a new foreground color using the Foreground Color box in the Toolbox, the Color palette, or the Swatches palette, and this new foreground color will be used as the type color, too.

Finally, you can select some type then press Alt+Backspace (Option+Delete on the Mac) to change the type to the current foreground color, or Ctrl+Backspace (⌘+Delete on the Mac) to change it to the current background color.

> **NOTE** When you create a new type layer, Photoshop uses the current foreground color as the default color for the type.

> **TIP** As with most of the options in the Character palette, you can change the color of existing text by selecting it first then picking a color, or you can choose a color for your text before you start typing it. If you change the color of selected text, you might want to press Ctrl+H (⌘+H on the Mac) to hide the highlight effect on the selected text, so you can see the selected text in its proper color.

Smoothing type with anti-aliasing

Although Photoshop stores type as resolution-independent vectors, at the end of the day the type still needs to be rendered as pixels on a bitmap display (your computer screen) or printed using a series of dots on the paper. The process of converting the vector type to pixels invariably introduces *aliasing*, or a jagged staircase effect, as each pixel has to approximate the smooth lines and curves of the vector type.

Fortunately, Photoshop provides a way to reduce the effect of these jagged edges: anti-aliasing. This works by blending the edge pixels of the type with the background to create the impression of a smoother edge.

Photoshop gives you no less than four different anti-aliasing methods, or you can opt for no anti-aliasing. To choose your method, use the Anti-Aliasing Method option in the Type tool's options bar or in the bottom right corner of the Character palette, shown in Figure 4.6. The options work as follows:

- **None:** This option turns off anti-aliasing altogether — your type will look as blocky as the day it was born.

- **Sharp:** This smoothes the type in a way that emphasizes the sharp edges of the characters.

- **Crisp:** This provides a similar effect to Sharp, but it's not quite so full-on.

- **Strong:** This option emphasizes the thick parts of the characters to produce a strong, slightly bold effect.

- **Smooth:** Use this option to give a smoother, more rounded appearance to the type.

Examples of some of these anti-aliasing methods are shown in Figure 4.16.

FIGURE 4.16

The same character with different anti-aliasing methods applied: None (left), Smooth (middle), and Strong (right). We've zoomed in so you can see the effect more clearly.

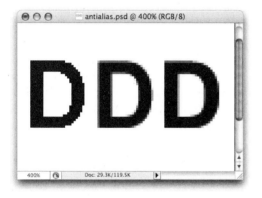

Usually, you'll want to anti-alias your type; however, the None option can be useful for very small font sizes, where anti-aliasing can muddy the text and reduce legibility. Another situation where anti-aliasing can cause problems is with saving images in GIF or PNG-8 format for the Web; anti-aliasing increases the number of colors in the image substantially, which can result in large file sizes when using these image formats.

NOTE The anti-aliasing setting applies to the whole of the type layer; you can't specify anti-aliasing on a character-by-character basis.

Controlling fractional widths

If you're working with on-screen fonts at small font sizes — 20 pixels or less, for example — you'll find that the gaps between letters aren't always consistent. Figure 4.17 shows an example of this. It's caused by Photoshop computing the gaps between letters using fractional numbers that then get rounded randomly up or down so that they can be displayed as pixels on the display.

FIGURE 4.17

Small type with fractional widths enabled (top) and disabled (bottom). Notice how the spacing between the bottom "tail" of one "a" and the start of the next "a" is consistent when fractional widths are turned off.

You can fix this by turning off fractional widths: Deselect the Fractional Widths option in the Character palette menu. The letters will now always line up evenly.

Using system text handling

This feature is handy if you design graphical user interfaces (GUIs) and need to match the text used by your operating system for rendering labels, menus, buttons, and other widgets. Enable it by selecting the System Layout option in the Character palette menu, and the currently selected type layer will be rendered using the operating system's text handling methods.

Preventing unwanted word breaks

Sometimes you want to make sure that certain groups of words stay on the same line, as shown in Figure 4.18. You can do this in Photoshop by selecting the words that you want to keep together and selecting No Break from the Character palette menu. Photoshop then makes sure that the group of words you select is not split at the end of a line, moving the entire group to the start of the next line if necessary.

Rotating letters in vertical type

Normally, Photoshop creates vertical type with each letter being the same way round as it is in horizontal type — that is, upright. Photoshop calls this Standard Vertical Roman Alignment.

If you prefer, you can rotate the letters by 90 degrees, so that they face down the page. To do this, deselect the Standard Vertical Roman Alignment option in the Character palette menu.

Figure 4.19 shows the difference between these two styles.

FIGURE 4.18

A paragraph with No Break disabled (top) and enabled (bottom). The text "Royal Society for the Protection of Type" was selected; then the No Break option was enabled.

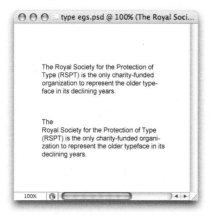

FIGURE 4.19

Type with Standard Vertical Roman Alignment disabled (left) and enabled (right)

Formatting Paragraphs

With Photoshop, you can apply a variety of word-processor-style paragraph formatting to your type. You can control the following:

- Alignment and justification of your type
- Left and right indents
- Paragraph spacing (the amount of space between paragraphs)
- Automatic word hyphenation
- Composition (how your paragraphs are laid out)
- Amount of spacing between words and letters
- Hanging punctuation (punctuation outside margins)

All these options are available via the Paragraph palette, as shown in Figure 4.20. To access this palette, click the Toggle Palettes button in the Type tool's options bar (shown in Figure 4.6) or choose Window ➪ Paragraph from the main menu. You can also access the text alignment options from the options bar.

 TIP If you want to access the Paragraph palette quickly while editing type, press Ctrl+M (⌘+M on the Mac). This only works if you're in Edit mode; outside of Edit mode, it displays the Curves dialog box.

FIGURE 4.20

The Paragraph palette (and duplicated alignment buttons in the options bar) allows you to control your paragraph formatting.

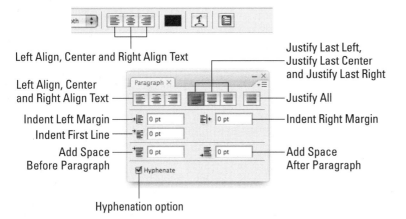

TIP As with the Character palette, you can access the Paragraph palette from within any tool. For example, from within the Brush tool you can change the justification of a type layer by selecting the layer then choosing a justification option from the Paragraph palette.

TIP You can quickly return the Paragraph palette to its default settings. To do this, choose Reset Paragraph from the Paragraph palette menu. (Make sure you haven't selected any type and that you don't have a type layer selected, unless you want to reset the selected type to the default settings, too.)

The paragraph formatting options in the Paragraph palette operate on whole paragraphs of text, not on individual characters. Click in the paragraph that you want to format, and select an option from the Paragraph palette. The formatting is then applied to that paragraph. To format more than one paragraph, select all the paragraphs with the keyboard or mouse; then select your formatting option from the palette.

Some of the Paragraph palette functions — such as justification and hanging punctuation — are only available when you edit paragraph type. If you're typing or editing point type they're disabled. If you want to use these functions, first convert your point type to paragraph type by choosing Layer ➪ Type ➪ Convert to Paragraph Text.

NOTE Each line in point type is treated as a separate paragraph for the purposes of paragraph formatting.

The following sections explore each of the formatting options in the Paragraph palette.

Aligning type

You can left-align, center, or right-align your type by clicking the alignment buttons in the options bar or in the Paragraph palette (shown in Figure 4.20).

Click the Left Align Text button to align your text on the left (this is the default alignment). The left-hand edge of the text lines up with the margin, leaving the right-hand edge ragged. You can also press Ctrl+Shift+L (⌘+Shift+L on the Mac) while editing text.

Click the Center Text button to center your text horizontally, leaving both edges of the paragraph ragged. You can also press Ctrl+Shift+C (⌘+Shift+C on the Mac) while editing text.

Click the Right Align Text button to align your text on the right. The right-hand edge of the text lines up with the right-hand margin, leaving the left-hand edge ragged. You can also press Ctrl+Shift+R (⌘+Shift+R on the Mac) while editing text.

NOTE If you're working with vertical type then the type is aligned vertically rather than horizontally, and the Left Align Text and Right Align Text buttons are replaced with Top Align Text and Bottom Align Text, respectively.

Justifying type

Justifying a piece of type means lining up both the left and right edges of the type with their respective margins, as shown in Figure 4.21. Photoshop is flexible in its justification options, giving you a lot of control over the look of your type. To control justification using the Justify buttons in the Paragraph palette (refer to Figure 4.20), do the following:

FIGURE 4.21

A paragraph of text with (top row, left to right) no justification, last left justification and last centered justification, and (bottom row, left to right) last right justification and all (force) justification.

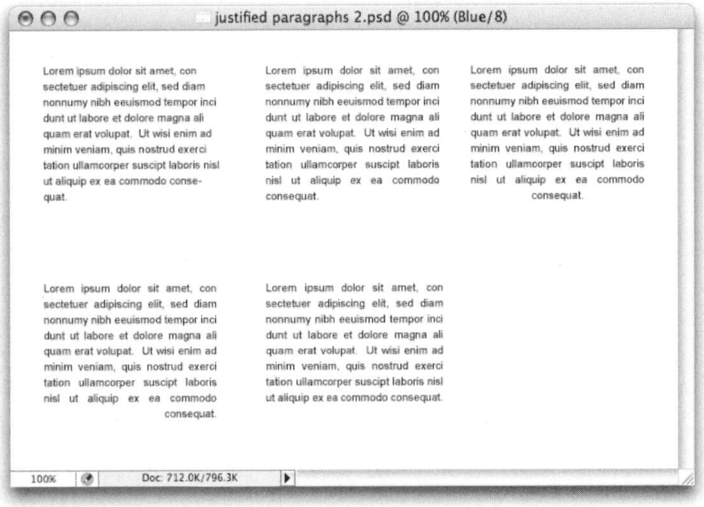

- Click the Justify Last Left button to justify all lines in the paragraph except the last line. The last line is aligned left instead.

- Click the Justify Last Centered button to justify all lines in the paragraph except the last; the last line is centered instead.

- Click the Justify Last Right button to justify all lines in the paragraph except the last one, which is aligned right instead.

- Click the Justify All button to justify all lines in the paragraph, including the last line. (This is also known as *force justification*.) If the last line is very short then this can produce odd results, with large gaps between words on the last line. However if you use it on a single-line paragraph then it can be a handy way to evenly space several words (or the letters of a single word) across the entire width of the paragraph.

TIP To remove justification from a paragraph, select one of the alignment buttons (left, center, or right) instead.

TIP You can enable Justify Last Left with the keyboard shortcut Ctrl+Shift+J (⌘+Shift+J on the Mac), and Justify All with Ctrl+Shift+F (⌘+Shift+F on the Mac). Only these two justification options have keyboard shortcuts.

Indenting paragraphs

Photoshop gives you control over indentation on a paragraph-by-paragraph basis. By using the Indent options in the Paragraph palette (refer to Figure 4.20), you can specify how much to indent the left margin of the paragraph, the right margin, and the first line of the paragraph. (The default values of 0 mean no indenting.) Try the following:

■ Type an amount to indent the left margin of the paragraph into the Indent Left Margin box and press Enter (Return on the Mac). The whole paragraph is indented by that amount relative to the left-hand edge of the bounding box.

■ Type an amount to indent the right margin into the Indent Right Margin box then press Enter (Return on the Mac). The paragraph is indented by that amount relative to the right-hand edge of the bounding box.

■ Type an amount to indent the first line of the paragraph into the Indent First Line box and press Enter (Return on the Mac). The left margin of the first line only is indented by that amount relative to the left-hand edge of the bounding box.

TIP You can also *outdent* (move outside the bounding box) the left margin, the right margin, or the first line. Simply type a negative value into the appropriate box. This is particularly handy for outdenting the first line of text, also known as creating a hanging paragraph.

NOTE All the values for indentation — and for paragraph spacing, which is described in the next section — are specified in the current type unit (pixels, points, or millimeters), but you can override the unit by typing px, pt, or mm after the value.

NOTE When working with vertical type, Indent Left Margin indents the top margin, Indent Right Margin indents the bottom margin, and Indent First Line indents the top margin of the first line.

Adjusting the space between paragraphs

You can also control the amount of vertical space before and after each paragraph of type. The default for both settings is 0, which means no space. The values add together, so if you have 10 pixels of vertical space below one paragraph and 10 pixels of space above the paragraph below, the total gap between the two paragraphs is 20 pixels. To add vertical space, do the following:

- Type the amount of vertical space to add before the paragraph into the Add Space Before Paragraph box in the Paragraph palette — shown in Figure 4.20 — then press Enter (Return on the Mac).

- To add vertical space after the paragraph as well, type the amount into the Add Space After Paragraph box in the Paragraph palette — shown in Figure 4.20 — and press Enter (Return on the Mac).

TIP   **You can quickly set the vertical space to the same amount for all paragraphs — which is usually what you want to happen — by selecting the type layer in the Layers palette then typing a value in one of the paragraph spacing boxes.**

Controlling hyphenation

Photoshop's hyphenation features can automatically insert hyphens to break certain words at the ends of lines, as shown in Figure 4.22. Depending on the family and size of font you're using, and the nature of the text you typed, this can result in a more pleasing look to the text. On the other hand, you probably don't want any hyphenation for short blocks of text, in which case you can turn automatic hyphenation off completely.

FIGURE 4.22

A paragraph of text without hyphenation (top) and with hyphenation enabled (bottom)

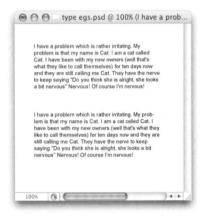

To turn hyphenation off or on, click the Hyphenate option at the bottom of the Paragraph palette, shown in Figure 4.20. As with most of the other paragraph formatting options, the Hyphenate setting applies to the paragraph that the cursor is currently in or, if you've selected multiple paragraphs or the whole type layer, it applies to all those paragraphs.

You can choose a dictionary to use for hyphenation (the same dictionary is also used for spell-checking). Naturally, this dictionary should be in the same language as the text you're typing for the hyphenation function to work properly. (Hyphenating a paragraph of English text using the Norwegian dictionary probably won't work out too well.) To choose the dictionary, flip over to the Character palette (Window ➪ Character) and pick a dictionary from the pop-up menu at the bottom of the palette, shown in Figure 4.6.

Generally, Photoshop does a good job of choosing when to hyphenate, but you can fine-tune its behavior by selecting Hyphenation from the Paragraph palette menu. This displays the Hyphenation dialog box, where you can tweak the following settings:

- **Words Longer Than:** This lets you specify the minimum word length (in letters) needed for hyphenation to occur. Words less than the specified length will never be hyphenated.

- **After First and Before Last:** Use these options to specify the minimum number of letters before and after a hyphen within a word. For example, a value of two letters for After First might hyphenate "elephant" as "el-ephant", whereas a value of three letters would force it to hyphenate on "ele-phant".

- **Hyphen Limit:** This setting controls how many consecutive lines can contain hyphens.

- **Hyphenation Zone:** With this setting you can control how close to the edge of the right margin a hyphen is allowed to get. For example, the default value of 3 picas ensures that Photoshop won't place a hyphen less than 3 picas from the right margin. This option only has an effect when using the Single-line Composer; the Every-line Composer does its own thing when it comes to placing hyphens near margins.

NOTE A *pica* is a typographic unit of measurement. There are 12 points in a pica and 6 picas in an inch.

- **Hyphenate Capitalized Words:** This specifies whether to allow hyphenation of words that start with a capital letter. You might want to turn this off to prevent proper names and words at the start of sentences from being hyphenated.

TIP You can see the effect of the values you're typing by selecting the Preview option in the dialog box. When enabled, glance at the document window to see how your new values will look when applied to your selected paragraph or paragraphs. When it's disabled you can see how your current hyphenation settings look for comparison.

Choosing a composition method

Photoshop can use one of two methods to decide when to break lines of text on the page: the Adobe Single-line Composer (which is the default) and the Adobe Every-line Composer. The difference between the two methods is quite subtle, and most of the time you'll probably be okay sticking with the default Single-line Composer, especially for short pieces of text. However, the Every-line Composer can give results that are more pleasing to the eye. Examples of the same paragraph with each composition method are shown in Figure 4.23.

FIGURE 4.23

A paragraph of text formatted with the Single-line Composer option (top) and the Every-line Composer option (bottom).

Both of these composition methods work in tandem with your chosen settings for hyphenation and justification.

To choose a composition method for a paragraph, select either Adobe Single-line Composer or Adobe Every-line Composer from the Paragraph palette menu.

The Single-line Composer

The Adobe Single-line Composer is the simpler of the two methods. It looks at individual lines of type in isolation to determine where to break lines.

First, it tries to tweak the spacing between words to fit the words on the line; if that doesn't work, it hyphenates the last word on the line. Finally, if hyphenation isn't appropriate it attempts to compress the spacing between letters or, as a last resort, expand the letter spacing.

The Every-line Composer

The more involved Adobe Every-line Composer looks at the "big picture" of the entire paragraph when deciding where to break lines. For example, it adjusts the line breaks near the top of the paragraph if it prevents a particularly hideous line break from occurring farther down the paragraph. This generally results in more even letter and word spacing throughout the paragraph, and requires less hyphenation.

The Every-line Composer tries to make the letter and word spacing in the paragraph as even as possible. However, it prefers creating uneven spacing to using hyphenation.

Adjusting word and letter spacing

Photoshop does its best to make the gaps between words and letters as sensible as possible; however, depending on the font, text size, and types of words you use you might want to tweak the amounts of word and letter spacing. This is especially true if you justify your type.

To control the word and letter spacing for a paragraph — or multiple paragraphs if you've selected a bunch of them or the whole type layer — choose Justification from the Paragraph palette menu. The Justification dialog box appears (shown in Figure 4.24), with options for minimum, desired, and maximum values for word spacing, letter spacing, and glyph scaling. There's also an Auto Leading box and a Preview option, which is covered in a minute.

FIGURE 4.24

The Justification dialog box gives you control over word and letter spacing in your paragraphs.

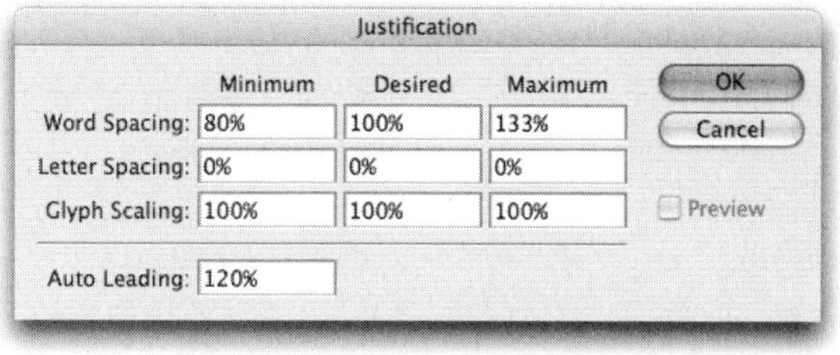

The Minimum, Desired, and Maximum boxes behave slightly differently, depending on whether the paragraph is justified or not:

- If the paragraph is justified, Minimum and Maximum specify the lowest and highest values that you're prepared to accept, respectively. Photoshop never goes outside these values. Desired is the value that you prefer; Photoshop does its best to stick to that value when justifying each line.

- If the paragraph isn't justified, Minimum and Maximum have no effect, while Desired can be thought of as Actual Value — the values you type for Desired are the values actually used in the paragraph. (The reason for this is that Photoshop doesn't need to juggle the values; it's not trying to stretch each line to fit the full width of the bounding box, so it can use the exact values you supply.)

Type values in the Word Spacing, Letter Spacing, or Glyph Scaling boxes to tell Photoshop how you want it to space the type:

- **Word Spacing:** This controls how much space Photoshop should place between each word. The default value of 100 percent equals one normal space character. You can type values from 0 percent (which means no space at all) up to 1000 percent (which means 10 times the normal spacing).

- **Letter Spacing:** This option lets you control the space between individual letters. The default is 0 percent, which means "don't add any extra spacing." You can type a value from -100 percent, which actually makes the letters overlap each other, all the way up to 500 percent, which adds, well, a lot of spacing.

- **Glyph Scaling:** Use this option to adjust the width of individual glyphs (characters). The default of 100 percent means that the glyphs are their normal width. You can type values from 50 percent (glyphs are scaled to half their normal width) up to 200 percent (glyphs are twice as wide as normal). You probably want to keep this value near 100 percent to stop your letters looking strange, but it can be a good way to help keep word and letter spacing nice and even in a paragraph.

> **NOTE**   Strictly speaking, a *glyph* is the representation of a particular character in a particular font. For practical purposes though, calling a glyph a character is near enough to the truth.

The Auto Leading setting is covered briefly earlier in the chapter. This setting controls how much leading is inserted between lines of text when you select the Auto value for Leading in the Character palette. The value is a percentage of the size of the font used at the time, with the default value being 120 percent (which is good for most purposes).

To see how your changes affect the type, select the Preview option in the dialog box. You can then see the effect in the document window. Toggle the Preview option off and on to compare the "before" and "after" states, so you can check that your changes are actually an improvement before clicking OK.

Specifying hanging punctuation

Normally, all characters in a block of paragraph type, including any punctuation marks, lie inside the bounding box. However, you can get Photoshop to place punctuation marks outside the bounding box if they happen to fall at the beginning or end of a line. This can create a pleasing effect, especially when using justification.

To toggle this effect on and off, choose Roman Hanging Punctuation from the Paragraph palette menu.

> **NOTE**   As you might imagine from the name, this effect is only intended for Roman fonts. If you're using Chinese, Japanese, or Korean fonts then use either Burasagari Standard or Burasagari Strong. These options are hidden by default; enable them by choosing Edit ➪ Preferences ➪ Type (Photoshop ➪ Preferences ➪ Type on the Mac) and selecting Show Asian Text Options.

Checking and Correcting Spelling

Photoshop's built-in spell checker is pretty good and worth using before sending that brochure off to the printers. It can check all the type layers in your document at once, but it ignores hidden layers, so make sure all the type layers you want to check are visible. Try the following options:

NOTE Make sure you use the right dictionary for the spell checker. To do this, display the Character palette (Window ➪ Character) and pick a language from the pop-up menu at the bottom of the palette.

- To check a selection of text within a layer, edit the type layer — for example, by selecting the Type tool then clicking in the text in the document window — and select the block of text you want to check. Choose Edit ➪ Check Spelling to display the Check Spelling dialog box.

- To check a whole type layer, select the layer. To check text from a certain point in the type layer to the end, edit the type layer and place the cursor where you want the checking to start. Choose Edit ➪ Check Spelling to display the Check Spelling dialog box.

- To check all visible type layers, select a type layer, make sure you're not in Edit mode and then choose Edit ➪ Check Spelling to display the Check Spelling dialog box. Make sure the Check All Layers option at the bottom of the dialog box is selected.

After you choose Edit ➪ Check Spelling, Photoshop displays the Check Spelling dialog box and it begins checking each word in your text against its dictionary. If it finds a word that's not in the dictionary, it flags it up in the Not In Dictionary box and offers its best guess at the correct word in the Change To box. If you're happy with its suggestion, click Change to change the current word to the word in the Change To box, or Change All to change all occurrences of the incorrectly spelled word to the word in the Change To box. You can also do the following:

- If you're not happy with Photoshop's suggestion, you can pick an alternative from the Suggestions list, or type the replacement word into the Change To box yourself. When you're satisfied, click Change or Change All.

- If you think Photoshop has flagged a word incorrectly, you can click Ignore to skip it and do nothing, or Ignore All to skip all occurrences of that word. If it's a word that you use a lot, you can add it to Photoshop's dictionary by clicking Add, and it will never query that word again.

After Photoshop finishes checking your text, a Spell Check Complete dialog box appears (click the Don't Show Again option if you find the dialog box annoying). Alternatively, you can end the spell check at any point by clicking Done in the Check Spelling dialog box, or simply by closing the dialog box.

Finding and Replacing Text

If you find yourself writing the next *War and Peace* in Photoshop (not recommended) or you've made the same mistake many times in your document, you'll probably need to search for, and possibly replace, some characters, words, or phrases within the text. Try these options:

- To search through a selection of text within a layer, edit the type layer and select the block of text you want to search. Choose Edit ➪ Find and Replace Text to display the Find And Replace Text dialog box.

- To search a whole type layer, select the layer. To search text from a certain point in the type layer to the end, edit the layer and place the insertion point where you want the search to start. Then choose Edit ⇨ Find and Replace Text to display the Find And Replace Text dialog box, and make sure the Forward option in the dialog is selected. (To search from the insertion point to the beginning of the text, deselect the Forward option.)

- To search all visible type layers, select a layer, make sure you're not in Edit mode, and choose Edit ⇨ Find and Replace Text to display the Find And Replace Text dialog box. Make sure the Search All Layers option at the bottom of the dialog box is selected.

NOTE Photoshop doesn't search hidden layers, so make sure you unhide all the layers you want to search before choosing Edit ⇨ Find and Replace Text.

After you choose Edit ⇨ Find and Replace Text, Photoshop displays the Find And Replace Text dialog box. Type the character, word, or phrase you want to search for in the Find What box.

Select Case Sensitive to take into account the case of the letters in the text as well (for example, "South" will only match "South", not "south"). Select Whole Word Only to match exact words (for example, "impress" will only match "impress," not "impressive").

If you just want to search for your text, click Find Next to find the next occurrence of the text. Keep clicking Find Next to find the remaining occurrences. After all are found, Photoshop displays a dialog box announcing it has finished (you can turn this off by selecting the Don't Show Again option). You can also end the search at any time by clicking Done in the Find And Replace Text dialog box or simply by closing the dialog box.

If you want to replace your search text with other text, type the replacement text in the Change To box. Click Find Next to find the next occurrence of the search text; then click Change to replace it with the text in the Change To box. You can then click Find Next again to find the next occurrence, and so on. Alternatively, click Change/Find to replace the text and move onto the next occurrence in one action. You can also click Change All to replace all occurrences of the search text instantly.

TIP You can search for any character or characters that you can type in the Find What box, not just letters or numbers. You can also select some text from a type layer (or even another application), copy it with Edit ⇨ Copy, then paste it into the Find What box by clicking in the box and pressing Ctrl+V (⌘+V on the Mac).

Creating Warped Type

With Photoshop, you're not limited to boring rectangles of text. You can bend your type layers into all sorts of interesting shapes by using the Warp Text feature. To begin warping your text, select the Type tool, select a type layer — you don't have to be editing the type itself — and click the Create Warped Text button in the options bar, as shown in Figure 4.25. You can also choose Layer ⇨ Type ⇨ Warp Text. You'll then see the Warp Text dialog appear, also shown in Figure 4.25.

Warping a type layer with the Warp Text feature. The effect is exactly the same as using the Warp command on a layer.

Create Warped Text button

The controls in this dialog work as follows:

- **Style:** Use this option to pick a basic shape to warp the text into.
- **Horizontal and Vertical:** This controls the orientation of the warp effect. The default is Horizontal; choose Vertical, and the warp shape gets flipped through 90 degrees.
- **Bend:** Use this to control the amount of warping. Negative values bend the text in the opposite direction to positive values. A value of 0 produces no warp.
- **Horizontal and Vertical Distortion:** Use these two options to apply a perspective distortion to the type. Positive Horizontal Distortion values make the right side of the text taller than the left side; negative values make the left side taller than the right. Meanwhile, positive Vertical Distortion values stretch the bottom of the text, while negative Vertical Distortion values stretch the top. A value of 0 produces no distortion.

Once you're satisfied with your warp effect, click OK to apply it to your type layer. The warping effect is dynamic, so you can go back and change its settings at any time by selecting the type layer and redisplaying the Warp Text dialog. You can also continue to edit the text in your type layer; the text gets rewarped as you type.

 The Warp Text feature does have a couple of limitations. For one thing, you can't warp a type layer that contains any faux bold character formatting — you'll see a warning dialog if you try — nor can you apply any faux bold formatting to already-warped text (you'll find the icon grayed out in the Character palette). In addition, Warp Text can't warp a type layer that uses any fonts that don't contain outline data, such as bitmap fonts. Again, you'll see a warning appear if you try to warp such a type layer or, if you've already applied warping to a layer, any incompatible fonts appear grayed out in the Font Family menu.

If you use the Warp command to warp layers, you might notice a striking similarity between the Warp Text dialog and the options in the Warp command's options bar. The Warp Text feature and the Warp command work identically; you can use either method to warp your type layer, and the results are exactly the same. (You can even access the Warp command while editing text by choosing Edit ⇨ Transform ⇨ Warp, although this does take you out of text editing mode.) In fact, Warp Text and the Warp command are interchangeable; if you warp your text using Warp Text, you can later edit your warp settings for that type layer via the Warp command, and vice-versa.

Unlike warping normal layers, shape layers or any other type of content, the effects of text warping are editable and reversible at any time. If you warp a pre-warped type layer using either the Warp Text feature or the Warp command, you'll see your original Style, Orientation, Bend, Horizontal Distortion and Vertical Distortion settings reappear in the dialog or options bar.

The other important difference between warping type layers and warping other layers is that, sadly, you can't apply custom warping to type layers.

 For more detail on the workings of the Warp command, flip back to Chapter 3.

To remove a warp effect completely from a type layer, bring up the Warp Text dialog and choose None for the Style option.

Creating Type on a Path

As well as warping your type into preset shapes with the Warp Text feature, you can also make your type twist and bend to any shape you want. If you can draw it, Photoshop can fit type along it!

In order to do this, start with a path, like the one shown in Figure 4.26. The path will be the template for the type; Photoshop flows the type along the curves and lines of the path.

You can create your path using whatever method you're comfortable with. Following are some examples:

- Draw the path using the Pen tool or Freeform Pen tool. (Make sure you select the Paths option in the tool's options bar.)

- Create the path using one of the shape tools. (Again, make sure you select the Paths option.)

■ Make a selection; then convert the selection to a path with the Make Work Path from Selection icon at the bottom of the Paths palette.

CROSS-REF For more on creating paths and shapes, see Chapter 5.

FIGURE 4.26

A simple open path. The path serves as a template for your flowing text.

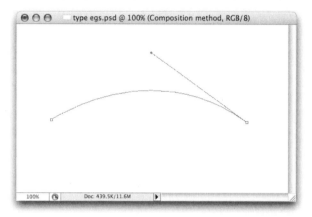

TIP This feature works best if your path is fairly smooth. If you have a lot of sharp corners or steep curves, the text jumps about madly as it tries to follow the path.

To place your type along the path, select the Type tool and move the cursor over a point on the path. The tool's I-beam cursor changes to an I-beam with a dotted line running through it.

Click where you want the type to start, and start typing. Photoshop flows the text along the path as you type, as shown in Figure 4.27.

NOTE Type always flows in the direction that the path was originally drawn; in other words, it follows the order of the anchor points used to create the path. So, if your path was created right to left, your text flows right to left (and is upside down to boot!). Never fear — you can easily flip the text the right way round. See the section "Flipping the type" to find out how to do this.

While you type, you can use all the regular formatting tools in the Character and Paragraph palettes to format your type. When you're happy with your type, commit it as normal (see the section "Adding a Type Layer" earlier in this chapter).

TIP If you want your type to sit above or below the path, rather than directly on it, adjust the baseline shift value in the Character palette. A positive value moves the type above the path, while a negative value drags the type down below the path.

FIGURE 4.27

Entering type along the path. The cross on the left indicates the starting point of the type, and the hollow circle on the right indicates the endpoint.

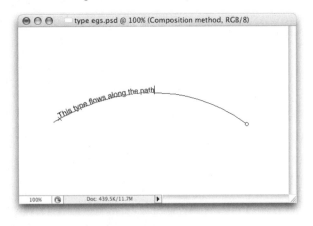

Positioning the type

When you first enter your type on the path, it starts at the point you clicked. You see a small cross at the start of the type, indicating the start point, and a hollow circle at the end of the path, indicating the endpoint. (If the text you type goes beyond the endpoint, it is chopped off.)

To change the start point of the type, select the Path tool or Direct Selection tool; then move the cursor over the type until you see the cursor change to a forward-pointing arrow. You can then click and drag to reposition the start point.

Similarly, to change the endpoint, select the Path tool or Direct Selection tool and move the cursor over the endpoint until it changes to a backward-pointing arrow; click and drag to reposition it.

TIP If you're in the process of editing your type, you can quickly position the start point or endpoint by holding down Ctrl (⌘ on the Mac), then clicking and dragging the start point or endpoint to move it.

Flipping the type

You might sometimes end up with your type upside down and facing backward. This can happen if, for example, the original path was drawn right-to-left.

To flip the type the right way up, select the start point or endpoint of the type as described in the section "Positioning the type," then drag the mouse so it crosses the line of the path, as shown in Figure 4.28. The type is then flipped to face the other way.

FIGURE 4.28

Flipping type on a path. Click a start point or endpoint; then drag across the line of the path.

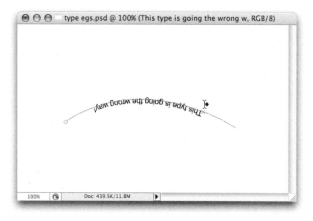

Reshaping the type

After you create your type on a path, you can go back and change the shape of the path later, and the type reflows along the new shape.

The important thing to remember is that, when you create your type layer, Photoshop creates a new path based on the original path. This special path is called a *type path*; you can see it by selecting the type layer then displaying the Paths palette. Type paths are automatically created, and the only way to delete a type path is to delete the corresponding type layer.

What this means is that, if you want to alter the shape of your type later, you need to edit this type path, not your original path.

To select the type path for editing, select the type layer, display the Paths palette, and click the type path in the palette to select it. (You can also select the type path automatically by reediting the text in the type layer.)

After you select the type path, you can use the pen tools and the other path tools — such as the Direct Selection tool — to reshape it just like any other path. The text automatically flows along the new shape of the path, as shown in Figure 4.29.

FIGURE 4.29

Reshaping the type path. As the path's shape is altered, the type reflows along the new contours of the path.

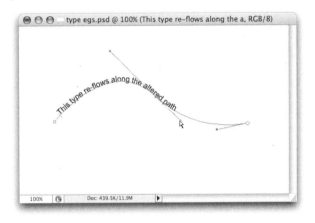

Creating type inside a closed path

If you're working with a closed path (a path without a start or end anchor point), you have a choice: You can either create the type along the edge of the path (as described earlier) or you can create the type inside the path, as shown in Figure 4.30.

FIGURE 4.30

Type inside a closed path

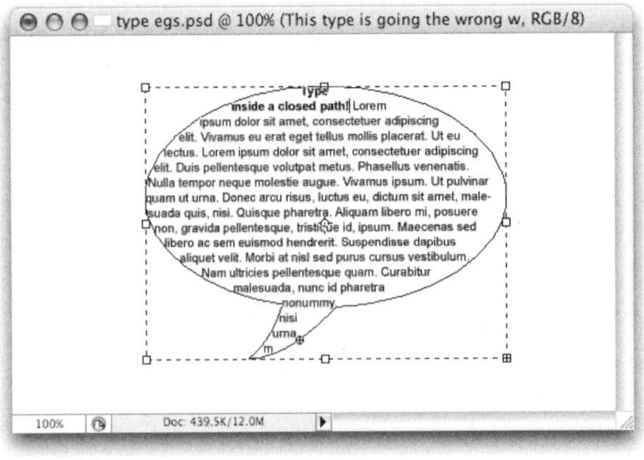

To create the type inside the path, select a type tool then move the cursor inside the shape of the path. The cursor changes to an I-beam with a dotted circle around it, which indicates that the type will be placed inside the path. Click with the mouse and begin typing; your type flows within the boundaries of the path. Pretty cool!

Shapes are ideal for this purpose, as they're essentially closed paths. Create the shape with the Paths option enabled in the Shape tool's options bar; then switch to the Type tool and click inside the shape to enter your type.

> **TIP** You can even create type inside the vector mask in a shape layer. It doesn't matter to Photoshop; as far as it's concerned, they're all just closed paths. Just make sure the vector mask is selected by clicking its thumbnail in the Layers palette — you'll see a highlight box around it if it's selected, and the vector mask path will appear in the document window. Then click inside the path to type your text.

> **CROSS-REF** As with type along a path, you can reshape the type path at a later point and the text reflows to fill the new shape. See the section "Reshaping the type" for more info.

Creating Bitmap Type Layers

At the start of this chapter, we talked about older versions of Photoshop that only let you create bitmap type layers. You may recall that the type in bitmap layers can't be reedited, nor can it be scaled or rotated without losing quality and detail.

So what's the point of a bitmap type layer, you may ask? Well, a bitmap type layer is essentially a normal layer (see Chapter 1), which means that you can do practically anything to it. For example, you can paint directly on the layer with any of the painting tools, allowing you to modify the individual pixels of the type — something you can't do with type layers. You can also apply filters and use transform commands such as Distort and Perspective, which can't ordinarily be used on type layers.

> **CROSS-REF** You can also convert your type layer — indeed, any kind of layer — to a Smart Object by choosing Layer ➪ Smart Objects ➪ Convert to Smart Object. You can then do a few things that you couldn't do with the standard type layer, such as applying Smart Filters. For more on Smart Objects, see Chapter 8.

How do you do it? Easy — select the type layer, then choose Layer ➪ Rasterize ➪ Type. The selected layer is instantly converted to a bitmap layer — the letter "T" disappears from the layer's thumbnail in the Layers palette and is replaced with a thumbnail of the layer contents. The layer is now a normal layer.

> **CAUTION** After you convert a type layer to a normal layer, there's no going back. You can't convert back to a type layer, nor can you edit the type ever again. If you've spent a lot of time creating your type layer or you think you might want to edit the type later, duplicate the layer first (by choosing Layer ➪ Duplicate Layer) so that you have an editable backup copy of it. You might want to hide the duplicate so it doesn't get in the way.

Figure 4.31 shows a type layer that's been converted into a bitmap layer and then had some artistic effects applied to it. (You can see that the bitmap layer has already started to lose some quality around the edges of the letters.)

A regular type layer (top) is converted into a bitmap type layer; then the Mezzotint and ZigZag filters are applied to the layer (bottom).

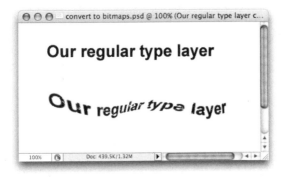

> **TIP** To save time, you can just go ahead and apply a filter to, or start painting on, a regular type layer. Photoshop automatically converts the type layer to a bitmap layer (after asking you for confirmation first).

Converting Type Layers to Shape Layers

Just as you can convert a type layer to a bitmap layer (see the previous section), you can also convert a type layer to a shape layer.

To convert a type layer to a shape layer, select the type layer, then choose Layer ⇨ Type ⇨ Convert to Shape.

> **TIP** If the path outlines around each letter bother you, hide them with View ⇨ Show ⇨ Target Path, or press Shift+Ctrl+H (Shift+⌘+H on the Mac).

Photoshop converts each letter in the type layer to a separate path within the shape's vector mask. This means that you can then go in and transform or reshape each letter individually using, for example, the pen tools, the Direct Selection tool, or Edit ⇨ Free Transform Path.

Converting type to shapes is also handy if you need to send your Photoshop files to a company for printing. There are three main benefits of this approach:

- The printing company can make last-minute changes to font sizes without having to ask you to resubmit all the artwork (though you may wish to do these tweaks yourself anyway).

- If the printing company doesn't have the correct font, there's a possibility that it will use a font it deems appropriate (but that you don't). This is undesirable from a design perspective, and can waste time in reproofing or reprinting.

- Sending fonts to printing companies is technically illegal (unless the printing company also owns a license for the font). Converting the text to shapes allows you remain on the correct side of the law, because you're not including the actual font files.

The main downside of converting to a shape layer is that, as with converting to a bitmap layer, your type is no longer editable as type. Best to keep a backup copy of your type layer if you think you might want to edit it later!

CAUTION   Some fonts cannot be converted to shape layers because they contain no outline data (for example, bitmap fonts). A warning dialog to this effect appears if you attempt to convert a type layer that contains such a font. Be wary of any font in the font menu that doesn't have some kind of symbol to the left of its name — such a font is usually a bitmap font.

Figure 4.32 shows a type layer converted to a shape layer, then manipulated to produce some interesting effects.

FIGURE 4.32

A regular type layer (left) is converted into a shape layer. The capital and lowercase "l"s are stretched and the dot above the "i" is replaced with a flower (right).

Creating Work Paths from Type Layers

As an alternative to converting your type layer to a shape layer, you can create a work path from the letters in the type layer. Unlike converting to a shape layer, this path is created in addition to your original type layer, so you don't need to make a backup of your type layer first.

After you create your work path you can treat it just like any other path; you can edit it with the pen tools and the Direct Selection tool, transform it with Edit ➪ Free Transform Path, and so on.

This feature is handy for creating a vector mask in the shape of your type. For example, in Figure 4.33 a work path is created from a type layer, then this path is used to mask another, normal layer with Layer ➪ Vector Mask ➪ Current Path.

FIGURE 4.33

A work path is made from the type layer (top). This path is then applied as a vector mask to a bitmap layer containing a photo, producing the end effect (bottom).

Creating Type as a Mask

You can create type as a mask (also known as a selection), rather than as a full type layer. To do this, click the Type tool icon in the Toolbox, hold down the mouse button, and select either the Horizontal Type Mask Tool or the Vertical Type Mask Tool option from the pop-up menu.

Text entry works in the same way as for the regular Horizontal and Vertical Type tools. Click in the document window with the mouse to create point type, or click and drag a bounding box to create paragraph type. You can also create a type mask on a path, and so on.

Figure 4.34 shows text being typed with the Horizontal Type Mask tool. While you type your text, a colored overlay appears over the document, indicating the masked-off (by default) areas of the image. When you commit your type, a selection is created instead of a type layer.

TIP The overlay color and behavior are taken from the Quick Mask options. To change these, double-click the Quick Mask icon at the bottom of the Toolbox; then adjust the options in the Quick Mask Options dialog box that appears. (For more on the Quick Mask mode, see Chapter 9.)

FIGURE 4.34

Entering type with the Horizontal Type Mask tool

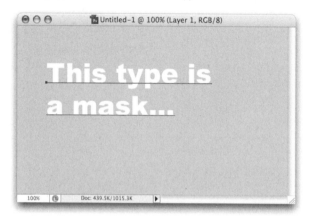

After you create your type mask, you can use it just like any other selection — fill it, stroke it, use it as a layer mask, and so on.

TIP The Type Mask tools are great for quickly creating a selection in the shape of some text. However, if you create a lot of text or you think you might want to go back and reedit the text later, it's best to create your text as a type layer using the standard Horizontal or Vertical Type tool. You can then make a selection based on your type layer at any time by Ctrl+clicking (⌘+clicking on the Mac) the type layer's thumbnail (letter "T") in the Layers palette. If you ever need to edit your text, just edit the original type layer; then make a new selection from it.

Understanding Type Aesthetics

So far, the nuts and bolts of creating and editing type in Photoshop have been covered. Let's take a diversion into the creative side of things at this point, and consider the aesthetic aspects of type. Which fonts are best for which situations? How can you retain a good balance of readability and visual appeal? What are the classic pitfalls that you should avoid?

In answering these questions, it's first worth noting that the study of type, or typography, is an art form in itself—don't expect to be an expert overnight! But don't despair; there are some basic rules of typesetting that you can pick up very quickly and easily. This section aims to give you a quick induction into the world of type. Type styles are many and varied, but there are some basic styles to be aware of. There's a good chance you have picked up some of this simply by immersion in books, magazines, advertising, and TV, but we try to put them into a little context here.

Serif type

Serif type forms are characterized by small flourishes on the ends of letters, or *serifs*. The style has been in existence since the fifteenth or sixteenth century, and was originally based on handwritten texts—mostly religious documents. You may have heard of a typeface called Garamond, which was created by Claude Garamond in Paris in the sixteenth century. When you use a typeface like this, you're using something that's essentially 400 years old!

The best known serif typeface is probably Times, depicted in Figure 4.35. It displays the classic lines of a serif typeface, with elegant flaring of the ends of the letters. As the name suggests, it was created for The Times newspaper and has been around since 1931.

FIGURE 4.35

The classic Times typeface. Note the serifs on the ends of the letterforms.

The serifs tend to allow easy reading of large bodies of text, and most novels are set in some form of serif typeface for this exact reason. This is a great technique to adapt to your own designs. A paragraph set in a serif face like Times is always nice and legible, especially when used in the context of a printed document.

Sans serif type

These typefaces are more modern than the serif faces, and do not have the serifs seen in Times and its ilk. One of the early sans serif fonts, Akzidenz Grotesk, released in 1896, is still in use today. You can see it in Figure 4.36.

FIGURE 4.36

Akzidenz Grotesk is an early sans serif typeface.

In terms of popularity, Helvetica is the de facto sans serif standard. It's a font you see everywhere, from signage to brochures and television, and it even has its own fan sites on the Web! Many designers, if left to their own devices, would use nothing but Helvetica, which probably explains why you see it around so much. Other fonts approximate Helvetica — for example, Arial and Swiss — and indeed they are somewhat interchangeable, as you can see from the examples in Figure 4.37. (The top example is Helvetica.)

Sans serif typefaces are often used as headlines or when sheer clarity is most important. Again, this is a technique you can use freely in your own work — no one was ever fired for using Helvetica as a headline font. They're also great when you want text to be read on-screen; Verdana is the classic on-screen sans serif font. While serif forms are great in print where the flourishes draw the eye across the page, they tend to lose definition when viewed on a low-resolution monitor, so use a sans serif font in this environment to maximize legibility.

NOTE Current monitors tend to run in much lower resolutions than printed materials. Monitor resolutions tend to be around 72-150 dots per inch (dpi), whereas print work is usually 300 dpi or higher. In practice, this means that letterforms are more clearly defined in print than on-screen.

FIGURE 4.37

Helvetica and Arial together

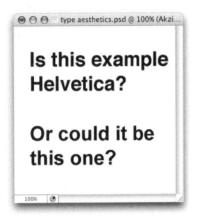

Display type

Display, or decorative, type is designed to add a decorative touch to the page, and is best used sparingly because it tends to be a little hard on the eye when used in bulk. It's often used to convey a particular topic or to evoke a particular mood. For example, one might use a Western font to add a decorative touch to a project concerned with a ranch, or a stencil font when you want to convey a sense of something being stamped. Figure 4.38 shows some examples of display fonts.

FIGURE 4.38

Some examples of display typefaces. These types of fonts are best used sparingly in the page.

Typeface tips

- **If you want classy, use the classics.** The reason these old fonts have stood the test of time so well is simply that people love them. It remains to be seen if the current crop of fonts has the staying power of a Bodoni or a Palatino. With that in mind, it's worth thinking about using these fonts when you create a design that requires a classy feel. You should find several classic fonts preinstalled on your computer. These include Times, Palatino and Arial (you can use Arial as a substitute for Helvetica).

- **Be consistent.** When you design a document of any description, it's important for the sake of a professional appearance to make sure your use of type is consistent. In particular, try to stick with just two typefaces per project — any more than that and it all starts getting a bit messy. Pick one for headings and one for the bulk of the text, and stick with those choices. Continuing the same principle, keep your use of colors, capitalization, spacing, and justification consistent, too. Photoshop's type tools allow a lot of tinkering with your text, and it's easy to create multiple looks within the same document. However, keeping type consistent pretty much assures you of a decent result, so don't go overboard.

- **Use space.** Musicians have a well-worn phrase: "It's not what you play, it's what you leave out." What these grizzled souls are outlining is the principle of space. Space in a document draws the eye to the content and imparts a feeling of calm elegance to the whole thing. It can be tempting to fill out a page with text right to the edges, but be generous with margins and the space around type elements. The extra space will really pay off. You can use Photoshop's guides and rulers to make sure that you line up all the elements nicely.

CROSS-REF Guides and rulers are explored in Chapter 2.

- **Keep it legible.** Text is only useful if the reader can read it. It sounds obvious, but it can be very tempting to overlay text on a disruptive background or photo, to use miniscule fonts or a very "distressed" typeface. In some circles it's perfectly acceptable to push the boundaries of type into some less legible areas, but generally, this is unlikely to win you many friends with readers.

- **Experiment.** The best way to learn about how to make type work for you is simply to dive in and start creating your own work. You might break some rules in the process, but some of the best typography has come from people breaking rules and creating fantastic work in the process. This is all meant to be fun, so try out ideas, tinker with your kerning and leading, and generally get your hands dirty making type come alive!

Tutorial: Bringing It All Together

This chapter has covered a lot of ground on type layers, so now it's time to put some of that theory into practice and see how all these techniques can be used in a project. The premise for this example is that you're laying out a page of a children's book called *Please Don't Call Me Fluff*, which concerns a somewhat distressed cat who doesn't like any of the names his owners choose for him!

Start with your basic page. In this case, the book will be in a 16cm square format. Because it will be printed, use a resolution of 300 dpi. Go ahead and create your basic document. Your New dialog box looks something like Figure 4.39.

Now add a very basic illustration. Add two shape layers — a rectangle created with the Rectangle tool and a cat shape created with the Custom Shape tool. Use the rectangle as a clipping mask for the cat. You can see the results in Figure 4.40.

CROSS-REF   You can find more information on shapes and clipping masks in Chapters 5 and 9.

FIGURE 4.39

The New dialog box shows your document size and resolution. Give your document the name "Fluff."

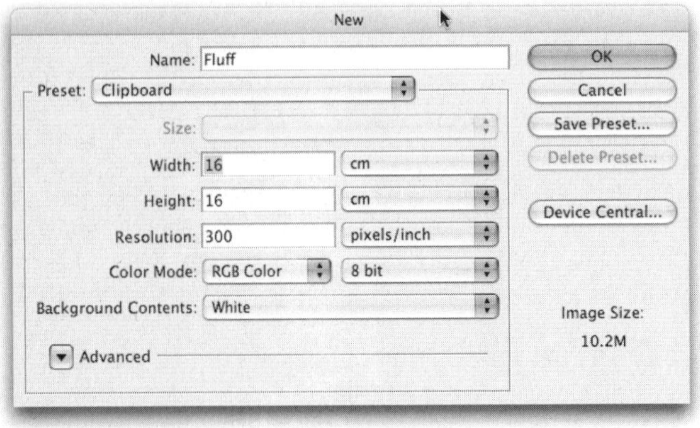

FIGURE 4.40

Your basic illustration, with a cat shape and a green rectangle shape. The rectangle is acting as a clipping mask for the cat layer.

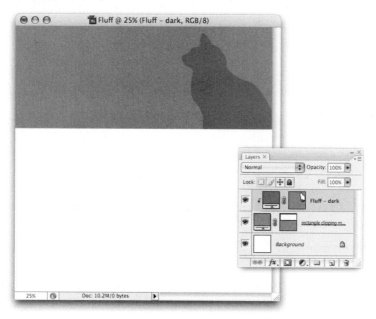

Adding a title

Now add some text to your illustration to give the page a title. To do this, follow these steps:

1. **Create the type layer.** Select the Horizontal Type tool, and make sure the top layer is active so that your type will be visible above the cat. Position the I-beam cursor roughly where you want the title to start, then click and type the title.

2. **Set the font and size.** The chances are that this text won't be in the font you're looking for, or the correct size, so select the text you entered by pressing Ctrl+A (⌘+A on the Mac) and use the Font Family and Font Size pop-up menus in the options bar. Experiment a little to find something that conveys the mood you're after. A font called "Geek a byte 2" is used here. It has a suitably cheerful feel to it, and a size of 30 points.

 The excellent "Geek a byte 2" font was created by Jakob Fischer, and is available from www.1001fonts.com/font_details.html?font_id=2633.

3. **Beef up the word "Fluff."** It would be good to have more impact on the word "Fluff" to communicate the cat's exasperation with his owners. Positioning the I-beam cursor at the start of the word "Fluff", drag to the right to highlight it, and cut it from the document using Edit ⇨ Cut. Click in the document window again, slightly away from the existing text; then choose Edit ⇨ Paste to paste the word into its own type layer. This allows you to treat this word independently of the rest of the sentence. You want it bigger, so highlight it again and increase the size to, say, 60 points.

4. **Reposition the type layers a little.** Select the "Please don't call me..." type layer and reposition it using the Move tool, moving it up to sit just to the left of the cat's chin. Then select the Fluff layer and position it below the first line and to the right, so the sentence is complete.

CROSS-REF You can read about the Move tool in Chapter 2.

5. **Resize the type layers.** The text sizes are now pretty good, but they could use some fine-tuning. Again, using the Move tool, enable the Show Transform Controls option in the options bar. This allows you to resize each layer more precisely than fiddling with font sizes; the font size automatically scales as you resize the layer. Holding down Shift to constrain the proportions of the type, drag the corner resize handles to make the "Please don't call me..." layer slightly smaller and the Fluff layer a bit bigger to fill the space nicely. Because you're using the Move tool, you can also reposition the text slightly as you do this. You can see the results in Figure 4.41.

FIGURE 4.41

Using the Move tool to resize and reposition the title elements

Creating the main text

Turn your attention to the large white space beneath the title, which will hold the start of the actual story. Use the technique of a *drop capital*, which is where the first letter of a paragraph is much bigger and bolder than the remainder. To do this, use the techniques discussed earlier in this chapter for applying text to a path. In this case, use a path as a container for your text.

Select the Pen tool from the Toolbox; then click the Paths icon in the options bar to ensure that you create a work path, rather than a shape or filled area. Now you can create the path that will contain the text, as shown in Figure 4.42. Make sure to leave a space for the drop capital. You might also like to use Photoshop's guides feature to help you line up the left and right edges of the path with the corresponding edges of the title.

> **TIP**
>
> Hold down Shift as you click with the Pen tool to ensure that the lines of the path snap to the horizontal and vertical.

When you finish drawing out the path, click the first point in the path to close it. You should now have a path in the Paths palette called Work Path.

FIGURE 4.42

Creating a closed path to contain the text

After you have the path, copy the story from your source document and paste it inside the path. To do this, follow these steps:

1. **Copy the source text from your text editing software using Edit ⇨ Copy.** This stores the text in your computer's clipboard, ready for pasting into Photoshop.

2. **Flip back to Photoshop and make sure the Work Path path is selected in the Paths palette.** You'll know it's selected if you can see its outline in the document window.

3. **Select the Horizontal Type tool, and position the cursor within the path in the document window.** The cursor changes to an I-beam with a dotted circle around it.

4. **Click to start placing the text, then choose Edit ⇨ Paste to paste the copied text into the new text layer.** The text flows nicely inside the contours of the path.

Set a font and size for your pasted text. Choose Edit ⇨ Select All to highlight all the text, then choose a suitable font and size in the options bar — Arial at 9pt is selected here, which fills the space well. The first letter "I" is also deleted from the text, because you'll be replacing that with a drop capital in the convenient gap at the top left of the path. Finally, commit your edits by pressing Ctrl+Enter (⌘+Return on the Mac) or clicking the check mark icon in the options bar.

You can go back and reshape the path at any time using the Direct Selection tool and pen tools. You might need to do this if you drew your path freehand. Any odd kinks in the lines can result in some very odd hyphenation from Photoshop, so these need to be straight. When you reshape the path, the text reflows within the new shape.

Figure 4.43 shows the current state of play.

FIGURE 4.43

Pasting the text into the path and tidying up the path outline

Adding the drop capital

The last thing you need to do is add your drop capital. Add it as a separate type layer. To begin, select the Horizontal Type tool, and choose an appropriate font and color using the options in the options bar. You might like to use the same font as used for the title text, and the same green that you used for the rectangle shape at the start of the example.

Add your letter "i" drop capital. Shift+click in the document window where you want to place the drop capital; then type your small letter "i." Confirm your edits to create the new type layer; then use the Move tool to resize and reposition the drop capital if required, as shown in Figure 4.44.

> **NOTE** Shift+clicking in the document window ensures that your type is created on a new layer. If you just click, Photoshop might assume that you want to edit the existing type layer instead.

All done! You now have a nicely laid-out page, with an eye-grabbing title and some beautiful flowed body text with a cute drop capital letter "i" at the start.

> **NOTE** The more observant reader will have noticed that the "drop capital" in the example is a lowercase letter "i," rather than a capital letter. The "drop capital" term is used though, because "drop lowercase" doesn't quite have the same ring to it.

FIGURE 4.44

The finished page, complete with cat graphic, funky title, and a nice drop capital in the body text

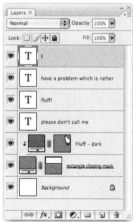

Summary

This chapter looked at type layers and explored Photoshop's impressive range of type editing and formatting features. You learned what a type layer is and how to create one, and also how to select type within a type layer for editing. The difference between point type and paragraph type was explained.

You explored all the character formatting features of Photoshop's Character palette, including setting the font, style, and size; controlling leading, kerning, and tracking; scaling characters; applying baseline shift; choosing font colors; and fine-tuning the anti-aliasing, or smoothing, of your type.

Similarly, the Paragraph palette was looked at, covering options such as alignment, justification, indenting, paragraph spacing, hyphenation, layout, and hanging punctuation.

You learned how to check and correct spelling of text within type layers, and also how to perform search-and-replace operations on your text. You also explored techniques for warping type, creating type on — and inside — paths, and creating bitmap type layers, and learned how to convert type layers to shape layers and paths.

Finally, we looked at creating type as a mask, or selection, touched on the aesthetic aspects of typography and choosing appropriate fonts depending on the situation, and ended with a complete example, showing how to use Photoshop's type layers to create and illustrate a page from a children's book.

Chapter 5

Working with Shape Layers

Photoshop has given you the ability to draw vector paths using the Pen tool since version 2, but since version 6 you can create *shapes*, which are essentially filled paths. Photoshop achieves this wondrous feat with a special kind of layer called a shape layer, which is really a fill layer (explained in Chapter 6) with a vector mask to define the shape.

So why bother with shape layers? Why not just draw shapes on normal bitmap layers? Well, as discussed in Chapter 1, vector shape layers can do a few things that normal bitmap layers can't. For example, you can go back and edit a shape layer at any time — maybe you forgot to add a little star to a logo, for example — without losing any quality. You can also stretch and squeeze a shape layer as much as you want, again without losing quality or ending up with jagged edges.

Because shape layers are essentially fill layers, you can change the fill color with a couple of clicks, or even swap the color for a gradient or pattern, all without touching the shape's outline or causing any loss of quality. See Figure 5.1 for an example.

Naturally, there also are disadvantages to shape layers, otherwise nobody would use normal layers anymore. The main disadvantage is that, as vector-based layers, they're not great at storing real-world images with lots of subtle changes in color, such as photographs. For these types of images, normal bitmap layers are far and away your best bet. However, shape layers (and vector paths in general) are great for clipping bitmap layers, because they have those wonderfully sharp, clean edges, no matter what the resolution.

You also need to be a bit careful when exporting layered documents containing shape layers to other software, as support for shape layers in other graphics packages is often limited, to put it mildly. You might want to convert your shape layers to normal layers using the Rasterize Layer command before exporting.

FIGURE 5.1

You can create shape layers using Photoshop's shape tools. In this example, the filled contents of a shape layer are swapped, all without having to touch the shape outline or lose any image quality.

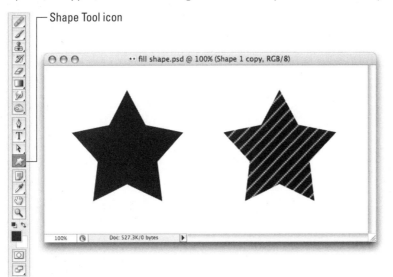

— Shape Tool icon

Adding a Shape Layer

There are many ways to create a shape layer (which are discussed later), but by far the easiest way is to use one of the shape tools. These come in two varieties: the basic shape tools for creating geometric patterns, and the Custom Shape tool for creating, well, all sorts of wacky things.

You can create a shape layer using the following steps:

1. **Select a shape tool.** Click the Shape Tool icon in the Toolbox (shown in Figure 5.1), and select a shape tool from the options bar. You can also choose a specific shape tool by pressing Shift+U to cycle through all the hidden shape tools until you find the one you want. Alternatively, Alt+click (Option+click on the Mac) the Shape Tool icon to cycle through the tools, or click and hold the mouse button on the Shape Tool icon to choose a tool from a pop-up menu.

NOTE The Shape Tool icon in the Toolbox updates to show the currently selected shape tool.

2. **Set options for the shape.** Use the options in the shape tool's options bar (described in the following list) to customize the shape.

3. **Draw the shape.** Click in the document window where you want your shape to appear, and drag out the shape.

TIP What if you started dragging out your shape in the wrong place? No problem — simply hold down the Spacebar while you drag to reposition the shape instead. Release the Spacebar to return to drawing the shape.

All the shape tools share a similar options bar, as shown in Figure 5.2. The available options include:

- **Shape Layers, Paths, and Fill Pixels buttons:** These let you choose the format of the shape. The default option — and the one covered the most here — is Shape Layers, which, as you'd expect, creates a new shape layer. The other two options — discussed later — create paths and draw directly on bitmap layers, respectively.

- **Pen Tool and Freeform Pen tool buttons:** These are quick ways to flip between the pen tools and the various shape tools. The pen and shape tools are very closely related, as you see later, because they both work with vectors.

- **Basic shape tool buttons:** These range from the Rectangle tool on the left to the Line tool on the right. They let you create basic geometric shapes such as rectangles, circles, polygons, lines, and arrows.

- **Custom Shape tool button:** Rather than creating just one kind of shape like each of the basic shape tools, the Custom Shape tool lets you choose from a library of different shapes, including fancy arrows, bullets, stars, and other icons.

- **Geometry Options button:** Click this little triangle to the right of the Shape tool buttons to display the tool's Geometry Options palette. This palette lets you specify options for the shape tool that you're using, such as its size, or whether its aspect ratio is constrained. The exact options vary from tool to tool.

- **Shape option:** This option varies depending on the shape tool you're using. For example, the Polygon tool gives you a Sides input box for selecting how many sides the polygon has; the Custom Shape tool has a Shape pop-up palette where you can choose the shape you want to draw, and so on.

- **Shape combination buttons:** These five buttons control what happens if you drag out a new shape on an existing shape layer. The first button, Create a New Shape Layer, simply adds a new shape layer and sticks the shape on that. The remaining options let you specify how the new shape should interact with existing shapes on the layer. These are covered in detail in the section "Editing Shape Layers" later in this chapter.

- **Link button:** If selected, the options you choose for Style and Color apply to the active shape layer as well as to any future shape layers you create. If you deselect this option, your Style and Color choices only apply to future shape layers; they don't touch the active layer.

- **Style menu:** This pop-up menu displays the styles in the Styles palette, letting you choose from a variety of preset layer styles to apply to your shape.

CROSS-REF Styles, including how to edit them and create your own, are covered in detail in Chapter 10.

- **Color box:** Click the color box to open the Color Picker dialog box and choose a fill color for your shape.

NOTE If you choose a style that features a Color, Gradient or Pattern overlay, the overlay overrides the fill color, so changing the fill color has no effect.

FIGURE 5.2

Specify options for your shape before you create it by using the settings in the shape tool's options bar.

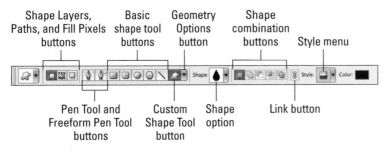

NOTE All of the options to the left of the Link button only work when creating new shapes. This means that you need to make your choices from among these options before you start dragging out your shape.

After you drag out your shape in the document window, release the mouse button. Photoshop creates your new shape layer for you, using your chosen shape options. If you want, you can then create new shapes by clicking in the document window and dragging again. Each time you create a new shape, Photoshop creates a new shape layer by default, but you can add shapes to an existing shape layer, too — see the section "Editing Shape Layers" later in this chapter for more details.

TIP To hide the vector mask path in the document window so you can see the shape more clearly, press Ctrl+Shift+H (⌘+Shift+H on the Mac), or choose View ➪ Show ➪ Target Path. Press the same key combination, or choose the same menu option, to redisplay the path.

You'll probably use the shape tools most often for creating shape layers (or working on existing shape layers), but they can be used to create other types of shapes, too:

- To create just a path without the associated shape layer, select a shape tool, click the Paths button in the shape tool's options bar, and drag out your shape. After you create the shape, it appears as a new work path in the Paths palette or, if you already have a path selected in the palette, the new shape is added to that path. Because a path is just an outline, you can't select options such as a fill color or style in this mode, but you can, of course, fill or stroke your path after you create it.

■ To paint directly onto a bitmap layer, select the layer, select a shape tool, and click the Fill Pixels button in the options bar. Create your shape as usual; Photoshop paints it onto the bitmap layer using the current foreground color as the fill. Because it's not a separate object, you can't apply a style to it as you can with a shape layer. You can choose a blending mode and opacity for it, however — specify these with the Mode and Opacity options in the options bar before creating the shape. You can also smooth the edges of the shape's pixels by selecting the Anti-Alias option.

Working with basic shape tools

Photoshop provides you with five basic shape tools that let you create simple geometric shapes: the Rectangle and Rounded Rectangle tools, the Ellipse tool, the Polygon tool, and the Line tool. This section explores these tools and their various options.

Drawing rectangles and squares with the rectangle tools

The two rectangle tools (Rectangle and Rounded Rectangle) let you create rectangles and squares. The only difference between the two tools is that the Rounded Rectangle tool produces rectangles with rounded corners (the Holy Grail of Web designers everywhere).

To add a rectangle to your document, select the Rectangle or Rounded Rectangle tool and then click in the document window and drag out the rectangle from one corner to the other. To constrain the rectangle to a square, hold down Shift as you drag. You can also click the Geometry Options button in the options bar and select the Square option from the Geometry Options palette.

By default, Photoshop draws the rectangle from corner to corner, but you can drag out a rectangle from its center, too. To do this, hold down Alt (Option on the Mac) while you drag, or select the From Center option in the Geometry Options palette.

CAUTION If your active layer isn't a shape layer, make sure you press Alt (Option on the Mac) after you start dragging, not before, or you get the Eyedropper tool instead.

To draw rectangles with curved corners, select the Rounded Rectangle tool, then use the Radius box in the options bar to specify the radius of the corners. Imagine that each corner is a quarter segment of a circle; the Radius value specifies the radius of the whole circle.

To specify additional options when creating rectangles, click the Geometry Options button in the tool's options bar (shown in Figure 5.2) to display a palette of options. The available choices are:

■ **Unconstrained:** Select this option to create the rectangle exactly as you drag it out.

■ **Square:** This option constrains the rectangle so its width and height are always equal, making a square. (You can also press Shift while dragging to do the same thing.)

- **Fixed Size:** This locks the rectangle to a fixed width and height, which you need to type in the W and H boxes next to the option. You can then click in the document window and drag with the mouse to position the rectangle.

- **Proportional:** This allows you to specify a fixed aspect ratio for the rectangle. After you select this option, type a relative width in the W box and a relative height in the H box. For example, if you type a value of 16 for W and 9 for H then your rectangle takes on the aspect ratio of a 16:9 widescreen TV. Now click and drag in the document window as normal. You'll notice that, while you can adjust the size of the rectangle with the mouse, it always maintains those 16:9 proportions.

- **From Center:** Select this option and you can drag your rectangle out from its center, rather than corner to corner. To do the same thing with the keyboard, press and hold Alt (Option on the Mac) after you start dragging with the mouse.

- **Snap to Pixels:** Because shapes are vectors, they're not locked to the pixels on your screen; they're *resolution-independent*. Normally this is a good thing, but it does mean that Photoshop has to approximate your shape using pixels. For example, if a vertical edge of your shape falls between two pixels, Photoshop smoothes the edge using a technique called anti-aliasing. This is usually what you want to happen; however, the effect can look odd with rectangles, which you'd expect to have hard edges, not smooth. No problem; just select the Snap to Pixels option and Photoshop makes sure that both your rectangle's width and height are a whole number of pixels, eliminating the need for anti-aliasing.

Drawing ellipses and circles with the Ellipse tool

You can use the Ellipse tool to draw both ellipses (with independent width and height) and circles (with constrained width and height). To do this, select the Ellipse tool; then click in the document window and drag. Release the mouse button to make your ellipse.

Photoshop creates the ellipse with one "corner" at the point where you start dragging, and the other "corner" where you finish dragging. Of course, ellipses and circles don't have corners, so imagine a bounding box surrounding the ellipse, touching its top, bottom, left, and right edges. The corners of this imaginary rectangle are the corners we're talking about here.

Creating ellipses like this can be counterintuitive and hard to judge; you'll probably prefer to create your ellipses by dragging from their centers instead. To do this, simply press Alt (Option on the Mac) after you start dragging, and hold it down. Alternatively, you can select the From Center option in the Geometry Options palette, which has the same effect.

To create a circle instead of an ellipse, hold down the Shift key while you drag, or select the Circle option in the Geometry Options palette.

The rest of the Ellipse tool's geometry options are identical to those of the rectangle tools — described earlier — so we won't go into them here. The only other difference is a lack of a Snap to Pixels option, which isn't so necessary when drawing round shapes such as ellipses.

Drawing regular polygons with the Polygon tool

With the Polygon tool you can draw any regular polygon, from a three-sided equilateral triangle all the way up to a 100-sided hectagon if you so desire (although with that many sides it'll probably look much like a circle). Simply select the Polygon tool, type the number of sides you want in the Sides box, then click in the document window and drag.

Unlike the other basic shape tools, the Polygon tool always creates shapes by dragging from the center. You can rotate the shape at the same time as dragging it out by moving the mouse cursor around the center point. To constrain the rotation to 45-degree steps, hold down Shift while dragging.

You can customize the polygon further with the options in the tool's Geometry Options palette, as follows:

- **Radius:** Normally, the radius (size) of the polygon is determined by how far you drag from the center point; however, you can lock the polygon to a specified radius by typing a value in this box. The mouse is then used only for rotating the shape.

> **TIP**   Don't forget that you can use any unit you want when typing length measurements in boxes. For example, to specify a radius of 7.5 centimeters, type 7.5 cm in the Radius box.

- **Smooth Corners:** Select this option to give the corners of the polygon a nice smooth shape; deselect it to leave them sharp and pointy. Unless you also enable Star (see the next item) this option works best on shapes with very few sides, such as three or four; any more and the polygon just starts to look like a circle.

- **Star:** Select this option to create a star: Photoshop indents each edge of the polygon in the middle to create a star shape.

- **Indent Sides By:** This option works in conjunction with Star, and lets you specify how much the centers of each side should be indented. The value is a percentage of the polygon's radius; you can type anything from 1 percent (hardly indented at all) to 99 percent (indented right down to the center of the polygon, producing an extremely spiky star).

- **Smooth Indents:** This setting does for the star indents what Smooth Corners does for the polygon's corners. Both options work independently, so you can have smooth corners and smooth indents, one or the other, or neither.

All these polygon options allow you a fair bit of creativity when using this tool. Figure 5.3 shows some of the tricks we managed to pull using various combinations of the previous settings.

FIGURE 5.3

Getting creative with polygons. Here various Polygon tool options are used to create a variety of different shapes.

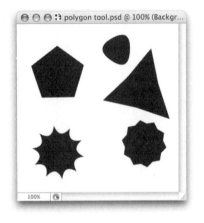

Drawing straight lines and arrows with the Line tool

The Line tool is great for drawing lines of any size and thickness, with or without arrowheads. To draw a line, select the Line tool then click in the document window where you want the line to start. Drag out the line; then release the mouse button to create it. Hold down Shift while dragging if you want to constrain the line's angle to 45-degree steps.

To change the thickness of the line, type a value in the Weight box in the options bar. For example, to create a line that's 5 pixels wide, type **5 px** in the box.

The options in the Line tool's Geometry Options palette let you add arrowheads to lines and control their appearance, as follows:

- **Start and End:** Select one or both of these options to add an arrowhead to the start or the end of the line, respectively. The start of the line is the point that you start dragging to create the line; the end is the point at which you release the mouse button.

- **Width and Length:** These options specify the width and length of the arrowheads; you can use these to alter their shape fairly dramatically. They're expressed as a percentage of the line weight, so if you create a line that's 10 pixels wide, a 200 percent wide arrowhead is 20 pixels wide. (A width of 100 percent and a length of 200 percent create something that looks rather convincingly like a pencil.)

- **Concavity:** Use this option to specify how convex or concave the arrowhead looks. It's expressed as a percentage of the arrowhead's length, and it affects the two edges of the arrowhead that join onto the line. Type a positive value to make these edges slope in toward the arrow point; type a negative value to make them slope out the other way, creating a diamond- or spear-shaped arrowhead.

Figure 5.4 shows some lines created with various weights and arrowhead settings.

> **TIP** Sadly, you can't draw curved lines directly with the Line tool, but there's a nifty way to turn straight lines into arcs. Create your straight line as normal, but make sure it runs horizontally from left to right (press Shift to constrain the line to the horizontal). Now choose Edit ⇨ Transform Path ⇨ Warp, and select the Arc option from the Warp pop-up menu in the options bar. Adjust the radius of the curve by dragging the handle in the warp grid up and down.

FIGURE 5.4

A few different lines drawn with the Line tool. The second and third lines from the top show how the size of the arrowheads is proportional to the line's weight.

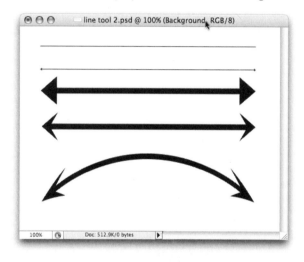

Working with the Custom Shape tool

The final shape tool in the list is the Custom Shape tool. Rather than working with a basic fixed shape like the other tools, the Custom Shape tool lets you choose from a wide variety of complex preset shapes, such as icons, decorative patterns, and bullets. There's even a radioactive warning symbol in there should you ever find yourself designing signage for nuclear power plants. And should you get bored with the available shapes, you can also create your own presets and add them to the palette.

To draw a custom shape, select the Custom Shape tool, choose a shape from the Shape pop-up palette, click in the document window, and start dragging. Don't forget that you can hold down the Spacebar as you drag to position the shape. When you're happy with the shape's size and position, release the mouse button to create the shape.

The Custom Shape tool also comes with some geometry options, as follows:

- **Unconstrained:** This option behaves much like it does with the other shape tools; when selected, the width and height of your shape are not constrained at all.

- **Defined Proportions:** Select this option to lock the shape's aspect ratio to that of the original shape preset. This is often a good idea as it maintains the correct look of the shape. For example, if you use the Cat preset with this option enabled, you won't accidentally draw a fat cat or a thin cat. Figure 5.5 shows this in action.

- **Defined Size:** This option, when selected, creates the shape with the exact width and height of the original preset. This means that your shape looks exactly as intended, but you're somewhat at the mercy of the designer of the shape preset; depending on the size of the image you work with, it could end up looking ridiculously big or small.

- **Fixed Size:** This behaves like it does for the Rectangle and Ellipse tools; type a width and height in the W and H boxes to lock the custom shape to those dimensions.

- **From Center:** Again, this option is identical to its counterpart in the rectangle and Ellipse tools; select it to drag the shape from its center, rather than from corner to corner.

FIGURE 5.5

Drawing a cat using the Custom Shape tool with Defined Proportions selected (top left) and deselected (bottom right).

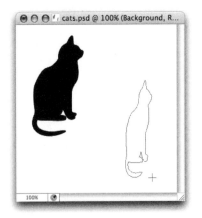

You can also create your own custom shape presets from an existing path or vector mask. To do this, select the path in the Paths palette, or the vector mask by clicking its thumbnail in the Layers palette, then choose Edit ➪ Define Custom Shape. Give your masterpiece a name, and Photoshop adds it to the Shape palette, ready for use when creating new custom shapes.

Other ways to create a shape layer

Although the shape tools are the most easy and convenient way to create new shape layers, you can use other techniques, too. Shapes are just fill layers with vector masks, so if you can create a vector path, you can create a shape layer.

You can use the pen tools to create shape layers. Select either the Pen or Freeform Pen tool in the Toolbox, and then make sure the Shape Layers option in the options bar is selected. After you start drawing, Photoshop creates a new shape layer, fills it with your chosen fill color and applies your chosen style. The pen and shape tools are closely related; you can think of the pen tools as do-it-yourself versions of the shape tools. Both sets of tools can be used to create either paths or shape layers. Only the shape tools can be used to fill pixels on an existing bitmap layer though.

What if you already have a path that you created or imported previously, and you want to turn it into a shape layer? There are a couple of ways to do this:

■ Select the path in the Paths palette and save it as a custom shape using Edit ➪ Define Custom Shape. Then select the Custom Shape tool, make sure the Shape Layers option is selected, and select your custom shape from the Shape pop-up palette. If you want the shape to have exactly the same dimensions as your original path, select the Defined Size geometry option. Click and drag in the document window to create your shape layer.

■ Alternatively, you can build up your shape layer piece by piece. First, create a new solid color fill layer by choosing Layer ➪ New Fill Layer ➪ Solid Color and picking a fill color. Select this new layer, then select your path in the Paths palette and choose Layer ➪ Vector Mask ➪ Current Path. This applies your path to the fill layer as a vector mask, effectively creating a shape layer. You can then choose a style for your shape layer by clicking a style in the Styles palette (Window ➪ Styles), or make up your own style by choosing options under Layer ➪ Layer Style.

The second approach is a bit more long winded than the first. However, it means you don't end up with lots of temporary shapes in your Custom Shapes palette, and it gives you a bit more flexibility, too. For example, you can create a shape based on a Gradient or Pattern fill layer this way — something you can't do directly with the shape tools. (If you want to do a similar thing with the shape tools, choose a Gradient or Pattern Overlay for the shape's Layer Style.)

Editing Shape Layers

You might think that, after you add your shape layer, the shape is set in stone. In fact, you can change pretty much every aspect of a shape layer at any point after you create it. At first glance it might not be immediately obvious how you can edit such a layer, but all is revealed in this section.

Editing a shape layer's style and content

What if you create your shape layer with a certain style, but you want to change it later? Simply select the shape layer; then pick a new style from the Styles palette by clicking the style in the palette. If you can't see the Styles palette, choose Window ➪ Styles to bring it forward.

You're not limited to the presets in the Styles palette, though. After you apply a preset to a shape layer, you can double-click the layer in the Layers palette (just make sure you avoid the thumbnails and layer name) to display the Layer Style dialog box, allowing you to tweak the layer's effects as much as you like. You can also right-click the shape layer in the Layers palette and choose Blending Options to display the same dialog box. Don't forget that you also can edit the shape layer's blending options, such as its blending mode and opacity. It is a layer, after all.

> **CROSS-REF** Layer styles are covered in detail, including how to create and edit effects, in Chapter 10. For details on the various blending options, see Chapter 7.

Want to change a shape's fill color? Just double-click the shape layer's thumbnail to display the Color Picker, and choose a new color. You can even change the plain color fill to a gradient fill or a pattern fill by choosing Layer ➪ Change Layer Content ➪ Gradient, or Layer ➪ Change Layer Content ➪ Pattern, respectively.

> **CAUTION** If the shape layer has a layer style applied that includes a color, gradient, or pattern overlay effect, then that overlay overrides any fill color, gradient, or pattern. So if you change the layer's fill and nothing seems to be happening, check which effects are being applied to the layer.

> **CROSS-REF** For more on filling layers with gradients and patterns, see Chapter 6.

Converting a shape layer to an adjustment layer

You may have noticed all the adjustment layer options under Layer ➪ Change Layer Content. Fill layers (which is what shape layers are, basically) and adjustment layers are very closely related, and, in fact, you can swap between the two easily. This is fantastic because it means you can use a shape to mask off an adjustment layer. Simply create your shape layer; then change it to an adjustment layer by choosing a layer type under Layer ➪ Change Layer Content. An example of this is shown in Figure 5.6.

Converting a shape layer to a normal bitmap layer

You can go a step further and convert a shape layer to a normal layer. This means that you retain the vector mask that defines the shape outline, but the inside of the shape is now a regular bitmap image, rather than a fill. This allows you to paint inside the shape using virtually any tool or use the shape's outline to mask an existing bitmap layer, such as a photo. In short, it gives you a lot of flexibility.

FIGURE 5.6

A new star shape layer is created here and then converted it into an Exposure adjustment layer. Photoshop applies the adjustment to the underlying layer using the chosen shape.

To convert the shape layer to a normal layer, select the layer then choose Layer ➪ Rasterize ➪ Fill Content. The contents of the fill are then turned into a bitmap image, and your shape layer becomes a regular bitmap layer. The layer's thumbnail in the Layers palette changes from displaying a fill layer icon to showing you the actual layer contents, as you can see in Figure 5.7.

NOTE You can't use Layer ➪ Rasterize ➪ Fill Content on an adjustment layer, so if you previously converted your shape's fill layer to an adjustment layer, you first need to convert it back with Layer ➪ Change Layer Content ➪ Solid Color.

FIGURE 5.7

Converting a shape layer (left) to a normal layer (right) with Layer ➪ Rasterize ➪ Fill Content. Notice how the layer thumbnail changes, letting you know that it's now a normal layer.

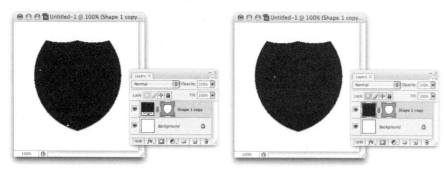

After you convert the shape layer to a normal layer, you can do practically anything to it. You can paint on the layer using a painting tool; use the Clone Stamp, Dodge, or Burn tools; or apply any filter under the Filter menu. Because your new normal layer retains the shape layer's vector mask, any content that you create or edit on the layer is masked off to fit the shape. You can now have fun filling your shape with whatever you want.

Applying a shape to an existing normal layer

What if you want an existing normal layer to take on the shape of a shape layer? There are a number of ways to do this; choose the method that works for you from the following list:

■ Click the shape layer's vector mask thumbnail and drag it on top of the normal layer in the Layers palette. This moves the vector mask from one layer to the other, so that the shape now clips your normal layer. (You'll probably want to delete the now de-masked shape layer.) Alternatively, you can copy the vector mask to the normal layer, preserving the original vector mask in the shape layer. To do this, hold down Alt (Option on the Mac) before you click and drag the vector mask.

■ Select the shape layer, then open up the Paths palette (Window ⇨ Paths). You'll see the shape's vector mask in there (imaginatively titled something like Shape 1 Vector Mask). Click that mask in the Paths palette and drag it down to the New Path icon at the bottom of the palette. This makes a duplicate called Path 1 (or something similar). Select this dupli-cate if it's not already selected, then select the normal layer in the Layers palette and choose Layer ⇨ Vector Mask ⇨ Current Path to apply the path as a vector mask to the normal layer. (You might want to delete that duplicate path from the Paths palette afterward.)

■ A variant on the previous technique: If you haven't yet created your shape layer, click the Paths option in the shape tool's options bar to create a working path instead of a shape layer. Draw your shape to create the path. Finally, select the path in the Paths palette, select the normal layer, then choose Layer ⇨ Vector Mask ⇨ Current Path.

> **TIP**   A handy shortcut for Layer ⇨ Vector Mask ⇨ Current Path is to Ctrl+click (Option+click on the Mac) the Add Layer Mask icon at the bottom of the Layers palette.

■ Another technique is to keep the shape layer as it is, and use it as a clipping mask to mask off the contents of the normal layer. To do this, position the normal layer above the shape layer in the Layers palette, select the normal layer, and choose Layer ⇨ Create Clipping Mask. Watch out for any effects applied to the shape layer, though, as these then appear on your clipped normal layer instead. (You might want to turn them off.) In addi-tion, if your clipped layer contains transparent areas, you might need to set the shape layer's Fill to 0 percent, and deselect its Blend Clipped Layers as Group blending option, to prevent the shape layer showing through. Finally, if you're happy to lose your shape layer, you can merge the two layers together: select both layers and choose Layer ⇨ Merge Layers.

Figure 5.8 gives you an idea of the power you can wield when you start masking normal layers with the vector masks from shape layers.

 **TIP** You can use the previous techniques to apply a shape to a type layer, too, thereby masking off parts of your type.

FIGURE 5.8

A spiky shape is applied as a vector mask to a normal layer to mask out the area around the turkey's head.

Moving and altering shapes

So far, only editing the content of the shape layer has been discussed; we haven't looked at editing the vector shape itself. It's easy to do this, though, because the shape is simply a path. This means that you can move the shape around, add and delete points on the shape, reshape segments, and so on, all by using the usual path-editing suspects: the Path and Direct Selection tools, the pen tools, and the anchor point tools.

How to select a shape

To select a whole shape within a shape layer, use the Path Selection tool (the one with the black arrow). To select this tool, click the Selection Tool (arrow) icon in the Toolbox. If the Direct Selection tool is currently selected (shown by a white arrow), hold the mouse button down over the icon in the Toolbox until a pop-up menu appears, then choose the Path Selection tool from the menu. After you select this tool, the mouse pointer changes to a black arrow.

A quicker way to select this tool is to press Shift+A until your mouse pointer becomes a black arrow. Alternatively, if you're currently using a shape tool or the Direct Selection tool, you can just hold down Ctrl (⌘ on the Mac) to access the Path Selection tool temporarily.

TIP   You can press Shift and a tool's shortcut key to cycle through any hidden tools that share the same space in the Toolbox. For example, as well as pressing Shift+A to cycle through the Path and Direct Selection tools, you can press Shift+U to cycle through the shape tools, or Shift+S to cycle through the stamp tools. In fact, if you choose Edit ➪ Preferences ➪ General (Photoshop ➪ Preferences ➪ General on the Mac) and deselect the Use Shift Key for Tool Switch option, you don't even have to press Shift.

After you select the Path Selection tool, click the shape in the document window to select it. Control points appear at the corners of the shape, indicating that it's selected.

To select more than one shape on the layer at the same time, Shift+click all the shapes you want to select. You can also drag a rubber band around shapes to select them.

NOTE   You can't select shapes on more than one shape layer at the same time with the Path Selection tool.

To deselect all shapes, click anywhere outside them in the document window.

 As well as selecting whole shapes, you can also select individual segments and anchor points within the shape. To do this, select the Direct Selection tool (the white arrow) in the Toolbox, or keep pressing Shift+A until the cursor changes to a white arrow. You can now click a segment or point within a shape to select it. A point changes from a hollow square to a solid one when it's selected.

If you want to select multiple segments or points, Shift+click each segment or point you want to add to, or remove from, the selection.

Moving shapes around

After you select a shape with the Path Selection tool, you can drag it around the document window to reposition it. Hold down Shift if you want to constrain the movement to 45-degree steps. You can also nudge the shape around 1 pixel at a time by using the arrow keys, provided you still have the Path Selection tool selected. (This means that if you're currently holding down Ctrl/⌘ to temporarily access the Path Selection tool from a shape tool, then you need to keep that key held down while using the arrow keys.) Hold down Shift as well to nudge the shape in 10-pixel steps.

Editing shapes

You can change a shape's, well, shape using the Direct Selection tool, the pen tools, and the anchor point tools. You won't get a detailed primer on these tools here, but this section should be enough to give you a general idea. Figure 5.9 gives an overview of the different types of points and segments that make up shapes and paths.

FIGURE 5.9

A shape or path usually consists of two or more anchor points — with or without direction lines — and some straight or curved line segments.

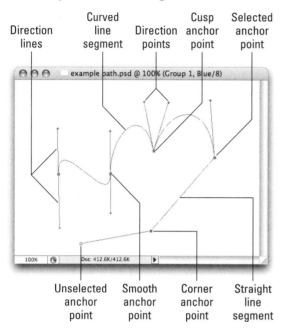

To move a segment or anchor point within a shape, select the segment or anchor point by clicking it with the Direct Selection tool, then drag it with the mouse, as shown in Figure 5.10. (To move a curved segment, Shift+click the anchor points at either end of the curve first to select them; otherwise you'll reshape the curve when you drag it, rather than move it.) You can also nudge anchor points a pixel at a time using the arrow keys (as always, hold down Shift to nudge in 10-pixel increments).

TIP When moving segments and points, you can constrain the movement to 45-degree steps by holding down Shift as you drag. This is useful if you want to move a segment or point in a straight line.

To add a new anchor point, select the shape's path using either the Path Selection tool or the Direct Selection tool. Then choose the Pen or Freeform Pen tool and make sure its Auto Add/Delete option is selected in the options bar. Now, click anywhere on a path segment in the shape to add a new point, as shown in Figure 5.10. To delete a point, follow the same steps, but click the point you want to remove instead. You can also delete a point or segment by clicking it with the Direct Selection tool to select it, then pressing Delete.

> **NOTE**   You can also add and delete points using the Add Anchor Point and Delete Anchor Point tools — available by holding down the mouse button over the Pen Tool icon in the Toolbox — but it's easier just to use the regular pen tools with Auto Add/Delete enabled.

FIGURE 5.10

To move a straight segment, simply drag it with the Direct Selection tool (left). To move a curved segment, select the anchor points at either end of the curve using the Direct Selection tool, then drag the curve (center). To add a new anchor point, select the path, then use the Pen tool with Auto Add/Delete enabled; click on the path where you want to add the new point (right).

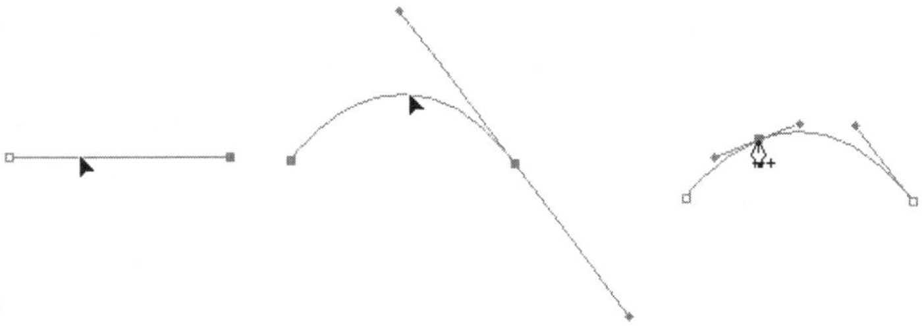

To convert a smooth point to a corner point without direction lines — that is, a corner point with straight line segments on either side — select the Convert Point tool in the Toolbox (it's grouped with the pen tools, and it looks like an open arrowhead), then click the point you want to convert. To convert the other way, click the corner point with the Convert Point tool and drag with the mouse to pull out the direction lines. Both these techniques are shown in Figure 5.11. To create a point with only one direction line, so that there's a curved segment on one side of the point and a straight line segment on the other, click the point with the Convert Point tool, then Alt+drag (Option+drag on the Mac) the point to pull the direction line out from the point. You can also drag a direction line back into the point to turn that side of the point back into a corner point.

> **TIP**   You can temporarily access the Convert Point tool from either pen tool by holding down Alt (Option on the Mac).

You can also turn a smooth point into a corner point with direction lines. This is known as a *cusp point*; that is, a corner with curves rather than a corner with straight lines. To do this, select the point, then click either of its direction points with the Convert Point tool, or Alt+click (Option+click on the Mac) a direction point with the Direct Selection tool. Drag the point around until you get the shape you want, as shown in Figure 5.11. You have now "broken" the direction lines so that they work independently of each other; the two curves enter and leave the points at different angles, creating a cusp. Compare this to the original smooth point, where the direction lines moved together and were at 180 degrees to each other, and the curves traveled smoothly through the point.

If you want to convert a cusp point back into a smooth point, select the Convert Point tool, then click the point and drag to pull out two symmetrical direction lines again.

186

TIP Whenever you think direction lines, think curves. The longer a direction line is, the more pronounced its corresponding curve at the time it leaves the anchor point. A very short direction line produces a curve that's almost a straight line. If you remove the direction line altogether, or drag it right into the anchor point, its corresponding line will be totally straight as it exits the anchor point.

FIGURE 5.11

Converting an anchor point in a path

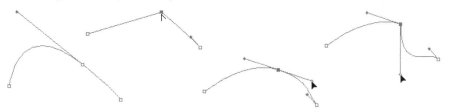

To reshape the curves on both sides of a smooth point, select the point, then click either of the point's direction points with the Direct Selection tool and drag. To reshape just one curve, "break" the direction lines as described earlier to make a cusp point, then click and drag the direction point of the curve you want to shape, using either the Direct Selection tool or the Convert Point tool. Figure 5.12 shows how to reshape both curves at a smooth point, and one curve at a cusp point, by dragging direction points.

To reshape both curves of a cusp point at the same time, select the Direct Selection tool, click the point, then Alt+click (Option+click on the Mac) either direction point and drag.

TIP You can also reshape a curve by clicking the curve itself with the Direct Selection tool and dragging. Figure 5.12 shows this in action.

FIGURE 5.12

Drag the direction points with the Direct Selection tool to reshape both curves at a smooth point (left) and one curve at a cusp point (middle). You can also reshape a curve by dragging the curve itself (right).

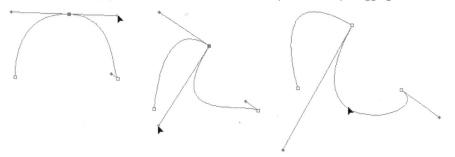

Cutting, pasting, duplicating, and deleting shapes

After you select a shape's vector mask path, or a segment within the path, you can cut or copy it then paste it into a new path, or you can simply delete it. You can also duplicate the entire path, if you want to use it for other purposes.

Cutting and copying works much like you'd expect. Select the path or segment you want to cut or copy, then choose Edit ➪ Cut, or Edit ➪ Copy (or use the equivalent keyboard shortcut). You can then paste the path or segment into the same vector mask, a different vector mask, or a different path. Simply select the mask or path you want to paste it into, then choose Edit ➪ Paste, or press Ctrl+V (⌘+V on the Mac).

To duplicate a shape's entire vector mask path, select the shape layer, open the Paths palette (Window ➪ Paths), find the shape's vector mask path in the palette, and then click it and drag it down to the Create New Path icon at the bottom of the palette. You can now use this path anywhere you want.

Transforming shapes

You can use all the transform commands under Edit ➪ Transform, as well as the Free Transform command, on shapes. When you transform a shape, you're really transforming its outline path (that is to say, its vector mask).

To transform a whole shape layer, select the layer; then choose Edit ➪ Free Transform, or select an option from under Edit ➪ Transform.

To transform shapes within a layer, use the Path Selection tool (see the section "How to select a shape" earlier in this chapter) to select the shape; then transform it using one of the transform commands. (When you do this, the transform commands change to Edit ➪ Free Transform Path, and Edit ➪ Transform Path, because you're now directly manipulating paths within the shape layer.)

You can even transform individual points within a shape. To do this, select the points using the Direct Selection tool, then choose Edit ➪ Free Transform Points, or choose an option from under Edit ➪ Transform Points. Any segments attached to the points are transformed as well.

TIP As you're only transforming the shape's vector mask, any fill pattern inside the shape does not get transformed at the same time. For example, you can stretch the shape layer as big as you want, but the pattern inside remains the same size; you just see it repeating more (see Figure 5.13 for an example). If you want to stretch the pattern as well, and the pattern is created as a Pattern fill layer, you first need to rasterize the shape layer with Layer ➪ Rasterize ➪ Shape. You can then transform the layer as a regular bitmap layer, so the pattern is transformed along with the shape. If the pattern is created as a Pattern Overlay effect though, you also need to rasterize the effect with Layer ➪ Layer Style ➪ Create Layer. Then select the newly created pattern layer and press Ctrl+E (⌘+E on the Mac) to merge the two layers. Finally, you can transform both shape and pattern with one of the transform commands. Phew.

FIGURE 5.13

Transforming a shape with the transform commands. Notice how the shape's fill pattern doesn't get transformed—only shape's outline.

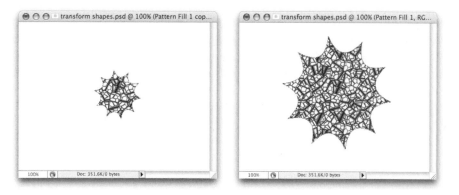

Combining Shapes on a Single Layer

So far we've talked about adding one shape per layer, but Photoshop lets you add as many shapes as you want to a single shape layer. Even better, you can choose how those shapes overlap. This allows you to create entirely new shapes in various ways—by adding shapes on top of each other; by using one shape to cut out another one; by intersecting shapes; and by cutting out shape intersections.

> **TIP** Having shapes on a single shape layer is also great for exporting to other packages such as Illustrator, because Photoshop only lets you export one shape layer at a time. If your shape is spread across more than one layer you have to export each layer separately, then realign them in Illustrator.

You can perform all these clever tricks using the five combination buttons available in each shape tool's options bar (refer to Figure 5.2).

> **NOTE** You can also use all of these buttons, apart from the first Add to Shape Area button, when creating paths with the shape tools. In that case you are combining paths, of course, rather than shapes. However, you can't use these buttons at all when using the Fill Pixels option. Even Photoshop has its limits.

If you're creating a new shape layer, or you haven't selected the vector mask of an existing shape layer to work on, then only the first option, Create New Shape Layer, is available. This option creates each new shape on a separate layer. This is often what you want to happen; shapes on separate layers are easier to manipulate independently, and they can all have their own styles, fills, and so on. However, if you want to combine your shapes in interesting ways, read on.

To use any of the other combination options, make sure an existing shape layer's vector mask is selected. This is the case if you've just created a new shape. You can tell if the vector mask is selected by looking at the layer's vector mask thumbnail in the Layers palette — if it has an outline rectangle around it, it's selected. If the vector mask isn't selected, click its thumbnail to select it.

After you select the vector mask, select a shape tool, click a combination option, then drag out your shape in the document window. Photoshop combines your new shape with existing shapes in the layer, using the combination method you select.

NOTE These combination tricks are generally designed to work on overlapping shapes, so you won't see much happening if you don't overlap them. However, the Subtract From Shape Area option can be a handy way to invert a stand-alone shape. (See the section "Recombining existing shapes on a layer.")

Adding shapes together

The next option along the options bar is Add To Shape Area. This option simply adds the new shape on top of existing shapes in the layer, combining the two shapes to create a bigger shape area. Use this if you want to add one shape to another, as shown in Figure 5.14. Click the Add To Shape Area button, then start drawing your shape.

TIP You can quickly select the Add To Shape Area option by pressing the plus (+) key. You can also hold down Shift before you start drawing your new shape to add it to the shape area; release Shift after you start drawing, unless you also want to constrain the shape's proportions or angle.

FIGURE 5.14

Adding shapes together using the Add To Shape Area option. The end result is a bigger shape area that encompasses both the original shapes.

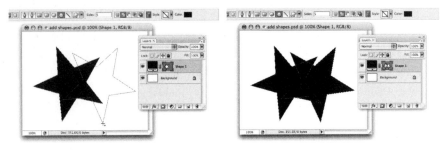

Subtracting shapes from each other

Subtract From Shape Area, the next option, uses your newly created shape to cut out areas of the existing shape layer. It's almost like using the shape as an eraser. Figure 5.15 shows how this works in practice. Select Subtract From Shape Area, draw your new shape, and Photoshop subtracts the shape you draw from the existing shape area.

TIP To quickly select Subtract From Shape Area, press the minus (-) key. Alternatively, hold down Alt (Option on the Mac) before drawing your shape to subtract it from the shape area. With some shape tools, you'll want to release the Alt/Option key after you start drawing, unless you want to drag out the shape from the center.

FIGURE 5.15

Creating a donut using the Subtract From Shape Area option. First, the big circle is created; then the little circle is added on top with Subtract From Shape Area selected.

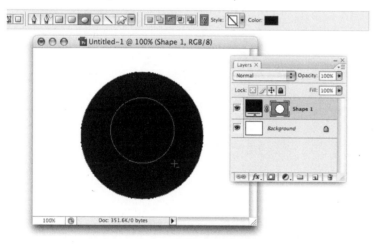

Intersecting and excluding overlapping shapes

You can also combine shapes so that just the intersecting areas of the shapes remain. To do this, select the Intersect Shape Areas option in the options bar, then draw your new shape. Any parts of the shape layer that don't overlap with your new shape are removed from the shape area. You can see an example of intersecting shapes in Figure 5.16.

The final combination option, Exclude Overlapping Shape Areas, has the opposite effect of the Intersect Shape Areas option. Rather than removing the parts of the shapes that don't overlap, this option removes the parts that do. Look at Figure 5.16 to see how this works.

To use this option, click the Exclude Overlapping Shape Areas button and then draw your shape. Photoshop removes any parts of the shape that overlap existing shapes from the shape area.

Here you can see the difference between the Intersect Shape Areas and Exclude Overlapping Shape Areas options. The first (left) leaves you with just the parts of the shapes that overlap, while the second (right) removes the overlapping parts from the shape area.

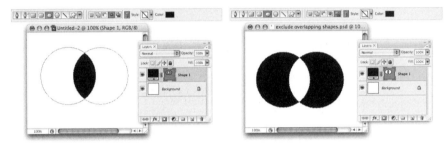

Recombining existing shapes on a layer

The choice you make when you add a shape to an existing shape layer isn't set in stone. Thanks to the joy of vectors, you can go back at any time and change the way the shapes on a layer interact, and the shape area adjusts itself accordingly.

However, it's not all a bed of roses. The main problem with this approach is that you can only change how a shape interacts with other shapes below it in the same layer, and you can't change the stacking order of shapes in a layer either — newer shapes always sit on top of older ones. The best approach is to be methodical in how you create your multishape layers, so you can get them to interact in the way you want.

To change a shape's combination method, select the shape's path using the Path Selection tool, then choose a new combination option — add, subtract, intersect, or exclude — using the buttons in the options bar. The shape layer immediately changes to reflect the new combination method that you select, as you can see in Figure 5.17. For example, if you change a shape's combination method to Subtract From Shape Area, the shape cuts a hole in any underlying shapes.

 Don't forget that you can temporarily access the Path Selection tool to select shapes while you're using a shape tool. To do this, hold down Ctrl (⌘ on the Mac).

You can use this approach to invert a shape area, so that everything that was inside the shape area moves outside, and vice versa. To do this, make sure the shape you want to invert is the only shape on the shape layer, select it, then click the Subtract From Shape Area button (or press the minus key). This subtracts the shape from nothing, leaving you with an inverted shape area. Figure 5.18 shows this handy trick in action.

FIGURE 5.17

In the original shape layer (left), the triangle is added to the square using the Add To Shape Area option. By selecting the triangle with the Path Selection tool and changing its combination method to Subtract From Shape Area, the triangle now cuts out a portion of the square (right).

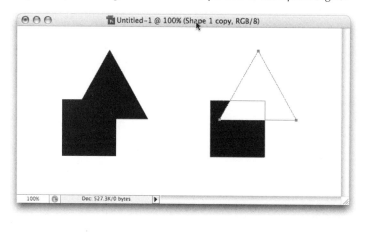

FIGURE 5.18

Want your shape's vector mask to mask off areas of your layer, rather than revealing them? Invert the shape area (left) by selecting the vector mask path and changing its combination method to Subtract From Shape Area (right).

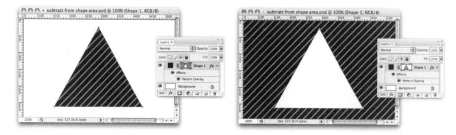

After your shapes are combined the way you want them, you can fuse them permanently into a single shape (technically a single *path component,* which means a distinct, separate series of path segments joined together). To do this, select the Path Selection tool (you need to actually select it from the Toolbox or with Shift+A, rather than temporarily accessing it), Shift+click all the shapes you want to combine, then click the Combine button in the options bar to permanently join them together into one shape.

Aligning and distributing shapes

You can align shapes with each other, or evenly distribute shapes throughout the shape layer, much as you can with layers themselves. To do this, select the Path Selection tool, select the shapes you want to align or distribute, then click one of the Align or Distribute buttons in the options bar, as shown in Figure 5.19.

 The Align and Distribute buttons in the Path Selection tool's options bar only work for shapes within a single shape layer. If you want to align or distribute shapes on separate shape layers, select the layers, then use the commands under Layer ⇨ Align, or Layer ⇨ Distribute.

 For more on aligning and distributing layers, see Chapter 2.

FIGURE 5.19

The Align and Distribute options in the Path Selection tool's options bar let you accurately rearrange the shapes in a shape layer.

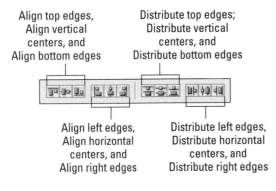

Align top edges, Align vertical centers, and Align bottom edges

Distribute top edges; Distribute vertical centers, and Distribute bottom edges

Align left edges, Align horizontal centers, and Align right edges

Distribute left edges, Distribute horizontal centers, and Distribute right edges

Tutorial: Shape Layers in Practice

We've covered a lot of ground in this chapter, and now we want to take you through a simple example of shape layers in action. In this example, you're going to create a new logo for a sushi restaurant. Shape layers are ideal for creating logos, because they can be scaled easily with no loss of quality. This means that, whether you want to use the logo on a Web site, for signage, or on the side of a bus, you won't have to redraw anything.

Start by creating a new document. Choose File ⇨ New to display the New dialog box, as shown in Figure 5.20. The precise document dimensions aren't particularly important, because shapes are resolution-independent, but give yourself some room to experiment. Use a document size of 800 x 800 pixels at 72 dpi.

Creating a document. Choose a reasonably big canvas, but note that the Width, Height, and Resolution settings aren't critical.

Adding the first shape

The idea is to create a logo for a sushi restaurant, so do a bit of brainstorming to think of suitable ideas. Bowls and chopsticks spring to mind, along with a funky feel. Rather than drawing these items explicitly, go for something a bit more abstract to evoke the feel of them rather than representing them accurately.

Start by selecting the Ellipse tool from the Toolbox. To do this, click and hold the mouse button over the Shape Tool icon and select Ellipse Tool from the pop-up menu. You can also press Shift+U until the Ellipse tool is selected, or click the Shape Tool icon in the Toolbox, then click the Ellipse Tool button in the options bar. So many choices.

Make sure the Shape Layers option is selected in the options bar, then draw a circle shape by holding down Shift and dragging in the document window.

Bowls have a bottom, so "cut" a bottom out of your circular bowl shape. To do this, click the Subtract From Shape Area button in the options bar, click inside the circle in the document window, and drag out a new circle, as shown in Figure 5.21. Photoshop uses your new circle to cut out an area of the original.

You can actually move the cutout circle around separately from the black circle because they're separate paths on the shape layer. To do this, select the Path Selection tool from the Toolbox and click the cutout circle to select it. You can then drag it around with the mouse until you get a result you like, as shown in Figure 5.22. This example goes for a slightly off-center cutout, which we like.

TIP If you want the second circle exactly centered within the first, select both paths using the Path Selection tool and click the Align Horizontal Centers and Align Vertical Centers buttons in the options bar to line them up.

FIGURE 5.21

Using the Subtract From Shape Area option to cut out part of the original circle

FIGURE 5.22

Moving the second path around. There's now a hole in the center of the original circle. The Background layer is hidden so you can see through the hole to the checkerboard pattern behind.

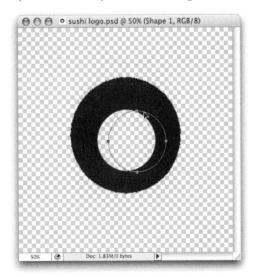

This effect is okay, but it's not very dynamic. Try using Photoshop's transform commands to give it something extra. First, select the whole shape layer by clicking it in the Layers palette. If the layer's vector mask is selected, with a rectangular border around its thumbnail, click its thumbnail to deselect it. Then choose Edit ➪ Free Transform, or press Ctrl+T (⌘+T on the Mac), to start transforming the shape layer.

TIP If you want to transform the two circles of the shape layer individually, click a circle in the document window with the Path Selection tool to select its path; then transform it with Edit ➪ Free Transform Path.

The Distort command is a great way of playing with the "planes" of a layer. To access it from within the Free Transform command, hold down Ctrl (⌘ on the Mac), then start dragging the edge or corner handles of the bounding box in the document window. As you move the handles, the shape starts to look like it's rocking backward or looming forward. In Figure 5.23, the Distort and Rotate commands are used to tinker with the shape layer; the Path Selection tool is also used to select the inner circle, which is then enlarged with the Scale command to produce a pleasingly dramatic effect.

CROSS-REF For more information on Photoshop's various transform commands, see Chapter 3.

FIGURE 5.23

Using the Free Transform command to add drama to the shape. The shape layer is rotated and distorted, and the inner cutout circle is enlarged slightly.

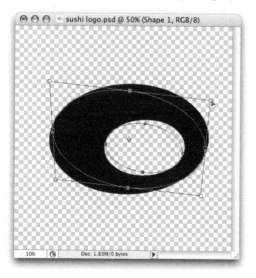

Adding the chopsticks

That's a nice shape to work with. Add another element to the logo: chopsticks. Start by creating a single chopstick; you can then duplicate this to make two. To create the chopstick, follow these steps:

1. **Switch to the Line tool.** Click and hold the Shape Tool icon in the Toolbox and choose Line Tool from the pop-up menu. Alternatively, if you still have the Ellipse tool selected you can click the Line Tool icon in the options bar.

2. **Type a weight of 10 pixels in the Weight box.** This gives you a pretty thick, chunky line to represent a chopstick.

3. **Make sure the Create New Shape Layer option is selected.** To do this, click the Create New Shape Layer button in the options bar.

4. **Click above the circles, then drag down below the circles.** This creates a vertical line to represent your chopstick.

Make the chopstick a bit more stylish by tapering the bottom end of it. To do this, select the Direct Selection tool and click the chopstick in the document window to select it. Small handles appear at each of the four corners of the chopstick. Click the bottom-left corner — it goes dark when selected — then drag it slightly to the right. Then click the bottom-right corner and drag it a bit to the left, as shown in Figure 5.24.

FIGURE 5.24

Tapering the chopstick using the Direct Selection tool

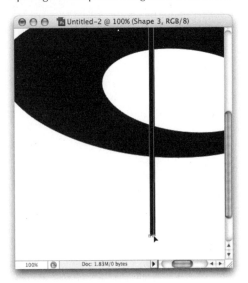

TIP It's much easier to see what you're doing if you zoom in a little. To do this, hold down Ctrl (⌘ on the Mac) and press the plus (+) key to zoom in and minus (-) to zoom out. You can move around the canvas by holding down the Spacebar, then clicking in the document window and dragging. Alternatively, display the Navigator palette (Window ⇨ Navigator); then drag the red square in the Navigator around.

You need two of these chopsticks to make your logo. One way to duplicate the chopstick is to duplicate the shape layer by choosing Layer ⇨ Duplicate Layer. For this example, though, duplicate the chopstick shape within its shape layer, so that you end up with both chopsticks on the same layer. To do this, select the chopstick using the Path Selection tool; while holding down Alt (Option on the Mac), drag the chopstick slightly to the right. Photoshop duplicates the chopstick's path as you drag, creating a new path on the same shape layer, as you can see in Figure 5.25.

FIGURE 5.25

Copying the chopstick using the Path Selection tool. Hold down Alt (Option on the Mac) as you drag the chopstick to duplicate the chopstick's path and position the duplicate path at the same time.

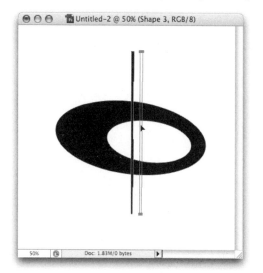

To add a little jauntiness to the pair of newly formed chopsticks, rotate your duplicate chopstick slightly. To do this, select it with the Path Selection tool (if it's not already selected), then enter Free Transform mode by choosing Edit ⇨ Free Transform Path, or pressing Ctrl+T (⌘+T on the Mac). Move the mouse cursor outside the chopstick's bounding box until it changes to a curved, double-headed arrow, then click and drag to rotate the chopstick slightly clockwise.

Your logo is finished. You can see the result in Figure 5.26. At first glance, the final article is simply a cool shape, but with a closer look you can see the concept behind it: a bowl and chopsticks. Just what you were aiming for.

FIGURE 5.26

The final logo. Your file has just three layers, including the Background layer.

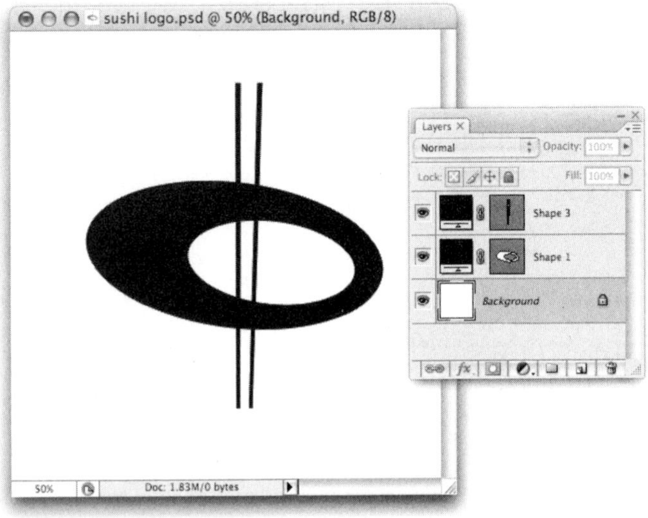

At some point you'll probably want to get your logo into Adobe Illustrator. Illustrator's support for Photoshop files is pretty good, but support for shape layers is less than elegant. You can't just open the PSD file in Illustrator and retain the ability to edit the shapes, so you need to find another approach.

Illustrator supports copy and paste for paths between open Photoshop and Illustrator documents, and that can be a fast and effective approach, because shapes are basically composed of paths. Use the Path Selection tool to select individual shapes in a layer, and select Edit ➪ Copy. In an Illustrator document, select Edit ➪ Paste. Your shape appears in the Illustrator document as a path, which you need to recolor. Because you're only bringing over the basic paths, you also lose any layer styles you applied.

This is a very good approach if all your shapes are on a single layer in Photoshop. However, if your design is split between multiple shape layers, as in the logo example here, it becomes a little trickier. Although you can select multiple layers in Photoshop, you can't select multiple paths across layers. To get around this issue, here are some alternative strategies you can try for exporting multi-layered shapes:

- Use the approach just outlined. Select the shapes on one shape layer using the Path Selection tool, and copy and paste them into Illustrator. Repeat for the other shape layer or layers, then realign and recolor your shapes in Illustrator. In this example, this approach is quite acceptable, because there are only two layers.

- Export the paths to Illustrator files. Again, using the Path Selection tool, select the shapes one shape layer at a time, but rather than copying and pasting, choose File ⇨ Export ⇨ Paths to Illustrator. This produces Illustrator (.ai) files that are saved to your hard drive, which can then be opened in Illustrator. You must save as many files as you have shape layers, then recompose and recolor the final design in Illustrator.

- Merge the vector mask paths on the separate shape layers together so that you have all your shapes in a single layer's vector mask. This gets around the problem discussed earlier, because you can then cleanly export the shapes as a single layer in one go.

To use this last approach with your logo example, follow these steps:

1. **Select the vector mask of the chopsticks layer.** To do this, click the layer's vector mask thumbnail in the Layers palette so that a border appears around the thumbnail.

2. **Choose Edit ⇨ Copy.** This copies the path that makes up the layer's vector mask and stores it in the clipboard.

3. **Select the vector mask of the circles layer.** Again, to select the vector mask, simply click its thumbnail in the Layers palette.

4. **Choose Edit ⇨ Paste.** The chopsticks layer's vector mask path is now pasted on top of the circles layer's vector mask path, combining the separate paths into a single path.

5. **Click the new "bowl and chopsticks" layer's vector mask thumbnail to deselect it, then click it again.** This ensures that all the path components of the vector mask — bowl and chopsticks — are selected.

6. **Choose Edit ⇨ Copy.** This copies the whole vector mask to the clipboard.

7. **Switch to Illustrator, create a new document, and choose Edit ⇨ Paste.** You've now pasted your whole logo — bowl and chopsticks — into Illustrator as a single, intact path.

Combining paths like this can sometimes produce unexpected results. For example, if you copy and paste the circles layer's vector mask thumbnail into the chopsticks layer, the part of the chopsticks going through the inner circle disappears! This is due to how the shape combining works. The inner circle is a subtractive element — remember that you created it with Subtract From Shape Area enabled. The paste action places the circles on top of the stack. The inner circle subtracts itself from any shape area underneath it, so it effectively knocks a hole in the underlying chopsticks shape. However, when pasting the chopsticks onto the circles, the chopsticks are above the circles in the stacking order, so they're not affected by the subtractive nature of that inner circle.

CROSS-REF For more on combining shapes and on shape stacking order, see the section "Combining Shapes on a Single Layer" earlier in this chapter.

Summary

This chapter has introduced you to a very versatile type of layer — shape layers. Because shape layers are vector-based, they can be stretched, squeezed, and otherwise manipulated as often as you want, with no loss of quality.

You looked at how to add shape layers using the shape tools — Rectangle, Rounded Rectangle, Ellipse, Polygon, Line, and Custom Shape — and also using the Pen and Freeform Pen tools. You also learned how to convert an existing path into a shape layer.

You learned how to edit a shape layer's style, and also how to change the content of a shape layer; you can turn it into an adjustment layer, convert it to a normal bitmap layer, or take a shape layer and apply its vector mask to an existing normal layer.

As well as altering a shape layer's style and content, you learned how to edit the shape itself through the use of the Path and Direct Selection tools, the Pen and Freeform Pen tools, and the Convert Point tool. You also looked at cutting, copying, and pasting individual shape paths, as well as deleting them, and you learned how to transform shapes using the transform commands, much like you can transform layers.

As well as creating shapes on separate shape layers, you can combine them within a single shape layer. You looked at how to add new shapes to a shape layer, subtract shapes from existing shapes within a layer, intersect overlapping shape areas in a layer, and exclude overlapping areas. You also learned about using the Align and Distribute buttons to align several shapes within a shape layer, or to distribute several shapes evenly across a layer.

Finally, you brought many of these concepts together into one practical example: designing a logo for a sushi restaurant using shape layers.

Chapter 6

Exploring Adjustment and Fill Layers

This chapter concentrates on a really useful layer type in Photoshop, the *adjustment layer*. This layer type was first introduced in version 4.0, and it offers a really flexible way to make color and tonal adjustments to your images.

You've probably used quite a few of the adjustment commands under the Image ⇨ Adjustments menu. These commands let you tweak various aspects of your image, such as brightness and contrast, hue and saturation levels, and color balance. Wonderful though these commands are, they're all *destructive*, which means they permanently alter the pixels of your image. Each time you go back and make another adjustment, you lose more and more image detail, and you can't reverse the effect of an adjustment, either.

You can, of course, use the History palette to jump back to a time before you made the adjustment, or you can keep multiple copies of your layer or document as a backup, but it's much better to use an adjustment layer. The great thing about adjustment layers is that they're *nondestructive*; your adjustments don't touch the underlying pixels of the image. So you can add, remove, and edit adjustment layers without worrying that you're committing to permanent changes. Fantastic stuff.

This chapter introduces you to adjustment layers, explains how they work, explores each of the adjustment layer types, and shows how you can really get the most out of these layers to produce great-looking images.

You also look at *fill layers*. These simple layers are closely related to adjustment layers, in that they apply an image-wide effect that you can control with a layer mask. In fact, you can easily turn an adjustment layer into a fill layer and vice versa. Fill layers are great for applying solid color, gradient, or pattern fills to areas of your image. Shape layers, which are covered extensively in Chapter 5, are essentially fill layers with vector masks.

Introducing Adjustment Layers

An adjustment layer is another of the layer types offered by Photoshop, and it shares many of the common properties of layers. For example:

- It appears in the Layers palette.
- You can rename, group, and reorder it just like a regular layer.
- You can control its opacity and blending mode.
- You can apply layer masks and vector masks to it.

One of the things you can't do with an adjustment layer is paint on it. In fact, adjustment layers are very closely related to fill layers, which are covered later in this chapter; both types of layers affect the whole image area (assuming you're not using a mask), and don't have any pixel content of their own. You can, however, paint on an adjustment layer's mask.

Instead of pixel content, an adjustment layer has, well, an adjustment. Examples of adjustments include Levels, Brightness/Contrast, and Hue/Saturation (you'll be exploring all the adjustment layer types later). You can see exactly which type of adjustment you're applying by looking at the layer's thumbnail in the Layers palette. Figure 6.1 shows the complete list of adjustment layers, along with their thumbnails.

It's important to remember that an adjustment layer applies its adjustment to all layers below it by default. Any layers above the adjustment layer remain unaffected.

FIGURE 6.1

Adjustment layers in the Layers palette. Each type of adjustment layer has its own thumbnail, so you can easily identify the adjustment that you're applying.

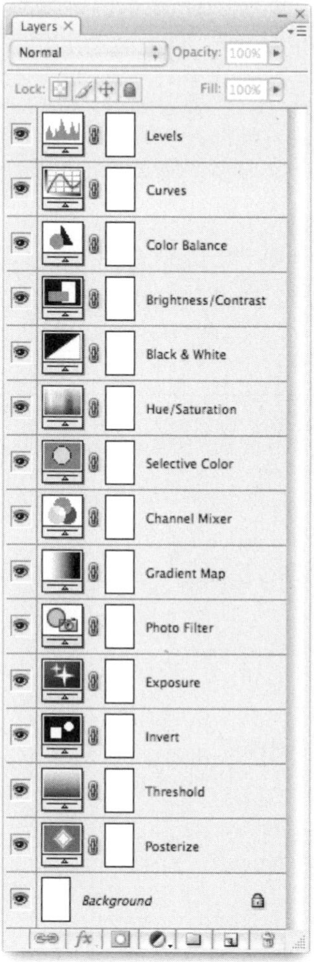

Creating an Adjustment Layer

Creating an adjustment layer is straightforward. To create a new adjustment layer, follow these steps:

1. **Click the Create New Fill or Adjustment Layer icon, as shown in Figure 6.2.** This displays a menu of available adjustment and fill layer types.

2. **Choose an adjustment from the menu.** The first three choices — Solid Color, Gradient, and Pattern — are fill layers, which are covered in detail toward the end of this chapter. The remaining options in the list are all adjustment layers. Simply click an option to create an adjustment layer of that type.

> **TIP**   You can also create a new adjustment layer by choosing an option under Layer ⇨ New Adjustment Layer.

FIGURE 6.2

Creating a new adjustment layer. You can choose an option from the top three in the list to create a fill layer, or pick one of the bottom 14 options to create an adjustment layer.

3. **Edit your adjustment.** After you choose an adjustment layer type, Photoshop creates the layer and displays a dialog box, allowing you to edit the adjustment. The exact dialog box

that appears depends on the type of adjustment; for example, creating a Curves layer displays the Curves dialog box, while creating a Brightness/Contrast layer displays the Brightness/Contrast dialog box. Use the dialog box to make your adjustment — make sure Preview is selected so you can see the changes you make — then click OK to apply the adjustment.

> **TIP** You can reset the settings in any of these dialog boxes back to their default values at any time. To do this, hold down Alt (Option on the Mac) while you're in the dialog box, and the Cancel button changes to Reset. Click Reset to reset the dialog box's settings.

Setting adjustment layer options

When you create a new adjustment layer by choosing an option under Layer ➪ New Adjustment Layer, Photoshop displays the New Layer dialog box, as shown in Figure 6.3. This dialog box gives you the following options for the new layer:

- **Name:** By default, Photoshop chooses a name that reflects the adjustment you're applying, but you can change this to a more memorable name if it helps.

- **Use Previous Layer to Create Clipping Mask:** This allows you to restrict the adjustment to just the active layer. See the section "Applying an adjustment to specific layers" for more on this feature.

- **Color:** You can use this to color-code your adjustment layer.

- **Mode:** Photoshop lets you apply blending modes to adjustment layers, just like regular layers. Find out more about this in the section "Using Blending Modes with Adjustment and Fill Layers" at the end of this chapter.

- **Opacity:** You can choose an opacity level for the adjustment layer. The amount of the adjustment that's applied mirrors the layer's opacity: the higher the opacity, the stronger the adjustment effect.

> **TIP** You can also access the New Layer dialog box by Alt+clicking (Option+clicking on the Mac) the Create New Fill or Adjustment Layer icon, then choosing an adjustment from the pop-up menu.

FIGURE 6.3

The New Layer dialog box allows you to specify additional options when creating an adjustment layer.

Previewing color changes with the Info palette

The Info palette contains some useful information when you work in an adjustment layer dialog box, as shown in Figure 6.4. Choose Window ➪ Info or press F8 to display it.

The Info palette gives you "before" and "after" snapshots of your color values when you're inside an adjustment dialog box.

The top two panes of the Info palette display the channel values of the color of the pixel under the mouse cursor. Move the mouse over an image in the document window to see this in action. In normal use, the left pane displays the channels of the color mode that you're working in — RGB, CMYK, or Lab, for example — while the right pane displays the CMYK equivalent along with any gamut warnings (shown as exclamation points next to the channel values).

TIP You can change which color modes are displayed in the left and right panes by choosing Palette Options from the palette menu and changing the Mode settings under First Color Readout and Second Color Readout.

When working with an adjustment layer dialog box, however, the Info palette shows two values for each color channel, separated by a slash (/). The first value represents the existing color of the pixel under the mouse cursor, while the second value shows what the color will be after the adjustment has been applied.

This feature is handy for seeing at a glance which areas of your image you might be clipping with your adjustment; if a lot of RGB color values are showing 0 or 255 then you're probably clipping quite a bit (unless your image is meant to have many areas of pure black or white). The Info palette is also useful for checking that your adjusted colors are within the CMYK gamut.

> **TIP** You're not limited to displaying just the color under the mouse cursor. While using an adjustment layer dialog box, Shift+click in the document window to create a color sampler; the sampler appears as a small crosshair where you clicked, and a new pane in the Info palette called "#1" tracks the "before" and "after" colors at this point. You can create up to four samplers. To move a sampler in the image, Shift+click it and drag; to delete it, Shift+click it and drag it outside the document window.

Applying an adjustment to specific layers

Normally when you create a new adjustment layer, Photoshop applies the adjustment to all layers below the adjustment layer in the Layers palette. If you prefer, you can limit the adjustment to just one layer. To do this, follow these steps:

1. **Select the layer to which you want to apply the adjustment.** The layer should be highlighted in the Layers palette.

2. **Create the adjustment layer using the New Layer dialog box.** To do this, choose an option from under Layer ⇨ New Adjustment Layer, or Alt/Option+click the Create New Fill or Adjustment Layer icon.

3. **Select the Use Previous Layer to Create Clipping Mask option.** You find this check box just below Name in the New Layer dialog box.

4. **Click OK.** Photoshop creates a clipping mask from the active layer, and adds the new adjustment layer to the clipping mask.

The adjustment layer now only affects the layer in the clipping mask.

You can also restrict an adjustment layer to a single layer after you create it, as follows:

1. **Position the adjustment layer so it's directly above the layer you want to apply it to in the Layers palette.** You can do this by dragging the layer in the Layers palette, or by selecting the layer and pressing Ctrl+[and Ctrl+] (⌘+[and ⌘+] on the Mac).

2. **Select the adjustment layer.** The layer should be highlighted in the Layers palette.

3. **Right-click the adjustment layer and choose Create Clipping Mask.** Photoshop creates a clipping mask from the adjustment layer and the layer below, and the adjustment is limited to that layer only.

> **TIP** You can also create the clipping mask by choosing Layer ➪ Create Clipping Mask, or pressing Ctrl+Alt+G (⌘+Option+G on the Mac).

You can restrict adjustments to multiple layers as well. Simply create your clipping mask as described previously and then drag other layers that you want to adjust into the clipping mask, as shown in Figure 6.5. You can even add multiple adjustment layers to the clipping mask; Photoshop applies the adjustments only to the layer or layers in the mask.

> **CROSS-REF** Clipping masks are covered in detail in Chapter 9.

FIGURE 6.5

Restricting adjustments to just a few layers using a clipping mask

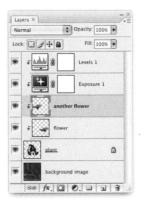

Another great way to restrict adjustments to specific layers is to use groups. Place the layers in a group, along with the adjustment layer or layers, then select any blending mode other than Pass Through for the group — Normal, for example. As always, make sure your adjustment layer is above the layers you want it to affect. This approach is simpler if you find clipping masks a bit much to cope with.

Editing Adjustment Layers

As mentioned already, the beauty of adjustment layers is that you can go back and edit the adjustment. And edit it again. And again.

Editing an adjustment is simplicity itself — simply double-click the adjustment layer's thumbnail. The relevant adjustment dialog reappears, allowing you to tweak the adjustment to your heart's content. When you're happy, click OK to apply the new adjustment, or click Cancel to revert to what you had before.

If you prefer, you can choose Layer ➡ Layer Content Options. This has exactly the same effect as double-clicking the layer thumbnail.

What if you've spent time creating and positioning your Levels adjustment layer, and you've lovingly crafted an intricate layer mask for it, but you decide you really should be using a Curves adjustment layer instead? No problem; simply choose Layer ➡ Change Layer Content ➡ Curves, and your Levels adjustment layer instantly turns into a Curves layer, mask and all.

CROSS-REF You can paint on an adjustment layer's layer mask, or edit its vector mask, to control which areas of your image are affected by the adjustment. Find out more about this in the section "Masking Adjustment Layers" toward the end of this chapter.

As well as using the previous techniques, you can manipulate an adjustment layer pretty much like any other layer: double-click its name to rename it, drag it around the Layers palette to reorder it, lock its position with the Lock Position icon in the Layers palette (which actually locks the position of its layer mask), and so on.

NOTE If you merge an adjustment layer with another layer (or layers), the adjustment is permanently applied to that layer. Generally, this is a bad idea unless you have a lot of adjustment layers with layer masks and you're very concerned about large file sizes.

Exploring Adjustment Layer Types

In this section, we take a look at the range of adjustments that you can apply using adjustment layers. All these adjustments are also available (as destructive versions) under Image ➡ Adjustments. However, it's worth noting that many of the adjustments under Image ➡ Adjustments, such as Match Color or Shadow/Highlight, aren't available as adjustment layers, at least in CS3. But one can dream.

Adjusting Levels

The Levels adjustment layer lets you creatively adjust the brightness and contrast, dynamic range, and color balance of your images. Levels adjustments are great for correcting underexposed or overexposed images, adjusting the balance of the midtones in an image, and correcting color casts.

To create a new Levels adjustment layer, choose Layer ➡ New Adjustment Layer ➡ Levels, or click the Create New Fill or Adjustment Layer icon and select Levels from the pop-up menu. After the layer is created, the Levels dialog box appears, as shown in Figure 6.6.

The main part of the dialog box contains a *histogram* of the image that you're adjusting. A histogram is a graph that shows you the distribution of dark, medium, and light pixels in your image. The x axis along the bottom represents all possible brightness values (0-255 for an 8-bit image), and the y axis shows you the number of pixels in the image that are at that brightness value.

FIGURE 6.6

The Levels dialog box is used when creating and editing Levels adjustment layers.

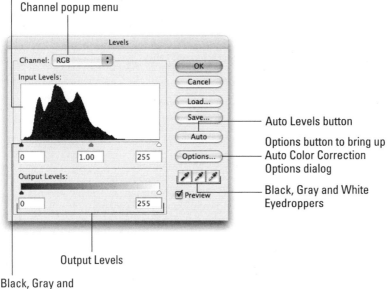

Histogram

Channel popup menu

Auto Levels button

Options button to bring up Auto Color Correction Options dialog

Black, Gray and White Eyedroppers

Output Levels

Black, Gray and White Sliders

A histogram is a great way to tell at a glance how wide the dynamic range of an image is. As a general rule, you want an image to have a good spread of brightness values all the way from 0 (black) up to 255 (white), as this gives you the highest possible contrast without *clipping* (losing detail). The exceptions are, for example, photos of misty landscapes where nothing is truly black or white, or where you want to have a lower-contrast image for artistic effect.

So the histogram for an image with too little contrast might look something like Figure 6.7. You can see a corrected version of the image, along with its histogram, in the same figure.

TIP You can view the histogram for an image by choosing Window ⇨ Histogram, which displays the Histogram palette. Provided the palette is visible while you're in the Layers dialog box, you can see the changes you're making "live" in the palette, which is a pretty useful reference.

The histogram also gives you other useful image information at a glance. For example, if there are a lot of pixels toward the dark end of the brightness range — noticeable by a big "bulge" on the left side of the histogram — then you know that you're working with a *low key* image, with most of the tones concentrated in the shadows. Conversely, a bulge on the right-hand side indicates a *high key* image that is concentrated more in the highlights.

FIGURE 6.7

A washed-out image with too little contrast, along with its histogram (left), and the corrected image and histogram (right)

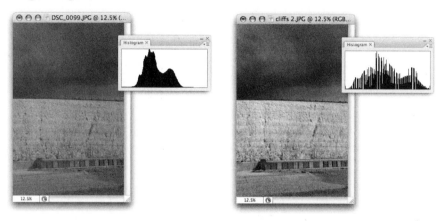

 The histogram in the Levels dialog box shows data just for the parts of the image that you're adjusting. So if you apply a Levels adjustment layer to a selected layer or layers, the histogram only shows data for those layers. Otherwise, the histogram shows data for all visible layers beneath the adjustment layer. Similarly, if you mask off parts of a Levels adjustment layer using its layer mask, the histogram only shows data for the pixels within the unmasked areas.

Adjusting input levels to control brightness and contrast

Below the histogram are three little sliders: a black slider on the left, a gray one in the middle, and a white one on the right. These are the Input Levels sliders; click and drag them around to control the range of brightness values in your image. Here's how they work:

- The black slider specifies the new black point in the image. All brightness levels in the image that are less than or equal to the value at the slider are mapped to the left-hand Output Levels value, which is 0 (black) by default. Drag the slider to a value of 100, for example, and all brightness values of 100 or less become black by default. The remaining brightness levels — the ones that were greater than 100 — are then stretched out over the full tonal range, 0 to 255, thereby giving you a higher-contrast image.

- The white slider behaves in the opposite way: it specifies the new white point. Brightness values equal to or greater than the white slider value are mapped to the right-hand Output Levels value, which defaults to 255 (white). So dragging the slider to 200 results in all brightness values greater than or equal to 200 being turned white by default, with the brightness levels below 200 being stretched out over the full range from 0 to 255.

- The gray slider in the middle is used for specifying the new mid-gray point of the image (brightness level 128); it allows you to lighten or darken the midtones without affecting the shadows or highlights too much. Drag to the left to make the midtones lighter; drag to the right to make them darker.

For example, in the low-contrast image in Figure 6.7, the black slider is dragged to the right until it reaches the left-hand edge of the histogram data (the lowest level used by pixels in the image), and the white slider is dragged to the right-hand edge of the data (representing the brightest pixels in the image). The end result is that the histogram is remapped from those two values to the full range from 0 to 255, making the histogram spread out to use the full available dynamic range and increasing the contrast of the image.

NOTE   You may be wondering: Why not just use the Brightness/Contrast adjustment layer (or Image ⇨ Adjustments ⇨ Brightness/Contrast) to adjust brightness and maximize contrast? You can, of course, and it generally does an adequate job, but it tends to mangle your levels a fair bit, and somewhat unpredictably. (This assumes you're using the CS3 Brightness/Contrast with the Use Legacy option disabled; if you enable the Use Legacy option, or use Brightness/Contrast with older versions of Photoshop, then the results are truly terrible.) The Levels adjustment gives you more precise control over the dynamic range of your image.

You can also type numeric values rather than clicking and dragging the slider, using the three boxes directly below the histogram. The left and right boxes represent the new black point and white point, respectively, measured from 0 (black) to 255 (white). The box in the middle represents the mid-gray point (also known as the gamma value), and is measured from 0.1 (black) all the way up to 9.99 (white). 1.0 represents exactly 50 percent gray (RGB 128,128,128, or #808080 if you're a Web type).

TIP   For precise control, click in one of the boxes and use the up- and down-arrow keys to increase or decrease the value in steps of one (black point and white point) or one hundredth (gray point). Hold down Shift at the same time to change the value in steps of 10 (black and white points) or 0.1 (gray point).

CAUTION   Be wary of altering the histogram too much when using Levels. If you stretch the histogram a lot you start to see "combing" in the histogram (lots of isolated spikes), and this means the image may start to look *posterized*— continuous tones start to appear as blocky areas of color. (Of course, if you use a Levels adjustment layer, then you're not making any permanent changes to the pixels themselves, which is a plus.)

Finding shadows and highlights in the image

One of the main uses of Levels is to remap the darkest point in an image to 0 and the lightest point to 255, thereby stretching the histogram over the whole dynamic range and increasing contrast. If you click and drag the black slider to the right of the darkest point, or drag the white slider to the left of the lightest point, then you're starting to clip parts of your image, which means you're discarding shadow tones darker than the black slider, or highlights lighter than the white slider.

Clipping sounds like a bad thing, and it usually is. But what if those extreme shadows and highlights don't contain anything useful? Maybe there's not much useful detail in them, and you'd rather lose them so that you can expand the dynamic range further and eke out a bit more contrast from the midtones.

Luckily, there's an easy way to find out exactly what detail you're losing from your image when you start to clip with the sliders. To do this, hold down the Alt key (Option on the Mac) and start dragging either the black slider from left to right, or the white slider from right to left. As soon as the slider hits the start or end of the histogram data, you start to see bits of the image appear, as shown in Figure 6.8. These are the parts of the image that are clipped when the slider is in that position. (A fully black or white image means that nothing is clipped.) This way, you can see precisely what detail is being lost through clipping. Very handy.

FIGURE 6.8

Finding the extreme shadows and highlights in an image by using the threshold mode in the Levels dialog box

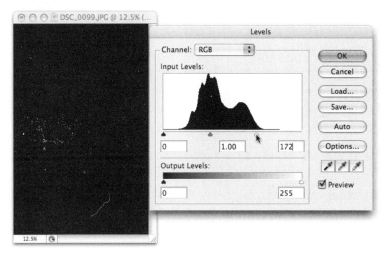

You can use this threshold technique in the RGB composite channel, in which case pixels appear the moment any one of the Red, Green, or Blue channels hits the threshold, or in individual color channels, where pixels only appear when the selected channel starts being clipped.

NOTE   This threshold function only works in RGB color mode; it's unavailable for CMYK or Lab mode.

Using output levels to reduce contrast

As mentioned earlier, the Output Levels figures represent the two brightness values that the black and white Input Levels are mapped to. Usually you probably want to leave these at 0 (black) and 255 (white), to make sure you get the most contrast you can out of your image without clipping. However, sometimes it's useful to map the black and white points onto a more limited range of values, resulting in a less contrasty image.

One common reason for doing this is to give your image more "headroom" if you plan to do more adjustments later. For example, if you know that you're going to really boost the brightness in one part of your image later on, click and drag the white Output Levels slider down a bit from 255 beforehand, so you have a bit of room to play with at the bright end of the range. If you don't do this, the bright parts of your image may be clipped when you boost the brightness later, resulting in loss of detail.

You can adjust the Output Levels values in much the same way as using the Input Levels controls. Click and drag the black slider, or type a value in the left-hand box below the slider, to set the new black point level. Drag the white slider, or type a value in the right-hand box, to set the new white point level. The values run from 0 (black) to 255 (white).

You can even push the black slider past the white slider, which starts to invert the image. In fact, if you push the black slider all the way to the right and drag the white slider all the way to the left, you're effectively performing exactly the same operation as Image ➪ Adjustments ➪ Invert.

Working on individual color channels

So far, you've been working on the composite RGB image, as indicated by the Channel option at the top of the dialog box being set to RGB. Working on all three color channels at once like this is the quickest way to adjust brightness levels in your image while maintaining the color balance. This is the mode you'll probably work in most often, but it can be handy to work on individual color channels, too.

For example, you can use the individual channel modes to correct color casts. First, choose the Red channel from the Channel pop-up menu, and adjust the black and white points until you have a good spread of red in the image. Repeat the process for the Green and Blue channels. You now have a fairly even spread of red, green, and blue in your image.

Adjusting levels and correcting colors with the eyedroppers

The black and white eyedroppers toward the bottom right of the Levels dialog box are an alternative to dragging the black point and white point sliders around the histogram. Rather than setting the black and white points using the histogram, you can use the eyedroppers to set these points by clicking directly on pixels in your image that should be pure black or pure white.

CAUTION   Using an eyedropper undoes any changes you make with the sliders, so you'll probably want to use the eyedroppers first, then use the sliders for fine-tuning afterward.

CAUTION   These eyedroppers are a nice rough-and-ready way to adjust the histogram, but it can be hard to find a decent black or white point in the image. You can also easily clip your histogram this way, so be careful. For example, if you don't click the whitest point in your image with the white eyedropper, all brightness values lighter than the level at that point get clipped to that level.

The gray eyedropper between the black and white ones behaves slightly differently. It lets you specify which area of your image should be neutral mid-gray (red, green, and blue values all equal to 128), without stretching the histogram — that is to say, without adjusting the brightness and contrast. This makes the gray eyedropper wonderful for color correction: Simply choose the gray eyedropper, find an area of your image that should be a neutral mid-gray, and click it. The color balance of the image changes in order to make that pixel a neutral gray, which usually sorts out the other colors in your image, too.

> **NOTE** The eyedroppers work by adjusting the black, gray, and white point sliders in the individual color channels (switch to the Red channel, then use an eyedropper and you'll see this in action). The overall changes are reflected in the RGB histogram, but the sliders in the RGB histogram don't move.

Although the eyedroppers default to mapping to black, mid-gray, and white, you can actually change these target colors to any color you want. This is handy if you want to tone down your image so that it doesn't contain pure black or white areas, or for adding or removing color tints. To do this, double-click one of the eyedropper icons to display the Color Picker dialog box, then choose an appropriate color.

Saving and retrieving Levels settings

When you're happy with the changes you've made in the Levels dialog box, you can save the settings in the dialog box to a file. You might want to do this if you think it's an adjustment that you'll make often.

To save your settings, click Save and choose a location and a file name for your settings file. Levels settings file names end in the .alv file extension.

To load your settings in the future, create or edit a Levels adjustment layer (or choose Image ⇨ Adjustments ⇨ Levels) to display the Levels dialog box. Click Load, and open the ALV file that you saved previously.

Getting Photoshop to do the hard work

The magic Auto button in the Levels dialog box behaves much like the Auto Levels command (Image ⇨ Adjustments ⇨ Auto Levels). You can also tweak the parameters of both the Auto button and the Auto Levels command through the Options button in the Levels dialog box (more on this button later).

To apply an automatic levels adjustment from within the Levels dialog box, simply click Auto. Photoshop automatically adjusts the black, white, and gray points for each of the color channel histograms, with the changes being reflected in the overall RGB histogram. If you select the Preview option, the results are seen in the document window.

Essentially, Auto Levels does what you'd do manually if you were using the Levels dialog box to expand the dynamic range. It puts the black point at the start of the histogram data, and the white point at the end of the data. It also discards (clips) a small percentage of the extreme black and white tones in the image. If you use the Auto button you can adjust the amount of clipping using the Options button (described later); with Image ⇨ Adjustments ⇨ Auto Levels, however, you're stuck with the defaults.

Auto Levels is great for making a quick levels adjustment to your image, and it usually does a pretty good job. Because it works on color channels individually, it works best for images that have a fairly even distribution of brightness values across all channels. However, if your image naturally contains a lot of red, for example, applying Auto Levels increases the levels of blue and green more than the red, resulting in a fairly major color shift. It's also not too hot for images that are meant to have areas of low contrast, as Auto Levels attempts to create the maximum amount of contrast it can.

Click Options, below Auto, to display the Auto Color Correction Options dialog box, as shown in Figure 6.9. The settings in this dialog box let you tweak the parameters used by the following:

- Auto Levels command
- Auto Contrast command
- Auto Color command
- The Auto button in both the Levels dialog box (described earlier) and in the Curves dialog box (described later in this chapter)

FIGURE 6.9

Tweaking Photoshop's automatic correction functions using the Auto Color Correction Options dialog box

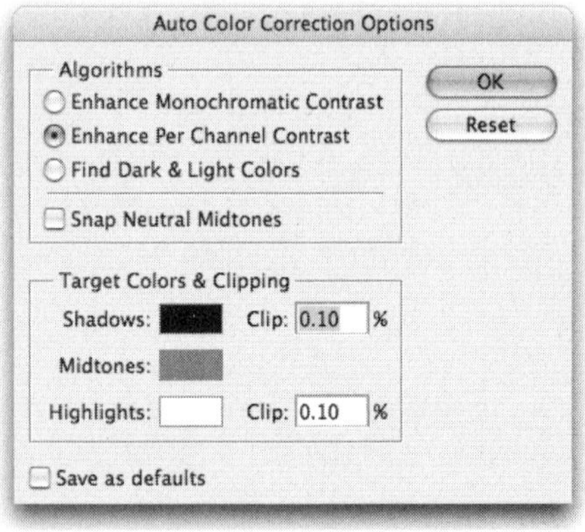

Here's how the options work:

- **Enhance Monochromatic Contrast:** This algorithm adjusts all color channels in the image by the same amount, thereby avoiding any color casting, as can happen with Auto Levels. This is the algorithm used by the Auto Contrast command (Image ⇨ Adjustments ⇨ Auto Contrast). Select this option to apply an Auto Contrast-like effect to the image.
- **Enhance Per Channel Contrast:** This option, which is the default algorithm, adjusts the color channels individually to maximize the contrast in each channel. This produces the

most pronounced contrast increase, but often results in color shifts (which may be a good thing if you want to correct a color cast). This algorithm is used by Auto Levels (described earlier), so choose this option if you want to apply Auto Levels to the image.

■ **Find Dark & Light Colors:** This algorithm looks for average dark and light points in the image and maps these to the shadows and highlights to increase the contrast while minimizing the amount of clipping. This algorithm, along with Snap Neutral Midtones, is used by the Auto Color command. Select both Find Dark & Light Colors and Snap Neutral Midtones if you want to apply an Auto Color correction.

■ **Snap Neutral Midtones:** Selecting this option tells Photoshop to guess which color in the image is supposed to be neutral gray; then adjust the gamma to make this color neutral gray. This option is designed for automatically removing color casts, and it generally does a pretty good job.

■ **Shadows:** Click the color box next to Shadows to pick a target color to map the black point to. This is much like double-clicking the black eyedropper to choose a target shadow color or adjusting the black Output Levels slider.

■ **Midtones:** Click the Midtones color box to choose a target color to use for neutral gray. It behaves much like double-clicking the gray eyedropper to choose a target neutral gray. This option works in tandem with the Snap Neutral Midtones option to help remove color casts.

■ **Highlights:** Click the color box to the right of Highlights to choose a target color for the white point. It's the equivalent of double-clicking the white eyedropper or dragging the white Output Levels slider.

■ **Clip values:** Use the Shadows and Highlights Clip values to specify how much of the darkest and lightest values Photoshop should ignore when selecting the black and white points. The higher you make these values, the more the histogram is clipped. The idea of the clip values is to remove the extreme dark and bright levels that are usually very noisy when captured by scanners or digital cameras. These days, however, scanners and cameras are a lot better than they used to be, so you might want to use a slightly lower value than the default of 0.1 percent to ensure you're retaining the maximum possible dynamic range.

■ **Save as Defaults:** Selecting this option permanently saves all the settings in the Auto Color Correction Options dialog box so that they're used for all future clicks of the Auto button (in both the Levels and the Curves dialog boxes). In addition, the Target Colors & Clipping settings are saved for use by the Auto Color, Auto Levels, and Auto Contrast commands in the future. This is handy if you have a batch of images that you want to correct in the same way; you only have to select Auto Color, Auto Levels, or Auto Contrast in the future to apply the same color correction settings.

■ **OK/Cancel.** Click OK to apply automatic color correction using the settings in the dialog box. Click Cancel to ignore the settings (including the Save as Defaults option) and return to the Levels dialog box.

 When using Save as Defaults, the saved algorithm is used only for the Auto button. The Auto Levels, Auto Contrast, and Auto Color commands still use their default algorithms. In addition, Auto Color always behaves as if the Snap Neutral Midtones option is selected.

 Some of the previous options are unavailable when working in CMYK or Lab color modes.

Fine-tuning contrast with Curves

Like the Levels adjustment layer, Curves allows you to adjust the range of brightness values and colors in an image. The main advantage of Curves is that it gives you more control over how you map the input (existing) brightness levels of the image to the output (new) levels. Its main disadvantage is that it's not as intuitive to use for making simple dynamic range adjustments; you're better off using Levels in that scenario.

Still, the Curves adjustment is very powerful because it lets you make contrast adjustments to specific tonal ranges in an image, as you'll see in a moment. It's well worth learning for those times when you really want to squeeze the absolute best from an image.

To create a new Curves adjustment layer, choose Layer ➪ New Adjustment Layer ➪ Curves. Alternatively you can click the Create New Fill or Adjustment Layer icon in the Layers palette and choose Curves from the pop-up menu. After you create the layer, the Curves dialog box (shown in Figure 6.10) appears.

The main part of the Curves dialog box is taken up by a graph containing — you guessed it — a curve. This curve maps input brightness levels along the bottom to output brightness levels up the left-hand side. The default "curve" is a straight diagonal line from bottom left to top right, which means that each input level is mapped to the same output level — for example, an input level of 100 maps to an output level of 100, 200 maps to 200, and so on. In other words, the input and output images are identical; no change is being applied.

As you move your mouse over the graph, you can see the Input and Output values below and to the left of the graph changing, showing you the location of the mouse pointer in terms of input and output levels. The input levels range from 0 (black) on the left to 255 (white) on the right; the output levels also range from 0 (bottom) to 255 (top).

This is the case for RGB images anyway. If you work in CMYK, the levels range from 0 percent ink coverage (bottom left) to 100 percent ink coverage (top right), and the curve is reversed. You can swap these two measurement methods at any time, though; simply expand the Curve Display Options by clicking the downward-pointing arrow in the dialog box, then select an option for the Show Amount Of setting.

For the sake of simplicity, assume in this chapter that you're working in RGB mode, with the brightness levels running from 0 to 255.

FIGURE 6.10

The Curves dialog box, which you use when creating and editing Curves adjustment layers

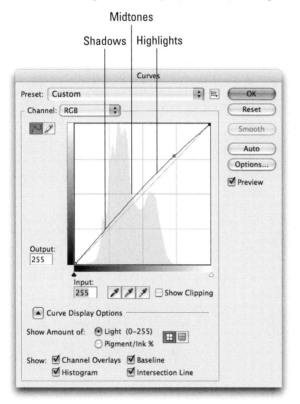

An easy way to understand how the graph relates to your image is to remember that the bottom-left part of the graph represents shadows, the middle part of the graph represents midtones, and the top right of the graph represents highlights, as indicated in Figure 6.10.

Editing the curve

To start shaping your curve, click a point on the diagonal line in the graph and a control point appears (a little black square). Click and drag this square to pull the curve around.

To get finer control over the shape of your curve, click another point on the curve; another control point appears that you can drag around independently of the first one. Notice how the shape of the curve is affected by the position of each and every control point. You can have up to 16 control points in your curve, including the black point on the far left and the white point on the far right (neither of which can be deleted).

To select a point you've already created, click it. It changes from a hollow square to a solid square to indicate that it's selected.

You can cycle through all the points in the graph with the keyboard. Press Ctrl+Tab to cycle forward through the points, or Ctrl+Shift+Tab to cycle backward.

If you've gone crazy and added way too many control points, you can easily delete them by doing one of the following:

- Drag the point out of the graph.
- Click the point to select it, then press Backspace or Delete (either Delete key on the Mac).
- Ctrl+click (⌘+click on the Mac) on the point.

You can select multiple points at once by Shift+clicking each point. Shift+click a point again to deselect it. (Click outside the curve to deselect all the points.) After you select multiple points, click one point and drag to move all the points together.

When you select a point, the Input and Output values below and to the left of the graph become editable. Type new values from 0 to 255 to move the position of the point precisely. For example, typing **128** into both boxes places the point squarely in the middle of the graph.

NOTE Because the curve always has to move from left to right (it can't double back on itself), you can't always position a point anywhere you like in the graph. If you try to position a point outside its allowed area when typing Input and Output values manually, Photoshop corrects you with a dialog box.

If you select multiple points, the Input and Output values both show zero. The values are then relative; for example, you can type **10** in the Input box to shift all selected points 10 pixels to the right, or type **-5** in the Output box to shift them down 5 pixels. This is great for making precise adjustments to the curve.

If you prefer, you can draw your curve directly in the graph, rather than creating and dragging points. To do this, click the Pencil icon to the left of the graph, then click and drag in the graph to draw the curve. This is a great way to quickly sketch the shape of curve that you're after, although it's not very precise. After you draw your curve, you might want to click Smooth to smooth things out a bit. If the curve still isn't smooth enough for you, keep clicking Smooth; each click smoothes the curve a bit more.

Switch back to points mode by clicking the Points icon next to the Pencil icon. You see that Photoshop has approximated your hand-drawn curve using points.

Locating tones in the image

So you've noticed an area of your image that could do with a bit of contrast adjustment. How do you find out where those tones are on the curve? Simply move the mouse over the document window (the cursor changes to an eyedropper), click a pixel in the document window and hold the mouse button down. A small circle appears on the curve back in the Curves dialog box that indi-cates the position on the curve of the tone represented by that pixel. Figure 6.11 shows this in action.

FIGURE 6.11

Finding a tone on the graph by clicking pixels in the image. The small circle on the curve indicates the input and output levels of the clicked pixel.

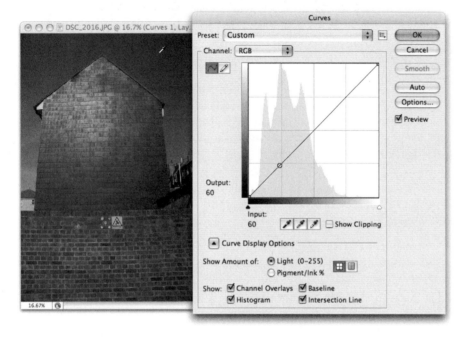

A good trick is to drag the mouse quickly around the general area you're interested in; the circle bobs up and down the curve, giving you a good idea of the part of the curve that you need to adjust.

You can also add control points to the curve by clicking in the document window. To do this, hold down Ctrl (⌘ on the Mac) and click a pixel in the image. Photoshop adds a control point to the curve at the point represented by that pixel's tone. (This only works for RGB images.)

NOTE Ctrl/⌘+clicking, as just described, adds the point to the curve of the current channel you're working on. For example, if you're working on the RGB composite channel it adds that point to the RGB curve; if you're working on the Blue channel it adds the point to the Blue curve, and so on. See the section "Editing individual channels" for more on working with individual color channels.

TIP You can use the previous method to add a point to all of the color channel curves at once (excluding the composite channel). To do this, Ctrl+Shift+click (⌘+Shift+click on the Mac) a pixel in the image. A big advantage of this method is that it also works in CMYK and Lab mode.

Editing individual channels

By default, you're working on the RGB (or CMYK) composite channel in the Curves dialog box, but you can work on an individual color channel by choosing the channel from the Channel pop-up menu. The composite curve can be edited independently of the individual channel curves, but both the composite and the individual channel curves interact to produce the overall adjustment.

Editing the curves of individual color channels can be useful for creating special color effects. It's also very handy if you happen to have a color cast in a particular tonal region in your image.

TIP If you have a color cast across the whole image, you're better off removing it with the Levels command, or using a command such as Image ⇨ Adjustments ⇨ Auto Color or Image ⇨ Adjustments ⇨ Color Balance, as they're much quicker and easier to use.

Changing the look of the Curves graph

The bottom of the Curves dialog box houses the Curve Display Options. By default, these are hidden from view; to expand them, click the button with the downward-pointing arrow to the left of Curve Display Options. A list of extra options appears, which you can see in Figure 6.10. The options work as follows:

- **Show Amount Of:** This was touched on earlier in the chapter. Click the Light option to display values running from 0 (black) to 255 (white); click the Pigment/Ink option to reverse the graph and display values from 0 percent (white) to 100 percent (black).

- **Grid buttons:** These buttons, to the right of the Show Amount Of option, let you change the grid size. Click the left-hand button to display gridlines in 25 percent steps; click the right-hand button to display a finer grid with 10 percent steps. You can also Alt+click (Option+click on the Mac) anywhere within the graph to toggle between the two settings.

- **Channel Overlays:** With this option selected, you can see the individual Red, Green, and Blue channel curves overlaid onto the composite (RGB) graph. This is great, because it gives you an at-a-glance view of your changes to both the composite and individual channel curves, all on the one composite graph. (To edit an individual color channel, you still need to flip to that channel's graph using the Channel pop-up menu.)

- **Histogram:** Select this option to overlay a histogram of the image on the graph, showing you the number of pixels in the image (y axis) at each brightness level (x axis). This is a histogram of the image before your curves adjustment is applied, so it doesn't change as you adjust the curve. The histogram is handy for checking if you're clipping the shadows or highlights of the image; for example, if the leftmost (black) control point is to the right of the leftmost point of the histogram data, you're clipping some of the shadow levels in your image. It also gives you a quick visual indication of the amount of pixels within the tonal range that you're adjusting within the curve, so you can tell how much of an impact your adjustment is likely to have on the image.

- **Baseline:** This option simply draws a diagonal reference line through the graph; the points on this line represent no change to the brightness levels. This gives you a quick visual clue as to how much you're altering the image; the further your curve is from that diagonal line, the bigger the adjustment that you're making.

- **Intersection Line:** With this option selected, Photoshop draws a set of crosshairs through a control point when you click and drag the point with the mouse. This lets you position the point more accurately with respect to other points on the curve or to the histogram.

NEW FEATURE The Curve Display Options are a handy new feature of CS3. Two of the options — the Show Amount Of option and the Grid buttons — are simply more intuitive reworkings of the CS2 interface; previously you had to click an obscure double-headed arrow icon at the bottom of the graph to change the Show Amount Of setting, and you could only Alt/Option+click in the graph to change the grid size. However, the four Show options are genuinely new to Photoshop, and are welcome additions — particularly the Channel Overlays and Histogram options.

Working with Curves presets

If you've made a Curves adjustment that you think you'll want to reuse in the future, you can save it as a Curves preset file. You can load the preset file later when you want to reapply the adjustment. You can also choose from a range of built-in presets to give you a head start with your Curves adjustments.

NEW FEATURE Photoshop CS3 introduces a range of built-in Curves presets that make great starting points for a range of common tasks. Presets include Color Negative, for accurately converting a scan of a color negative to a positive image; and Cross Process, for emulating the artistic effect of processing E-6 film in C-41 chemicals. These built-in presets are all available from the Preset pop-up menu in the Curves dialog box.

To save your current Curves adjustment as a preset, click the Preset Options icon to the right of the Preset menu at the top of the Curves dialog box, and choose Save Preset. Choose a folder to save the preset file to — the default is the Curves folder within Photoshop's Presets folder — and give the file a name. Photoshop saves your preset to the file and also adds the preset to a special section of the Preset pop-up menu, below the main list of built-in presets, allowing you to access it quickly in the future.

TIP You can save your preset file anywhere you want; however, if you save it in Photoshop's Curves presets folder, the preset is permanently added to the Preset pop-up menu. This is handy if you've made a Curves preset that you're likely to use again and again.

To load a preset that you saved earlier, click the Preset Options icon and choose Load Preset. Find the preset file in the file selector dialog, and click Load. Photoshop loads the preset and updates the Curves dialog with the preset's settings. You can also access your loaded preset by choosing its name from the Preset pop-up menu.

To delete a preset, select the preset from the Preset menu. Click the Preset Options icon to the right of the menu, and choose Delete Current Preset. This not only removes the preset from the Preset menu, but also deletes the preset file from your hard drive, so be careful! You can't delete built-in presets this way; you can only delete presets that you've created yourself.

Other controls in the Curves dialog box

The remaining controls in the Curves dialog box — Auto, Options, and the Eyedropper icons — behave much like their counterparts in the Levels dialog (see the section "Adjusting Levels" earlier in this chapter), so we just cover the differences here.

- **Auto:** As with Levels, Photoshop applies the auto color corrections to the individual color channels. Unlike Levels, where you can see the changes in the RGB histogram, you won't see the changes in the RGB curve; it remains as (or reverts to) a diagonal straight line. However, if you select the Channel Overlays option you can see the changes that Photoshop has applied to the individual color channels, overlaid on top of the RGB graph.

- **Eyedroppers:** Again, these are applied to the individual color channel curves; the RGB composite curve remains as a straight line.

Understanding Curves in action

Whereas Levels only allows you to adjust the overall contrast of your image, Curves allows you to selectively increase or decrease contrast across several different tonal ranges of your image at the same time. For example, with Curves you could decrease the contrast in the shadows of your image (where you may not have much detail), while at the same time increasing contrast in the upper midtones of your image (which might include a person's face).

The important thing to remember is that, while you can increase contrast in some areas and decrease it in others, there's only so much contrast to "go around," as you only have a fixed range of brightness values to work with (0-255 for an RGB image). So as you increase the contrast in one area of the curve, you inevitably decrease it in another area.

TIP The exception to the previous rule is when your image isn't using the full dynamic range — that is, its histogram doesn't stretch fully from level 0 on the left to level 255 on the right. In this situation, you can create a net increase in contrast, because you have some "headroom" to play with. You can happily sacrifice some of the extreme shadows and highlights — probably creating something that looks like the "extreme S-curve" described in the following paragraphs — to gain contrast in other tonal ranges, because there's no detail in those shadows and highlights. When you do this, you effectively expand the dynamic range of your image. Alternatively, you may prefer simply to increase the overall contrast of the image using the black and white Input Levels sliders (described in the section "Adjusting Levels" earlier in this chapter), but then you lose your headroom for making local contrast adjustments via Curves. It's your choice.

To increase contrast in a region of tones in the image, make the curve steeper at that region. To decrease contrast, make the curve shallower. This makes sense when you think about it; for example, if you make the curve steeper for a range of tones, you increase the difference in brightness between the dark (on the left) and the light (on the right) portions of that range.

There are a couple of common curve shapes that are worth knowing; in fact, you've probably created these curves yourself if you've used the Curves dialog box a fair bit. These curves are known as the *S-curve* and *inverted S-curve* (from their shapes), and you can see them in action in Figure 6.12.

FIGURE 6.12

Adjusting an image's contrast using an S-curve (top) and an inverted S-curve (bottom)

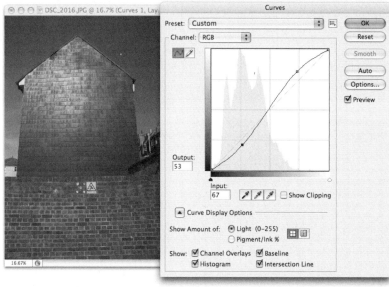

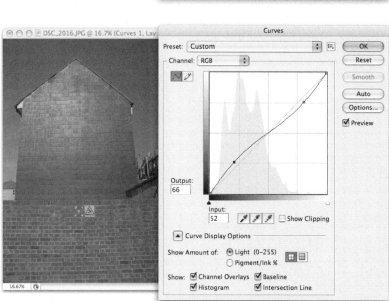

These two curve types work as follows:

- An S-curve increases the slope across the midtones, increasing the midtone contrast at the expense of some contrast in the shadows and highlights. This generally results in an apparently higher-contrast image, because most of the detail is usually concentrated around the midtones.

- An inverted S-curve does the opposite — it produces a gradual slope over the midtones, resulting in flat midtones and high-contrast shadows and highlights. The end result is usually the appearance of a lower-contrast image.

NOTE These two curves highlight an important advantage that the Curves adjustment has over Levels: you can increase the apparent contrast in an image without resorting to clipping. For example, if you try to increase the contrast in the midtones using Levels, you inevitably end up clipping some of the shadows and highlights at the same time as you move the black and white point sliders closer together. With Curves, you merely increase midtone contrast at the expense of contrast in the shadows and highlights; provided you don't push the curve to extremes, or move the black and white points, you're not clipping the shadows or highlights at all.

To create an S-curve, click a point in the shadows (bottom-left) portion of the curve and drag downward (or to the right), then click somewhere in the highlights (top-right) portion of the curve and drag upward (or to the left). To create an inverted S-curve, do the opposite: drag up in the shadows and drag down in the highlights.

It's also worth mentioning that you can create an "extreme S-curve" by clicking the black point in the bottom-left corner and dragging right, then clicking the white point in the top-right corner and dragging left. This is exactly the same as dragging the black and white Input Levels sliders in the Levels dialog box (see the section "Adjusting Levels" earlier in this chapter). If you drag these points into the histogram data then you start to clip the extreme shadows and highlights.

NEW FEATURE Photoshop CS3 adds a black and a white slider below the x-axis of the graph, linked to the black point and white point, respectively. These let you easily control the horizontal placement of these points, which makes them great for creating the "extreme S-curves" described earlier — it's almost like having a simplified Levels dialog box within the Curves dialog box. To complement these sliders, you can select the Show Clipping option, which behaves in the same way as Alt/Option+dragging the black and white sliders in the Levels dialog box. See the section "Finding shadows and highlights in the image" earlier in the chapter for details on this feature. In fact, you can also Alt/Option+drag the black and white sliders in the Curves dialog box to temporarily show the clipped shadows and highlights, just like you can in the Levels dialog box.

Generally you only need to make small adjustments to the curve to achieve your desired results. Big adjustments result in extreme increases or decreases in contrast, resulting in the appearance of posterization and unwanted artifacts in the image.

TIP If you need more subtlety than you can get from tweaking the curve alone, use the Curves adjustment layer's Opacity slider to decrease the opacity down from 100 percent, thereby reducing the effect further.

You'll also find that, for normal uses, you want the curve to have a positive gradient — that is, the curve always travels upward as it moves from left to right. If you start dragging points so far down that the curve starts to head downhill to the right, you'll notice that your image starts to become more and more surreal. This is because you're starting to invert parts of the image at that point — you're mapping dark values (toward the left) to light values (higher up) and vice versa. This can be wonderful if you're after that kind of special effect, though.

Tweaking colors with Color Balance

The Color Balance adjustment layer is great for making quick, simple adjustments to the color makeup of an image. It allows you to shift the color balance across three broad areas of your image — the shadows, midtones, and highlights. (Photoshop decides which parts of your image fall into these three categories.)

CROSS-REF If you want more fine-grained control over tonal ranges than Photoshop's arbitrary shadows, midtones, and highlights give you, check out the Curves adjustment layer described earlier in this chapter.

To create a new Color Balance adjustment layer, choose Layer ➪ New Adjustment Layer ➪ Color Balance, or click the Create New Fill or Adjustment Layer icon in the Layers palette and choose Color Balance from the pop-up menu. After you create the layer, the Color Balance dialog box, shown in Figure 6.13, appears.

FIGURE 6.13

The Color Balance dialog box is perfect for quick and easy color adjustment.

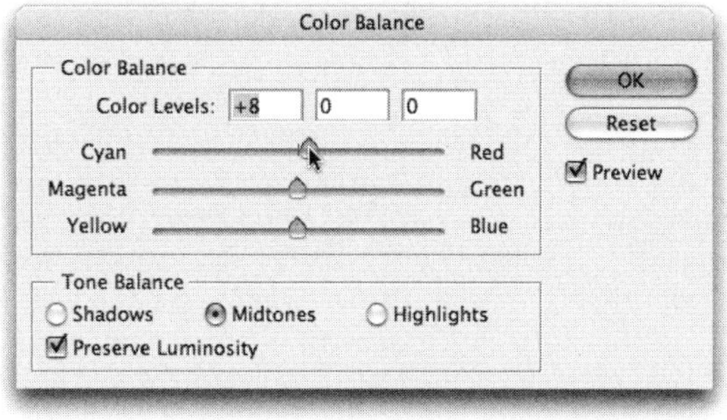

To adjust the color balance of your image, choose a range of brightness values that you want to adjust — shadows, midtones, or highlights — by selecting an option under Tone Balance. Then click and drag one of the color sliders toward a color to shift the color balance closer to that color and away from the opposite color. For example, drag the Cyan/Red slider toward Red to increase the amount of red and reduce the amount of cyan.

You'll probably want to select the Preview option so you can see what's going on in your image. Toggle it to compare the original image with your new color-adjusted version.

What you're actually doing with the color sliders is either increasing the brightness levels of the Red, Green, or Blue channel (when you drag to the right), or decreasing the brightness of these channels (when you drag to the left). As you'd imagine, moving these sliders to the right increases the overall brightness of the image, while dragging to the right decreases it.

The Preserve Luminosity option, which is selected by default, compensates for this and ensures that the brightness levels in the image are not so dramatically affected by the color correction. This is usually what you want, but if you prefer not to use this compensation, deselect the option. You can see the difference in Figure 6.14.

You can also type values numerically using the three Color Levels boxes at the top of the dialog box. The left-hand box represents Cyan/Red, the middle box Magenta/Green, and the right-hand box Yellow/Blue. Values range from -100 (the maximum amount of cyan/magenta/yellow) to 100 (the maximum amount of red/green/blue). A value of 0 means no change in that color channel.

TIP As with most numeric values in Photoshop, you can change the values in the boxes in steps by using the arrow keys. Click in one of the boxes and use the up- and down-arrow keys to increase or decrease the value in steps of 1, or press Shift+up arrow and Shift+down arrow to change the value in steps of 10.

NOTE If you work in Lab mode, you'll see the a and b channel sliders in the dialog box instead (Green/Magenta and Blue/Yellow, respectively).

Altering brightness and contrast

The Brightness/Contrast adjustment layer is fairly self-explanatory. You can use it to increase or decrease the amount of brightness and/or contrast in your image.

NEW FEATURE With Photoshop CS3, Adobe has reworked the Brightness/Contrast adjustment to make it much more useful. In earlier versions, Brightness simply upped or reduced the brightness levels of each pixel in the image across the board, while Contrast stretched or squeezed the whole dynamic range. The inevitable results were either clipping, or a very flat-looking image, making Brightness/Contrast almost useless for professional work. The new Brightness/Contrast is much more intelligent. Brightness now adjusts the spread of the brightness levels across the shadows, midtones, and highlights to create a more high-key or low-key image, in a similar way to using the gray point slider in Levels, while Contrast increases or decreases the contrast across the midrange, much like using an S-curve or inverted S-curve in the Curves dialog. While not as precise as using Levels or Curves, it's certainly much better than what we had before, and most important, it no longer results in any clipping of the shadows or highlights. If you're really keen to mess up your image, though, feel free to select the Use Legacy option in the dialog box, which makes Photoshop use the pre-CS3 Brightness/Contrast method instead.

FIGURE 6.14

Adjusting the color balance of an image's midtones, with Preserve Luminosity selected (top) and dese-lected (bottom)

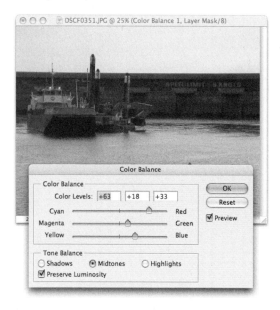

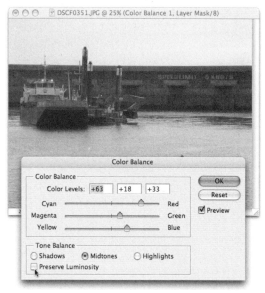

To make a new Brightness/Contrast adjustment layer, simply choose Layer ➪ New Adjustment Layer ➪ Brightness/Contrast, or click the Create New Fill or Adjustment Layer icon in the Layers palette and choose Brightness/Contrast from the menu. After you create the layer, the Brightness/Contrast dialog box (shown in Figure 6.15) appears.

FIGURE 6.15

The Brightness/Contrast dialog box lets you easily tweak the overall brightness and contrast of your image.

Click and drag the Brightness slider to the right to increase the overall brightness of the image; drag it to the left to decrease the brightness. Likewise, drag the Contrast slider to the right to add contrast, or drag it to the left to produce a less contrasty image. Select the Preview option to see the effect that your adjustments are having on the image.

You can also change values by clicking in the Brightness and Contrast boxes and typing new values. Type -**100** to decrease the brightness or contrast by the maximum amount, or **100** to increase them to the max. A value of 0 means no change. As with the Color Balance dialog box (described earlier), you can also use the arrow keys to change the values in steps of 1.

Converting an image to black and white

NEW FEATURE   New in Photoshop CS3 is an addition that will be very welcome to many photographers: the Black & White adjustment layer. Black and white conversion of color photos is the topic of much Photoshop voodoo, with multiple approaches being championed by different pundits. This has come about because almost all digital cameras only have a color mode, so to get a black-and-white image from a digital photo requires a conversion. Previously, Photoshop hasn't really had a dedicated way to approach this; there's the Channel Mixer approach, the Lab color approach, the simple Desaturate command, and the list goes on. The new Black & White adjustment layer offers a dedicated solution to this conundrum for the first time.

To create a new Black & White adjustment layer, choose Layer ➪ New Adjustment Layer ➪ Black & White, or simply click the Create New Fill or Adjustment Layer icon in the Layers palette and choose Black & White from the menu. The former approach displays a dialog box where you can name your new adjustment layer and choose a blending mode and other options, and the latter simply takes you straight to the Black and White dialog box, as shown in Figure 6.16.

FIGURE 6.16

The Black and White adjustment layer dialog box gives you direct control over the luminosity of each color channel in the image.

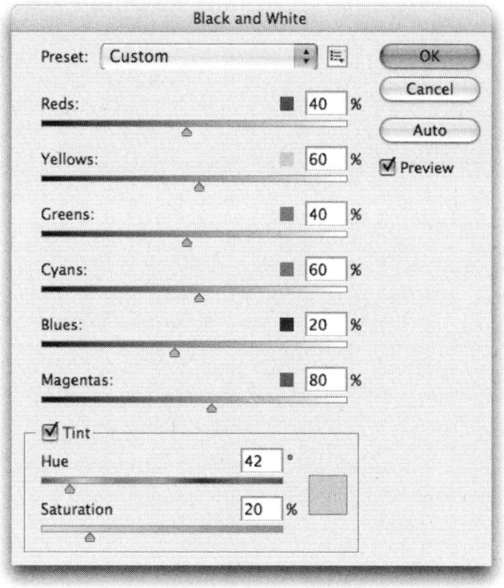

The basic controls in this dialog box are quite simple. Here's how they work:

- **Preset:** This offers a selection of photography-related presets. You can also save any changes you make to the adjustment layer as additional presets (in the BLW file format), so that you can reapply them to other images, which is great if you have to perform multiple conversions from a single shoot.

CROSS-REF These presets work in a similar way to the Curves presets. See the section "Working with Curves presets" earlier in this chapter.

- **Color sliders:** Although it may seem odd to have color controls within a black-and-white conversion utility, these are, in fact, very helpful. The sliders control the amount of each color that contributes to the luminosity of the final black-and-white image. This allows you to mimic the effects of using colored filters on a camera loaded with black-and-white film. Traditionally, for example, black-and-white photographers have used a red filter on their cameras to darken blue skies, which is great for landscapes. Alternatively, thinking of it from a nontraditional standpoint, you can emphasize the original colors within the context of a black-and-white image.

To reduce the luminosity of a color, click and drag the slider to the left; to increase it, drag it to the right. As with most values in Photoshop, you can also type your own values, from -200 percent to 300 percent, into each color's numerical entry box. Increasing positive values contribute more and more from that channel to the final brightness levels; negative values start to subtract that channel from the end result.

> **TIP**   You can also adjust the color sliders by clicking and dragging in the document window. Click a pixel in the image, and drag left and right. Photoshop adjusts the color slider that best approximates the color of that pixel.

- **Tint:** The Tint options allow you to introduce a color cast to your images. Think sepia or platinum print techniques. This option has sliders for both Hue and Saturation. Click the checkbox next to Tint to select these options and apply a tint. Pick the color you want to introduce with the Hue slider, and choose the amount of that color to apply with the Saturation slider. This feature is best used sparingly and is useful for adding just a touch of life to a fully black-and-white image. The color box on the right shows the tint you're using; you can also click this color box to pick a color directly, using a Color Picker dialog box.

- **Auto:** This gives Photoshop control over the conversion process. It tries to create a good balance across the tonal ranges, which may or may not be what you're looking for. If you don't like the result, you can, of course, tweak the effect afterward by clicking and dragging the color sliders.

So how does this new adjustment layer work in practice? If you've used the Channel Mixer to perform black-and-white conversions, you may be somewhat familiar with the approach. You still have control over the Red, Green, and Blue channels, but the Black & White adjustment layer adds a second tier of colors—yellows, cyans, and magentas—to allow for much more flexibility in the conversion process.

Within the Channel Mixer, the Red, Green, and Blue values should add up to 100 percent to avoid blown highlights and posterization. However, the Black & White adjustment isn't nearly so fussy on this front, so you don't have to worry about making your sliders add up to anything. In practice, this gives you more control, and causes less worrying about the technicalities of blown highlights and clipped shadows.

Having said that, it is easy to introduce a good deal of noise when using the sliders, so err on the side of caution.

To illustrate the use of the color sliders, you'll look at converting a color image of a lamppost and the sea to black and white. In Figure 6.17, you can see the photo, converted with the default settings for the Black & White adjustment layer. It's done an adequate job of this, and the channels are well balanced. In the original photo, the sky is a definite blue, and the top of that lamppost is actually red due to having colored glass. Say you want to emphasize these elements by darkening the blue skies, and drawing attention to the original color of the glass.

The default settings of the Black & White adjustment layer are fine as far as they go, but the conversion is flat and lacks drama.

To darken the sky, you can click and drag the Blues slider left, reducing the Blue channel's luminosity. You also balance that by increasing the Red channel to 150 percent to make the glass in the lamppost more prominent.

You can further emphasize the sign on the lamppost (originally yellow) by increasing the Yellows value to 120 percent. Meanwhile, dropping the Magentas value to 30 percent brings back a little detail in the glass of the lamppost. Lastly, drop the Cyans slider to 50 percent to further darken the sky a little. The final conversion is shown in Figure 6.18.

FIGURE 6.18

The image is now much more dramatic than the one produced by the initial conversion. It really brings out the colors of the original photo.

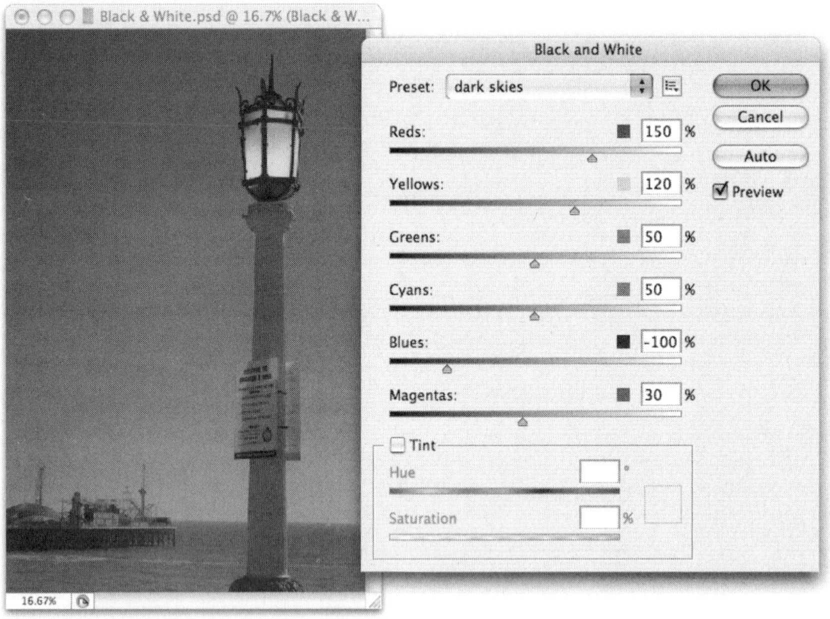

Adjusting colors using Hue/Saturation

Another weapon in Photoshop's color-correction arsenal is the Hue/Saturation adjustment layer. With Hue/Saturation, you can adjust the hue, saturation, and lightness across the whole image or across specified color ranges. You can also colorize the entire image, which is handy for adding color tints to black-and-white photos.

To create a Hue/Saturation adjustment layer, choose Layer ➪ New Adjustment Layer ➪ Hue/Saturation, or click the Create New Fill or Adjustment Layer icon in the Layers palette and choose Hue/Saturation from the menu. After you create the layer, the Hue/Saturation dialog box appears, as shown in Figure 6.19.

FIGURE 6.19

The Hue/Saturation dialog box and adjustment layer offer you a fine degree of control over your color adjustments.

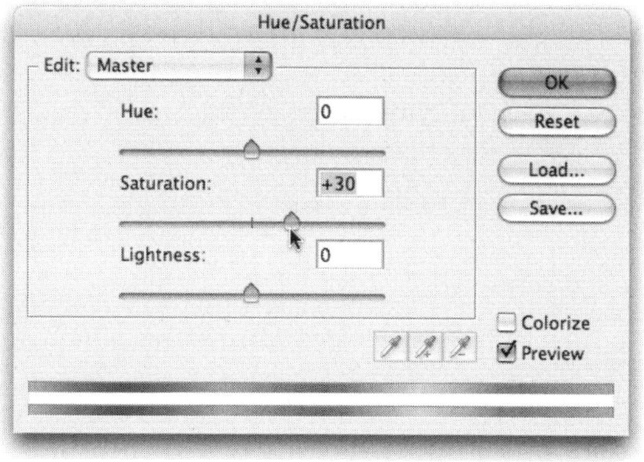

The main controls in this dialog box are the Hue, Saturation, and Lightness sliders, which work as follows:

- **Hue:** The Hue slider lets you move the hues in the image around the color wheel. If you're not familiar with the color wheel, think of a clock face with red at the 12 o'clock position (0 degrees), green at 4 o'clock (120 degrees), and blue at 8 o'clock (240 degrees). Click and drag this slider to shift all the colors in the image. Positive values shift the hues clockwise around the wheel; negative values shift them counterclockwise. For example, dragging the slider to a value of +30 shifts the reds in the image toward orange, the greens toward cyan, and the blues toward magenta.

- **Saturation:** This slider controls how *saturated*, or colorized, the colors in the image appear. Click and drag it all the way to the left (-100) to completely desaturate the image; all color information is removed from the image, leaving only the luminance values. Drag it all the way to the right (+100) to boost your color values to the max. Unless you're creating special effects, you'll want to make more subtle changes — between around -30 and +30 — to avoid removing or adding too much color detail.

- **Lightness:** The Lightness slider increases or reduces the amount of lightness in the image by adding white to lighten the image, or adding black to darken it. Clicking and dragging the Lightness slider all the way to the left (-100) results in a 100 percent black image; dragging it all the way to the right (+100) produces a 100 percent white image.

CAUTION Be careful when adjusting the Saturation and Lightness sliders, as it's very easy to clip your image and lose detail. In fact, you're nearly always better off using Levels, Curves, or Brightness/Contrast to alter brightness and contrast, rather than using Lightness. If you do use the Saturation and Lightness sliders, keep an eye on the image's histogram (Window ➭ Histogram) as you adjust them, so you can see exactly how your changes are affecting the dynamic range of the image.

The bottom of the Hue/Saturation dialog box contains two color bars, one below the other. These color bars serve two purposes:

- They provide an at-a-glance view of your slider adjustments. The top bar represents the hues on the color wheel before you've applied your adjustments, and the bottom bar shows how the color wheel has been changed by your adjustments. Shift the hues with the Hue slider and you'll see the bottom bar slide along, showing how your old hues are mapping to the new ones. Likewise, drag the Saturation and Lightness sliders and the bottom bar shows you how the colors are being affected by your changes.

- When working with color ranges (see the section "Adjusting specific color ranges"), sliders appear between the two color bars, allowing you to specify the range of hues you want to adjust.

> **TIP**   The top color bar defaults to showing reds in the middle with blues and greens off to the left and the right. This is all very well, but what if you're working on a range of greeny-blues and you want to see what's going on properly? Simply hold down Ctrl (⌘ on the Mac) and move the mouse over either color bar. The cursor changes to a hand. You can now click the color bar and drag it left or right to "spin the color wheel" until the color range you're working on is in the middle.

Adjusting specific color ranges

The Edit pop-up menu at the top of the dialog box lets you choose a range of colors to work on. The default, Master, works on the entire image, but you probably won't use it that often unless you're colorizing or desaturating an image. Why? Well, shifting all the hues in the image tends to produce some pretty odd effects. Clicking and dragging the Hue slider to the right might be great for making the sky in a photo a nice blue, but people in the same photo start to look a bit unwell as their skin tones start to become more and more greeny-yellow.

The answer to this problem is to bring into play the really powerful part of the Hue/Saturation dialog box: the ability to work only on a selected color range (or even on a bunch of ranges at the same time).

To enable this feature, choose any color range from the Edit pop-up menu apart from Master. Some interesting figures and sliders appear toward the bottom of the dialog box; more on these in a minute. For example, if you want to work on just the sky in your photo, you might choose Cyans or Blues. Any adjustments that you now make with the Hue, Saturation, and Lightness sliders now only affect that range of colors.

Better yet, you can adjust several ranges of colors independently. Choose another color range from the Edit menu and drag the sliders to adjust that color range. Photoshop remembers the adjustments you made to the first color range. In this way you can adjust several color ranges at the same time.

You're probably wondering what happens if you want to adjust a range of colors that doesn't neatly match any of the options in the Edit menu. In fact, this is usually the case, and this is where those extra sliders between the color bars at the bottom of the dialog box come into their own. Figure 6.20 shows the Hue/Saturation dialog box when you're editing a color range.

FIGURE 6.20

Adjusting a color range with the Hue/Saturation dialog box

Drop-off

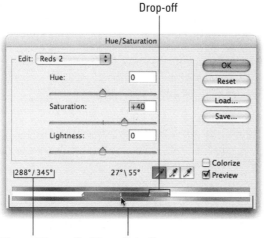

Size and Drop-off of the   Color Range
color range represented
numerically in angles
around the color wheel

With these sliders, and the associated eyedropper icons above the color bars, you can specify exactly which range of colors you want to work on. You can also control the size and, therefore, steepness of the drop-off at each end of the range. Generally, you want to allow a reasonable amount of drop-off, so that your adjustment blends gradually into areas outside the range. If you have a sharp drop-off at the start or end of the range, you'll probably notice some jagged transitions appearing in your image.

Here's how the color range sliders and eyedroppers work:

- To select a different color range, click the dark gray bar in the center of the sliders and drag left or right. The top color bar shows you the range of colors that you selected. Alternatively, click the left eyedropper icon and click a color in the image. This changes the color range so that the clicked color is in the center of the range.

- To widen or narrow the color range, click one of the lighter gray bars and drag left or right. For example, drag the left bar to the left to increase the color range; drag it to the right to decrease the range. Alternatively, click the middle eyedropper (with the plus sign) and click a color in the image to expand the range to include that color. Conversely, click the right-hand eyedropper (with the minus sign), then click a color in the image to contract the range so that it no longer includes that color.

- To increase or decrease the size of the drop-off at either end of the range, drag one of the four little sliders that lie between and around the gray bars. For example, to make the left-hand edge of the color range drop off sharply, click and drag the two sliders on the left closer together. To make a gentler, wider drop-off, drag the sliders apart. The outer triangular sliders change the drop-off without affecting the color range; the inner rectangular sliders change both the drop-off and the range.

TIP   While the left-hand eyedropper icon is selected, you can Shift+click a color in the image to expand the color range, or Alt+click (Option+click on the Mac) a color to contract the color range. This saves you from having to keep clicking the other two eyedropper icons.

If you choose a preset color range from the Edit menu then move the range into a different part of the color wheel, the menu option changes to reflect the new color range. If a preset color range with that name already exists, Photoshop adds a number after the name of the range. You can replace all six of the preset ranges with your own custom ranges in this way.

For example, say you select the Reds preset and click and drag it toward yellow. The Edit menu option will be renamed Yellows, and the existing Yellows option will be renamed Yellows 2. If you then select the Greens preset and drag that toward yellow, too, it will be renamed Yellows 3, and so on.

While you're altering a color range, the four values above the color bars show you the size and drop-off of the range numerically. The values are all in degrees and represent angles around the color wheel, as described earlier. As you might imagine, the four values reflect the positions of the four sliders between the color bars.

TIP   For even more fine-grained control over the parts of the image you're adjusting, select an area to work on with one of the selection tools, then create your Hue/Saturation adjustment layer. Photoshop automatically applies the selection as a layer mask to restrict your adjustments to that selected area. You can then narrow down the area to work on even further by using a color range.

Colorizing images

Selecting the Colorize option in the dialog box switches the Hue/Saturation layer into Colorize mode. This behaves quite differently to the normal mode; in Colorize mode, all existing color information is replaced by the values of the Hue and Saturation sliders, allowing you to give a single, uniform tint to the image.

Because of this, the Hue and Saturation values become absolute, rather than relative. The Hue slider now runs from 0 (red) up to 360 degrees (which, of course, is also red), covering the full color spectrum in between. Saturation now goes from 0 (completely desaturated) to 100 percent (fully saturated). The Lightness slider behaves as usual: -100 is 100 percent black, while +100 is 100 percent white.

As you might imagine, the Colorize option is most useful for colorizing grayscale images. It can also be handy if the colors in the image look terrible but the basic luminance detail is sound; simply use the Colorize option to wipe out the existing color information and add your own.

> **TIP** You can't select a color range when Colorize is enabled (presumably because it's prima-rily designed to work on grayscale images). If you want to colorize different areas of your image with different colors, create several Hue/Saturation adjustment layers and use their layer masks to select the areas you want to colorize. (More on masking adjustment layers later in this chapter.)

Correcting out-of-gamut colors

One very useful application of the Hue/Saturation adjustment layer is to eliminate out-of-gamut colors from an image. A *gamut* is a range of colors that a particular output device or color space is capable of displaying or representing. In Photoshop, *out-of-gamut* usually refers to colors in the RGB or Lab modes that can't be represented in the CMYK mode. This happens quite a lot because CMYK has a smaller gamut than either RGB or Lab; for example, CMYK can't handle pure red (255, 0, 0).

This means that, when you convert your RGB or Lab image to CMYK to send to the printers, some of the colors in your original image are lost in the conversion. The trick is in how you manage that loss.

The gung-ho approach is simply to convert to CMYK (Image ➪ Mode ➪ CMYK Color) and let Photoshop deal with it. Unfortunately it doesn't always do a great job, leaving you with quite a dull-looking image and losing color detail in key parts of your image. You can help it along a bit by picking a different Rendering Intent setting in the Customize Proof Condition dialog box (View ➪ Proof Setup ➪ Custom) but this still doesn't give you much flexibility.

Another approach is to use the Sponge tool on the out-of-gamut areas of the image. Set its mode to Desaturate and use a low flow (say, 5 or 10 percent). Turn on the gamut warning by choosing View ➪ Gamut Warning or pressing Ctrl+Shift+Y (⌘+Shift+Y on the Mac) to see the out-of-gamut pixels in gray (by default). Gently sponge over those pixels until the gray spots are removed. Don't overdo it or you'll desaturate your image too much.

A much quicker (and also nondestructive) way of correcting out-of-gamut colors is to use — you guessed it — a Hue/Saturation adjustment layer. The trick is to use the Saturation slider in the dialog box to reduce saturation for the out-of-gamut color ranges.

To do this, follow these steps:

1. **Set up soft proofing for CMYK.** To do this, choose View ➪ Proof Setup ➪ Working CMYK. (You can instead choose any of the other "Working..." options in the menu as required.)

2. **Turn on the gamut warning.** Choose View ➪ Gamut Warning or press Ctrl+Shift+Y (⌘+Shift+Y on the Mac). Out-of-gamut pixels in the image now appear gray (by default).

3. **Create a new Hue/Saturation layer.** Make sure the layer is above your image layer in the Layers palette.

4. **Pick a color range from the Hue/Saturation dialog's Edit menu.** Choose a range that approximates a color that's showing as out-of-gamut in the image. (You may want to tog-gle the gamut warning on and off so you can see the original colors; luckily Photoshop lets you do this even within the Hue/Saturation dialog.)

5. **Fine-tune the range.** Click on other out-of-gamut pixels of similar color with the middle (plus) eyedropper, then click on nearby in-gamut pixels with the right (minus) eyedropper.

6. **Reduce the saturation.** Gradually click and drag the Saturation slider to the left until most of the pixels are in-gamut (you should see just a smattering of gray gamut warning pixels now).

7. **Pick another color range.** If other significant out-of-gamut areas of the image remain, choose another color range from the Edit menu and repeat the above process.

8. **Save the results.** When you're happy with the results, click OK to close the dialog box. (You can, of course, go back and reedit the saturation levels by double-clicking on the adjustment layer's thumbnail.)

9. **Convert to CMYK.** Finally, choose Image ➪ Mode ➪ CMYK Color to convert your corrected image to CMYK. Photoshop now moves any remaining out-of-gamut colors into the CMYK gamut, and you're good to go. Because you moved most of the out-of-gamut colors yourself, the results usually look significantly better than using the fully automated approach.

By the way, the reason reducing the saturation fixes gamut problems is that that most of the colors that CMYK can't represent are highly saturated ones. By reducing the saturation of these colors, you can squeeze them into the CMYK gamut.

TIP The other solution, of course, is to scan using CMYK in the first place. However, this isn't always an ideal option; for one thing, you can do a lot more manipulation in the RGB color space than you can in CMYK.

Changing CMYK values with Selective Color

Photoshop's Selective Color adjustment layer lets you adjust the hue and lightness of color ranges using CMYK sliders. Although you can use Selective Color in any color mode, it really comes into its own when working with CMYK images. Because the sliders adjust the cyan, magenta, yellow, and black components of each color range, it gives you direct control over the amount of each ink used in the CMYK printing process.

Selective Color is great for removing color casts introduced by the conversion to CMYK; for example, if your blues look a bit too green in CMYK mode then you can pull back the yellow component in the Blues color range.

You don't have to use it just on CMYK images — it can be a handy way to selectively alter colors in any image, although you may find that Hue/Saturation works better for you.

Create a Selective Color adjustment layer by choosing Layer ➪ New Adjustment Layer ➪ Selective Color. You can also click the Create New Fill or Adjustment Layer icon in the Layers palette and choose Selective Color from the menu. After you create the adjustment layer, the Selective Color Options dialog box appears, as shown in Figure 6.21.

FIGURE 6.21

The Selective Color Options dialog box alters the color balance of selected color ranges through the use of Cyan, Magenta, Yellow, and Black sliders.

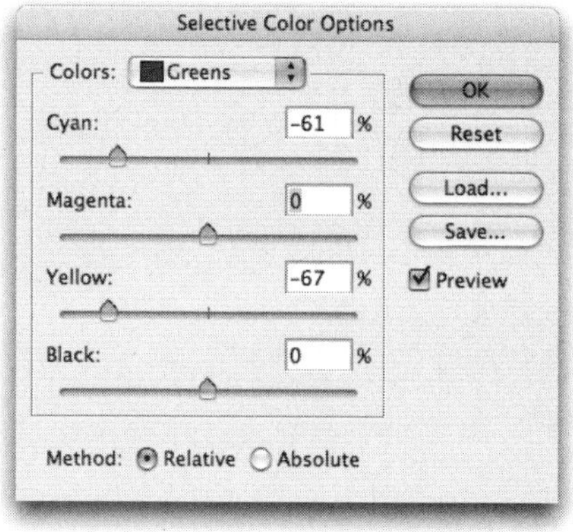

Use the Colors pop-up menu to choose a color range to work on. As well as the six additive and subtractive primaries, you can choose from Whites, Neutrals (mid-grays), and Blacks. This is what the "selective" of Selective Color refers to — you can adjust the CMYK process colors in just the red components of the image, for example, without touching any of the other components.

After choosing a color range, use the Cyan, Magenta, Yellow, and Black sliders to adjust the amount of CMYK inks for that color range. You can click and drag the sliders or type values in the boxes above each slider; a value of 0 means no change, a negative value decreases the amount of that ink, and a positive value increases it.

The slider values are all measured in percentages of ink coverage. If you use the default Method option, Relative, then the percentage used is relative to the amount of that ink already in each pixel. For example, if you set the Cyan slider to 10 percent then a pixel that previously contained 50 percent cyan now contains 55 percent cyan (10 percent of 50 percent is 5 percent). If you select the Absolute option instead, the slider values are independent of the existing pixel color; for example, setting the Cyan slider to 10 percent increases the same pixel's cyan component from 50 percent to 60 percent. As you might imagine, the Absolute setting tends to have a more dramatic effect than Relative.

Mashing up colors with the Channel Mixer

With the Channel Mixer adjustment layer you can radically alter the color makeup of your image. The main uses of the Channel Mixer are to creatively convert color images to black and white, and to add special color effects to images.

CROSS-REF When it comes to converting color images to black and white, the Channel Mixer has largely been superseded by the new Black & White adjustment layer in Photoshop CS3, described earlier in this chapter, although the Channel Mixer arguably produces better results in the right hands.

To create a Channel Mixer adjustment layer, choose Layer ➪ New Adjustment Layer ➪ Channel Mixer, or click the Create New Fill or Adjustment Layer icon in the Layers palette and choose Channel Mixer from the menu. After you create your adjustment layer, the Channel Mixer dialog box, shown in Figure 6.22, appears.

FIGURE 6.22

With the Channel Mixer dialog you can mix various amounts of the original color channels together for each output channel.

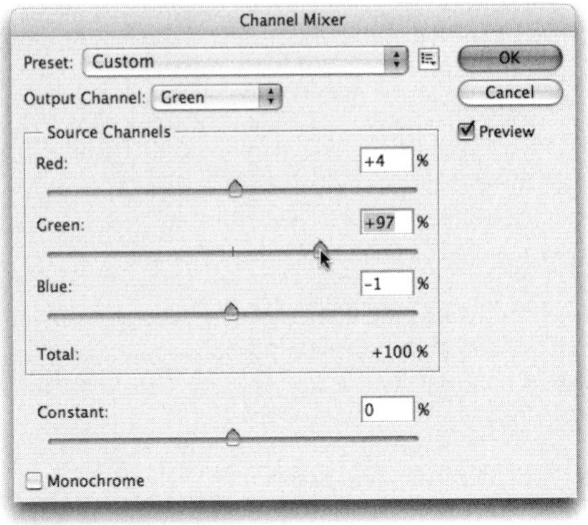

NOTE The Channel Mixer adjustment layer is not available in Lab mode.

To start using the Channel Mixer, choose an output channel from the Output Channel pop-up menu. The available channels depend on the color mode you're working in: for example, you'll see Red, Green, and Blue in RGB mode.

Initially, Photoshop is sending 100 percent of the Red source channel to the Red output channel, 100 percent of the Green source channel to the Green output channel, and 100 percent of the Blue source channel to the Blue output channel. In other words, the output channels (the end result) are identical to the input channels (the original image); no mixing is taking place.

To mix the channels, click and drag the Red, Green, and Blue sliders around, or type values in the boxes above each slider. For example, to introduce some green from the image into the Red output channel, choose Red from the Output Channel menu then drag the Green slider to the right. If you drag the Green slider to the left past 0 so that the value turns negative, Photoshop starts subtracting the Green source channel's value from the output channel.

Pick a different output channel, and you can set the source channel sliders for that output channel, too. Each output channel has its own set of sliders, so you can choose different source channel mixes for each of the Red, Green, and Blue output channels.

You get the best results if all your sliders add up to 100 percent for each output channel, as the resulting image is then roughly the same brightness as the original. You can also adjust the overall brightness of each output channel by clicking and dragging the Constant slider or typing a value into its associated input box. Zero means no change, 200 percent makes the output channel completely white, and -200 percent makes the output channel completely black.

NEW FEATURE   Photoshop CS3 makes it easy for you to check that your sliders add up to 100 percent with the new Total display below the sliders. This shows you the sum total of the channel slider values. If this sum exceeds 100 percent, a little warning triangle appears to remind you that you're losing detail in the image.

Converting to black and white

If you want to convert a color image to black and white, the Channel Mixer is a great tool for the job. To do this, select the Monochrome option at the bottom of the dialog box. The Output Channel menu changes to contain just one option: Gray. You can now use the Source Channel sliders to specify how much of the original color channels go into making up the grayscale image. Again, for best results, all the channel values should add up to 100 percent.

A good way to convert to black and white is first to look at each color channel in isolation as a black-and-white image to see which channel looks best. There are a couple of different ways you can do this:

- If you're not currently in the Channel Mixer dialog box, display the Channels palette (Window ⇨ Channels) and use the eye icons next to each channel to hide all channels except Red. Take a look at the image in the document window. You're now looking at how the image will look in black and white if you just use the Red channel. Repeat with the Green and Blue channels to see which one you like best.

NOTE   If the image in the document window looks red, green, or blue rather than grayscale, choose Edit ⇨ Preferences ⇨ Interface (Photoshop ⇨ Preferences ⇨ Interface on the Mac) and deselect the Show Channels in Color option.

- If you're already in the Channel Mixer dialog box, select the Monochrome option, then set the Red source channel value to 100 percent and the other two channels to 0 percent. Next, set the Green channel to 100 percent and the other two to 0 percent. Finally, try the Blue channel at 100 percent and the others set to 0. See which one you prefer.

After you decide which channel you like the most, open the Channel Mixer dialog box by creating a new Channel Mixer adjustment layer or editing an existing one, and set your preferred channel to, say, 80 percent and the other two channels to 10 percent each. Tweak the values until you get a result you like.

NOTE You might be wondering why you can't just choose Image ⇨ Adjustments ⇨ Desaturate to convert an image to black and white. Actually, you can, but the results don't tend to look that great. Photoshop does a fairly good job of estimating how much of each color channel to use, but the best values vary from photo to photo and it's no substitute for your eye. Another advantage of using the Channel Mixer is that it's available as an adjustment layer, allowing you to convert to black and white nondestructively.

Channel Mixer presets

You can save Channel Mixer settings as preset files for later reuse. Channel Mixer preset file names end in .cha. To load, save, and delete presets, click the Preset Options button to the right of the Preset menu and use the options in the pop-up menu that appears. These options work in exactly the same way as their equivalents in the Curves dialog box; see the section "Working with Curves presets" earlier in the chapter, for details.

The built-in Channel Mixer presets relate to converting photos to black and white. Most of the presets mimic the effects of different colored filters on the lens of a camera when using black and white film. The Black & White Infrared preset instead mimics the use of black and white infrared film.

Using Gradient Map to colorize images

The Gradient Map adjustment layer takes a grayscale version of your image and maps the brightness levels in the grayscale version to the colors of a gradient to produce the final result. For example, if you use a gradient that runs from red on the left to yellow on the right, the shadows of the image appear red, the highlights appear yellow, and the midtones appear orange. The fun part about Gradient Map is that you can use any gradient you want as the map, allowing you to produce some pretty far-out effects.

To create a new Gradient Map adjustment layer, choose Layer ⇨ New Adjustment Layer ⇨ Gradient Map; alternatively, click the Create New Fill or Adjustment Layer icon in the Layers palette and choose Gradient Map from the pop-up menu. After you create the layer, the Gradient Map dialog box, shown in Figure 6.23, appears.

This dialog box is very easy to use. Click the downward-pointing arrow to the right of the gradient in the dialog box, and the Gradient Picker, containing a list of available gradients, appears. Choose a gradient from the list to apply that gradient to your image. You can pick a different set of gradients by clicking the right-pointing arrow in the pop-up list of gradients, then choosing a set from the list toward the bottom of the pop-up menu.

FIGURE 6.23

Gradient Map lets you map the grayscale values of your image onto a gradient, creating some interesting colorizing effects.

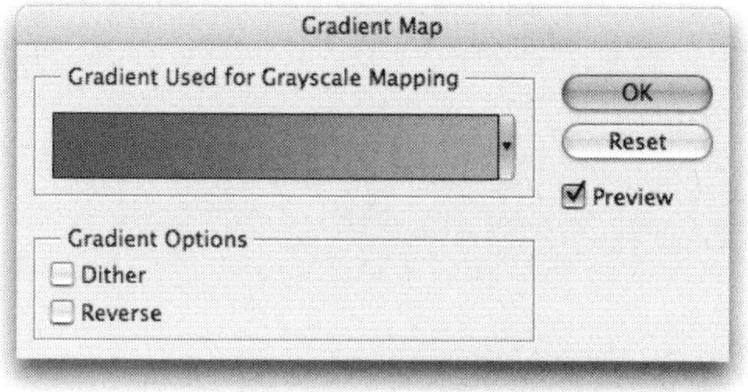

To make a custom gradient, click the gradient in the Gradient Map dialog box to display the Gradient Editor dialog box. You can then edit the gradient and use it as the gradient map. You can also save your edited gradient as a preset by clicking New, or choose another gradient from the list of presets.

CAUTION Gradient Map doesn't really work with gradients containing transparency. Well, it works, but the transparency is ignored, so it's not much use.

You can create some dramatic color effects using Gradient Map. For example, choose the Spectrum gradient in the default list to produce a fairly psychedelic tie-dyed effect, or choose the Copper gradient to give the effect of the photo being etched out of a copper sheet, as shown in Figure 6.24. (No prizes for guessing what the Black, White gradient looks like.)

TIP For an interesting pointillistic effect, choose the Noise gradient type in the Gradient Editor and play with the Roughness slider.

Of the remaining options in the Gradient Map dialog box, Dither adds dithering to the gradient effect to help reduce banding effects in the image, while Reverse swaps the order of the gradient — for example, if your gradient runs from black to white, selecting Reverse makes it run from white to black instead. Preview behaves as always, allowing you to toggle the "before" and "after" images in the document window.

CROSS-REF For more on gradients and the Gradient Editor, see the section "Making gradients with Gradient fill layers" toward the end of this chapter.

FIGURE 6.24

You can produce some interesting color and tonal effects using Gradient Map. Here, the Copper gradient is used to produce an "etched-out-of-metal" effect.

Simulating lens filters with Photo Filter

Many photographers alter the color balance of their photos using filters in front of the lens. Sometimes these filters are used for artistic effect; often they're used to compensate for different lighting conditions. The Photo Filter adjustment layer lets you simulate these filters from within Photoshop, which is much easier than lugging a bunch of filters around.

To add a Photo Filter adjustment layer to your image, choose Layer ➪ New Adjustment Layer ➪ Photo Filter, or click the Create New Fill or Adjustment Layer icon in the Layers palette and choose Photo Filter from the menu. After you create your adjustment layer, the Photo filter dialog box appears (see Figure 6.25), allowing you to choose a filter and adjust various settings.

FIGURE 6.25

Use the Photo Filter dialog box to simulate various lens filters, enabling you to correct colors and add special effects to your images.

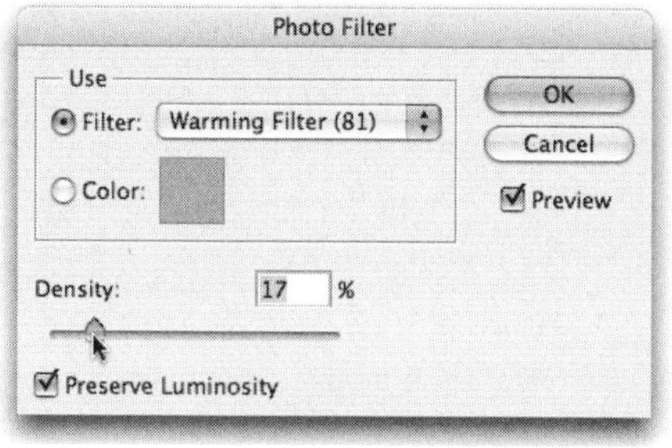

You can either choose a preset filter from the Filter pop-up menu, or make up your own filter using the Color box. The preset filters include the following:

- **Warming Filter (85) and Warming Filter (LBA):** These two filters are designed to correct the white balance in a photo taken under high-temperature (blue) light, such as daylight. Such photos can often have a blue color cast, particularly if tungsten film is used. These two filters add orange to the image, thereby correcting the blue tint.

- **Cooling Filter (80) and Cooling Filter (LBB):** These filters perform the opposite functions to the 85 and LBA warming filters. They correct the white balance of a photo that has an orange tint by adding blue. Such photos often result from shooting indoors under a tungsten light while using a daylight film.

- **Warming Filter (81) and Cooling Filter (82):** These two filters warm and cool the image in a similar way to the previous filters, but their effect is more subtle. They're good for making minor color-balance adjustments.

- **Sepia:** This is great for those old-school sepia-toned effects. You'll probably want to increase the Density setting (described in a moment) above 50 percent to create the desired effect.

- **Underwater:** This filter adds an aqua tint to the photo, as if it was taken under the sea.

The remaining preset filters offer a range of standard colors from red through magenta, as well as Deep Red, Blue, Emerald, and Yellow for more pronounced effects.

You can also choose your own custom filter color. Click the Color box to display the Color Picker; then select the color you want to use for your filter.

The Density slider and associated input box let you specify the strength of the filter effect. The default of 25 percent produces a pretty subtle color shift, while the maximum of 100 percent creates a very strong effect.

The Preserve Luminosity option, which is selected by default, ensures that the image's luminosity remains constant through the filtering process. Deselecting this option results in a darker image.

Making tonal adjustments with Exposure

NEW FEATURE This is another new adjustment layer in Photoshop CS3, and will appeal to those who have cameras that tend toward a slight underexposure, as well as designers given under-exposed images to work with. Originally found in CS2 under Image ⇨ Adjustments, the new nonde-structive adjustment layer version is a welcome addition.

The Exposure adjustment layer allows you to compensate for under- or overexposed images using a metaphor familiar to photographers: stops. To create a new Exposure adjustment layer, choose Layer ⇨ New Adjustment Layer ⇨ Exposure. A dialog box appears where you can name your new adjustment layer and choose a blending mode, as well as other options. You can also click the Create New Fill or Adjustment Layer icon in the Layers palette, and choose Exposure from the pop-up menu, which simply takes you straight to the Exposure dialog box, as shown in Figure 6.26.

FIGURE 6.26

The Exposure dialog box. Use this adjustment layer to correct underexposed or overexposed photos.

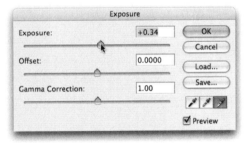

The controls for this adjustment layer work as follows:

- **Exposure:** This slider allows you to set a positive or negative exposure value for the image. Clicking and dragging the slider to the left results in a darker, less exposed image, and dragging it to the right gives you a lighter, more exposed result. You can also type a value directly in the box above the slider. This value is measured in *stops*. A stop is a pho-tographic term; an increase of 1 stop represents a halving of the amount of light hitting the camera sensor. In the Exposure dialog box, the effect is reversed — presumably to make it more intuitive for nonphotographers — so higher values result in a brighter image. Also, unlike using a real film camera, the Exposure slider lets you set exposure values not just in whole stops, but in hundredths of a stop.

- **Offset:** Here, you can adjust the brightness of the shadows with minimal effect on the highlights. Click and drag to the left to darken shadows, and to the right to lighten them.

- **Gamma Correction:** This allows you to lighten or darken the midtones of the image without greatly affecting the shadows or highlights. Click and drag to the left to lighten the midtones; drag to the right to darken them. It's much like dragging the gray slider in the Levels dialog box (see the section "Adjusting Levels" earlier in this chapter).

TIP   With all three controls just described, you can set values numerically by clicking in the boxes above the sliders and typing new values.

- **Eyedroppers:** You can use the eyedroppers to define your black, white, and mid-gray values visually by clicking on the corresponding areas of the image. Clicking a pixel with the black eyedropper adjusts the Offset value, setting the pixel that you click to black. Clicking with the gray and white eyedroppers controls the Exposure value, setting the pixel that you click to mid-gray and white respectively. In practice, it can be tricky to get the exposure right with these eyedroppers; the sliders usually produce a more pleasing result.

- **Load and Save buttons:** These two buttons offer a way to save settings that you're likely to use again. Click Save to save a setting as an EAP (Exposure preset) file to your hard drive; click Load to retrieve a previously saved setting.

The following example shows what an Exposure adjustment layer can achieve with a slightly underexposed photo. In Figure 6.27, you can see a goose that is presumably a little uptight because his photo is going to be underexposed. Luckily, you can salvage the shot (and the goose's pride) with an Exposure adjustment layer.

FIGURE 6.27

Your sadly underexposed goose

First, click and drag the Exposure slider to the right to enhance the overall image. As you do this, it's important not to go too far or you introduce clipping into the highlights and lose detail. As with many Photoshop adjustments, less is more, and in this case, a good setting is around 1.3 stops.

Darken the shadows a little using the Offset slider. Less is very definitely more here, and it just needs a little nudge to the left to add a value of around -0.0221.

Lastly, the midtones could be a little brighter, so click and drag the Gamma Correction slider a little to the left to a value of 1.15.

As you can see in Figure 6.28, the improvements are quite dramatic, and the goose should now feel a lot happier about his representation.

FIGURE 6.28

The image is now more fully exposed and shows how the Exposure adjustment layer can produce very natural looking results, just as if you had used the correct in-camera exposure.

Inverting an image's colors

The Invert adjustment layer is one of the simplest ones available — in fact it doesn't even have a dialog box. All it does is invert the color values of each color channel for every pixel in the image. *Invert* in this sense means that dark color values become bright and bright values become dark.

> **NOTE** What Photoshop actually does is subtract each channel's color value from 255. So a color value that was white (255) becomes black (0), and vice versa.

To add a new Invert adjustment layer, simply choose Layer ➪ New Adjustment Layer ➪ Invert, or click the Create New Fill or Adjustment Layer icon in the Layers palette and choose Invert from the pop-up menu.

If you invert a grayscale image, as shown in Figure 6.29, the result is much as you'd expect — dark areas become light and light areas become dark, while midtones don't change as much. If you try it on a color image, though, you may be surprised by the result. The reason the colors look so odd is that each color channel is being inverted, and what you see is the combined results of those color channel inversions. For example, a yellow pixel becomes blue because the Red and Green channels of the pixel invert to become black, while the Blue channel inverts to become white.

FIGURE 6.29

Inverting a grayscale image (left) using the Invert adjustment layer produces a "negative" version of the image (right).

And before you ask — no, unfortunately you can't just apply an Invert adjustment layer to turn a scan of a color negative into a positive image. While this works for black-and-white negatives, color negatives have an orange mask that turns blue when inverted, and the end result usually has low contrast. However, you can fix this up using Levels and Curves adjustment layers (see earlier in this chapter) to remove the cast and boost the contrast; you can also try using the Auto Levels or Auto Contrast commands, which usually do a pretty good job.

NEW FEATURE Photoshop CS3 now includes a handy Curves preset — Color Negative — that you can use as a basis for the conversion.

Apart from creating cool effects and turning negatives into positives, Invert has other uses. For example, it's often used to invert masks, making previously masked areas visible, and vice versa — although, as you can't easily apply an adjustment layer to a mask, this usually tends to be done by choosing Image ➪ Adjustments ➪ Invert.

Applying a threshold

The Threshold adjustment layer reduces your image to just two colors — black and white — based on the brightness levels of the original image. The clever bit is that you can choose the brightness level that separates the blacks from the whites, hence the "threshold" name. This makes Threshold handy for a couple of things, which are discussed shortly.

To add a Threshold adjustment layer to your document, choose Layer ➪ New Adjustment Layer ➪ Threshold, or click the Create New Fill or Adjustment Layer icon in the Layers palette and choose Threshold from the options in the pop-up menu. After you create your adjustment layer, the Threshold dialog box appears, as shown in Figure 6.30.

FIGURE 6.30

The Threshold dialog box allows you to choose a threshold brightness level that separates the black pixels from the white.

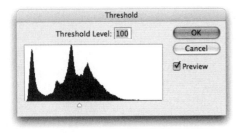

The dialog box contains a histogram showing you how many pixels in your image are using each of the available brightness levels from 0 to 255. Black (0) is shown on the left-hand side of the histogram; white (255) is shown on the right. So if, for example, the histogram has quite a big "hill" toward the right-hand side, it means that your image contains a lot of bright pixels.

CROSS-REF Find out more on image histograms in the section "Adjusting Levels" earlier in this chapter.

NOTE If you're working with a color image, the brightness levels in the histogram represent the average of the individual channel levels. So if you're working with an RGB image and you see a high peak at level 200, for example, that means that there are a lot of pixels in the image whose color channel levels equal 200 when averaged together.

When you first create a Threshold adjustment layer, Photoshop puts the threshold value right in the middle of the histogram at value 128 (mid-gray). This means that any pixels darker than mid-gray now appear as black in your image, and any pixels with a brightness level equal to or greater than 128 appear as white. (Select the Preview option to see the effect while the Threshold dialog box is open.)

To change the threshold, either click and drag the slider below the histogram to the left or right, or type a new threshold value (from 1 to 255) in the Threshold Level box. As you alter the threshold, your image changes to show more white (if you drag the slider to the left) or black (if you drag to the right).

You'll probably find that the threshold looks best with a fairly equal amount of black and white. To achieve this, drag the slider so that approximately half the total area of the histogram graph is to the left of it, and half is to the right, as shown in Figure 6.31.

FIGURE 6.31

The Threshold effect often looks best when there is roughly the same number of pixels to the left of the slider as there is to the right.

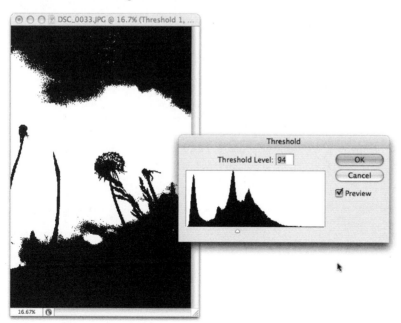

You can create some nice special effects using Threshold. Try adding a Threshold adjustment layer then applying the Gaussian Blur filter (Filter ➪ Blur ➪ Gaussian Blur) to the underlying layer to produce some great "organic" shapes like those in Figure 6.32. Or merge the adjustment layer with the underlying layer, then apply the Gaussian Blur to create a soft threshold effect. Other filters also produce interesting results when combined with Threshold.

Of course, Threshold is handy if you need to convert an image to black and white — for example, if you know you'll be printing it using a process that only works with two levels. Simply create a Threshold adjustment layer, then click and drag the slider until you get a result you're happy with.

Threshold serves another very useful purpose: You can use it to identify the shadows and highlights in your image. This is handy if you want to work on the shadows and highlights using, for example, the Curves or Levels adjustment layers. Not only can you use Threshold to see where the shadows and highlights are in your image, but you can also find out their brightness levels too. To do so, follow these steps:

1. **Create a Threshold adjustment layer.** Select the layer you want to identify the shadows and highlights in; then create a Threshold layer above it by choosing Layer ➪ New Adjustment Layer ➪ Threshold.

2. **Locate the shadows.** In the Threshold dialog box, click and drag the slider all the way to the left so that the image in the document window becomes completely white (make sure Preview is selected). Now, slowly drag the slider to the right until you start seeing a few clumps of black pixels. These are your shadows.

3. **Record the shadows.** Make a note of the brightness value at the slider in the Levels dialog box or, for more precision, Shift+click one or two clumps of black in the image to create color samplers. You can then read the color values of the shadows in the Info palette.

4. **Locate the highlights.** Click and drag the Threshold slider to the right — the image should now be completely black. Slowly drag the slider to the left until a few clumps of white appear. You've found your highlights.

5. **Record the highlights.** Note the brightness value and/or Shift+click the highlights in the image to create color samplers, as described in Step 3.

If you've created color samplers, you now have an instant visual record of the darkest and lightest points in your image, and you know their exact brightness levels, too.

Posterizing an image

The last adjustment layer in the list, Posterize, reduces the number of colors in your image in a similar way to Threshold. The advantage of Posterize is that you can choose the number of levels in the final image; you're not limited to two levels like you are with Threshold. On the other hand, Posterize doesn't let you specify a threshold level; the colors in your image are simply divided equally.

Using a Threshold adjustment with various Gaussian Blur radius values on the underlying layer creates these organic shapes.

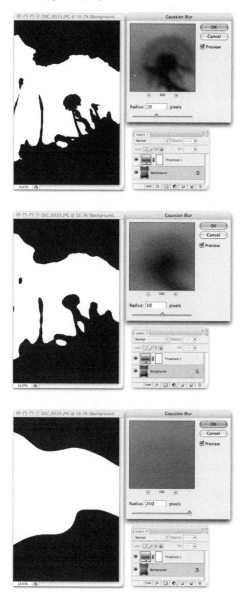

To create a Posterize adjustment layer and effect, choose Layer ➪ New Adjustment Layer ➪ Posterize, or click the Create New Fill or Adjustment Layer icon in the Layers palette and choose Posterize from the menu. After you create the Posterize layer, the Posterize dialog box (shown in Figure 6.33) appears.

FIGURE 6.33

Reduce the number of colors in your image using Posterize to create some interesting special effects.

Posterize is very simple to use; in fact, its only option is Levels, which you use to control the number of color levels in your final image. Type any value you want from 2 to 255, make sure Preview is selected, and the results appear in the document window. (A value of 255 produces hardly any change in the image because the original image has 256 available levels.)

If you're working with an RGB color image, you may be wondering why a Levels value of 2 appears to produce up to eight colors in the final image (including black and white). The reason is that Posterize works on a per-channel basis: when you specify two levels, Photoshop uses two levels (black and white) for the Red channel, two for the Green channel, and two for the Blue channel, making a total of eight possible channel combinations. If you try Posterize on a grayscale image, so there's only one color channel, the number of grayscale levels in the final image does indeed match the value you choose for Levels.

NOTE Using Posterize with a Levels value of 2 on a grayscale image has exactly the same effect as using Threshold on the same image with a Threshold Level value of 128, in case you were wondering.

You can use Posterize on its own to create special effects, or combine it with filters and other adjustment layers, much like you can with Threshold. Figure 6.34 shows an example of this in action.

FIGURE 6.34

Using a Posterize adjustment layer with the Mosaic filter to create a cool effect

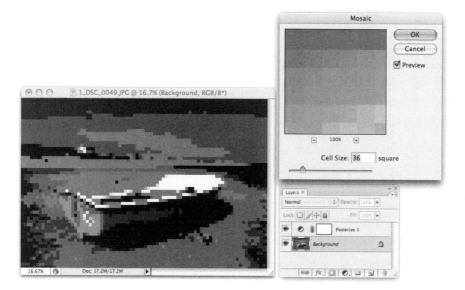

Creating Filled Areas with Fill Layers

After exploring adjustment layers in depth, you now move onto another layer type: fill layers. Fill layers are included in the same chapter as adjustment layers because the two layer types are quite closely related, and also because there isn't a great deal to say about fill layers—not enough to warrant their own chapter, at least.

You can use fill layers to fill your document with areas of solid color, with gradient fills, or with pattern fills. Fill layers are similar to adjustment layers because both layer types apply an effect that always spreads across the whole image width and height. If you want to limit the fill to a specific part of your image you need to use the layer's layer or vector mask. Fill layers are also nondestructive like adjustment layers; you can go back and reedit a fill layer's content at any time. In fact, the only significant difference between fill layers and adjustment layers is that a fill layer's content is a solid color, gradient, or pattern fill that works independently from other layers, whereas an adjustment layer's content is an adjustment that applies to one or more of the layers below it.

> **NOTE**   Shape layers, discussed in detail in Chapter 5, are simply fill layers with vector masks and (potentially) layer styles applied. Knowing this fact might help you get your head around shape layers — or fill layers, for that matter.

Adding a fill layer

To add a new fill layer to your document, click the Create New Fill or Adjustment Layer icon at the bottom of the Layers palette, then choose Solid Color, Gradient, or Pattern, as shown in Figure 6.35. You can also create a new fill layer by selecting an option under Layer ➪ New Fill Layer.

FIGURE 6.35

To create a new fill layer, click the Create New Fill or Adjustment Layer icon and choose one of the top three options.

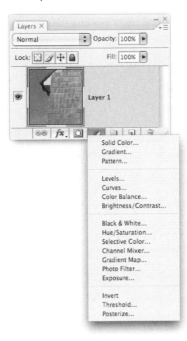

After you choose a fill layer type from the menu, Photoshop creates the fill layer and a dialog box appears that you can use to customize the fill. Choosing Solid Color simply displays a Color Picker dialog box that you can use to choose the fill color; choosing Gradient or Pattern displays a dialog box that lets you customize the gradient or pattern fill, respectively. These dialog boxes are explored in more detail in a moment.

If you select an option under Layer ➪ New Fill Layer, or create a fill layer by Alt/Option+clicking the Create New Fill or Adjustment Layer icon, Photoshop displays the New Layer dialog box. This dialog box allows you to customize a few options for the new layer. These options work in the same way as they do for adjustment layers; for more information, see the section "Setting adjustment layer options" earlier in the chapter.

Select the Use Previous Layer to Create Clipping Mask option to make the fill layer take on the shape of the layer below it. Fill layers behave like any other layer in a clipping mask; their contents are clipped by the shape of the base layer in the mask.

CROSS-REF Look at the section "Applying an adjustment to specific layers" earlier in this chapter for hints on using clipping masks with adjustment layers. The same techniques also apply to fill layers. For more on clipping masks in general, see Chapter 9.

After you create your fill layer, you can double-click its thumbnail to display its dialog box for reediting. In fact, all the methods for editing adjustment layers described in the section "Editing Adjustment Layers" earlier in this chapter also apply to fill layers. You can control the shape of your fill by editing its layer or vector mask; see the section "Masking Adjustment and Fill Layers" later in this chapter for more on these techniques.

Creating blocks of color with Solid Color fill layers

The Solid Color fill layer type is very easy to use; the only decision you need to make is what color to use for the fill. Create a new Solid Color fill layer, or double-click an existing layer's thumbnail to edit it, and Photoshop displays the Color Picker dialog box. Choose the color you want to use for the fill, and click OK. That's all there is to it.

As you'd imagine, Solid Color fill layers are useful for those times when you need to fill an area with a single color. They're best used in conjunction with vector masks — in other words, shape layers — but occasionally it's useful to fill the whole image with a single color. For example, if you want to apply a tint or color correction to a photo, create a new Solid Color layer on top of the photo layer, then you can tweak the color and opacity of the layer until you get a result you like.

Making gradients with Gradient fill layers

You can use a Gradient fill layer to fill an area with a smooth gradient that fades between two or more colors (or between one or more colors and transparency). This is great for adding subtle shading to an area of your image; for creating illustrative elements, for example sun rays; and for adding texture to an illustration.

When you create a Gradient layer, or double-click a Gradient layer's thumbnail to edit it, Photoshop displays the Gradient Fill dialog box, as shown in Figure 6.36. You can use this dialog box to customize the look of your gradient.

FIGURE 6.36

The Gradient Fill dialog box allows you to edit the look of your gradient fill layers.

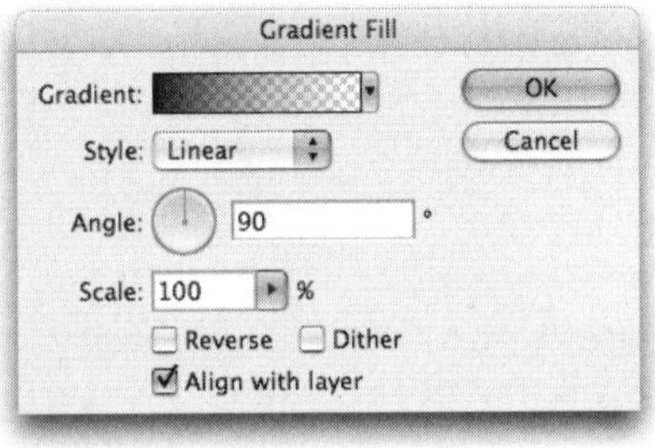

The options in the Gradient Fill dialog box work as follows:

- **Gradient:** Use this option to choose the gradient to use. Click the downward-pointing arrow to the right of the Gradient box to open the Gradient Picker; click a preset gradient in the list to use it. You can also click the little arrow in the top-right corner of the picker to display a menu that allows you to create, load, and save gradient presets, as well as change the appearance of the picker. To edit the current gradient, click in the Gradient box to display the Gradient Editor dialog box. The Gradient Picker and Gradient Editor are covered in more detail in the following sections.

- **Style:** The Style option lets you control how the gradient is applied. Linear applies the gradient in a straight line (for example, from top to bottom or right to left). Radial applies the gradient from the center to the edge in a circular pattern. Angle applies the gradient in a clockwise sweep around the center. Reflected applies the gradient in a straight line like Linear does, but it draws the gradient in both directions, starting from the center. Finally, Diamond creates a diamond pattern using the gradient, with the start of the gradient in the center. You can see all these different styles in Figure 6.37.

- **Angle:** The Angle setting controls the angle that at which the gradient is applied. Click and drag in the Angle circle, or type a value in degrees in the box to the right. For the Linear and Reflected gradient styles, Angle determines the direction that the gradient moves in. For the Angle style, the Angle option sets the start angle of the sweep. For the Diamond style, Angle sets the angle of one of the points of the diamond.

- **Scale:** This setting lets you adjust the size of the gradient fill. Click and drag the slider to the left to make the gradient smaller; drag it to the right to stretch the gradient. You can also type a percentage value in the box on the right; values range from 10 percent of the original size up to 150 percent.

- **Reverse:** Selecting this option simply reverses the direction of your chosen gradient. For example, a gradient that normally runs from black to white will run from white to black when this option is selected.

- **Dither:** Select this option if you notice bands of color appearing in your gradient. It randomly shifts around some of the pixels in the gradient to help smooth over the transitions, and therefore reduces the banding effect.

■ **Align with Layer:** When this option is selected, Photoshop aligns the gradient fill to the boundaries of the fill layer's layer mask or vector mask. This means that the center of the unmasked portion is used as the center point of the gradient, and the gradient is stretched or squashed so that it exactly fills the unmasked portion. In addition, if you click and drag the layer or vector mask around the document window, the gradient moves with it. If you deselect the Align with Layer option, Photoshop locks the gradient to the overall document instead; the center point of the gradient becomes the center of the document, and the gradient stretches to fill the whole document. The layer or vector mask also moves independently of the gradient; if you drag the mask with the Move tool, the gradient stays where it is.

FIGURE 6.37

Here you can see examples of the five available gradient styles in action. From left to right, they are Linear, Radial, Angle, Reflected, and Diamond.

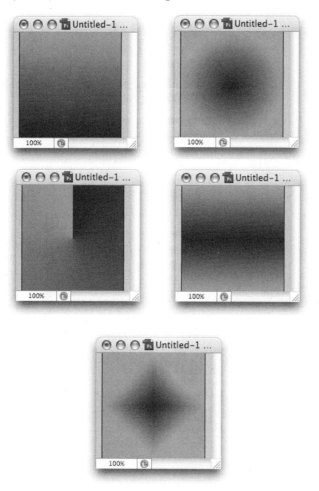

While the Gradient Fill dialog box is displayed, you can position the gradient fill in the document window; simply click in the window and drag. By dragging like this, and using the Angle and Scale options in the dialog box, you can position the gradient pretty much any way you want.

Choosing gradient presets with the Gradient Picker

Photoshop provides you with a range of useful preset gradients that you can use in your fill layers. To pick a gradient preset, click the downward-pointing arrow to the right of the Gradient box in the Gradient Fill dialog box. This displays the Gradient Picker, as shown in Figure 6.38. Select a preset to use by double-clicking its thumbnail icon in the Gradient Picker. You can also click the icon once then click outside the Gradient Picker, or press Esc, to close the picker. Finally, you can also pick a preset by using the arrow keys to scroll through the presets, then pressing Enter (Return on the Mac) when the preset you want is selected.

FIGURE 6.38

The Gradient Picker lets you browse and choose from the available gradient presets, as well as save and load presets.

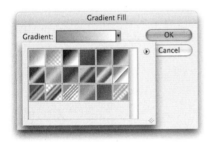

> **TIP** Hold the mouse cursor over a preset's icon to view the name of the preset as a tooltip.

By default, Photoshop displays the presets in the Gradient Picker as a list of small thumbnail icons, but you can change the appearance of the presets. To do this, click the small arrow in the top right of the Gradient Picker window; then choose one of the following options from the drop-down menu that appears:

- **Text Only:** This displays the presets as a list of names, without the icons. It's a nice and compact way of viewing the presets, but not much help if you can't remember what a particular preset looks like.

- **Small Thumbnail:** This is the default option; Photoshop displays the presets as a series of small icons.

- **Large Thumbnail:** This option makes the icons twice as wide and tall. It's handy if you have a lot of complex, detailed gradient presets in the list.

- **Small List:** This displays each preset as a tiny icon followed by its name.

- **Large List:** This option is similar to Small List, but the icons are the same size as they are for Small Thumbnail. If you like seeing the preset names, and you don't mind the extra space this option takes up, then it's arguably the best option of the lot.

TIP If you have a lot of gradient presets loaded, you can expand the Gradient Picker window by clicking and dragging the resize handle in the bottom-right corner of the window. Photoshop handily remembers the size of the window, too, so next time you use the Gradient Picker the window is the same size.

Loading and saving gradient presets

Using the Gradient Picker, you can save the current set of presets to a special gradient preset library file. You can also load a set of presets from a library or replace the current set of presets with those in a library file.

To save the current presets, click the arrow in the top right of the Gradient Picker and choose Save Gradients from the menu that appears. A dialog box appears that asks you to choose where to save the presets. Choose a folder and a name for your library file, and Photoshop saves the presets to that file.

NOTE Gradient preset library file names end in the .grd extension.

CAUTION If you make any custom gradient presets (see the section "Creating custom gradients") that you want to keep, make sure you save the presets before replacing them with those from a library file. In fact, Photoshop offers you the chance to save your set of presets first if you previously customized them.

NOTE The current set of gradients remains in place even if you restart Photoshop. However, if you ever delete your Photoshop settings file — hold down Ctrl+Alt+Shift (Command+Option+Shift on the Mac) immediately after launching Photoshop — the gradients, and indeed all other presets in Photoshop, revert to their factory defaults.

About the Preset Manager

Under the Gradient Picker's menu (and indeed the menu of all other similar pickers in Photoshop), you can select the Preset Manager option to open Photoshop's Preset Manager. You can also access the Preset Manager by choosing Edit ➪ Preset Manager.

The Preset Manager gives you a convenient way to organize your various presets — Brushes, Swatches, Gradients, Styles, Patterns, Contours, Custom Shapes, and Tools — all in one place. You can view the list of available presets for each preset type; rename and delete presets; reorder presets in the list; and load and save presets from and to preset libraries. Use the Preset Manager to do the following:

- **View the currently loaded presets of a particular type**. Choose a preset type from the Preset Type menu at the top of the dialog box. You can change the way the presets are displayed by clicking the triangle to the right of the Preset Type menu and choosing from the first five options in the menu that appears. (Each preset type has its own, independent display setting.)

- **Select presets.** Click a preset's icon or name in the list to select it. Photoshop also lets you select multiple presets in the list for reordering, renaming, deleting, or saving. To do this, Ctrl+click (⌘+click on the Mac) a preset's icon or name to add it to, or remove it from, the selection. You can also select a range of presets by clicking the first preset in the range and Shift+clicking the last. To select all the presets of a particular type, press Ctrl+A (⌘+A) on the Mac). To deselect all presets, press Ctrl+D (⌘+D on the Mac).

- **Reorder a preset.** To reorder a preset, select it and drag it to its new position.

- **Rename and delete presets.** To rename or delete a preset, right-click the preset's icon or name and choose Rename or Delete from the pop-up menu. This also works inside the various pickers in Photoshop, such as the Gradient Picker, Pattern Picker, and Contour Picker. You can also rename or delete a preset by selecting it and clicking Rename or Delete on the right-hand side of the dialog box. Another quick way to delete a preset is simply to Alt+click (Option+click on the Mac) its icon or name.

- **Load the presets in a preset library.** To do this, click Load and choose a library file. Photoshop places the loaded presets after any existing presets in the list. Alternatively, you can replace the current set of presets with those from a library by clicking the triangle to the right of the Preset Type menu and choosing Replace.

- **Reset the list of presets to the factory defaults.** To reset the presets, click the triangle to the right of the Preset Type menu and choose Reset. Photoshop then offers you the choice of replacing the current presets with the defaults or appending the defaults to the end of the current list.

- **Save one or more presets as a new library.** To do this, select the preset or presets and click Save Set. Choose a folder in which to save the library, give the library file a name, and click Save. This allows you to create your own custom libraries of presets for later use.

To load a set of presets from a library file, click the arrow in the top right of the Gradient Picker and choose Load Gradients from the menu. Navigate to your library file and open it to load the presets. They're added to the end of the list in the Gradient Picker.

Alternatively, you can replace the current presets with those in a library file. To do this, click the arrow in the top right of the Gradient Picker and choose Replace Gradients. Find and open your library file to load the presets. The current gradients in the Gradient Picker are removed and replaced with the ones in the loaded library.

By default, Photoshop comes with a list of just 15 preset gradients, but there are nearly 100 more presets in eight library files inside the Presets/Gradients folder within the Photoshop program folder. To load a library, choose Load Gradients or Replace Gradients, select one of the library files, and click Load. The libraries in the Presets/Gradients folder also appear at the bottom of the Gradient Picker menu; simply click a library to load it; then choose either Append to add the presets to your existing list, or OK to replace your existing presets with those in the library.

If you want to reset the gradients in the Gradient Picker to the factory defaults, click the arrow in the top right of the Gradient Picker and choose Reset Gradients from the menu. Photoshop gives you the choice of appending the factory defaults to your current set or simply replacing your current set altogether with the defaults.

Creating custom gradients

The gradient preset library files that ship with Photoshop give you a huge range of gradients to pick from. It doesn't stop there, though; Photoshop, flexible in all things, lets you create you own, unique custom gradients.

It's all done through the Gradient Editor dialog box. To access this dialog box, click the gradient inside the Gradient box within the Gradient Fill dialog box. Figure 6.39 shows the Gradient Editor in all its glory.

> **TIP**   You can also access the Gradient Editor by clicking the Gradient box in the Gradient tool's options bar, in the Gradient Overlay layer style options, or in the Gradient Map dialog box.

> **TIP**   You can make the Gradient Editor dialog box bigger by clicking and dragging the resize handle in the bottom-right corner of the dialog box. This is great if you have a long list of presets loaded or if you want finer control over editing your gradient.

The top Presets area of the dialog box shows you the list of currently loaded gradient presets, much like working with the Gradient Picker described earlier. You can also click the little triangle above the Presets area on the right to access a similar menu to the Gradient Picker's menu. Use this menu to change how the presets are displayed (this setting works independently of the setting in the Gradient Picker), reset the presets to the default list, and load preset libraries.

FIGURE 6.39

Click the gradient inside the Gradient box within the Gradient Fill dialog box to display the Gradient Editor, which you can use to create and edit your own gradients.

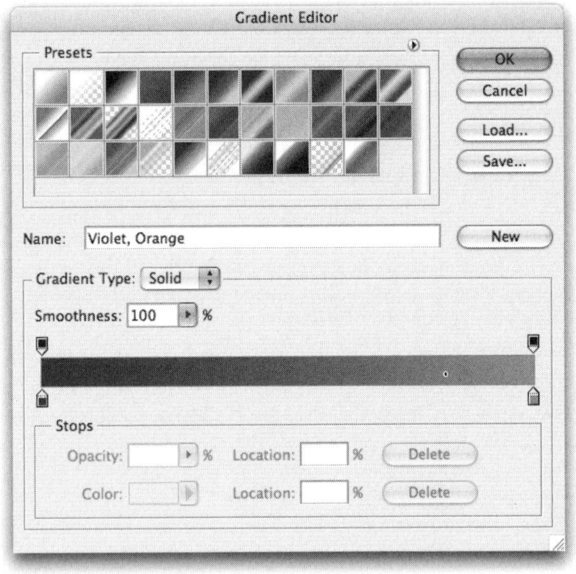

Click a preset in the list to display it for editing. The preset's name appears in the Name box. It's a good idea to name your preset before you start editing it, then click New to add the preset to the list.

CAUTION   If you edit a preset without naming it and clicking New, Photoshop names the preset Custom. If you then select a different preset without clicking New first, the preset you were editing is lost forever, without warning.

After you create and name your custom gradient, use the options in the bottom half of the dialog to customize it.

There are two distinct types of gradient that you can create in Photoshop: *solid* gradients, which are the type you'll probably use most often, and *noise* gradients.

Creating solid gradients

A solid gradient is a gradient that moves smoothly between two or more solid colors (or between one or more colors and transparency). All the presets in the factory default set are solid gradients.

To create a solid gradient, make sure Solid is selected for the Gradient Type option in the dialog box. You'll see the controls shown in Figure 6.40 appear in the bottom half of the dialog.

FIGURE 6.40

Editing a solid gradient. Use the gradient bar and associated controls to customize the look of the gradient.

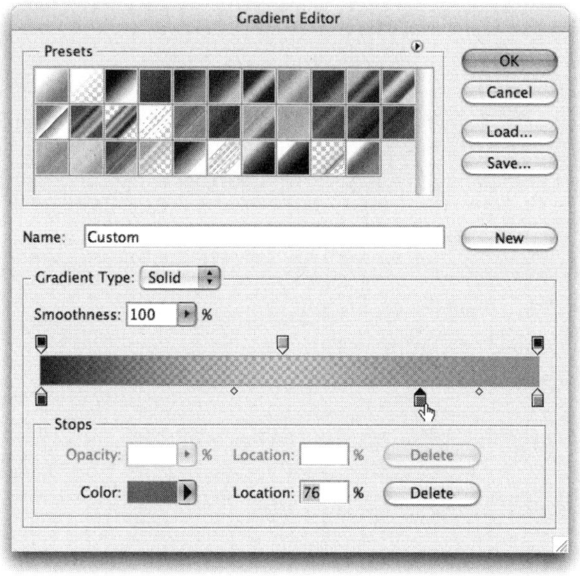

Most of the action revolves around the gradient bar in the center of the dialog box. This bar gives you a visual representation of your gradient, from start (left) to end (right), and lets you customize the colors and areas of transparency within the gradient.

Above the gradient bar are at least two *opacity stops*, and below the bar are at least two *color stops*. These stops are what you use to customize the gradient. Each opacity stop represents a particular opacity level within the gradient, while each color stop represents a certain color in the gradient. Photoshop smoothly blends the opacity levels or colors between one stop and the next, creating the smooth gradient effect.

To customize the gradient, you create, move, and delete these stops. In addition, you can specify the opacity level or color at each stop. You can add as many stops as you can fit into the gradient bar, giving you a pretty good level of control over the subtleties of your gradient.

> **TIP** If you want to produce a gradient with lots and lots of colors, see the section "Creating noise gradients."

Unless you're creating a lot of semitransparent gradients, you'll probably be using the color stops rather than the opacity stops most of the time. Here's how to work with the color stops:

■ To create a new color stop, simply click below the gradient bar where you want the stop to appear. You can then click and drag the stop around the gradient to position it as you want; as you drag, Photoshop updates the gradient bar accordingly. You can also duplicate an existing color stop; to do this, Alt+click (Option+click on the Mac) the stop, and drag.

NOTE The stop initially takes on the color of the previously selected stop — or the foreground color if no stop was previously selected. If the previously selected stop is the foreground or background color, the stop is filled with a gray and white checkerboard pattern, with the top-left square (in the case of the foreground color) or the bottom-right square (in the case of the background color) being filled with black. Quite what the point is of this checkerboard pattern is anybody's guess; maybe it's just to remind you that you're initially working with the foreground or background color. As soon as you move the stop or edit it in any way, the checkerboard is replaced with the actual color.

TIP The fill layer also updates in the document window as you edit the gradient. This is very handy, as you can see exactly how your gradient will appear in your final image.

■ To select a color stop, click it. The triangle above the stop changes from hollow to solid, indicating that the stop is selected.

■ To remove a color stop from the gradient, click and drag it away from the gradient bar. You can also remove it by selecting it, then clicking the active Delete button at the bottom of the dialog box, or by pressing Backspace or Delete (Win) or either Delete key (Mac).

■ To change the color of a color stop, select the stop, then click the Color box in the bottom left of the dialog. Alternatively, simply double-click the stop. A Color Picker dialog box appears that lets you select the color you want to use. You can also pick a color from the document window or from the gradient bar itself. To do this, select the stop, then move the mouse over the document window or gradient bar — the mouse cursor changes to an eyedropper — and click a pixel to use its color for the stop.

■ You can also use either the current foreground or background color for the color stop. To do this, select the stop, then click the arrow to the right of the Color box in the bottom left of the dialog box, and choose either Foreground or Background from the pop-up menu.

NOTE Photoshop doesn't "remember" the fact that you chose the foreground or background color for the stop; it merely uses whatever your foreground or background color happens to be at the time. So if you later change your foreground or background color, don't expect the gradient to update as well.

■ By default, Photoshop blends the colors together evenly across the distance between two color stops, but you can change this by clicking and dragging the small midpoint diamond that sits between the stops. The midpoint defines the point that contains 50 percent of one color and 50 percent of the other. Click either color stop to select the stop, and the midpoint diamond appears between the two stops. Drag the diamond to the left to make the gradient transition more sharply toward the right-hand color, and vice versa.

■ For greater precision, you can change the position of a color stop or midpoint diamond numerically. To do this, select the color stop or midpoint — midpoints change from hollow to solid diamonds when you select them — then type a percentage value in the Location box at the bottom of the dialog box. Values for color stops range from 0 percent (on the left-hand side of the gradient bar) to 100 percent (on the right of the bar). Fifty percent places the stop right in the middle of the bar. Values for midpoints range from 5 percent (close to the left-hand stop) to 95 percent (close to the right-hand stop). A value of 50 percent places the midpoint exactly midway between the two stops, resulting in an even transition from one color to the next.

> **TIP** As with most numeric fields in Photoshop, you can adjust the Location value in steps of 1 percent by clicking in the Location box and pressing the up- and down-arrow keys. Hold down Shift as well to adjust the value in steps of 10 percent.

As well as specifying the colors in the gradient using the color stops below the gradient bar, you can also choose to make some areas of the gradient translucent or transparent using the opacity stops above the bar.

These opacity stops work in much the same way as the color stops; you can add, move, and delete them using the techniques described earlier. The main difference is that you're working with opacity levels rather than color values. An opacity level of 100 percent makes the gradient completely opaque at that point, while an opacity level of 0 percent makes the gradient completely transparent. Values in between result in varying degrees of translucency at that point in the gradient. The gradient bar shows transparent and translucent areas by displaying a checkerboard pattern: the stronger the pattern, the more transparent the gradient at that point.

Like their color stop cousins, opacity stops have midpoint diamonds between them. A diamond between two opacity stops represents the opacity level midway between the level at one stop and the level at the other stop. Click and drag the diamond to make the transition between opacity levels occur more abruptly toward one stop or the other.

In addition to editing the color and opacity stops, you can control the smoothness of the gradient with the Smoothness option above the gradient bar. As you might imagine, a Smoothness value of 100 percent produces a gradient with smoother transitions than a value of 0 percent does. Click the arrow to the right of the Smoothness option to display a slider that you can click and drag to adjust the value, or simply click inside the Smoothness box and type a numeric value from 0 to 100 percent.

Creating noise gradients

The other type of gradient that you can produce in Photoshop is the noise gradient. Noise gradients take a different approach to solid gradients; rather than specifying color stops for the gradient to transition between, you specify an overall range of color values, and Photoshop randomly transitions the gradient from one end of the range to the other. You can control the roughness of this transition, which gives you quite a lot of flexibility in the effects that you can produce.

Noise gradients are a great way to add a random element of interest to a gradient. Rather than transitioning smoothly from one color to the next like solid gradients do, noise gradients can be full of subtle variations, which can give them a more natural, organic quality.

To create a noise gradient, select Noise for the Gradient Type option in the Gradient Editor dialog box. The controls below Gradient Type change to those shown in Figure 6.41, allowing you to customize the noise gradient.

FIGURE 6.41

Editing a noise gradient. Adjust the color range using the sliders at the bottom of the dialog. You can also control the roughness or smoothness of the gradient's transitions using the Roughness control.

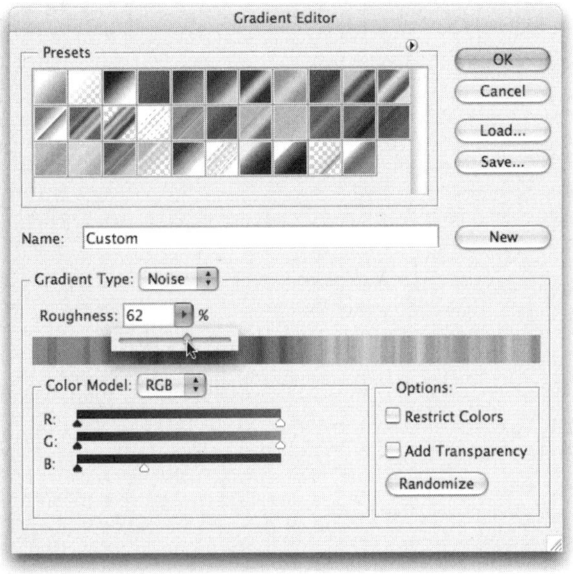

The first thing you'll probably want to do is set a rough color range for the gradient. To do this, choose a color mode from the Color Model menu — RGB, HSB, or LAB — then for each of the three color range bars, click and drag the black start slider and white end slider to limit the range of color values that Photoshop has to work with. For example, if you select HSB for the Color Model, and click and drag the black Hue slider to the right so that it's pointing at the pink range of the spectrum, Photoshop will be forced to choose colors within the range of pink to red.

However, Photoshop doesn't use the whole range of color values that you specify; instead, it chooses a random sample from within that range. This is where the Randomize button comes into play; each time you click it, Photoshop chooses a new random sample from within your chosen color ranges. If you're not happy with the exact range that Photoshop chooses, keep clicking Randomize until you get a result you like.

After you find a range that you like, try fiddling with the Roughness slider. Click the arrow to the right of the Roughness field to display the slider; click and drag the slider left and right to get an effect you're happy with. Alternatively, click in the Roughness field and type a value from 0 to 100 percent. A Roughness value of 0 percent produces a smooth transition from one color to the next, much like creating a solid gradient. The more you increase the Roughness value, the more Photoshop randomizes the colors in the transition. By the time you get to 100 percent, it's no longer really a transition; the colors in the gradient are completely randomized.

You can select the Restrict Colors option to tone down the colors and make them a bit less saturated. Select Add Transparency to add random opacity levels to the gradient, too; if you disable this option, the gradient is 100 percent opaque across the board.

> **TIP** To get an idea of the kind of effects you can achieve with noise gradients, check out the Noise Samples preset library, which is available in the Presets/Gradients folder of your Photoshop application folder, or via the pop-up menu in the Gradient Picker and Gradient Editor.

Filling with a pattern using Pattern fill layers

As well as applying a solid color or a gradient fill using fill layers, you can also create pattern fills. A *pattern* is simply a small bitmap image that is repeated horizontally and vertically, or *tiled*. You can use one of the 200-odd patterns that come shipped with Photoshop, or you can create your own.

To create a Pattern fill layer, click the Create New Fill or Adjustment Layer icon at the bottom of the Layers palette, then choose Pattern near the top of the menu. Photoshop displays the Pattern Fill dialog box, as shown in Figure 6.42, that you can use to select the pattern to use for the fill and to set various options for the fill.

FIGURE 6.42

Creating or editing a Pattern fill layer with the Pattern Fill dialog box. Choose the pattern to use, set various options for the fill, and you're all set.

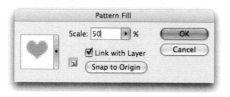

While you're in the Pattern Fill dialog box, you can position the pattern exactly how you want it by clicking and dragging in the document window.

Here's how the various options in the Pattern Fill dialog box work:

- **Pattern box:** The big box on the left side of the dialog box is where you choose the pattern that you want to use for the fill. Click either the pattern in the box or the downward-pointing arrow to the right of the box to display the Pattern Picker, where you can choose a different preset pattern to use.

CROSS-REF The Pattern Picker works in exactly the same way as the Gradient Picker; you can select, add, rename, and delete pattern presets; load and save presets using preset library files; and so on. Pattern preset library files have a .pat extension. See the sections "Choosing gradient presets with the Gradient Picker" and "Loading and saving gradient presets", as well as the sidebar "About the Preset Manager", for more info.

- **Scale:** Use this setting to increase or decrease the size of the pattern in the fill. Note that this doesn't change the size of the filled area; it merely changes the size of the pattern tiles that make up the fill. Click the arrow to the right of the Scale field to make a slider appear. Click and drag the slider to the left to make the pattern smaller; drag it to the right to stretch the pattern. You can also type a percentage value in the field; values range from 1 percent all the way up to 1000 percent, or ten times the original pattern size.

- **Link with Layer:** Selecting this option causes the pattern to move with the layer mask when you move the mask around with the Move tool. If you prefer the pattern to remain fixed, deselect this option, and you can move the mask around without affecting the position of the pattern. Regardless of this setting, you can always move the pattern around independently of the layer mask by clicking and dragging in the document window while the Pattern Fill dialog box is open.

- **Snap to Origin:** If you've moved the pattern from its original position by dragging in the document window, click this button to reset the pattern's position back to its origin.

- **New icon:** Click this icon to the right of the Pattern box to add the current pattern as a new preset.

TIP To create a new pattern, use the Rectangle Marquee tool to select the area of your image that you want to turn into a pattern. Then choose Edit ⇨ Define Pattern, give your pattern a name, and click OK. You can also use the Pattern Maker filter to help you make seamless repeating pattern tiles; to use it, choose Filter ⇨ Pattern Maker, then select an area of your image to turn into a pattern. Both of these pattern-making techniques only work on bitmap layers.

Masking Adjustment and Fill Layers

You've probably noticed that each adjustment layer or fill layer you create comes with its own layer mask, as shown in Figure 6.43. By default, the mask is pure white, which means that the whole of the adjustment effect or fill is visible. If you start painting on the mask with a color other than white then you start to partially obscure the adjustment or fill. If you paint with pure black on the mask then the adjustment effect or fill is completely hidden in the black areas, allowing the original underlying layers to show through.

Masks applied to fill layers let you create filled shapes, which is indeed how shape layers, described in Chapter 5, work; these use a vector mask to define the shape. In the case of an adjustment layer, masks let you restrict the adjustment to specific parts of your image, which is very useful. For example, if you have a photo with a dark foreground and a bright sky, you can add an Exposure adjustment layer to make the foreground lighter, but mask off the sky using the adjustment layer's mask to prevent it from also being lightened.

FIGURE 6.43

An adjustment layer with its associated layer mask

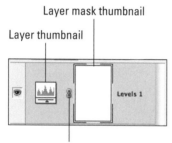

Layer mask thumbnail

Layer thumbnail

Levels 1

Link Mask icon

Figure 6.44 shows this principle in action. A Levels adjustment layer is added above the image layer. The adjustment layer's mask is then painted on to mask off the adjustment in a specific area of the image.

TIP   To quickly create a new adjustment or fill layer that only affects part of an image, select that part of the image using one of the selection tools, then create the layer. Photoshop uses the selection to create a layer mask for the layer that masks off the unselected parts of the layer's contents.

As with any normal layer mask, you can disable an adjustment or fill layer's mask by Shift+clicking the mask's thumbnail image (which makes the layer affect the whole image), add the layer mask to a selection by right-clicking its thumbnail and choosing Add Layer Mask to Selection, and so on. You can also unlink the layer mask from the layer by clicking the link icon between the layer and mask thumbnails, allowing you to use the Move tool to move the mask around separately from the layer. This is only really useful for gradient and pattern fill layers, as these are the only ones whose content you can move around.

You're not limited to bitmap layer masks with adjustment layers and fill layers; if you prefer to use a vector mask, go right ahead. Select the layer, then choose Layer ➪ Vector Mask ➪ Reveal All, or Layer ➪ Vector Mask ➪ Hide All. You can then draw on the vector mask with the Pen or Shape tool to create filled shapes and alter the mask. Bitmap and vector masks can both be applied at once and, if the masks are linked, moving the bitmap mask moves the vector mask along with it.

FIGURE 6.44

Painting on an adjustment layer's mask restricts the adjustment effect to specific areas of the image.

CROSS-REF   Layer and vector masks are covered in detail in Chapter 9.

Using Blending Modes with Adjustment and Fill Layers

One of the many wonderful things about adjustment and fill layers is the fact that they're layers, just like normal layers or type layers. This means that you can even apply blending modes to them. Not only does this combination of adjustments, fills, and blending modes let you create some fantastic effects, it's also pretty handy for color correction, as you see in a moment. And, of course, because both these layer types, as well as blending modes, are nondestructive, you can change the layer or the blending mode any time you want. Hours of fun!

On the special effects front, try a few of these:

- Create a Threshold adjustment layer above your image layer, then give it a blending mode of Soft Light to create an effect similar to the Cutout filter, as shown in Figure 6.45. Click and drag the slider in the Threshold dialog box until you get a result you're happy with. For a more pronounced effect, try using the Darken or Lighten blending mode instead.

- Create a Hue/Saturation adjustment layer above your image and click and drag the Saturation slider down to 0 to create a grayscale version of the original image. Then select a blending mode of Hard Light for the adjustment layer to create a high-contrast, old silvery photo effect (great for wedding photos).

- Try using the Invert adjustment layer with a Difference blending mode to add colorful chrome effects to an image.

- Create a Gradient fill layer above a photo layer; then set its blending mode to Color Dodge or Vivid Light to add an interesting "burned-out" effect to the photo.

FIGURE 6.45

Using a Threshold adjustment layer with a Soft Light blending mode to create a cutout effect

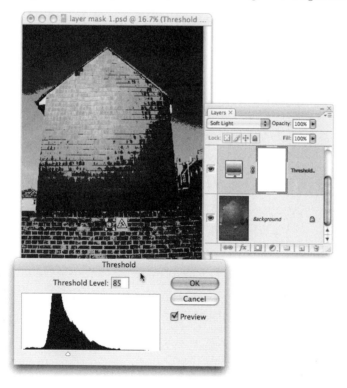

If you're correcting colors or adjusting contrast using adjustment layers, you may want to restrict the adjustment to just the color or luminance component of the image. This is where the modes at the bottom of the Blending Mode pop-up menu are very useful. For example, use a Curves adjustment layer with a blending mode of Luminosity to ensure you only affect the brightness levels of the image without touching the colors. Conversely, try creating a Hue/Saturation adjustment layer and setting its blending mode to Color to ensure that you're not accidentally lightening or darkening the image.

> **TIP** If you're used to switching to Lab mode to work on the colors or luminance channels of your image independently, try the previous techniques as an alternative. You can achieve a similar effect without having to leave RGB mode (unless you're the kind of person who prefers always working in Lab mode, of course).

Another handy trick with adjustment layers and blending modes takes advantage of the fact that an adjustment layer with no adjustment applied acts as a duplicate of the layer beneath. This is great for those times when you want to "duplicate" a layer and apply a blending mode to a duplicate. The adjustment layer takes up less RAM and hard drive space than physically duplicating the layer, and it automatically updates if you edit the original layer, too. For example, create a Levels adjustment layer above a photo layer, and just click OK to close the Levels dialog box. You can then choose a blending mode of, say, Color Dodge for the adjustment layer to add some extra punch and saturation to the photo.

Summary

In this comprehensive chapter on adjustment and fill layers, you've taken a good look at the features offered by both these very useful layer types. It kicked off with a look at the advantages of adjustment layers, including the fact that they're nondestructive, as well as the fact that they can be manipulated much like normal layers. You then learned how to create an adjustment layer, how to preview color changes using the Info palette, and how to limit an adjustment effect to specific layers.

You took a look at editing adjustment layers, both in terms of reediting the adjustment effect and also by manipulating the layer itself. You then explored each adjustment layer type in depth — from Levels and Curves for advanced contrast and dynamic range adjustments, to Hue/Saturation and Color Balance for adjusting colors, and two new welcome additions in CS3: the Exposure and Black & White adjustment layers.

You learned the nitty-gritty of creating and editing Solid Color, Gradient, and Pattern fill layers, including how to edit a gradient and define a pattern. After that, you learned how to apply layer masks and vector masks to adjustment and fill layers in order to restrict the adjustment or fill to specific areas of your image. Finally, you learned how applying blending modes to fill and adjustment layers can be used to create some advanced effects.

Part III

Advanced Layer Features

Chapter 7

Combining Layers with Blending Modes

Blending modes are a great feature of Photoshop that really exploit the concept of layers to its fullest. They allow you to mix the pixels of different layers together in all sorts of interesting ways to produce some great special effects. Take a look at Figure 7.1 to see some examples of blending modes in action. In each case, the layers that make up the image haven't been touched; only the blending mode is changed.

The other great thing about layer blending modes is that, like adjustment layers and layer styles, they're nondestructive. You can change a layer's blending mode at any time without permanently affecting the pixels of any of the affected layers.

Most folks use Photoshop's blending modes to create artistic effects and make layers merge together in a funky and pleasing manner. The classic strategy here is the *scattershot* approach, where you start at the top of the list of blending modes and work your way through to see which mode works best! Although the blending modes in Photoshop all have a mathematical basis, the results are often unpredictable. The best way to learn about and use blending modes is to experiment with them. Play with different modes and opacity values for each layer until you get a result you're happy with.

Having said that, in this chapter you learn exactly what these most mysterious of Photoshop features actually do to your pixels, which should make this process slightly less hit and miss.

NOTE Although blending modes can often have unpredictable effects, frequently producing "happy accidents," it's also possible to use them in a very premeditated manner to achieve a known result. An example of this is the practice of sharpening a photo by duplicating its layer, then running a High Pass filter over the duplicate layer and setting its blending mode to Soft Light.

IN THIS CHAPTER

Setting a layer's blending mode

Exploring each blending mode in turn

Summarizing the modes

Choosing which color channels get blended

Using one layer to knock out layers below

Controlling how interior effects and clipping masks blend

Turning off a layer's transparency mask

Altering how layer and vector masks interact with layer effects

Controlling the blend based on brightness and color ranges

Working with the blending modes of individual layer effects

Blending modes appear in two main areas of Photoshop:

- **Layers:** Each layer in a document — apart from fully locked layers or the Background layer — can have a specified blending mode applied to it, which affects how that layer blends with everything below it. This chapter focuses on layer blending modes.

- **The painting tools:** The blending modes for painting tools, such as the Brush and Clone Stamp tools, allow you to control how new pixels that you paint on a layer blend with existing pixels on the layer. For the most part, these behave the same as the layer blending modes, but there are a couple of additional modes for some tools, which are covered later in the chapter.

FIGURE 7.1

Here you can see a couple of layers blended with different blending modes. The Layers palette (left) shows the two original image layers. The flowers layer's mode is then set to Darken (center) and Linear Dodge (Add) (right). Notice how changing the blending mode can really alter the whole look of the image!

 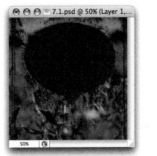 

Choosing a Blending Mode

To pick a blending mode for a layer, select the layer that you want to change; then choose an option from the Blending Mode pop-up menu at the top of the Layers palette, as shown in Figure 7.2. All blending modes except Darker Color and Lighter Color also have keyboard shortcuts; these are covered in the section "Summarizing the blending modes" later in the chapter. (Note that if you're using a painting tool then the keyboard shortcut sets the tool's blending mode in the options bar, not the layer's blending mode.)

 You can also quickly change a layer's blending mode by pressing Shift and + (plus) to move down the list, or Shift and - (minus) to move up the list.

CROSS-REF Although you can't set the blending mode for multiple selected layers at once, you can set the blending mode for a layer group. For more on groups, see Chapter 2.

FIGURE 7.2

Choosing a blending mode from the Blending Mode pop-up menu

Understanding Blending Modes

A layer's blending mode interacts, on a pixel-by-pixel basis, with the layers below it. These layers may in turn have their own blending modes interacting with each other, and so on. The final composite image that you see on the screen is the combined result of each layer blending with the layers below.

The following terms are used in this chapter when talking about how blending modes work:

- **Top layer:** The layer to which you're applying the blending mode.
- **Bottom layer:** The visible layer underneath the top layer or, if there is more than one layer underneath, the combined result of all the underneath layers (as if you'd flattened them).
- **Blend color:** The color of a pixel in the top layer or, when painting, the new color of a pixel being painted.
- **Base color:** The color of the corresponding pixel in the bottom layer or, when painting, the layer being painted on.
- **Result color:** The result of combining the blend and base color. It's the color that you actually see on the screen as a result of the blending mode.

If you're working with a color image — for example, an image in RGB format — you probably know that the image is composed of different color *channels*: Red, Green, and Blue in the case of RGB images. It's worth noting that nearly all the blending modes work on each channel independently, then combine the separate result color channels to produce the final result color. The exceptions to this rule are Darker Color and Lighter Color, and the Component blending modes; these modes work individually on other components of the image such as the hue, saturation, and luminosity.

For example, look at the Darken blending mode. If you apply it to a layer in an RGB image, Darken compares first the Red channels of the base and blend colors, and chooses whichever channel is darker to produce the red result channel. It then does the same with the Green and the Blue channels. Finally, it combines the three Red, Green, and Blue result channels to get the final result color. This explains why you often end up with radically different colors from the base and blend colors when you use blending modes.

Exploring the Blending Modes

Photoshop CS3 features a grand total of 25 blending modes that can be applied to layers, plus two additional modes that only work with certain painting tools and options. This section looks at each blending mode in turn, in the order that they appear in the Blending Mode pop-up menu.

The layer blending modes are grouped into Simple, Darkening, Lightening, Light, Difference, and Component. (These are just names that we've found useful — there aren't any "official" names so feel free to use your own!) This grouping is reflected in the Blending Mode pop-up menu in Photoshop's Layers palette; you can see horizontal separators between each group in the menu.

Simple blending modes

There are four blending modes in this category: Normal, which leaves things as they are; Dissolve, which randomly mixes pixel colors from the base and blend colors; Behind, which adds new pixels behind existing ones; and Clear, which erases existing pixels.

Normal

The default blending mode is Normal. It does pretty much what you'd expect it to do; the pixels in the top layer sit on top of the pixels in the bottom layer without interacting with them. If the top layer's opacity is set to 100 percent, the layer's pixels completely obscure the bottom layer; for opacity values lower than 100 percent, the pixels of the bottom layer start to show through. You can see the effect of different opacities when using the Normal blending mode in Figure 7.3.

The top layer in this example is using a Normal blending mode, with its opacity set to 100 percent (left) and 50 percent (right). Notice how the pixels of the bottom layer show through at 50 percent opacity.

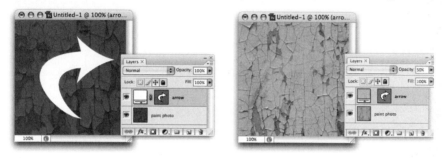

Dissolve

Rather than smoothly combining the base and blend colors of semitransparent pixels like Normal does, the Dissolve blending mode works by randomly picking either the base color or the blend color for each pixel, resulting in a speckled effect.

Dissolve only affects semitransparent pixels, so if your top layer only contains opaque pixels, with no feathering around the edges of the content, you won't see any effect with Dissolve. You can see an example of this in Figure 7.4; the layer with no semitransparent pixels shows no change, whereas the layer with some feathering round the edges dissolves into the bottom layer. Another way to think of Dissolve is that it dithers the semitransparent areas of the image.

The Dissolve blending mode tends to produce a very rough, noisy appearance, which can be handy for giving the impression of rough surfaces, for example.

TIP If you want to create this effect on a layer with fully opaque pixels, lower the layer's opacity a bit. As soon as you drop the opacity below 100 percent, the Dissolve effect kicks in.

Behind

This mode is not available via the Blending Mode option in the Layers palette. Instead, you can use it with the Brush and Pencil tools, the Clone and Pattern Stamp tools, the History Brush tool, the Gradient and Paint Bucket tools, and the shape tools when working in Fill Pixels mode. It's also available in the Fill and Stroke dialog boxes (Edit ➪ Fill, and Edit ➪ Stroke, respectively).

As the name suggests, the Behind mode adds new pixels so that they appear behind existing ones. Painting over 100 percent opaque pixels has no effect. Painting over semitransparent pixels mixes the base and blend colors. Painting over transparent pixels fills them with the blend color.

FIGURE 7.4

Examples of layers using the Dissolve blending mode. The top layer in the first example (left) is completely opaque, so Dissolve has no effect. The top layer in the second example (right) was produced by applying a Gaussian Blur filter to the square. This means that it now contains semitransparent pixels, which the Dissolve blending mode has mixed randomly with the base colors of the bottom layer.

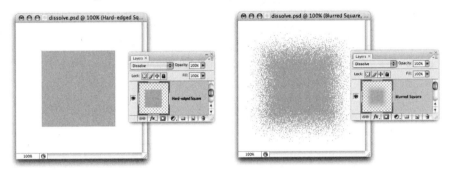

To use Chapter 1's "sheets of acetate" analogy for layers, it's the equivalent of painting on the reverse side of the acetate. This makes it great for creating hand-drawn outlines around your layer contents, for example.

Figure 7.5 shows the effect of painting on top of a layer using the Behind blending mode.

FIGURE 7.5

Painting on top of a layer using the Behind blending mode. Notice how the added pixels appear to be behind the existing pixels on the layer.

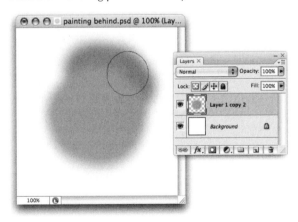

Clear

As with Behind, you can't apply Clear to a layer itself. It works with the Brush and Pencil tools, the Paint Bucket tool, and the shape tools when working in Fill Pixels mode. You can also use it when filling regions via the Fill dialog box (Edit ➪ Fill), and when creating borders via the Stroke dialog box (Edit ➪ Stroke).

Clear effectively turns the tool you're using into an eraser, clearing pixels that would normally be painted and turning them transparent. This is handy if you want to erase areas of the image more creatively than simply using the Eraser tool. It's also useful in conjunction with the Paint Bucket tool or the Fill command, as it gives you a quick way of erasing a large area of your image.

Figure 7.6 shows how part of a layer can be erased by using the Clear mode with the Pencil tool.

FIGURE 7.6
_____

Erasing part of a layer using the Clear blending mode with the Pencil tool. With this blending mode, the pencil acts as an eraser, taking pixels back to transparency.

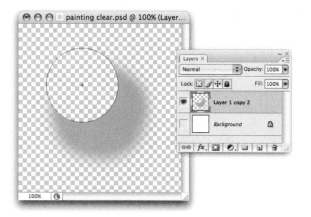

NOTE As you might imagine, Behind and Clear are not available if the layer's transparency is locked (in fact they're grayed out in the pop-up menu in this case). This also explains why you can't use these modes on the Background layer. You need to convert the Background layer to a normal layer first, then you can paint on the layer using Behind or Clear.

Darkening modes

As the name suggests, the five darkening blending modes, Darken, Multiply, Color Burn, Linear Burn, and Darker Color, all mix the base and blend colors to produce a darker result color. This means that your final image tends to be darker than either of the individual layers. The darkening modes can be a great way to add moody effects to your image.

Darken

The Darken blending mode is simple enough: For each pixel in the image, it looks at the base color and the blend color and uses whichever is the darkest for the result color. In other words, for any given pixel, the top layer's color is only used if it's darker than the color of the bottom layer. If it's lighter, the bottom layer's pixel shows through instead.

Characteristics of the Darken blending mode include the following:

- The order of the layers doesn't matter.
- A black base or blend color produces black.
- A white base or blend color produces no change in the other layer.

The end effect is usually a fairly sharp transition between the blended layer and the underlying layers, as shown in Figure 7.7.

FIGURE 7.7

In this example of the Darken blending mode, notice how the darker areas of each layer — such as the lead in the window, and the shadows in the leaves — tend to override lighter areas in the opposite layer.

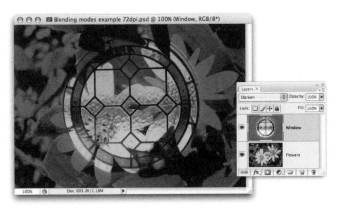

Multiply

Multiply takes the base and blend colors for each pixel and multiplies them together to get the result color. Two colors of the same brightness multiply together to produce a darker color. If one of the base or blend colors is white, then the result color will be the same as the other color. On the other hand, if either the base or the blend color is black, the result will be black.

This means that, unless one of the two starting colors is white, Multiply always results in a darker result color; therefore, the image is pretty much guaranteed to be darker overall.

The Multiply blending mode behaves in the following manner:

- The order of the layers doesn't matter.
- A black base or blend color produces black.
- A white base or blend color produces no change in the other layer.

Multiply generally produces a more pleasing darkening effect than Darken, with the overall image being darkened and the top and bottom layers merging more gently into one another. You can see this effect in Figure 7.8.

FIGURE 7.8

Multiply produces a similar effect to Darken, but it's generally softer and more natural looking (although often darker overall). Notice how more of the hues and detail in the bottom layer have been retained when compared with Darken, particularly in the yellow petals outside the window.

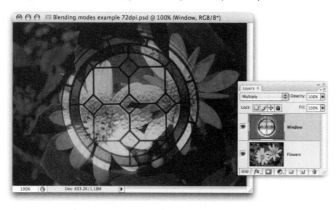

Color Burn

This blending mode takes the base color and darkens it by decreasing its brightness and increasing its contrast, looking at the blend color as a guide. If the blend color is dark, the base color is darkened a lot; if the blend color is light, the base color is only slightly darkened. This darkened base color is used for the result color.

To summarize, Color Burn works as follows:

- The order of the layers does matter.
- A black blend color produces black.
- A white blend color produces no change in the bottom layer.

The overall effect of Color Burn is usually a high-contrast, vibrant, and colorful darkening effect, as you can see in Figure 7.9.

FIGURE 7.9

Applying Color Burn to your top layer mixes the layers in a strong, vibrant way. The results may not be particularly natural in appearance, but they certainly catch the eye!

Linear Burn

The Linear Burn blending mode is similar to Color Burn, but it darkens the base color by decreasing its brightness only; it doesn't touch the contrast.

The characteristics of the Linear Burn mode are as follows:

- The order of the layers doesn't matter.
- A black base or blend color produces black.
- A white base or blend color produces no change in the other layer.

Linear Burn tends to produce a darker, yet gentler effect than Color Burn, as illustrated in Figure 7.10. The result isn't so contrasty.

Darker Color

NEW FEATURE This blending mode, along with Lighter Color — described later in the chapter — is a new addition in CS3.

Darker Color is simply a composite version of the Darken blending mode. Much like Darken, it works by using whichever is the darkest of the base and blend colors as the result color. The difference is in how Photoshop determines which of the base and the blend colors is the darkest, and in how it combines the result. With Darken, each color channel is compared separately, with the darker channel taken in each case. The three resulting channels are then combined to produce the final color. With Darker Color, however, the luminance channels of the pixels are compared instead; Photoshop then simply uses the composite channel of the darker of the two pixels for the result color.

Linear Burn produces a less contrasty, more blended darkening effect than Color Burn, though the end result is often darker.

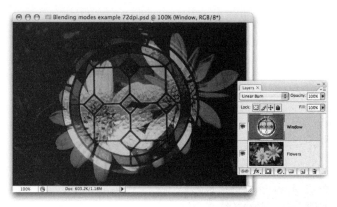

Darker Color produces the following effects:

- The order of the layers doesn't matter.
- A black base or blend color produces black.
- A white base or blend color produces no change in the other layer.

Figure 7.11 shows Darker Color doing its stuff. As you might imagine, the effect is similar to Darken, but preserves the colors of the original layers. It can produce fairly sharp transitions between the layers though, as base color abruptly gives way to blend color and vice-versa.

The Darker Color blending mode in action. It's preserved more of the original colors in the window, but the transitions between the layers are sometimes quite harsh — for example, around the top of the red band in the window, and in the leaves.

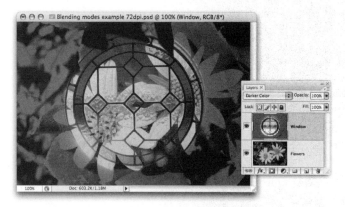

Lightening modes

Photoshop's five lightening blending modes—Lighten, Screen, Color Dodge, Linear Dodge (Add), and Lighter Color—are the mathematical counterparts of the darkening modes just described. Each lightening mode mixes the base and blend colors to produce a lighter result color, creating a lighter overall image.

Lighten

The Lighten blending mode produces a simple lightening effect by preserving the light pixels in the top layer and losing any pixels that are darker than those in the bottom layers, allowing those bottom-layer pixels to show through instead. For each pixel, it looks at the base color and the blend color, and uses whichever is the lightest for the result color.

The Lighten mode has the following attributes:

- The order of the layers doesn't matter.
- A black base or blend color produces no change in the other layer.
- A white base or blend color produces white.

You can see the effect of Lighten in Figure 7.12. It can produce fairly surreal results with a kind of "cut-out" effect.

FIGURE 7.12

Our stained glass window with the Lighten blending mode applied. The results are certainly lighter, if slightly surreal in places, particularly the petals.

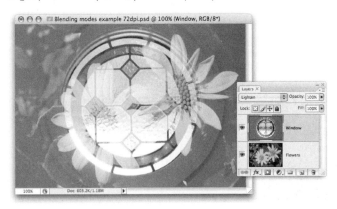

Screen

Screen, the lightening counterpart to Multiply, takes the inverse of the base and blend colors for each pixel and multiplies them together to get the result color. Two colors of the same brightness multiply together to produce a lighter color.

Unless one of the two starting colors is black, Screen always results in a lighter result color. This means that the resulting image is nearly always lighter after Screen has been applied.

The Screen blending mode has the following characteristics:

- The order of the layers doesn't matter.
- A black base or blend color produces no change in the other layer.
- A white base or blend color produces white.

The effect of the Screen blending mode is shown in Figure 7.13. The effect is generally more natural looking than Lighten, and usually produces a brighter overall image.

FIGURE 7.13

The effect of the Screen blending mode is similar to Lighten, but the layers tend to blend together a bit more naturally.

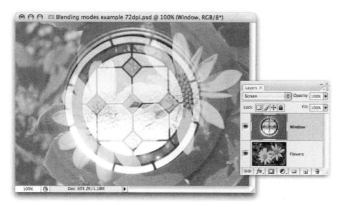

Color Dodge

The Color Dodge mode — the counterpart of Color Burn — lightens the base color of each pixel by increasing both its brightness and contrast. The amount of lightening is worked out by looking at the blend color; a light blend color results in a lot of lightening, while a darker blend color won't have so much effect. The lightened base color is used as the result color.

A blend color of black produces a result color that is the same as the base color (no lightening), while a blend color of white produces a result color of white (100 percent lightening).

To summarize the effects of Color Dodge:

- The order of the layers does matter.
- A black blend color produces no change.
- A white blend color produces white.

Color Dodge tends to produce quite a dramatic, high-contrast "bleaching" effect on both the blended layer and the underlying layers, as shown in Figure 7.14.

FIGURE 7.14

Color Dodge has pushed up the brightness and contrast of both layers, resulting in an oversaturated, vibrant look.

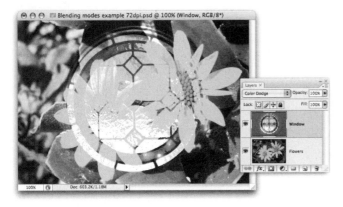

Linear Dodge (Add)

This blending mode is the lightening equivalent of Linear Burn. It produces the result color by increasing the brightness of the base color; unlike Color Dodge the contrast is unaffected.

Linear Dodge (Add) produces the following effects:

- The order of the layers doesn't matter.
- A black base or blend color produces no change in the other layer.
- A white base or blend color produces white.

You can see the effect of Linear Dodge (Add) in Figure 7.15. The overall effect is similar to that of Color Dodge, but smoother, with a gentler blending of the layers. The colors are also closer to those of the original layers.

FIGURE 7.15

Linear Dodge (Add) is still bleaching your layers like Color Dodge, but the effect isn't quite so "in-your-face." Overall brightness levels are higher, but the layers blend together more naturally, retaining more of their original colors.

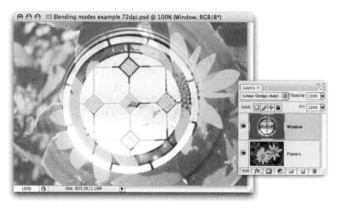

Lighter Color

NEW FEATURE This blending mode, along with Darker Color, is a new addition in CS3.

Just as Darker Color is a composite version of Darken, Lighter Color is a composite version of Lighten. Photoshop compares the luminance channels of the base and blend colors, and uses the composite color of whichever is the brighter of the two pixels as the result color.

Lighter Color can be summarized as follows:

- The order of the layers doesn't matter.
- A black base or blend color produces no change in the other layer.
- A white base or blend color produces white.

As you can see in Figure 7.16, the effect of Lighter Color is fairly similar to Lighten. As with Darker Color, Lighter Color doesn't skew colors as wildly as its non-composite counterpart, though it does create a more extreme cut-out effect.

FIGURE 7.16

An example of the Lighter Color blending mode. This has taken the cut-out effect of Lighten up a notch — the petals have been almost completely divorced from their leafy background. The original colors of the layers are preserved, however.

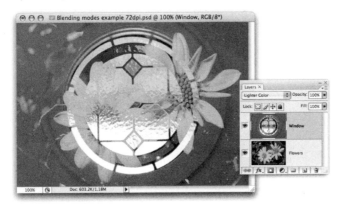

Light modes

Photoshop features seven light modes, which all tend to blend the layers in ways that increase the contrast of the final image. Although they share this contrast-increasing property, their effects can be radically different. The light modes are useful for a wide range of applications, from simulating lighting conditions through to sharpening techniques and special effects.

Overlay

The Overlay blending mode works by darkening the darker base colors using Multiply and lightening the lighter base colors using Screen. The end result is increased contrast by emphasizing the darker and lighter parts of the bottom layer.

Overlay works on your layers as follows:

- The order of the layers does matter.
- A black blend color produces a highly darkened bottom layer.
- A white blend color produces a highly lightened bottom layer.

You can see in Figure 7.17 how the underlying layer shows through quite strongly compared to the blended layer.

Soft Light

This blending mode produces a slightly more subtle effect than Overlay. It works by applying the Darken or Lighten blending mode to each pixel depending on the brightness of the blend color. Bright blend colors result in a lightening of the image, while dark blend colors result in darkening.

FIGURE 7.17

When applying the Overlay mode, the underlying flowers layer predominates and overall contrast increases. The top layer tends to take on the colors of the bottom layer.

Soft Light produces the following effects:

- The order of the layers does matter.
- A black blend color produces a somewhat darkened bottom layer.
- A white blend color produces a somewhat lightened bottom layer.

The overall effect can be likened to shining a diffused spotlight onto the image. You can see Soft Light in action in Figure 7.18.

FIGURE 7.18

This example of the Soft Light blending mode provides a nice gentle effect, with the two layers merging naturally. It's less contrasty than the Overlay mode.

297

Hard Light

The Hard Light blending mode behaves in a similar way to Overlay, except that Photoshop uses the blend color to determine whether to apply Multiply or Screen, rather than the base color. This results in more of an emphasis on the top layer than the bottom layer. In fact, applying Hard Light to the top layer has exactly the same effect as swapping the layers over and applying Overlay to the top layer.

The effects of Hard Light are summarized below:

- The order of the layers does matter.
- A black blend color produces black.
- A white blend color produces white.

The overall effect of Hard Light is one of shining a hard-focused spotlight onto the image. Figure 7.19 shows an example of Hard Light doing its stuff.

FIGURE 7.19

With Hard Light, the top layer predominates in the end result. The hues in the final image are heavily influenced by the colors in the window layer.

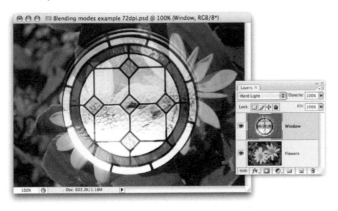

Vivid Light

This blending mode dodges or burns each pixel depending on the brightness of the blend color. If the blend color is lighter than 50 percent gray, then the Color Dodge blending mode is applied to create a lighter result color. On the other hand, blend colors darker than 50 percent gray invoke Color Burn to produce a darker result color.

Vivid Light has the following characteristics:

- The order of the layers does matter.
- A black blend color produces black.
- A white blend color produces white.

The end result of the Vivid Light blending mode is a high-contrast image, often with very saturated colors. It's great if you need that eye-popping, glow-in-the-dark effect! Figure 7.20 shows Vivid Light in action.

FIGURE 7.20

With Vivid Light, the colors in both layers have become very saturated, and the overall effect is very high contrast.

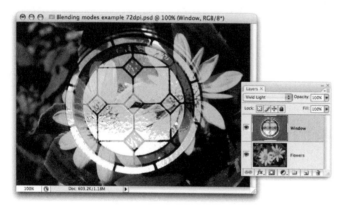

Linear Light

Linear Light is very similar to Vivid Light; the only difference is that Linear Light uses Linear Dodge (Add) and Linear Burn instead of Color Dodge and Color Burn. As you might imagine, this produces a less full-on effect than Vivid Light does. In fact, it's often quite similar to Hard Light.

The Linear Light mode works as follows:

- The order of the layers does matter.
- A black blend color produces black.
- A white blend color produces white.

You can see an image with the Linear Light blending mode applied in Figure 7.21.

FIGURE 7.21

Linear Light has produced a similar effect to Hard Light with the two layers, but it's slightly darker and higher in contrast. The colors are also somewhat more unnatural than with Hard Light.

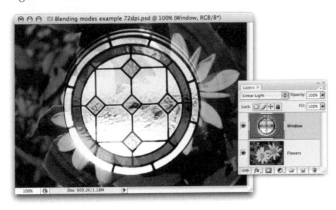

Pin Light

Like many of the other Light blending modes, Pin Light looks at the brightness level of the blend color to determine what action to take, but also compares the blend color with the base color and then decides which to use.

If the blend color is brighter than 50 percent gray, and the base color is darker than that blend color, then the blend color is used; otherwise the base color is used instead. Similarly, if the blend color is darker than 50 percent gray and the base color is also lighter than the blend color, then the blend color is used; otherwise the base color is used.

Pin Light produces the following effects:

■ The order of the layers does matter.

■ A black blend color produces black.

■ A white blend color produces white.

The overall effect of Pin Light is that very light or very dark colors in the top layer are kept, while midtones and nonsaturated colors tend to turn transparent, allowing the bottom layer to show through. A 50 percent gray pixel in the top layer becomes completely transparent, with opacity decreasing as the color tends toward black or white.

Figure 7.22 shows the effects of Pin Light on a real-world example.

FIGURE 7.22

The Pin Light blending mode in action. Notice how some midtone areas of the top layer—particularly the area around the outside edge of the window—have become nearly transparent, allowing the flowers layer to show through.

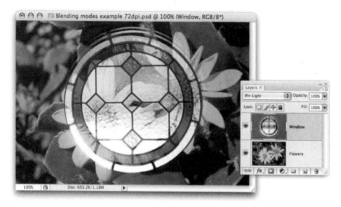

Hard Mix

The no-compromise Hard Mix blending mode sets each of the color channels to either full black or full white, depending on the ratio of that channel in the base and blend colors. The net result of this is that the image is boiled down to just eight colors: the six primary and secondary colors (red, green, blue, cyan, magenta, yellow), black, and white. This means that you get a harsh, posterized image that's guaranteed to give your eyeballs a good workout. Figure 7.23 shows Hard Mix applied to the example images (sunglasses recommended for viewing).

Hard Mix can be summarized as follows:

- The order of the layers does matter.
- A black blend color produces a very dark posterized bottom layer.
- A white blend color produces a very light posterized bottom layer.

It may seem like a fairly pointless blending mode, but Hard Mix has its uses—it's quite handy for image sharpening, for example.

FIGURE 7.23

The window and flowers example becomes almost unrecognizable with Hard Mix, as all the colors in the image are boiled down to just eight distinct tones.

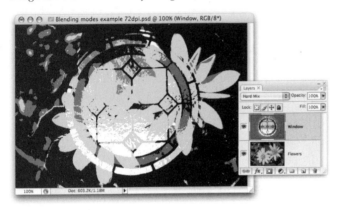

Difference modes

Photoshop's two difference modes, Difference and Exclusion, work by looking at the difference between the top and bottom layers. The end results are not particularly aesthetically pleasing as a rule, but these blending modes do have their place, particularly when combined with other modes, adjustment layers, and layer effects.

Difference

The Difference mode is a simple subtraction of one layer from the other: The value of the base color is subtracted from the value of the blend color, and the absolute value returned is used for the result color.

As you might imagine, Difference produces the following effects:

- The order of the layers doesn't matter.
- A black blend color produces no change.
- A white blend color inverts the bottom layer.

You can see the result of applying the Difference mode in Figure 7.24.

> **TIP** Difference produces quite an odd effect, but it's a handy way to compare two images to see if they're identical. Put one image in one layer and the second image in a layer above the first. Apply the Difference mode to the top image, and, if the two images are identical, you'll see black. Any discrepancies between the two images appear as colored pixels.

FIGURE 7.24

With the Difference blending mode, the two layers are subtracted, producing an odd effect. Because each of the three color channels are subtracted individually, the combined result is a fairly radical shift in hues.

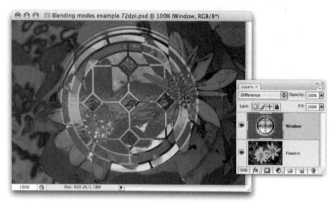

Exclusion

The Exclusion blending mode is similar to Difference, in that it compares the difference between the two layers. It's a modified version of Difference that results in an image with less contrast. While black and white still result in no change and inversion, respectively, midtones in one layer result in a decrease in contrast in the other layer. 50 percent gray in one layer results in zero contrast in the other, with the contrast increasing as the color channel tends toward either black or white.

The effects of Exclusion can be summarized as follows:

- The order of the layers doesn't matter.
- A black blend color produces no change.
- A white blend color inverts the bottom layer.

Figure 7.25 shows the Exclusion mode in action. While you can't use it to compare two images like you can with Difference, it's arguably the more useful of the two modes from an artistic point of view.

FIGURE 7.25

Exclusion produces a similar effect to Difference, but the result is somewhat gentler and, arguably, more pleasing to the eye.

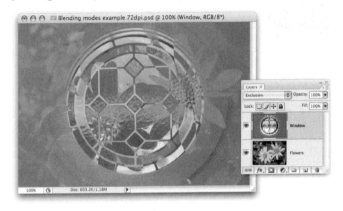

Component modes

The final four blending modes — Hue, Saturation, Color, and Luminosity — all work their magic using one or more of the hue, saturation, and luminance components of the image. This is in contrast to most of the other modes, which work on the color channels of the image (for example, Red, Green, and Blue for RGB images). Obviously, the component modes are really only useful for color images, although Luminosity sort of works on a grayscale image.

NOTE With all of the component modes, the order of the layers is significant; if you swap the layers and reapply the blending mode to the top layer, the results will be different. To get a better idea of how these modes function, take a look at the color insert.

Hue

This blending mode is pretty straightforward; it takes the hue component of the blend color and combines it with the saturation and luminance of the base color. In other words, the end result is a version of the bottom layer that takes on the hue of the top layer.

You can see an example of the Hue mode doing its stuff in Figure 7.26.

Saturation

Much as the Hue mode adds the hue component of the blend color to the base color, the Saturation mode mixes the saturation component of the blend color with the hue and luminance of the base color. This means that you end up with a somewhat strange effect, with the bottom layer taking on the saturation values of the top layer.

Figure 7.27 shows the Saturation blending mode being applied to a couple of layers.

The Hue blending mode in action. The flowers have taken on the beige, red, blue, and yellow hues of the top window layer.

Here the Saturation mode is applied to a pair of layers. The center areas of the flowers layer have become desaturated, due to the lack of color in the window glass.

Color

The Color blending mode is a combination of the Hue and Saturation modes, applying both the hue and saturation components of the blend color to the base color. This makes Color a good way to apply the color elements of one layer to another — for example, you can colorize a black and white photo on the bottom layer by painting onto the top layer.

In Figure 7.28, the Color blending mode is used to apply the colors from one layer to another in order to produce quite an interesting effect.

FIGURE 7.28

The Color blending mode combines the Hue and Saturation modes. The flowers have taken on both the hues and the saturation values of the stained glass window layer.

Luminosity

The Luminosity mode is the opposite of the Color mode; rather than applying the blend color's color components (hue and saturation) to the base color, it applies the brightness (luminance) component instead.

The end result is one of the top layer being colorized by the bottom layer, as you can see in Figure 7.29.

FIGURE 7.29

The example layers with the Luminosity blending mode applied. Although the hue and saturation components of the flowers layer are retained, the image is now taking its brightness levels from the window layer, producing quite an odd result.

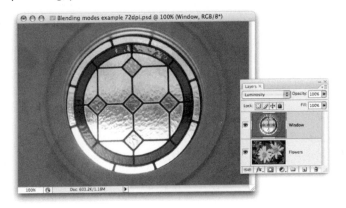

Summarizing the blending modes

Table 7.1 outlines the key features and differences of each blending mode in Photoshop. Each blending mode is shown with its keyboard shortcut. To use the shortcut, hold down Alt+Shift (Win) or Option+Shift (Mac) and press the appropriate key to set the active layer's blending mode.

NOTE If you're using a painting tool, the keyboard shortcut sets the tool's blending mode in the options bar, not the layer's blending mode.

The Available for column indicates the situations when each blending mode is available. Layers and painting tools means that you can use the blending mode on layers and also use the blending mode with certain painting tools. Painting tools only means that the blending mode is reserved for use with certain painting tools only, such as the Brush tool or the Gradient tool.

TABLE 7.1

Summary of Photoshop Blending Modes

Blending mode and shortcut	Description	End effect	Available for
Normal (N)	Normal blending between the base and blend colors.	No effect.	Layers and painting tools
Dissolve (I)	Randomly chooses either the base color or the blend color for each pixel.	Speckled, noisy effect of the top layer dissolving into the bottom layer.	Layers and painting tools
Behind (Q)	Paints behind transparent and semitransparent pixels in the layer.	Transparent and semitransparent areas are painted on; opaque areas are untouched.	Painting tools only
Clear (R)	Clears pixels instead of painting them.	Opaque and semiopaque pixels that would normally be painted on are made transparent.	Painting tools only
Darken (K)	Uses either the base color or the blend color for the result color, whichever is darkest.	Darker areas of the top layer remain visible, while the bottom layer shows through the lighter areas.	Layers and painting tools
Multiply (M)	Multiplies the base and blend color to produce a (usually) darker result color.	Similar to Darken, but generally a more blended effect. The overall image is usually darkened.	Layers and painting tools

continued

TABLE 7.1	*(continued)*		
Blending mode and shortcut	**Description**	**End effect**	**Available for**
Color Burn (B)	Darkens the base color by decreasing brightness and increasing contrast to get the result color. The amount of change is determined by the blend color.	High-contrast, colorful, extreme darkening effect.	Layers and painting tools
Linear Burn (A)	Darkens the base color by decreasing brightness to get the result color. The amount of change is determined by the blend color.	Similar to Color Burn but darker and less extreme.	Layers and painting tools
Darker Color (no key)	Composite version of Darken. Compares the luminance channels rather than the color channels, and uses the composite value of the darkest pixel.	Darker areas of the top layer remain visible, while the bottom layer shows through the lighter areas.	Layers and painting tools
Lighten (G)	Uses either the base color or the blend color for the result color, whichever is lightest.	Lighter areas of the top layer remain visible, while the bottom layer shows through the darker areas.	Layers and painting tools
Screen (S)	Multiplies the inverse of the base and blend color to produce a (usually) lighter result color.	Similar to Lighten, but generally a more blended effect. The overall image is usually lightened.	Layers and painting tools
Color Dodge (D)	Lightens the base color by increasing brightness and contrast to get the result color. The amount of change is determined by the blend color.	High-contrast, colorful, extreme lightening effect.	Layers and painting tools
Linear Dodge (Add) (W)	Lightens the base color by increasing brightness to get the result color. The amount of change is determined by the blend color.	Similar to Color Dodge but lighter and less extreme.	Layers and painting tools

Blending mode and shortcut	Description	End effect	Available for
Lighter Color (no key)	Composite version of Lighten. Compares the luminance channels rather than the color channels, and uses the composite value of the brightest pixel.	Lighter areas of the top layer remain visible, while the bottom layer shows through the darker areas.	Layers and painting tools
Overlay (O)	Darkens the darker base colors using Multiply, and lightens the lighter base colors using Screen.	Increased contrast by emphasizing the darker and lighter parts of the bottom layer.	Layers and painting tools
Soft Light (F)	Applies the Darken or Lighten mode to each pixel depending on the brightness of the blend color.	Similar to Overlay, but more subtle.	Layers and painting tools
Hard Light (H)	Darkens the darker blend colors using Multiply, and lightens the lighter blend colors using Screen.	Increased contrast by emphasizing the darker and lighter parts of the top layer.	Layers and painting tools
Vivid Light (V)	Dodges or burns each pixel depending on the brightness of the blend color.	A high-contrast image with very saturated colors.	Layers and painting tools
Linear Light (J)	Uses Linear Dodge (Add) or Linear Burn on each pixel depending on the brightness of the blend color.	An effect somewhere between Hard Light and Vivid Light.	Layers and painting tools
Pin Light (Z)	Lightens or darkens the image based on the ratio of the base and blend colors.	Midtones of the top layer tend toward transparent.	Layers and painting tools
Hard Mix (L)	Sets each channel to either black or white, depending on the ratio of that channel in the base and blend colors.	A posterized image with just eight colors: the six primaries and secondaries, black and white.	Layers and painting tools

continued

TABLE 7.1	(continued)		
Blending mode and shortcut	**Description**	**End effect**	**Available for**
Difference (E)	Subtracts the value of the base color from the value of the blend color and uses the absolute value as the result.	The difference between one layer and the other. If the two layers are identical, it produces black.	Layers and painting tools
Exclusion (X)	A modified version of Difference. Midtones in one layer result in reduced contrast in the other layer.	A similar effect to Difference, but more subtle.	Layers and painting tools
Hue (U)	Combines the hue of the blend color with the saturation and luminance of the base color.	The bottom layer takes on the hue of the top layer.	Layers and painting tools
Saturation (S)	Combines the saturation of the blend color with the hue and luminance of the base color.	The bottom layer takes on the saturation of the top layer.	Layers and painting tools
Color (C)	Combines the hue and saturation of the blend color with the luminance of the base color.	The bottom layer takes on the color of the top layer.	Layers and painting tools
Luminosity (L)	Combines the luminance of the blend color with the hue and saturation of the base color.	The bottom layer takes on the luminance of the top layer.	Layers and painting tools

Fine-Tuning a Blend Effect

If the wealth of available blending modes combined with the Opacity and Fill sliders still doesn't offer you enough creative control, Photoshop has another trick up its sleeve. This is the Blending Options section within the Layer Style dialog box, as shown in Figure 7.30.

CROSS-REF The Layer Style dialog box controls much more than the blending options. It allows you to apply a range of effects to your layers, from shadows through to glows and embossing effects. To find out more about layer effects and styles, see Chapter 10.

To display the Layer Style dialog box for a layer, select the layer and then do any one of the following:

- Double-click the layer thumbnail in the Layers palette (this only works for normal layers).

- Double-click elsewhere in the layer in the Layers palette (this works for all layer types, but make sure you don't double-click the layer name or a mask thumbnail).

- Choose Layer ➪ Layer Style ➪ Blending Options.

- Right-click the layer in the Layers palette and choose Blending Options from the pop-up menu.

- Choose Blending Options from the Layers palette menu.

- Click the Add a Layer Style icon at the bottom of the Layers palette, then choose Blending Options from the pop-up menu.

- Right-click in the document window and select Blending Options from the pop-up menu. This only works if you're using one of the selection tools (except the Magic Wand tool) or the Crop tool, which limits its usefulness somewhat.

After the Layer Style dialog box appears, the Blending Options are the first item at the top of the list on the left. Photoshop automatically selects this item when you first display the dialog box, but if you select one of the other items in the list, simply click the Blending Options item to reselect Blending Options.

FIGURE 7.30

Use the Blending Options section at the top of the Layer Style dialog box to fine-tune the way your layers blend.

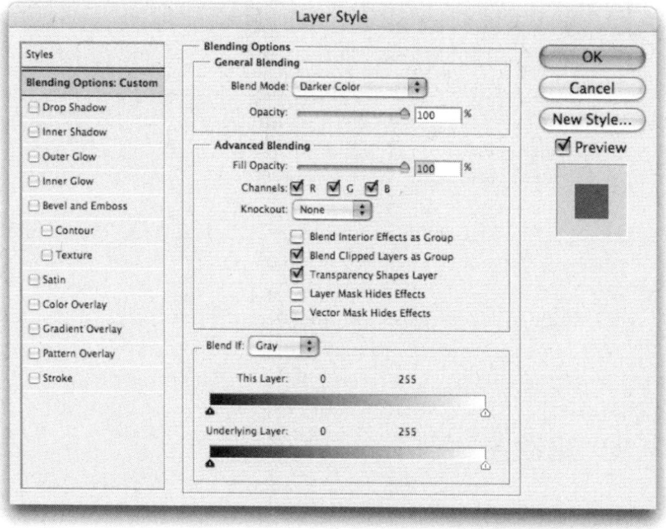

The first three blending options in the dialog box — Blend Mode, Opacity, and Fill Opacity — behave exactly like their counterparts in the Layers palette. Blend Mode has already been dealt with in this chapter, and Opacity and Fill Opacity are explained in detail in Chapter 2, so they aren't covered here.

This section explores the remaining blending options in the list. With these options you can remove one or more color channels from the blend; create *knockouts* that let a top layer punch through other layers to reveal a lower layer; control the way layer effects are blended; and specify how the top and bottom layers are blended based on color ranges.

Excluding color channels from the blend

As mentioned earlier in the chapter, Photoshop usually blends the top and bottom layers together by blending each color channel, then compositing the channels together to get the final image. However, you can actually control which color channels from each layer are involved in the blending process.

To do this, deselect one or more color channels in the Channels blending option (below Fill Opacity). For example, if you deselect the Red (R) channel in an RGB image, the red component of the active layer is excluded from the blend.

You can use these check boxes to get an extra degree of control over how your layer blends with the layers below. It's good for adding just a red tint to the underlying layers, for example. You can also try combining these settings with the Blend Mode option to produce some interesting special effects.

Creating knockouts

Knockouts let you use the shape of one layer to bore a hole through one or more lower layers, revealing the bottom layer through the hole. This is great for creating interesting effects, especially within complex, multilayered images, where revealing lower layers in the stacking order creates a feeling of depth and complexity. Figure 7.31 shows a knockout in action.

> **NOTE** It takes a few tries to get the hang of knockouts, as they aren't the most intuitive things in Photoshop, so don't worry if they don't seem to work the first time you try them out.

We'll explain how to create knockouts in the sections below, but here's a quick overview of how knockouts work. Creating a knockout involves setting the Knockout option for the layer that you want to use as the knockout shape — call this the *knockout layer* — to either Shallow or Deep. Generally speaking, Shallow knocks through to the first visible underlying layer that's not part of the knockout, while Deep knocks through to the Background layer.

FIGURE 7.31

A knockout uses the shape of its top layer to burrow through one or more underlying layers, revealing a layer underneath. In this case the Heart layer knocks out the Circle layer to reveal the Background layer.

Knockout layer

The knockout layer's shape burrows through the white Circle layer to the rose on the Background layer.

In addition, there are three key things to bear in mind when creating knockouts, as follows:

- Because the shape of the knockout layer's nontransparent pixels acts as the template for the knocking out, you need to use a knockout layer that doesn't fill the whole document. If you use a whole-document knockout layer, the knockout obliterates all pixels in the knocked-out layers (which probably isn't what you want).

- For the knockout effect to work, the knockout layer's Fill Opacity needs to be less than 100 percent, or its blending mode needs to reveal some of the underlying layers. This is because a fully opaque knockout layer won't allow any of the knocked-out layers to show through.

- Finally, and perhaps most importantly, the way you arrange the layers in your knockout has a big influence on how the knockout effect turns out. All knockouts work in essentially the same way — the knockout layer bores a hole through one or more layers below to reveal an underlying layer — but exactly which layers are bored through and which are revealed depends on the way your layers are arranged.

The next sections explain the three different ways that you can arrange your layers and create knockouts.

Creating a knockout with layers in a group

In many ways, this is the easiest and most straightforward approach. You need at least two non-Background layers in the knockout — the upper knockout layer that will do the knocking out, and one or more underlying layers that will be bored through.

Place all the layers that you want to be part of the knockout effect on top of each other, select them all, and group them by pressing Alt+G (⌘+G on the Mac). Double-click the top layer in the group — the knockout layer — to display its Layer Style dialog box, and choose either Shallow or Deep for the Knockout option:

- Choosing Shallow causes the knockout layer's shape to bore through the other layers in the group to reveal the first visible layer below the group. (If that first visible layer happens to be the Background layer, then Shallow produces the same result as Deep.)

- Choosing Deep bores through every single layer below to reveal the Background layer. If there's no visible Background layer, it bores through to transparency. The exception to this rule is if the group's blending mode is set to anything other than Pass Through; in that case, the knockout behaves as if Shallow was selected.

Figure 7.32 shows a knockout effect that uses layers in a group, with the Knockout option set to both Shallow and Deep.

NOTE Remember that you need to reduce the knockout layer's Fill Opacity setting down from 100 percent, or choose a blending mode that reveals some of the underlying layers, for the knockout effect to work.

Creating a knockout with layers in a clipping mask

The slightly more complicated way of creating a knockout is to use a clipping mask.

CROSS-REF If you're not familiar with the way clipping masks work, have a thorough read of Chapter 9 first. It will make things a lot clearer.

Again, for this to work you need at least two non-Background layers, and you need to stack your layers one on top of the other in the Layers palette. Then select all these layers except the bottom-most layer — which becomes the base layer of the mask — and choose Layer ⇨ Create Clipping Mask, or press Ctrl+Alt+G (⌘+Option+G on the Mac).

The next thing you'll probably want to do is double-click the base layer of your clipping mask — the layer with the underlined name — to display its Layer Style dialog box, and deselect the Blend Clipped Layers as Group option (it's selected by default). If you leave it selected, the knockout only bores down far enough to reveal the base layer, regardless of your knockout layer's Shallow or Deep setting. However, if this is the result you're after, then just leave this option selected.

FIGURE 7.32

A knockout created using layers in a group. Notice how the Shallow setting (a) knocks through to the layer immediately under the knockout group — the blue Color Fill layer — while the Deep setting (b) burrows all the way through to the Background layer.

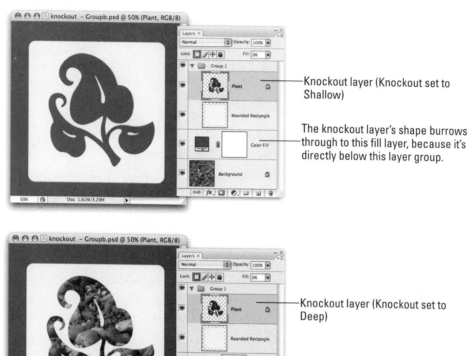

Knockout layer (Knockout set to Shallow)

The knockout layer's shape burrows through to this fill layer, because it's directly below this layer group.

Knockout layer (Knockout set to Deep)

The knockout layer's shape burrows through to the stones on the Background layer.

315

CAUTION If your clipping mask only has two layers in it — the top, knockout layer and the base layer — you definitely need to deselect the base layer's Blend Clipped Layers as Group option. If you don't do this, your knockout won't work at all.

Now you can double-click the top layer in the clipping mask — the knockout layer — and, in its Layer Style dialog box, choose either Shallow or Deep for the Knockout option to create the knockout. Assuming you deselected the Blend Clipped Layers as Group option for the base layer, the options behave as follows:

- Shallow causes the knockout layer to bore down through the other layers in the clipping mask to reveal the first visible layer below the base layer of the mask. (As with group knockouts, if the first visible layer is the Background layer, then the effect of Shallow is identical to that of Deep.)

- Deep makes the knockout layer drill right down through to reveal the Background layer; if the Background layer is hidden or not present, it drills through to reveal transparency.

NOTE Don't forget that, for the knockout to work, you need to reduce the knockout layer's Fill Opacity setting below 100 percent, or choose a blending mode that reveals some of the underlying layers.

In Figure 7.33 you can see a knockout created using a clipping mask, with both Shallow and Deep Knockout settings for the knockout layer.

Creating a knockout with layers that aren't in a group or clipping mask

You can also create a knockout even if your layers are not in a group or a clipping mask. However, in this case the knockout always bores down to the Background layer, regardless of the knockout layer's Shallow or Deep setting. If there's no visible Background layer in the document, it bores down to transparency.

To create the knockout, simply place your layers in order in the Layers palette, double-click the top layer — the one you want to do the knocking out — and select either Shallow or Deep for the Knockout option in the Layer Style dialog box. As usual, you'll need to set the knockout layer's Fill Opacity below 100 percent, or choose a blending mode that reveals the underlying layers, for the knockout to work.

Figure 7.34 shows such a knockout in action.

FIGURE 7.33

Using a clipping mask to create a knockout. Shallow (a) reveals the layer immediately below the base layer of the clipping mask — in this case the blue Color Fill layer — while Deep (b) reveals the Background layer.

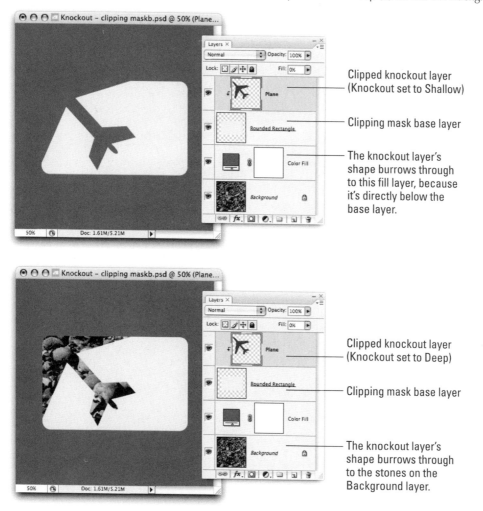

Clipped knockout layer (Knockout set to Shallow)

Clipping mask base layer

The knockout layer's shape burrows through to this fill layer, because it's directly below the base layer.

Clipped knockout layer (Knockout set to Deep)

Clipping mask base layer

The knockout layer's shape burrows through to the stones on the Background layer.

FIGURE 7.34

When you create a knockout with layers that aren't in a group or clipping mask, the knockout layer's shape always burrows down to the Background layer, regardless of the knockout layer's Knockout setting.

Kncokout layer (Knockout set to Deep)

The knockout layer's shape burrows
through the Polygon and Color Fill
layers to the stones on the Background layer.

Blending interior effects

Some of the effects that you can apply to layers in the Layer Style dialog box are known as *interior effects*. These effects only work on the opaque pixels of the layer; unlike the other effects they never spill out into transparent areas. The interior effects are:

- Inner Glow
- Satin
- Color Overlay
- Gradient Overlay
- Pattern Overlay

By default, all effects — including interior effects — are unaffected by the layer's blending mode and Fill Opacity setting. For example, if you choose a blending mode of Hard Light for a layer, the pixels in the layer interact with the layers below to produce the Hard Light effect, but any effects added to the layer display as normal. Similarly, if you decrease the Fill Opacity of a layer, the layer's pixels gradually become more transparent, allowing the underlying layers to show through, but any effects applied to the layer remain at their original opacity levels.

However, by selecting the Blend Interior Effects as Group option — right below the Knockout option in the Layer Style palette — you can get Photoshop to include any interior effects in the blend. This means that changing the layer's blending mode or Fill Opacity setting alters the interior effects as well as the layer's pixels. (Normal effects still remain unaltered.)

You can see an example that uses the Blend Interior Effects as Group option in Figure 7.35.

Blending interior effects. With Blend Interior Effects as Group unselected (a), the Drop Shadow and Pattern Overlay are unaffected by the layer's Hard Mix mode. With Blend Interior Effects as Group selected (b), the interior Pattern Overlay effect takes on the layer's Hard Mix mode. The regular Drop Shadow effect remains untouched.

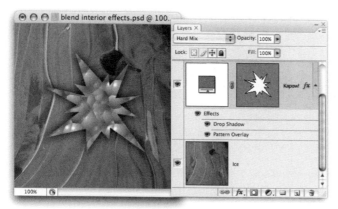

Controlling the blending of a clipping mask

When you create a clipping mask, the layers in the mask are blended in the following way by default:

- First, the masked layers are blended together using their selected blending modes and blending options.
- The group of masked layers is then blended with the pixels below the clipping mask using the blending mode of the base layer.

This is controlled by the Blend Clipped Layers as Group option in the Layer Style dialog box. (You find this option below Blend Interior Effects as Group.) It's enabled by default on the base layer, which creates the behavior just described.

If you prefer, you can make the layers in the clipping mask blend independently of the base layer. To do this, select the base layer, display its Blending Options in the Layer Style dialog box, and deselect the Blend Clipped Layers as Group option. All the layers in the clipping mask, including the base layer, now blend individually, as they would if they were not part of a clipping mask.

Figure 7.36 shows this option in action.

NOTE Changing the opacity of the base layer still affects the opacity of the clipped layers, even with Blend Clipped Layers as Group deselected. This is because the layers are still behaving as a clipping mask, with the transparent (and semitransparent) pixels in the base layer masking off the pixels in the masked layers above. However, if you reduce the Fill opacity of the base layer, provided Blend Clipped Layers as Group is deselected, the clipped layers remain unaffected.

CROSS-REF Find out all about clipping masks in Chapter 9.

Disabling a layer's transparency mask

As mentioned in Chapter 2, each layer has an invisible transparency mask associated with it, defined by the transparent areas of the layer's contents. Normally, Photoshop constrains any layer effects to this transparency mask, which is why your drop shadow follows the edges of your layer content, for example.

You can disable a layer's transparency mask (from a layer effects point of view) by deselecting the Transparency Shapes Layer option, below the Blend Clipped Layers as Group option, in the Layer Style dialog box. Layer effects now use the whole image, rather than being restricted to the opaque or semiopaque areas of the layer.

If you deselect this option when using effects such as Color or Gradient Overlay then the overlay fills the whole layer, effectively giving you a fill layer. However, effects such as Drop Shadow disappear, because these effects need an opaque area to work on.

FIGURE 7.36

Use the Blend Clipped Layers as Group option to control how a clipping mask blends with the layers below. When it's selected for the base layer (a), the layers in the mask are blended together, and the result is blended with the layers below using the base layer's mode (Color Dodge in this case). When it's not selected (b), the layers in the mask blend as individual layers, so the Pattern layer blends with the layers below using the Screen mode.

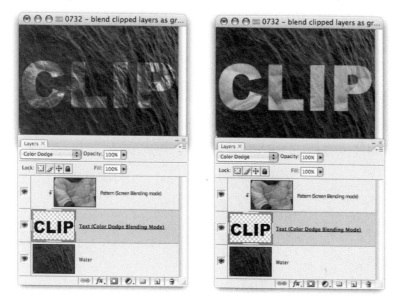

There's another benefit to disabling the layer's transparency mask. This relies on the fact that layer masks and vector masks also control which areas of a layer are opaque, and therefore which areas are acted on by layer effects. So if your layer has a layer or vector mask, and you deselect Transparency Shapes Layer, you're effectively handing control of the shape of the effect over to the layer or vector mask.

Figure 7.37 makes this a bit clearer. By default, Transparency Shapes Layer is enabled, so the drop shadow follows the opaque areas of the masked layer. By deselecting Transparency Shapes Layer, the drop shadow instead follows the contours of the layer mask.

NOTE This setting also applies to knockouts. If Transparency Shapes Layer is selected for the knockout layer, the knockout effect is restricted to the knockout layer's transparency mask, which is usually what you want to happen. If it's deselected, the entire knockout layer acts as a knockout, wiping out everything in the knocked-out layers below (unless the knockout layer also has a layer or vector mask applied to it).

FIGURE 7.37

With Transparency Shapes Layer enabled (left), the drop shadow follows the shape of the layer's pixels (including those pixels masked off by the layer mask). With this option disabled (right), the shadow now follows the outline of the layer mask instead.

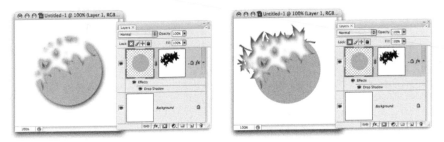

Hiding effects with layer and vector masks

If your layer has a layer or vector mask (or both) applied, and you add a layer effect, Photoshop normally applies the mask first to mask out the unwanted opaque areas of the layer, then applies the effect to the opaque pixels that are left.

You can reverse this behavior by enabling the Layer Mask Hides Effects or Vector Mask Hides Effects option (or both) in the Layer Style dialog box. When enabled, Photoshop first applies any effects to the layer as if the mask isn't there, then applies the mask to both layer and effects. The net result of this is that, rather than helping to define the shape of the layer and therefore the effects, the mask is now used to mask off areas of both the layer and the effects.

Figure 7.38 illustrates the Layer Mask Hides Effects option with an example.

FIGURE 7.38

When Layer Mask Hides Effects is disabled, the layer mask is used to help define the opaque pixels that the drop shadow is applied to (left). When it's enabled, the layer mask is instead used to mask off both the layer's opaque pixels and the drop shadow (right).

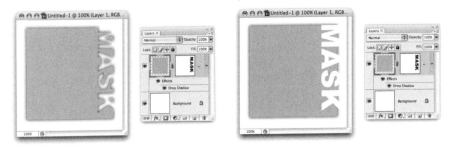

CROSS-REF Find out more about layer masks and vector masks in Chapter 9.

Blending by color range

The final bunch of controls under Blending Options gives you a lot of creative control over how your top and bottom layers blend together. You can use these options to specify which pixels in each layer appear in the blend, based on their color or brightness. For example, you can keep just the bright blue sky in a top layer, or force through the lush green grass in a bottom layer.

Here's how it works. You have two sliders: This Layer and Underlying Layer. This Layer controls how much of the top layer is blended (shown), while Underlying Layer controls how much of the bottom layer is blended (hidden). The default — assuming you're using the Normal blending mode — is for all nontransparent pixels in the top layer to be blended (shown), and all of the bottom layer to be blended (hidden). In other words, the default slider settings result in opaque pixels in the top layer completely covering the bottom layer, which is what you'd expect.

Hiding parts of the top layer

To start dropping out pixels from the top layer, drag the little black and white sliders below the This Layer bar, as follows:

- **Click and drag the black slider to the right to lose pixels darker than the color at the slider position.** You can see the black slider position by looking at the first value to the right of This Layer — the values go from 0 (black) to 255 (white). For example, if you drag the black slider to the midpoint (128), all colors in the top layer that are darker than mid-gray are excluded from the image.

- **Click and drag the white slider to the left to remove pixels lighter than the selected color.** This color is indicated by the second value to the right of This Layer. For example, if you drag the white slider from 255 down to 200, all pixels in the top layer with brightness values greater than 200 are dropped.

Figure 7.39 shows these sliders in action.

Punching through parts of the bottom layer

To start forcing pixels of the bottom layer through, so that they show through the top layer, drag the sliders below the Underlying Layer bar, as follows:

- **Click and drag the black slider to the right to punch through any pixels darker than that color.** The first value to the right of Underlying Layer indicates the threshold color that you selected. Any pixels darker than that color are removed from the blend and displayed regardless. For example, dragging the black slider to 128 forces pixels from the bottom layer that are darker than mid-gray to be displayed.

- **Click and drag the white slider to the left to punch through pixels lighter than the selected color.** The selected color is shown by the second value to the right of Underlying Layer. For example, if you drag the white slider down to 200, all pixels from the bottom layer with brightness values greater than 200 show through.

FIGURE 7.39

Hiding darker parts of the top layer by dragging the black This Layer slider

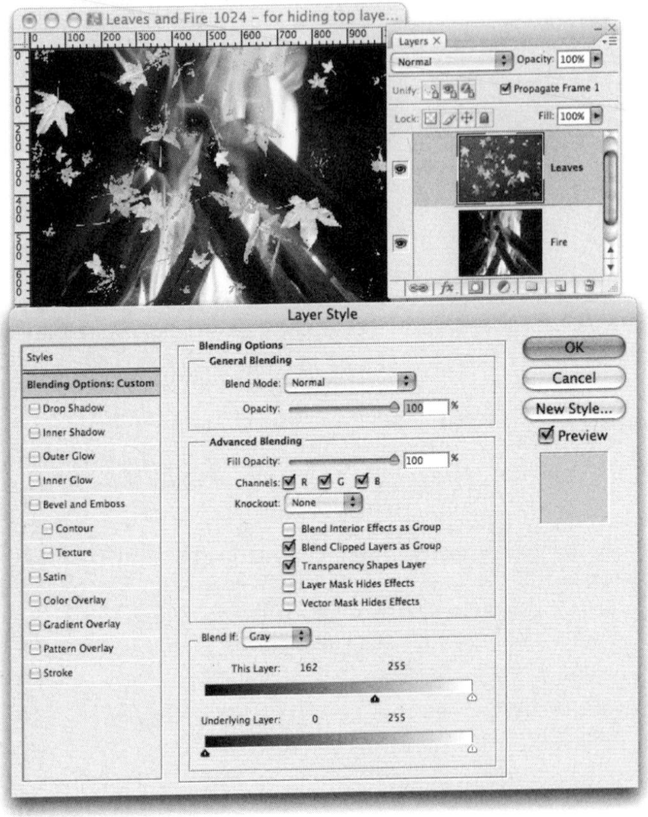

You can see the Underlying Layer sliders working their magic in Figure 7.40.

Smoothing the transitions

These sliders are pretty cool, but when you work with images containing lots of colors — photos spring to mind — the results can be somewhat jagged and blocky. The reason for this is that the color values you choose with the sliders are hard cutoff points. For example, if you work with a photo of a sunset on your top layer and you drag the black This Layer slider to a point within the range of oranges of the sunset, you see the sunset being rudely cut off, with a jagged edge along the color threshold that you selected.

Adobe thought this through, of course, and sensibly provided the ability to define a soft threshold for each of the four sliders rather than the default hard thresholds. Here's how it works:

FIGURE 7.40

Forcing through the darker areas of the bottom layer using the black Underlying Layer slider

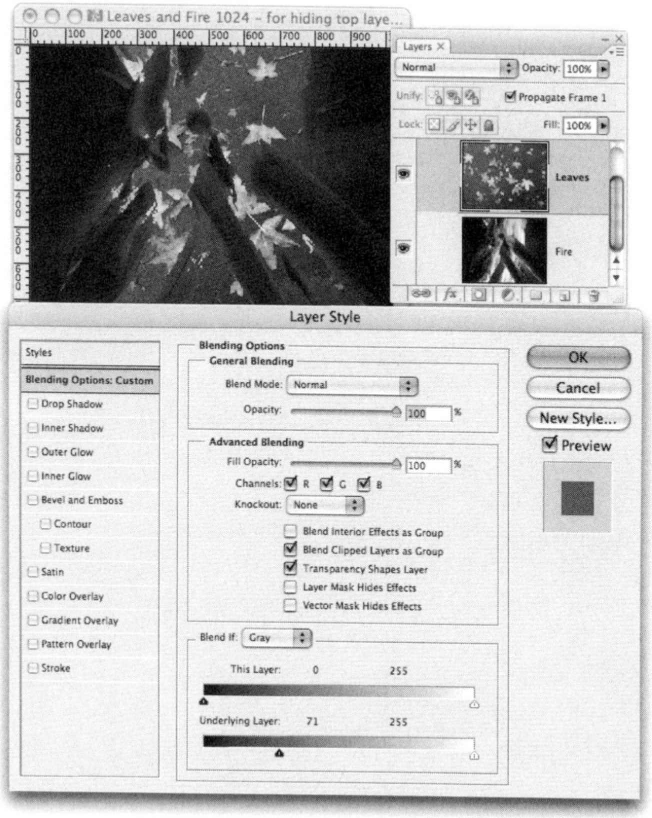

1. **Move the mouse over either the left or the right half of a slider triangle, hold down Alt (Win) or Option (Mac), click, and drag.** You'll see the slider split into two halves. The corresponding number to the right of This Layer or Underlying Layer now shows two values, separated by a '/', representing the lower and upper values of the soft threshold.

2. **Click and drag the two halves around.** (You don't need to hold down Alt/Option anymore.) The bigger the gap between the two halves, the more gentle the threshold becomes.

3. **To join the two halves together again, click and drag one half on top of the other.** The two halves merge to form the original slider triangle, and you're back to a hard threshold again.

An example clarifies these soft thresholds. In the top image in Figure 7.41, you see two photos in separate layers. The top layer, a landscape photo of a range of mountains, is set to an Overlay blending mode, which then interacts with the plant life and reflections in the layer below. To bring through more of that bottom layer in the sky of the landscape, you click and drag the white This Layer slider to the left to hide the lightest parts of the top layer. This results in the lower layer showing through in the skies, but in a very hard-edged, jagged way.

To get around this, you can split the white This Layer slider to create a more subtle effect. In the bottom image, you can see that, with the two halves of the slider separated, the mountains of the top layer merge with the colors of the bottom layer much more smoothly.

FIGURE 7.41

Soft thresholds in action. In the first example (left), the This Layer slider is dragged to bring through the bottom layer, but the results are somewhat jagged. Splitting the slider creates a soft threshold, resulting in a much smoother effect (right).

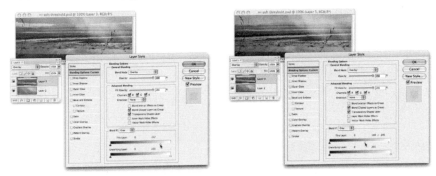

> **TIP** With both the This Layer and Underlying Layer controls, you can actually click and drag the black slider to the right of the white slider (or the white slider to the left of the black slider). This reverses the effect of the blend; pixels that would have been taken from the top layer for that selected range are now taken from the bottom layer and vice versa. This can add a whole new dimension to the blend.

Blending based on color

By default, the This Layer and Underlying Layer sliders control blending based on the overall brightness levels of the pixels in the top and bottom layers. However, you can also adjust sliders for individual color channels by choosing different channels for the Blend If option. For example, if you choose Red, the This Layer and Underlying Layer sliders control the blending based only on the Red channel of each pixel. To return to the default composite sliders, choose Gray.

You can control the sliders for each of the Blend If channels independently, and the sliders also interact. For example, if you set one range using the This Layer slider for the Gray channel and then set another range using the This Layer slider for the Red channel, Photoshop only uses a pixel from the top layer if both of the following occur:

- The pixel's overall brightness sits between your Gray slider triangles.
- The brightness of the pixel's Red channel sits between your Red slider triangles.

Blending by color channel gives you finer control over exactly which pixels are selected for the top and bottom layers, as you can select based on hue as well as by brightness. This is great if you want to keep just the bright blue sky of a layer, for example.

Applying Blending Modes to Layer Effects

You may have noticed that each of the effects in the Layer Style dialog box has its own Blend Mode option, usually toward the top of the dialog. An effect's blending mode applies only to that effect. Therefore you can have several blending modes in action for a layer — one for the layer itself, and one for each effect you've enabled.

Photoshop sets the effect blending modes to sensible values by default; for example, Drop Shadow uses Multiply to darken and blend with the background, Outer Glow uses Screen to lighten the background and create a nice glow, and so on.

Although these default blending modes are best suited to their effects, there's nothing to stop you sticking with them. Try picking different blending modes for some interesting artistic effects; the Dodge, Burn, and Hard Mix modes are quite fun to use with Outer Glow, for example. Figure 7.42 shows some of the tricks you can achieve by fiddling with the effect blending modes.

CROSS-REF Layer effects are covered in detail in Chapter 10.

FIGURE 7.42

Tweaking the blending modes of various layer effects to create some interesting results

Summary

In this chapter, you explored Photoshop's powerful, and sometimes mysterious, blending modes that let you mix your layers together in many interesting and fun ways. You looked at the sort of effects you can achieve with blending modes, learned how to set the blending mode for a layer, and briefly explored some of the science behind these curious creatures. You then dived headlong into a detailed explanation of each of Photoshop's 27 blending modes with plenty of examples to illustrate the modes.

Next, you looked at the additional blending options you can apply to a layer, such as choosing which color channels to include in the blend; creating knockouts; controlling how effects interact with layer, vector and clipping masks; disabling a layer's transparency mask; and choosing the mix of pixels from the top and bottom layers based on their brightness and color. Finally, you took a brief look at how you can apply blending modes to individual layer effects, in addition to the layers themselves. And who said Photoshop was just a paint program?

Chapter 8

Exploring Smart Objects

Smart Objects, first introduced in Photoshop CS2, behave in a similar way to regular layers at first glance. The key difference is that Smart Objects act as containers for other content. That other content can be practically anything that can be rendered as an image, including:

- A bunch of other Photoshop layers, whether they're normal bitmap layers, type layers, shape layers, adjustment layers, or fill layers
- Artwork created in Illustrator, then pasted into a document in Photoshop
- A separate image file, such as a JPEG, a TIFF, an Illustrator AI file, an EPS file, a PDF, or even another Photoshop PSD file

A Smart Object appears in the Layers palette, just like a regular layer, as shown in Figure 8.1. You can edit the contents of a Smart Object at any time — either in Photoshop or, in the case of vector Smart Objects, within Illustrator — and the Smart Object updates to reflect your changes.

When you create a new Smart Object, you're essentially creating a "virtual" document that contains the Smart Object's content. Photoshop embeds this document within the main document. When you edit a Smart Object's content — in Photoshop or Illustrator — you edit it as if it were a separate document; when you save the document, the Smart Object is updated.

So what can you use Smart Objects for? Here are some of the advantages of using Smart Objects:

- You can transform bitmap layers nondestructively. Each time you scale, rotate, skew, or warp a Smart Object, it applies the transform to a fresh copy of the original Smart Object content. The original content remains untouched.

- Use the same Smart Object more than once in the same document. Edit the contents of one copy of the Smart Object, and all the other copies are changed automatically.

- As we mentioned earlier, you can use a Smart Object to embed Illustrator artwork, or any supported image file, as a layer inside a Photoshop document. You can then reedit the original content at any time.

- Smart Objects are the gateway to one of the most eagerly awaited new features in Photoshop CS3: Smart Filters. Convert one or more layers to a Smart Object, and you can apply "live," editable filters to them.

In this chapter, you look at how to create and edit Smart Objects, and you explore some useful applications of these handy creatures. The chapter finishes with a practical example that demonstrates the power of Smart Objects.

FIGURE 8.1

A Smart Object in the Layers palette. The thumbnail has a little icon in its bottom-right corner to indicate that it's a Smart Object.

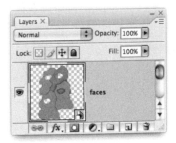

Creating a Smart Object

Photoshop gives you a few different ways to create Smart Objects. The exact method you use depends on the format of your source material. You can turn existing layers in your document into Smart Objects; you can copy and paste, or drag, artwork from Illustrator; and you can import image files in a variety of formats.

Creating a Smart Object from one or more layers

You can take one or more layers in your document and turn them into a Smart Object. The Smart Object then behaves as a single-layer composite version of your original layers.

To create a Smart Object this way, select the layer or layers you want to convert and then do one of the following:

- Choose Layer ➪ Smart Objects ➪ Convert to Smart Object.
- Right-click the layer or layers in the Layers palette and choose Convert to Smart Object.
- Choose Convert to Smart Object from the Layers palette menu.

Photoshop converts your selected layer or layers to a Smart Object, as you can see in Figure 8.2.

FIGURE 8.2

Converting layers into a Smart Object. Select the layers (left), and choose Layer ➪ Smart Objects ➪ Convert to Smart Object. The Smart Object replaces the layers in the Layers palette (right).

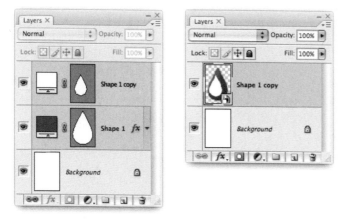

CAUTION   There's one major caveat with creating Smart Objects from layers: Any clipping masks in the original layers are released during the conversion process. This means that, if you mask off one layer with the contents of another using a clipping mask, your masked layer is no longer masked in the Smart Object. To fix this, edit the contents of the Smart Object (this process is described in a moment), and re-create the clipping mask.

Because this process is a conversion, you lose your selected layers from the document. Never fear, however; the layers are still there, they're just embedded in the Smart Object. You see how to get at them shortly.

NOTE When you create a Smart Object this way, Photoshop creates an embedded PSB document containing your Smart Object's content. The PSB format, also known as the Large Document Format, is a special Photoshop document format designed for holding files over 2GB in size. Not that your Smart Object is likely to reach anywhere near 2GB in most circumstances.

Creating a Smart Object from Illustrator artwork

You can import Illustrator artwork into Photoshop as a Smart Object. When you do this, the original Illustrator vector artwork is embedded inside the Photoshop document, which means you can reedit it in Illustrator at any time. You can also use Photoshop to scale, rotate, skew, and warp the Smart Object as much as you want; Photoshop works from the original vector artwork, so your smooth lines and curves are always preserved.

To get the Illustrator artwork into Photoshop as a Smart Object, follow these steps:

1. **Open your documents.** Open your Photoshop document in Photoshop, and your Illustrator document in Illustrator.

2. **Set clipboard preferences in Illustrator.** To make sure the artwork is transferred as a Smart Object and not as a bitmap layer, make sure a couple of preferences are set correctly in Illustrator. To do this, choose Edit ➪ Preferences ➪ File Handling & Clipboard (Illustrator ➪ Preferences ➪ File Handling & Clipboard on the Mac), and make sure both the PDF and AICB (no transparency support) options are checked.

3. **Copy the artwork.** Select your artwork in Illustrator, and choose Edit ➪ Copy, or press Ctrl+C (⌘+C on the Mac).

4. **Paste the artwork.** Switch to your document in Photoshop, and choose Edit ➪ Paste, or press Ctrl+V (⌘+V on the Mac). The Paste dialog box, shown in Figure 8.3, appears. Select the Smart Object option.

5. **Position the artwork.** Your Illustrator artwork appears in the document window, with a bounding box, transform handles and a blue cross through the middle of the artwork. You're now in Free Transform mode, and you can move, scale, rotate, skew, or warp the artwork as you see fit, as shown in Figure 8.3. When you're happy with the appearance of the artwork, press Enter (Return on the Mac) to place the artwork and create the Smart Object.

CROSS-REF For more on the Free Transform command, see Chapter 3.

You can also click and drag artwork from Illustrator into Photoshop as a Smart Object. To do this, first make sure your Illustrator clipboard preferences a set as described above, with both the PDF and AICB (no transparency support) options checked. Then select the artwork in Illustrator, and drag it across to your Photoshop document. Photoshop imports the artwork, allows you to position it as described in step 5, and creates a Smart Object for it.

FIGURE 8.3

Copying and pasting Illustrator artwork as a Smart Object. First, select and copy the artwork in Illustrator (left), then select the Smart Object option when pasting into Photoshop (center). Finally, position and transform your artwork as required (right), and press Enter (Win) or Return (Mac) to place the artwork.

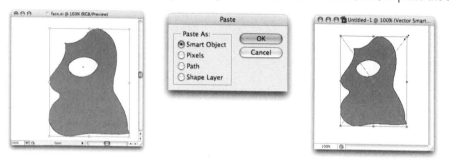

Creating a Smart Object from an image file

The final way to create a Smart Object is to import an image file into Photoshop. To do this, choose File ⇨ Place; then choose the image file that you want to import, and click Place. The image appears in the document window with a bounding box; you can then position and transform your image as described in the section "Creating a Smart Object from Illustrator artwork." After you position your image, press Enter (Return on the Mac) to place the image and create the Smart Object.

You can create a Smart Object from virtually any kind of image file this way, including other Photoshop documents, JPEGs, GIFs, TIFFs, PDFs, EPS files, and Illustrator AI files. A copy of the file is embedded within your Smart Object. You can edit this copy at any time in its original format. For example, you can edit a Photoshop document embedded within a Smart Object as if it were a separate, layered document, or edit an Illustrator document embedded within a Smart Object as a separate document in Illustrator. (Editing Smart Objects is covered in a bit.)

Placing an Illustrator AI file or a PDF file involves an additional step. After you click Place in the file chooser, the Place PDF dialog box, shown in Figure 8.4, appears.

Select Page to display a list of pages in the file. You can then choose the page that you want to load as a Smart Object by clicking its thumbnail in the list below. Alternatively, select Image to display a list of images embedded within the file; then choose an image to import from the list. To change the size of the thumbnails in the list, choose an option from the Thumbnail Size menu at the bottom of the dialog box.

NOTE If you're importing an Illustrator AI file, select Page. There will only be one page, of course, because you can't create multipage documents in Illustrator.

FIGURE 8.4

When you place a PDF or Illustrator AI file, Photoshop displays the Place PDF dialog box, allowing you to choose which parts of the artwork to import and how you want the artwork to be cropped.

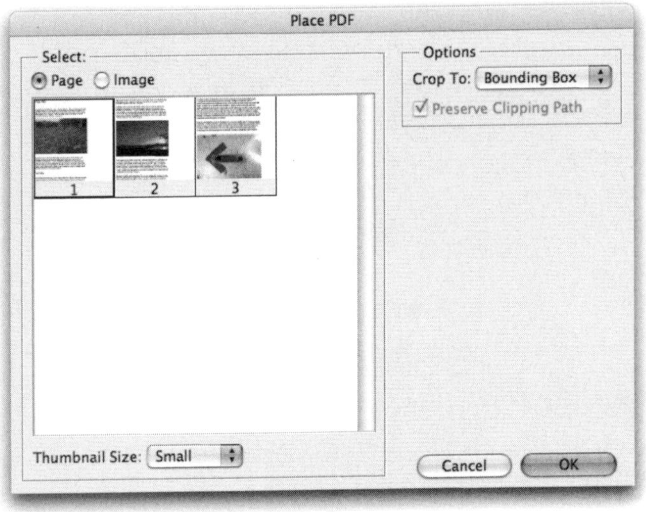

If you select the Page option, you can specify how you want the imported page to be cropped using the Crop To menu. The options in the list work as follows:

- **Bounding Box:** If you select this option, Photoshop automatically trims the image to include just the text and graphics in the page, removing extra white space. This is the default setting.

- **Media Box:** Select this option to import the whole of the page.

- **Crop Box:** This option crops the image down to the region within the crop margins specified within the file (also known as the clipping region).

- **Bleed Box:** The Bleed Box is often slightly larger than the Crop Box to allow for inaccuracies in the printing process. Printing outside the cropped region (known as *bleeding*) ensures that your ink goes right to the edge of the cropped region. Select this option to crop the imported image to the Bleed Box.

- **Trim Box:** This is the area that the creator of the image has defined as the final area of the page after trimming. It may be smaller than the Media Box to allow for crop marks, registration marks, and so on.

- **Art Box:** The Art Box represents the extent of the meaningful page content, as defined by the creator of the page. This may include intended white space around the content.

If you select the Image option, on the other hand, you can select the Preserve Clipping Path option to ensure that the imported image is clipped to any defined clipping path in the source image. Alternatively, deselect this option to import the entire unclipped image.

NEW FEATURE The Preserve Clipping Path option is new to Photoshop CS3. Previously, in CS2, the entire image was imported, regardless of any clipping path.

After you make your choices in the dialog box, click OK to place the imported image in the document as a Smart Object, as described earlier.

Editing Smart Objects

A Smart Object behaves much like a regular layer. For example, you can rename a Smart Object, reorder it in the Layers palette, change its Opacity and Fill settings, and apply layer effects to it. You can also transform the Smart Object using the transform commands under Edit ➪ Transform, apart from Distort and Perspective (which are grayed out). When you use a transform command on a Smart Object, it always works on a fresh copy of the original Smart Object content, meaning that you can transform a Smart Object as many times as you want without progressively degrading the image — even if that image is a bitmap.

At some point, though, you'll probably want to edit the contents of the Smart Object itself. To do this, double-click the Smart Object's thumbnail in the Layers palette, or right-click the Smart Object in the Layers palette and choose Edit Contents. You can also select the Smart Object in the Layers palette, and choose Layer ➪ Smart Objects ➪ Edit Contents, or simply choose Edit Contents from the Layers palette menu.

Exactly how you edit your Smart Object's contents depends on the contents themselves. For example, if your Smart Object contains Illustrator vector artwork, Photoshop fires up, or switches to, Illustrator and opens the Smart Object in that. If your Smart Object contains a layered Photoshop document or a flat image, Photoshop opens the contents as a separate Photoshop document for you to work with.

Before letting you edit the Smart Object's contents, though, Photoshop displays a handy reminder dialog box, as shown in Figure 8.5. This dialog box points out that you're actually editing a separate document and that you need to save any changes you make to this document before the changes appear in the original Smart Object. In addition, make sure that you save the document with the same file name and in the same folder, so that Photoshop picks up the changes. After you get the hang of this point, however, you'll probably want to select the Don't Show Again check box in the corner of the dialog box.

FIGURE 8.5

Before you start editing a Smart Object's contents, Photoshop displays this warning dialog box to remind you to save your changes.

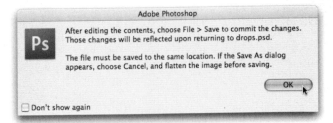

Click OK to close the dialog box, and the contents of your Smart Object appear, ready for editing. Make your changes to this document, then save it by choosing File ⇨ Save. You can close it too if you like. Switch back to your original Photoshop document, and you see that the Smart Object is updated with your edits, as shown in Figure 8.6.

NOTE What's happening behind the scenes here? When you edit a Smart Object, Photoshop extracts the embedded file containing the Smart Object's content and saves that file to your computer's temporary folder (for example, within the /var/tmp folder on Mac OS X, or within the Documents and Settings folder on Windows). You then work on that file in Photoshop or Illustrator. When you then save — and, optionally, close — that file, Photoshop reembeds the saved file back in your original document, and the Smart Object updates to show the changes.

FIGURE 8.6

Editing a Smart Object. Double-click the Smart Object's thumbnail (left) to open its contents in a new document window (center). Make your changes and save the file; the Smart Object updates to include the changes (right).

NOTE It's worth pointing out that, if you crop or resize a Photoshop document containing a Smart Object, the embedded contents of the Smart Object aren't cropped or resized. For example, if your 300 dpi document contains a Smart Object with a 300 dpi photo inside, and you resize the document to 72 dpi, the photo inside the Smart Object remains untouched at 300 dpi. So if you're ever wondering why a document that you scaled down to 72 dpi is still 20MB, this could be the reason!

Duplicating Smart Objects

When you duplicate a Smart Object, you link the duplicate with the original. This means that if you make any changes to the contents of one of the Smart Objects, the other Smart Object changes as well, as shown in Figure 8.7. This holds true for each and every copy that you make, even if it's a copy of a copy.

NOTE Only the Smart Objects' contents are linked like this. You can still change other properties of the Smart Objects independently, such as their names, opacities, blending modes, layer effects, and so on.

NOTE This linking only happens if you duplicate a Smart Object within the same document. If you drag a Smart Object to a different document, the two Smart Objects are not linked at all.

You can duplicate a Smart Object in the same way you duplicate a layer. For example, you can:

- Click and drag the Smart Object in the Layers palette down to the New Layer icon at the bottom of the palette.
- Right-click the Smart Object in the palette and choose Duplicate Layer.
- Select the Smart Object and choose Layer ➪ Duplicate Layer (or choose Duplicate Layer from the Layers palette menu).

CROSS-REF Duplicating layers, as well as other layer operations, are covered in Chapter 2.

FIGURE 8.7

When you duplicate a Smart Object (left), the duplicate is linked with the original. If you change the contents of either Smart Object, the other Smart Object updates to reflect your changes (right).

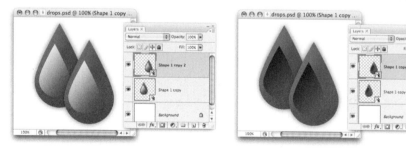

If you'd rather make a completely separate, independent copy of a Smart Object, select the Smart Object and choose Layer ➪ Smart Objects ➪ New Smart Object via Copy. You can also right-click the Smart Object in the Layers palette and choose New Smart Object via Copy. You can now edit the contents of this duplicate Smart Object without affecting the original.

Nesting Smart Objects

If you create your Smart Object by converting one or more Photoshop layers, or by placing a Photoshop document as described in the section "Creating a Smart Object from an image file", your Smart Object contains a layered Photoshop document. You can then create one or more Smart Objects inside this embedded document, effectively nesting the Smart Objects inside the parent Smart Object.

Figure 8.8 shows this technique in action. First, a layer is selected and turned into a Smart Object by choosing Layer ➪ Smart Objects ➪ Convert to Smart Object. The Smart Object's layer thumbnail is double-clicked to edit the Photoshop document inside it. Finally, the layer inside this Photoshop document is converted to a Smart Object, and the document is saved. The first document now contains a Smart Object that, in turn, contains another Smart Object. You can continue nesting Smart objects like this as many times as you want.

TIP You can also go the other way — select a layer and choose Convert to Smart Object, then select the converted Smart Object and choose Convert to Smart Object again. You've now created a Smart Object within a Smart Object.

CROSS-REF Nesting Smart Objects is a great way to add multiple copies of an item to a document. In fact, the example at the end of this chapter shows how you can use nesting to quickly produce a totally reeditable cluster of heart shapes.

FIGURE 8.8

How to nest Smart Objects. Here, a layer in the Untitled-1 document is turned into a Smart Object. The Smart Object is then edited as Shape 1.psb, and the layer inside is turned into another Smart Object (Shape 1).

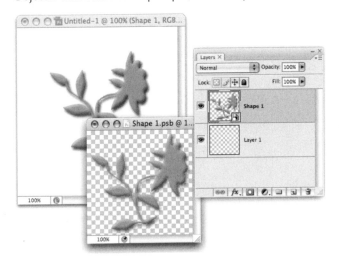

Converting and deleting Smart Objects

You can convert a Smart Object into a normal bitmap layer at any time. This is handy for saving RAM and hard drive space, particularly if your Smart Object contains several high-resolution layers. It's also useful if you want to do a Distort or Perspective transformation on a Smart Object (although you could always do the transformation on its contents at a pinch). Bear in mind, though, that you lose the original editable content inside the Smart Object when you convert it to a normal layer.

Photoshop gives you a few ways to convert a Smart Object into a layer:

- Right-click the Smart Object in the Layers palette and then choose Rasterize Layer from the pop-up menu.
- Select the Smart Object and then choose Layer ➪ Smart Objects ➪ Rasterize.
- Select the Smart Object and then choose Layer ➪ Rasterize ➪ Smart Object.

These all accomplish the same thing. Photoshop converts the Smart Object to a normal layer by rasterizing and/or flattening the Smart Object's contents as appropriate, then discards the Smart Object's contents.

CAUTION When you convert a Smart Object like this, any Smart Filters are permanently applied to the Smart Object as it is rasterized. There's no going back and editing the Smart Filters after you convert to a normal layer.

Deleting a Smart Object is, as you'd imagine, much like deleting a layer. You can click and drag it to the trash icon at the bottom of the Layers palette; right-click it and choose Delete Layer; and so on. Of course, when you delete a Smart Object, its embedded contents — whether a layered Photoshop document or vector artwork created in Illustrator — are deleted along with it.

Working with Smart Filters

NEW FEATURE Smart Filters are a new — and most welcome — addition to Photoshop. Finally, you have the ability to apply any Photoshop filter nondestructively, allowing you to go back and edit — or even remove — the filter at any time, without touching the pixels of your underlying image.

Much as the introduction of layer effects in Photoshop 6.0 allowed you to apply styling such as drop shadows to your layers nondestructively, Smart Filters let you apply any of Photoshop's available range of filters in a nondestructive, reeditable way. The catch is that you can only apply Smart Filters to Smart Objects; hence the reason they are covered in this chapter. If you want to apply a Smart Filter to a regular layer, you first need to turn it into a Smart Object.

Adobe does more than just give you "live" versions of filters, though. Each Smart Object comes with its own special mask just for filters, giving you creative control over which areas of your image are affected by the filters. You can also change the stacking order of filters within a Smart Object, effectively letting you apply the filters in any order you want. This makes it really easy to experiment with a huge range of filter combinations. Finally, each filter can even have its own blending mode and opacity, adding yet another dimension to the creative process.

> **CAUTION** One gotcha with Smart Filters revolves around resizing your image. Unlike a layer effect, whose size scales along with the image size, most Smart Filters are unaffected by resizing the image. For example, you might apply an Unsharp Mask Smart Filter to your 300 dpi image, setting the Radius option to a value that works well for that image — say, 4 pixels. If you then resize that image to 72 dpi, the Unsharp Mask radius remains at 4 pixels, resulting in a drastically oversharpened image. You need to reedit the Smart Filter and bring the radius down to a value more appropriate for your lower-resolution image.

Applying a Smart Filter

Applying a new Smart Filter to a Smart Object is simply a matter of choosing a filter from under the Filter menu. If your layer isn't already a Smart Object, you first need to turn it into one; see the section "Creating a Smart Object from one or more layers" earlier in this chapter for more info. Alternatively, simply select your layer; then choose Filter ➪ Convert for Smart Filters. A dialog box pointing out that your layer is about to be turned into a Smart Object appears; select the Don't Show Again option in the dialog box if it bugs you.

After you choose a filter from the Filter menu, you usually see a dialog box appear that allows you to tweak various settings for the filter, much like using the filter in "destructive" mode. Make your changes — remembering that you can always go back and change them later — and click OK to apply the filter. You might want to select the Preview option in the dialog box while you're making your changes, so that you can see them reflected in the document window.

Now that you've applied your Smart Filter, you see that the Smart Object in the Layers palette has changed, as shown in Figure 8.9. First of all, a small lens filter icon appears within the Smart Object, indicating that the Smart Object has Smart Filters applied. The little arrow to the right of the icon allows you to show or hide the Smart Filters, as well as any layer effects associated with the Smart Object. A Smart Filters item also appears below the Smart Object. This item has its own thumbnail — the filter mask thumbnail — that is explained in a moment. Finally, below the Smart Filters item you can see the name of the filter that you added, along with an eye icon for toggling the effect of the filter on and off, and a sliders icon that you can use to adjust the filter's blending options.

Editing Smart Filters

After you add your Smart Filter to your Smart Object, you can tweak the filter's settings at any time simply by double-clicking the filter name in the Layers palette. Alternatively, right-click the filter name and choose Edit Smart Filter from the pop-up menu. The filter's dialog box reappears; make your changes to the filter's settings, then click OK to apply the new settings, or Cancel to back out and return to the previous settings.

FIGURE 8.9

A Smart Object in the Layers palette with a Gaussian Blur Smart Filter applied

Smart Object   Filter mask thumbnail

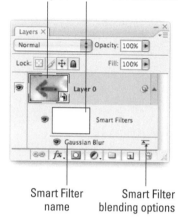

Smart Filter   Smart Filter
name   blending options

TIP   You can also hold down Alt (Option on the Mac) to turn the Cancel button into a Reset button; click this button to return the filter settings to the state they were in when you first displayed the dialog.

As you'd expect, you can click the eye icon next to a filter in the Layers palette to disable the filter temporarily. Click the eye icon again to reenable it. If you prefer, you can right-click the filter name in the palette and choose Enable Smart Filter or Disable Smart Filter from the pop-up menu.

You can also click the eye icon next to the Smart Filters item to disable all filters for that Smart Object; click the eye icon again to reenable those filters that were previously enabled. Alternatively, select the Smart Object; then choose Layer ➪ Smart Filter ➪ Disable/Enable Smart Filters.

To delete a Smart Filter altogether, click and drag its name in the Layers palette down to the trash icon at the bottom of the palette, or right-click it and choose Delete Smart Filter from the menu. To delete all Smart Filters for a Smart Object, click and drag its Smart Filters item to the trash icon, or right-click the Smart Filters item and choose Clear Smart Filters from the pop-up menu. You can also select the Smart Object and choose Layer ➪ Smart Filter ➪ Clear Smart Filters.

CAUTION   Using Clear Smart Filters, or deleting the last Smart Filter for a Smart Object, also destroys the filter mask associated with the Smart Object. (More on filter masks in the section "Masking Smart Filters.")

One great feature of Smart Filters is that you can reorder them within a Smart Object in the Layers palette, thereby changing the order that the filters are applied to the Smart Object. For example, add an Unsharp Mask filter to a photo to sharpen it, then add a Lens Flare filter on top; Photoshop applies the Lens Flare after the Unsharp Mask. You can then reverse this order by clicking and dragging the Unsharp Mask filter above the Lens Flare filter in the Layers palette. Now the Unsharp Mask filter sharpens both the photo and the Lens Flare filter. After you add three or four filters to the mix, you have a lot of room for experimentation.

Reordering Smart Filters is simply a case of clicking a filter name in the Layers palette and dragging it to its new position. As you drag, a thick black horizontal bar appears in the Layers palette, indicating where the filter will be placed when you release the mouse button. Hold down Alt (Option on the Mac) to copy your filter to its new location, rather than moving it.

NOTE If you edit a Smart Filter that sits underneath one or more other filters in the same Smart Object, the filters above that Smart Filter are temporarily disabled while you edit it. This is also true if you edit the Smart Filter's blending mode (which you get to later in the chapter). This means that you can only preview the Smart Filter you're editing, along with any filters below. Photoshop displays a dialog box warning you of this when you try to edit the Smart Filter; as always, select the Don't Show Again check box if the dialog box annoys you.

Speaking of dragging Smart Filters, you can change the Smart Object that a Smart Filter is applied to by dragging the filter from one Smart Object to another in the Layers palette. This moves the filter; if you'd rather duplicate it, hold down Alt (Option on the Mac) before you drag. To move or copy all filters from one Smart Object to another — including the filter mask — drag or Alt/Option+drag the Smart Filters item (not the filter mask thumbnail).

NOTE Some filters — and therefore some Smart Filters — don't work in all color modes or color depths. For example, if you convert a document containing Smart Filters from one color mode to another — say, from RGB to Lab — and you don't rasterize your Smart Objects during the conversion, you may find that some Smart Filters no longer have any effect. You'll see a little warning triangle appear next to each errant Smart Filter in the Layers palette, alerting you to the problem.

Masking Smart Filters

Each Smart Object comes with its own special mask — known as the *filter mask* — that you can use to shape the effects of any Smart Filters that you apply to the Smart Object. You can move or edit the mask at any time to change which areas of the image are affected by the filters.

NOTE This is a very handy feature unique to Smart Filters, although with a bit of work you can get similar results with regular filters. To do this, duplicate your layer, move the duplicate above the original in the Layers palette, add a layer mask to the duplicate, then apply your filters to the masked layer. You can then edit your layer mask to restrict the filters to certain parts of the image. (Masked-off areas reveal the lower unfiltered image layer.)

Masking off filters is great for situations such as sharpening foreground detail without touching soft background detail, thereby adding more punch to your images. Or try adding an artistic Smart Filter such as Watercolor, filling the filter mask with black, then painting on the mask with white at 10 percent opacity to gradually add the watercolor effect to areas of the image.

The filter mask has its own thumbnail, which you can see next to the Smart Filters item in the Layers palette (shown in Figure 8.9). This mask behaves much like a layer mask. It's white by default, which means that the filters apply to the whole image.

CROSS-REF To find out more about layer masks — which work in a similar way to filter masks — see Chapter 9.

To work on the mask, click its thumbnail to make the mask active; a border appears around the thumbnail. You can now paint on the mask with black or shades of gray to mask off areas of the image from the filter effects. To return to working on the Smart Object, click the Smart Object's thumbnail to make it active, or simply click away from the filter thumbnail in the Layers palette.

You can see an example of Smart Filter masking in Figure 8.10. A Torn Edges Smart Filter is used to add a little "dirt" to the black-and-white photo. The effect is a little strong in certain areas of the image, so large black brushes at around 20% opacity are used to paint onto the filter mask to lessen the effect of the filter in those areas.

FIGURE 8.10

Smart Filter masking in action. The effect of this Torn Edges Smart Filter on the sea, the stones, and the shadow is lessened by painting onto the filter mask using semitransparent black brushes.

CAUTION If your filter mask is active, don't forget that all edits you make are made to the mask, not the Smart Object. This includes adding (destructive) filters! It's quite easy to accidentally add a destructive filter to the mask, when in fact you meant to add a new Smart Filter to the Smart Object. To add the Smart Filter, click away from the filter mask thumbnail first.

You can view the filter mask on its own by Alt+clicking (Option+clicking on the Mac) the mask's thumbnail in the Layers palette. Alt/Option+click the thumbnail again to return to viewing the image. To view both mask and image at the same time, Alt+Shift+click (Option+Shift+click on the Mac) the mask thumbnail. The mask appears as a color overlay, much like working with the Quick Mask mode. To return to viewing just the image, Alt+Shift+click (Option+Shift+click on the Mac) the mask thumbnail again.

To change the appearance of the mask's overlay, double-click the mask thumbnail. You can change the color of the overlay by clicking the Color box and choosing a color in the Color Picker dialog box that appears. You can also change the overlay's opacity setting using the Opacity box, which allows you to choose how much of the underlying image shows through the overlay. Values range from 0 percent (an invisible overlay) up to 100 percent (a solid overlay).

NOTE   These settings only change the appearance of the overlay; they don't touch the underlying mask or filters.

Just as a layer mask has its own alpha channel, so does a filter mask. You can view this mask in the Channels palette; select the Smart Object in the Layers palette, then view the Channels palette by choosing Window ➪ Channels. You see the mask at the bottom of the palette; it has the same name as the Smart Object, with the words "Filter Mask" tacked onto the end of the name. You can work with this channel just like any other alpha channel in Photoshop. You only see the channel in the Channels palette while its associated Smart Object is active; if you want to save a copy of the channel on a more permanent basis, click and drag the channel down to the New icon at the bottom of the palette.

CROSS-REF   Alpha channels are explored in more detail in Chapter 9.

You can load a filter mask as a selection by Ctrl+clicking (⌘+clicking on the Mac) the mask thumbnail in the Layers palette. For more fine-grained control, you can do the following:

- Ctrl+Shift+click (⌘+Shift+click on the Mac) the mask's thumbnail to add the mask to an existing selection. Or you can right-click the thumbnail and choose Add Filter Mask to Selection.

- Ctrl+Alt+click (⌘+Option+click on the Mac) the thumbnail to subtract the mask from an existing selection. Alternatively, right-click the thumbnail and choose Subtract Filter Mask from Selection.

- Ctrl+Alt+Shift+click (⌘+Option+Shift+click on the Mac) the thumbnail to load the intersection of the mask and an existing selection. Or right-click the thumbnail and choose Intersect Filter Mask with Selection.

You can temporarily disable a filter mask, allowing the filters to affect the whole area of the image. To do this, Shift+click the mask thumbnail, or right-click the thumbnail and choose Disable Filter Mask from the pop-up menu. To delete a filter mask altogether, click and drag its thumbnail to the Delete Layer (trash) icon at the bottom of the Layers palette, or click the mask thumbnail to make it active and click the Delete Layer icon. You can also right-click the thumbnail and choose Delete

Filter Mask. Use whichever method is quickest for you. If you later want to add a filter mask again, right-click the Smart Filters item and choose Add Filter Mask from the pop-up menu.

Setting Smart Filter blending options

Another great benefit of using a Smart Filter is that you can apply any of Photoshop's range of layer blending modes to it and also adjust its opacity, giving you even more creative control over your filters. It's a great way to add subtlety and depth to the effect of a filter. For example, in Figure 8.11 a Pin Light blending mode is used on a Grain Smart Filter to soften the effect of the filter.

FIGURE 8.11

Tweaking filter effects using blending modes. In the first example (left), the Grain Smart Filter is applied at full opacity with a Normal blending mode. In the second case (right), the filter's blending mode is set to Pin Light and its opacity reduced to 45 percent. The effect with the Pin Light mode applied is much less intense.

When it comes to blending, a Smart Filter behaves as if it were a layer on top of its Smart Object. The filter effect blends with the Smart Object below, using your chosen blending mode and opacity setting, to produce the final result. For example, choose a Luminosity blending mode for the filter, and Photoshop applies only the brightness values of the filter to the Smart Object's contents, ignoring any hue and saturation components of the filter effect.

CROSS-REF For more on how blending modes work as well as a detailed description of each mode, refer to Chapter 7.

The blending mode of a Smart Filter defaults to Normal. To change the filter's mode, as well as set its opacity, proceed as follows:

1. **Display the Blending Options dialog box.** Double-click the little sliders icon to the right of the filter name in the Layers palette, as shown in Figure 8.9. You can also right-click the filter name in the palette, and choose Edit Smart Filter Blending Options from the pop-up menu. The Blending Options dialog box, as shown in Figure 8.12, appears.

FIGURE 8.12

The Blending Options dialog box lets you change the Smart Filter's blending mode and opacity.

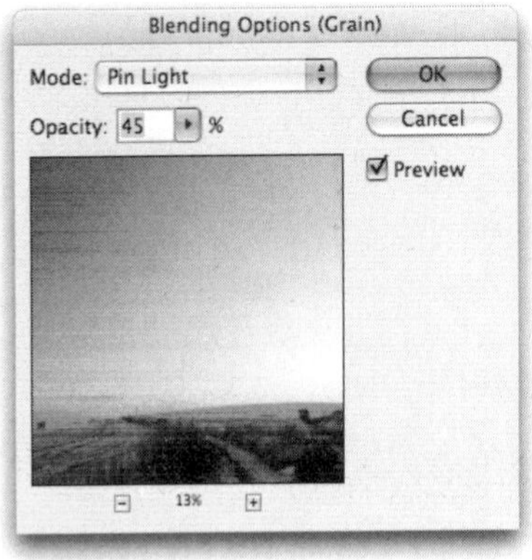

2. **Adjust the filter's blending mode and opacity.** Use the Mode option to change the blending mode of the filter; use the Opacity setting to adjust the opacity of the filter. An opacity of 100 percent — the default — displays the full effect of the filter on the Smart Object, while a value of 0 percent renders the filter invisible.

3. **Preview your changes.** You'll see the preview image in the dialog update to reflect your chosen settings. If you select the Preview option, you can also see your new settings applied in the document window. Click the plus (+) and minus (-) buttons at the bottom of the dialog box to zoom in and out of the image in the preview window; click in the document window to move the preview window around the image. You can also drag the preview window itself to move the preview around.

4. **Commit or cancel your changes.** Click OK to commit your changes, click Cancel to back out, or Alt+click (Option+click on the Mac) Cancel to reset the dialog box to the state it was in when it first appeared.

Exporting and Replacing Smart Objects

If you want to work with the contents of a Smart Object on their own, you can export them to a separate document. To do this, select the Smart Object and choose Layer ⇨ Smart Objects ⇨ Export Contents. A Save dialog box appears that allows you to choose a name and location for the exported document; by default, Photoshop names the document after the Smart Object. Click Save to finish the export.

Smart Objects with content created in Photoshop are exported as a PSB (Large Document Format) file, while Smart Objects containing vector content — such as that produced in Illustrator — are saved as a PDF file.

You can also replace the contents of a Smart Object with the contents of another file. This is much like using the Place command (File ➪ Place) to place a file as a new Smart Object, except that you're replacing the content in an existing Smart Object instead. When you do this, Photoshop automatically stretches or squeezes the file's contents to fill the space taken up by the previous contents. In addition, all linked Smart Objects are updated with the new contents, making it a great way to swap out an image across the board.

To replace a Smart Object's contents, select the Smart Object and choose Layer ➪ Smart Objects ➪ Replace Contents. You can also right-click the Smart Object in the Layers palette and choose Replace Contents from the pop-up menu. A file chooser appears. Select the file that you want to use — you can import any file format that Photoshop recognizes — and click Place to replace the contents.

Tutorial: Using Smart Objects in Practice

In this tutorial, you look at Smart Objects in action, and create a "flock" of love hearts floating in the sky. Smart Objects are great for this kind of application, as you can make edits to the original Smart Object and see your changes update across all occurrences of the object.

Start by creating a document to work on. Choose File ➪ New, and create a document 400 pixels square at 72 pixels/inch.

Create your basic heart as follows:

1. **Create the heart shape.** Select the Custom Shape tool and, in the options bar, make sure the Shape Layers option is selected. Click in the Shape box and choose a love heart shape from the picker. Make the foreground color a nice, warm pink. An RGB value of 242, 25, 96 is good. Now, in the document window, click and drag out the heart shape while holding down Shift to constrain the proportions. Make it a good size; about a quarter to a third of the height of the document window is about right.

2. **Add a drop shadow.** Click the Add a Layer Style button in the Layers palette and choose Drop Shadow from the pop-up menu. The Layer Style dialog box appears with the Drop Shadow effect active. You just want a simple drop shadow with an Opacity of 60 percent, a Distance and Spread of 0, and a Size of 13 pixels.

3. **Add a bevel.** While in the Layer Style dialog box, select the Bevel and Emboss option to add a sense of 3-D to the heart. Set Style to Inner Bevel, Technique to Smooth, and Depth to 21 percent. Choose Up for the Direction, and set the Size to 54 pixels and the Soften option to 6 pixels. Set Angle to 130 degrees and Altitude to 48 degrees. Leave the other settings at their defaults. When you finish, click OK to close the dialog box.

4. **Add some highlights.** Click the New Layer icon in the Layers palette, and select the Brush tool. Make the foreground color white. In the options bar, click the Brush box and set the brush diameter to around 25 pixels. Now draw a highlight on the top left of the heart, as shown in Figure 8.13. Set that layer to have a blending mode of Soft Light. This extra highlight gives the heart a slightly cartoony feel.

5. **Make the heart a Smart Object.** Select both the heart and the highlight layers by Ctrl+clicking (⌘+clicking on the Mac) both layers in the Layers palette. Choose Layer ➪ Smart Objects ➪ Convert to Smart Object. Your layers are grouped into a new Smart Object in the Layers palette. Double-click the Smart Object's name and rename it **Heart**.

FIGURE 8.13

Adding a highlight to the heart using the Brush tool

Great, your first Smart Object is in place. Now create a duplicate heart in the same document, and edit it so that you have two slightly different versions, as follows:

1. **Copy the heart Smart Object.** Normally, if you duplicate a Smart Object by clicking and dragging to the New Layer icon, the two copies are linked together. If you then edit either the copy or the original, both update to reflect your changes. In this case, though, you want to create an independent copy. To do that, select the Smart Object in the Layers palette, and choose Layer ➪ Smart Objects ➪ New Smart Object via Copy.

2. **Reposition and resize one of the hearts.** Using the Move tool, position one of the hearts behind the other, with some of the underlying heart showing. You want the bottom heart to be just a little smaller than the top, so scale it down by choosing Edit ➪ Transform ➪ Scale.

3. **Open the underlying heart for editing.** Here comes the clever bit. Double-click the thumbnail of the underlying heart in the Layers palette. Photoshop displays a dialog box with some instructions about how to edit Smart Objects. Click OK to continue. The

Smart Object opens as a new Photoshop document, with both the original layers intact and ready to edit. It opens as a PSB file. This is because your Smart Object is really just a Photoshop file embedded into your document, albeit a PSB file rather than a PSD.

4. **Edit and save the heart.** Within the opened Smart Object, double-click the layer thumbnail of the shape layer, and change its fill color to a darker pink, say RGB 213, 3, 71. Save and close the PSB file. In the original document, the heart at the back changes to a darker pink than the one in front, while the topmost heart remains unchanged.

This darker heart adds depth to the composition. Double-click the darker heart Smart Object's name in the Layers palette; rename it **Darker Heart**.

You now have two separate Smart Objects with which to build your flock of hearts, as shown in Figure 8.14.

FIGURE 8.14

These two heart Smart Objects — one based on the other, but separately editable — form the basis for your composition.

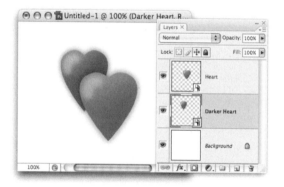

You can now start to duplicate the Smart Objects to form clusters of hearts. First, take a copy of the Heart Smart Object by clicking and dragging it to the New Layer icon in the Layers palette. Using the Move tool with the Show Transform Controls option selected, reposition and resize the duplicate to be smaller than, and slightly away from, the original heart. Do the same for the Darker Heart Smart Object.

When you have four hearts, select all four Smart Objects in the Layers palette, and choose Layer ➪ Smart Objects ➪ Convert to Smart Object. You now have a single Smart Object containing four other Smart Objects. Rename this new Smart Object **Cluster 1**. You can see your new Cluster 1 Smart Object in Figure 8.15.

FIGURE 8.15

The Cluster 1 Smart Object contains two copies each of your Heart and Darker Heart Smart Objects, making four heart shapes in all.

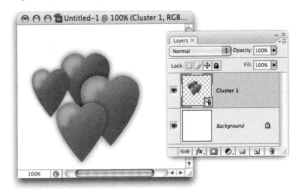

Now, duplicate the Cluster 1 Smart Object by selecting it and choosing Layer ➪ Smart Objects ➪ New Smart Object via Copy. Rename this new Smart Object **Cluster 2**. Using the Move tool, reposition Cluster 2 so that it sits on top of, but away from, the original cluster of hearts. It's looking pretty good at this point, but you can tell that it's a copy of the original. Luckily, you can now edit Cluster 2 to move and resize the elements inside it without affecting Cluster 1, because you chose the New Smart Object via Copy when creating the duplicate.

In the Layers palette, double-click the Cluster 2 Smart Object, and click OK to close the informational dialog box that appears. (You can turn this off by selecting the Don't Show Again check box if you've got the hang of the idea.) The original four Smart Objects appear in the document window, ready for repositioning and resizing. Use the Move tool with the Show Transform Controls option selected to quickly reposition and resize the hearts. Remember, you're working with Smart Objects here, so you can transform the hearts as many times as you want with no loss in quality. You can even duplicate some of the hearts further, so that each cluster has a different number of hearts, as shown in Figure 8.16.

When you're happy with your edits, save and close the file. Your changes are reflected in the main document.

You can now use a nice feature of Smart Objects and apply a layer style to the whole of Cluster 2. To do this, select Cluster 2 in the Layers palette, and click the Add a Layer Style icon at the bottom of the palette. Choose Drop Shadow from the pop-up menu. We want a big, diffuse shadow, so set Distance and Spread to 0 and Size to around 40 pixels, and click OK to apply the effect. You'll see that the shadow has been applied to the whole of Cluster 2.

FIGURE 8.16

Repositioning and resizing the hearts inside Cluster 2, the copied cluster of hearts. An extra heart — Heart Copy 2 — has also been created by duplicating the original Heart Smart Object. You can see the main document in the background as Cluster 2 is being edited.

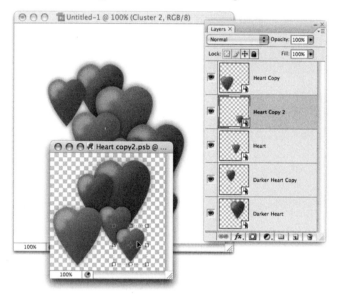

To really fill out the image, make and edit another copy based on Cluster 1. To do this, follow these steps:

1. **Copy the Cluster 1 Smart Object.** Select Cluster 1 in the Layers palette, and choose Layer ⇨ Smart Objects ⇨ New Smart Object via Copy. Rename this Smart Object **Cluster 3**.

2. **Reposition the copy.** Use the Move tool to position the cluster slightly away from the other two.

3. **Edit the copy.** Double-click the thumbnail of Cluster 3 in the Layers palette to edit the Smart Object in a new window. Using the Move tool, reposition and resize the individual Heart and Darker Heart Smart Objects, and their copies, until you have a good spread of hearts. When you're happy, save and close the file. The Cluster 3 Smart Object in the main document updates to reflect your edits.

You can now create more depth to the composition by clicking and dragging this new Smart Object upward in the Layers palette to sit on top of the others. Remember, you can go back at any point and tinker with the positions and sizes of the hearts, which makes for a very flexible approach. You could even continue to cluster the hearts, creating a really dense image using just those two original hearts. The final design can be seen in Figure 8.17.

FIGURE 8.17

The final design, using multiple nested Smart Objects to create a cluster of hearts

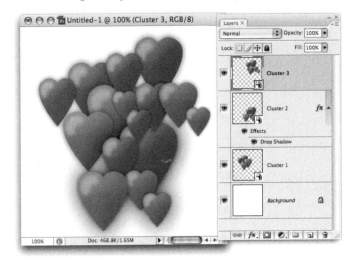

Summary

In this chapter on Smart Objects, you learned what Smart Objects are and why they're useful; not only do they allow you to transform bitmaps nondestructively, but you can link Smart Objects together so that you only have to worry about updating one Smart Object. They're also a great way to embed other content, such as Illustrator artwork, as a layer inside your Photoshop document. Smart Objects also allow you to apply Smart Filters — a new technology in Photoshop CS3 that lets you apply "live," reeditable filters to your images.

You learned how to create a Smart Object from an existing layer or layers, from Illustrator artwork, and from any image file. You looked at how to edit the contents of a Smart Object, as well as duplicating Smart Objects and nesting Smart Objects inside each other, opening up a world of creative possibilities. How to convert a Smart Object back into a regular bitmap layer and, of course, how to delete Smart Objects were also covered.

Next, you took a good look at Smart Filters and how you can apply them to your Smart Objects, mask them off, and change their blending modes. You also learned how to export the content embedded in a Smart Object to a separate document and how to replace the contents of a Smart Object with those in an external image file. Finally, all this knowledge was brought together in a practical example that showed you how to use nested Smart Objects to create a versatile, completely reeditable "flock" of love hearts.

Chapter 9

Working with Masks

asks are one of those areas of Photoshop that you can happily ignore for years and yet still be perfectly productive. Once you start delving into them, though, they can open up a whole new world — a world where selections are easier to make, and where layers become much less cumbersome to work with.

Broadly speaking, masks in Photoshop are used for two distinct purposes. First, they can be used in the same way as selections, allowing you to work on selected areas of your image while masking off, or protecting, other areas from editing. This is a bit like using masking tape to protect areas that you don't want to paint on. Second, you can use them to hide unwanted areas of your image, while still keeping those areas available for later use or editing. Think of adding a sheet of acetate on top of your layer, then painting black onto the sheet.

Photoshop gives you various types of masks to play with, including Quick Masks, alpha channels, layer masks, vector masks, and clipping masks. Quick Masks and alpha channels are more commonly used to make selections, while the other types of masks tend to be used to hide areas of an image. It's important to remember, though, that masks are fundamentally the same, regardless of which use you put them to. You can use a mask as a selection one minute, then use the same mask to hide parts of your image the next.

This chapter takes you through all the different types of masks available in Photoshop, concentrating mainly on masking layers with layer masks, vector masks, and clipping masks. Along the way, various masking techniques are explored with some practical examples.

Types of Masks

As mentioned earlier, a mask can be used to protect certain areas of your image so that you can't accidentally modify them, or it can be used to hide areas of your image. All masks in Photoshop share these basic concepts, but you can use different types of masks to achieve different things.

There are two fundamental types of masks in Photoshop:

- **Bitmap mask:** This is by far the most common mask type. In fact, bitmap masks are so common that they're often just referred to as masks. A bitmap mask is simply a grayscale image, with the same width and height as the image it's masking. The exact shade of gray of each pixel in the mask determines whether or not that pixel is masked off in the image. If the pixel is black, the image pixel is masked off. If it's white, then the image pixel isn't masked off. If it's gray, then the image pixel is partially masked off, creating semitransparent areas of the mask — perfect for creating feathered edges, for example. As you see in a moment, when you make a selection with one of the selection tools, you essentially create a bitmap mask behind the scenes. The selected areas map to white in the mask; unselected areas map to black; feathered edges map to various shades of gray.

- **Vector mask:** As you might imagine, vector masks use vector paths to mask off areas in the image. Rather than drawing on the mask using the bitmap painting tools, you draw on it using the pen or shape tools. Create a closed path, and all the parts of your image inside the path are revealed, while all the parts outside it are hidden. In Photoshop, you can store vector masks as paths in the Paths palette, just like you can store bitmap masks in the Channels palette.

You can see a bitmap mask and a vector mask being edited in Figure 9.1.

All the types of masks discussed in the following sections are based on these two fundamental mask types. They're pretty much all bitmap masks, with the exception of vector masks (naturally).

FIGURE 9.1

Editing a bitmap mask — in this case, a layer mask (left) — and reshaping a vector mask (right). You alter bitmap masks with brushes and the other painting tools; you shape vector masks using the pen tools, shape tools, anchor point tools, and the Path and Direct Selection tools.

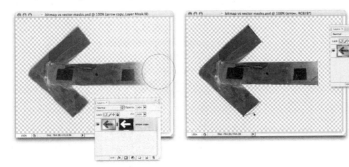

General masks

There are a couple of mask types that aren't directly connected to layers, but they are covered in this chapter, partly because they serve as a good introduction to masks in general, and partly because they're pretty essential reading in their own right:

- **Selection masks:** Whenever you make a selection in Photoshop, you create a selection mask behind the scenes. This type of mask is used by Photoshop to remember which parts of your image you've selected, and which parts you haven't.

- **Alpha channels:** These are channels that appear in the Channels palette, much like the regular color and composite channels. Their main purpose is to store masks, and they're often used to save selections permanently along with the document.

Selection masks and alpha channels work on the whole image, independently from any layers in the document. Both of these masks, as well as Photoshop's handy Quick Mask mode, are covered in some detail in the section "Exploring Selection Masks and Alpha Channels" later in this chapter.

These mask types are commonly used to create, edit, and store selections. Photoshop lets you easily convert from a selection to a mask, and vice versa. In fact, you can think of masking as the inverse of selecting. When you select part of an image with a selection tool, you're really masking off the unselected parts. Similarly, when you paint on a mask to hide areas of your image, you're selecting the parts you haven't painted on.

So why not just stick with normal selections? After all, Photoshop gives you a range of wonderful selection tools, from the basic Marquee tools for selecting geometric shapes through to the Lasso and Magic Wand tools that, with a bit of practice, you can use to select all sorts of awkward and esoteric shapes. You can draw a precise path with the Pen tool and turn that into a selection. So why do you need masks as well?

Well, there are many selection tasks that these tools just can't cope with. The classic one is selecting wispy, wavy hair on a person's head; this is notoriously difficult to do. Or consider trying to select natural objects, such as a tree, or hundreds of blades of grass. If you try that with the Lasso tool you'll be there well into the night.

Here are some of the great things masks can offer that the regular selection tools can't:

- You can paint on a mask with any paint tool, apply filters to the mask, and even select parts of the mask with the selection tools. In fact, virtually anything that you can do to a regular image, you can do to a mask.

- You can easily work right down to the pixel level, which gives you really fine control over reshaping your selection.

- Because you can use practically any tool to modify a mask, they're very easy to edit. For example, it's usually easier to add an irregular-shaped area to a mask using the Eraser tool than it is to use the Lasso tool.

- Feathering a selected area with a mask is as simple as painting on it with shades of gray. This gives you much finer control over feathering than the selection tools do; for example, one edge of your selected area can be hard and the opposite edge can be feathered.

Masks specific to layers

The remaining mask types in Photoshop are all related to layers in one way or another. They all work on individual layers or bunches of layers, rather than applying to the whole image.

Layer-specific masks include:

- **Layer masks:** (The name is a bit of a giveaway.) A layer mask is a bitmap mask channel tied to an individual layer, and it masks off parts of the layer it's associated with.

- **Vector masks:** These are the vector-based equivalent of layer masks. Like layer masks, a vector mask is associated with an individual layer, but rather than using pixels to mask off areas of the layer, it uses vector paths to define the boundaries of the mask.

CROSS-REF You can have both a layer mask and a vector mask on a single layer, which gives you a lot of flexibility with your masking. Learn how to do this in the section "Combining Layer and Vector Masks" later in this chapter.

- **Clipping masks:** Instead of using a separate mask channel or path to do its masking, a clipping mask uses the transparency mask of one layer to mask off areas of one or more layers above it. They're the "masks you don't have to make".

- **Transparency masks:** Each layer has an invisible transparency mask that defines which pixels in the layer are opaque and which are transparent (or semitransparent). Like selection masks, you don't see these masks in everyday use; they kind of lurk behind the curtain, minding their own business. But without them, layers wouldn't be much use at all.

TIP You can actually load a layer's transparency mask as a selection by Ctrl+clicking (⌘+clicking on the Mac) the layer's thumbnail. See? Transparency masks really do exist. While you're at it, you can add the mask to an existing selection by holding down Shift also; subtract the mask from a selection by holding down Alt (Option on the Mac) also; and for a real finger-twister, hold down Ctrl+Alt+Shift (⌘+Option+Shift on the Mac) to load the intersection of the mask and selection. All these options are also available by right-clicking the thumbnail to bring up a pop-up menu. Choose Select Pixels to load the mask as a selection, Add Transparency Mask to add the mask to a selection, Subtract Transparency Mask to subtract the mask from a selection, or Intersect Transparency Mask to load the intersection of mask and selection.

Although these mask types are fundamentally similar to selection masks and alpha channels, they're normally used in a very different way. Rather than selecting areas of your image for editing, they're used to hide unwanted areas. The difference is sometimes subtle, though, and you can easily switch between both uses — which, of course, is what makes masks so wonderfully flexible.

Exploring Selection Masks and Alpha Channels

Let's dive into masks and masking techniques by taking a look at a couple of mask types: selection masks and alpha channels. Although these two mask types aren't directly related to layers, they're pretty important in Photoshop, and they're a good way to help you understand how masking works in general. So pull up a chair and begin.

Using selection masks and the Quick Mask mode

Selection masks are one of the easiest types of masks to understand. Whenever you create a selection in Photoshop using one of the selection tools, you create a selection mask. You don't normally see it, but it's there.

The selection marquee (or "marching ants") around your selection defines the boundaries between the selected (white) areas of the selection mask and the unselected (black) areas of the mask. You can see this in Figure 9.2, which shows a selection marquee and its corresponding selection mask.

FIGURE 9.2

A selection marquee (left) and its equivalent selection mask (right)

As mentioned earlier, feathered areas of a selection are represented by gray pixels in a mask. Figure 9.3 shows a feathered selection and its selection mask. Here, the same selection that was made previously is feathered by choosing Select ➪ Feather (a feather radius of 30 pixels is used). Although the selection marquee still has a hard edge to it, the mask clearly shows the feathering as various shades of gray.

FIGURE 9.3

Here is the same selection feathered. Notice how the selection marquee still has a hard edge (left) but the selection mask now shows the feathered areas as shades of gray (right).

NOTE   You may be wondering why the marquee still has a hard edge, even though the selection is feathered. The selection marquee represents the boundaries between areas of the selection mask that are darker than 50 percent gray, and areas that are lighter than (or equal to) 50 percent gray. In your original selection, the marquee exactly follows the boundary, because a non-feathered selection transitions sharply from white (selected) pixels to black (unselected). When you feather your selection, you're blurring the darker and lighter pixels on either side of the boundary, but the mid-gray point on the boundary stays the same. Hence the marquee retains its hard edge.

Using the Quick Mask mode

Now that you know a selection is essentially a mask, wouldn't it be good if you could actually view this selection mask and edit it, too? This is exactly what the Quick Mask mode is for.

Correcting the contrast of a washed-out photo with a Levels adjustment layer.
On the left, the original photo, and on the right, the corrected version.

Blending modes let you combine two or more layers together in a variety of interesting ways.
The-left hand images below are the two original photos used in all the blending mode examples. To the right of these are examples of the Darken and Multiply blending modes.

The Two Original Photos

Read about blending modes in Chapter 7.

Darken

Multiply

Blending Modes: Color Burn, Linear Burn, and Darker Color.

Color Burn

Linear Burn

Read about blending modes in Chapter 7.

Darker Color

Blending Modes: Lighten, Screen, and Color Dodge.

Lighten

Screen

Read about blending
modes in Chapter 7.

Color Dodge

Blending Modes: Linear Dodge (Add), Lighter Color, and Overlay.

Linear Dodge (Add)

Lighter Color

Read about blending modes in Chapter 7.

Overlay

Blending Modes: Soft Light, Hard Light, and Vivid Light.

Soft Light

Hard Light

Read about blending
modes in Chapter 7.

Vivid Light

Blending Modes: Linear Light, Pin Light, and Hard Mix.

Linear Light

Pin Light

Read about blending
modes in Chapter 7.

Hard Mix

Blending Modes: Difference, Exclusion, and Hue.

Difference

Exclusion

Read about blending
modes in Chapter 7.

Hue

Blending Modes: Saturation, Color, and Luminosity.

Saturation

Color

Read about blending
modes in Chapter 7.

Luminosity

__Painting on a layer mask with various shades of gray to control transparency.__

Get to know masks
in Chapter 9.

Removing a background and creating a composite image using a layer mask.

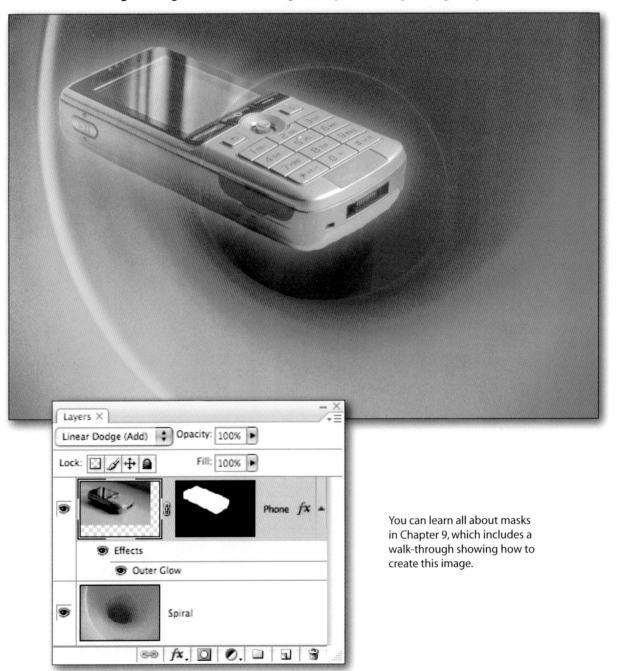

You can learn all about masks in Chapter 9, which includes a walk-through showing how to create this image.

Creating a logo using layer styles and shape layers.

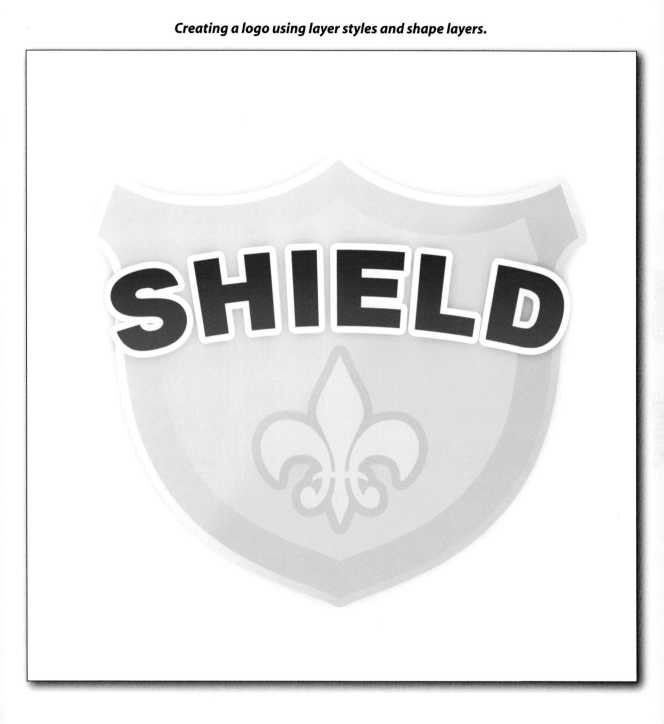

Read the full tutorial and all about layer styles in Chapter 10.

Creating a mixed-media illustration using scanned material.

Sharpen your pencils and read all about it in Chapter 14.

Retouching a landscape using layer masks and adjustment layers.

The top image is the starting point, and the bottom one is the final result.
Learn how to achieve this in Chapter 15.

Fixing color casts in a photo using a Levels adjustment layer.

The original image above, with the corrected version on the right. Learn more about adjustment layers in Chapter 6, and read the full tutorial for this example in Chapter 15.

Retouching a portrait using adjustment layers, masks, blending modes, and Smart Objects.

The image on the left is the starting photo, and the image below shows the portrait after retouching. This kind of work is certainly not to everyone's tastes, but it's useful to know how to apply the techniques when necessary! Read the full tutorial in Chapter 15.

Get the lowdown on how to create this poster in Chapter 16.

To use Quick Mask, make a selection using one of the selection tools; then click the Quick Mask button in the Toolbox, as shown in Figure 9.4. To switch back to standard selection mode with the marquee, click the Quick Mask button again. You can also press Q to toggle quickly between Standard and Quick Mask modes.

NEW FEATURE Older versions of Photoshop featured a separate Standard Mode button that you'd use to flip back to the standard selection mode. In CS3, Adobe has sensibly done away with this waste of screen space, and simply made the Quick Mask button a toggle instead.

FIGURE 9.4

Switching to Quick Mask mode. Select an area using a selection tool (left) and then switch to Quick Mask mode (right). The mask appears as a red translucent coating over the image.

When you switch to Quick Mask mode, you'll see your selection represented by the selection mask instead of the regular marching ants. The mask appears as a red overlay on top of the image. The red areas of the overlay represent the unselected, black areas of the mask, and the transparent areas represent the white, or selected, areas of the mask. If you feather your selection, the Quick Mask mode shows the feathered areas as semitransparent red areas.

NOTE Why red, semitransparent red, and transparent? Well, this is just the way the mask appears; it's really grayscale (black to white). Apart from being easier to see over the top of the image than black or gray, the red comes from real-world masking film, commonly red in color, which is laid over an image acetate. Pieces are then cut out of the red sheet, and the whole thing exposed to light-sensitive film. The red sheet prevents light getting through to the film, literally masking off those areas. Meanwhile, the white areas of the Quick Mask show as transparent, to make it clear that those are the selected parts of your image. If they were white, well, you wouldn't be able to see your image, would you?

Now that you're in Quick Mask mode, you can edit your selection as a mask, rather than using the standard selection tools. Try painting on the mask with the Brush tool or removing areas of the mask with the Eraser tool. Masks are grayscale images, so the foreground and background colors change to black and white; if you try painting with a color, it will come out as a shade of gray.

NOTE   As you probably know, the Brush tool always paints with the foreground color, and the Eraser always paints with the background. So if you have a white foreground and black background (the opposite of the default) then the Brush actually "erases" areas of the mask (that is, paints on it with white), while the Eraser "paints" black onto the mask.

You can also fill the mask with a pattern or gradient, or transform the mask using the commands under Edit ➪ Transform. Pretty much anything's possible when working on a mask. Don't worry about affecting your underlying image, either — all the edits you're making only affect the shape of the mask, and therefore the shape of the selection. The image itself remains untouched.

You can also select areas of the mask using any of the selection tools. When you do this, you effectively select parts of the original selection, or "mask the mask." If this all sounds a bit much, try to focus on the mask rather than on the original image; you're painting on the mask, and selecting parts of it, just as if it were an image in its own right. Use any tools that you need to get the mask into shape.

The important thing to remember about the selection mask — and indeed any bitmap mask in Photoshop — is that the areas of the mask that you paint on with black become unselected (masked) in the underlying image, while the areas that you erase, or paint on with white, become selected (unmasked) in the image.

When you're happy with your selection mask, click the Quick Mask Mode button again to return to the normal selection marquee. Notice how the marquee changes to reflect the edits you make to the mask in Quick Mask mode, as shown in Figure 9.5.

NOTE   If you happen to have the Channels palette open when using Quick Mask mode, you may notice that a channel called Quick Mask appears in the palette. It's just a temporary channel to store the mask, and it only appears while you're in Quick Mask mode, so it's not that useful in itself (although you can save a permanent copy of it by dragging it to the New icon at the bottom of the palette). However, it does illustrate an important point: bitmap masks in Photoshop are actually stored as channels. Its thumbnail in the Channels palette illustrates another point, too: The red parts of the mask really are black, and the transparent parts really are white.

Changing the appearance of the Quick Mask

Although the Quick Mask starts off as a translucent red covering over the masked areas of your image, you can change its appearance to suit the image you're working with, or just to suit your tastes (maybe you hate red — who knows?).

To display the Quick Mask Options dialog box, as shown in Figure 9.6, double-click either the Quick Mask button in the Toolbox or the Quick Mask channel in the Channels palette.

FIGURE 9.5

After painting on the mask using the Brush tool (left), we flipped back to the standard selection mode by clicking the Quick Mask Mode button again. You can see that the marquee has now changed to reflect the new mask shape (right).

FIGURE 9.6

The Quick Mask Options dialog box allows you to customize the appearance of the Quick Mask's color overlay.

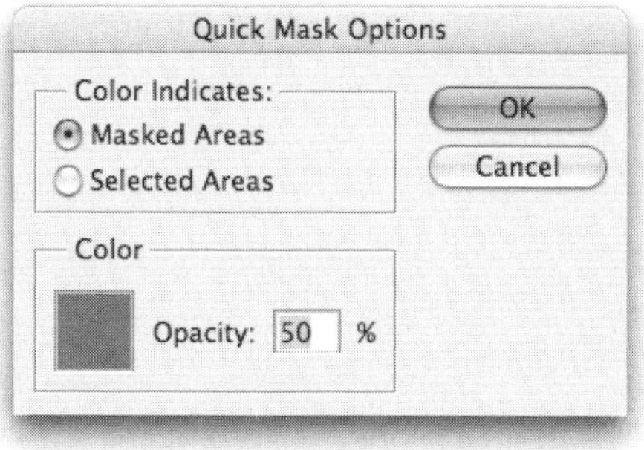

We told a bit of a white lie (pun intended) when we mentioned earlier that white always represents unmasked (selected) areas in a mask and black always represents the masked (unselected) areas. You can, in fact, swap these over, and this is what the options in the Color Indicates section are for:

- **Masked Areas:** This is the default option, with black representing masked areas and white representing selected areas. When selected, the Quick Mask button in the Toolbox becomes a white circle on a gray background.

- **Selected Areas:** This reverses the effect, so that black represents selected areas and white represents masked areas. When you select this option, the Quick Mask button in the Toolbox changes to a gray circle on a white background.

Use whichever option makes more sense to you, but you'll probably want to stick with your choice throughout, or you might start getting really confused. If you do mix and match, keep a close eye on the Quick Mask button so you know which mode you're in. For the purposes of this book, we'll be working with the Masked Areas option selected unless indicated otherwise.

> **TIP** You can quickly toggle between the Masked Areas and Selected Areas options at any time while in Quick Mask mode. To do this, Alt+click (Option+click on the Mac) the Quick Mask button in the Toolbox.

If you're not happy with the default red color used for the black areas of the mask, click the Color box and choose a different value. For example, if your image contains a lot of red areas then you'll have a hard time distinguishing the red overlay from the red parts of the image, so you might want to choose a different color.

The final setting in the dialog box, Opacity, lets you specify how opaque the red overlay is. The default is 50 percent. Change it to 100 percent to make it completely opaque, which lets you see the mask more easily, but at the cost of no longer being able to see the masked-off areas of your image. You can choose any value between 0 percent and 100 percent; set it to 0 percent to make it completely transparent (rather pointless, we're sure you'd agree).

It's important to understand that neither the Color nor the Opacity options affect the mask itself; they merely change the appearance of the mask. For example, just because you increase the overlay's Opacity setting from 50 percent to 100 percent doesn't mean that the mask itself has become more opaque.

Saving selections as alpha channels

It's already been mentioned briefly that most bitmap masks in Photoshop are stored in channels. Some channels are only temporary, such as the Quick Mask channel, which only appears while you're in Quick Mask mode. However, you can save selections and masks to more permanent channels that get saved along with the image. These channels are called *alpha channels*. Photoshop very generously allows you to save over 50 of these channels in each document. (The total number of channels allowed, including the color channels themselves, is 56.)

> **NOTE** The term "alpha channel" comes from the computer graphics technique used to overlay two images on top of each other, known as *alpha compositing*. The alpha channel of the top image determines which pixels should be transparent, allowing the bottom image to show through, and which should be opaque, covering over the bottom image. Because an alpha channel is a separate grayscale channel that sits alongside the color channels of an image, each pixel in the alpha channel can have one of 256 levels of transparency, from fully transparent to fully opaque, in addition to its usual color information. Alpha compositing was developed back in the late 1970s and early 1980s, and it's pretty fundamental to the way that graphics software such as Photoshop functions. In fact, without it Photoshop wouldn't have layers, this book wouldn't exist, and the world would be a frightfully dull place.

Saving a selection

To save your current selection permanently to an alpha channel, choose Selection ➪ Save Selection. The Save Selection dialog box appears, as shown in Figure 9.7, letting you choose where, and how, to save the selection:

- **Document:** This menu lets you choose which document to save the selection in. Usually you'll want to save it as an alpha channel in the current document, which is selected by default. However, you can pick another document from the list, or create a new multi-channel document and create the alpha channel in that; to do this, choose the New option in the menu.

CAUTION Because masks and selections fill the entire image area, you can only save a selection to another document if it has exactly the same width and height as the current image.

- **Channel:** This is where you choose the alpha channel that you want to save the selection to. The default option, New, creates a brand-new alpha channel from your selection.

- **Name:** If you've elected to create a new alpha channel, you can type a name for the new channel here. Go on, you know you want to. If you don't, Photoshop will call it something dull, like Alpha 1.

- **Operation:** If, on the other hand, you decide you want to place your selection into an existing alpha channel, then Photoshop needs to know how you want the selection and channel to be merged. Replace Channel obliterates any existing pixels in the channel with your new selection mask. Add to Channel adds the selected pixels in your selection mask to the channel, turning black pixels white. Subtract from Channel does the opposite, subtracting the selection from the channel and turning white pixels black. Finally, Intersect with Channel deselects (turns to black) everything except the selected areas in both your selection mask and the channel.

TIP The Operation setting can be handy if, for example, you've already selected a tree in a photo, but then you want to add some grass to the same selection so that you can manipulate tree and grass together.

Click OK and Photoshop saves your selection as a new alpha channel, which you can see in the Channels palette (Window ➪ Channels). It also preserves your active selection, so if you've finished with it for now, press Ctrl+D (⌘+D on the Mac) to deselect. Save your document and your selection is now preserved, safe and sound, in that alpha channel.

NOTE You can save your document as a Photoshop file, or as a PDF or a TIFF file, and the alpha channels will be preserved. These three file formats all support up to 56 channels. If you try to save using an image format that can't preserve your alpha channels, Photoshop warns you with a little warning triangle next to Alpha Channels in the Save As dialog box.

FIGURE 9.7

The Save Selection dialog box allows you to save a copy of your current selection mask as an alpha channel, which is then saved along with the image.

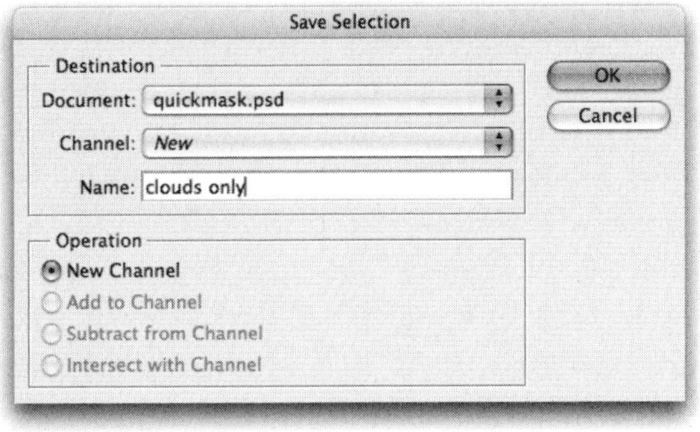

There's also a much quicker way to save your selection to a new alpha channel: simply click the Save Selection as Channel icon at the bottom of the Channels palette. Photoshop then saves your current selection mask as a new alpha channel in the same document. Alt+click (Option+click on the Mac) the Save Selection as Channel icon to set options for the new channel at the same time.

Loading a selection

After you create your alpha channel, what then? Well, you can load the channel as a selection again at any time. The thorough, if slightly long-winded, way to do this is to choose Select ➪ Load Selection, which gives you a dialog box not unlike the Save Selection dialog box, with the following options:

■ **Document:** Again, you can choose which document you want to load the selection into. The default is the current document, which is usually what you want.

■ **Channel:** Pick the channel you want to load. If you already had a channel selected in the Channels palette, this is used as the default.

■ **Invert:** Select this option to invert the channel before you load it into the selection. White, unmasked areas of the channel become black, while the black, masked areas become white.

■ **Operation:** If you already have a selection active for the document, you can choose New to trash that selection and replace it with the loaded selection, or you can choose one of the other three options to merge the selections together; these work just like their counterparts in the Save Selection dialog box described earlier. If you don't already have an active selection, you can only choose New.

There are many quick ways to load an alpha channel as a selection, including the following:

- Select the channel in the Channels palette and then click the Load Channel as Selection icon at the bottom of the palette.

- Just as you can Ctrl+click (⌘+click) a layer's thumbnail in the Layers palette to load its transparency mask as a selection, you can load an alpha channel as a selection by Ctrl/⌘+clicking its thumbnail. (This, and the following shortcuts, even work for paths in the Paths palette.)

- To add an alpha channel to the current selection, Ctrl+Shift+click (⌘+Shift+click on the Mac) its thumbnail in the Channels palette.

- To subtract an alpha channel from the current selection, Ctrl+Alt+click (⌘+Option+click on the Mac) its thumbnail.

- Finally, to intersect an alpha channel with the current selection, Ctrl+Shift+Alt+click (⌘+Shift+Option+click on the Mac) its thumbnail.

> **TIP** You can load any type of channel in the Channels palette as a selection by using the previous shortcuts. For example, you can load any of the color channels, the composite channel, or a spot color channel. This can be handy for isolating certain areas in your image based on color.

Working on alpha channels

You don't have to keep loading alpha channels as selections in order to edit them; you can edit an alpha channel directly as a mask, much like you do in the Quick Mask mode (which we covered earlier in the chapter).

To do this, make sure your composite channel (called "RGB" in RGB mode) in the Channels palette is visible; it should have an eye icon to the left of its thumbnail. Next, click the eye icon next to your chosen alpha channel's thumbnail in the Channels palette to make it visible, too. You'll see a red coating appear over your image, representing the masked areas of the channel, just like the Quick Mask mode. Select the alpha channel by clicking it in the Channels palette, and you can edit it just like a normal image, as shown in Figure 9.8. For example, you can paint on it with a painting tool or fill it with the Gradient tool.

> **TIP** Don't forget to select the channel you want to work on before you start painting. The active channel (highlighted in the Channels palette) is the one that your edits will affect, even if another channel happens to be visible at the time.

If you want to go back to viewing just your image, click the eye icon next to the channel's thumbnail again to hide it. You can also view the alpha channel in isolation, without viewing the image at the same time. To do this, hide all channels except the channel you want to work on by clicking their eye icons. When just one channel is visible, you can see it in its true colors: black, white, and shades of gray.

FIGURE 9.8

Editing an alpha channel directly as a mask.

TIP To toggle the image channels on and off — that is, the composite channel and color channels — press the ~ (tilde) key. This lets you quickly flip between viewing a mask in isolation and viewing the mask with the image. It also works even if you don't have the Channels palette open, which is another plus.

When you're happy with your newly edited channel, you can load it as a selection again as described earlier, then use the selection as you like.

As with the Quick Mask mode, you can select parts of the alpha channel you're working on by using the selection tools, then work on just that part of the channel. You can even go one stage further, and edit that selection in Quick Mask mode — simply click the Quick Mask Mode button in the Toolbox as usual. You're now editing the selection mask of a selection that you made on an alpha channel mask, that in turn may well have come from a selection. Confused yet? You may want to set different overlay colors for the channel and the Quick Mask, if only for your own sanity. If you're really keen, you could save your new selection as a separate alpha channel, then work on that. That's one to impress your friends with.

As if Photoshop's alpha channels weren't powerful enough, you can view, and even edit, multiple channels at the same time. To view more than one channel, make the channels visible using their eye icons in the Channels palette. You'll see the color overlays for each channel appear in the document window, laid on top of each other. Again, you might want to choose different color overlays for each channel, to avoid hurting your brain.

NOTE Somewhat confusingly, the stacking order of channels in the Channels palette works in the opposite direction to the order in the Layers palette. So the image channels at the top of the palette are always on the bottom, and a channel at the bottom of the palette is overlaid over all the other channels.

If you want to edit more than one channel at once, Shift+click all the channels you want to work on in the Channels palette. Now when you paint or use any other editing tool, the edits affect all the channels at once, as shown in Figure 9.9. You probably won't use this feature much, but it can be handy if you need to select an area of your image that is currently masked off by more than one mask, for example.

FIGURE 9.9

Editing multiple alpha channels at once. As you edit one channel, the same edits are applied to the other selected channels.

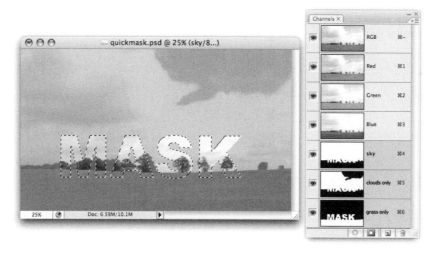

You don't have to create alpha channels from a selection. You can create a new alpha channel from scratch and start editing it directly to create your mask, then load it as a selection when you finish. To quickly create a new alpha channel, simply click the Create New Channel icon at the bottom of the Channels palette. Alternatively, to display the New Channel dialog box so you can give it a name and customize its appearance (see the section "Changing alpha channel appearance"), Alt+click (Option+click on the Mac) the Create New Channel icon. You can also click the Palette Menu icon in the top-right corner of the Channels palette, and choose New Channel from the pop-up menu.

A handy trick is to duplicate one of the color channels in your image and use that as a mask. For example, if the contrast between an object you want to select and its background is greatest in the Red channel, click and drag the Red channel in the Channels palette down to the Create New Channel icon at the bottom of the palette to duplicate it. You can then use the painting tools to refine your mask until you've accurately masked off the background. Then load the channel as a selection to select just the object you were after.

Changing alpha channel appearance

You can customize the appearance of alpha channels in much the same way as you can with the Quick Mask. If you want, you can even set different options for every alpha channel in your document.

367

To customize a channel, double-click the channel thumbnail in the Channels palette to display the Channel Options dialog box. For more info on what the options in the dialog box mean, see the section "Changing the appearance of the Quick Mask" earlier in this chapter. There's also a Name box so you can rename your channel at the same time. (You can also rename channels by double-clicking their names in the Channels palette, much like layers in the Layers palette.)

Using Layer Masks

Now that you've learned the basics of masking by looking at selection masks and alpha channels, you can focus on the mask types that are specific to layers.

This section explores layer masks. These are bitmap masks, much like selection masks and alpha channels. The important difference with a layer mask is that it's tied to a specific layer, and it only masks the pixels on that layer. Also, as mentioned earlier, layer masks — as well as the other layer-specific masks described in the rest of this chapter — are normally used to reveal and hide areas of your layers; selection masks and alpha channels are more commonly used to make selections.

Creating layer masks

You can add a layer mask to a layer in a number of different ways, including the following:

- Select the layer; then click the Add Layer Mask icon at the bottom of the Layers palette (indicated in Figure 9.10). This creates a fully white layer mask (so no pixels of the layer are masked) and attaches it to the layer. Alternatively, choose Layer ➪ Layer Mask ➪ Reveal All.

- Select the layer, then Alt+click (Option+click on the Mac) the Add Layer Mask icon. This creates a fully black layer mask; all pixels of the layer are masked, effectively making the layer completely transparent (or hidden — whichever way you prefer to look at it). To do the same thing via the menu, choose Layer ➪ Layer Mask ➪ Hide All.

- Make a selection using one of the selection tools (or choose Select ➪ Load Selection), then select the layer and click the Add Layer Mask icon. Photoshop creates the layer mask based on your selection, so any selected pixels of the layer remain opaque, while unselected pixels are masked off and appear transparent in the layer. You can also create a layer mask this way by choosing Layer ➪ Layer Mask ➪ Reveal Selection. To do the opposite and create a layer mask that hides the selected areas of your selection, Alt+click (Option+click on the Mac) the Add Layer Mask icon. Alternatively, choose Layer ➪ Layer Mask ➪ Hide Selection.

> **TIP** You can also create a layer mask (or a vector mask — see the section "Using Vector Masks" later in the chapter) for a layer group. Simply select the group in the Layers palette; then use one of the previous methods to create a mask for the group. Photoshop applies the mask to the combined result of all the layers in the group (including the effects of any layer masks associated with those layers).

After you create a layer mask, an extra thumbnail appears to the right of the layer thumbnail, as shown in Figure 9.10. This thumbnail represents the layer mask. The thumbnail has a rectangular border around it, indicating that it's active; any edits you carry out while the mask is active are performed on the mask, not on the layer contents.

FIGURE 9.10

A layer mask gets its own thumbnail in the Layers palette, to the right of the standard layer thumbnail. The border around the thumbnail indicates that it's active; any edits you make will affect the mask, not the layer.

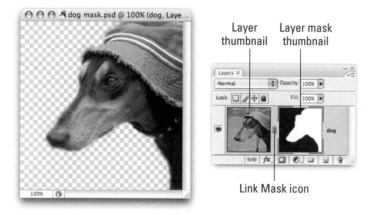

To return to working on the layer contents rather than on the mask, click the layer thumbnail, or press Ctrl+~ (⌘+~ on the Mac). The rectangular border moves from the mask thumbnail to the layer thumbnail. Click the mask thumbnail, or press Ctrl+\ (⌘+\ on the Mac) to switch back again.

The other thing you may notice when you create a layer mask is that a new channel appears in the Channels palette. It has the same name as the layer, with the word "Mask" after it. This is an alpha channel that stores the layer mask itself and, as such, you can manipulate it using most of the usual alpha channel techniques described earlier in the chapter. However, it's only visible in the Channels palette while that layer is active; switch to a different layer and it disappears from the palette. If you want to save a copy of it to work on separately, click and drag it down to the Create New Channel icon at the bottom of the palette.

Editing layer masks

To edit your layer mask, make sure it's active by clicking its thumbnail in the Layers palette, then modify pixels in the mask using your tools of choice. As with any bitmap mask, you can use practically any tool or command you like on the mask, ranging from the brush tools and retouching tools through to the filters in the Filter menu and the transform commands under Edit ➪ Transform.

If you paint black onto the mask, you mask off the corresponding areas of the layer, allowing the underlying layers to show through. If you paint using white, you unmask those areas of the layer, making them opaque and blocking out the underlying layers. Painting with shades of gray makes the corresponding pixels in the layer semitransparent — a bit like adjusting the layer's Opacity slider, but on a pixel-by-pixel basis. You can see these effects in Figure 9.11, which shows a layer mask that's been painted on using black, white, and gray.

FIGURE 9.11

By painting on a layer mask using black, white, and various shades of gray, you can control the amount of opacity applied to the corresponding pixels in the layer.

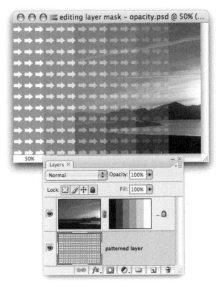

Although you can see a thumbnail version of the layer mask in the Layers palette while you're painting on it, it's not very practical if you want to see what you're doing in detail. To view the layer mask on its own in the document window, Alt+click (Option+click on the Mac) the layer mask's thumbnail in the Layers palette. Alt/Option+click the layer mask thumbnail again to return to viewing the image.

To view the layer mask and the image at the same time, Alt+Shift+click (Option+Shift+click on the Mac) the layer mask thumbnail. The layer mask appears as a color overlay, much like the Quick Mask mode described earlier in this chapter. To return to viewing the image on its own, Alt+Shift+click (Win) or Option+Shift+click (Mac) the layer mask thumbnail again.

> **TIP** An even quicker way to view the active layer with its mask is simply to press the \ (backslash) key. After you have both layer and mask visible, you can also press ~ (tilde) to toggle between layer and mask, and layer only.

Figure 9.12 shows a layer mask being edited in all three modes: image only, layer mask only, and image with layer mask.

NOTE All these mode-changing techniques are really doing is changing the visibility of the image and mask channels. If you view the Channels palette (Window ⇨ Channels) while using these techniques, you can see the eye icons change as you flip between the modes.

You can change the appearance of the layer mask's color overlay by double-clicking the layer mask thumbnail, or by right-clicking the thumbnail and choosing Layer Mask Options from the pop-up menu. Click the Color box to choose a color for the overlay; set its opacity from 0 percent to 100 percent using the Opacity box. (The Opacity setting merely affects the appearance of the overlay; it doesn't change the opacity of the mask or the layer.)

FIGURE 9.12

Viewing the layer mask in different ways. In the first image (left), you're painting on the layer mask in the normal way, with the layer itself visible in the document window. Alt/Option+click the layer mask thumbnail to view the mask in isolation (center). Alt/Option+Shift+click the thumbnail to view the layer and its mask at the same time (right).

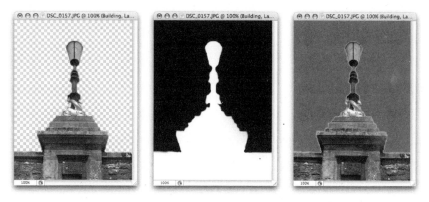

Applying a layer mask permanently to a layer

If you're happy with the way your layer is being masked by its layer mask, you can apply the layer mask permanently to the layer, deleting masked areas of the layer and leaving unmasked areas alone. Photoshop deletes the mask at the same time. This is a good way to reduce your document's file size and save disk space.

To do this, select the layer; then choose Layer ⇨ Layer Mask ⇨ Apply. If you prefer, you can right-click the layer mask thumbnail in the Layers palette and choose Apply Layer Mask from the pop-up menu. You can also use one of the methods described in the section "Deleting a layer mask."

CAUTION   Applying a layer mask deletes the mask and permanently alters the layer it was associated with. You can't go back and separate the layer from the mask later. It's best to only apply a layer mask if you really need to save disk space and you're sure you won't ever want the original layer and mask back.

Deleting a layer mask

Layer masks are stored, along with their layers, when you save your document, so they're around as long as you need them. If you decide you no longer need a layer mask, or you need to save some disk space, you can delete the mask by selecting the layer then choosing Layer ➪ Layer Mask ➪ Delete. You can also right-click the layer mask thumbnail in the Layers palette, and choose Delete Layer Mask from the pop-up menu.

You can delete the layer mask using the Layers palette's Delete Layer icon, too. Click the layer mask thumbnail to make it active; then click the Delete Layer icon. You can also click and drag the layer mask thumbnail down to the icon. When you delete a layer mask in this way, a message box appears asking if you want to apply the mask to the layer before deleting it, thereby permanently deleting the masked areas of your layer. Click Apply to do this, or Delete to just delete the mask. Press Cancel if you get cold feet.

TIP   If you're more of a channels type of person, you can also delete a layer mask by selecting its alpha channel in the Channels palette and clicking the Delete Current Channel icon at the bottom of the palette.

Using Vector Masks

Like layer masks, vector masks are tied to layers, and they only affect the pixels on the layer they're associated with. The main difference between the two mask types is that vector masks use vector paths to define the selected and masked areas of the layer, whereas layer masks use pixels to do their job.

Vector masks share many of the advantages of their vector-based cousins: shape layers, type layers, and paths. They're resolution-independent, so you can scale them up and down or transform them with no loss of quality. You can go back and edit a vector mask as many times as you want — again, with no reduction in quality or sharpness. Finally, a vector mask usually takes up a lot less RAM and disk space than the equivalent layer mask.

The main disadvantage of vector masks is that you can't create semitransparent masks; everything in the layer is either completely masked or completely selected. This also means that you can't feather the edges of selected areas when using vector masks; these masks always produce hard edges.

Creating vector masks

You can create a vector mask using similar techniques to creating a layer mask. The main difference is that, whereas layer masks can be created from selections, vector masks can be created from paths or shapes.

To create a new vector mask for a layer, use any of the following techniques:

- Select the layer, then Ctrl+click (⌘+click on the Mac) the Add Layer Mask icon at the bottom of the Layers palette. This creates a vector mask where no pixels in the layer are masked off, and attaches the mask to the layer. You can do the same thing by choosing Layer ➪ Vector Mask ➪ Reveal All.

- Select the layer, then Ctrl+Alt+click (⌘+Option+click on the Mac) the Add Layer Mask icon to create a vector mask with all pixels in the layer masked off, making the layer completely transparent. Alternatively, choose Layer ➪ Vector Mask ➪ Hide All.

- Create a new path with the pen or shape tools, or select an existing path in the Paths palette, then Ctrl+click (⌘+click on the Mac) the Add Layer Mask icon. Photoshop uses the path to create the vector mask; anything inside the shape of the path is selected in the layer, while anything outside the path is masked off. You can also create a vector mask this way by choosing Layer ➪ Vector Mask ➪ Current Path.

CROSS-REF To find out how to apply a shape layer's vector mask to another layer, refer to Chapter 5.

Vector masks have their own thumbnails in the Layers palette, much like layer masks do. The thumbnail shows you which parts of the layer are revealed (in white) and which parts are masked off (in gray). The rectangular border around the thumbnail tells you that it's active; you'll also see the path outline appear in the document window while the mask is active, as shown in Figure 9.13. You can then edit the mask using any of the techniques described in the section "Editing vector masks."

FIGURE 9.13

A vector mask thumbnail shows the path that makes up the mask. White areas of the mask represent unmasked areas of the layer; gray areas are the masked-off parts of the layer.

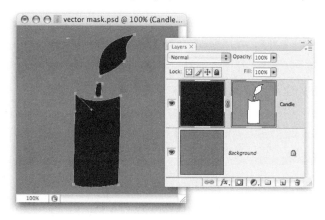

TIP   To toggle the path outline on and off in the document window, press Ctrl+Shift+H (⌘+Shift+H on the Mac).

As with layer masks, click the layer thumbnail to return to working on the layer. Click the mask thumbnail to switch back to editing the mask (you also need to switch to a path editing tool, of course). Unfortunately, there are no keyboard shortcuts for flipping between a layer and its vector mask.

Whereas a layer mask is represented by a channel in the Channels palette, a vector mask shows up as a path in the Paths palette. For example, if you add a vector mask to a layer called Teddy Bear, a new path called Teddy Bear Vector Mask magically appears in the Paths palette. This path only appears while that layer is active; select a different layer and the path vanishes from the palette.

TIP   Although the mask path only appears temporarily in the Paths palette, you can, if you want, grab a permanent copy of it that you can then edit separately. To do this, click the vector mask path in the Paths palette and drag it to the Create New Path icon at the bottom of the palette. Alternatively, double-click the path in the palette, and type a name for the duplicate path in the dialog box that appears.

Editing vector masks

Because vector masks use paths rather than bitmap images, you can't edit them using the standard painting tools. Instead, use one or more of the following path editing tools and commands:

- **The Pen and Freeform Pen tools:** Use these tools to draw your own paths on your vector mask.

- **The shape tools:** With these tools you can easily create all sorts of shapes to use for your vector mask.

- **The Path Selection and Direct Selection tools:** Use these to select and edit paths, segments, and points in your vector mask.

- **The Transform Path and Free Transform Path commands:** Available under Edit ⇨ Transform Path and Edit ⇨ Free Transform Path, you can use these commands to stretch, rotate, and bend your vector mask in exactly the same way as the regular transform commands.

CROSS-REF   Paths and shapes are covered in more detail in Chapter 5, including the basics of editing paths.

To edit a vector mask, activate it by clicking its thumbnail in the Layers palette. You can then change the mask using one of the tools and commands described in the previous list.

Within a vector mask, everything inside a path is revealed in the layer, while everything outside it is masked off. At least, this is the default. If you want to flip this around, select the Path Selection tool, select the path in the document window by clicking it (if the vector mask contains multiple paths, Shift+click each path to select them all), then click the Subtract From Shape Area button in the options bar. Now, everything outside the path or paths is revealed, and everything inside is masked off, as shown in Figure 9.14.

FIGURE 9.14

By selecting a path component (left) with the Path Selection tool then clicking the Subtract From Shape Area button, you can invert the path, so that what was revealed becomes masked, and vice versa (right).

Subtract From Shape Area button

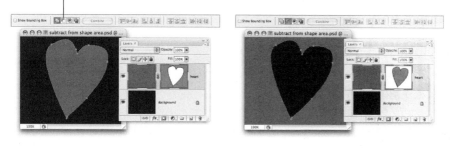

> **TIP** If you ever need to view a vector mask without its associated layer, select the layer and hide it by clicking its eye icon, then click the vector mask thumbnail in the Layers palette (or its path in the Paths palette) to select it.

Turning a vector mask into a layer mask

If you want to paint on a vector mask or use any other bitmap editing tools on it, Photoshop gives you the option of converting the vector mask into a regular layer mask. This process, called *rasterizing*, involves approximating the lines and curves of the vector mask's path as black and white pixels in the layer mask: black pixels for the parts of the mask outside the path and white pixels for the parts inside. (Photoshop also anti-aliases the edges where black meets white, producing a few grayscale pixels.)

> **CAUTION** Rasterizing a vector mask has the same disadvantages as rasterizing a type layer. You're taking that smooth, resolution-independent path and approximating it with pixels, so you're locking the mask to a particular resolution, and also making the shapes in the mask much harder to edit. It's a one-way process, too, although at a pinch you can use the Magic Wand tool to select the shape or shapes in the layer mask, then turn the selection back into a path using the Make Work Path From Selection icon at the bottom of the Paths palette. It probably won't be identical to the original mask shape, though.

Turning a vector mask into a layer mask couldn't be simpler. Select the layer containing the vector mask; then choose Layer ➪ Rasterize ➪ Vector Mask. You can also right-click the vector mask's thumbnail in the Layers palette, and select the Rasterize Vector Mask option. Photoshop swaps out the vector mask for its layer mask equivalent, and you're good to go.

CROSS-REF For more on working with layer masks, see the section "Using Layer Masks" earlier in this chapter.

Applying a vector mask permanently to a layer

To apply a vector mask to a layer, making the masking effect permanent, you first need to rasterize the mask, then apply the rasterized version as follows:

1. **Select the layer.** Click the layer in the Layers palette whose vector mask you want to apply.

2. **Rasterize the vector mask.** Choose Layer ➪ Rasterize ➪ Vector Mask to turn the vector mask into a layer mask.

3. **Apply the layer mask.** Choose Layer ➪ Layer Mask ➪ Apply. The layer mask is applied to the layer; Photoshop deletes the layer mask afterward.

CROSS-REF For more on applying layer masks, see the section "Applying a layer mask permanently to a layer" earlier in the chapter.

Applying a vector mask isn't such a dramatic saver of disk space as applying a layer mask, because vectors take up a lot less space than bitmaps. So unless the vector mask bugs you for some reason, you're probably better off leaving it as it is.

Deleting a vector mask

To delete an unwanted vector mask, select the layer containing the vector mask and choose Layer ➪ Vector Mask ➪ Delete. You can also right-click the vector mask's thumbnail and choose Delete Vector Mask, or drag the thumbnail down to the Delete Layer icon. (You can also click the vector mask thumbnail then click the Delete Layer icon.) Photoshop asks you to confirm that you want to delete the mask; click OK to continue. The vector mask vanishes, and the full layer is revealed again.

TIP You can also delete a vector mask without confirmation by selecting its thumbnail in the Layers palette, or its path in the Paths palette, and pressing Backspace (Delete on the Mac).

Managing Layer and Vector Masks

This section looks at some of the tricks you can perform with layer and vector masks, including moving and copying masks between layers; converting a mask into a selection; unlinking a mask from its layer so you can move mask and layer around independently; and temporarily disabling masks.

Moving a mask to a different layer

To move a layer or vector mask from one layer to another, click the mask's thumbnail in the Layers palette and drag it to the target layer. To copy the mask rather than moving it, hold down Alt (Option on the Mac) before you click and drag.

Loading a mask as a selection

Just as you can load a layer's transparency mask (or any other type of mask) as a selection, you can load a layer mask or vector mask as a selection by Ctrl+clicking (⌘+clicking on the Mac) the mask's thumbnail in the Layers palette. You can also do the following:

- Ctrl+Shift+click (⌘+Shift+click on the Mac) the mask's thumbnail to add the mask to an existing selection.

- Ctrl+Alt+click (⌘+Option+click on the Mac) the thumbnail to subtract the mask from an existing selection.

- Ctrl+Alt+Shift+click (⌘+Option+Shift+click on the Mac) the thumbnail to load the intersection of the mask and an existing selection.

> **TIP** For layer masks only, you can also right-click the mask thumbnail and choose Add Layer Mask To Selection, Subtract Layer Mask From Selection, or Intersect Layer Mask With Selection. (For some reason, these menu options aren't available for vector masks.)

Linking and unlinking a mask

The little link icon between the layer thumbnail and the mask thumbnail (shown in Figure 9.10) tells you that the layer and its mask are linked. This means that if you move the layer's contents around with the Move tool, the contents of the mask move along with it, and vice versa. This way, the mask is always masking the same areas of the layer contents.

To unlink the mask from the layer, click the link icon so that it disappears, or choose Layer ➪ Layer Mask ➪ Unlink, or Layer ➪ Vector Mask ➪ Unlink. Now the layer and mask can be moved independently. Click the layer thumbnail; then use the Move tool to move the layer around. The mask stays in the same place, and the layer contents move around under the mask. This is great for positioning an image within a frame defined by the mask, as you can see in Figure 9.15.

Similarly, if you click the mask thumbnail, you can drag the mask contents around without moving the layer. Use the Move tool if it's a layer mask or the Path Selection tool if it's a vector mask.

> **CROSS-REF** You can also move the layer or its layer mask (but not a vector mask) by Ctrl+dragging (Option+dragging on the Mac) in the document window. For more on the Move tool and its range of handy shortcuts, see Chapter 2.

To link the layer and mask again, click the space between the layer and mask thumbnails in the Layers palette, or choose Layer ➪ Layer Mask ➪ Link, or Layer ➪ Vector Mask ➪ Link. The link icon reappears, indicating that layer and mask are linked.

> **NOTE** Sadly, you can't link a Smart Object to its layer or vector mask. The mask always moves independently of the Smart Object.

FIGURE 9.15

By unlinking a layer from its mask, you can drag the layer around underneath the mask using the Move tool.

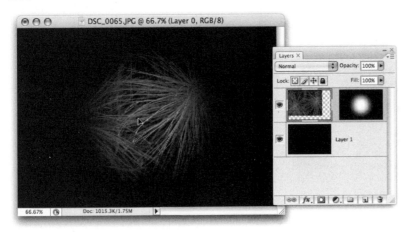

Disabling a mask

You might want to turn off a layer or vector mask temporarily so that you can see the whole layer again. To do this, Shift+click the mask thumbnail in the Layers palette, or right-click the thumbnail and choose Disable Layer/Vector Mask from the pop-up menu. A red X appears over the mask thumbnail, indicating that it's disabled and the masking effect is temporarily removed from the layer. Click or Shift+click the mask thumbnail again, or right-click it and choose Enable Layer/Vector Mask, to bring the mask back into action.

Combining Layer and Vector Masks

You may have thought by now that layer masks and vector masks are an "either/or" proposition — that you have to choose either one or the other when masking your layer — but, in fact, Photoshop lets you add both a layer mask and a vector mask to the same layer.

Why would you want to do this? Well, as you can see in Figure 9.16, it's perfect for those times when you want to use a hard-edged vector shape — in this case, a keyhole — along with a soft-edged bitmap, such as the blurred vignette mask used in the example. Furthermore, as they're separate masks, you can move both keyhole and vignette around independently, until you get the effect you're after.

When you stack masks like this, Photoshop always puts the layer mask thumbnail on the left (to the right of the layer thumbnail) and the vector mask thumbnail on the right. First, the layer mask is applied to the layer, and then the vector mask is applied on top.

FIGURE 9.16

Adding both a layer mask and a vector mask to a layer. Here we've taken an image of a wall and added a layer mask and a vector mask to the layer to simulate the effect of looking through a keyhole. The layer mask provides the darkening vignette element and the vector mask provides the keyhole itself. They're unlinked, so that we can easily recompose the image nondestructively.

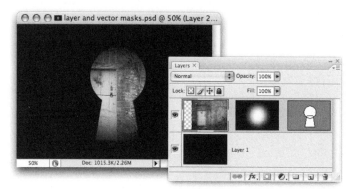

When your layer contains a layer mask and a vector mask, there are two link icons within the layer in the Layers palette: one between the layer thumbnail and the layer mask thumbnail, and another between the layer mask and vector mask thumbnails. The link icon on the left controls whether or not the layer mask moves in unison with the layer, much as it does when you only have a single mask. However, the icon on the right links the vector mask with the layer also, not with the layer mask as you might imagine.

Confused? Maybe this list will help explain everything:

- With just the left link icon showing, select the layer or the layer mask and drag with the Move tool. The layer and layer mask move together; the vector mask stays where it is. Select the vector mask and drag with the Path Selection tool, and only the vector mask moves.

- With just the right-hand link icon showing, select the layer and drag with the Move tool. The layer and its vector mask move together; the layer mask stays put. However, drag with the Direct Selection tool and only the vector mask moves; both the layer and the layer mask stay still.

- With both link icons showing, select either the layer or the layer mask, and drag with the Move tool. The layer and both masks move in unison. However, if you drag with the Direct Selection tool then only the vector mask moves — almost as if it has a mind of its own.

- Of course, with neither link icon showing, the layer and its masks can each be moved around independently.

> **TIP**
> Don't forget that you can also Shift+click either of the mask thumbnails to temporarily disable just that mask, or Shift+click both thumbnails to disable both masks.

> **NOTE**
> You're probably wondering what happens if you rasterize the vector mask on a layer that contains both a vector mask and a layer mask. The answer is that the vector mask gets rasterized into a bitmap mask which is then added to the existing layer mask, effectively stamping the rasterized vector mask onto the layer mask. Clever Photoshop.

Masking Layers with Clipping Masks

Our final mask type behaves a bit differently to the other types of masks looked at in this chapter. The mask of a clipping mask doesn't really exist in its own right; there's no separate channel or path storing the mask. A clipping mask simply takes the transparency mask of one layer and applies it, as if it were a layer mask, to one or more layers above it. In other words, you can use the shape of one layer to mask off the contents of one or more other layers.

An example makes this clearer. In Figure 9.17, a clipping mask consisting of three layers has been created. The bottom layer of the clipping mask is called the *base layer*; Photoshop helpfully underlines the name of the base layer so you can spot it easily. The two layers above the base layer are both part of the clipping mask, which means they are masked, or clipped, by the base layer. Photoshop indents the thumbnails of clipped layers in a clipping mask and also adds a downward-pointing arrow to the left of each thumbnail.

FIGURE 9.17

A clipping mask in action. This promo box for a Web site has a photo on top and a blue rectangular area on the bottom. The rounded rectangle base layer at the bottom of the clipping mask clips, or masks, the layers above it, shaping the layers and allowing the Background layer to show through.

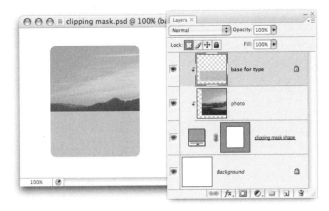

Because the clipping mask works by using the base layer's transparency mask to mask the upper layers, your base layer needs to have some opaque pixels on it if you want parts of the upper layers to show through. If your base layer contains nothing—that is, if it's completely transparent—the upper layers appear transparent, also.

NOTE Unlike regular masks, where the masking effect is determined by whether the pixels in the mask are black or white (or somewhere in between), clipping masks work on the transparency levels of the pixels in the base layer instead. A completely transparent pixel in the base layer masks (clips) the corresponding pixels in the upper layers; a completely opaque pixel allows the corresponding upper-layer pixels to show through. A partially transparent base-layer pixel results in a partially transparent upper-layer pixel. You can think of the upper layers in the clipping mask as "taking on the shape" of the base layer.

The layers in a clipping mask have to be directly on top of each other in the Layers palette. This means that you can't create a clipping mask that has unclipped layers interleaved with clipped layers. If you need to do this, duplicate the base layer and apply two clipping masks, one to each set of layers.

Clipping masks are handy because you can use the shape of an existing layer to do your masking without having to worry about creating additional masks. This also makes clipping masks great for using type as a mask. Because your original type layer remains intact, you can go back and edit the type at any time, and the clipped layers automatically change to reflect the new shape of the type layer.

Creating a clipping mask

The simplest clipping mask contains just two layers: the base layer and the clipped layer. The easiest way to create such a clipping mask is to follow these steps:

1. **Make sure the base layer is directly under the layer to be clipped.** If necessary, reorder the layers in the Layers palette so that the layer to be clipped is directly above the base layer.

2. **Hold down Alt (Option on the Mac) and move the mouse over the horizontal line between the layers in the Layers palette.** The mouse cursor changes to a left-pointing arrow and two overlapping circles.

3. **Click the mouse.** Photoshop creates the clipping mask, as shown in Figure 9.18.

Another way to create a clipping mask is to select the layer that you would like to be clipped (the top layer) and choose Layer ➪ Create Clipping Mask. Photoshop creates the clipping mask out of your selected layer and the layer directly below it. You can also access this menu option by right-clicking the top layer in the Layers palette or via the Layers palette menu. Or simply press Ctrl+Alt+G (⌘+Option+G on the Mac) to do the same thing.

FIGURE 9.18

Creating a clipping mask. Alt+click (Option+click on the Mac) the horizontal line between two layers (left) to create the mask (right).

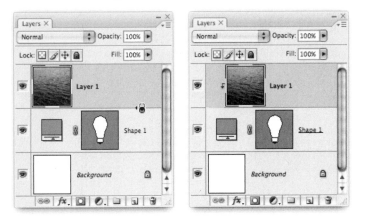

NEW FEATURE In Photoshop CS3, you can quickly create a clipping mask out of three or more layers. Stack the layers on top of each other, with the base layer on the bottom. Select all the layers above the base layer that you want to be clipped, and choose Layer ➪ Create Clipping Mask. Earlier versions of CS2 don't let you create a clipping mask out of multiple layers like this; instead you need to add the layers to the mask one at a time, as described in the section "Editing clipping masks."

Editing clipping masks

Now that you've created a clipping mask, you can use the Move tool to drag the individual layers around. For example, drag an upper (masked) layer around to reposition it within the mask, or drag the base layer to move the mask around.

You can also move the layers within a clipping mask up and down in the Layers palette. However if you move a layer so that it is no longer directly above or below another layer in the mask then it is removed from the mask. If you want to move the whole clipping mask around the Layers palette, select all the layers in the mask, then click and drag, as shown in Figure 9.19. Photoshop preserves the clipping mask provided you include at least the base layer and one other layer in your selection. You can also Alt+drag (Option+drag on the Mac) the selected layers to duplicate the clipping mask.

To add more layers to a clipping mask, simply drag them between existing layers in the mask in the Layers palette. You can also move the layer directly above the topmost layer in the mask, then use one of the methods described in the section "Creating a clipping mask" to add the layer to the mask.

FIGURE 9.19

Repositioning a clipping mask. Select all the layers in the mask, and then click one of the mask layers in the Layers palette and drag to the new position.

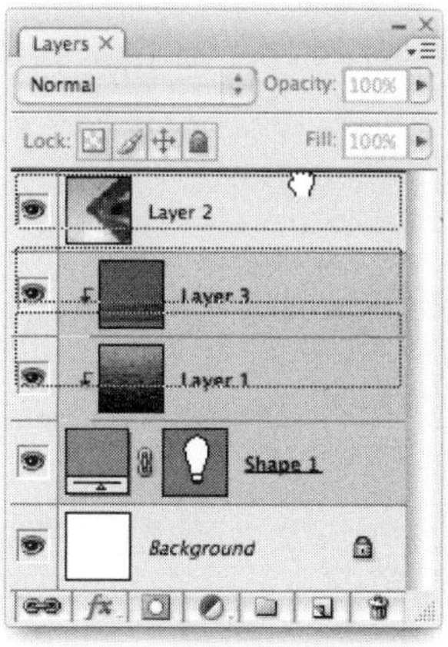

To remove layers from a clipping mask, do one of the following:

- Hold down Alt (Option on the Mac) and move the mouse between the layer you want to remove and the layer below in the Layers palette. The mouse cursor changes to a left-pointing arrow and two overlapping circles. Click to release the layer from the clipping mask.

- Select the layer you want to remove; then choose Layer ➪ Release Clipping Mask. (You can also select this menu option by right-clicking the layer in the Layers palette, or from the Layers palette menu). Alternatively, select the layer then press Ctrl+Alt+G (⌘+Option+G on the Mac).

When you remove a layer from a clipping mask, any clipped layers above that layer are also removed from the mask.

To release all layers from a clipping mask, effectively removing the clipping mask entirely, select the layer immediately above the base layer; then release that layer from the mask by choosing Layer ➪ Release Clipping Mask.

CROSS-REF By default, the layers in a clipping mask blend with other layers in the document using the blending mode of the base layer. However, you can change this so that each layer in the clipping mask blends using its own blending mode. Find out how to control the blending of clipping masks in Chapter 7.

If you add layer effects to your base layer — for example, a drop shadow or an inner glow — Photoshop overlays the effects on top of the clipped layers. This means that you can clip all your layers with a clipping mask, then add effects to the clipped result by adding the effects to the base layer. Figure 9.20 shows an example of this.

If your clipped layers contain any layer effects, then the base layer clips these effects along with the layer contents.

FIGURE 9.20

You can add effects to the base layer of the clipping mask to spice up your clipped layers.

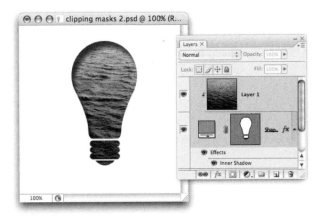

Tutorial: A Complete Example

In this example, you use masks to process two source photos and create a header image for a Web site. The photos — shown in Figure 9.21 — are of an abstract spiral shape and a cell phone. Your first aim is to combine the two images in a pleasing manner by masking off the background of the phone and superimposing it on the spiral. You then use a clipping mask to create the final header image.

Creating the mask for the cell phone

The first step is to isolate that cell phone by masking off its background. Use a bitmap layer mask for this, rather than a vector mask, since you want to preserve something of a soft edge to the mask. Using a vector mask would give a hard edge, making it trickier to blend the two images together. To create the mask, try using a combination of the Quick Selection tool and brushes. The Quick Selection tool gives a rough cutout that you can fine-tune with the brushes. Let's bring up the cell phone image into Photoshop and start work. Here are the steps required to create the cell phone mask:

FIGURE 9.21

The source photos. You combine the spiral image and the cell phone to create a header image for a Web site.

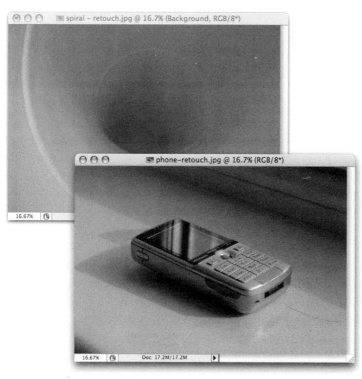

1. **Convert the photo image's Background layer to a normal layer.** To do this, double-click the Background layer in the Layers palette. This displays the New Layer dialog. Name the new layer **Phone** and click OK.

2. **Make an initial selection of the phone with the Quick Selection tool.** Select the Quick Selection tool from the Toolbox — it's in the same group as the Magic Wand tool — and choose a medium brush size by clicking the Brush option in the options bar. Try a Diameter setting of around 70 pixels.

   This new tool in CS3 allows for a very good selection in areas of low contrast, which is perfect for this image. All you have to do is hold down the mouse button and run the brush around the inside edge of the object you want to select in the document window. The best approach is to make the selection in stages, rather than just circling the object in one go. It can take some trial and error to get the selection right, and you might find that the tool selects areas you didn't want it to. To fix this, hold down Alt (Option on the Mac) to temporarily switch to the Subtract From Selection mode, and brush over a selected area. You can see this process in Figure 9.22.

TIP   If you're using a version of Photoshop earlier than CS3, you can use the Magic Wand tool to make the selection instead, but be aware that it's not as efficient as the newer Quick Selection tool.

FIGURE 9.22

If the Quick Selection tool has been a bit overzealous in what it's selected, Alt+click (Option+click on the Mac) the undesired areas to remove them from the selection.

3. **Take a snapshot of the selection.** After you have your basic selection, it's worth saving a snapshot of the selection as a channel by choosing Select ➪ Save Selection. This allows you to revert to this stage at any time, which is handy if the following steps don't go according to plan!

4. **Turn the selection into a layer mask.** You can now create your layer mask for the Phone layer. With your selection active, simply click the Add Layer Mask icon at the bottom of the Layers palette. The background disappears, leaving just the phone itself. The background is still there, of course; it's just hidden by the mask.

   At this stage, it's likely that your phone mask is slightly rough around the edges, with some elements selected when you don't want them to be, and vice versa.

5. **Refine the layer mask.** Use the Brush tool to "paint" onto and refine the mask. You want to soften the edges slightly where they're a little hard, and you're also looking to reveal any areas missed by the Quick Selection tool. Conversely, you also need to paint out any unwanted areas. Here that might be the shadow beneath the phone, which has confused the Quick Selection tool somewhat in the example.

Use a white brush to reveal areas — try a brush with a Diameter of 60 pixels and a Hardness of 70 percent — and a black brush at the same size to hide elements. A quick way to select a white and black brush is to press D while the layer mask is active to reset the foreground and background colors to white and black, respectively. You can then press X to flip between a white and a black brush. Running the white brush around any hard edges will help to smooth these edges out.

TIP
It can be hard to see what you're doing at this point. To help make your life easier, press \ (Backslash) to display the colored mask overlay, then double-click the layer mask thumbnail in the Layers palette and set its Opacity to 100 percent. This shows you the edges you're creating very nicely. Press \ again to hide the overlay.

You might find yourself running over the edges occasionally, so press X to flip the foreground and background colors, and repair any damage as you go. Keep the strokes short; if you need to choose Edit ⇨ Undo to undo a mistake, you don't want to be undoing a lot of work for the sake of one slip. As you can see in Figure 9.23, it can help to zoom in on the image as you do this, so you can really see what you're doing.

FIGURE 9.23

Zoom right into the image to tidy up that layer mask!

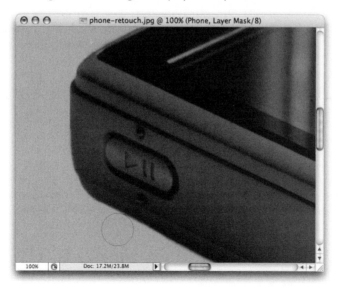

After completing these steps, you should have a well-masked cell phone, ready for inclusion in the final image.

Putting the elements together

Now open the spiral image in Photoshop, and simply click and drag the cell phone layer, mask and all, into the spiral. To do this, click the cell phone layer's thumbnail in the Layers palette — not the mask thumbnail — and drag it across to the spiral's document window. You now have a nice composite image, as shown in Figure 9.24. Notice how the layer mask is preserved along with the layer as it's copied to the new document.

The phone is now within the spiral image, with the layer mask perfectly intact.

The initial results of the composition are somewhat unpromising; the phone seems very alienated from the spiral image. You're going to fix this by using a blending mode to allow the phone to sit better within the image. Select the phone layer in the composite image and choose Linear Dodge from the Blending Mode menu at the top of the Layers palette. Now the phone sits much more elegantly in the composition and seems more part of the spiral.

To bring the phone out of the spiral a little, add an Outer Glow effect to the phone. Select the phone layer, click the Add a Layer Style icon at the bottom of the Layers palette, and choose Outer Glow from the pop-up menu. In the Layer Style dialog box, select a soft glow by clicking and dragging the Size slider to the right, and choose an appropriate color by clicking the Color box. Note that the glow follows the contours of the revealed phone area you created with the layer mask.

Figure 9.25 shows the two images coexisting much more happily. It's a good idea to save the image as a Photoshop file at this point.

FIGURE 9.25

With the addition of a Linear Dodge blending mode and an Outer Glow effect, the phone now blends nicely with the spiral image.

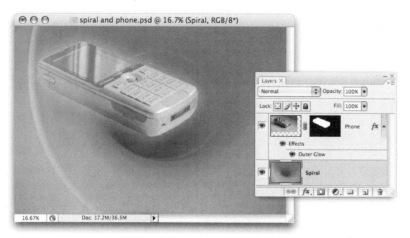

Creating the final header image

The image you created is destined to become part of a Web page, and the prebaked page is shown in Figure 9.26 with a conspicuous gap at the top where the image will go. The area at the top is a shape layer, and you'll be using this as the base layer for a clipping mask to shape the header image.

The phone-and-spiral image is at a much higher resolution than you need in this case. Creating the image at a high resolution is actually good practice, because it allows more flexibility for repurposing the image later. Right now, though, reduce the size of the image so that it fits into the header area. The area that it needs to fit within is 750 pixels wide, so the image needs to be just a little wider than that; say, 850 pixels. This gives you some leeway in terms of composition.

Resize the phone-and-spiral image by choosing Image ➪ Image Size. Resize it from its native size of 3000 pixels wide at 300 dpi, to a more Web-friendly 850 pixels wide at 72 dpi. After the image is at the new, smaller size, save it as a new Photoshop file to give you two versions of the image: one at the original high resolution and one at the lower Web resolution.

You're now ready to bring the image into your Web layout. Open both documents in Photoshop, and select both the phone and spiral layers in the first document by Ctrl+clicking (⌘+clicking on the Mac) each layer in the Layers palette. Now simply drag the layers over to the Web layout document. Again, the phone layer comes through with its layer mask intact.

FIGURE 9.26

A basic Web page layout, ready to receive the images into the header area at the top

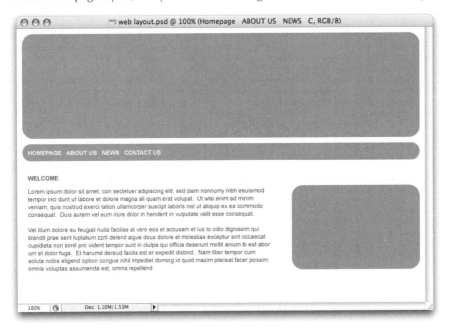

You'll find that the image layers completely cover the whole area of the layout, but that's where the clipping mask comes in. In the Layers palette, select the imported phone and spiral layers, if they're not already selected, then drag them through the stacking order until they're just above the rounded-rectangle header shape layer. Now, with those two layers still selected, create a clipping mask by choosing Layer ⇨ Create Clipping Mask. The images are now masked by the header shape layer, which becomes the base layer of the clipping mask.

One of the great things about clipping masks is that you can now select the spiral and phone layers and, using the Move tool, move them around within the clipping mask to recompose the image to best fit the new space. Because the individual layers are retained, you can also experiment with the position of the phone independently of the spiral layer.

Even at this stage, the phone's layer mask is intact, and if you want, you can paint on it to tweak any remaining rough edges, or even change it dramatically to fade the phone image further into the background, as seen in Figure 9.27.

FIGURE 9.27

In the final incarnation of the Web page, the phone is flipped and repositioned. The phone's layer mask is edited using a large soft brush.

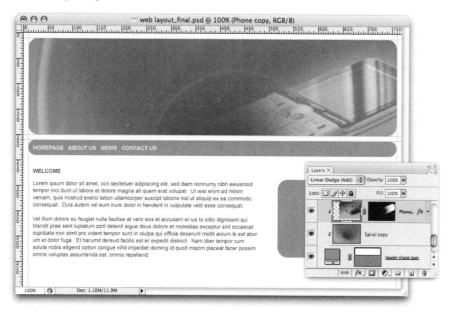

Summary

In this chapter, you've taken a comprehensive tour of Photoshop's various masking features. It started with a brief explanation of masks, and the advantages they offer over selections. You then got an overview of the different mask types: bitmap versus vector masks, and masks that can be used anywhere versus masks that are specific to layers.

You then embarked on a journey through selection masks, the Quick Mask mode, and alpha channels. While not directly related to layers, these types of mask are pretty essential tools in Photoshop, and they also give a good grounding in masking techniques, which is invaluable when working with the more layer-specific masks.

Speaking of layer-specific masks, you then moved into a detailed discussion of layer masks, which let you mask off layer content using pixels; and vector masks, which you can use to create precise, resolution-independent masks for your layers. You then looked at how to manage layer and vector masks, as well as how to use both types of mask in the one layer.

The last mask type you explored was the clipping mask, which lets you use the transparent areas of one layer to mask off one or more layers above it. You finished with a detailed example that employed both layer masks and clipping masks to produce an eye-catching Web site header image.

Chapter 10

Discovering Layer Styles

It's 1997, and a designer is busily working at her desk. Her boss comes over and asks her to add a drop shadow to the company logo. In Photoshop 4, she opens the logo document and selects the opaque pixels of the logo layer by ⌘+clicking the logo layer's thumbnail in the Layers palette.

Next, she creates a new layer and fills the selection with black. She then drags the new layer underneath the logo layer in the Layers palette, and nudges the layer a few pixels down and to the right. Now she blurs the new layer slightly by choosing Filter ➪ Blur ➪ Gaussian Blur. After setting the layer's blending mode to Multiply and tweaking its opacity a bit, it's done — a beautiful drop shadow. Time to go to lunch.

Fast-forward ten years, and the same designer needs to do another drop shadow for the company logo. After opening the logo document in Photoshop CS2, she double-clicks the logo layer, checks the Drop Shadow layer effect box, tweaks the opacity, and clicks OK. Coffee time.

You get the message by now — Photoshop's layer effects and styles are wonderful time-saving inventions, leaving you with more time to think creatively, finish the job, and drink coffee.

Here are some other great advantages of layer styles:

- They're totally reeditable at any point — much as type layers are, for example. If you decide that your drop shadow doesn't quite have the right "oomph" when you return to the document weeks later, you can change it in a flash.

- Even if you change the layer's content — for example, if you edit some type, or you rotate a logo — the layer style keeps pace with your changes, updating itself in real time to match the new content.

- Because they're re-created dynamically each time you make a change to the layer, layer effects don't lose quality, no matter how many times you stretch or squeeze the layer.

- You can apply layer effects and styles to any type of layer, from normal layers through to type layers and shape layers, and even to fill and adjustment layers (should you so desire).

- Photoshop lets you mix and match different effects on the same layer — for example, a drop shadow and a bevel — and then save the result as a preset style. Reuse that style as often as you want, across layers and across documents. Photoshop also ships with more than a hundred preset styles that you can use in your own images.

This chapter explains how to create and use layer styles, and explores each layer effect in depth. It finishes with a simple tutorial that shows you how to design a logo using layer styles.

Adding a Layer Style

A layer style encompasses everything that you can tweak in the Layer Style dialog box (which is described in a moment). This includes nondestructive layer effects, as well as settings such as the layer's blending mode, opacity, and other blending options.

Each layer comes with a default style, which contains no effects and has default blending options (such as a Normal blending mode, an Opacity of 100 percent, and so on). You can add a custom style to any layer apart from the Background layer and fully locked layers. When you customize a layer style, you usually enable and edit one or more effects within the style. You can change the layer's blending options and make them part of the custom style, too, if you like. (More on this in the section "Editing and Managing Layer Styles.")

True to form, Photoshop gives you a million and one ways to add a custom style to a layer. Choose the one that works for you:

- Double-click the layer in the Layers palette. Be careful to click away from the thumbnail, name, and link icon.

- Right-click the layer in the Layers palette, and choose Blending Options from the pop-up menu.

- Select the layer and then choose Blending Options from the Layers palette menu.

- Select the layer, click the Add a Layer Style icon (the *fx* symbol) at the bottom of the Layers palette, then choose an effect to add from the pop-up menu, or choose Blending Options at the top of the menu.

- Select the layer; then choose an effect to add from the available options under Layer ➪ Layer Style.

- Select the layer; then choose Layer ➪ Layer Style ➪ Blending Options.

After you finish one of these actions, Photoshop presents you with the majestic Layer Style dialog box, as shown in Figure 10.1. The various parts of the dialog box work as follows:

- **Styles:** Click this section in the top left of the dialog to display a list of all loaded style presets and then click a preset to use it on the current layer.

- **Blending Options:** This section below Styles lets you tweak the blending settings for the layer, including the blending mode, opacity, and advanced blending options.

CROSS-REF Blending options are covered in detail in Chapter 7.

- **Effects:** The list of available effects runs down the left-hand side of the dialog box. Select the check box next to an effect to enable it; click the effect name to see and customize the effect's options.

- **Effect Options:** The main part of the dialog box is taken up with an array of options for your currently selected effect (or for the Blending Options, if that's what you've selected).

- **New Style button:** With this button you can create custom style presets and save them to the Styles palette.

- **Preview:** Select this option to see how your custom style looks in the document window. You can also preview your style by looking at the thumbnail below the Preview option.

When you're happy with your settings, click OK to apply the new style to the layer.

TIP To back out of any changes you've made in the Layer Style dialog box, click Cancel. You can also hold down Alt (Option on the Mac) to turn the Cancel button into a Reset button. Click Reset to return the dialog box's options to the state they were in when you first opened the dialog.

You can also apply one of Photoshop's many preset styles to a layer. To do this, select the layer, then pull up the Styles palette (Window ➪ Styles) and click the style you want to apply. You can also click and drag a preset from the Styles palette to a layer in the Layers palette to apply it to that layer, or drag it to the document window; Photoshop applies the style to the topmost layer under the mouse cursor in the window.

TIP When you apply a preset style to a layer, Photoshop deletes any existing effects in the layer by default. To preserve the existing effects, hold down Shift while you click or drag the style preset.

FIGURE 10.1

The Layer Style dialog box. In this example, a Drop Shadow effect is being edited.

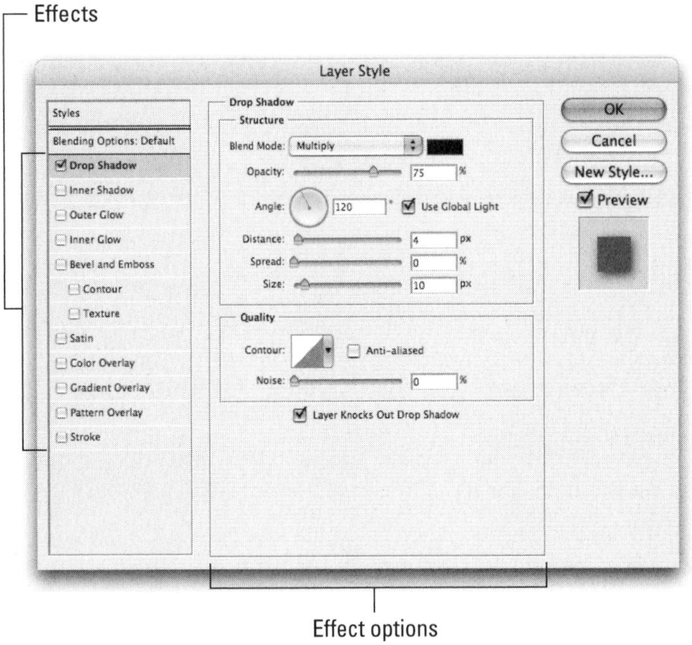

Effects

Effect options

Editing and Managing Layer Styles

After you add a custom style to a layer, you can go back and edit the style at any time. To do this, select the layer, then display the Layer Style dialog box using one of the techniques described in the section "Adding a Layer Style." When the dialog box appears, make your changes to the effects and blending options, and click OK to apply the new style to the layer.

If you add any effects to a layer, you'll notice a little *fx* symbol appear on the right-hand side of the layer in the Layers palette, as shown in Figure 10.2. Click the downward-pointing arrow to the right of the symbol to display the list of effects attached to the layer.

To jump straight to a particular effect and edit it, double-click its name in the Layers palette. Photoshop opens the Layer Style dialog box and takes you straight to your chosen effect.

FIGURE 10.2

Each effect in a layer style is displayed individually in the Layers palette.

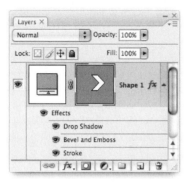

Disabling, hiding, and deleting effects

You can turn off an effect by clicking its eye icon in the Layers palette. The eye icon disappears and the effect no longer appears in the document window. You can also turn off an effect by deselecting the check box next to its name in the Layer Style dialog box. Click the eye icon again or select the check box to turn the effect back on.

To turn off all effects for a layer, click the eye icon next to the Effects item under the layer in the Layers palette. Click it again to turn them back on. You can also turn all effects for a layer off and on by right-clicking any effect under the layer in the Layers palette and choosing Disable Layer Effects or Enable Layer Effects from the pop-up menu.

You can also choose Layer ➪ Layer Style ➪ Hide All Effects to temporarily hide all effects in the entire document. Choose Layer ➪ Layer Style ➪ Show All Effects to reveal them again.

NOTE When you choose Show All Effects, any effects that were previously disabled by clicking their eye icons or choosing Disable Layer Effects remain disabled. In other words, disabling and enabling an effect works independently from the Hide All Effects and Show All Effects commands.

To delete an effect entirely from a layer, click it in the Layers palette and drag it down to the Delete Layer (trash can) icon at the bottom of the palette. To delete all effects from a layer, drag the Effects item under the layer to the Delete Layer icon.

NOTE Even if you delete a layer effect from a layer, Photoshop remembers its settings for that layer. So if, for example, you delete a Drop Shadow effect from a layer, then later decide to add the Drop Shadow effect back in for that layer, your previous Drop Shadow settings appear in the Layer Style dialog box by default. This holds true unless you delete all the effects in a layer by dragging its Effects item to the trash icon, or unless you clear a layer style completely.

To clear a layer style completely, removing all effects and returning the layer's Blending Options to the factory defaults, select the layer and choose Layer ➪ Layer Style ➪ Clear Layer Style. You can also right-click the layer in the Layers palette and choose Clear Layer Style from the pop-up menu. If the Styles palette is open, you can also click the Clear Style icon at the bottom of the palette.

Moving and duplicating effects and styles

You can move an effect from one layer to another. To do this, first reveal the list of effects for the source layer by clicking the downward-pointing arrow next to its *fx* icon in the Layers palette. Click the effect you want to move, and drag it to the target layer in the Layers palette. To copy the effect rather than move it, hold down Alt (Option on the Mac), then click the effect and drag.

You can also move or duplicate all effects in a layer at once. To move them, reveal the list of effects in the source layer, then click and drag the Effects item to the target layer in the Layers palette. To duplicate all effects, hold down Alt (Option on the Mac) before you click and drag.

As well as dragging effects to a layer in the Layers palette, you can also click the effect you want to duplicate in the Layers palette and drag it straight into the document window. Release the mouse button, and Photoshop copies the effect onto the topmost layer under your mouse cursor. (You can only duplicate effects with this method; you can't move them.)

Photoshop also lets you copy and paste an entire layer style from one layer to another. This includes all effects, as well as any custom blending options in the style. To do this, select the layer from which you want to copy the style and choose Layer ➪ Layer Style ➪ Copy Layer Style. You can also right-click the layer in the Layers palette, then choose Copy Layer Style from the pop-up menu. Select the layer to which you want to copy the style, and choose Layer ➪ Layer Style ➪ Paste Layer Style, or right-click the layer and choose Paste Layer Style.

CAUTION When you move or copy all effects from one layer to another, any existing effects in the target layer are deleted. Similarly, if you copy and paste a whole layer style from one layer to another, the entire layer style of the target layer is overwritten. You might want to duplicate your target layer first so you have a backup of its effects. You can then click and drag any effects back into the target layer afterward.

Creating and managing preset layer styles

As we mention earlier, you can save a layer's style as a preset that you can then use on any layer, at any time. (To find out how to apply an existing preset style to a layer, see the section "Adding a Layer Style" earlier in this chapter.)

There are a few ways to create a new style preset:

- Display the Styles palette by choosing Window ➪ Styles, select the layer that has the style you want to save and then move the mouse to an empty space in the Styles palette; the cursor changes to a paint bucket icon. Click the mouse button to add the style.

- Rather than clicking in an empty space in the Styles palette, you can simply click the Create New Style icon at the bottom of the palette, or choose New Style from the Styles palette menu.

- Select the layer whose style you want to save, then display the Layer Style dialog box and click the New Style button.

After you do any of these, the New Style dialog box appears, as shown in Figure 10.3. It contains a small preview of your style, followed by a Name box where you can type a name for your new style. Select Include Layer Effects if you want any layer effects in the layer style to be preserved. You can also select Include Layer Blending Options to preserve any blending options such as the layer opacity and blending mode. You need to select at least one option, otherwise there's nothing to save. (By default, Photoshop selects Include Layer Effects if you add any effects to the layer, and Include Layer Blending Options if you change any of the layer's blending options from the default.) When you finish, click OK to create your new style; it appears in the Styles palette.

> **TIP** If you're in a hurry, you can bypass the New Style dialog box by Alt+clicking (Option+clicking on the Mac) the Create New Style button in the Styles palette. Photoshop uses sensible defaults for Include Layer Effects and Include Layer Blending Options, as previously described, and gives it an exciting name such as Style 1. Never fear — you can change the preset's name later. See the following for details.

FIGURE 10.3

The New Style dialog box lets you create a new style preset from the active layer's style.

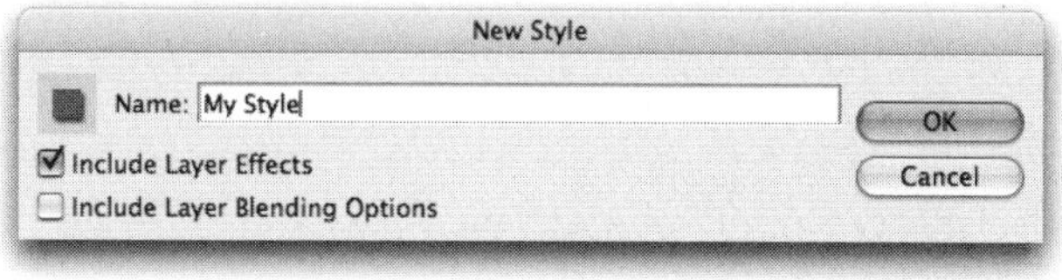

To rename a preset style, double-click it in the Styles palette. If you're viewing your presets in a list format — more on this later — then the style name becomes editable; just type your new name and press Enter (Return on the Mac). If you're viewing the presets in thumbnail mode, a Style Name dialog box appears that allows you to edit the name. You can also right-click a style and choose Rename Style from the pop-up menu. When viewing the Styles palette embedded within the Layer Style dialog box, you can select a style then choose Rename Style from the palette menu (click the little triangle to the top right of the palette within the dialog box).

Deleting a preset is simply a matter of clicking it in the Styles palette and dragging it to the Delete Style icon at the bottom of the palette. You can also right-click it and choose Delete Style from the pop-up menu or, if you're viewing styles within the Layer Style dialog box, select the style and choose Delete Style from the palette menu.

> **TIP**   You can also rename and delete styles when using a shape or pen tool in Shape Layers mode. Click the Style option in the options bar to display the Styles pop-up palette, right-click a style, and choose Rename Style or Delete Style, or click a style to select it then choose Rename Style or Delete Style from the palette menu. You can also load and save styles via this pop-up palette, too; see the next paragraph for more on saving and loading.

Styles can also be saved to and loaded from disk. To save the current preset styles in the Styles palette, choose Save Styles from the palette menu. Styles are saved in a special style presets file that ends with the .asl extension. To load a batch of styles into the palette, choose Load Styles from the palette menu and choose an ASL file; the styles are added to the end of the current list of styles in the palette. If you prefer to replace all the current styles with the loaded batch, choose Replace Styles instead.

Photoshop comes with a wealth of preset styles designed for a range of uses, including photographic effects, text styles, and Web buttons. You can pick from these presets by choosing an option from the lower half of the Styles palette menu. Photoshop asks whether you want to replace your current set of styles with the ones you're loading (just click OK) or add them to the end of your current set (click Append).

> **TIP**   If you save a batch of styles in Photoshop's Styles folder (inside the Presets folder), that batch will appear in the list at the bottom of the Styles palette menu the next time you start Photoshop.

If you start getting a bit overwhelmed by all the styles you've accumulated in your Styles palette, you can reset the list to a minimal set of styles by choosing Reset Styles from the Styles palette menu.

By default, styles in the Styles palette are displayed as tiny thumbnails, but you can change this. Choose Large Thumbnail from the palette menu to make the thumbnails bigger, or choose Text Only to view the styles as a plain text list with no thumbnails. Small List displays each style as a really tiny thumbnail followed by its name, while Large List displays the styles using a bigger thumbnail and font size.

> **CROSS-REF**   Style presets are particularly useful when creating new shape layers. For more on this topic, see Chapter 5.

Converting a layer style to individual layers

If you need more control over your layer effects than the Layer Style dialog box gives you, you can always convert the effects to separate layers. You can then tweak those layers as much as you want; for example, you can transform them, paint on them, or apply filters to them.

To do this, select the layer; then choose Layer ⇨ Layer Style ⇨ Create Layer(s). As you can see in Figure 10.4, Photoshop creates one or more extra layers to re-create your chosen effects and removes the effects from the layer itself. Sometimes it creates a layer below the active layer (for example, when converting the Drop Shadow effect); sometimes it creates a clipping mask with the active layer as the base layer and adds the effect layers to the mask. After Photoshop creates the layers, you're free to edit, move, or delete them.

CAUTION Photoshop doesn't always do a perfect job of this conversion; some of the layer effects simply can't be rendered accurately using separate layers. You get a warning about this when you choose Layer ➪ Layer Style ➪ Create Layer(s). If you don't like the results you can always undo the operation with Edit ➪ Undo Create Layers and return to your original layer with its effects intact. Note that you can't convert the layers back into layer effects further down the line; it's strictly a one-way operation.

FIGURE 10.4

When you apply the Create Layers command to your active layer with effects (left), Photoshop renders the effects as individual layers and removes the layer effects from the active layer (right).

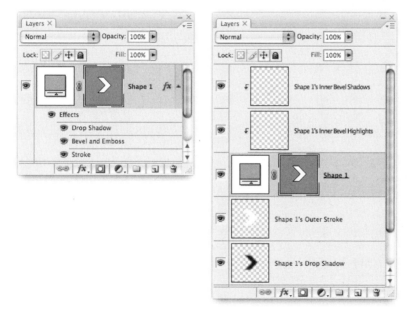

Exploring Layer Effects

Now that we've covered the basics of adding styles and effects to your layers, let's look at each of the available layer effects in detail. For each effect, you learn what it does, how you can use it, and how all its options work. The following options are common to all effects, so we'll get them out of the way here:

- **Blend Mode:** Unlike the blending mode pop-up menu in the Layers palette, which controls how the active layer blends with the layers below, this Blend Mode option controls how the effect blends with the active layer or with the underlying layers. Generally, the default blending mode used by each layer effect works best, but you may want to tweak the blending mode to produce some unique results.

NOTE If the effect appears on top of the layer, such as with Inner Shadow, then the effect blends with the active layer. On the other hand, if the effect is outside the layer boundary — this happens with Drop Shadow, for example — then the effect blends with the layers below the active layer instead.

CROSS-REF For more on how blending modes work, see Chapter 7.

- **Opacity:** As with the Blending Mode option, this controls the opacity of the effect, rather than the opacity of the layer. Reduce the Opacity slider to make the effect more transparent and, therefore, more subtle. If the effect appears on top of the active layer, more of the active layer shows through; if the effect is outside the layer boundary, then more of the underlying layers show through.

NOTE The term *layer boundary* refers to the edges between the nontransparent and transparent pixels in the layer; in other words, the edges of the layer contents. If all pixels in the layer are nontransparent, the layer boundary is effectively the same as the document boundary.

These two options behave the same for all of the effects discussed in the following sections, so they won't be mentioned again.

Drop Shadow and Inner Shadow

The first two effects in the list, Drop Shadow and Inner Shadow, let you add a variety of shadow effects to your layers. Drop Shadow produces a shadow that lies behind the contents of the layer, making the layer appear to jump out from the image, while Inner Shadow produces a shadow that lies inside the edges of the layer contents, making the layer appear recessed, or cut out, from the image. Figure 10.5 shows the difference between a drop shadow and an inner shadow.

The Drop Shadow and Inner Shadow effects have practically identical options, as follows:

- **Color box:** Click the color box to choose a color for the shadow. The default is black, and that's probably what you want most of the time. Other colors tend to look a bit unnatural, but might be useful if you're after a particular effect.
- **Angle:** Use this control to set the direction of the light source that casts the shadow. You can click and drag in the circle to change the angle, or type a value in degrees in the box to the right of the circle. As you move the angle, the direction of the shadow changes. While the shadow effect is highlighted in the dialog box, you can also click the shadow in the document window and drag it around to change its position — this affects both the Angle and the Distance settings. This is great if you want to quickly and visually position a shadow.

Here a moon shape layer is created with the Moon preset shape and a Drop Shadow (left) and an Inner Shadow (right) effect is applied to it.

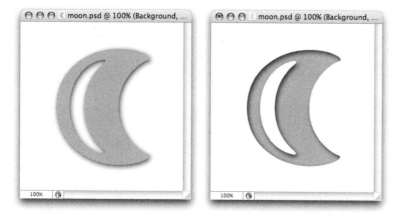

- **Use Global Light:** Select this option to use the global light angle for the shadow effect. This is generally a good plan, as it means that all the effects in your document are using consistent lighting. If you change the value of Angle with this option enabled, the global light angle changes as well. You can learn more about this feature in the sidebar "Global Light."

- **Distance:** This is the distance of the shadow from the layer content, in pixels. Click and drag the slider to select a distance from zero all the way up to 30,000 pixels (the slider starts to increase in bigger jumps as you move it farther to the right). You can also type a value in the box to the right of the slider. A zero value aligns the shadow exactly with the layer; you'll probably want to set a fairly large Size value to see the shadow properly in this case. You can also drag the shadow around in the document window to change its distance and angle, as long as the shadow effect is highlighted in the dialog box.

- **Spread (Drop Shadow) and Choke (Inner Shadow):** These options control how much of the shadow is blurred and how much is fully opaque. The values are expressed as a percentage of the total shadow size, defined by the Size option (see the next item). As with Distance, you can click and drag the slider or type a value in the box to the right. A value of zero results in the whole shadow being blurred, while a value of 100 percent results in no blurring at all. These options effectively adjust the sharpness of the shadow.

- **Size:** Use this option to control the size of the shadow in pixels. For example, a Size of 10 extends the shadow 10 pixels from the layer boundary. Use the slider to increase the size from zero — the same size as the layer content — up to 250 pixels, or type a value in the box to the right of the slider.

- **Contour:** When creating a shadow, Photoshop fades the shadow pixels from opaque to transparent. By default, this transition moves gradually from opaque, at the layer boundary, to transparent, at the edge of the shadow. You can choose a different transition by picking a contour from the Contour box. Click the downward-pointing arrow next to the box to pick a preset contour graph, or click the graph in the box to create your own. Think of the graph as moving from the layer boundary (on the right) to the edge of the shadow (on the left), with opacity increasing as you move from bottom to top.

NOTE   The contour only controls the blurred part of the shadow, not the fully opaque part defined by the Spread or Choke value.

CROSS-REF   For more on using contours, as well as creating your own, see the section "Using Contours" later in the chapter.

■ **Anti-Aliased:** If you're using a contour with lots of steep hills and valleys, and you use a small shadow size, you might find that the transitions in the shadow have quite jagged edges. If so, select the Anti-Aliased option to help smooth out the edges, as shown in Figure 10.6.

■ **Noise:** Clicking and dragging the Noise slider to the right introduces random elements into the opacity levels of the pixels in the shadow. The more you drag to the right, the more pronounced the random elements become. You can also type a percentage value in the box to the right, where 0 percent means no noise and 100 percent gives the most pronounced effect. This option is great for creating rough-looking shadows and also for reducing banding effects when exporting your images for the Web.

■ **Layer Knocks Out Drop Shadow:** This option, only available for the Drop Shadow effect, is selected by default and works in conjunction with the layer's Fill Opacity setting. It ensures that the pixels of the layer content always sit on top of any pixels in the drop shadow. For example, in Figure 10.7 the layer in both images has a Fill Opacity of 25 percent. Deselecting Layer Knocks Out Drop Shadow causes the drop shadow to show through.

FIGURE 10.6

The Anti-Aliased option in action. A 30-sided star shape is created and a small drop shadow with the Ring — Double contour is added (left). Selecting the Anti-Aliased option (right) reduces the jaggies.

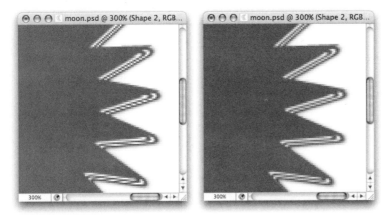

Global Light

The Drop Shadow, Inner Shadow, and Bevel and Emboss effects all have the option to use a global angle and, for Bevel and Emboss, an altitude setting. These two settings are collectively called the Global Light setting, and it applies across the whole document. By setting your effects to use the Global Light setting, you can make sure that they're all using the same angle and altitude values, resulting in a consistent look to your effects.

To change the Global Light angle or altitude, you can either use the controls within a Drop Shadow, Inner Shadow, or Bevel and Emboss effect—provided its Use Global Light option is selected—or you can choose Layer ⇨ Layer Style ⇨ Global Light, and set the angle and altitude in the dialog box that appears.

FIGURE 10.7

A drop shadow is added to the moon and the moon's Fill Opacity is set at 25 percent.

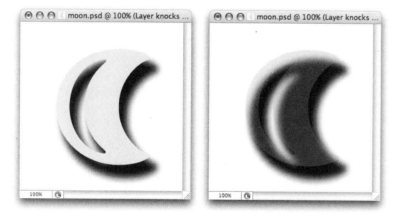

Outer and Inner Glow

In many ways, the Outer Glow and Inner Glow effects are the counterparts of Drop Shadow and Inner Shadow. Rather than creating shadows around the edges of the layer content, they create light instead. Outer Glow creates a halo of light directed outside the layer content, while Inner Glow directs the light inward toward the center of the content, as you can see in Figure 10.8.

FIGURE 10.8

Applying Outer Glow on the Moon shape (left) produces a glowing halo round the outside of the shape. On the other hand, Inner Glow (right) directs the glowing light inward, toward the center of the shape.

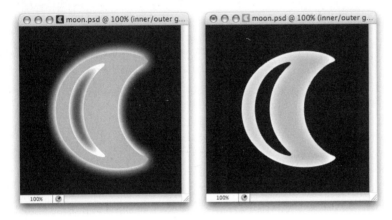

The options for Outer and Inner Glow are almost exactly the same. The only difference is that Inner Glow allows you to control the direction of the glow with the Source option. The various options work as follows:

- **Noise:** Increasing this slider adds more random elements to the transparency levels of the pixels in the glow. This works in the same way as the Noise option for shadows — see the section "Drop Shadow and Inner Shadow" earlier in the chapter for more info.

- **Color box:** To choose a solid color to use for the glow, click the color box. You can also choose a gradient for the glow instead by clicking the downward arrow to the right of the Gradient box, and picking a gradient from the list. Alternatively, click in the Gradient box to edit the current gradient. Photoshop then uses the gradient to color the glow, with the left-hand edge of the gradient coloring the glow nearest to the edge of the layer content, and the right-hand edge coloring the part toward the edge of the glow. For example, to create a warm, fiery glow, try using the Orange, Yellow, Orange gradient.

CROSS-REF For more information on gradients, see Chapter 6.

- **Technique:** You can choose from two different techniques for generating the glow effect. Softer creates the effect by applying a blur; it produces a gentler, more natural-looking glow, but doesn't preserve the detail of the layer that well. On the other hand, Precise follows the contours of the layer accurately. Precise is good for applying glows to type layers — particularly when using small Size values — but it can look somewhat unnatural when used with large glow sizes.

■ **Source (Inner Glow):** This option allows you to specify whether the glow emanates outward from the center of the layer content (Center) or inward from the layer boundary (Edge).

■ **Spread (Outer Glow) and Choke (Inner Glow):** Use these options to control how much of the glow effect is blurred (diffused), and how much is fully opaque (solid) — in other words, how sharp the glow's cutoff is. Click and drag the slider to change the spread or choke, or type a value in the box to the right. The values range from 0 to 100 percent, where 0 produces a fully blurred glow and 100 produces a totally solid glow. These values don't change the size of the glow; that's controlled by the Size option. They merely control how much of the glow's radius is blurred, and how much is opaque.

■ **Size:** This option adjusts the size of the outer or inner glow, measured in pixels from the layer boundary. You can choose values from zero — which produces virtually no glow effect — all the way up to 250 pixels. Use the slider to adjust the value, or type a value in the box to the right.

■ **Contour:** Use this option to specify how the glow effect transitions from opaque at the layer boundary (or at the center of the layer content if using an Inner Glow with the Center setting) to transparent at the edge of the glow. Pick a contour from the Contour box, and the glow follows that contour, working from the layer boundary (or center) on the right to the edge of the blur on the left. The higher the point on the curve, the more opaque the result. Choose from a preset contour by clicking the downward-pointing arrow next to the box, or create your own contour by clicking the graph in the box.

■ **Anti-Aliased:** This option smoothes the transitions between opaque and transparent areas of the glow. It's useful if you're using a glow contour with a lot of variations, as it prevents jagged edges from appearing in the glow.

■ **Range:** This controls both the position of the contour within the range of the glow, and the size of the contour within that range. A value of 50 percent places the contour bang in the middle of the glow range, with the contour spread across the whole range of the glow; 1 percent moves the contour to one edge of the glow and makes the contour take up only 1 percent of the overall glow size; and 100 percent makes the contour stretch to twice the size of the whole glow.

NOTE The position and size of the contour are also affected by the Spread or Choke setting. The higher the Spread or Choke value, the smaller the range taken up by the contour, and vice versa.

■ **Jitter:** The Jitter option works in conjunction with the Gradient option (see the "Color box" description), so you need to choose a gradient for Jitter to have any effect. The option adds random elements to the spread of colors and opacity levels across the gradient to produce an effect similar to Noise that applies across the whole gradient. The more you drag to the right, the more pronounced the effect becomes. You can also type a percentage value in the box to the right. 0 percent has no effect, while 100 percent gives the most pronounced effect. You can use this option to reduce banding effects when working with indexed-color images, such as GIFs.

Jitter has no effect when using the Foreground to Background gradient preset. You either need to use a gradient with two or more (nontransparent) colors for Jitter to work, or you need to have at least three opacity stops in the gradient.

Bevel and Emboss

Moving farther down the list of available effects, you come to Bevel and Emboss. This versatile effect lets you add various beveling and embossing effects to your layer, imparting a three-dimensional element to the layer. Figure 10.9 shows some of the effects you can achieve with Bevel and Emboss.

FIGURE 10.9

Various Bevel and Emboss effects are applied to the moon shape: Inner Bevel (left), Emboss (center), and Pillow Emboss (right).

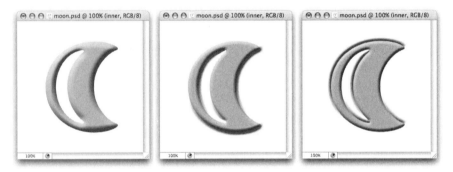

The main Bevel and Emboss options work as follows:

- **Style:** This is where you choose the type of beveling that you want to apply. Outer Bevel adds a bevel outside the layer boundary, giving the impression of the layer being raised from its background. Inner Bevel adds the bevel inside the layer boundary instead, making the layer itself look beveled and three-dimensional. Emboss adds a bevel across the layer boundary, giving the impression of the layer being stamped on the underlying layers, while Pillow Emboss adds shading to both the inside and outside of the layer boundary to make the layer look like it's embedded in the underlying layers. Finally, Stroke Emboss adds embossing to the layer's Stroke effect only. (You need to have applied a Stroke effect for the embossing to be noticeable.)

- **Technique:** This option lets you tweak the method that Photoshop uses when forming the beveling effect. Smooth applies a small amount of blur to the effect to produce a softer result, but it doesn't follow the contours of the layer boundary particularly well, resulting in a loss of detail when using large Size values. Chisel Hard hugs the contours of the layer boundary much more accurately, preserving features from the layer contents, making it great for type layers. Chisel Soft is a compromise between Chisel Hard and

Smooth; it usually doesn't follow the contours as accurately as Chisel Hard, but it produces a gentler effect. It does tend to introduce quite strong artifacts, or ridges, in the bevel, though.

- **Depth:** This option specifies the contrast of the shading used for the effect. A high value results in a high level of contrast, producing a pronounced, or deep, bevel. A low value produces low-contrast shading, giving the impression of a shallow bevel.

- **Direction:** This option controls whether the beveling effect makes the layer appear raised (Up) or indented (Down). It's the equivalent of rotating the Angle setting by 180 degrees.

- **Size:** Use this option to control the size of the bevel in pixels. Click and drag the slider to change the size, or type a value from 0 to 250 pixels in the box to the right of the slider. For example, a Size value of 10 pixels makes the effect extend 10 pixels from the layer boundary.

- **Soften:** This option is great for smoothing over artifacts caused by using either of the Chisel techniques. It adds a touch of blurring to the effect to help smooth things out. Adjust the radius — and therefore the amount — of the blur by clicking and dragging the slider or by typing a value between 0 and 16 pixels in the box to the right.

- **Angle and Altitude:** Use the Angle option to adjust the direction of the light source used for the bevel effect. Click and drag the little crosshair in the circle, or type a value (in degrees) in the Angle box to the right. As you adjust the angle, you can see the effect change direction in the document window. You can also adjust the altitude of the light source; drag the crosshair toward the center to move the light source directly overhead and high up (much like the midday sun); drag it toward the edge to move the source more toward the horizon. You can also type a value for the light source altitude, in degrees, in the Altitude box; 0 degrees puts the light source on the horizon, while 90 degrees puts it directly overhead.

- **Use Global Light:** This option locks the effect's Angle and Altitude settings to the Global Light settings. This means that this effect, and all other effects in your document that have Use Global Light selected, use the exact same lighting settings, thereby guaranteeing a consistent look to the effects. If you change the effect's Angle and Altitude settings with Use Global Light selected, the Global Light angle and altitude also are changed.

- **Gloss Contour:** This option controls how the highlights and shadows that make up the effect are mapped across the range of the effect. Choose a preset contour by clicking the downward-pointing arrow next to the box, or create your own contour by clicking the graph in the box. The Input values along the bottom of the graph represent the areas in shadow in the effect (on the left) to the areas in the light (on the right). The Output values up the side of the graph represent the amount of shadow (at the bottom) or highlight (at the top) to apply. So the default Linear gradient exactly maps shadowed areas to shadows, and lit areas to highlights. By varying the curve within the graph, you control how the "dark" and "light" areas of the bevel are shaded. For example, if you choose the Cone contour, the areas of the bevel that are supposed to be in extreme darkness or light appear dark, while the areas in between appear bright (assuming default settings of the Highlight and Shadow options). The net result of all this is that using anything other than the Linear gradient tends to produce a glossy, metallic effect, with localized shadows and highlights.

- **Anti-Aliased:** If you use a fairly complex Gloss Contour graph, with lots of spikes, then you'll probably notice that the glossy effects appear jagged in the image, particularly if your original layer is quite small or detailed. By selecting the Anti-Aliased option, you can smooth out these transitions, resulting in a less jagged effect.

- **Highlight Mode, Color box, and Opacity:** These settings control the blending mode, color, and opacity to use for the Highlight shading in the effect. To create the bevel, Photoshop applies a Highlight and a Shadow. These are usually applied to the "light" and "dark" areas of the effect, respectively, but you can change this mapping using the Gloss Contour option. Use the Highlight Mode menu to select a different blend mode; click the Color box to pick a different color to use for the highlight; click and drag the Opacity slider (or type a value in the box to the right) to control how opaque or transparent the highlight is. The default values usually work pretty well, but you can experiment with the options here to create different effects. For example, if you choose a Highlight Mode of Multiply and set its Color to Black, your "highlights" will become shadows. The Opacity sliders are also a great way to fine-tune the overall impact of the effect.

- **Shadow Mode, Color, and Opacity:** As you might imagine, these controls apply to the Shadow shading used for the effect and behave much like their Highlight counterparts described previously.

If all the previous options still don't give you the control you need, Photoshop has two more tricks up its sleeve: the Contour and Texture subeffects under the Bevel and Emboss effect. Contour allows you to sculpt the shape of the bevel itself, while Texture lets you apply a pattern as a bumpy texture to the layer contents. In short, Contour and Texture give you a lot of control over the three-dimensional aspect of the effect. Figure 10.10 shows a couple of examples of Contour and Texture in action.

FIGURE 10.10

The Contour and Texture subeffects doing their stuff. In the first example, (left) the Ring-Double contour is applied to the moon shape using the Contour subeffect, while the second example (right) uses the Texture subeffect to apply the Optical Checkerboard pattern as a texture to the moon.

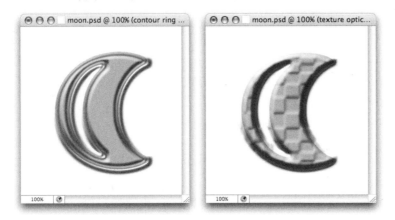

As with the regular effects in the dialog box, select the check box to the left of Contour or Texture to enable the subeffect, or click the subeffect name itself to both enable the subeffect and edit its options. Note that the Contour and Texture subeffects only work in conjunction with the Bevel and Emboss effect; if Bevel and Emboss isn't enabled, these sub-effects don't do anything.

The options for the Contour subeffect work as follows:

- **Contour:** The contour you choose here affects the shape of the raised and lowered parts of the bevel effect around the edge of the layer contents. Think of the bevel as a three-dimensional shape viewed from above, with the contour being a cross-section of that shape as viewed from the side; if you could cut through the bevel at any point with a saw, you'd see your selected contour shape. The default contour, Linear, produces a standard, 45-degree sloping bevel — which is the same as not enabling the Contour subeffect at all — but you can get some great effects with the other presets. For example, **Cove:** Deep produces a nice curved, hollowed-out bevel like a quarter pipe (you could almost skate up it), while Rounded Steps adds four "steps" to the contour, giving it a ridged effect. Choose a preset by clicking the downward-pointing arrow next to the box, or create your own contour by clicking the graph in the box.

> **TIP** The shape of the bevel, as defined by the chosen contour, is most obvious when using the Chisel Hard technique.

- **Anti-Aliased:** The Anti-Aliased option is particularly useful for this effect, because it's very easy to produce quite jagged-looking bevels, especially with some of the spikier contours. Simply select this option to smooth out all those nasty jagged bits, and create a nice smooth beveling effect.

- **Range:** Use this option to adjust the position and size of the contour within the bevel's cross-section. If you click and drag the slider all the way to the left, or type a value of 0, the contour is pushed to one edge of the bevel and only takes up a tiny proportion of the bevel; the rest of the bevel defaults to the standard 45-degree slope. If you drag the slider all the way to the right, or type a value of 100 percent, the contour stretches to fill out twice the width of the bevel. The default value of 50 percent sits the contour nicely in the middle of the bevel, exactly filling the bevel's width.

While the Contour subeffect lets you shape the bevel effect, Texture lets you add a three-dimensional bumpy texture to the layer contents themselves, using a technique known as *bump mapping*. Photoshop then adds shading, including any beveling that you specify, to this newly textured layer. The exceptions to this rule are Outer Bevel, where only the bevel is textured; and Stroke Emboss, where only the stroke effect is textured.

You can control the texture using the following options:

- **Pattern:** This option lets you choose a pattern to use for the texture. Click the pattern to display the pop-up Pattern picker; then click the pattern you want to use. You can also click the triangle in the top right of the Pattern picker to bring up the palette menu — this lets you create and delete patterns; change the appearance of patterns in the palette; load and save patterns; and pick from a range of pattern presets. By default, darker pixels in the pattern correspond to higher points in the texture, and lighter pixels correspond to lower points, but you can change this with the Invert option. Photoshop spreads the texture across the whole layer, repeating it as necessary. While the Texture subeffect is highlighted in the dialog box, you can move the texture around the layer by clicking and dragging in the document window, which is handy if you need to align the texture with the layer contents.

CROSS-REF   For more on patterns and the Pattern picker, see Chapter 6.

- **Snap To Origin:** If you have moved the texture from its original position by clicking and dragging it in the document window, you can move the texture back to its default position by clicking this button.

- **Scale:** By clicking and dragging this slider — or typing values in the box to the right of the slider — you can control the size of the texture as it appears in the effect. This is useful because the resolution of the pattern probably won't match the resolution of your document. By adjusting the scale of the texture, you can make the texture match the layer contents to give a pleasing result. Photoshop lets you scale the texture from 1 percent of its original size all the way up to 1000 percent.

- **Depth:** This option lets you control how much the texture is "raised" or "lowered." Click and drag the slider, or type values in the box to the right. Positive values raise the texture, so that dark pixels in the pattern correspond to high points in the texture and light pixels correspond to dark points; negative values reverse this mapping, so that dark maps to low points and light maps to high points. The higher the positive value, or the lower the negative value, the more the texture is raised or lowered. A value of zero results in a completely flat, and therefore invisible, texture. Depth values can range from -1000 percent (fully lowered) to 1000 percent (fully raised).

- **Invert:** This option simply inverts the high and low points of the texture, so that dark pixels of the pattern map to low points in the texture and light pixels map to high points. This is handy if your texture is based on a black background rather than a white one, for example.

NOTE   A Depth value of 50 percent with Invert disabled has the same effect as a Depth value of -50 percent with Invert enabled. In other words, Invert effectively flips the Depth setting from negative to positive, and vice versa.

- **Link with Layer:** Selecting this option causes the texture to move with the layer contents when using the Move tool, which is usually what you want to happen. Disable this option, and the texture remains fixed relative to the document window.

Satin

The Satin effect adds some dark (by default) internal shading to the layer, based on the shape of the layer boundary, to create the effect of a satin coating over the layer. In many ways it's like a gentler, simplified version of Inner Glow, with control over angle and distance. It's quite a subtle effect, but it can produce some nice results. Figure 10.11 shows some examples of Satin doing its stuff.

FIGURE 10.11

The Satin effect is applied here to the Moon shape, using various settings.

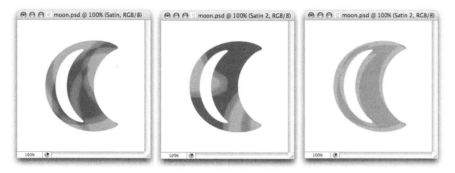

You can tweak the Satin effect fairly radically using its various options, as follows:

- **Angle:** This specifies the angle of the shading relative to the layer. Click and drag the little pointer in the circle to change the angle, or type a value in the box to the right. Values of 0, 90, or 180 degrees produce fairly boring results where the shading just heads straight in from the layer boundary horizontally or vertically; other angles are more interesting.

NOTE This Angle setting behaves independently of the Global Light Angle setting; one does not affect the other.

- **Distance:** This setting controls how far the shading extends inward from the layer boundary. Click and drag the slider, or type a value (in pixels) in the box to the right of the slider. Values range from 1 pixel to 250 pixels. For added interest, increase the distance until the lines of the shading start to cross over each other.

- **Size:** This option affects both the size and the blurriness of the shading. Click and drag the slider to the left to tighten the shading and make it more precise; drag the slider to the right to create a softer effect spread over a wider area. Size values can range from 0 pixels up to 250 pixels.

- **Contour:** Much as the Contour option for Inner Glow shapes the opaque and transparent areas of the glow, this option lets you control the opaque and transparent parts of the satin shading. Choose a contour preset from the list by clicking the downward-pointing arrow next to the box, or create your own preset by clicking the graph in the box. By default, Photoshop uses the Gaussian contour preset, which produces a soft, gentle effect, but if you're after something with a bit more pizzazz, try the Ring and Ring - Double presets.

- **Anti-Aliased:** Use this option to smooth over any jagged areas of the satin shading. Unless you're using one of the spikier contours with a very small Size setting, you're unlikely to need this option much.

- **Invert:** This option simply inverts the satin shading, so that dark areas become light and light areas become dark. It's on by default, which tends to put the dark areas of shading in the center of the layer and the lighter areas around the edge. Experiment with both settings to find the one that suits your layer the best.

Color, Gradient, and Pattern Overlay

The next three effects in the list are Color Overlay, Gradient Overlay, and Pattern Overlay. As their names imply, these effects all place an overlay on top of your layer, effectively "filling" the layer. The shape of the overlay exactly follows the shape of the layer contents (in tech-speak, the overlay is clipped by the layer's transparency mask). The simplest effect, Color Overlay, lets you add a solid color overlay to the layer. Gradient Overlay creates the overlay as a gradient, with control over the gradient used, as well as the shape, angle, and size of the gradient. Pattern Overlay lets you choose a pattern to overlay onto the layer; you can tweak the size of the pattern to match the layer.

CROSS-REF   These three Overlay effects behave in a similar way to their fill layer equivalents. Find out more about these in Chapter 6.

Figure 10.12 shows some examples of these overlay effects.

NOTE   Photoshop applies any interior effects — such as Inner Shadow, Inner Glow, Inner Bevel, and Satin — after the overlay. This means that you can, for example, add a Gradient Overlay effect to your layer and then add a Satin effect on top. You can also add one overlay effect on top of another; if you do this, you need to reduce the top overlay's opacity if you want the underlying overlay to show through.

FIGURE 10.12

In this example, the Color, Gradient, and Pattern Overlay effects are used to fill the Moon shape with a solid color (left), a gradient (center), and a pattern (right), respectively.

The options for these effects work as follows:

- **Color box:** This option within the Color Overlay effect lets you choose the color to use for the overlay. Click the box and pick a color from the Color Picker dialog box.

- **Gradient:** Use this option to choose the gradient to use for the Gradient Overlay effect. To do this, click the downward-pointing arrow to the right of the Gradient box to open the Gradient Picker, then click a preset gradient in the list. You can also create, load, and save gradient presets using the Gradient Picker — click the little arrow in the top-right corner of the picker to display a menu for this — and create your own gradients via the Gradient Editor by clicking in the Gradient box.

CROSS-REF For information on the detailed workings of the Gradient Picker and Gradient Editor, see Chapter 6.

- **Reverse:** This option, available for the Gradient Overlay effect, reverses the direction of the selected gradient.

- **Style:** The Style option for Gradient Overlay controls how Photoshop applies the gradient to your layer. Linear applies the gradient in a straight line, while Radial applies the gradient in a circular pattern from center to edge. Angle creates the gradient as a clockwise sweep around the center. Reflected draws the gradient in a straight line in both directions, starting from the center. Diamond uses the gradient to draw a diamond pattern around the center.

- **Align with Layer:** When this Gradient Overlay option is enabled, the gradient is aligned relative to the layer contents. The center of the gradient sits in the center of the layer contents, and the gradient fills the contents. Click and drag the layer around the document window, and the gradient moves with it. When this option is disabled, Photoshop aligns the gradient to the document; the center point of the gradient sits in the center of the document, and the gradient stretches out to fill the whole document. The layer and the gradient move independently; if you drag the layer around, the gradient remains stationary.

TIP Although Photoshop centers the gradient in the layer or image by default, you can reposition the gradient by dragging it in the document window while Gradient Overlay is highlighted in the Layer Style dialog box.

- **Angle:** The Angle setting, available for Gradient Overlay, controls the angle of the gradient. Click and drag the line around in the circle, or type a value in degrees in the box to the right. For the Linear and Reflected gradient styles, Angle determines the direction that the gradient moves in. For the Angle style, the Angle option sets the start angle of the sweep. For Diamond, this setting controls the angle of one of the points of the diamond, letting you rotate the diamond as you see fit. As you'd expect, Angle has no rotation effect on the Radial style.

NOTE For both the Radial and Diamond styles, the Angle setting also affects the size of the gradient somewhat. There's probably a very good reason for this, but it's not a particularly useful feature.

- **Scale:** This setting, available for both the Gradient and Pattern Overlay effects, lets you adjust the size of the effect. Click and drag the slider to the left to shrink the effect; drag it to the right to stretch it. Alternatively, type a percentage value in the box on the right. Values for Gradient Overlay range from 10 percent of the original gradient size up to 150 percent, while values for Pattern Overlay vary from 1 percent up to 1000 percent, or 10 times the original size.

- **Pattern:** Moving on to the options unique to the Pattern Overlay effect, you start with Pattern, which lets you choose the pattern to overlay on top of your layer. This option works in pretty much the same way as its counterpart in the Texture subeffect, described in the section "Bevel and Emboss" earlier in this chapter. After you select your pattern, you can click and drag it in the document window to reposition it whenever Pattern Overlay is highlighted in the Layer Style dialog box.

- **Snap to Origin:** Again, this works in the same way as it does within the Texture subeffect. Click the button to return the pattern back to its default position.

- **Link with Layer:** The final Pattern Overlay option also behaves like its equivalent in the Texture subeffect. Select this option, and the pattern moves around the document with the layer. Deselect it, and the pattern remains fixed relative to the document.

Stroke

The final effect in Photoshop's effects armory is Stroke. With this effect you can automatically draw a line around the edge of your layer contents. You can control the size and position of the line, and choose to draw the line using a solid color, a gradient, or a pattern. Figure 10.13 shows some examples of different stroke styles.

FIGURE 10.13

Here, a line is drawn around the Moon shape using the Stroke effect with various different options.

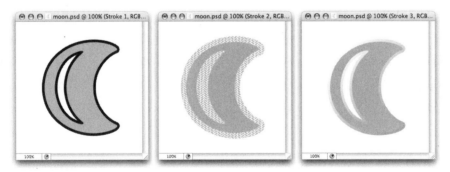

You can adjust the Stroke effect using the following options:

- **Size:** Use this setting to control the width of the line. You can click and drag the slider to alter the width, or type a value in the box. Values can range from 1 pixel wide up to 250 pixels wide.

- **Position:** Choose Outside to draw the line around the outside of the layer boundary, or Inside to draw it around the inside. Center places the line squarely on top of the boundary.

- **Fill Type:** This option lets you choose from three styles of fill for the line. The default, Color, simply uses a solid color for the line, but you can also choose Gradient to fill the line with a gradient fill, or Pattern to fill the line with a pattern. The options available below the Fill Type option behave exactly like their counterparts in the Color, Gradient, and Pattern Overlay effects, described earlier in this chapter.

Using Contours

Most layer effects feature a Contour option, allowing you to use a contour graph to fine-tune the effect. For example, with the Drop Shadow effect, you can use a contour to vary the opacity of the drop shadow as it drops away from the layer, while the Contour option in the Contour subeffect allows you to sculpt the shape of your bevels.

Working with contour presets

The Contour option within each layer effect shows you the current contour being used for the effect as a little graph. To change to a different contour preset, click the downward-pointing arrow to the right of the graph to display the Contour Picker, as shown in Figure 10.14. You can then select a preset to use by double-clicking its graph in the Contour Picker. Alternatively, click the graph once, then click outside the Contour Picker or press Esc to close the picker. You can also pick a contour preset by using the arrow keys to scroll through the presets, then pressing Enter (Return on the Mac) after you select your preset.

You can also use the Contour Picker to save and load presets to special contour library files; these files have an .shc extension. Photoshop comes with 12 built-in contours, but you'll find a bigger set of interesting presets inside the Presets/Contours folder within your Photoshop program folder. They're stored in a file called Contours.shc. This file contains the original 12 presets plus 18 new ones, making a total of 30 presets. Choose Load Contours or Replace Contours to load them. Unless you've added custom contours of your own, you'll probably want to use Replace Contours to replace the current set; otherwise, you'll end up with duplicates.

CROSS-REF The Contour Picker works in almost exactly the same way as the Gradient Picker, which is described in detail in Chapter 6.

FIGURE 10.14

The Contour Picker lets you browse and choose from the range of loaded contour presets, as well as save and load batches of presets.

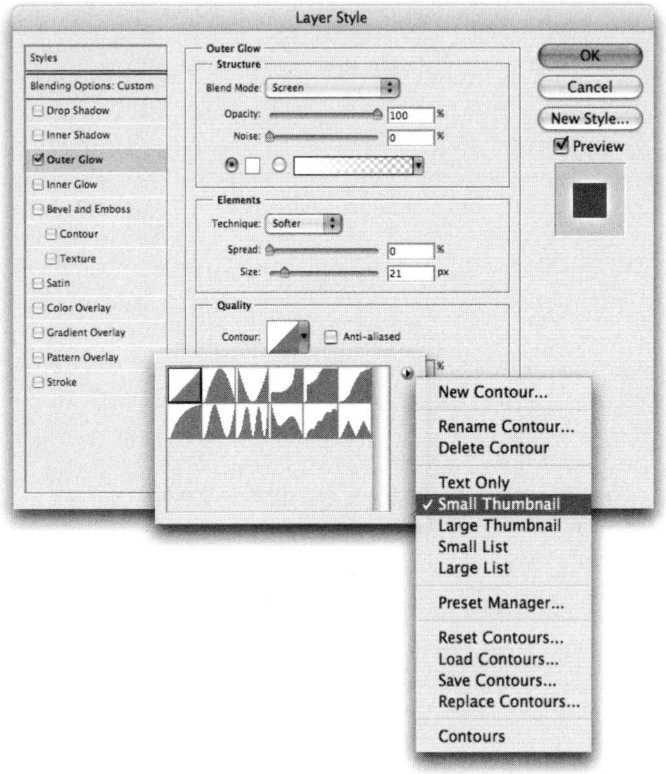

Creating your own contours

As well as using preset contours, you can also create your own contour shapes. To do this, choose an existing contour to work on and then click the contour graph in the Contour box. The Contour Editor dialog box, shown in Figure 10.15, appears, allowing you to edit the contour and, optionally, save it as a new preset.

By default, you're editing the contour preset you clicked on, but you can change this by choosing a different preset from the Preset menu at the top of the dialog box. If you start editing a contour, the value in the Preset menu changes to Custom.

FIGURE 10.15

Click the contour graph in the Contour box to access the Contour Editor, where you can create, edit, load, and save contour presets.

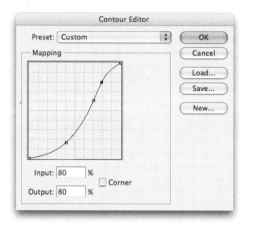

Editing a contour works in a similar way to using the Curves dialog box (see Chapter 6 for more on the Curves adjustment layer). Click the curve inside the Mapping box to add a new control point; you can then drag this control point around to shape the curve. You can keep adding more points to get finer control over the shape of the curve; Photoshop lets you add up to 16 points. To delete a point, Ctrl+click it (⌘+click it on the Mac), or drag it outside the graph.

Click a point to select it, and you can then drag it with the mouse or use the arrow keys to move it around. You can also type values in the Input and Output boxes to move the point. Shift+click multiple points to select them.

TIP To change the size of the grid lines in the Mapping box, Alt+click (Option+click on the Mac) anywhere inside the box.

By default, the control points are smooth; the curve passes smoothly between them. To turn a smooth point into a corner point with straight lines, select the point then select the Corner check box. This means you can create sharp corners and drop-offs in the contour.

NOTE As you edit the contour's curve, you can see the new shape reflected in the contour graph icon in the Contour box. The effect in the document window also updates in real time as the contour changes.

When you're happy with your new contour, you can save it to the current list of loaded presets by clicking New and giving it a name. Alternatively, you can save the contour to a contour preset library file by clicking Save and choosing a folder and name for the file. This creates a library file with just the one preset in it; if you want to save the current set of presets, use the Save Contours option in the Contour Picker, or the Save Set button in the Preset Manager dialog box.

CROSS-REF For more on the Preset Manager, see Chapter 6.

You can also load a contour from a contour library file into the dialog box for editing. To do this, click Load in the dialog box, and choose a library file. Note, however, that Photoshop only loads the first preset in the library, which really only makes it useful for loading single-preset libraries, such as those made by clicking Save in the dialog box. If you want to load a whole library of presets, select the Load Contours option in the Contour Picker, or click Load in the Preset Manager dialog box.

Tutorial: Creating a Logo Using Layer Styles

Layer styles can transform the most mundane designs into something very pleasing, and you'll prove this point in this tutorial by creating a logo from distinctly unpromising ingredients. The logo you'll create is for a mythical company called Shield, an imaginary Web-based security firm. The logo should be modern, slick, and simple. It'll be used primarily on the Web, so don't worry about how it looks in print.

Begin by creating a new Photoshop document of 400 pixels square at 72 pixels/inch (screen resolution).

The next step is to create a shield shape. Luckily, Photoshop ships with a few shield shapes in its Custom Shape presets. Select the Custom Shape tool in the Toolbox, and click the Shape option in the options bar. Choose one of the shield presets — Sign 5 is used here.

TIP If you can't see the Sign 5 shape, click the small arrow in the top right of the picker and choose All from the pop-up menu. Click Append or OK in the confirmation dialog box. Photoshop then loads all its shape presets, including the Sign 5 shape.

Change the foreground color to black. It doesn't really matter what color you choose at this point, since you'll be changing the shield's color using layer effects, but you do need to be able to see what you're drawing. Hold down Shift to constrain the shape's proportions, and click in the top left of the document window. Drag down and to the right to create your shield; make it around two-thirds of the size of the window. When you make the shape, double-click the shape layer's name in the Layers palette, and rename it **Shield**.

Now you have a large, black shield, which is very unpromising, but start adding some layer effects. Double-click the layer in the Layers palette, avoiding the name, thumbnail, and vector mask thumbnail. This displays the Layer Style dialog box.

First, add a gradient. Click the Gradient Overlay effect in the list on the left side of the dialog box to select and enable this effect. Now click inside the Gradient box to display the Gradient Editor. Customize the gradient as follows:

1. **Set the left color stop.** Click the left color stop, and click in the Color box below to display the Select Stop Color dialog box. Choose a slightly muted lime green — RGB 197, 204, 2 is fine.

2. **Set the right color stop.** Select the right color stop and, again, click the Color box to access the Select Color Stop dialog box. Choose quite a definite yellow this time, say RGB 239, 242, 6.

3. **Steepen the gradient.** You've produced a gradual gradient, but this logo calls for something that feels a little shinier, which requires a steeper gradient. Click and drag the left color stop to the right until it's approximately in the center. Drag the right-hand midpoint diamond so that it's close to the center stop, as shown in Figure 10.16. You should see the gradient become less gentle as you do this. Click OK to close the Gradient Editor and return to the Layer Style dialog box.

FIGURE 10.16

The Gradient Editor showing the two color stops and the midpoint slider, as well as the document window in the background. You can see that you've created quite a hard gradient.

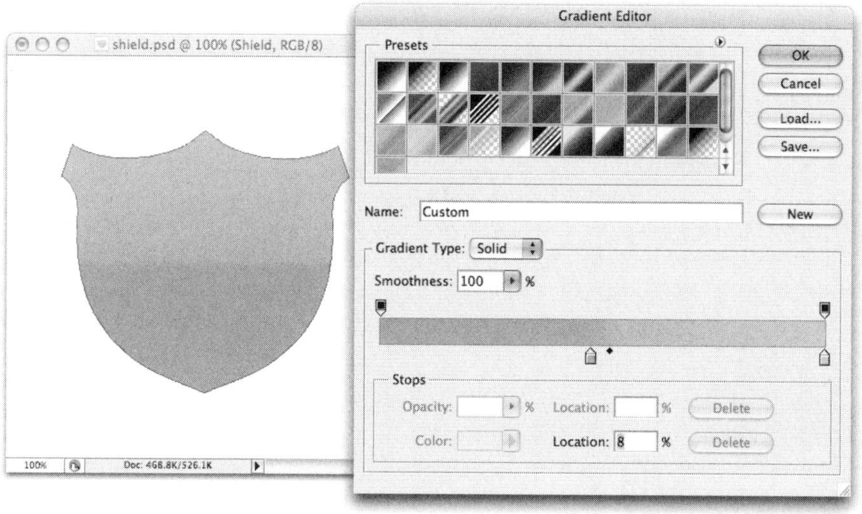

Back in the Layer Style dialog box, you want to change the direction of the gradient so that the darker green color is off to the right and heading toward the bottom. To do this, simply click and drag the line within the circle of the Angle option. As you do this, you'll see the gradient rotate in the document window. A setting of about 140 degrees is good.

That's a good start to the logo, but add a drop shadow to bring the shield off the page a little. Still in the Layer Style dialog box, select the Drop Shadow effect. You want quite a subtle drop shadow,

421

so set Opacity to 50 percent, Distance to 0 pixels, Spread to 0 percent, and Size to 21 pixels. Other settings can remain as they are. This produces a gentle, all-round shadow.

The last task for this stage of the logo is to add a Stroke effect to the outside of the shield. Still in the Layer Style dialog box, click Stroke at the bottom of the list on the left. You'll add quite a wide stroke to the shield. Choose a Size of 6 pixels, and make sure Position is set to Outside and Blend Mode is set to Normal. Reduce the Opacity setting to 20 percent to produce a gentle effect.

A gradient-filled stroke will look good here, so choose Gradient from the Fill Type menu. You'll then be presented with the options for editing a gradient. Click in the Gradient box, select the Black, White preset in the Gradient Editor dialog box, and click OK to close the dialog box. Keep Style set at Linear, and select the Align with Layer option. Set Angle to be the same as your main gradient on the shield: 140 degrees. This reinforces the impression of a single light source. Set Scale to 60 percent.

You can now click OK to close the Layer Style dialog box. Your shield should look like the one in Figure 10.17.

FIGURE 10.17

The basic shield with Drop Shadow, Gradient Overlay, and Stroke effects applied

To impart further depth to the shield, you're going to copy the Shield layer and apply different effects to the copy. In the Layers palette, click and drag the Shield layer to the New Layer icon to duplicate it. Rename the new layer to something sensible like **Shield Highlights**.

The new shield needs to be smaller and sit within the original. Make sure the Shield Highlights layer is active, and choose Edit ➪ Transform ➪ Scale. Hold down Shift as well as Alt (Option on the Mac) to keep the Shield Highlights layer centered, and click and drag a corner resize handle to reduce the size, as shown in Figure 10.18. Double-click the shield, or press Enter (Return on the Mac) to commit the transform.

Resizing the Shield Highlights layer

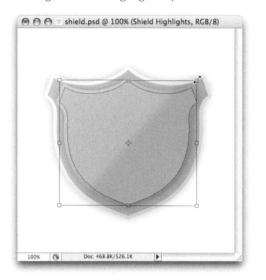

You don't want either the Drop Shadow or the Stroke effects in the Shield Highlights layer, so get rid of them. In the Layers palette, click and drag both of these effects to the trash icon, leaving only the Gradient Overlay effect in place. Right now, your gradient is invisible because it's retained the original Shield layer's gradient, so you need to edit it. Double-click the Shield Highlights layer's Gradient Overlay effect in the Layers palette to display the Layer Style dialog box; then click in the Gradient box to access the Gradient Editor.

You want to keep the structure of the gradient, but change the colors of the left and center color stops. Select the center stop, and change its color to a lighter version of the existing color — RGB 220, 223, 4 is fine. Now select the left stop and set it to the same color values. Click OK to close the Gradient Editor; then click OK to also close the Layer Style dialog box.

You can see the new-look shield in Figure 10.19.

FIGURE 10.19

With the new gradient settings, the Shield Highlights layer provides a nice depth to the whole design.

Add some text to the design. Select the Type tool and, in the options bar, select Arial Black as the font for a good heavy effect, and choose a font size of 60 pixels. Choose a foreground color you can see, such as black. The exact color doesn't matter, as you'll be applying an overlay to the type in a moment that will override its color. Click near the top left of the shield design, and type **SHIELD**. Don't commit the type just yet.

You'll give the type an arc shape, so that it creates a feeling of being pushed out by the shield, and adds a bit of a heraldic feel. To do this, click the Create Warped Text button in the options bar, which displays the Warp Text dialog box. Choose Arc from the Style menu, and make sure the Horizontal option is selected. A Bend value of +17 percent is fine. Keep the Horizontal and Vertical Distortion sliders at 0 percent. You can see our settings in Figure 10.20. Click OK to close the dialog box, and press Ctrl+Enter (⌘+Return on the Mac) to commit the type. The type layer's thumbnail in the Layers palette changes to reflect the fact that the text is now on an arc.

You need to reposition and resize the text, so select the Move tool and select the Show Transform Controls option in the options bar. Position the text so that it's sitting near the top of the shield, just under the shield's "shoulders" and overlapping the left edge of the shield slightly. Hold down Shift to constrain the proportions, and resize the type so that it's just overlapping the right side of the shield by a similar amount, as shown in Figure 10.21. Double-click the shield to commit the scaling operation.

FIGURE 10.20

The Warp Text dialog box

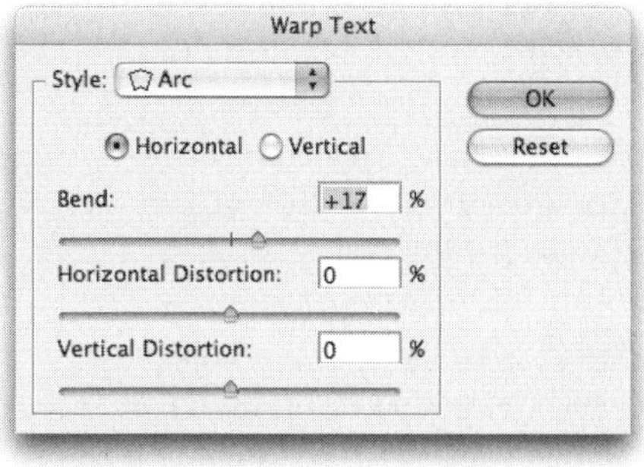

FIGURE 10.21

Resizing and repositioning the type using the Move tool

Now bring layer effects back into play. Double-click the type layer in the Layers palette — being careful to avoid the name or thumbnail — to display the Layer Style dialog box again. You're going to apply some effects to bring the type to life. Follow these steps:

1. **Apply a Gradient Overlay.** Click the Gradient Overlay effect in the Layer Style dialog box, and click in the Gradient box to access the Gradient Editor. Choose a dark to light blue gradient to complement the yellows in the shield. Set the left color stop to a really vibrant blue; RGB 23, 60, 246 is good. Set the right stop to a much darker version, for example RGB 3, 47, 137. Click OK to close the Gradient Editor. Back in the Layer Style dialog box, set the Blend Mode to Normal, the Opacity to 100 percent, the Style to Linear, and the Angle to 90 degrees.

2. **Add a Stroke.** Still within the Layer Style dialog box, click the Stroke effect, and set Size to 4px, Position to Outside, Blend Mode to Normal and Opacity to 100 percent. Under Fill Type, choose Color; then click in the Color box to change the color to white. You now have a chunky white border around the type.

3. **Apply a Drop Shadow.** You're going to give the text a very gentle drop shadow to lift it off the shield a touch. Click the Drop Shadow effect in the Layer Style dialog box. Set Distance to 0, Spread to 0 percent, and the Size to 10 pixels. All other settings can remain at their defaults. Click OK to close the Layer Style dialog box.

You should now have a type layer that looks somewhat like the one in Figure 10.22.

FIGURE 10.22

The type layer with Gradient Overlay, Stroke, and Drop Shadow effects applied

To really set the design off, add a further heraldic element below the text using a shape layer. Select the Custom Shape tool and, in the options bar, click the Shape option and choose Fleur-De-Lis from the picker. Choose a variant of the darker areas of the shield colors as the foreground color — something like RGB 204, 211, 4.

Hold down Shift to constrain the proportions of the shape and, in the document window, click and drag the shape out so that it sits within the shield, below the text. Using the Move tool, line up the fleur-de-lis so that it's on the horizontal center line of the shield. Rename the shape layer in the Layers palette to something memorable, like **Fleur-de-Lis**.

Now in the Layers palette, select a Blending Mode of Overlay for the Fleur-de-Lis layer. This has the effect of brightening the color, and it also lets some of the gradient beneath through into the shape.

Finally, apply a Stroke effect to the fleur-de-lis. Double-click the Fleur-de-Lis layer in the Layers palette — remembering to click in a blank area of the layer — to display the Layer Style dialog box. Click the Stroke effect. Set Size to 6 pixels, Position to Outside, Blend Mode to Normal, and Opacity to a gentle 10 percent. Choose Color for the Fill Type, click the Color box, and set the color to black. Click OK to close the Layer Style dialog box.

TIP The trick with applying layer styles is to be restrained with the effects you introduce. It's easy to go crazy with them and create something over the top.

Your logo is now complete; you can see the finished design in Figure 10.23. Remember, though, that all the layer effects you applied are completely reeditable, so if you later decide that you want the shield to be orange, you can reedit each of the Gradient Overlay effects to change their colors. Of course, you can change the Drop Shadows and the Strokes, too. All the shape and type layers are also still editable, so you can tweak these elements too if you wish; the layer styles automatically update to reflect any changes that you make.

FIGURE 10.23

The final Shield design, with its attendant Layers palette

Summary

In this chapter, you explored layer styles, a great feature of Photoshop that lets you add a range of dynamic, flexible effects to your layers. Because layer styles and effects are generated on the fly, you can easily go back and edit the style later on. In addition, when you edit your layer's contents, the layer effects update automatically.

You learned how to add layer styles to layers, and how to edit and manage those styles and work with style presets. You also learned how to turn individual effects on and off via the Layers palette, and also how to break a layer style out into separate layers for further editing.

You explored each of the effects that you can apply to layers, including shadows, glows, bevels, embossing effects, satin effects, overlays, and strokes. You also took a detailed look at the Contour Editor, which you can use to create your own contours for various effects, giving them a unique touch. Finally, all this knowledge was brought together with a great example that puts Photoshop's layer styles through their paces.

Chapter 11

Using Layer Comps

L ayer comps, first introduced in Photoshop CS, are a great way to try out different compositions of your layers (hence the name). You can think of layer comps as snapshots of the state of your layers. For example, you can create a layer comp that records the current arrangement of your layers, rearrange a few layers to form a new composition, and then save that snapshot as a new layer comp. You can then flip between the two comps and decide which one you like best.

Photoshop lets you create as many layer comps as you want in a document. Layer comps merely record information such as layer positions and settings, so they don't add much to your document's file size.

Such convenience comes at a price, however. As layer comps don't record everything about your layers, they can be quite restrictive. For example, they don't track the following:

- The stacking order of your layers within the Layers palette.

- Any edits to the actual contents of a layer, such as painting on a layer, using a retouching tool on a layer, editing the type in a type layer, or transforming the contents of a layer with a transform command. However, they do record the horizontal and vertical position of a layer's contents.

- Any Smart Filters that you apply to Smart Objects.

These limitations can sometimes be frustrating; however, once you're aware of what layer comps can and cannot do, they can be a very useful tool, both for artistic experimentation and also for those all-important client demos. This chapter walks you through the features of layer comps and offers some hints and tips on the best way to use them.

Introducing the Layer Comps Palette

Most activities involving layer comps revolve around the Layer Comps palette, shown in Figure 11.1. To display this palette, choose Window ➪ Layer Comps.

The Layer Comps palette allows you to view and work with all layer comps in your document.

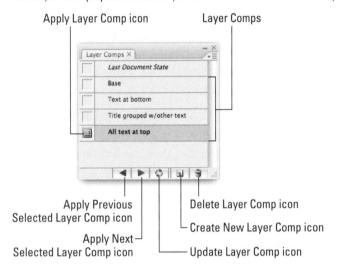

Each layer comp is shown as a separate item in the Layer Comps palette. To the left of each comp is a space for a square icon, known as the Apply Layer Comp icon. This icon shows you which comp is currently *applied*; that is, which comp you're looking at in the document window.

At the top of the palette is a special item called Last Document State. This records the last state of your layers before you applied a layer comp. Every time you make a change to your layers that results in the currently applied comp becoming out of date, the Apply Layer Comp icon flips back to Last Document State.

When it comes to manipulating comps, the Layer Comps palette behaves much like the Layers palette. Select a bunch of layer comps that are next to each other in the palette by clicking the top comp and Shift+clicking the bottom comp. If you want to select comps that aren't next to each other, Ctrl+click (⌘+click on the Mac) each comp. To rename a comp, double-click its name in the Layer Comps palette and type a new name.

You can reorder comps in the palette by clicking and dragging a comp from one position to the other. Unlike reordering layers, this doesn't have any effect on the appearance of the comps in the document window; it's purely so that you can organize your comps to suit your taste. It's also handy for flipping through your various comps when you show them to your client; this is discussed later in the chapter.

Creating and Deleting Layer Comps

To create a new layer comp recording the current state of your layers, first make sure the Layer Comps palette is visible by choosing Window ➪ Layer Comps. Click the Create New Layer Comp icon at the bottom of the Layer Comps palette. The New Layer Comp dialog box appears, as shown in Figure 11.2.

FIGURE 11.2

Creating a new layer comp. You can give your layer comp a name, choose which layer properties you want the comp to restore, and add a comment to describe the comp.

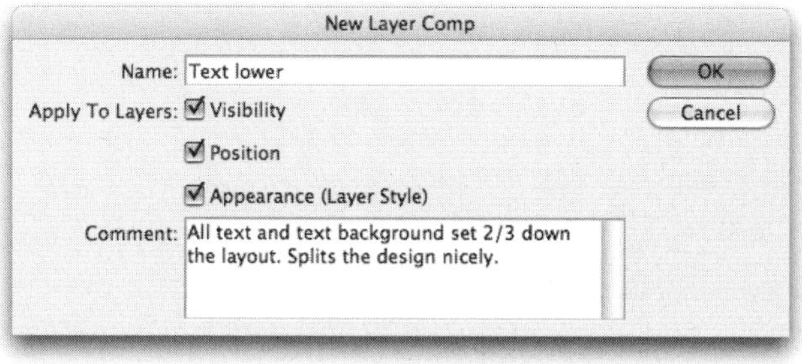

Type a name for your new comp in the Name box. This works much like a layer name; the name you type here appears in the Layer Comps palette, allowing you to identify the comp.

The next three options let you tell the layer comp which aspects of your layers it should restore whenever it's reapplied. They work as follows:

- **Visibility:** Select this option to restore the state of the eye icons next to each layer and group in the Layers palette. This option also restores the status of any layer and vector masks in the Layers palette; that is, whether each mask is enabled or disabled. It also restores the status of the link icons for any layer and vector masks; that is, whether the mask position is locked to the layer position or not.

CROSS-REF To enable or disable a layer mask or vector mask, Shift+click its thumbnail in the Layers palette. For more on masks, see Chapter 9.

■   **Position:** Selecting this option restores the position of the contents of layers within the document window. For example, if you have a layer positioned in the top-left corner of your document at the time you create the comp, and you later move the layer with the Move tool, reapplying the comp moves the layer back to the top-left corner.

CAUTION   Layer comps only record the horizontal and vertical positions of layer contents. They can't track anything else, such as transformations, or the effects of any of the painting tools. If you make changes such as these, they're effectively applied across all layer comps.

TIP   If you want to change the layer contents themselves from one comp to the next — for example, to change the font used in a type layer, or the rotation of an element in the layer — duplicate the layer, then make your changes to the duplicate. Now, create your first comp with the original layer visible and the duplicate hidden, and create the second comp with the original hidden and the duplicate visible. You can then toggle between the comps to view both versions. (Make sure the Visibility option on each comp is selected, of course.)

■   **Appearance (Layer Style):** With this option selected, the layer comp restores all the settings within the Layer Style dialog box for each layer. We're talking all layer effects, as well as everything in the Blending Options section of the dialog box: Opacity and Fill Opacity, knockouts, and so on. It even restores details such as the exact shape of any contours you use within the layer's effects.

CAUTION   Unfortunately, layer comps don't record or apply Photoshop CS3's Smart Filters. Any changes you make to a Smart Object's Smart Filters are applied across all comps regardless.

You can also type a comment in the Comment box to help you remember more about the snapshot that you're creating. If you add a comment, a right-pointing triangle appears next to the comp in the Layer Comps palette; click this triangle to reveal the comment within the palette.

Click OK to create the new layer comp, recording the current state of your document. Its name appears in the Layer Comps palette, along with an Apply Layer Comp icon next to the comp, indicating that it's currently applied: The state of the comp matches the state of your document window.

NOTE   When you create a layer comp, Photoshop remembers the Visibility, Position, and Appearance settings that you used. The next layer comp that you create defaults to these remembered settings.

If you now change any aspect of your layers that have been recorded by your new layer comp, such as changing the visibility of a layer, the Apply Layer Comp icon moves from the new layer comp back to Last Document State at the top of the palette, indicating that the layer comp's recorded snapshot is now out of sync with the current state of your layers. You can now create another new comp to record the current state. You can also reapply the comp to revert your layers back to the comp's snapshot, or update the comp to reflect the new state of your layers. Applying and updating comps are explained in the following sections.

 You can also create a new layer comp by duplicating an existing comp. This is handy if, for example, you want to go back and create variations based on a certain comp. To duplicate a comp, click and drag it to the Create New Layer Comp icon in the Layer Comps palette, or right-click it in the palette and choose Duplicate Layer Comp.

TIP To quickly create a new layer comp without displaying the New Layer Comp dialog box, Alt+click (Option+click on the Mac) the Create New Layer Comp icon.

To delete a layer comp, select it in the Layer Comps palette and click the Delete Layer Comp icon at the bottom of the palette. You can also drag the comp down to the icon. To delete more than one comp at once, select the comps, then click the Delete Layer Comp icon or drag them onto the icon. If you prefer, you can right-click a comp in the palette and choose Delete Layer Comp.

TIP You can also access all of the options in the right-click pop-up menu from the Layer Comps palette menu.

Flipping Between Layer Comps

After you create a few layer comps, you can flip between them by clicking their Apply Layer Comp icons in the Layers palette. When you click a comp's Apply Layer Comp icon, your document's layers step back in time to the state they were in when that comp was created or last updated. This means that you can quickly flip between your various comps as you showcase them to your client, for example.

An even quicker way to flip between the comps is to use the left- and right-arrow icons at the bottom of the Layer Comps palette. By default, this cycles through all the comps in the palette. If you'd rather cycle through just a few of your comps, select them by Ctrl+clicking (⌘+clicking on the Mac) or Shift+clicking them in the palette, and then click the arrow icons.

In Figure 11.3, we're flipping between three layer comps. Notice how the document window changes in each case. The Apply Layer Comp icon always shows the currently-applied comp.

As well as flipping between the comps, you can flip back to the state that your layers were in before you applied a layer comp. To do this, click the Apply Layer Comp icon next to the Last Document State item in the Layer Comps palette, or choose Restore Last Document State from the Layer Comps palette menu.

FIGURE 11.3

Flipping through layer comps

Updating Layer Comps

What if you create a layer comp and later realize that you want that type layer just a few pixels to the left in the comp? No problem. Photoshop lets you update an existing layer comp to record the current state of your layers.

To do this, select the layer comp by clicking it in the Layer Comps palette. If you want to make your changes based on this comp, click its Apply Layer Comp icon to revert your document window and Layers palette to that comp's state. Now make your layer adjustments. Finally, with the layer comp still selected in the Layer Comps palette, click the Update Layer Comp icon at the bottom of the palette, as shown in Figure 11.4. The layer comp updates to reflect your changes.

 When you update a layer comp to the current state of your layers, Photoshop moves the Apply Layer Comp icon to the updated comp. This makes it clear that the updated comp now matches your current document state.

TIP You can also update multiple layer comps to match the current document state. To do this, select all the comps you want to update, and then click the Update Layer Comp icon.

FIGURE 11.4

Updating an existing layer comp. Select the comp (left), and, if desired, click its Apply Layer Comp icon to load its snapshot. Make changes to your layers — here we toggled some layer visibilities (center) — then, with the comp still selected, click the Update Layer Comp icon. The comp updates to record the current state of the layers (right).

> **TIP**
>
> To copy a snapshot of your layers from one comp to another, start by clicking the first comp's Apply Layer Comp icon to set the layers to that comp's snapshot. Then click the second comp to highlight it, and click the Update Layer Comp icon at the bottom of the palette to record the snapshot in the second comp.

Changing Layer Comp Options

You can reedit a layer comp's options at any time. This allows you to change which layer properties the comp restores, as well as edit the comp's name and comments. To do this, double-click the comp in the Layer Comps palette, or right-click it and choose Layer Comp Options. The Layer Comp Options dialog box — which bears more than a passing resemblance to the New Layer Comp dialog box, shown in Figure 11.2 — appears. Make your changes; then click OK to save the changes to the comp and close the dialog box.

> **NOTE**
>
> Even if you reedit a layer comp's options and disable the Visibility, Position, or Appearance settings, the comp still remembers those layer properties; it just doesn't reapply them when you click the comp's Apply Layer Comp icon. You can reenable the option at a later date and then click the Apply Layer Comp icon to restore the corresponding layer properties.

Understanding Layer Comp Warnings

Handy though layer comps are, they can't record all aspects of your document. As already mentioned, changes such as painting and Smart Filters aren't recorded by layer comps.

In addition, some operations can "break" layer comps, meaning that they can no longer fully restore the state of your layers. This can happen if you make any of the following changes to a layer (or layers) whose state was recorded by a layer comp:

- **Delete a layer.** Layer comps only store and record the properties of a layer; they can't store a backup copy of the layer itself. So when you delete a layer, it's gone; the layer comp can't recover it.

- **Merge one or more layers.** If the merge results in a recorded layer being deleted, then the layer comp that recorded that layer's properties can, of course, no longer restore its snapshot.

- **Convert a layer to the Background layer.** Converting a layer to the Background layer removes its layer style; any effects that were applied to the layer are rasterized, and options such as Opacity and Fill Opacity are disabled. The process also locks the layer so that its contents can't be repositioned. Therefore, any affected layer comps are no longer able to restore any of these properties.

NOTE   You can convert the Background layer to a normal layer without breaking an associated layer comp, because a normal layer has all the recordable properties of the Background layer and more.

- **Convert your document to a different color mode.** If you change color modes by choosing an option under Image ⇨ Mode, then your layers are usually flattened into a single layer. Naturally, this drastic step breaks any layer comps that were recording those layers, as they can no longer restore the state of any of the layers.

TIP   You can still convert between some color modes — such as RGB to CMYK — without flattening your layers. To do this, select the Don't Merge or Don't Flatten option in the warning dialog box that appears. However, be aware that this can put your layers somewhat out of whack; it's best to flatten if at all possible, especially if you're sending your file off to be printed.

If you perform any of the four actions just described, a little yellow caution triangle appears on the right-hand side of one or more comps in the Layer Comps palette. These warnings are there to let you know that those comps are now "broken" — they can no longer fully restore their layer snapshots. At this point, you have four choices:

- **Do nothing.** You can carry on regardless and leave the caution triangle in place, but bear in mind that the affected comp can no longer restore its intended state, somewhat limiting its usefulness.

- **Clear the comp warning.** This is essentially the same as doing nothing; all it does is remove the caution triangle. To do this, click the triangle to display the explanatory dialog box shown in Figure 11.5; click Clear to remove the triangle.

TIP   You can also clear a layer comp warning by right-clicking the caution triangle and choosing Clear Layer Comp Warning from the pop-up menu. Alternatively, to clear the warnings of all layer comps in one fell swoop, choose Clear All Layer Comp Warnings from the pop-up menu.

- **Undo the operation.** You might not have realized that merging or deleting a particular layer would break the layer comp. Unless you have a real need to merge or delete that layer, you're probably better off pressing Ctrl+Z (⌘+Z on the Mac) to back out of the change, thereby returning all your layer comps to a working state.

- **Update the affected comp.** Your final option is to select the affected comp and click the Update Layer Comp icon at the bottom of the Layer Comps palette. This resets the comp to match the current document state. Of course, this loses the comp's previous recorded state, but it does at least bring the comp up to date with the new state of your layers, thereby "fixing" the comp.

Click a layer comp warning triangle to display this dialog box. Click Clear if you want to remove the warning.

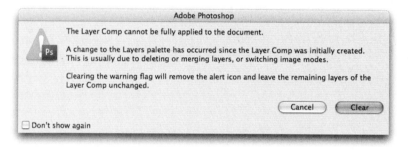

Exporting Layer Comps

As well as cycling through your layer comps in Photoshop, you can export the comps to a series of flat image files, a PDF file, or a Web Photo Gallery (WPG). This is great for showcasing your comps to clients remotely, particularly if they don't have a copy of Photoshop on hand.

Exporting comps to flat image files

To export your layer comps to a series of flat image files, choose File ➪ Scripts ➪ Layer Comps to Files. A dialog box appears, as shown in Figure 11.6, allowing you to choose a folder to save the files in, as well as specify various options for the export, as follows:

- **Destination:** Type the path to a folder where you want to save your exported image files. You can also click Browse to locate the folder or create a new folder.

- **File Name Prefix:** Photoshop uses the characters in this box as the basis for each of the exported image file names (it also adds a serial number and the layer comp name). It defaults to the name of your Photoshop document.

- **Selected Layer Comps Only:** You can choose to export just some of your layer comps, rather than all comps in the document. To do this, select the comps in the Layer Comps palette, and when you export the comps, select this option.

- **File Type:** Choose a file format to save the exported images in. Depending on your choice, various options appear in the box below. Choose BMP or Targa and Photoshop asks you to choose a color depth for the images. Choose JPEG, and you can specify the JPEG quality level; values range from 0 to 12, with 0 being the lowest quality, and 12 being the highest (with the largest file size). The PDF option exports the comps as individual PDF files and allows you to specify whether the images should be encoded in ZIP or JPEG format; choose JPEG and you can also set the JPEG quality level, as just described. PSD exports the comps as individual Photoshop files; select the Maximize Compatibility option to ensure that the file can be read by other applications and earlier versions of Photoshop, at the expense of larger file sizes. Finally, when you export as TIFF files, you can choose from no image compression, LZW compression, ZIP compression, or JPEG compression. JPEG gives you a Quality setting, as described previously. For maximum compatibility, choose no compression or LZW compression.

■ **Include ICC Profile:** Select this option to embed your document's ICC color profile in the exported images. This is generally a good idea, as it means the colors in the files will look the same on any properly calibrated display — provided, of course, your display is properly calibrated!

Exporting layer comps to image files using the Layer Comps To Files dialog box

After you select your options, click Run to begin the export. You should see a few flickering windows, followed by a dialog proclaiming the success of the export. Take a look at the destination folder on your hard drive, and you should see each layer comp lovingly exported as a flat image file, ready for sending to your client.

Exporting comps to a PDF file

Photoshop lets you export all your layer comps, or a selection of comps, to a single PDF file, with one comp per page. You can also choose to enable a slide-show option, letting viewers of the PDF view the comps as a slide show when using software that supports it, such as Adobe Reader.

To export your comps to a PDF, choose File ➪ Scripts ➪ Layer Comps to PDF. The Layer Comps To PDF dialog box appears, as shown in Figure 11.7. Select from the following options for the export:

- **Destination:** Choose a path and file name for the exported PDF, either by typing in the Destination box or by clicking Browse and using the file chooser.

- **Selected Layer Comps Only:** Select this option if you've selected just some of your layer comps to export in the Layer Comps palette. If this option is not selected, Photoshop exports all the comps in the document.

- **Slideshow Options:** If you want to enable the slide-show feature in the PDF reader, select the Advance Every *X* Seconds option, and type a value in the box — this value is the delay, in seconds, before moving from one comp to the next. Select the Loop After Last Page option to display the comps in a continuous loop.

Click Run to export the comps. After a few flickering windows, a success dialog box should appear, and you'll find the PDF file saved in the destination folder on your hard drive. Open the PDF and you'll see that each comp is displayed on its own page in the PDF. This is very handy for e-mailing to clients.

FIGURE 11.7

The Layer Comps To PDF dialog box lets you create a single PDF file from your layer comps, with one comp per page.

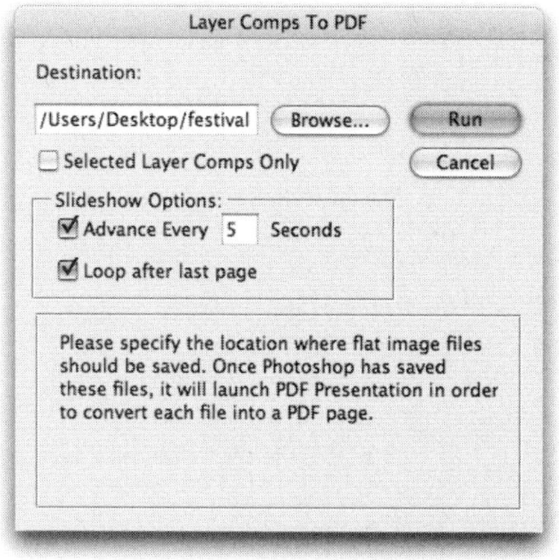

NOTE Layer Comps to PDF exports your layer comps as pages in a single PDF file. If you prefer to have one PDF per comp, use the Layer Comps to Files script just described, and choose PDF for the File Type option.

Exporting comps as a Web photo gallery

To make life even easier for your clients, you can export your layer comps as standard Web pages, ready to be uploaded to your Web site for viewing. To do this, choose File ➪ Scripts ➪ Layer Comps to WPG. The Layer Comps To Web Photo Gallery dialog box appears as shown in Figure 11.8, allowing you to choose a couple of options for your gallery:

- **Destination:** This is the path to the folder where you want to create the gallery's HTML and image files. Click Browse to locate the folder or create a new folder.

- **Style:** Use this box to choose a look for the gallery. Unfortunately, this option is a text box, not a menu, which means you have to type the exact name of the style. You can view a list of preset styles by choosing File ➪ Automate ➪ Web Photo Gallery and browsing the Styles menu at the top of the dialog. Alternatively, look in the Presets/Web Photo Gallery folder inside your Photoshop application folder; each style is listed as a folder named after the style.

TIP You can also create your own Web Photo Gallery styles by copying one of the folders inside Presets/Web Photo Gallery, renaming the copied folder, and editing the files inside.

After you choose a destination and style, click Run to create the gallery. When the script finishes, the gallery appears in a browser window. To publish your gallery on the Web, upload the gallery folder to your Web server.

FIGURE 11.8

Use the Layer Comps To Web Photo Gallery dialog box to export your comps to a mini-Web site, ready for uploading to your Web server.

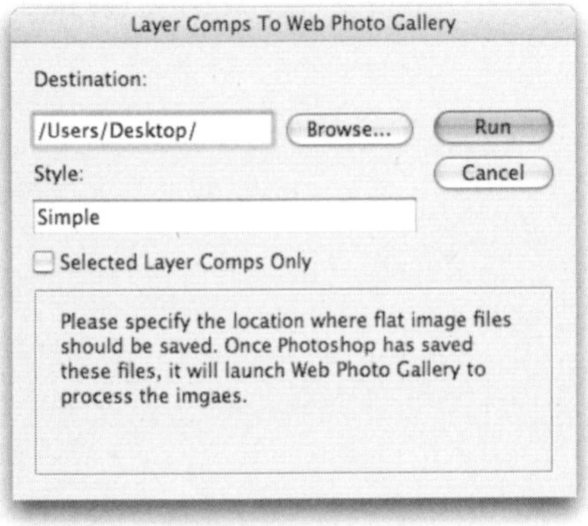

Layer Comps To Web Photo Gallery

Destination:

/Users/Desktop/ [Browse...] (Run)

Style: (Cancel)

Simple

☐ Selected Layer Comps Only

Please specify the location where flat image files should be saved. Once Photoshop has saved these files, it will launch Web Photo Gallery to process the imgaes.

Summary

Layer comps are a great way to view and showcase different versions of your work, all within one Photoshop file. In this chapter, you explored the ins and outs of layer comps. We looked at the aspects of your document that can be recorded in layer comp snapshots, and also mentioned those facets of your layers that comps can't track. You explored the Layer Comps palette and learned how to create and delete layer comps, as well as control the aspects of your layers that each layer comp restores when it's applied.

You learned how to apply — or flip between — different layer comps, and also how to bring a layer comp up to date with the current state of your layers. You also learned how you can change a comp's options after the comp has been created. You explored the concept of layer comp warnings, and looked at what you can do about them. Finally, you learned how to export your layer comps to flat image files, PDF files, and Web photo galleries to give them a life outside Photoshop.

Part IV

Using Layers in Real-World Situations

Chapter 12

Exploring Layer Strategies

This chapter, the first in the "Real World" part of the book, takes a wide view of layers in the real world. While it's important to know how layers work and how to manipulate them in Photoshop, it also helps to be aware of wider issues such as document management and working in a team. Essentially, you can view this chapter as a discussion of best practices.

You look at ways to keep your layers organized, and how to create multiple versions of your Photoshop files to help you refine your designs. The chapter also looks at techniques for organizing your Photoshop files on disk, so that you can easily find the files you need when working on a project.

Photoshop provides many features to help you edit your images nondestructively, and this chapter explores some ideas to help you do this. You'll also look at situations where you might want to flatten your Photoshop files to save space.

The chapter also takes a look at using layers in real-world situations. You'll learn some tricks to help you work better in a team, and you'll explore some common workflow situations. Finally, the chapter shows how you can use radically different approaches with your Photoshop layers to achieve similar results.

Organizing Layers for Clarity

Here's a scenario: You create a Photoshop document composed of, say, 50 layers. After you finish, you know your way around it like the back of your hand. The whole thing makes perfect sense to you at that moment, so you don't bother to organize your layers at all. A month passes, and now you need to reedit that document; when you open it you're presented with something that looks like Figure 12.1.

FIGURE 12.1

The document itself looks good, but it was created without once giving thought to the layer structure, resulting in a pretty incomprehensible mess. You can't see all the layers here, but you can see from the size of the scrollbar that there are lots more of them!

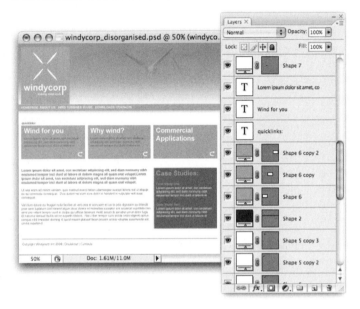

You have no idea which layer is which, and you spend a good half hour just coming to grips with the file. The following sections look at what can we do about this sorry state of affairs.

Naming your layers

Naming layers is the first step to sanity within multilayer documents, so here's how you might do that in the context of this Web site design example. It's pretty intimidating when you're confronted with this many layers, so where do you start?

The ever-useful Move tool can come to your aid here. Select the Move tool, select the Auto-Select option in the options bar, and choose Layer from the menu next to the Auto-Select option. You might also want to deselect the Show Transform Controls option, if it's selected, as it can get in the way in this case. Now, when you click an item in the document window, Photoshop automatically selects the corresponding layer in the Layers palette, as seen in Figure 12.2.

FIGURE 12.2

With the Move tool selected and Auto-Select: Layer enabled, clicking an item in the document window automatically selects the corresponding layer in the Layers palette. Here a part of the logo is selected.

After selecting the layer, you want to name it for future reference. To do this, double-click the layer's name in the Layers palette, and type a meaningful name. In the previous figure, the top-right blade of the propeller in the logo is selected, so this layer might become Propeller Blade Top Right — a great improvement over the previous name, Shape 5 copy.

When naming layers, try to name them so that the name actually means something when you come back to it. You could have called the layer Prop Shape Layer 1, which is okay, but it has some drawbacks, including the following:

- It may not be immediately obvious that "prop" means "propeller."
- You don't need to be told that it's a shape layer — the icons remind you of that.
- "1" doesn't convey which part of the propeller it is.

Be succinct with your layer names, but also be as clear and meaningful as possible. Now select and name all the layers in your document in turn.

Type layers are interesting. You might think that, because what you type becomes the layer name, it's going to be easy to identify the type layer in the future. When designing, though, you often use the same dummy text for each component. The example contains multiple layers starting with "Lorem ipsum dolor sit amet" — a popular dummy Latin text — and you can't tell which layer represents which block of text. Luckily, although the text you type when creating a type layer is reflected in the layer's name, this does not hold true in reverse — you can rename a type layer without affecting its content. Name type layers according to their position on the page or within page elements. So your block of text to the left of the page might become Main Body Text, and the descriptive text within the center promotional box might become Promo Center Description.

When you finish, you should have a much better idea about which layer is which, and a Layers palette that looks more like the one in Figure 12.3. This is so much easier to find your way around; you'll thank yourself for it!

FIGURE 12.3

All the layers in the document are now clearly named.

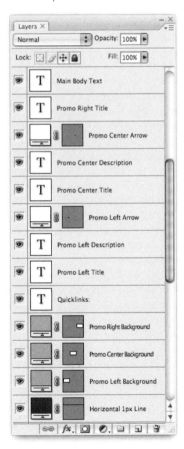

Grouping layers by content

Of course, having sensibly named layers really helps with navigating a Photoshop file, but you can go one step further and use layer groups to organize your layers by content. This technique is especially useful when you're working with a large number of layers, since you can see at a glance which group relates to a particular area of your document. You can also nest groups within each other to create a highly structured document.

CROSS-REF You can find more information on creating and using layer groups in Chapter 2.

In the continuing example of the Windycorp Web site, for example, you might start by grouping layers into four main sections:

- Header elements
- Promotional areas
- The main body of the page
- The footer of the page

When naming groups, it's best to use the same semantic approach as you use when naming layers. You might name your four groups as follows:

- Header
- Green Promo Items
- Body Elements
- Footer

You can see the results of your layer grouping in Figure 12.4.

FIGURE 12.4

Now all your layers are grouped into four main sections. Because the groups relate directly to elements on the page, you can see at a glance which group you need to edit.

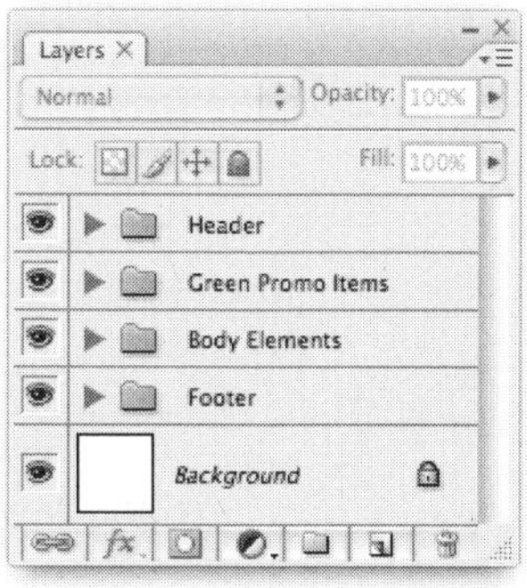

> **TIP**   If you're designing something like a Web page that contains elements positioned one after the other, such as a header, body text, and footer, it can help you navigate the Layers palette if you reorder your groups in the palette until they roughly mimic the page layout.

As mentioned earlier, you can nest groups within one another. This can be a great help in situations like the Windycorp example, as you can subdivide the main sections into smaller groups of elements. Currently, within the Green Promo Items group, you have lots of layers that, although named, are still quite hard to navigate. You can break this down into three subgroups, representing the left, center, and right promotional boxes.

Furthermore, you can split the header into Menu, Logo, and Header Image groups, while the Body Elements group can have all the elements for the case studies grouped together. The final layout of the Layers palette, containing all these nested groups, looks like Figure 12.5. You can see which group corresponds to which section of the page, and the individual layers inside the groups are, of course, sensibly named.

FIGURE 12.5

All layers are grouped into content-specific layer groups. The document is now easy to navigate.

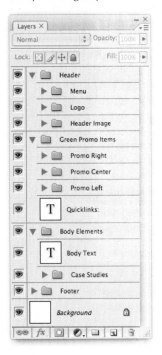

Storing Different Versions of Documents

Whatever you create in Photoshop, there's a good chance you'll to want to keep more than one version of each file as you work. Keeping different versions means storing many similar files for the same job. This can quickly eat hard drive space, so why would you want to do it? Versioning lets you revert to an earlier version of your file — great if you need to backtrack — and it also lets you retain different treatments of a design to see which you like best.

Versioning is often used in a commercial design environment to present alternate versions of a design to clients, and it's a common tactic with photographers and illustrators, too. In a home environment, saving a design at various stages along the way brings the same benefits — you have historical backups of your work, and you can easily go back to an earlier version if you decide you don't like the one you're working on.

NOTE While a file is still open, you can revert to earlier editing stages using the History palette. To display this palette, choose Window ⇨ History. The History palette allows you to step back through the various actions that you've performed on a document. You can think of it as a more fully featured Undo command with multiple levels (Photoshop only has one level of undo in the conventional sense). You can also save snapshots. A snapshot is a "freezing" of the state of your document. To save a snapshot, display the History palette, and click the Create New Snapshot icon at the bottom of the palette. Your new snapshot appears at the top of the palette. You can save multiple snapshots for ongoing reference, and you can revert to a saved snapshot at any time while the document's open.

CAUTION When the document is closed, its history and snapshots are lost forever; they're only available while the document is open. This means that they're really only useful while you're working on a document; you can't rely on the History palette as a versioning system.

As you work on a Photoshop file, you'll hopefully reach a point where you're basically happy with the design you're working on. This is the time to save your first version, preserving your document's layers precisely as they are. As you work through a project, you'll likely want to retain several different versions of a design so you can refer to them, or even revert back to them if need be. The following sections outline some ways to store and track versions of a design.

Using layer comps

You can use layer comps to record different versions of your layers within a single document. A little like the History palette, layer comps take snapshots of the state of your layers. However, unlike the History palette, layer comps are saved with the document. They're a great way to investigate the possibilities of a design after the individual elements are in place.

CROSS-REF You can find more info on layer comps in Chapter 11.

Layer comps only take notice of three features of your layers: visibility, position, and layer style. That means that if you tweak the content or size of a type layer, for example, that change is reflected across all layer comps. So layer comps don't really function as a true versioning system. However, they're great when, for example, you've finished your basic design, and you want to see what the logo looks like on the top right rather than the top left.

In Figure 12.6, you can see some layer comps in action. This is a poster design with three layer comps for experimenting with different layer positions. The second version is similar to the first; some space is added around the type, and the background image is shifted slightly. In the third version, the image is dramatically repositioned to create a much more striking feel. At the end of the design process, you can go back and step through the comps to get an overview of the progress of the design.

FIGURE 12.6

Three versions of the same poster, created using layer comps. If you simply need to tweak position, visibility, and layer styles, layer comps are great.

Using Version Cue

Version Cue is Adobe's own file versioning system. It comprises two elements. The first is the Version Cue server, which can run locally on your computer or over a network. The second is the connectivity built into the CS3 applications.

The server component is shipped with most Adobe Creative Suites, but not stand-alone versions of Photoshop, although the stand-alone versions can still access Version Cue servers. Version Cue integrates closely with the full range of CS3 applications, and is best suited to a team-based environment because you can run the central Version Cue server to manage all the assets for a project — photos, Photoshop files, and so on — across all team members. For example, with three designers working on a project, one member can check out a Photoshop file from the server to avoid the potential problem of two people overwriting the same file.

NOTE You may notice that, when you open and save files in Photoshop, there's an option called Use Adobe Dialog within the file selector dialog boxes. If you select this option, an alternate version of the dialog box is presented from which you can access the Version Cue server. To use Version Cue, you need to be using your dialog boxes in this mode.

Alternate Version Cue versions are saved within a single PSD file, which is in turn stored in a Version Cue project. Projects are managed from within Bridge, Adobe's asset management application that ships with Photoshop. Each Version Cue project can contain multiple assets, mixing flat images with layered Photoshop files. In Figure 12.7, you can see a project set up within Bridge. There are just two files here: the original photo used to create the background image and a single PSD file.

FIGURE 12.7

Here you can see Bridge showing assets relating to a project called "Brighton Theatre Poster." The single file on the right — "theatre poster final.psd" — contains three versions of the document, shown on the left, with alternative treatments and additions.

— File information

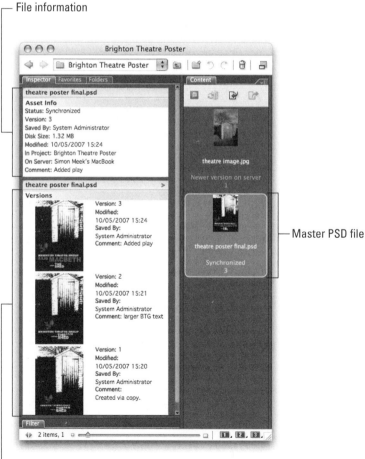

— Master PSD file

— The three versions of the master file

Each Photoshop file within Version Cue can contain multiple versions of the document, and each version can have its own comments. The last version — Version 3 in this example — is the one you see when you open the file in Photoshop. However, if you decide that an earlier version was much better, you can *promote* that older version to be the current version instead. You can do this either within Bridge or in Photoshop itself. To do it within Bridge, right-click the file and choose View Versions from the pop-up menu. Bridge presents you with all the versions of the file as thumbnails. Right-click the version you want to promote, and select Promote To Current Version. A Check In dialog box appears that offers to create a new version based on the selected version, letting you add a comment to the new version as you go.

To promote a version from within Photoshop itself, first open the file in Photoshop. Click the right-pointing arrow at the bottom of the document window and choose Versions. In the Versions For dialog box that appears — shown in Figure 12.8 — select an older version, then click Promote To Current Version to promote it. This creates a new version based on your selected version, and you're prompted to add a comment to this new version. By the way, you can also view different versions within Photoshop by selecting the version and clicking View Version.

FIGURE 12.8

The Versions For dialog box within Photoshop. Note the Promote To Current Version button for promoting the selected earlier version to the current version.

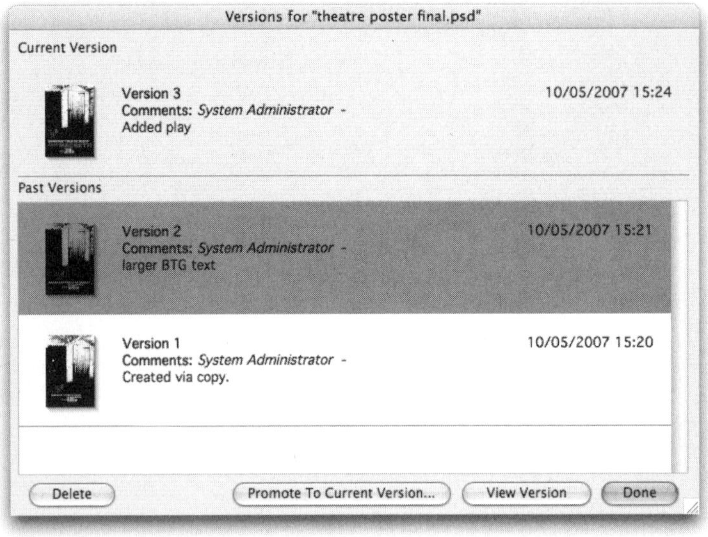

NOTE You can access versions stored in Version Cue projects from within any of the CS3 applications. For example, if you want to place a PSD file in an InDesign project, you can import the PSD from the Version Cue server from within InDesign. You can also promote versions of a PSD file from within any Version Cue enabled CS3 application, just as described for Photoshop. So if you decide that an older version of a PSD file is more suitable for your final InDesign project, you can promote that version from within InDesign. The CS3 versions of Illustrator, Photoshop, InDesign, Acrobat, Flash, InCopy, and Bridge can all work in tandem with Version Cue.

Creating your own versioning system

You can also create your own system for versioning your Photoshop files. This has the benefit that you can tailor it exactly to the way you like to work. Plus, you don't have to buy and learn an additional piece of software to use it.

How might you go about keeping your own versions of your Photoshop files? There's no correct way as such, but here are some good guidelines to follow:

- **Keep it simple.** Avoid getting bogged down with very detailed organizational systems, but look at how you really like to work, and build the system around that. It may be that your particular needs require a very detailed system. Don't feel duty-bound to create something very complex if you don't need to, however.

- **Use a consistent naming system.** After you have a naming system in place, stick with it, or it'll prove to be a headache down the line when you come back to edit old files.

- **Keep a consistent folder structure.** Keep different types of files — PSDs, RAW camera files, exported JPEGs, and so on — in their own subfolders, and keep the same folder structure across projects. That way, you'll be able to find files quickly as you move from project to project.

CROSS-REF Naming conventions and file organization are covered in more detail in the next section.

The versioning system you choose probably depends on the way you work. If you're working in a team, Version Cue is likely to be your best bet, because the process of checking files in and out saves any mishaps with overwriting files. When working on your own, where file overwriting is less of an issue, it's probably simpler to create your own system. This approach also has the advantage that you're not tied to Version Cue as a system, allowing you greater flexibility with your file structure.

Managing Documents

If you use Version Cue, as described in the previous section, the software manages your documents for you to a large extent. In the scenario where you create your own document system, however, it's helpful to think a little about how to organize all those layered Photoshop files.

Naming your files

When you begin a design, you'll likely start by creating a few rough designs to choose from. These might be very different, but as you develop a particular idea, you'll probably concentrate on just one or two designs and tweak those until you're happy with them. This development period can generate a lot of files; it's quite likely that you'll create at least ten versions of a file before the design is perfected, especially in a commercial environment. Keeping track of these files requires a robust naming system.

A good approach is to number your initial designs. In Figure 12.9, you can see three starting designs for a Web site for the Brighton Theatre Group example. They're simply named "v1," "v2," and "v3" (version 1, version 2, and version 3). You could also add a date to each file name, if that's useful for you.

FIGURE 12.9

A simple but effective start to managing initial designs, with numbered versions

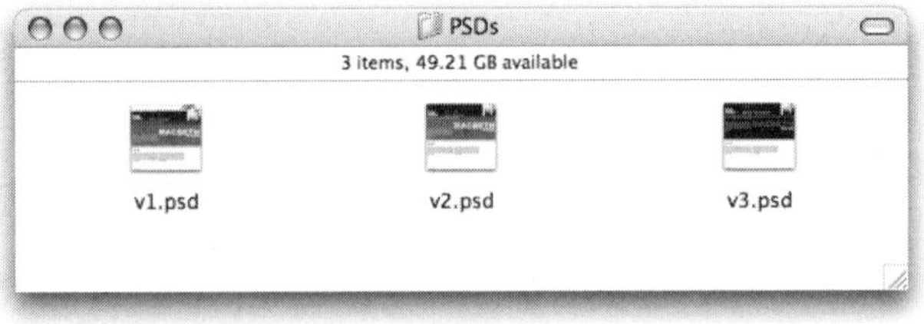

As you progress through the design, you might well find yourself refining just one of these versions. To keep the file naming consistent for each new iteration of the design, you can add a second tier to your versioning system by adding a letter to each file name: "v1b.psd", "v1c.psd", and so on. In this way you create an easy-to-follow set of files, allowing you to see the development process at a glance.

Organizing your files

The trick with organizing files is to use folders to separate out the various types of file. For example, in the Brighton Theatre Group example, you might start with a project folder, into which you can place the various elements grouped within their own folders. In Figure 12.10, you can see that the project folder contains subfolders for all the elements of the poster and Web site designs, as well as extra folders for supporting documentation and original photos. The Web site files are split further into two folders: PSDs, which contains the numbered, layered Photoshop files; and Flat Visuals, which contains nonlayered versions of the files to be sent to the client for approval.

FIGURE 12.10

The project folder contains all the elements for the project, nicely segregated into easy-to-find subfolders. All the layered Photoshop files are contained in a single folder, separate from other elements.

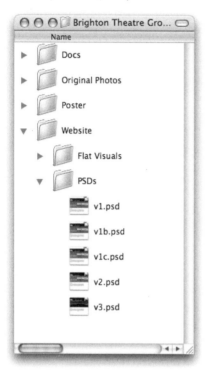

Keeping all your layered Photoshop files separate from other project elements makes it easy to keep track of the various iterations of your files, without extra elements like Word files, photos, and flattened versions getting in the way. Furthermore, the less clutter you create, the less likely you are to mistakenly delete important files, and the less time you'll spend looking for them. To prove the point, consider Figure 12.11, in which all the layered Photoshop files for the Web site are mixed up with the poster files, some Word documents, photos, and flattened JPEGs. This version is hard to navigate, and you can't easily tell at a glance what each file contains. In this kind of environment, it's easy to delete, or save over, the wrong file. This is a small project, too; if you were to have many more versions and supporting files, you could easily create a project that's impossible to work with!

FIGURE 12.11

Putting all the files for the project together in a single folder makes it hard to navigate.

Backing up

Hard drives fail. You've spent hundreds of hours on a project, tweaking your layer styles over multiple documents, only to lose everything when your hard drive starts making unpleasant clicking noises and finally dies. In that scenario, everything on that drive is lost unless you spend a small fortune on data recovery. To protect those precious files, don't rely on one hard drive; you need to back up the files. If you take on-board nothing else from this chapter, please heed this!

There's an old saying in the IT world: Digital data doesn't exist unless it exists in three places at once. This is good advice. Keep one set of files on your computer and another set on an external backup drive, and ideally archive each project to CD or DVD when complete and send those archives somewhere else, like a friend's or colleague's house. Sending files offsite means that, should the worst happen, and the house or office burns down, you still have those files. The same goes for photo libraries.

Nondestructive Editing

One of the great things about using layers is that you can make nearly all your edits without altering the original image directly. For example, adjustment layers and Smart Objects allow you to edit a photo quite dramatically without ever touching the original. This section looks at some advantages of, and strategies for, nondestructive editing.

Nondestructive editing offers you the following benefits:

- **Increased flexibility during editing:** You're bound to change your mind about elements as you work on a photo or design. If you apply a Gaussian Blur filter to a normal layer, it's pretty much set in stone. Apart from the History palette, there's no way back. However, if you make that photo a Smart Object first, Photoshop applies the blur as a Smart Filter — assuming you're using CS3 — and you can reedit the parameters of the blur as you work.

- **The ability to revise edits over time:** Inevitably, you'll realize weeks later that you can improve on your edits to a design or photo. Non-destructive editing means that you don't have to start from scratch each time you do this.

- **You can easily remind yourself of the original image:** When you're working on a file, especially a photo, it's useful to know where you've come from. Hiding your ten adjustment layers to reveal the original photo lets you see quickly how far you've come, and whether you're overdoing your treatments.

CAUTION While this kind of editing is a great idea, you should never work on the original photo file. Always make a copy first. Accidents happen!

Layers give you lots of ways to edit your files nondestructively. If you're careful, and you're aware of the tools available, you should be able to go through the entire editing process without ever touching the original image. Here are some of the features of layers that you can use to achieve this goal.

Editing with adjustment layers

Adjustment layers are one of the most flexible ways to edit your photos. These layers apply nondestructive versions of most of the adjustments found under the Image ➪ Adjustments menu option. Adjustment layers allow you to experiment a great deal with your images as you edit them.

CROSS-REF You'll find a thorough treatment of adjustment layers, describing each adjustment in detail, in Chapter 6.

It's the flexibility of adjustment layers that makes them so special. You can achieve similar results using the destructive versions of the adjustments, but you won't be able to go back and tweak your adjustments later. In Figure 12.12, for example, a basic black-and-white conversion of a photo is carried out by applying Black & White and Levels adjustments in two ways. The first example uses the destructive adjustments found under Image ➪ Adjustments, and the second uses adjustment layers. As you can see, the results are pretty much identical.

FIGURE 12.12

Two versions of the same photo. On the left, the Black & White and Levels adjustments are applied directly to the photo using the commands under Image ➪ Adjustments. On the right, adjustment layers are used to achieve the same effect. You can see the unchanged image at the bottom of the Layers palette.

So, the two approaches don't yield any difference in image quality, but look at what you might want to do next. Maybe you decide that you've overdone the emphasis on the bike's frame — originally red — when doing the original conversion. In the first image, where edits are applied destructively, changing this is very tricky. To change the emphasis on the frame of the bike, you have to select the frame, which is going to be a long-winded process in itself, and use Levels or Curves to de-emphasize that area. In the example with adjustment layers, you can simply edit the Black & White layer and move the Red slider a little to the left — merely a few moments of work.

If you decide that you want to try a super-desaturated look with just a touch of the original colors showing through, the first image is again problematic. You have to import a new version of the color photo, and position the color image beneath the black-and-white version in the Layers palette. This is tricky because the photo is already cropped, and you have to match the cropping exactly. You then need to reduce the opacity of the black-and-white version's layer a touch to achieve the results you want. In the second image, you just have to drop the opacity of the Black & White adjustment layer by around 20 percent, and you're there in less than 5 seconds.

So, although it's possible to achieve similar results with both destructive and nondestructive edits, you lose a lot in terms of flexibility when you edit destructively, and the process offers no advantage in terms of image quality. Adjustment layers allow you to try things very quickly to see if the results are pleasing, and discard the edits just as quickly. This inevitably leads to more experimentation and is more likely to produce a better end result from an artistic standpoint.

Using Smart Objects and Smart Filters

New in Photoshop CS3 is the ability to apply filters nondestructively to a Smart Object, leaving the original image unaltered. This is a major step forward for so many reasons. You can apply dramatic filters to a photo without touching the original beneath. In Figure 12.13, Torn Edges and Crystallize filters are applied to a photo of an old door to produce an edgy, funky background. To make sure the filters are applied as Smart Filters, the photo is first converted to a Smart Object.

FIGURE 12.13

This funky background image was created using two Smart Filters on a photo converted to a Smart Object.

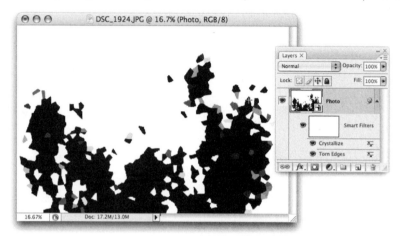

CROSS-REF You can find more on Smart Objects and Smart Filters in Chapter 8.

Smart Filters remain completely editable after you create them, and you can also alter the blending modes and opacities of the filter effects at any time. Like adjustment layers, the reeditable nature of Smart Filters lends itself to experimentation; if you decide that you've gone too far with the Torn Edges filter, for example, you can go back and reedit it to suit. In previous versions of Photoshop, you would have had to start again with the original image, so this really is a massive timesaver.

Because the filters are stacked in the Layers palette, you can click and drag them above and below each other in the stacking order to create quite different effects. This "live" interaction between filters is something never seen before in Photoshop, and it provides lots of opportunities for fun experimentation!

Using layer masks and clipping masks

If you're looking to remove an area of an image, there are two main routes you can follow: you can select the area you want to remove and delete it, or you can use a layer mask. The latter approach has the benefit that, if you later need to reintroduce some of the area you masked off, you can. If you delete it, on the other hand, it's lost for good, and you'll have to go back to the original image and create a new selection.

CROSS-REF Layer masks and clipping masks are covered in detail in Chapter 9.

In Figure 12.14, a design for a Web site header has been created, consisting of a Background layer, a shape layer forming the basic shape of the header, and two illustrative elements taken from different photos. Two kinds of masks are used in the process: layer masks on the two illustrative elements and a clipping mask to bind these two elements to the shape layer below.

FIGURE 12.14

In this design for the header of a Web site, the use of two layer masks and a clipping mask allows you to easily reedit and reposition the elements.

The layer mask on the Plants layer is masking out a large chunk of the layer to allow for that text on the right side of the design. The masking means that the text doesn't have to compete with the patterns that would otherwise sit underneath it. Meanwhile, the layer mask on the Church layer masks out a small part of the branches to produce a more natural, ragged effect. If you decide that you want the branches in the Church layer back, all you have to do is paint white on its layer mask and they'll return. By the same token, if you want more of the Plants layer to show through, you could paint gray on the right side of its layer mask to reveal more plants beneath the text.

The clipping mask clips the illustrative elements to the outline of the Box shape layer. You can freely reposition the illustrations within that shape, because both images in the two illustration layers remain intact; they're merely masked off.

Contrast this flexible approach with the alternative. To achieve the same effect without using masks, you'd have to erase parts of the Plants and Church layers with the Eraser tool, and accept that you couldn't change those edits thereafter. To keep these two layers within the bounds of the Box shape layer, you'd have to select the pixels within the layer by Ctrl+clicking (⌘+clicking on the Mac) the vector mask for that layer, invert the selection, then use that selection to delete the areas of the Church and Plants layers that fall outside the boundaries of the shape. At that point, your composition would be fixed; you'd have no way of experimenting with it. If you decide you don't like the effect after a couple of days, you're back to square one. Not good.

Once again, these nondestructive approaches give you much more flexibility with a design, allow you to experiment with ideas, and save you time when reworking those ideas.

Copying layers

If all else fails and you have to make a destructive edit for whatever reason, it's a good idea to copy the layer you're going to be working on before you start and then work on the copy. This gives you a fallback if you decide you don't like the effect that your edit has produced.

To copy a layer, simply click and drag it to the New Layer icon in the Layers palette. If you find yourself having to do this several times within a document, create a new group called something like **Originals**, and place the untouched versions in there. This makes sure you don't inadvertently edit the original layer. When you're happy with all the edits, you can either delete the backup layers or save them with the file for future reference.

Flattening an Image

Flattening your layered image is a dramatic and very final option. All the layers in your image are combined into the one Background layer, and all your work tweaking adjustment layers and fine-tuning your type layers is frozen into one single layer. If you then save over your layered file, the layer information is lost forever.

To flatten a layered image, choose Layer ➪ Flatten Image. If any of your layers are hidden, you'll be asked to confirm that you want to delete those layers before flattening.

There are several reasons why you may choose to take this step. For example:

- **You want to save disk space.** If your file is really huge, flattening the image dramatically reduces its size. You can read more about this issue in a moment.

- **Your computer is having trouble working with a really big file.** If you have a lot of layers in a document, you may want to flatten the image before starting on further design work, or flatten an illustration in stages as you work on it. This is especially true when dealing with a large, high-resolution photo.

- **You need to save the file in a format that doesn't support layers.** This may be the case if you're sending someone a JPEG file, for example.

In the second and third scenarios, the best option is to save a copy of the layered file before you flatten it. You can then work on the flattened version of the file. Remember, if you flatten an image, you can't go back and tweak it afterward, so keeping a layered version in reserve is a good insurance policy. If the second scenario really gives you trouble, try adding more RAM to your computer. If the computer is getting a little old, however, it may be worth upgrading it (if funds permit) to save your own sanity!

A layered Photoshop file can get very big very quickly. In Figure 12.15, you can see a photo that has been converted to black and white. Although the original photo was 6 megapixels, it has been cropped to a panoramic format, so this version is smaller than the photo's original dimensions. The photo is converted to a Smart Object, and a Gaussian Blur Smart Filter applied. Several adjustment layers are also used: a Levels layer, two Exposure layers, a Black and White layer, and a Photo Filter layer. Last, a frame is added around the whole thing. The original JPEG from the camera was 2.5MB. The final Photoshop file on the hard drive is more than 45MB.

FIGURE 12.15

A 2.5MB color digital photo, with a few adjustment layers added, is now 45.6MB in size. (You can see the computer reporting the on-disk file size in the background.)

At this point, we're happy with the image, for now. There's a temptation to flatten the image to save the hard drive space — after all, the photo is complete, and the flattened file size for this particular image is only 12MB. However, if you decide later that the frame is not up to par, or you want to readjust the Red channel in the Black and White adjustment layer, you would have to go back to the original photo and re-create the whole thing, which would be time consuming and frustrating. It's far better to keep the layered version intact if possible.

Your files are priceless, so data storage is very inexpensive in comparison. Just about the cheapest component you can add to your computer is storage. If you have a hard drive with a small capacity, say 40GB, it will fill up quite soon when creating files like this example.

> **TIP** You can add another drive, or an external drive, very cheaply these days. At the time of writing, a 250GB external USB hard drive can be had for around $95. If you tend to create a lot of large files and want to retain the flexibility that layers offer, a drive like this is a great investment. Ideally, you'd have two external drives that mirror each other, so that if one fails you still have the full data on the other. At this price level, it seems like a sensible move for peace of mind.

As an example of how you can use (and use up!) disk space, some professional photographers use a few large drives for each photo shoot, each drive containing the same information. One drive is at the photographer's studio for easy access; one might be at the photographer's house; and a third might be at an assistant's or friend's house. In this way, the full layered Photoshop files exist in three different places at once, and if any of the locations burn down, or a disk is stolen or fails, the data is still safe. The price of retaining the information is very small in comparison to the total cost of the shoot, so it makes perfect financial sense for the peace of mind it allows.

Working in a Team

Up to now, this chapter has concentrated on situations where you're working on your own, but there might come a time where you have to work within a team — maybe at a design or advertising agency, or just with a group of friends. A team might have two or three designers, all working on the same files at different times. That means Photoshop files can come from any member of the team, and each member will be unfamiliar with the files he or she receives from other members. This section looks at how to make this process of transferring files between team members as painless as possible.

Creating self-documenting files

Throughout this book, the importance of keeping your layers organized is often emphasized. This becomes even more important when you work within a team. Other people need to get to work on your designs quickly and with the minimum of fuss.

We already looked at the importance of naming and organizing your layers earlier in the chapter, but it's worth restating that the better your files are organized, the easier others will find them to work with. When time is of the essence in a professional environment, an hour spent coming to grips with a badly organized Photoshop file of a hundred layers can make the difference between hitting and missing a deadline. In turn, this will make the creator of such a file very unpopular!

There are other strategies you can employ, too. One great feature of Photoshop is the ability to add notes to a file. A note is a nonprinting approximation of a sticky note that exists right within the document window, but above all your layers, as shown in Figure 12.16. You can leave notes for others to refer to when working on the file. To create a new note, use the Notes tool. Click the Notes Tool icon in the Toolbox, and then click in the document window to add a note.

You can collapse the note into a small icon by clicking the small square at the top left of the note. You can also highlight the note and press Ctrl+W (⌘+W on the Mac). Double-click the icon to expand the note again. You can add as many notes as you want to a file.

FIGURE 12.16

A note communicating an issue with the menu in a Web site layout

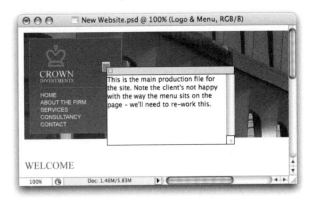

To delete a note, click the note to highlight it and press Backspace (Delete on the Mac). You'll be asked if you really want to delete the note; click OK or Cancel accordingly. If you want to hide notes so they don't get in the way when working on a file, choose View ➪ Show ➪ Annotations. To show your notes again, choose the same option.

There are some options for the Notes tool in the options bar:

- **Author:** You can add an author field to the note so that others know who wrote it. The author appears in the title bar of the note window when it opens. It also appears as a tooltip when you hover over the note icon in the document window.

- **Size:** This controls the size of the text in the note, from Smallest to Largest in five steps. The default value is Medium.

- **Color:** You can change the color of the note from the default yellow.

- **Clear All:** This button deletes all the notes from a document.

There's also an option for creating audio notes in a file; you need a microphone and speakers on your computer to make it work. The Audio Annotation tool is found under the Notes tool icon in the toolbox. Watch out, though; using this tool is unlikely to win you friends in a quiet office environment!

Another strategy is to create a markup layer or group. This is an overlay that sits above all other layers in the stacking order and contains production notes for the file. For a Web site, you might create layers that measure out the pixel dimensions of the various elements, plus color swatches and font information. This is a very effective method of communicating with others. You can see an example of this in Figure 12.17. The actual design is "dimmed" with a pure black layer, and the markup information is added on top in white to make it stand out clearly.

A markup group, containing notes, dimensions, and color information. Note that the group has been made a different color and labeled clearly to make sure there's no risk of the markup getting exported along with the design.

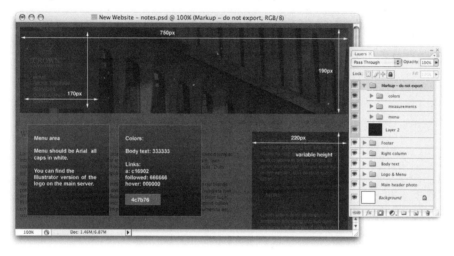

These techniques will help you communicate with others on your team, and the clearer you can be, the more they'll thank you.

Making sure your files are accurate

It's easy to put together a Photoshop file that looks great, but that's not the end of the story. When you hand it over to others for further work or for printing, it should also be accurate in terms of resolution, measurements, color, typefaces, bleeds (for print work), and so on. Resolution and measurements are arguably the most important of these because they're very hard to correct if you get them wrong.

You can check your document's resolution by clicking the right-pointing arrow at the bottom of the document window and choosing Show ➪ Document Dimensions. On-screen work should be at least 72 dpi, and print work should be based on the target resolution of the final print run; call the printer to find out what it should be before you start. If you get this wrong, and you later have to scale up your design for a higher resolution, you'll kick yourself when you have to re-create all your bitmap layers because they look terrible when scaled up.

Measurements will likely need to be determined before you start, and you can use Photoshop's guides, rulers, and the Ruler tool to make sure that everything on the page is pixel-perfect before sending it on to others. Related to this, make sure that elements align correctly on the page. You can use the Align and Distribute commands — available under the Layer menu — to make sure all your layers align and space out perfectly.

CROSS-REF   You can find more on guides and measuring, as well as aligning and distributing layers, in Chapter 2.

The basic rule is to check your files thoroughly against the initial specifications and the brief for accuracy before sending them on to others. Then check them again.

Abiding by the rules

When you work in an organization, you'll find it has its own way of doing things. That applies to how coffee is made, what goes where in the fridge, and the structure of the files on the server. You might find that there's no real rhyme or reason to the file structure on the server and that no one ever names a single layer (it happens). Even if there is a structure in place, it may well not be what you're used to.

The important thing is to learn how the organization works and fit in with it, at least in the short term. Don't start imposing your own file structure on someone else, even if you think yours is better. Organizations work in strange ways, but if a system has worked well enough for ages, no one is going to thank you for tinkering with it to the extent that they don't know where any files are anymore. Some firms have their own unique ways to organize their layers, and again, you should learn and respect these ways, prescriptive though they may be.

Getting hired with layers

Will being great with layers get you hired into your dream job? Sadly, no. Creatives are hired mostly on the strength of their ideas and how well the interviewer feels they'll fit into the existing team. Indeed, the sobering truth is that many creatives are hired based on who they know and who they've worked for previously.

Having said all that, it never hurts to project an organized image in this ultracompetitive marketplace. Part of that is your personal presentation and the work you show to people, but it also extends to how files and layers are organized. If you're up against someone with similar creative skills, it's going to come down to the little things. If you're showing someone your work and it contains a beautifully ordered Layers palette, it can only help.

Exploring Common Workflow Scenarios

When working on a project, layered Photoshop files are almost always part of an overall process. This process is called your workflow, and it covers the steps of your project from start to finish. This section looks at some example workflows and the role of layers within them.

Photography

Let's look at a simple workflow for cataloging and processing digital photos. This workflow starts from the perspective of having a memory card full of images, rather than exploring the photography process itself, because here you're concerned with what happens in and around Photoshop. You can see a diagrammatic version of the workflow in Figure 12.18.

FIGURE 12.18

The steps involved in a photography workflow

Import photos to computer.
↓
Compare and sort photos. Choose photos to process.
↓
Take a temporary copy of the photos to be processed.
↓
Process photos in Photoshop and save full size PSDs back to catalog.
↓
Prepare for output by copying and resizing PSDs.
↓
Sharpen according to output media.
↓
Save resized/sharpened PSDs.
↓
Print photos, or output to Web.
↓
Save flat versions of PSD files as TIFF/JPEG images, if sending to clients.
↓
Back everything up.

The end result of this workflow is that you have a repository of your original, untouched photos to work from. In addition, you create a single, full-size, layered Photoshop master file for each processed photo; copies of this file provide resized and sharpened versions for output to various media.

The role of layers

In the photography workflow scenario just described, layers are likely to be central to the process. The processed photo in Photoshop probably has several different kinds of layer applied to it: adjustment layers, Smart Objects (with Smart Filters), maybe a type layer for a credit and copyright notice, and maybe a shape layer for a frame.

The layers are preserved from the creation of your master file right through to the resized copies that you use for various output scenarios. You may be wondering why the sharpening step is right at the end of the process, rather than at the point where the master file is created. Sharpening has different effects at different resolutions, so applying sharpening at the master stage would have an undesirably intense effect at lower Web resolutions. You need less sharpening at lower resolutions, so it's best to do this step right at the end of the chain.

A photography workflow example

Here's a simple example to back up the theoretical points just covered. In Figure 12.19, you can see the results of a shoot. There are 60 photos here, from which one or two are picked to be processed in Photoshop. How you compare and contrast photos is a matter of personal choice. Some people like to use dedicated cataloging software; some prefer to just use the basic organizational tools that came with the computer. These original files should be regarded as "untouchable" in terms of editing.

FIGURE 12.19

A folder of images, with two chosen for processing in Photoshop. Note that the chosen images are copied into a separate folder to make sure only copies, not the original files, are worked on.

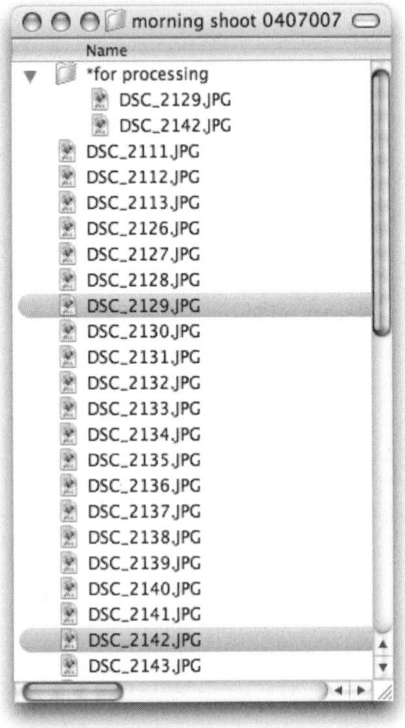

You can see that the chosen photos are copied into a separate folder to make sure the original files aren't touched. This is purely a safeguard measure, and the folder can be deleted once processing is complete.

Once the photos you want to work on are isolated, you can open them in Photoshop and start to apply your processing using adjustment layers. This is really a mini-workflow in its own right, starting with basic changes, and evolving as you process the file to fine-tune the adjustment layers and layer masks.

We now have two photos with full sets of layers, as shown in Figure 12.20, which we can save back to the shoot folder. We'll create a new subfolder inside the shoot folder called "processed" and save the Photoshop files in there.

FIGURE 12.20

The two layered files are opened in Photoshop. In the background, you can see the project folder with the two PSD files saved inside.

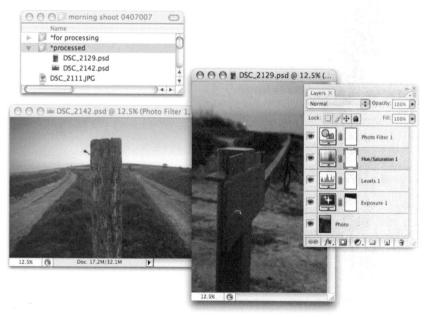

Imagine now that you want to upload these photos to an online photo-sharing site like Flickr. The current photo files are approximately 2000 x 3008 pixels at 300 dpi. Using Edit ⇨ Image Size, you can reduce the resolution for both files to 72 dpi, resulting in files of 480 x 722 pixels, which is about right for Flickr. Save them as additional Photoshop files, adding "_72dpi" to the end of each file name to indicate its resolution. This means you still have your full-size PSD files in reserve.

Now's the time to apply sharpening to the files. For each photo, convert the photo layer to a Smart Object and add a Smart Sharpen Smart Filter to provide a reeditable sharpening effect. After the sharpening is in place, you can save each image as a JPEG file, ready for upload.

You can now delete the "for processing" folder containing the duplicates of the chosen photos. This folder was really only in place to make sure you weren't editing the originals, thereby reducing the potential of overwriting an original file.

You've now ended up with the original photo files, two "master" full-resolution layered Photoshop files, and two separate layered 72 dpi Photoshop files for export, as well as flat, exported JPEG versions of the photos. You can see how the final files are organized in Figure 12.21. The separate PSD files allow you to go back and edit the photos at any point in the future.

FIGURE 12.21

In the final organization of the files, the "for processing" folder is deleted now that the files are processed.

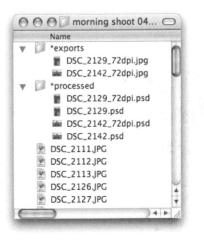

CAUTION   Backups should be a part of every workflow. Wherever you store your photo catalog, make sure it's included in any backup routine you have in place.

Web design

If you're a Web designer using Photoshop, your workflow is likely to be very much centered around the application. From initial ideas to the final Web image files, most of the visual process will revolve around Photoshop and the Layers palette. Only after the design is finalized does the process move beyond Photoshop. In Figure 12.22, you can see a visual representation of a typical workflow.

FIGURE 12.22

A typical workflow for a Web designer

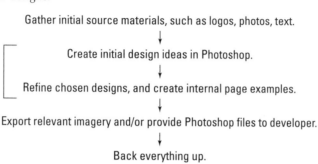

Gather initial source materials, such as logos, photos, text.
↓
Export flat versions of the design as JPEG/PNG/GIF files for viewing by client (unless you're doing your own site).
Create initial design ideas in Photoshop.
↓
Refine chosen designs, and create internal page examples.
↓
Export relevant imagery and/or provide Photoshop files to developer.
↓
Back everything up.

As discussed earlier in the chapter, this workflow will probably result in several alternate versions of a design. It's worth keeping all these unused designs in case you need to refer to them or roll back a design to an earlier version.

The role of layers

Because the bulk of your time as a Web designer will be spent in Photoshop, layers are integral to your workflow. When building page elements, you'll probably use many techniques outlined in the book including the shape tools, the Type tool, adjustment layers for photo editing, clipping masks, and layer styles.

CROSS-REF You can find a full walkthrough of a Web page design process in Chapter 14, covering many aspects of layers from a Web design perspective, such as slicing and exporting.

A Web design workflow example

Let's illustrate the above workflow with an example. You might start by organizing the supporting materials. You've probably been given some photos, the logo for the company you're working for, and the basic text for the Web site.

The next step is to create rough ideas for the site design. You can make several versions of these, as described earlier in the chapter. After the client agrees to a design, it's time to refine the design and double-check the layouts to make sure they're pixel-perfect in preparation for building the site. You might also create further page mockups for various areas of the site to work out any kinks in the design before the build process begins. You can see the kinds of files you might end up with in Figure 12.23.

FIGURE 12.23

Final site designs for a mythical cruise company, Red Star Cruises. In the background, you can see the "sources" folder that contains the company logo, text copy for the site, and photos for inclusion in the design, all supplied by the client.

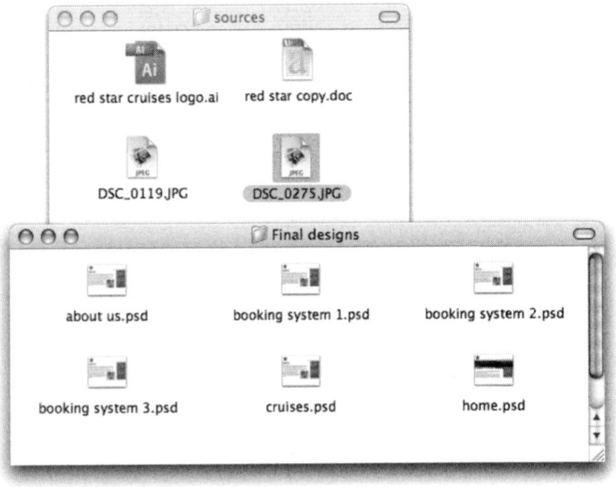

Unless you're making a site for yourself, you'll be exporting flattened, non-layered images at all stages to send to others for approval. A quick way to do this is simply to choose File ➪ Save for Web & Devices to save a JPEG file of the entire page.

At the end of this process, you should have a series of layered Photoshop files covering the main sections of the site. At this stage, you can either start the build yourself or, if you're working in a team, document the files and hand them over to a Web developer.

The final stage involves slicing and exporting individual elements such as the logo, ready to include in the Web pages. For this reason, and to make your documents useful as a reference when building the site, it's important to make sure that the Photoshop files you create are pixel-perfect at this stage.

As always, back up those precious files!

Print design

Although Photoshop is perfectly capable of outputting print-ready files, if you work regularly in a print design environment you're likely to use it differently. Traditionally, print work is done in layout packages like QuarkXPress or, more recently, Adobe's InDesign. Adobe Illustrator is another popular choice for print jobs that don't require multiple pages. In this context, Photoshop is merely a part of your workflow, and not the application in which you spend most of your time. Figure 12.24 shows an example workflow for a print environment.

FIGURE 12.24

This workflow shows how you might use Photoshop in a print setting.

Gather initial source materials, such as logos, photos, text.

↓

Start working on designs using a layout package such as InDesign, QuarkXpress or Illustrator.

↓

Create illustrative elements or edit photos in Photoshop.

↓

Import Photoshop files into your layout package.

↓

Finalize designs and output to print.

↓

Back everything up.

As you can see, in this scenario Photoshop is somewhat demoted to what amounts to a high-end image editor, rather than being used as a design tool in its own right. Remember, though, that any photos used in a print workflow have probably already been through the photography workflow outlined earlier.

The role of layers

When you import a Photoshop file into a page layout program such as InDesign or QuarkXPress, you're really linking to the file on the hard drive. Rather than editing the Photoshop layers in the page layout program, you edit them by opening the linked Photoshop file within Photoshop. When you save the PSD file in Photoshop, your changes are reflected in the layout program. In Figure 12.25, you can see an InDesign layout window. The photo within the brochure is a layered Photoshop file placed into the InDesign layout. In turn, the Photoshop file contains a photo layer, along with two adjustment layers (Exposure and Hue/Saturation) to correct exposure and enhance colors.

CROSS-REF For more on how QuarkXPress and InDesign handle Photoshop files, see Chapter 13.

Of course, even as a print designer, you must come to grips with many of Photoshop's layer features, if only to knock photos into shape. You probably won't use the Type tool very much, though, because type is very much the province of layout software.

FIGURE 12.25

In this layout in Adobe InDesign, the photo is a layered Photoshop file, linked to from within the layout. If you make changes to the Photoshop file from within Photoshop, the InDesign file updates itself accordingly.

Choosing a Strategy

In common with many professional applications, Photoshop often provides more than one method to achieve the same goal. For example, to create a simple square, you could fill a rectangular selection or use the Rectangle tool. You could create a four-sided shape using the Polygon tool. In a pinch, you could even use the Line tool with a very heavy weight. Any of these methods results in a square, and they're all valid approaches. (Of course, there's greater scope for editability with shape layers, and you'd have to be pretty insane to create a square with the Line tool.)

When editing photos, there are also multiple approaches you can take. For example, if you want to make a black-and-white image from a color photo, you can choose from three different adjustment layers: Black and White, the Channel Mixer, or Hue/Saturation. By the same token, you can also make contrast adjustments using any one of three adjustment layers: Levels, Curves, or Brightness/Contrast. In both scenarios, you can also perform the same edits, albeit destructively, using the adjustments found under the Image ➪ Adjustments menu.

The point is that the method you use will be a function of the results you're trying to achieve coupled with personal preference. This section looks at some alternative methods for working in Photoshop, and tries to come to some conclusions about best practices.

Navigating your document's layers

When working with Photoshop, there are many different ways to navigate and interact with your main organizational tool — your layers. To select a layer, you can simply click the layer in the Layers palette, or you can use Move tool with Auto-Select enabled. Some people rarely go near the Layers palette; they prefer instead to use the Move tool to select everything, and have this down to a fine art. Others find that this method is difficult to use and are always selecting the wrong layer.

By the same token, in the Layer menu there are many options for working with layers — as you might expect — but some folks almost never go anywhere near it, preferring instead to work with the corresponding options in the Layers palette, or use keyboard shortcuts.

Speaking of which, Photoshop is full of keyboard shortcuts. If you can do it with the mouse, there's usually a way to do it with the keyboard. If you become good at these and have a good memory, you can work very fast indeed, but most people get by with a smattering of keyboard shortcuts, using point-and-click for everything else. This is perfectly fine, and you shouldn't feel bad about it!

CROSS-REF You can find a long list of layer-based shortcuts in Appendix B.

Knowing your tools

While it's okay to use quirky methodologies for doing things in Photoshop, the state you should be striving for is a *mind like water*. This is a term derived from martial arts and refers to a position of perfect readiness. This is what you should be aiming for with your Photoshop skills: perfectly ready to meet any challenge thrown at you. When you have your skill set down, the software should feel like an extension of your brain; at that point, the main focus of your time becomes simply creating, rather than wondering how to achieve a particular effect.

Inevitably, there will be times when the dark recesses of Photoshop throw you a little, but you want to keep this to a minimum. The best way to do this, like any other skill, is simply to practice. If you use Photoshop professionally, the clients will keep you practicing just fine; if not, try to find the time to use it as much as you can — the more you practice, the more you learn, and the faster and easier each successive project becomes.

Precisely because Photoshop gives you multiple ways to achieve similar results, you should always be open to new ways of working. Don't assume that your way is best, just because it's the way you've always done things!

Keeping an eye on the final result

The really important thing about any creative project is the final result. Photoshop allows for a great deal of experimentation and wacky effects, especially in the realms of layer styles and Smart Filters, but that doesn't mean you should always use these features. Think instead about what's best for the actual design and what result you want to see, and then try to achieve that result.

This constant evaluation of the desired end result helps to keep the project on track and encourages you to produce output that reflects your taste, rather than letting Photoshop's feature set shape your creativity.

Three ways to a similar result

In this example, you're going to look at a fairly common process in Photoshop: adding a frame to a photograph. You'll go through three different ways to add a small black frame to a photo. Each method has a different approach, and produces a slightly different effect. Figure 12.26 shows the basic photo. It's been manipulated, converted to a black-and-white image, and resized ready for upload to the Web.

FIGURE 12.26

A moody seaside scene converted to black and white, ready for framing

One approach is to add a very simple straight black frame to the photo. To do this, you can use layer styles to add a Stroke effect around the photo layer.

CROSS-REF You can find more information on layer styles and effects in Chapter 10.

NOTE Make sure you convert your photo's Background layer to a normal layer first — you can't apply a layer style to the Background layer.

Double-click the photo layer in the Layers palette and choose the Stroke effect in the Layer Style dialog box. Set the stroke's Position to Inside, because you're effectively adding a stroke to the edge of the document. Set the size to 6 pixels to give a slim but definite frame. Leave Blend Mode at Normal and Opacity at 100 percent. With the Fill Type set to Color, choose black for the fill color. This provides the result in Figure 12.27.

FIGURE 12.27

Using a Stroke layer effect to add a basic black frame to the photo

This is fine, but maybe a little too precise. What if you wanted an approximation of the effect of scanning a 35mm negative, which produces a frame with slightly rounded inner corners? This requires a little more thought. The obvious answer is to use the Rounded Rectangle tool to create rounded edges. Here's how you might do that, based on the original photo layer without the Stroke effect:

1. **Create a fully black shape layer.** Select the Rectangle tool, and make sure the foreground color is black. Drag the new shape out across the full extent of the document window, until the whole photo is covered.

CROSS-REF You can investigate Shape Layers more fully in Chapter 5.

2. **Create the frame.** Make sure the vector mask thumbnail for the previous step's shape layer is selected. Now select the Rounded Rectangle tool, and give it a Radius of 10 pixels. Select the Subtract From Shape Area option. Position the cursor just inside the document bounds at the top-left corner, then click and drag down and to the right until you reach a

point just inside the bottom right of the image. This second shape that you've created knocks out the center of the original shape.

3. **Refine the position of the inner shape.** If you want to tweak the position of the inner shape to make sure the frame is even (or possibly uneven), select the Path Selection tool and click the center of the image, which selects the inner shape. Use the arrow keys to nudge the shape around until you're happy.

You can see the final results in Figure 12.28.

FIGURE 12.28

In this example, a shape layer is used to add a rounded element to the inner corners of the frame.

Great, you now have a decent approximation of the feel of a scanned 35mm negative. It's still a bit pristine and artificial, though. Real scans of this type actually have a slightly soft inner edge, with the photo bleeding into the frame, rather than the hard edge you see here. How can you achieve this effect?

Shape layers are great for a hard-edged, precise feel, but not so good for the soft edge you're looking for here. They can still help you create the look you're after, though. Here's how — again, we're starting with the original photo layer here:

1. **Create a rounded rectangle shape.** Select the Rounded Rectangle tool with a Radius of 10 pixels and a foreground color of black. Click just inside the top-left corner of the image. Drag down and to the right, stopping just inside the bottom-right corner. This should produce a black, rounded rectangle over the bulk of the image, leaving just the outer areas showing the actual photo — almost a "negative" of the frame.

2. **Select the pixels of a new shape.** Ctrl+click (⌘+click on the Mac) the vector mask thumbnail for the shape layer; this selects the shape's pixels. You'll see "marching ants" around the edge of the shape layer.

3. **Feather the selection.** To get the soft-edged effect you're looking for, feather the edges of the selection. Hide the shape layer, leaving just the selection active. Choose Select ➪ Modify ➪ Feather and, in the Feather Selection dialog box, type a radius of 3 pixels. Click OK to close the dialog box.

4. **Invert and fill the selection.** Choose Select ➪ Inverse to invert the selection. You'll see the selection change to form the basis of the frame. Create a new layer by clicking the New Layer icon in the Layers palette. Last, fill the selection by choosing Edit ➪ Fill and selecting Black as the fill color. Click OK to apply the fill. Press Ctrl +D (⌘+D on the Mac) to deselect the area. You should be left with a black frame around the photo, with a soft, feathered feel to the inner edge. This looks much more like a scan of a 35mm negative, and has a pleasing, organic quality to it, as you can see in Figure 12.29. You can now discard the original shape layer you created.

FIGURE 12.29

The third technique has produced a frame with a soft inner edge, creating a retro effect by mimicking the effect of a 35mm negative scan (a). A detail is also shown at 200 percent (b) to illustrate the effect more clearly.

This example shows three techniques for creating a simple black frame around a photo. Each technique has its own merits, and the example serves to illustrate that the tools you choose are a function of the desired end result. The frames are only subtly different, but you had to change techniques at every step to achieve those different effects.

Summary

This chapter covered a lot of ground relating to using layers and Photoshop files in the real world. It started off with a detailed look at how to organize your layers with layer naming and layer groups. It also investigated how to create different versions of your files when working on a particular job, and how you might go about managing the resulting proliferation of layered Photoshop files.

You explored the benefits of nondestructive editing using a variety of layer strategies to make sure your original images always remain untouched, and some advice was offered on flattening your PSD files.

You looked at how to keep your team happy with your work, and then learned how layered Photoshop files can fit into your workflow. Finally, you learned that there isn't always a "proper" way to achieve a particular result, and you explored different ways to approach Photoshop's many layer-related tools.

Chapter 13

Using Layers in Other Applications

This book has looked at layers in great detail, and now it's time to investigate the Photoshop document format itself, and how it interacts with other applications.

Photoshop's first release was in 1988 for the Apple Macintosh only. Since then, the application has come a long way, adding major features such as layers and layer styles, which means that the Photoshop file format now has to support many more features than it did then.

This long history, coupled with consistently innovative updates, led to Photoshop becoming the market leader and industry standard it is today. In turn, the PSD file has become a ubiquitous format that nearly all other image editors have to support to one degree or another.

This chapter looks at the Photoshop PSD format in some detail, and also shows how to tweak the way Photoshop saves and handles files. You'll learn about other file formats that support Photoshop layers. Finally, the chapter looks at a range of other applications, from Illustrator through to Flash and QuarkXPress, and reveals how these applications deal with layered Photoshop files.

It's not very glamorous stuff, but it's useful nonetheless. Sure, a file format doesn't have the appeal of an elegant drop shadow or a really nice piece of typography, but at 2 a.m. one day, when you're trying to work out how to save a layered TIFF file to send to your printers, this chapter might just save you!

Understanding the PSD Format

The PSD (Photoshop Document) file format is the native format for saving documents in Photoshop. It has a .psd file extension, hence the name. Saving in the PSD format preserves all the features of your Photoshop document, including layers, layer styles, channels, masks, and so on. Although Photoshop can read and write many other image formats, only the PSD format — and its close cousin, the PSB format (more on this format later) — perfectly preserve the original state of your document.

The PSD format is a *lossless* file format. This means that, when you save an image, Photoshop doesn't remove any data from the image file. By contrast, a *lossy* format, like JPEG, selectively removes subtle image data each time the file is saved in order to reduce the file size. The PSD format is not overly concerned with preserving file size; its mission in life is to retain all information.

PSD files can handle bit depths of 8, 16, or 32. *Bit depth* refers to how much color information is stored within each pixel in an image. An RGB 8-bit file has 256 possible values for each of the three channels, and hence can store and display up to 16 million possible colors. In Photoshop, 32-bit files are most commonly used to store High Dynamic Range (HDR) images. HDR images store a much bigger range of brightness values than regular 8-bit or 16-bit images, and can represent the full range of brightness levels found in the real world. A photographer can capture multiple exposures of the same subject — for example, one exposure for highlights, one for midtones, and one for shadows — and merge the exposures together to form a single HDR image.

Layers are, of course, saved within a PSD file, and only PSD (and PSB) can support all the layer features in Photoshop; no other file format can do this. To preserve all your layer styles, type layers, masks, adjustment layers, and so on, you need to save in the PSD format. Furthermore, only Photoshop can read PSD files 100 percent accurately, although as you'll see later in the chapter, other image editors can also handle the format with varying degrees of success.

There is one other native Photoshop format: PSB (Photoshop Big), more commonly known as the Large Document Format. This supports all the features of PSD, and also allows files of over 2GB to be saved. It's also the format used to store Smart Objects. A PSB file can only be opened in Photoshop CS or later. You rarely have to use the PSB format, unless you're exporting Smart Objects or working with very large-scale graphics.

CROSS-REF   Smart Objects are covered in detail in Chapter 8.

Setting File Handling Preferences

You can modify the way Photoshop saves and handles files in the File Handling section of the Preferences dialog box, as shown in Figure 13.1. To access these preferences, choose Edit ➪ Preferences ➪ File Handling (Windows), or Photoshop ➪ Preferences ➪ File Handling (Mac).

FIGURE 13.1

Photoshop's file handling preferences. These are the default values in Photoshop CS3.

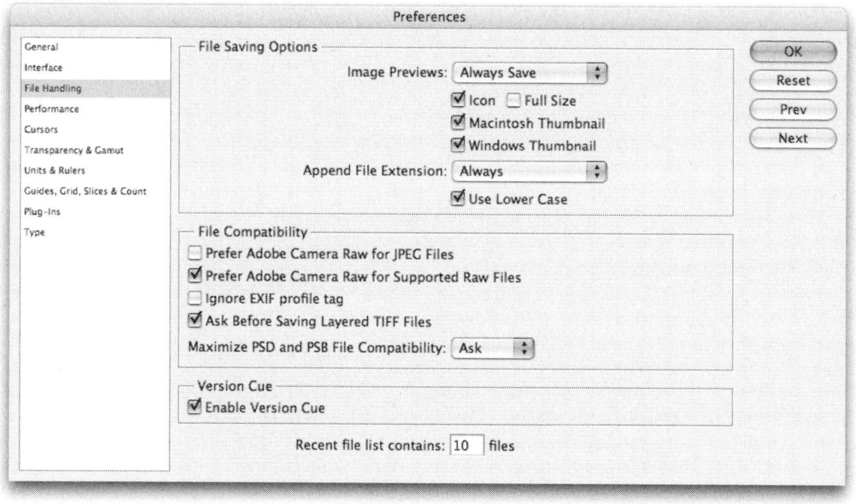

The first group within the dialog box — File Saving Options — lets you specify how your files are saved, as follows:

- **Image Previews:** This option governs how Photoshop saves small composite versions of your file to display in file browsers, such as Windows Explorer or the Mac's Finder. Image previews allow you to see a pictorial representation of each file as you browse it on your computer, which makes it a lot easier to find things. The default option — Always Save — always saves a preview along with an image, but you can also choose never to save previews (Never Save), or to have Photoshop ask you each time a file is saved (Ask When Saving). In the latter case, the Image Previews options appear in the Save or Save As dialog box when you save a file. It's probably fair to say that the default option — Always Save — is best for almost all circumstances.

- **Icon/Full Size/Macintosh Thumbnail/Windows Thumbnail (Mac only):** These options allow you to include a Finder preview icon, a low-resolution full-size composite preview image, a Mac thumbnail image, and/or a Windows thumbnail image inside the saved file. Enabling the Icon and two Thumbnail settings gives you the best chance of seeing icon previews of your files across both platforms, with minimal effect on file size. The Full Size option is only supported by certain applications and is best left disabled unless you know you're going to need it, as it can greatly increase your file sizes and slow down the file-saving process.

- **Append File Extension (Mac only):** Use this option to control whether Photoshop saves files with a file name extension or not. (The Mac uses a different method for determining file types, so it doesn't necessarily need file extensions.) The default setting is Always; you should probably leave it at that, because again you're likely to swap files between platforms at some point. There are two other settings — Never, and Ask When Saving — which do exactly what you'd expect.

- **File Extension (Windows only):** This option lets you choose whether to use upper- or lowercase file name extensions when saving files. (Windows always saves files with a file name extension.)

- **Use Lower Case (Mac only):** If you elect to save your files with file name extensions, select this option to ensure that lowercase letters are used for the extensions. Deselect this option to save files with uppercase file name extensions.

The second major group of options, File Compatibility, controls how Photoshop opens and saves specific file formats. The options include the following:

- **Prefer Adobe Camera Raw for JPEG Files:** Select this option to automatically open JPEG files in Camera Raw, Adobe's raw format conversion and manipulation plug-in. With this option disabled, JPEGs open directly in Photoshop by default.

NEW FEATURE   The Camera Raw plug-in built into previous versions of Photoshop was limited to handling images in raw format, leaving users of cameras that only produce JPEG images somewhat in the dark. Photoshop CS3 dramatically improves the situation, allowing you to open and process JPEG files in Camera Raw, too. You can choose whether to open a JPEG file within Camera Raw or directly within Photoshop at the time you open it. If you use Windows, choose File ⇨ Open As, select the file you want to open, and choose Camera Raw from the Open As menu at the bottom of the dialog box. On Mac OS, choose File ⇨ Open, select the JPEG file; then choose Camera Raw from the Format menu at the base of the dialog.

- **Prefer Adobe Camera Raw for Supported Raw Files:** This option, selected by default, makes Adobe Camera Raw the default plug-in for RAW files. If you deselect this option, and you have another RAW conversion plug-in installed, Photoshop defaults to using the third-party plug-in instead. You'll probably want to select this option if you prefer using Adobe Camera Raw for all your RAW images.

NEW FEATURE   The ability to choose the default plug-in that opens RAW files is a new and most welcome addition to Photoshop CS3. In previous versions, Photoshop always defaulted to the relevant third-party plug-in for RAW files.

TIP   When you open a RAW file, you can choose whether to open it in Camera Raw or in an installed third-party converter plug-in. In Windows, choose File ⇨ Open As, select the file to open, and choose either Camera Raw or your third-party plug-in from the Open As menu at the bottom of the dialog box. On Mac OS, choose File ⇨ Open, select the file; then choose either Camera Raw or your third-party plug-in from the Format menu at the base of the dialog box.

- **Ignore EXIF Profile Tag:** This option allows you to avoid potential issues with color profile information from a digital camera. EXIF information is metadata stored by digital cameras in each file they produce. Part of that information is the color space in which the camera records the photo, for example Adobe RGB. If you're working in a different color space within Photoshop — sRGB, for example — and want to preserve that when opening photos, you can select this option. Photoshop then opens the file using your working color profile, rather than the color profile defined in the EXIF information.

■ **Ask Before Saving Layered TIFF Files:** TIFF is one of the few non-Photoshop formats to support layers. Select this option, and Photoshop always asks you whether you want to preserve your layers by displaying the TIFF Options dialog box when you first save a layered TIFF file that was previously nonlayered. This topic is touched on again in the next section of the chapter.

■ **Maximize PSD and PSB File Compatibility:** A file saved with "maximized" compatibility includes a full-resolution flattened image along with the layer information. This makes for big files, and disabling this option reduces file sizes significantly. However, it means that older versions of Photoshop, as well as some other image editors, can't read much of the data within files saved in newer versions of Photoshop. You can choose from among Never, Always, and Ask. Never and Always are self-explanatory, while Ask displays a dialog box each time you save a new PSD file.

NOTE Each successive version of Photoshop adds more features for the PSD format to support, which makes swapping PSD files between versions of Photoshop somewhat fraught with issues. As a rule, if a saved file contains new features — for example, Smart Filters in CS3 — these elements are simply discarded by older versions of the software.

The next section of the dialog box, Version Cue, contains a single option: Enable Version Cue. Deselecting this option removes access to the Adobe file browser dialog boxes — and therefore any Version Cue projects — within Photoshop, and also removes access to Version Cue from within your copy of Adobe Bridge. (Any Version Cue servers remain running — you just won't have access to them.)

CROSS-REF Version Cue is covered in a bit more detail in Chapter 12.

The last option in the dialog box, Recent File List Contains, lets you specify how many files appear in the recent file list under the File ➪ Open Recent menu. Type a value from 0 up to 30. Zero means that the recent file list is always empty.

All recent files opened in Photoshop — not just PSD files — appear under File ➪ Open Recent.

Working with Other Layered File Formats

As mentioned previously, the only formats to support Photoshop layers natively are PSD and PSB. You can save images from Photoshop using other formats such as BMP, JPG, or GIF, but most of these formats don't know anything about layers; Photoshop flattens your layers in the saved file. However, there are a couple of other formats that do support Photoshop layers — TIFF and Photoshop PDF.

Using TIFF

TIFF was originally designed to solve problems relating to proprietary file formats, and to allow all image-manipulation software to exchange files more easily. TIFF has been very successful in this respect, and most image-editing software supports the format.

TIFF is a complex format and can contain information that's proprietary to a certain application or company. This feature allows it to support Photoshop layers. You can save a layered document as a TIFF file by choosing TIFF from the Format menu in Photoshop's Save As dialog box. When you do this, Photoshop gives you the option to save it with layers intact, as shown in Figure 13.2.

FIGURE 13.2

In Photoshop's Save As dialog box, you can save a layered document as a TIFF file. Note that the Layers option is selected.

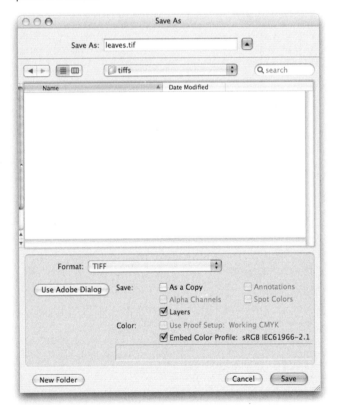

After clicking Save in the Save As dialog box, Photoshop displays an extra TIFF Options dialog box, as shown in Figure 13.3. The options in this dialog box work as follows:

- **Image Compression:** You can select a compression option for reducing the size of the TIFF file. The available options are NONE, LZW, ZIP, and JPEG. Only JPEG compression results in data loss; when you select this option you can specify a JPEG quality level from 0 (very lossy) to 12 (slightly lossy). LZW and ZIP compression both compress the file without losing any data. It used to be the case that saving with LZW compression caused problems when sending your file to be commercially printed, but these days this is much less of a problem. When you select ZIP compression, Photoshop warns you that ZIP is not supported in older TIFF readers and that saving the file may take more time. In practice, using ZIP compression within your own workflow should be fine. Generally, when moving files between systems, it's safest to go with the default option, NONE.

- **Pixel Order:** These two options let you choose between Interleaved (RGBRGB) or Per Channel (RRGGBB) pixel order. Currently, the Interleaved option seems best supported, but the Per Channel format can theoretically be saved and opened a little faster and offers better compression.

- **Byte Order:** PCs and older Macs store multi-byte numbers in opposite orders: PCs store the least significant (smallest) byte first; PowerPC Macs store the most significant (biggest) byte first. In reality, most modern image editors can read either one with no trouble, and the newer Intel Macs now behave in the same way as PCs anyway. However, if you're exporting TIFFs to a troublesome application, and the source and target computers have different types of processors, you might want to select a specific option here.

- **Save Image Pyramid:** This wonderfully named option has nothing to do with Egypt and everything to do with saving different-resolution versions of the image in the same file. This is handy for some applications such as image library servers, as it saves them having to re-create smaller versions of high-resolution images for thumbnails and previews.

NOTE If you use Photoshop to open a multiresolution TIFF file, Photoshop just reads the high-resolution image and ignores all the lower-resolution versions.

- **Save Transparency:** This option preserves the transparent pixels in your document in a separate alpha channel. Applications — including Photoshop — can then read this channel when opening the image, thereby re-creating the image's transparent areas.

- **Layer Compression:** As well as compressing the composite image using the Image Compression options at the top of the dialog box, Photoshop can also compress the individual layers in the TIFF. The default option — RLE, or Run Length Encoding — is a very simple method of compression, and extremely fast. ZIP compression is slower, but can result in smaller file sizes. If you prefer to just flatten the image and forget about layers, select Discard Layers and Save a Copy.

When you finish, click OK to save your document as a TIFF.

FIGURE 13.3

In the TIFF Options dialog box, you can specify how your TIFF file is saved, including file and layer compression options.

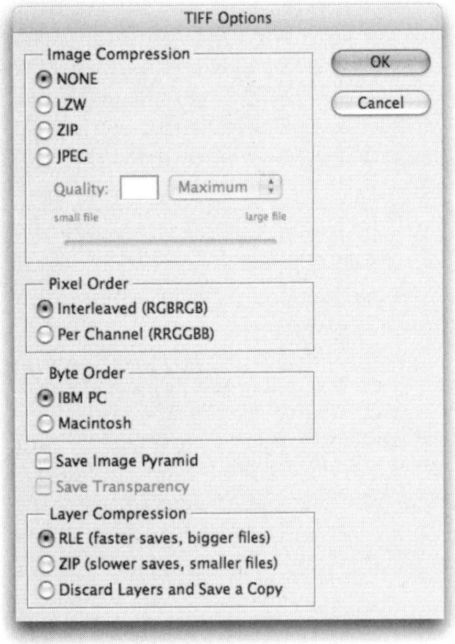

In reality, although it seems like TIFF ought to be a great option for making layered Photoshop files accessible across image editors, it doesn't work so well in practice. Other applications still need to be able to read that proprietary layer information or they just show the flat, composite version of the file. And, of course, if the other application can read layer information, it can probably read PSD files, too, in which case you may as well go with the default PSD format.

Working with Photoshop PDF

The PDF (Portable Document Format) file format has become something of a standard for imaging, and is very closely tied in with the whole Adobe software range. PDF supports many useful options, including alpha channels, spot colors, annotations, and, of course, layers. It's often used for sending files to print.

You can choose to preserve layers when you save a Photoshop file as Photoshop PDF. To save a file in this format, choose File ➪ Save As, and choose Photoshop PDF for the Format option in the dialog box. To preserve your document's layers, select the Layers option.

When you click OK, a warning dialog appears reminding you that any settings you choose in the upcoming Save Adobe PDF dialog box can override the settings you just selected. It's worth knowing, but if it gets annoying, select the Don't Show Again option. As prophesized by the warning dialog box, the next dialog box — as shown in Figure 13.4 — deals with the intricacies of the PDF export. From a layers perspective, the interesting element here is the Preserve Photoshop Editing Capabilities option within the General section of the dialog box. This preserves your layer data intact and is selected by default. If you deselect this option, you lose the ability to reedit the layers in the PDF.

FIGURE 13.4

In the Save Adobe PDF dialog box, if you disable Preserve Photoshop Editing Capabilities, you lose your layer data.

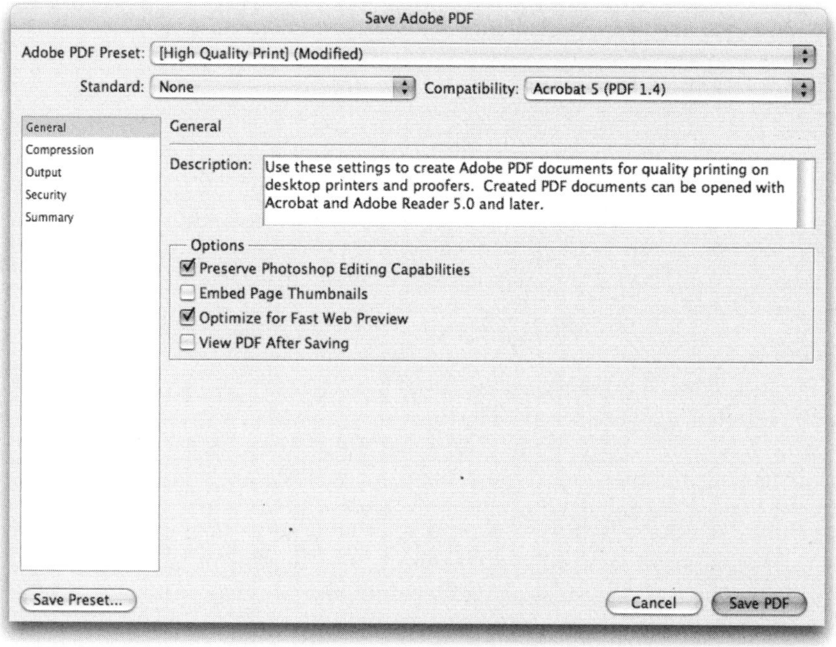

Using Layers in Other Applications

Photoshop, of course, does not exist in a vacuum. At some point you're probably going to want to move files to a different application or simply send a file to someone who uses different software. At that point it's useful to know which features of the Photoshop file will be seen by the target application. This section goes through some applications that support layers in some way, shape, or form. There are three basic ways in which applications tend to support layered Photoshop files:

- **A simple preview:** Some applications will open a layered PSD file but provide only a composite preview of the image. For example, InDesign can place a fully layered PSD file in a layout, but the PSD can't be edited from within the application.

- **As a "round trip" editing tool:** In certain applications, Photoshop is used as an external image editor. For example, in Adobe Lightroom, photos can be sent to Photoshop for editing and the results recombined with the photo catalog in Lightroom when the file is saved in Photoshop.

- **Full support for editing layers:** In some cases, an application provides support for editing layered Photoshop files directly. For example, you can open, edit, and save a layered PSD file in Adobe Fireworks.

This section takes a look at how specific applications support layered Photoshop files. Because Photoshop is the industry-standard image editor, nearly all other image editors support the PSD format in some way.

Using the Adobe Creative Suite

The Adobe Creative Suite 3 (CS3) comprises multiple applications that all use their own native format for saving files. For example, Illustrator uses AI files and InDesign uses INDD files. That said, support for Photoshop's PSD format is good throughout the suite. The suite is designed to work as a whole, so you'll find that there's no support for directly editing PSD files in the CS3 applications, with the exception of Fireworks. Instead, applications use a combination of previews and round-trip editing to support the PSD format.

Illustrator CS3

Illustrator has a long and venerable history, and the software is a powerhouse of vector illustration. It's also the market leader and industry standard by some margin. Its only true competitor was Macromedia Freehand, which was officially discontinued as part of Adobe's acquisition of Macromedia. You can think of Illustrator as a massive expansion of Photoshop's path and shape tools, and it's designed from the ground up to work with vector graphics.

Illustrator has its own Layers palette, which functions in a similar "stacking" manner to the Photoshop version. Layers appear as a stack within the palette, and you can move them up and down to control which layer is in front of which in the document window. Of course, you can also add and delete layers as in Photoshop. Other features of the Illustrator Layers palette, though, are somewhat different. For example, alongside the more familiar New Layer and trashcan icons, there's a New Sublayer icon (more on this later) and a Make/Release Clipping Mask icon. The Illustrator Layers palette menu also contains different options to Photoshop's.

Illustrator functions around a system of *objects*. An object is anything you draw in the document window — for example, a line or a shape. You can draw multiple objects on a single layer. Illustrator also splits layers into two basic types: top-level layers and sublayers. Top-level layers are a little like Photoshop's layer groups in that they can have sublayers nested inside them.

When importing a Photoshop file into Illustrator, you can either link to the file or embed it. When you link to a file, Illustrator references the original Photoshop file on your hard drive and displays a composite image representing the file inside your Illustrator document. When you embed a Photoshop file within an Illustrator document, on the other hand, Illustrator converts the Photoshop layers to Illustrator format, and they become part of the Illustrator document. As you might expect, embedding results in a larger Illustrator file than linking does.

You can import Photoshop files into an existing Illustrator document by choosing File ⇨ Place. As you choose the file to import in the Place dialog box, notice the Link option at the bottom of the dialog box. This option works as follows:

- Select the Link option to link to the Photoshop file on your hard drive, using a flat composite image to display the Photoshop file within the Illustrator document. (To edit the PSD file, you need to go back to Photoshop.)

- Deselect the Link option, and Illustrator embeds the Photoshop file directly in the Illustrator document, converting the Photoshop layers in the file to Illustrator layers wherever possible (unless you then select the Flatten Photoshop Layers to a Single Image option, described in a moment).

After you choose the Photoshop file to import and decide whether to link to or embed the file, click Place to move on to the Photoshop Import Options dialog box, as shown in Figure 13.5. This dialog box lets you control how Illustrator treats the Photoshop file on import. Not all options are selectable in the dialog box; exactly which options are available depends on whether you select the Link option in the Place dialog box or not. This is covered in more detail in a moment.

FIGURE 13.5

The Photoshop Import Options dialog box. In this example, the When Updating Link option is unavailable because the Link option is deselected in the previous Place dialog box.

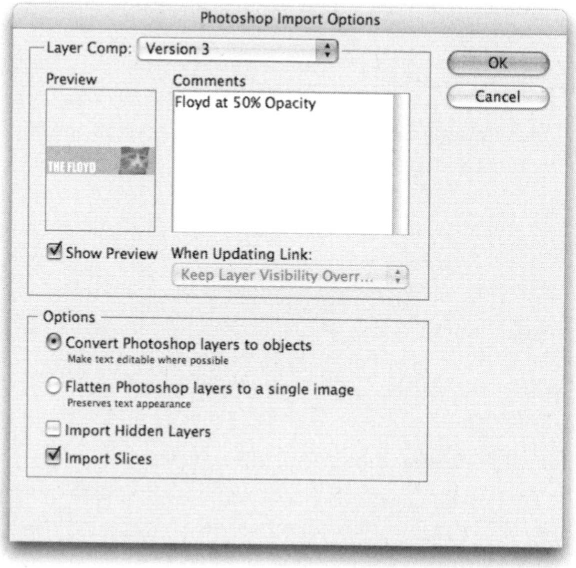

TIP   If you don't see the Photoshop Import Options dialog box, it's probably because your Photoshop and Illustrator files are using different color modes — for example, the Photoshop file might be in RGB mode while the Illustrator file uses CMYK. If possible, convert your Photoshop file so it matches the Illustrator document's color mode before you import.

The Photoshop Import Options dialog box is split into two groups. The top group deals with importing layer comps, while the bottom group handles layers and slices.

The layer comp options work like this:

- **Layer Comp:** If the Photoshop file contains layer comps, you can specify which version of the file to import by choosing a comp from this drop-down list.

- **Comments:** If the file contains layer comps, any comments for the chosen comp appear here.

- **Preview and Show Preview:** The Preview area shows a composite preview of the file (and layer comp, if selected) you're importing. The Show Preview option simply shows or hides the preview.

- **When Updating Link (only available if Link is selected in the Place dialog box):** When you use Photoshop to change the visibilities of one or more layers within a layer comp in your linked PSD file, Illustrator handles those changes in one of two ways, depending on your choice for this option. Keep Layer Visibility Overrides keeps the state of each layer's eye icon as it was when you originally imported the file, regardless of any visibility changes you later make via layer comps in Photoshop. Use Photoshop's Layer Visibility, on the other hand, always updates the imported file with any changes you make to the eye icons within a layer comp.

NOTE   The When Updating Link option only relates to layer comps. Any change you make to the state of a layer's eye icon outside of a layer comp is always reflected in Illustrator, regardless of the previous setting.

The bottom group of options in the dialog box works as follows:

- **Convert Photoshop Layers to Objects (only available if Link is not selected in the Place dialog box):** This option attempts to convert each Photoshop layer to a corresponding Illustrator object. Type layers are retained as editable text where possible, and each converted Photoshop layer is placed on its own Illustrator layer. Illustrator also groups all the imported objects together. Where it can't reproduce the exact effect of one or more Photoshop layers, Illustrator merges and/or rasterizes the affected layers.

- **Flatten Photoshop Layers to a Single Image:** Select this option, and your layered Photoshop document gets flattened into a single Illustrator object. (If you're linking your Photoshop document rather than embedding it, this option is automatically selected, because you're always working with a flattened composite image.)

- **Import Hidden Layers (only available if Convert Photoshop Layers to Objects is selected):** When selected, any nonvisible layers in the Photoshop file are imported along with the visible layers.

- **Import Slices (only available if Link is not selected in the Place dialog box):** If there are slices present in the Photoshop file, select this option to import the slices, too. Illustrator has a slicing tool very similar to that of Photoshop, and imported Photoshop slices retain their editability in Illustrator. If there are no slices in the Photoshop file, this option is unavailable.

When you're happy with your choices, click OK to complete the import.

How well does Illustrator's PSD handling work in practice? Take a look at the Photoshop file in Figure 13.6. It takes the form of a header design for a Web site showcasing our lovely cat, Floyd. The file contains the following:

- A lime green Background layer.
- A normal bitmap layer for the cat. This layer has a layer mask to remove the original background of the image. The layer also has a Hard Light blending mode applied to it.
- A type layer for the "THE FLOYD" header text.
- Three layer comps for various alternative designs.
- A layer-based slice for the type layer.

FIGURE 13.6

The example Photoshop file, showing the document window, the Layers palette, and the Layer Comps palette

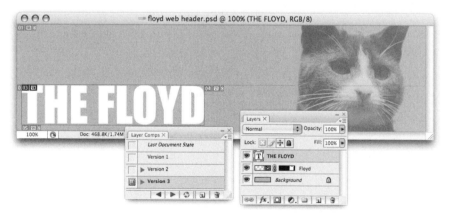

Figure 13.7 shows the file imported into Illustrator with the Link option deselected and the Convert Photoshop Layers to Objects and Import Slices options selected. The layers in the Photoshop file have been converted into Illustrator layers. Illustrator has managed to retain the Hard Light blending mode on the Floyd layer, thanks to its support for the majority of Photoshop's blending modes. Furthermore, the type layer is still editable, and the slice for the type layer that was created in Photoshop has come through as an Illustrator slice.

FIGURE 13.7

The Photoshop file imported into Illustrator. All the Photoshop layers have been converted to separate Illustrator sublayers.

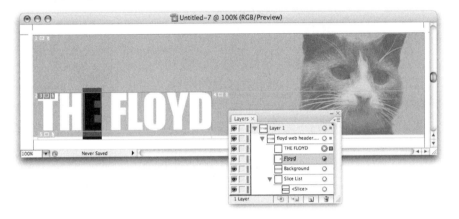

 To change the blending mode of an imported Photoshop layer, you first need to ungroup the imported objects. Initially, all the objects created by importing the Photoshop layers are grouped together across their sublayers, which prevents you from selecting an individual object to set its blending mode. To ungroup the objects on the sublayers, select the group by clicking any part of the group in the document window and choose Object ➪ Ungroup. Now select an individual object. Display the Transparency palette by choosing Window ➪ Transparency. You can now use the Blending Mode option in the palette to apply any blending mode supported by Illustrator to the object: Normal, Darken, Multiply, Lighten, Screen, Color Dodge, Overlay, Soft Light, Hard Light, Difference, Exclusion, Hue, Saturation, Color, or Luminosity.

NOTE If you import a Photoshop layer that uses a blending mode not supported by Illustrator, the resulting Illustrator object's blending mode gets set to Normal.

If you select the Link option in the original Place dialog box, the Convert Photoshop Layers to Objects option is dimmed, meaning you have to import the PSD file as a single flattened image. However, it does mean that you can reedit the PSD within Photoshop at any time. To do this, click the Edit Original icon within the Links palette in Illustrator, which reopens the file for editing in Photoshop. Make your edits within Photoshop and save the file. Flip back over to Illustrator, which displays a warning dialog box asking if you want to update the changed file. Click Yes, and the composite image in Illustrator updates to reflect the changes you made in Photoshop.

TIP You can also choose to open a Photoshop file directly in Illustrator without placing the PSD within an existing Illustrator document. To do this, choose File ➪ Open, and pick your Photoshop file in the Open dialog box. Click Open, and the Photoshop Import Options dialog box appears. In this case, you can still choose which layer comp you want to import, and you can also select either the Convert Photoshop Layers to Objects option or the Flatten Photoshop Layers to a Single Image option. You can also choose to import slices if you want. Click OK, and Illustrator imports your Photoshop file, converting it to an Illustrator document as it goes.

As well as placing and opening Photoshop files in Illustrator, you can also save layered Photoshop files from artwork created in Illustrator and open them in Photoshop. To do this, choose File ➪ Export, and choose Photoshop (PSD) for the Format option in the resulting Export dialog box. Click OK to display the Photoshop Export Options dialog box, as shown in Figure 13.8. The options in this dialog box work as follows:

- **Color Model:** This option allows you to set the color model — color mode in Photoshop-speak — of the exported PSD file. You can choose from RGB, CMYK, and Grayscale.

CAUTION If you choose a different color model from that of the Illustrator artwork, Illustrator writes out the image as a flat file, and the Write Layers option below is dimmed.

- **Resolution:** Here you can choose the resolution of the exported Photoshop file. You can choose from Screen (72 ppi, or pixels per inch), Medium (150 ppi), High (300 ppi), or Other, where you can define your own custom resolution.

- **Flat Image:** Selecting this option results in a flat, nonlayered image.

- **Write Layers:** If you select this option, Illustrator attempts to write out its objects as separate Photoshop layers.

- **Preserve Text Editability:** This works in conjunction with the Write Layers option. If you select this option, Illustrator preserves any type layers in the Illustrator file as type layers in Photoshop. If you find that your Illustrator type layers don't look right in Photoshop, deselect this option.

- **Maximum Editabiliy:** This option also works in conjunction with Write Layers. It writes each Illustrator sublayer to a separate Photoshop layer, with top-level layers re-created as Photoshop layer groups.

- **Anti-alias:** Illustrator, as a vector-illustration package, creates hard-edged, smooth line art. However, converting such line art to bitmap Photoshop layers inevitably results in jagged edges. Select this option to anti-alias any such rasterized elements, thereby alleviating the jaggies in Photoshop.

- **Embed ICC Profile:** When selected, this option embeds the color profile of your current Illustrator working space in the exported Photoshop file. You can see your current profile to the right of this option.

FIGURE 13.8

The Photoshop Export Options dialog box in Illustrator

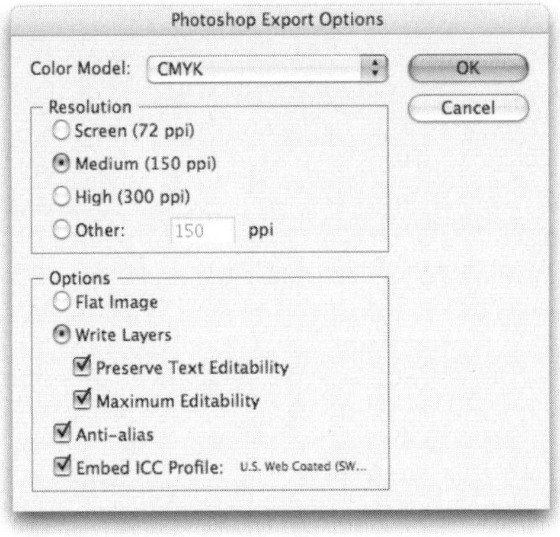

InDesign CS3

InDesign is a desktop publishing (DTP) application launched in 1999 to take on the industry standard DTP package, QuarkXPress. Due to some great features, Creative Suite integration, and some lackluster updates from Quark, the software now has a good share of the print industry.

CROSS-REF   QuarkXPress is covered in greater depth later in the chapter.

InDesign's Photoshop support revolves around linking to Photoshop files from within an InDesign layout. To reedit a linked PSD file, reopen it within Photoshop. When you save the PSD in Photoshop, it updates automatically within InDesign. Although InDesign has its own Layers palette, Photoshop layers in an imported PSD are not shown there. InDesign does have some other layer-related tricks up its sleeve, however, that you see in a moment.

To import a PSD into InDesign, choose File ➪ Place to display the Place dialog box. There's an option in the Place dialog box entitled Show Import Options. If you select this option, you can tell InDesign exactly how you want to import the PSD, as described in a moment. Alternatively, leave this option deselected to apply the options used for the last import, or sensible defaults, as appropriate. Find the Photoshop file to which you want to link, and click Open.

If you select Show Import Options in the Place dialog box, the Image Import Options dialog box appears, as shown in Figure 13.9. Here you can define options for how to import the Photoshop file. The dialog box consists of an image preview area and three tabs across the top. The tabs are:

- **Image:** If your Photoshop document contains a clipping path, you can select the Apply Photoshop Clipping Path option to transfer the clipping path to InDesign. You can also clip the imported image to the contents of an alpha channel in the Photoshop document by selecting the channel from the Alpha Channel menu.

- **Color:** Select the Profile option to pick the color profile that was used to create the document you're importing. Usually the profile is already embedded in the document, in which case Use Document Default is automatically selected; this is the best option to use, if possible. Meanwhile, Rendering Intent allows you to choose how InDesign reduces the document's colors to fit the (usually smaller) gamut of your printer or other output device. This option works in a way similar to the Rendering Intent option used in Photoshop to view proofs (View ⇨ Proof Setup ⇨ Custom). If you import photographic images, Perceptual is usually the best approach. The remaining options are better for areas with large amounts of solid color.

- **Layers:** This tab controls how the Photoshop layers in the imported document are handled. Show Layers lets you choose which layers are visible in the InDesign document; click the eye icons to hide the layers you don't want to see. (By default, hidden layers in the Photoshop file appear as hidden in the Show Layers list.) Use Layer Comp to pick which layer comp (if any) in the Photoshop document to import. Finally, When Updating Link controls how future changes to layer visibilities in Photoshop are reflected in the InDesign document. Select Use Photoshop's Layer Visibility, and any visibility changes you make in the linked Photoshop file within Photoshop are reflected in InDesign. Alternatively, select Keep Layer Visibility Overrides to preserve the layer visibilities that you specify in InDesign, regardless of any changes you later make in Photoshop.

FIGURE 13.9

The Image Import Options dialog box, showing a Photoshop file ready to be imported

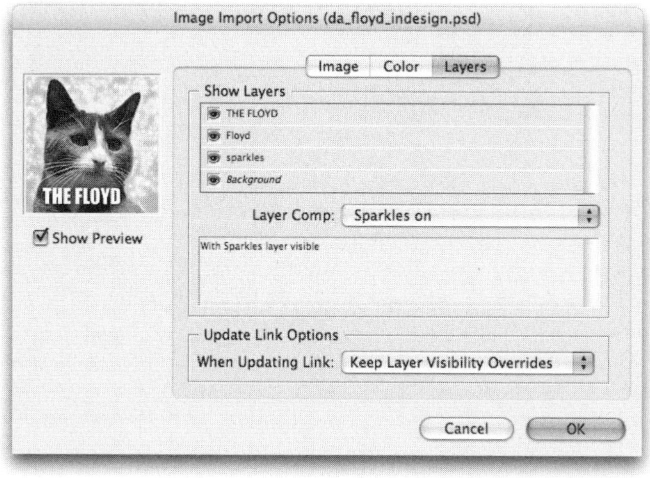

When you're happy with your options, click OK.

After you've opened the file to import and, optionally, set options for the import using the Image Import Options dialog box, the Loaded Graphics icon appears under your cursor, with a small preview of the file. Click a point in the layout to place the imported file at that point. Figure 13.10 shows a Photoshop file successfully placed in InDesign.

FIGURE 13.10

A Photoshop file placed within an InDesign layout

Great, you've now placed your Photoshop file within the InDesign document. The PSD comes across fine, although as it's really just a composite image, you can't edit the Photoshop layers themselves directly in InDesign. You can, however, edit the linked file in Photoshop and see it updated within InDesign without having to reimport it. To do this, select the imported image in your InDesign layout using the Direct Selection tool, then right-click the image and choose Edit Original from the pop-up menu. The PSD file opens in Photoshop for editing. Make your edits and save the file. When you flip back to InDesign, the image automatically updates to show your changes.

InDesign's talents do not stop at elegant round-trip editing, though. You can also toggle the visibilities of the Photoshop layers directly in InDesign, as well as flip between any layer comps embedded in the Photoshop file. To do this, right-click the placed Photoshop image and choose Object Layer Options to display the Object Layer Options dialog box, as shown in Figure 13.11. The options in the dialog box work in exactly the same way as their equivalents in the Image Import Options dialog box covered earlier. Select the Preview option to view your changes in the InDesign document window.

> **NOTE** Showing and hiding layers in the Object Layer Options dialog box doesn't affect the layer visibilities in the Photoshop file itself; these settings are stored wholly within the InDesign document.

FIGURE 13.11

The Object Layer Options dialog box allows you to toggle the visibilities of the original Photoshop layers within InDesign.

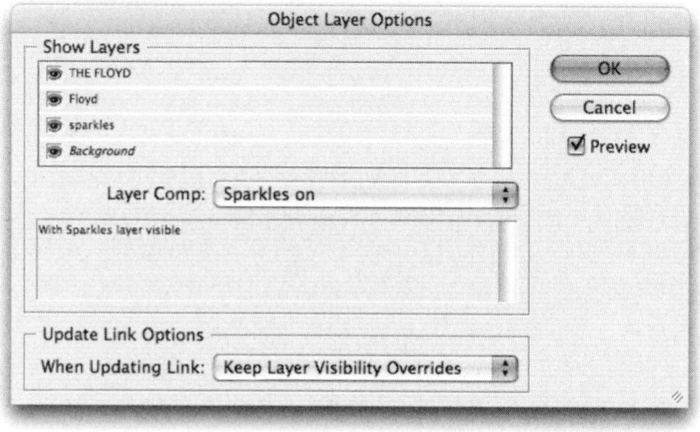

The Object Layer Options dialog box is slick, but you can't use it to edit the Photoshop layers directly. You can't change the stacking order of the layers, for example, or move the contents of different layers independently of one another. Neither can you see individual preview thumbnails of each layer.

You can set the Photoshop file's blending mode in InDesign. However, this merely affects how the composite image blends with the pixels below it in the InDesign document; you can't change the blending modes of the individual Photoshop layers this way. To set the blending mode, select the placed Photoshop file using the Direct Selection tool, and display the Effects palette by choosing Window ➪ Effects. You can then choose a mode from the Blending Mode menu.

NOTE InDesign supports the following blending modes: Normal, Multiply, Screen, Overlay, Soft Light, Hard Light, Color Dodge, Color Burn, Darken, Lighten, Difference, Exclusion, Hue, Saturation, Color, and Luminosity.

You can also set transparency effects — the InDesign equivalent of Photoshop layer effects — for the placed file. As with blending modes, these apply to the whole composite image, and cannot be set for individual Photoshop layers. To access these effects, select the imported Photoshop image using the Direct Selection tool, and click the *fx* button in the Effects palette. A pop-up menu appears, showing a range of options akin to Photoshop's own layer effects: Transparency, Drop Shadow, Inner Shadow, Outer Glow, Inner Glow, Bevel and Emboss, Satin, Basic Feather, Directional Feather, and Gradient Feather. Click an option to apply the effect to the placed Photoshop file.

Here's a great feature of InDesign's Photoshop integration. In Figure 13.10, earlier in the section, the text is flowing round the whole Photoshop document, but wouldn't it be great if it could flow around the cat itself? InDesign lets you create such an effect by flowing the text over the transparent areas of the image. To do this, start with a basic InDesign document with two text columns, and follow these steps:

1. **Place the Floyd Photoshop file.** You'll find it on the accompanying CD-ROM. The file contains — from the bottom up — a green Background layer, a layer containing some sparkles, the cat layer itself, and a THE FLOYD type layer. Alternatively, use your own layered PSD file. Choose File ➪ Place, and select the PSD file you want to import. Make sure the Show Import Options check box is deselected, and click Open. The Loaded Graphics icon appears under your mouse cursor, showing a small translucent preview of the file. Click in the layout where you want to place the file; InDesign then inserts the image at that point.

2. **Hide the underlying layers.** Select the placed document with the Direct Selection tool, then right-click the placed document and choose Object Layer Options to display the Object Layer Options dialog box. Hide the Background and Sparkles layers by clicking their eye icons in the dialog box, leaving just the Floyd and type layers visible, with a transparent area around the image. Click OK to close the dialog box.

3. **Set the transparent area as the clipping path.** Make sure the placed PSD is selected and choose Object ➪ Clipping Path ➪ Options. In the resulting Clipping Path dialog box, choose Alpha Channel from the Type menu. Click OK to close the dialog box then, from InDesign's Control Bar, select the Wrap Around Object Shape option. This wraps the text around the shape of the cat, as defined by the transparent area in the Photoshop image; a very elegant way of doing things. You can see the results in Figure 13.12.

NOTE If you've read both the Illustrator and InDesign sections, you should be starting to see a pattern as to how the components of the Creative Suite interact, with Photoshop as a cornerstone of the process.

FIGURE 13.12

Here the transparent area of the Photoshop image is used as a clipping path in InDesign. The text now flows elegantly around the cat.

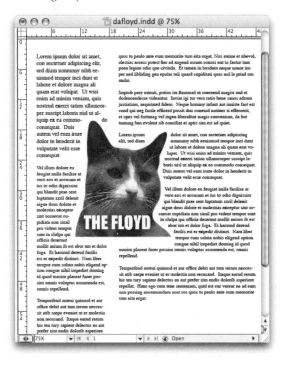

Fireworks CS3

Fireworks is an image editor similar to Photoshop, but it very much concentrates on Web site production. It effectively replaces the Web-centric ImageReady application, which was dropped from Photoshop CS3. Fireworks is a relative newcomer to the Adobe stable, having been bought from Macromedia in 2005 along with Dreamweaver, Flash, and various other pieces of software. These ex-Macromedia tools now form the Web arm of Adobe's Creative Suite.

Fireworks uses PNG — Portable Network Graphics — for its native file format, with added metadata to support Fireworks's own brand of layers. Photoshop layer support in Fireworks CS3 is much improved from earlier versions, and Photoshop files opened in Fireworks retain much of the editability found in the Photoshop version. To prove the point, Figure 13.13 shows the example "cat" Photoshop file opened in Fireworks by choosing File ➪ Open. The text remains editable, even with those layer effects applied to the type layer, and the layer mask is also intact.

FIGURE 13.13

The "Floyd" Photoshop document opened in Fireworks. Text remains editable, even with layer effects applied to the type, and the layer mask and blending mode are also retained.

Adobe has built in support for many of the layer effects and blending modes found in Photoshop. If you use Fireworks to open a Photoshop file containing layer effects, you'll see a section within the Filters area of the Properties palette called Photoshop Live Effects, as shown in Figure 13.14. Click the little i icon in the Properties palette to display the Photoshop Live Effects dialog box, which pretty much exactly mirrors the Layer Styles dialog box in Photoshop.

Fireworks also supports Photoshop's layer blending modes, which is why the Hard Light blending mode in this example is preserved.

When you try to save a PSD file in Fireworks by choosing File ➪ Save, Fireworks prompts you to save the document in its native PNG format instead. You can, however, choose File ➪ Save As to save it as a Photoshop file, and the Fireworks edits come through fine when opened in Photoshop.

FIGURE 13.14

The Photoshop Live Effects dialog box in Fireworks. In the background, you can see the Properties palette showing that Photoshop Live Effects is active on your open document.

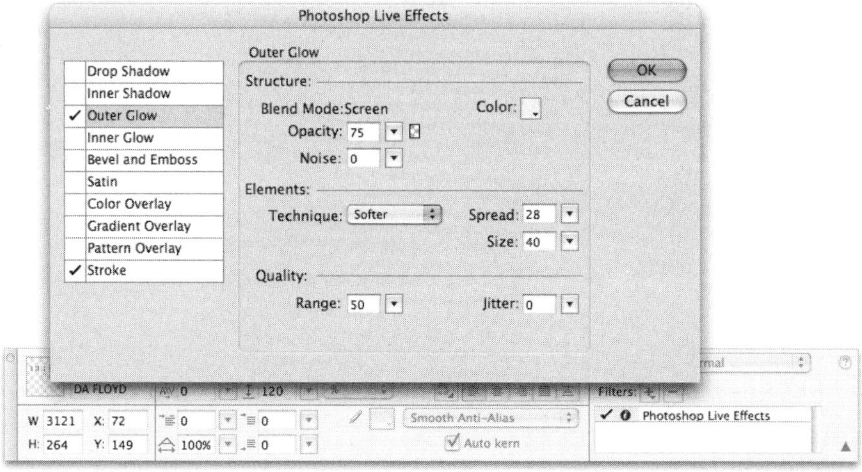

Native Fireworks files created entirely in Fireworks can also be saved as Photoshop files using Save As. In Figure 13.15, a simple Web site header is created in Fireworks. To save as a Photoshop file, you can choose File ➪ Save As and select Photoshop PSD from the Save Copy As menu. When opened in Photoshop, the PSD file saved from Fireworks renders perfectly.

NOTE Perfectly, that is, apart from the occasional glitch with fonts. As you can see in Figure 13.15, the PSD is showing the wrong font for the type layers in Photoshop. When the PSD is opened in Photoshop, a warning dialog box appears, pointing out that some text layers need to be updated. Click Update, and the result is the document in Figure 13.15. To fix these type layers, update them by selecting the Type tool in Photoshop, double-clicking the layer thumbnails in the Layers palette, and reselecting the correct font and size from the options bar. (This is not a Fireworks-to-Photoshop issue as such, but part of a wider issue with the Photoshop type engine.) Alternatively, you can click No in the warning dialog box when you first open the PSD, which retains the correct fonts in your type layers, but if you ever try to edit the text in those layers they flip over to the wrong font, and you need to set the correct font again as just described.

FIGURE 13.15

A Web site header. The original file was created in Fireworks (top), and then saved as a PSD file and opened in Photoshop (bottom). The document retains the layer structure in Photoshop, although, as occasionally happens when opening a PSD file, it hasn't retained the correct font for the type layers.

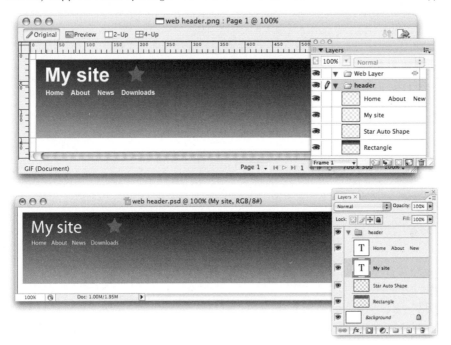

Flash CS3

Flash is another of the applications inherited by Adobe during the acquisition of Macromedia, and is at heart a platform for building dynamic and animated Web sites. Your Web browser renders exported Flash (SWF) files using the Flash plug-in, which is installed in the majority of browsers.

Before the release of CS3, Flash had little native support for Photoshop files, but all that is changed now. PSD files are supported very well within Flash CS3, and if you're used to designing in Photoshop and having to rebuild the design in Flash when creating a site, you have a treat in store!

To import a PSD into Flash, first create or open a document in Flash. Now choose File ⇨ Import ⇨ Import to Stage, select the Photoshop file to import, and click Import. You're greeted by the Import to Stage dialog box, as shown in Figure 13.16, which allows you to choose how the layers are imported. Here's how the options in the dialog box work:

■ **Layers list:** The big box on the left of the dialog box shows you all the layers in your Photoshop document. Select a check box next to a layer to import it; deselect to exclude it from the import. Click a layer to select it, and the import options to the right of the box change depending on the layer type (each of these options is described in a moment). You can select multiple layers by Ctrl+clicking (⌘+clicking on the Mac) or Shift+clicking them; if you do this, you see only the options common to your selected layers. It's a great way to quickly specify options for lots of layers at once, though — all text layers, for example. You can also merge layers together into a composite bitmap at the time of the import by selecting the layers you want to merge — they need to be next to each other in the stacking order and in the same layer group — then clicking Merge Layers below the box. This is useful if you have multiple Photoshop layers that can sensibly be combined into a single image within Flash. (If you change your mind, select the resultant Merged Bitmap layer and click the Separate button below the box.)

NOTE Fill layers and Smart Objects are treated as normal bitmap layers for the purpose of importing. Adjustment layers don't appear in the list; however, their effects are applied to any imported layers, if those layers are imported as Flash bitmaps.

FIGURE 13.16

The Import to Stage dialog box in Flash. Here, a native Photoshop file is being imported.

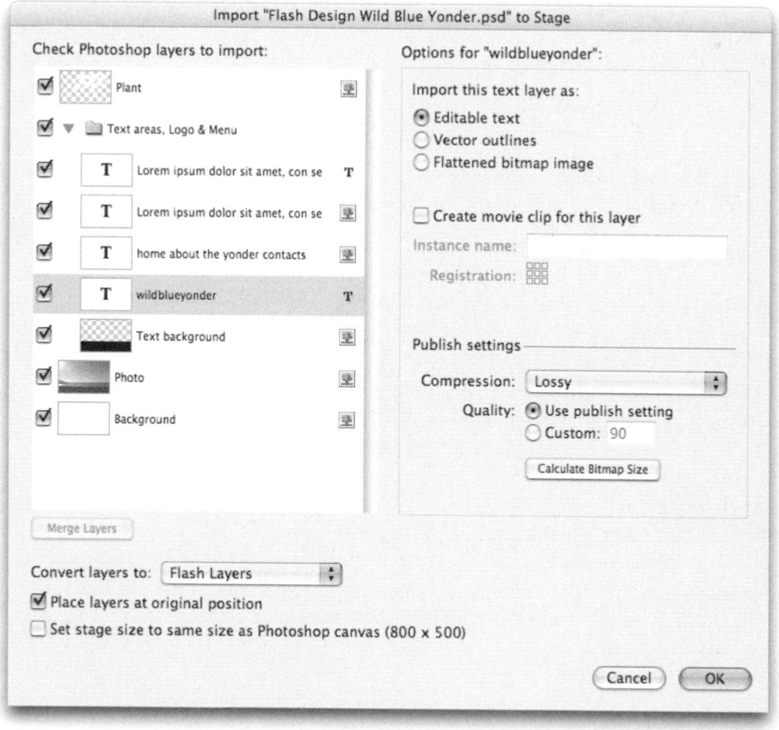

- **Import This Text Layer As (available if a text layer is selected):** You can choose to import the selected text layer in one of three ways. Editable Text converts the text in the Photoshop text layer to static text in Flash, but you lose any layer styles on the text layer, leaving bare, but editable, text. It does preserve the font and size, however, as well as any character and paragraph formatting. Vector Outlines renders the text as a movie clip containing vector shapes, which is great if you plan to animate letterforms within Flash. It also retains certain aspects of the layer style, such as blending mode and opacity (known as *alpha* in Flash-speak), in the movie clip. However, if your text contains any layer effects at all, both text and effects are rendered as bitmaps inside the movie clip. Therefore, if you want to retain your text as editable paths, you need to remove these effects in Photoshop first by clicking and dragging the layer's Effects item to the Trashcan icon in the Layers palette (sadly, just deleting the effects themselves doesn't cut it). Finally, Flattened Bitmap Image flattens the layer, layer style and all, perfectly reproducing the layer as a Flash bitmap; however, you won't be able to edit the text itself or any layer style you apply to the text layer in Photoshop.

- **Import This Shape Layer As (available if a shape layer is selected):** You have two options for importing a shape layer. Editable Paths and Layer Styles converts the layer to a movie clip containing the shape's vector path as a Flash drawing object. Some editable aspects of the layer style, such as the blending mode and opacity (alpha), are preserved for the movie clip. Exterior layer effects, such as drop shadows, come through as separate Flash bitmaps within the movie clip. However, if your Photoshop layer contains any interior effects, such as Satin or Gradient Overlay, then the whole shape is rasterized into a Flash bitmap inside the movie clip, leaving the shape uneditable. Meanwhile, Flattened Bitmap Image rasterizes the layer, applying the layer style (including any effects), and imports the rasterized layer as a Flash bitmap. You won't be able to edit any aspects of your Photoshop layer style after rasterizing the layer in this way, but at least you end up with a pixel-perfect rendition of your Photoshop layer in Flash.

- **Import This Image Layer As (available if a normal layer is selected):** You have two ways to import normal layers. Bitmap Image with Editable Layer Styles creates a movie clip containing the layer as a Flash bitmap. Exterior layer effects, such as drop shadows, are converted to separate bitmaps within the movie clip, while interior layer effects, such as Satin, are permanently stamped onto the layer bitmap. This option preserves the editable blending mode and opacity (alpha in Flash) of the layer in the Flash movie clip. Flattened Bitmap Image, on the other hand, rasterizes all aspects of the layer, including the blending mode, opacity settings, and all layer effects, into a single Flash bitmap. This is useful if you have problems importing a particular layer, but of course, you can't then edit any aspects of the Photoshop layer's style once it's in Flash.

CAUTION   Flash only supports the following Photoshop blending modes in editable form: Normal, Darken, Multiply, Lighten, Screen, Hard Light, Difference, and Overlay. If your selected import option results in Flash trying to preserve an unsupported blending mode in editable form, the blending mode is reset to Normal in the movie clip. However, if Flash is rasterizing your imported layer into a bitmap, the effects of even unsupported blending modes are retained in the bitmap.

TIP   To edit the blending mode within Flash, select the movie clip then choose from the Blend menu in the Property inspector. Likewise, you can alter the movie clip's alpha setting — the equivalent of Photoshop's opacity — by selecting Advanced for the Color option in the Property inspector, then clicking Settings to the right of Color and adjusting the Alpha value in the Advanced Effect dialog box.

NOTE   The effect of a layer's Fill setting is preserved whenever the layer is rendered as a bitmap in Flash. However, if you convert a shape layer to a vector Flash drawing object, or a text layer to vector shapes or static text, the Fill setting is lost (that is, it's set back to 100 percent). There's no way to edit the Fill setting of a movie clip in Flash.

■ **Create Movie Clip For This Layer:** Select this option to create a Flash movie clip in which to store the resulting bitmap; deselect it to import it as a bare bitmap. This option is only available if you select Flattened Bitmap Image, or if you click a layer group in the list on the left side of the dialog box. Otherwise, it's grayed out, and Flash always creates a movie clip for the layer.

NOTE   You can import layer groups via the Import to Stage dialog box. By default, Flash imports the layers inside the group as separate Flash layers nested inside a layer folder in the Timeline. However, if you select the Create Movie Clip For This Layer option for the group, Flash creates a movie clip for that group and embeds the imported Photoshop layers inside that movie clip.

■ **Instance Name:** If you create a movie clip for the selected layer, you can type a name for the instance of the movie clip here.

■ **Registration:** If you create a movie clip, you can change the registration point using a small grid. The registration point is the point around which the movie clip rotates in Flash. The default is the top-left corner, but you can, for example, choose the center point to rotate the movie clip around the center of the image instead.

■ **Compression:** This drop-down list has choices for the type of compression to apply to the layer's image when the SWF movie file is exported in Flash. (This setting doesn't have any effect during this import process; Flash always imports the layer without any compression.) Lossy compresses the image in JPEG format, losing some data from the image, while Lossless compresses using the PNG or GIF formats.

■ **Quality:** This option, available if you select Lossy from the Compression drop-down list, lets you set the JPEG quality level of the exported image. The Use Publish Setting option uses the quality setting in Flash's Publish Settings dialog box. Selecting the Custom option lets you override the quality setting on a layer-by-layer basis; type a value from 1 to 100 in the box to the right. Higher values result in better image integrity but larger file sizes.

TIP   You can always change a bitmap image's compression settings after the import by double-clicking the bitmap's icon in the Library and using the Compression option in the ensuing Bitmap Properties dialog box.

■ **Calculate Bitmap Size:** Click this button to reveal the number of bitmaps required to export the image, along with the compressed size of the exported image. The number of bitmaps depends on the nature of the layer you're importing. For example, if you import a bitmap layer containing a Drop Shadow effect, and you select the Bitmap Image with Editable Layer Styles option, Flash exports the resulting movie clip as two bitmaps: one for the image itself and one for the drop shadow. Use the Compressed Size value to get an idea of how big the resulting image will be using your chosen compression method; if it's huge, you might want to select Lossy and reduce the Quality value somewhat.

NOTE The Compression and Quality settings only affect bitmaps. If you convert a layer to purely editable text or vector shapes, these settings have no effect, and Calculate Bitmap Size reports no bitmaps and a compressed size of 0.0K.

■ **Convert Layers To:** Use this drop-down list to specify how the Photoshop layers are imported into Flash. Flash Layers creates a new Flash layer for each imported Photoshop layer; the Flash layer contains the imported layer in movie clip or bitmap form. Keyframes, on the other hand, places each imported Photoshop layer into its own keyframe within a single Flash layer, which is handy if you want to create animation or rollover effects from your Photoshop layers.

■ **Place Layers at Original Position:** This option controls the layout of the imported layers within Flash. Select this option to retain the absolute horizontal and vertical position of each layer as it was in the Photoshop document, relative to the top-left corner of the document. Deselect the option, and the individual layers retain their horizontal and vertical positions relative to each other, but the layers are placed at the center of the current stage view in Flash. Generally, you want to leave this option selected when importing a full design, but if you want to import just some layers from a Photoshop document and place them in the middle of your current stage view, deselect this option.

■ **Set Stage Size to Same Size as Photoshop Canvas:** Select this option, and the Flash stage is resized to exactly fit the imported Photoshop document's pixel dimensions.

TIP As well as importing a PSD directly into the stage, you can just import the PSD's layers into the Library without placing the assets on the stage. To do this, choose File ➪ Import ➪ Import to Library. Select your PSD, and an Import to Library dialog box appears. This works pretty much like the Import to Stage dialog box just described; the only difference is that this dialog box omits the two options at the bottom that deal with positioning the layers and setting the stage size.

TIP You can also set default options for importing Photoshop image, text, and shape layers by choosing Edit ➪ Preferences (Flash ➪ Preferences on the Mac) and clicking the PSD File Importer category in the left column. The options you set in this dialog box are then used for all future PSD imports by default (though you can still override the defaults in the Import to Stage and Import to Library dialog boxes).

After you click OK, your selected Photoshop layers are imported into Flash.

Let's see how well Flash's PSD import feature works in practice. In Figure 13.17, a design is created as the basis of a Flash site within Photoshop. It's made up of a type layer and multiple shape layers, with various layer effects applied to some of the layers.

FIGURE 13.17

The basis for the Flash Web site, designed in Photoshop

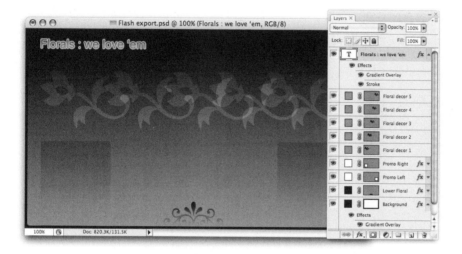

Next, a new document is created in Flash, and the PSD file imported using the Import to Stage dialog described previously. You can see the resulting Flash document in Figure 13.18. Flash does a pretty good job of the conversion process; it even preserves attributes such as the Overlay blending modes on the decorative floral layers. Because the type layer was imported as editable text, the layer effects haven't been retained, but similar effects can be produced using the Filters found in Flash's Property inspector.

This approach really is a massive timesaver, because you can now design in Photoshop and import all your work into Flash directly without having to rebuild the design from scratch within the Flash environment.

FIGURE 13.18

Flash has reproduced the Photoshop layout pretty faithfully. Note that the floral shapes retain their blending modes, as shown in the Property inspector.

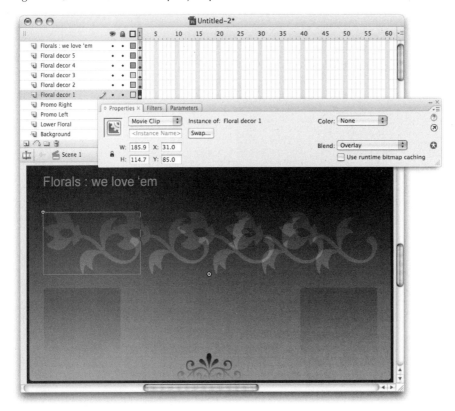

Dreamweaver CS3

Dreamweaver, another former Macromedia application, is something of a standard in the world of Web authoring. It's one of the few heavyweight Web authoring environments available, with only Microsoft FrontPage — and now potentially Expression Web — really in the running. To underline this, Adobe abandoned the inclusion of its GoLive Web development application in the CS3 bundles and includes Dreamweaver instead. (A new stand-alone version of GoLive is in the works at the time of writing.)

Dreamweaver's Photoshop support isn't as refined as Flash's, but Dreamweaver CS3 does have some support for Photoshop, revolving around copy and paste. While it doesn't take advantage of Photoshop's layer features as such, it's included in this section on the CS3 applications for completeness. In addition, if you're a Web designer using both Photoshop and Dreamweaver, you'll find the following technique very useful.

NEW FEATURE The ability to copy and paste graphics directly from Photoshop, as outlined in a moment, is a new feature in Dreamweaver CS3.

As an example, in Figure 13.19 you can see a basic Web site design created in Dreamweaver. Beneath the menu, a space is reserved for a promotional image.

FIGURE 13.19

A basic Web site design taking shape in Dreamweaver. Note the reserved space for a promotional area beneath the left menu.

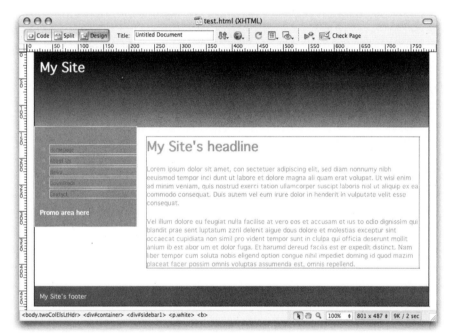

A mockup of the whole page, including the promo area, is created in Photoshop, as shown in Figure 13.20. In earlier versions of Dreamweaver, you had to export the promo item from Photoshop using File ➪ Save for Web and add it into the site design in Dreamweaver. In Dreamweaver CS3, it's a simpler copy-and-paste operation. Just follow these steps:

1. **Copy the promo box in Photoshop.** Select the area of the promo box you want to export, and choose Edit ➪ Copy Merged. This copies all the layers within the selected area. You can see the original layers intact in Figure 13.20; you don't have to flatten the image before exporting.

FIGURE 13.20

The Photoshop mockup for the site. Select the area to copy, and choose Edit ➪ Copy Merged to copy all the layers at once.

2. **Paste the promo box into Dreamweaver.** In Dreamweaver, place the cursor at the point where you want the image to appear. In this example, it replaces the holding text beneath the menu. Choose Edit ➪ Paste. The Image Preview dialog box appears, as shown in Figure 13.21.

3. **Select options for the imported image.** The Format option in the Image Preview dialog box lets you choose which Web image format to save the imported image as: JPEG, GIF, an animated GIF, or one of three PNG formats. You can also choose additional image options, depending on the format you select — these behave much like their equivalents in Photoshop's Save for Web & Devices dialog box — and see a preview of the Web image in the box on the right of the dialog box. Under the File tab in the top left of the dialog box, you can choose to scale the image with the Scale option. Type a percentage value for the scaling in the % field, or type an exact width and height in the W and H fields. Select the Constrain option to retain the image proportions. You can also make fine adjustments to the cropping using the Export Area options. The X and Y fields specify the top-left

corner of the crop area, while the W and H values let you choose the width and height of the crop area. You can also judge the impact of your chosen settings on image file size and download time (on a 56 Kbps modem) by checking the estimates above the preview area. When you're happy with your choices, click OK.

> **NOTE** If you're wondering why the Animation tab in the dialog is grayed out, it's because the Animation options don't apply when you import Photoshop images.

4. **Save the image.** You see a Save Web Image dialog box appear. Choose a location for the file — which will likely be the "images" folder within your Web site — and give the file a name. Click Save. A dialog box appears that asks you to provide Alt text for your image. Alt text is text that briefly describes the image; a Web browser displays this text in place of the image if the image doesn't load for some reason. After you type your Alt text, click OK. Dreamweaver places the image into the design at the point you clicked.

FIGURE 13.21

Dreamweaver's Image Preview dialog box shows the promotional item copied from the Photoshop layered document. Here, it's being saved as a GIF file.

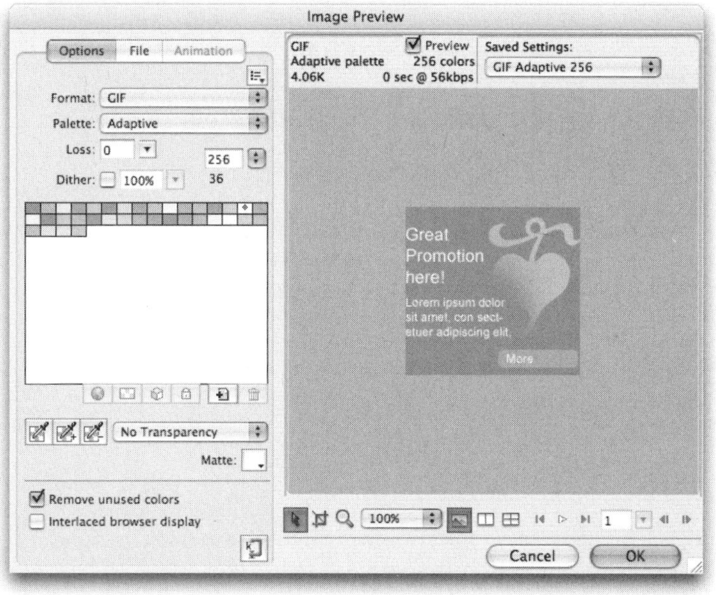

> **NOTE** The Image Preview dialog box in Dreamweaver is actually quite powerful, reproducing most of the options found in Photoshop's own Save for Web & Devices dialog box.

This approach is great if you're a habitual Photoshop and Dreamweaver user. It saves you having to export your slices from Photoshop as Web images and add them by hand into a Web page.

Using PSD files with photo editing tools

Photoshop may be the king of image editors, but there are lots more editors out there that support layered Photoshop files to one extent or another. This section looks at some of these editors, and how well they support Photoshop's layered PSD format.

Corel Paint Shop Pro Photo XI

Paint Shop Pro Photo — originally called just Paint Shop Pro — has a long history as a popular entry-level image editor. Originally a JASC product, it's now owned by Corel and has basic support for Photoshop layers and the PSD format in general.

Figure 13.22 shows a Photoshop file opened in Paint Shop Pro Photo. The file contains a photo with a layer mask and Hard Light blending mode, and a Background layer. Paint Shop Pro Photo has retained the layer structure, as well as the layer mask and blending mode on the photo. The Layers palette in Paint Shop Pro Photo shows the layer mask in a different way to Photoshop — as part of a Paint Shop Pro "group" — but it's definitely intact. The type layer, however, is rendered as a bitmap layer and is no longer editable.

FIGURE 13.22

A test Photoshop file opened in Corel Paint Shop Pro Photo XI. Paint Shop Pro Photo renders the type layer as a bitmap layer, but has done well otherwise.

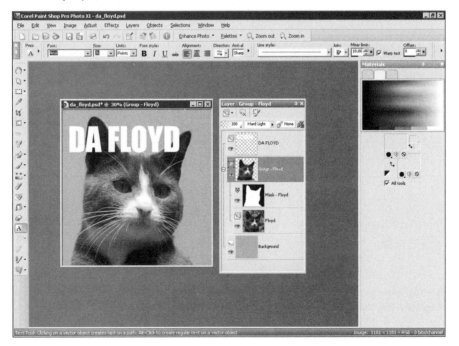

Paint Shop Pro can also save documents in the PSD format. In the example in Figure 13.23, a very simple Paint Shop Pro document is exported by choosing File ⇨ Save As, and selecting Photoshop from the Save As Type menu. Paint Shop Pro displays a warning message indicating that some vector data might be lost. Click Yes to go ahead and export anyway.

FIGURE 13.23

Exporting a simple Photoshop file from Paint Shop Pro. Note the warning message.

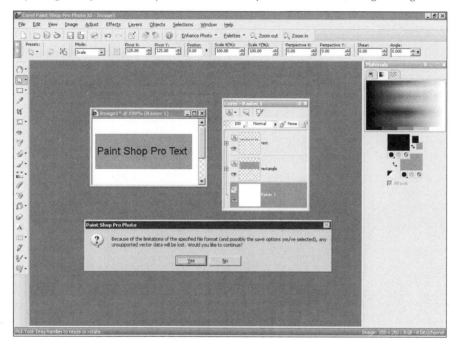

In the original file, the rectangle and text are both vector layers (Paint Shop Pro renders text as vectors to allow for resizing). Opened in Photoshop, however, both the rectangle and text are rendered as bitmap layers, although the structure of the layers is retained.

Adobe Photoshop Elements 5

Born in response to Paint Shop Pro's entry-level challenge, Photoshop Elements is Adobe's cut-down version of Photoshop. It's primarily designed for photographers, but it retains many useful design features, too. The interface is made less pro and more welcoming than the full Photoshop, and some of the tools common to both applications have different icons in each app. A lot of the basic functionality is very similar, though. It also possesses some great features that have since made it into the full version of Photoshop, such as the red-eye removal tool. It also has the very useful Photo Bin to store open documents. If you have many files open at once, this is great, and would be a useful feature in the full version, too.

Opening the previously-used test Photoshop file, you can see that Elements does a pretty immaculate job of handling Photoshop layers. The type layer remains editable, with all layer effects intact. The photo layer retains its layer mask and blending mode. You can see the file opened in Elements in Figure 13.24.

FIGURE 13.24

The test file opened in Photoshop Elements 5. Photoshop Elements does a great job of handling Photoshop files. In this case, all Photoshop layers come through unscathed.

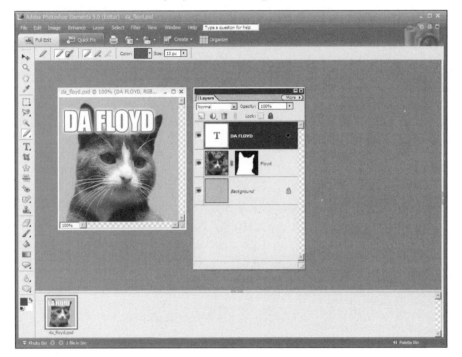

Saving PSD files from Elements is also simple, because PSD is its native format. PSD files saved from Elements should open in Photoshop CS3 with few surprises.

Adobe Photoshop Lightroom 1

Lightroom is Adobe's professional photography application. At the time of this writing, it's a pretty new product. Designed to be a competitor to Apple's Aperture — covered later — Lightroom is based around the workflow of cataloging, processing, and outputting photos. Its editing tools are very good, but sometimes you might want to edit a photo in Photoshop, maybe to add a mask or filter effect. Luckily, support for Photoshop files is built into Lightroom, as you might expect from an Adobe product.

Lightroom supports Photoshop files through the concept of round-trip editing. You pick a file to edit and send it to Photoshop for editing. When you save the file in Photoshop, the image updates itself back in Lightroom. Take a look at this in practice. In Figure 13.25, you can see the Lightroom environment. We've picked a photo to edit. Lightroom doesn't support the concept of masks, and this photo could badly do with an Exposure adjustment layer applied just to the foreground area — a feat that needs layer masks to accomplish.

FIGURE 13.25

Viewing an example photo in Photoshop Lightroom. You can't increase the exposure across the whole image because you would blow out the sky highlights in doing so. Adjustment layers and layer masks to the rescue!

To open the image in Photoshop, choose Photo ➪ Edit in Adobe Photoshop CS3. A dialog box appears (see Figure 13.26) that invites you to choose the mode to edit the photo in. The options in the dialog box work as follows:

- **Edit Original:** This opens the original photo in Photoshop for editing, and is probably best avoided from the perspective of keeping the original file as a "negative."

- **Edit a Copy:** Selecting this option opens a copy of the original photo in Photoshop, leaving the original file untouched.

- **Edit a Copy with Lightroom Adjustments:** This opens a version of the photo that includes any Lightroom adjustments you've already made. In this case, this option is selected because the photo has previously been warmed up a little in Lightroom.

- **Stack with Original:** Select this to add the edited photo to a stack along with the original. A *stack* is Lightroom's method of grouping similar or related photos. (If you select the Edit Original option, this option is not available.)

FIGURE 13.26

The Edit Photo dialog box in Photoshop Lightroom lets you choose which version of the photo you want to edit.

Once open in Photoshop, you can make your adjustments, which in this case involves applying an Exposure adjustment layer, along with a layer mask to constrain the effect to the foreground. When you're happy, you can save the file and flip back over to Lightroom. The library now contains the original photo and the edited version grouped together in a stack. You can see this in Figure 13.27.

If you want to reedit the already-edited photo, select it in Lightroom and choose Photo ➪ Edit in Adobe Photoshop CS3. If you select the Edit a Copy with Lightroom Adjustments option, you'll find that you're editing a flat version of the file. If you want to reedit the version containing the adjustment layer, select Edit a Copy instead.

FIGURE 13.27

The original photo (left) and the edited image (right), back in Lightroom's library

Apple Aperture 1.5

Apple's Mac-only Aperture software is similar conceptually to Adobe Lightroom in that it's designed for professional photographers and manages the cataloging, processing, and outputting of large numbers of photos. Like Lightroom, it has support for round-trip photo editing in Photoshop.

NOTE   To use Photoshop as an external image editor in Aperture, choose Aperture ⇨ Preferences. In the Output section, click Choose under the External Image Editor option. This displays the Select Application dialog, which presents you with a view of your Applications folder in column view. Navigate to the Adobe Photoshop CS3 folder and click the folder to find Adobe Photoshop CS3 (the application) within. Click the application to highlight it; then click Select to set Photoshop as Aperture's image editor.

The process of editing a photo from Aperture — shown in Figure 13.28 — is simple. Right-click the photo you want to edit and choose Open with External Editor. Aperture creates a copy of the photo, and opens the copy in Photoshop.

FIGURE 13.28

Apple's Aperture software in action. As soon as you choose to edit a photo in Photoshop, Aperture creates a new version of the image, seen here on the right.

Make your changes in Photoshop, then save the file. For example, you could apply some very silly changes to the seagull image shown in Figure 13.28 using a Smart Object and the Liquify filter. Back in Aperture, the version updates to show the edits applied to the poor seagull (see Figure 13.29).

If you want to make some more edits in Photoshop, simply select the previously edited photo and open it again in Photoshop. Aperture immediately creates another new version of the image for editing. All of your previous edits and layer features are preserved in the reopened version of the file.

The GIMP 2.2

The GIMP (GNU Image Manipulation Program) is a popular open-source image editor. It's available across Windows, Mac, and Linux. The great news is that it's free, but it does have an interface that you might describe as quirky, which takes some getting used to. That said, it's a powerful image editor, with many of the features you might find in Photoshop, including layers.

FIGURE 13.29

Back in Aperture, the seagull edited in Photoshop (on the left) now has a very odd-shaped neck.

So how well does this darling of the open-source community support files created in the decidedly non-open-source Photoshop? Pretty well, actually. In Figure 13.30 you can see the test Photoshop file opened in The GIMP 2.2. The photo layer comes across well, with the layer mask and blending mode preserved. The type layer is rendered as a bitmap layer, however, and all layer effects are lost. The GIMP has also introduced a small new area of photo across the top of the image. This is because it's lost a small strip of the layer mask.

The GIMP can also write layered Photoshop files. In Figure 13.31, a new file is created in The GIMP and saved as a Photoshop document. The original file has a Background layer, two rectangle bitmap layers — one with opacity at 50 percent and the other at 100 percent — and a type layer with a Multiply blending mode. The figure shows the document opened in both The GIMP and Photoshop. You can see that The GIMP generally does a pretty good job of saving the PSD; everything is retained in Photoshop except the editable type layer.

FIGURE 13.30

In the test Photoshop file opened in The GIMP, Floyd the cat is largely intact, though some of the layer mask at the top of the image is lost, and the type layer is rendered as a bitmap layer.

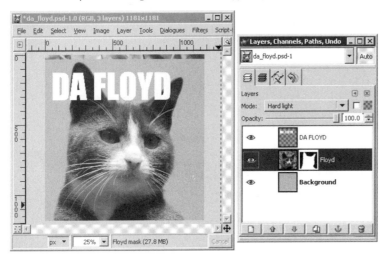

FIGURE 13.31

The original file within The GIMP (a) and the saved file opened in Photoshop (b). Everything but the editability of the type layer is retained, including the Multiply blending mode and opacity settings applied in The GIMP.

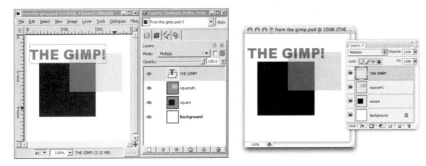

Exploring Photoshop layer support in QuarkXPress 7

QuarkXPress is the granddaddy of DTP software. Nearly everyone in the print industry has used it at some point, even if they've now moved to InDesign. It's the standard against which all comers are judged, but how well does it support our beloved Photoshop files?

Start with a basic test: importing an example Photoshop file into a QuarkXPress 7 layout. Create a simple layout in Quark with some text columns and a picture box. Next, import the PSD file into the picture box by selecting the box and choosing File ➪ Import Picture. In the Import Picture dialog box, select the PSD file to import. Click Open. The results of this can be seen in Figure 13.32.

 When you choose File ➪ Import Picture, Quark links to the PSD file on the hard drive; it doesn't embed the file itself in your Quark document.

 A picture box is a container for images. To create a picture box, select the Rectangle Picture Box tool from the Toolbox and click and drag within the document window. Text automatically flows around a picture box.

FIGURE 13.32

Here is an attempt to import a test PSD file into Quark. We run into problems, and Quark is using the embedded composite image instead of the layered version of the file. The problem stems from the use of layer effects on the type layer in Photoshop.

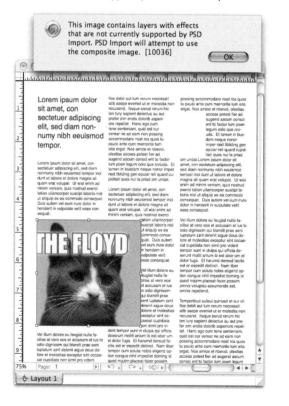

There is a slight snag, though. Because of the layer effects applied to the type layer within Photoshop, Quark can't import the individual layers of the Photoshop file, so it's imported the composite image instead.

To get around this problem, save a new version of the Photoshop file with no effects applied and reimport the file into Quark. To reimport the file, select the Content tool from the Quark Toolbox and click in the picture box to select the image. Press Backspace (Delete on the Mac) to delete the image from the picture box, and import the file again using File ➪ Import Picture.

The file now imports with no problems, and you can then use one of the great features of QuarkXPress 7: the PSD Import palette. To access this palette, choose Window ➪ PSD Import. This palette is effectively a cut-down version of Photoshop's Layers palette, and allows you to manipulate the Photoshop file directly with Quark. There are tabs for layers, channels, and paths. Select your placed Photoshop file, and the palette updates to show the Photoshop layers in the file, as shown in Figure 13.33. As you can see, the PSD Import palette honors the blending mode of the Floyd layer, as well as the layer mask. You can also disable the layer mask by Shift+clicking its thumbnail in the palette, just like you would in Photoshop.

FIGURE 13.33

Here, the layer effects from the type layer in the PSD are removed; then the PSD is reimported into Quark. This time the file imports with no warning dialog box. You can then use the PSD Import palette in Quark to change the visibility, blending mode, and opacity of each layer, much like using the Layers palette in Photoshop.

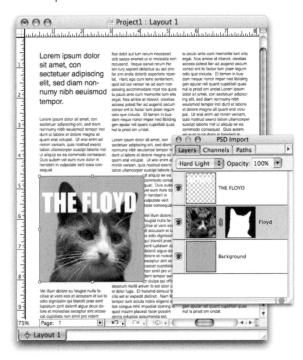

The PSD Import palette does have some limitations. For example, you can't create new layers or reorder layers. You can't edit the layer mask, and the text is imported as a bitmap image, so you can't edit that, either. That said, this is a very slick addition to QuarkXPress's handling of Photoshop files.

Suppose you want to change the color of that background behind the cat. First, in the PSD Import palette, hide the type and Background layers by clicking their eye icons, leaving just the Floyd layer visible. You can now specify your own background color by editing the picture box within Quark. To do this, select the picture box using the Item tool, then choose Item ➪ Modify to display the Modify dialog box, as shown in Figure 13.34. Click the Box tab to display options for the picture box. On the right of the dialog, there's a section called Box with a Color option inside. There are some preset colors already in the list — choose the Magenta preset. If desired, you can also choose the shade and opacity for the color at this point from those options below the list. (A shade in Quark-speak is a lighter version of the selected color, chosen by defining a percentage of the full color.)

FIGURE 13.34

Here, the Modify dialog box is used to change the background color of the picture box within QuarkXPress. As you can see in the PSD Import palette, the type and Background layers are hidden, leaving just the Floyd layer visible.

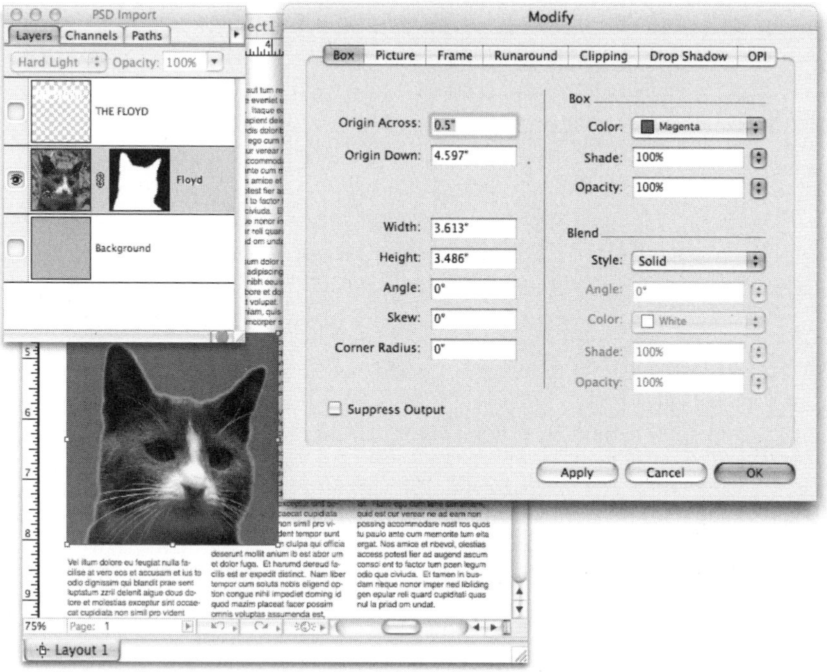

Even though the Floyd layer still has its Hard Light blending mode applied, this only has an effect on layers inside the Photoshop document; it doesn't blend with the picture box background color. However, the layer mask is very much intact, allowing you to see the color of the picture box around the cat.

You can also use the transparency of the Floyd layer mask to flow the text around the cat. First, remove the Magenta color applied earlier by selecting the picture box, choosing Item ➪ Modify, clicking the Box tab, and selecting None for the Color option, leaving you with a transparent picture box.

Currently, the text is flowing around the edges of the picture box. To make the text flow around the cat instead, display the Measurements palette by choosing Window ➪ Measurements. This palette is context-sensitive, so its contents depend on what you select in your document. Click the picture box; the Measurements palette changes to display options for controlling the runaround effect.

NOTE   A runaround in Quark is the effect of text flowing around a picture box.

In the Measurements palette, choose Alpha Channel from the Type menu on the left. An Alpha menu appears in the palette, just below the Type option, containing a list of all alpha channels embedded in the Photoshop file. In this case, there is only one alpha channel — the layer mask — that appears in the Alpha pop-up menu as Alpha Mask 1. Quark automatically selects this channel in the list. Now the text flows around the cat, rather than around the picture box itself, as shown in Figure 13.35. You can also move the PSD around within the picture box to create a more pleasing runaround. To do this, select the Content tool in the Toolbox and click and drag the cat around.

You can also adjust the gap between the cat and the text flowing around it by changing the Outset option to the right of the Type option in the Measurements palette. A value of 10 points creates a pleasing gap between cat and text.

You can still edit the Photoshop file back in Photoshop. To do this, right-click the picture box in the document and select Edit Original. The original Photoshop file opens in Photoshop. Edit and save the file and return to Quark. Right-click the Photoshop file in the Quark document and choose Update.

In the example in Figure 13.36, Floyd sports some rather silly sunglasses. This is created by dragging a photo of some shades into the Photoshop file, placing the shades layer at the top of the layer stack. Using a layer mask, the background is cut out, leaving the shades perched on Floyd's nose.

When the file is saved and then updated in Quark, the PSD Import palette changes to reflect the new Shades layer, and the document updates to show the sunglasses, as shown in Figure 13.36. Note that Quark remembers the position of the PSD file within the picture box from the previous edits with the Content tool, and that the visibilities of the type and Background layers are retained in the transition from Quark to Photoshop and back again.

FIGURE 13.35

The text now flows around the cat itself, rather than around the picture box. Note the Measurements palette showing Alpha Mask 1 on the left. This is the alpha channel that stores the layer mask for the Floyd layer in the Photoshop file.

TIP You may have noticed in Figure 13.36 that Quark is still using the cat layer's layer mask for the runaround, resulting in quite a narrow gap between the sunglasses and the text. If you want Quark to follow the contours of both cat and shades, create a new alpha channel in Photoshop that's a composite of the two layer masks, then use that alpha channel in the Measurements palette in Quark.

NOTE Photoshop adjustment layers are not supported within Quark. The layers themselves show up, but they have no effect on the image.

The PSD Import dialog box, introduced in version 6.5, is a very helpful addition to Quark's arsenal of tools and makes PSD handling much easier than in previous versions of the software.

FIGURE 13.36

Here, Floyd gets a makeover by reediting the PSD file in Photoshop and adding some sunglasses. After right-clicking the image in Quark and choosing Update, the updated PSD appears within the Quark document.

Other applications

Photoshop files are widely used across a variety of other applications, too. Photoshop is used for video, 3-D, and architectural work, as well as scientific and medical applications.

In the world of video editing, Photoshop plays an important role as an image editor for compositing live action with still images. It's also useful for creating titles for use with video-editing packages. For example, Adobe Premiere Pro can directly import layered Photoshop files to "tracks," including all alpha channels. You can even animate the layers within Premiere. Photoshop files are also well supported in Adobe After Effects, a motion graphics tool used in video production. Apple's Final Cut Pro also supports layered Photoshop files, although layer effects are not supported.

3-D applications use Photoshop extensively to create textures for 3-D objects. Indeed, some apps support reading and writing Photoshop files in this context. An example is Autodesk Maya, which has very tight Photoshop support. You can use any Photoshop file as a texture in Maya. You can also create layered PSD files in Maya that reflect different texture characteristics such as color and *bump* (a term referring to the relief of a texture). Similar to how DTP software like InDesign and QuarkXPress works, you can also edit any PSD file used in Maya within Photoshop and see the saved changes updated within Maya.

Lastly, a note about Microsoft Office: There is basic support for Photoshop files within Office in the sense that you can insert a PSD file into an Office document. However, there's no support for reediting the PSD in Photoshop again, and no layer support as such. Office simply uses the composite image to display the file.

Summary

In this chapter, you looked at the native file format of Photoshop — the PSD file — and how this format interacts with the world around it. We covered a couple of alternative layered formats in the shape of TIFF and Photoshop PDF files, and investigated how to use Photoshop's file handling preferences to change the way that Photoshop deals with opening and saving files. You also looked at maximizing your chances of getting a recent Photoshop file to work with earlier versions of Photoshop and other editors by means of the Maximize PSD and PSB File Compatibility option.

You took a detailed look at how layered Photoshop files interact with the other members of the Adobe CS3 suite of applications. Not surprisingly, the Adobe applications have the best support for the PSD format, and this makes for a rewarding and swift experience moving between the different applications in the range, which is, of course, exactly how Adobe wants it to be.

Finally, you looked at how well other image editors, DTP applications, and Web-authoring software work with the PSD format. You also took a brief look at some more specialized software that offers PSD support, including 3-D and video applications.

Chapter 14

Designing with Layers

In previous chapters, you looked mostly at the technical side of layers in Photoshop. In this chapter — along with the two following chapters — you're going to look at the practical side. Within this chapter are four example scenarios that might confront you as a designer. You work through these scenarios using Photoshop's layers in different ways, and learn how layers can help you with the design process.

This chapter covers the following:

- **Tweaking photos from a design perspective.** You use adjustment layers and layer masks to prepare a photo for a design layout.

- **Creating a Web site layout.** A lot of ground is covered here, from shape layers through to slicing the layout for export, as well as a foray into grid-based design.

- **Creating a montage.** You look at integrating several photos into a single image using layer masks and blending modes.

- **Putting together a mixed-media illustration.** Have you ever wanted to integrate hand-drawn elements into a design within Photoshop? You learn how, using layer techniques extensively as you go.

Instead of concentrating on the theory behind layers, layer masks, and blending modes, you'll investigate how to apply these tools to the practical, everyday situations just outlined. What do you do if the photos you're given for a job are washed out? How do you create a Web site design? How can you add your own drawings to a photo? How do you blend photos together? These questions are answered in detail, with cross-references to the chapters in the book that deal with the technical side of the tools used.

Although the examples here are biased toward designers, the techniques used here are useful to anyone wanting to see how Photoshop can be used practically. For example, if you're a photographer you may be interested to know how a montage is created.

ON the CD-ROM If you're following along with these examples, the Photoshop files used in them are found on the CD-ROM that comes with the book.

Tweaking Photos in a Design Environment

In this example, you work with a photo of an office building that is intended to form part of either a Web site or a brochure for a corporate real estate company. Some fairly simple techniques are used to get the photo to a high enough level of quality to feed into the layout.

In a typical workplace scenario, the photographer probably sends you a selection of photos on a CD after the client chooses his or her preferred shots. In this situation, there's a good chance you'll be getting the images straight from the camera, with only a minimum of processing applied. This is a good thing, because you usually want the processing of the photos to be under your control. This gives you the best chance of making the images look good in the context of the work. As a designer, it's your job to get these photos as good as they can possibly look. After all, you're selling the client's business here.

NOTE You'll probably receive images taken with a digital SLR camera. Images like these are generally less color-saturated and sharp than those from a small consumer digital camera. This is because the manufacturers of digital SLRs assume the photographer or designer wants full control over how the images turn out. A digital SLR does only a small amount of processing in-camera. If you're really lucky, you might get RAW files, which are captured with no processing at all, but you're likely to end up with JPEG (.jpg) or TIFF (.tif) files.

The first thing to do is simply to look at the photo, so open it in Photoshop. Figure 14.1 shows the starting photo, straight from the photographer.

The photo's basically pretty good, with only a couple of issues to correct. First, it's a little washed out and could do with a little more contrast and saturation. Second, the left-hand wall is very much in shadow; it would be good if you could tame that a bit.

You'll be looking at ways to correct these issues and create a photo that can be used for the next stage of the creative process. Corrections will be applied using Levels adjustment layers and layer masks.

FIGURE 14.1

The starting photo isn't bad, but it's a bit washed out, and the left-hand wall is a tad too dark.

Adding a Levels adjustment layer

Looking at your photo, it lacks a bit in the contrast department. You want an image with a little more contrast and "punch," and the Levels adjustment is ideal for this. You can, of course, use the Levels command (by choosing Image ➪ Adjustment ➪ Levels), but this works on the actual pixels of the photo. You want more control and flexibility, so use a Levels adjustment layer. To add a Levels layer, click the Create New Fill or Adjustment Layer icon at the bottom of the Layers palette and choose Levels. The Levels dialog box appears, as shown in Figure 14.2.

CROSS-REF You can find detailed information on Levels in Chapter 6.

Looking at the histogram in the Levels dialog, it looks like the highlights may have been clipped a bit, because the histogram ends abruptly at its right-hand edge. This is usually a sign that there were some more highlights outside the range of the histogram, so you've lost some detail in your highlights. It also looks as though the shadows could do with a bit of remapping to set them closer to zero, thereby increasing the contrast by stretching the histogram across the full tonal range. Although technically it seems like some highlights are lost, realistically the problem is minimal in this case. There's probably no reason to worry about it if it wasn't picked up by the photographer or client.

FIGURE 14.2

The Levels dialog box, showing slightly clipped highlights

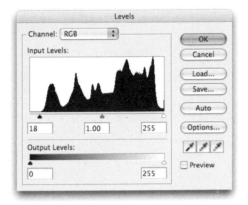

So, leave the white slider where it is because you don't want it to clip any more, and click and drag the black slider to the right until it touches the very start of the histogram data. As you do this you can see the image changing to give you instant visual feedback. (If you don't see this, make sure the Preview option in the dialog box is selected.) You'll see the blues in the sky darkening, along with the building. Now toggle the Preview check box off and on a few times to see how it looks. Remember that this is a subjective thing you're doing here. If it looks right, it probably is right — don't look only at the histogram.

TIP Clipping the shadows and highlights just a touch as you adjust things can sometimes pay off in terms of getting a really powerful effect. It's not "correct" as an approach, and again, these things are subjective, so use this technique with caution, especially in a commercial environment.

A basic Levels adjustment has been applied to the image, and already it looks punchier. Looking at the Layers palette, you can see that the adjustment layer is sitting nicely above the Background photo layer. If you hide the adjustment layer by clicking its eye icon in the Layers palette, as shown in Figure 14.3, you can see that the original image is untouched.

CROSS-REF You can accomplish the same effect using a Curves adjustment layer. Photoshop CS3 gives you the option of displaying a histogram within the Curves graph, which makes these kinds of adjustments much easier and more precise. You can also use a Brightness/Contrast adjustment layer, but a good result is more difficult to achieve that way despite the simplicity of its name. You can find more information on these and the other adjustment layer types in Chapter 6.

FIGURE 14.3

Hiding the adjustment layer reveals the untouched image below.

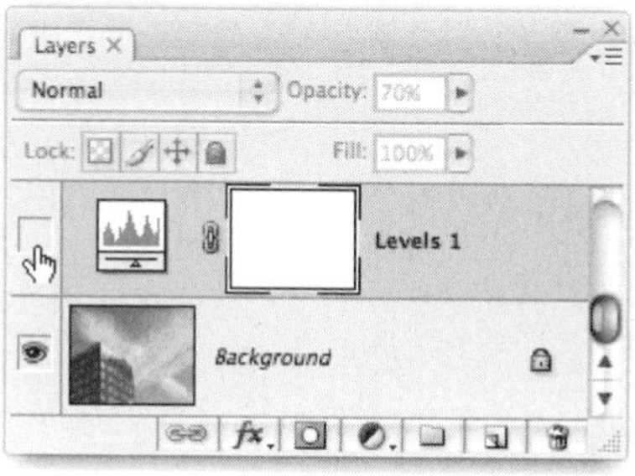

Making selective adjustments with a layer mask

Looking again at the image in Figure 14.1, you can see a very strong shadow on that wall to the left. This is, of course, down to the angle of the sun when the original photo was taken. It would be nice if you could reduce the brightness of the photo to make the sky and the other wall darker to match. However, if you did, the left-hand wall would also darken to the point of becoming too dark. How can you get around that?

What you want to do is work on only the sky and the lighter wall, and you can achieve this easily by using layer masks.

CROSS-REF You can find more detail on layer masks in Chapter 9.

To make this adjustment, follow these steps:

1. **Create a Levels adjustment layer.** Create a new Levels adjustment layer as before by clicking the Create New Fill or Adjustment Layer icon at the bottom of the Layers palette and choosing Levels from the pop-up menu. For now, just click OK to close the Levels dialog box — you don't want to do any adjusting for the moment.

2. **Choose a brush.** Select the Brush tool in the Toolbox and choose a fairly hard-edged black brush. To do this, click the Brush option in the options bar to display the Brush Preset picker. A list of thumbnails for choosing brush presets appears together with sliders for Master Diameter and Hardness. The Master Diameter slider increases the size of the brush as you click and drag it to the right; dragging it left decreases the size. The Hardness slider increases and decreases the feathering of the brush; the edge becomes softer the farther to the left you drag it. Set Master Diameter to around 100 pixels and Hardness to around 80 percent.

3. **Display the layer mask overlay.** So that you can see your layer mask as you paint on it, make the mask's channel visible. To do this, make sure the new Levels adjustment layer is active, then display the Channels palette (Window ➪ Channels). A channel at the bottom of the palette appears that represents the Levels layer's mask (it will probably be called something like Levels 2 Mask). Click the empty box to the left of the channel in the Channels palette so that its eye icon appears. The mask is now visible as you paint on it; colored areas of the mask show up as a red overlay.

TIP   You can also quickly toggle the red overlay for a layer mask on and off by pressing \ (Backslash). When the overlay is active, the eye icons in the Layers palette become grayed out.

4. **Paint on the layer mask.** To the right of the layer thumbnail in the Layers palette is the layer mask thumbnail, and this is what you're now interested in. You want to "paint out" any Levels effect on that darker wall using the layer mask, which leaves you free to push the levels a little on the other elements. Click the layer mask thumbnail to make sure the mask is active. Because you don't want the Levels adjustment to apply to the darker wall, you'll paint that area black to mask it. Reselect the black brush if need be, and start to paint in the document window over that darker left wall. As you do, the areas you paint turn red, indicating they're now masked. Keep painting with the brush until you cover all of the darker wall. If the Layers palette is displayed, you can see the results as you go in the layer mask thumbnail. Don't worry if you feel like you're going over the edges a bit — you can rectify that later. When you finish, your layer mask thumbnail should look something like the one in Figure 14.4. When you're happy with the mask, turn off the mask channel's visibility again in the Channels palette, or press \ (Backslash), to get rid of the red areas.

TIP   Here you're painting on your mask with a black brush, but you could also use any of the selection tools to create a selection, then fill the selection with black. The end result is the same.

FIGURE 14.4

The layer mask thumbnail showing your painted-out area

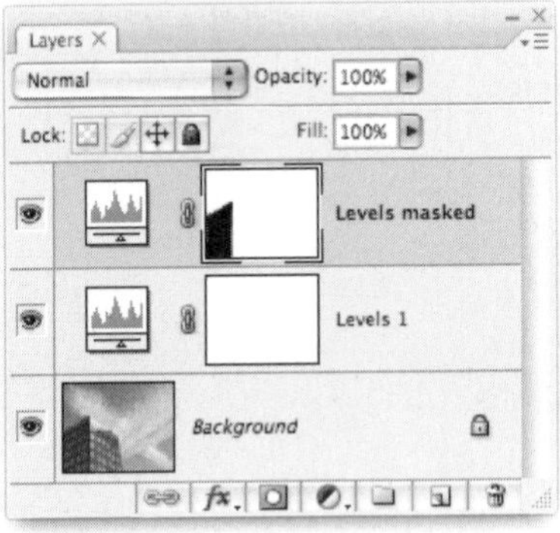

5. **Make the adjustment.** Now here's the magic: Double-click the second Levels layer's thumbnail to display the Levels dialog box. Start to drag the black slider in toward the right a little. The sky and the lighter wall darken, but the darker wall is left alone — it's been masked out. Now the two walls are closer to each other's tonal range, and the sky is rich with deep blue colors.

You may notice that the image histogram now has a little bit of a "combing" effect, with vertical gaps scattered throughout the graph. It's not too extreme, though; again, the important thing is to use your eyes to determine whether the image is becoming unacceptably posterized.

TIP A clever trick here is to reduce the layer opacity of the second Levels adjustment layer slightly to diminish the effect a little. It has a "taming" effect on the Levels adjustment because it makes the effect of the adjustment weaker. This approach can give you a nicely subtle level of control. It's also a great way to experiment and mix adjustments if you're working with multiple adjustment layers at once.

Tidying up the mask

If your mask has a few rough edges, you can easily go back and tidy them up. The mask in Figure 14.5 has some pretty rough areas. The mask has crept into the sky at the top, therefore that part of the sky is not being affected by the Levels adjustment. This results in a weird band of slightly lighter blue in the sky.

FIGURE 14.5

The slightly slapdash mask has leaked into the sky, resulting in part of the sky being masked off from the Levels adjustment along with the left-hand wall.

To fix this, paint on the mask in white around the edges of the building to tidy up that edge. Painting in white unmasks an area, just like painting in black masks it. If you paint in white over that bit of sky, you unmask it again, and it is again affected by the Levels adjustment.

TIP   If your foreground and background colors are black and white, you can press X to quickly flip them over and start painting with white. Press X again to flip back to painting with black. Alternatively, press E to flip to the Eraser tool; when working with a mask, the Eraser paints with the background color, which should be white. You can then press B to flip back to the Brush tool and return to painting with black.

You could have used many different methods to create your mask. For example, because this wall is straight-edged, it's a perfect candidate for a selection with the Polygonal Lasso tool. To try this out, follow these steps:

1. **Create a Levels adjustment layer.** Hide the second Levels adjustment layer by clicking its eye icon, then create a new Levels adjustment layer, and click OK to close its Levels dialog box.

2. **Make a polygonal selection.** Select the Polygonal Lasso tool from the Toolbox and trace the edge of the building, as shown in Figure 14.6. You can see that, unlike the normal Lasso tool, the Polygonal Lasso produces selections with straight edges, making it perfect for this application.

FIGURE 14.6

Tracing the edge of the building using the Polygonal Lasso tool

3. **Fill the selection.** When the selection is in place, click the new Levels layer's mask thumbnail to make sure it's active, and fill the selection with black by choosing Edit ➪ Fill and choosing Black for the Use option. Keep the Mode setting on Normal and the Opacity setting at 100 percent, and click OK. This fills the selected area of the mask with

black, masking off that area. If you don't see any change, press \ (Backslash) to display the masked area in red.

4. **Make the Levels adjustment.** Now press Ctrl+D (⌘+D on the Mac) to deselect the area, then double-click the new Levels layer's thumbnail to display the Levels dialog box. Click and drag the black slider slightly toward the right to darken the sky and right-hand wall again. This time, the left-hand wall is much more accurately masked, and the whole sky darkens.

Applying adjustments to other photos in a batch

There's a good chance that you'll receive several similar photos from the same batch when you work on a project, and often you'll need to apply similar adjustments to many or all of these images. The good news is that you don't have to start from scratch each time. Just like other types of layers, you can drag adjustment layers between documents, too. This means that you can get all your adjustments right on the first photo, and then quickly apply the same adjustments to the others.

To do this, open your next photo in Photoshop. Go back to the original and select all the adjustment layers you want to bring across by Shift+clicking or Ctrl+clicking (⌘+clicking on the Mac) the layers in the Layers palette. Now you can just drag your adjustment layers to the next photo to copy them across, and you can see the effects instantly, as shown in Figure 14.7.

CROSS-REF For more on selecting multiple layers at once, see Chapter 2.

FIGURE 14.7

Dragging multiple adjustment layers from one image to another

> **CAUTION** Bear in mind that you'll have to discard the layer masks of the adjustment layers in the new document, or you'll end up masking off the wrong areas in the new image.

Although you will probably need to tweak the adjustments a bit and, of course, create new layer masks, this is a great timesaving approach, and you'll finish with a more consistent set of images.

In this example, we looked at tweaking images for use in the design process by applying adjustment layers and layer masks. These are important concepts to grasp when retouching images in Photoshop, and a thorough knowledge of them can make a big difference in the quality of your output.

Designing a Web Site with Layers

In this example, you learn how to lay out a Web page design in Photoshop using layers. Many of the concepts discussed in the book are brought together, including clipping masks, the Move tool, the transform commands, layer styles, shape layers, and type layers. You'll also learn how best to organize the proliferation of layers that a Web project often creates, and how to export the final images.

The design brief for this example is to create a Web page layout for a fictitious investment banking company, Crown Investments. Investment banks generally don't go for cutting-edge designs, and this bank is no exception. The brief is to create a design that is conservative and reflects the bank's brand and culture. The design should allow for easy editing of the final site and also provide areas for cross-promotion. This means having an area on the page where the bank can link to other sections of the site that are of particular note.

It's likely that the structure of the site will be decided before the design process begins, so you know what the menu options will be before you start. It's important to know this in advance if possible so that, as a designer, you can provide space for the options within the visuals.

Most Web designers lay out Web site designs in Photoshop or a similar graphics package before any site building takes place. This is because it's quicker to get a feel for the visuals of a site, and to experiment with layouts, in a graphics package than it is in a Web page editor. This is especially true in the professional arena, where you need to get client approval on the visual and brand elements before committing to the build. Even when you work on your own Web presence, it's a great way to experiment with various looks before starting to build your site.

Although when creating the layouts in Photoshop you'll be working with a full page design, there's a good chance that only some elements will be exported when creating the final site. This is because Web sites are made from a combination of images and HTML markup, and elements like the text and menu are likely to be firmly on the markup side of the fence. You can read more about this in the section "Export Strategies."

Creating a new document

Create a new document for your layout. Choosing a size for this new document is part of the battle. Display the New dialog box by choosing File ➪ New. Follow these steps to set options for your new document and choose its dimensions:

1. **Type Crown Investments Website in the Name box.** You're building a site for Crown Investments, so this seems like as good a name as any. It pays to make your document name as meaningful and complete as possible for ease of reference; it's also handy if you ever need to search for the file by keyword.

2. **Make sure the Units menu to the right of the Width text box is set to Pixels.** Web sites are designed to be viewed on-screen, and pixels are the best unit of measurement to use when working with on-screen images.

3. **Type 770 in the Width box and 700 in the Height box.** Web sites can be designed to fit into different screen resolutions, and this affects what pixel dimensions you choose for the layout. You're going to design for a basic 800-x-600-pixel screen. This is often the default size for Web sites, because it's the "lowest common denominator" screen size. However, although the screen size might be 800 x 600 pixels, you won't actually create that size for your layout. You need to take into account scrollbars and the fact that people are used to scrolling Web sites vertically. With that in mind, use 770 x 700 pixels for this example.

> **NOTE** Screen size is given as two numbers that relate to how many pixels your screen displays horizontally and vertically. Common resolutions are 800 x 600, 1024 x 768, 1280 x 800, and so on. Modern PCs usually have displays of 1024 x 768 or higher. The bigger the numbers, the more your PC can fit on its screen. It's not a function of how physically big your screen is — you can run a 20-inch monitor at a number of different resolutions.

> **NOTE** Web sites can be fixed width or fluid width when viewed in a Web browser. Fixed-width sites are always the same width regardless of how wide your browser window is, and fluid-width sites stretch horizontally to fill the browser window as it's resized. Within Photoshop, of course, the layout is always fixed, but it's good to be aware whether your final site will be fixed or fluid width.

4. **Set the Resolution to 72 pixels/inch.** This is a good setting to use for building Web sites, as it approximates the resolution of most monitors.

5. **Set the Color Mode to RGB Color and the Background Contents to White.** RGB is the best mode to work in for on-screen images, and you're going to design the site with a white background.

Figure 14.8 shows the New dialog box with your settings for the new Web page. When you're happy, click OK to create the document.

FIGURE 14.8

Creating a new document for a Web layout

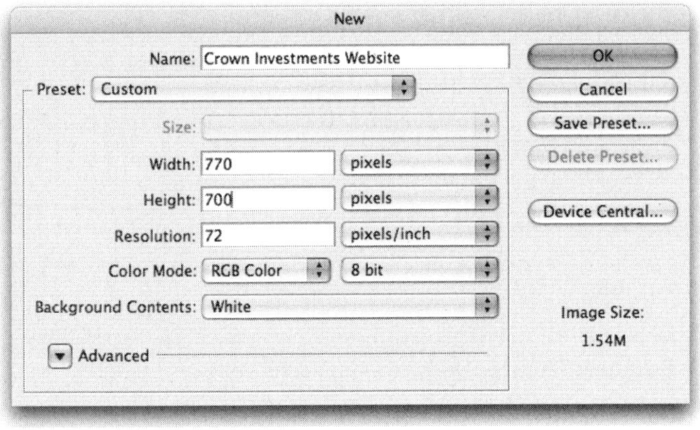

Using a design grid

When we talk about a grid in this context, it refers to a standard graphic design technique of dividing the page into evenly spaced areas. Design grids are used to make sure that all your layout elements line up, and to provide a clear, predictable visual structure for your design. For example, a newspaper layout generally uses a complex grid of columns and rows to create the basic areas in which text and images fit. Your site will use a much simpler grid structure.

NOTE In this context, a grid is not the same thing as Photoshop's grid feature, which overlays a standard set of divisions on your document. Your grid is user-defined to fit a particular project. However, you can use Photoshop's grid to help you lay out your design grid. Turn it on by choosing View ➪ Show ➪ Grid, or by pressing Ctrl+' (⌘+' on the Mac). You can define the grid's size, color, and appearance by choosing Edit ➪ Preferences (Photoshop ➪ Preferences on the Mac), and flipping to the Guides, Grid & Slices section in the Preferences dialog box. Make sure your grid is set to use pixels.

A quick and easy way to define a visual grid is to use Photoshop's guides feature. Guides are horizontal and vertical lines that you can overlay on top of your document, but are not part of the image in the sense that they don't appear when you print or otherwise export your document. They're simply visual clues that you can use to line elements up.

CROSS-REF You can read more about Photoshop's grid and guides features in Chapter 2.

Setting up the grid

To create a new guide, display Photoshop's rulers by choosing View ➪ Rulers or pressing Ctrl+R (⌘+R on the Mac), and do one of the following:

- To create a vertical guide, click inside the left ruler and drag to the right, into the document.

- To create a horizontal guide, drag down from the top ruler into the document.

Enable snapping (View ➪ Snap) and hold down Shift as you drag the guides to snap them to the tick marks on the rulers. You can move your guides at any time by holding down Ctrl (⌘ on the Mac) and positioning your mouse directly over a guide; when you do this, the mouse cursor changes to a double-line arrow. You can then click the guide and drag it to a new location. (If you need to delete a guide, simply drag it outside the document window.)

TIP To toggle your guides on or off, choose View ➪ Show ➪ Guides. If you can't see any guides, but you know they should be there, choose View ➪ Show and make sure the Guides option is selected. You can also show and hide your guides much more quickly by pressing Ctrl+; (⌘+; on the Mac).

For this example, you're going to create areas for a header image and menu, a main text area on the left, and a right-hand column for promotional items. You'll also give the whole page a border of 10 pixels. Create your guides as shown in Figure 14.9. The Web page now has a clearly defined structure.

FIGURE 14.9

Here a basic grid structure using guides is created. No actual design work yet though!

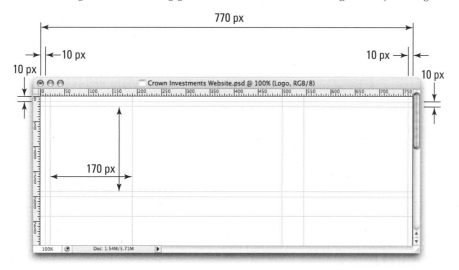

Creating the header image

You're going to put a nice photo of some office buildings in that top area, and to do that you're going to use a shape layer as a clipping mask.

CROSS-REF You can find more information about shape layers in Chapter 5. Clipping masks are covered in Chapter 9.

To place the photo, follow these steps:

1. **Create your shape.** To do this, click the Shape Tool icon in the Toolbox, and then click the Rectangle Tool icon in the options bar. Next, make sure you're going to create a new shape layer by clicking the Shape Layers icon on the left of the options bar, if it's not already selected. Enable snapping to the guides (View ➪ Snap To ➪ Guides). Now position the cursor on one of the corners of the header area, as defined by your guides, and click and drag toward the opposite corner to form a large rectangle at the top of the page. It doesn't matter at all what color you use to fill the shape because you'll be putting a photo over the top.

2. **Add the photo.** Now, add the photo to this header area. To do this, open the photo as a new document, then select its Background layer and drag it across to the layout document. There's a good chance that it will completely cover the page when you do this, but don't panic — clipping masks are about to save you!

3. **Create a clipping mask.** Look at the Layers palette. If the photo layer isn't directly above the rectangle shape layer you just created, drag it up so it is. Make sure this photo layer is selected, then choose Layer ➪ Create Clipping Mask, or press Ctrl+Alt+G (⌘+Option+G on the Mac). As you can see in Figure 14.10, the photo layer indents slightly in the Layers palette, and a small right-angled arrow appears next to the layer thumbnail, pointing to the shape layer below. You can see that the photo is now the same size as the rectangle in the document window; it's masked by the shape layer below it.

FIGURE 14.10

The header image is in place in your layout document. A clipping mask is used to mask the photo using the "photo area" shape layer underneath.

TIP There's a good chance that the photo is the wrong size and in the wrong place, but that's fine. You can still use the Move tool and the transform commands to move and resize the photo, even when masked like this. Indeed, this is one of the main benefits of using clipping masks; the photo retains its ability to be moved around within the clipped area, so you can change the photo's effective "crop" as you work.

Adding the menu

You're going to create a navigation menu that visitors to the Web site can use to flip between the main sections of the site. Although the text options in the menu will ultimately be built using HTML markup, it still helps to include the menu in the Photoshop layout so that you can get an idea of how it's going to look in the final site.

Creating the menu background

The menu will sit within the header image as text within a square background area, so start by creating that square area using Photoshop's ever-reliable shape layers. When you added the guides earlier, you created an inner square area on the left hand side of the header; this forms the basis for the menu area.

Select the Rectangle tool again, and make sure the Shape Layers option is selected in the options bar. Enable snapping to guides (View ➪ Snap To ➪ Guides). Position the mouse cursor at one corner of the inner area, and click and drag toward the opposite corner to form a square, as shown in Figure 14.11. Release the mouse button, and Photoshop creates your new square shape layer.

FIGURE 14.11

Dragging out a square for the menu background

You're now going to use a layer style to apply two varieties of effect to this shape: a gradient overlay and a stroke effect.

> **CROSS-REF** You can find out more about layer styles in Chapter 10.

To display the Layer Style dialog box, double-click an empty part of the square layer in the Layers palette, or select the square layer, click the *fx* button at the bottom of the Layers palette, and choose Blending Options from the pop-up menu that appears.

The two effects you're interested in are Gradient Overlay and Stroke. Look at the overlay first. You're looking for a simple gradient that moves from a darker shade of green to a lighter shade as it moves from the top to the bottom of the square. To create this gradient, follow these steps:

1. **Select the Gradient Overlay option on the left side of the dialog box.** The Gradient Overlay options appear in the main part of the dialog box, and the square in the document window is now filled with a gradient.

2. **Make sure Blend Mode is set to Normal and Opacity is set to 100 percent.** These are the default settings.

3. **Click inside the Gradient box.** The Gradient Editor dialog box appears.

4. **Choose the Black, White gradient preset from the list of presets at the top of the dialog box.** This is a simple two-color gradient that you'll use as a starting point. This preset is usually third in the list; if you don't see it, click the arrow at the top right of the dialog box and choose Reset Gradients.

5. **Click the left-hand color stop and choose a color by clicking the Color box at the bottom of the dialog box; repeat for the right-hand stop.** You can see this in action in Figure 14.12. The start color is a muted green (RGB values of 77, 124, 119), and the end color is a slighter darker green (RGB values of 56, 96, 92). The document window updates to show you the gradient with your new settings.

> **CROSS-REF** For more on editing gradients, see Chapter 6.

6. **Set the Style option to Linear, and make sure Align with Layer is selected.** This produces a simple, linear gradient effect and ensures that the effect stretches across the whole dimensions of the square.

7. **Choose an angle for the gradient using the Angle option.** Ninety degrees, or bottom to top, works nicely for this, but go with whatever you think looks best. You can either type this numerically in the text area, or just click and drag the line within the circle until it looks nice.

8. **Leave the Scale option set at 100 percent.** This makes sure the effect fills the whole square from bottom to top.

The Gradient Overlay effect in the dialog box now looks like Figure 14.13, and you can see the gradient applied to the square in the document window.

FIGURE 14.12

Editing the gradient. Click each color stop in turn, and choose a color for each stop by clicking the Color box at the bottom of the dialog box.

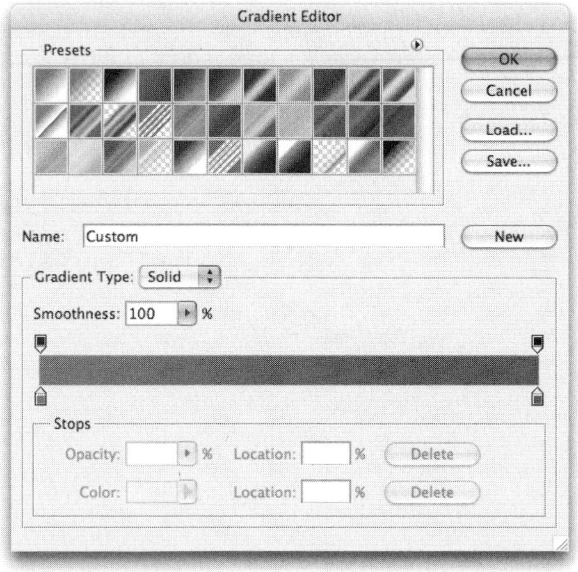

FIGURE 14.13

The settings of the finished Gradient Overlay effect in the Layer Style dialog box

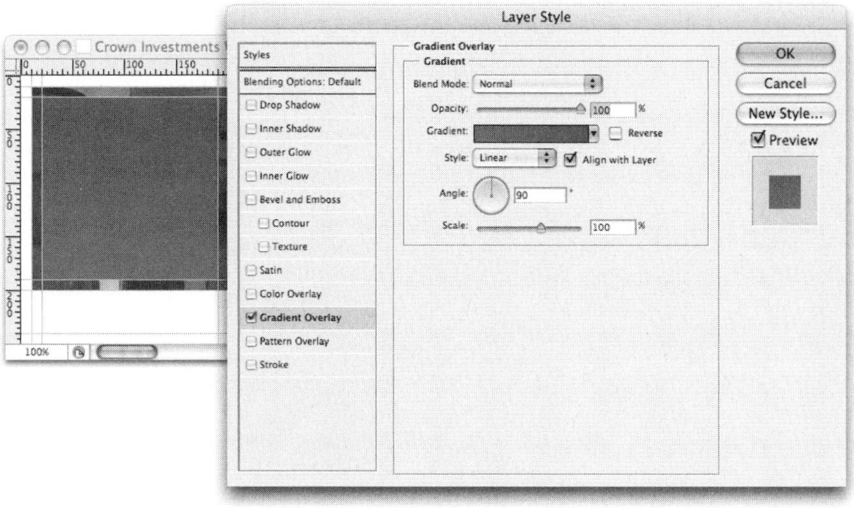

Next, add a border to the square using a Stroke effect. You might need to hide the guides first so you can see the effects of the stroke; to do this, press Ctrl+; (⌘+; on the Mac).

The steps for creating the border are as follows:

1. **Select the Stroke option on the left side of the dialog box.** The main part of the dialog box changes to show the options for the Stroke effect, and a border appears around the square in the document window.

2. **Set the Size option to 1 pixel.** You can do this by clicking and dragging the Size slider, or by typing **1** in the box. You want a nice, thin 1-pixel border around the box. The border in the document window changes as you drag the slider.

3. **Set the Position option to Inside.** You want the whole square to sit within your guides, so make sure the border sits within the square.

4. **Leave the Blend Mode and Opacity settings at their defaults of Normal and 100 percent, respectively.** This ensures that the border is created using a solid line.

5. **Set the Fill Type option to Color, and click the Color box beneath to set the color of your line.** This example uses a slightly lighter green (RGB values of 88, 40, 135) than either of the gradient colors, which just outlines the square slightly.

Figure 14.14 shows the Layer Style dialog box with the chosen Stroke settings, along with the menu square, complete with gradient and border.

FIGURE 14.14

The final Layer Style dialog box with Gradient Overlay and Stroke effects applied, and the finished square

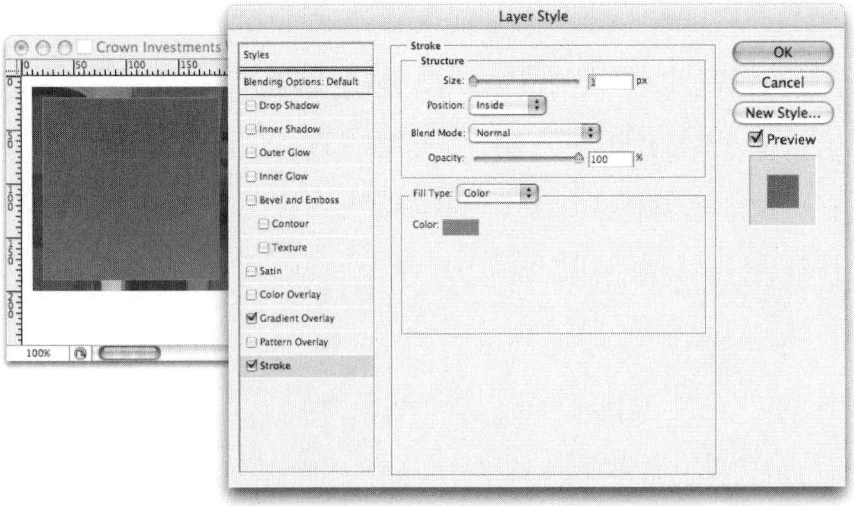

Adding the menu itself

Creating the menu is a simple process. It sits within the square you just created in the header.

Use the Type tool to create the text for the menu. First, select the Type tool by clicking its icon in the Toolbox, or by pressing T. Next, choose a suitable font, size, and color using the options in the Type tool's options bar. Try Arial with a size of 10 points and a text color of white.

The menu options will look good in all capitals, so press Caps Lock, or display the Character palette (Window ⇨ Character) and choose All Caps from the palette menu.

CROSS-REF You can find more information on the Type tool in Chapter 4.

Now position the cursor roughly where you want the menu to start. A position about half-way down the square is good, to allow room for the logo above. Click with the mouse, and start to type the menu options. After each option, press Enter (Return on the Mac) to put each option on a new line. When you're happy with your options, commit your edits by clicking the Commit button in the options bar or by pressing Ctrl+Enter (⌘+Return on the Mac). You can see the new type layer in the Layers palette.

There's a good chance the menu won't be in exactly the right place. You can use the Move tool to position it more accurately, or nudge the layer by holding down Ctrl (⌘ on the Mac) and using the arrow keys.

Figure 14.15 shows the menu in place.

FIGURE 14.15

The menu in place inside the square in the header

TIP It's common practice these days for the menu of a Web site to be created as an HTML list element rather than rendered as images. Therefore, it's a good idea to use system fonts such as Arial, Verdana, or Times to lay the menu out in the document, because these fonts are available on most PCs. This means that, when defined in the Web site's style sheet, your font is likely to look roughly the same for all visitors to the site. Of course, it's possible to use images as menu options if it's essential to the project, in which case the menu options will look identical on all computers.

Adding the logo

In a commercial environment, you'll probably receive the logo for the firm you're working for in one of the many common image formats, most of which can be opened in Photoshop. You can then resize the logo to 72 dpi and drag the relevant layers across to your layout document. For this example, however, you'll create the logo using shape layers and type layers.

The logo will be a crown, because in this imaginary example the client's name is "Crown Investments." It's not terribly imaginative, but it will suffice for these purposes. It consists of a graphical crown, the name of the firm, and a dividing line to separate the logo from the menu.

Create the logo as follows:

1. **Choose a crown shape.** You'll use a shape layer to create the crown element. To do this, click the Shape Tool icon in the Toolbox, then click the Custom Shape Tool icon in the options bar. Make sure the Shape Layers option is selected in the options bar. Now click the downward arrow inside the Shape option in the options bar to open the Custom Shape picker, and choose your favorite crown shape from the list.

TIP If you don't see any crown shapes in the list, click the arrow in the top-right corner of the Custom Shape picker, choose Objects from the pop-up menu, and click Append in the dialog box that appears. Photoshop loads the Objects shape library, which includes a few crown shapes, into the list.

2. **Draw the crown.** Choose a suitable foreground color by clicking the Color box in the options bar. You might want to use the same light green used for the border around the square. Now click in the top-left corner of the square in the document window, and drag out your crown. Hold down Shift as you drag to make sure the crown retains the right proportions. Release the mouse button to create the shape layer. If the crown is a little off-center, you can reposition and resize it as required using the Move tool and Edit ➪ Transform ➪ Scale.

3. **Choose a font for the text.** Select the Type tool and choose your favorite font, size, and color in the options bar. Times New Roman at around 17 points with a color of white is used here.

4. **Add the text.** Position the cursor below the crown, click the mouse button, and type the word **CROWN**. Press Ctrl+Enter (⌘+Return on the Mac) to commit the edit and create the type layer, then click below the CROWN text and type the word **INVESTMENTS**. Again, commit your edits to create the second type layer. You now have two separate type layers, one for each word, which makes it easy for you to resize the two words independently.

5. **Move and resize the text.** With the INVESTMENTS layer selected, choose Edit ⇨ Transform ⇨ Scale, or press Ctrl+T (⌘+T on the Mac), and drag the INVESTMENTS layer in the document window so it sits nicely underneath the CROWN text. Use the resize handles to resize the INVESTMENTS text so that it spans the same width as the CROWN text. Hold down Shift as you resize to maintain the correct proportions of the font.

TIP When moving and resizing the INVESTMENTS layer, you may need to zoom in a bit so that you can see what you're doing. To do this, press Ctrl+= (⌘+= on the Mac). To drag the image around the document window, hold down Shift and drag in the window. To zoom out again, press Ctrl+- (⌘+- on the Mac). You can use all these shortcuts even while you're using the transform command.

6. **Align the text with the crown.** Now the two type layers are aligned nicely with each other. However, you may need to resize both of them together so that they sit properly below the crown. To do this, Ctrl+click (⌘+click on the Mac) both layers in the Layers palette, then press Ctrl+T (⌘+T on the Mac) and resize the layers appropriately.

7. **Create a separator bar between the logo and the menu options.** To do this, click the Shape Tool icon in the Toolbox, make sure Shape Layers is selected in the options bar, and click the Line Tool icon, also in the options bar. Click the downward-pointing arrow to the right of the shape tool icons in the options bar to display the Arrowheads palette, and make sure both the start and end arrowheads are turned off. Set the Weight to 1 pixel, pick an appropriate color — in this example, the same color as the border around the square is used — and drag in the document window to create the line. Hold down Shift as you drag to keep the line to the horizontal. If you find you need to resize your line after you create it, simply press Ctrl+T (⌘+T on the Mac) to activate the Free Transform command, and drag the left and right resize handles until the line is the right width.

The logo and menu are finished. You can see the whole kit and caboodle in Figure 14.16.

FIGURE 14.16

The final square box, with the logo, company name, separator bar, and menu all in place

Laying out the rest of the page

The page header area is now complete, so move on to the rest of the page. You're going to create a right-hand column for sidebar text, and then add the main text area and a page footer.

Adding the right column

For the right-hand column, start by creating a box for the text. Click the Shape Tool icon the Toolbox, then click the Rectangle Tool icon in the options bar. Next, choose a color for the rectangle by clicking the Color box in the options bar. The same green as the lighter color stop from the menu background gradient is used in this example to keep the look consistent. Using the guides you created earlier, position the cursor at the top-left corner of the rectangle area, and drag downward and to the right, as shown in Figure 14.17. Release the mouse button to create the rectangle shape layer.

 Enable snapping to guides (View ⇨ Snap To ⇨ Guides) to help accurately position your page elements.

FIGURE 14.17

Using the Rectangle tool to create a box for the right column

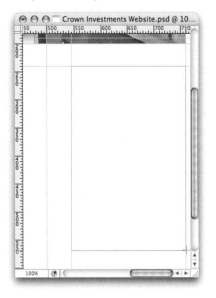

Homepages of Web sites tend to have a few promotional items, flagging up specific content deeper within the site. Add two promo items within the sidebar box. Use Arial for the text, a ubiquitous system font that's safe to render using markup within the page. It's a sans serif font, which makes

for easier on-screen reading than serif fonts such as Times. So select the Type tool in the Toolbox, and choose Arial for the Font Family option in the options bar. Set the font size to 11 points, and choose white for the text color by clicking the Color box in the options bar.

You're looking to create a paragraph of text here, so drag out a paragraph bounding box rather than simply clicking in the document window. Now you can copy and paste (or type) the text, and Photoshop flows the text inside the bounding box. When you finish, press Ctrl+Enter (⌘+Return on the Mac) to commit your edits.

CROSS-REF Find out more about point text and paragraph text in Chapter 4.

TIP The Lorem Ipsum Latin text, which is used in the example, is a standard text used throughout the publishing industry for laying out designs that haven't yet had the final text or "copy" written. This text serves a dual purpose. First, the designers can start to lay out pages before all the copy is created, making for faster, earlier development of the design. Second, it means that when clients see the designs, they're not worrying about the copy; it becomes almost invisible, allowing clients to concentrate on the design itself.

Create a More button that visitors to the site can click to get to the page you're promoting. You can easily create buttons in Photoshop using a combination of a shape layer and some layer effects. Follow these steps to create the button:

1. **Select the Rounded Rectangle tool.** Click the Shape Tool icon in the Toolbox and select the Rounded Rectangle tool in the options bar.

2. **Set options for the button shape.** Further along the options bar, there's a Radius option for setting the corner radius of the rectangle. As you might expect, this gives you control of how rounded the corners will be. For these purposes, 10 pixels is a good number, so type **10px** in the Radius box. You want to create a shape layer, not a path, so make sure the Shape Layers option is selected in the options bar. Finally, choose a color for the shape — for example, a dark green — by clicking the Color box in the options bar.

3. **Draw the button.** Positioning the cursor in the right column, drag out the rectangle until it looks like a button shape, then release the mouse button to create the shape layer.

Great, that's the basic shape, but you want to add a little depth and "buttony-ness" to it. To do this, add a drop shadow and a gradient to the button.

Making sure the button layer is active in the Layers palette, click the Add a Layer Style (the *fx*) button at the bottom of the palette and select Drop Shadow from the pop-up menu. The Layer Style dialog box appears with the Drop Shadow effect active.

You want the drop shadow to be pretty subtle, so try reducing the default opacity a little — down to, say, 60 percent — then set Distance to zero and Size to 4 pixels. You can leave everything else as it is, but feel free to experiment. Provided the Preview option is selected in the dialog box, you can see how your shadow looks in the document window. When you're happy, keep the Layer Style dialog box open.

The drop shadow hasn't really given the button much in the way of depth, so add something more tactile — a simple gradient, which should make the button look more three-dimensional. Follow these steps to add the gradient:

1. **Click the Gradient Overlay option in the Layer Style dialog box.** The effect should automatically turn on when you do this — the check box next to the effect becomes checked — but if it doesn't, click the check box to select it.

2. **Click the gradient inside the Gradient box.** This displays the Gradient Editor dialog box.

3. **Click the left-hand color stop, then click anywhere in the right-hand column box in the document window.** You can see this in action in Figure 14.18. This sets the left-hand stop to be the same color as the box background.

4. **Click the right-hand color stop, then click the Color box at the bottom of the dialog box to display the Select Stop Color dialog box, and choose a darker shade of the same color.** The easiest way to do this is first to click that box background in the document window again to get the right hue, then click the B (Brightness) option in the Color Picker. You can then click and drag the vertical brightness slider down slightly to produce a darker shade of the same hue.

FIGURE 14.18

Choosing the left color stop color using the Select Stop Color dialog box and clicking the right column box in the document window

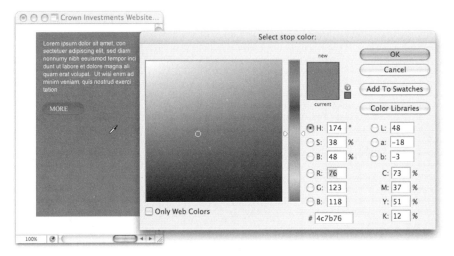

Click OK to close the Select Stop Color dialog box; then click OK again to close the Gradient Editor. Finally, click OK in the Layer Style dialog box. You should now be the proud owner of a nice tactile button.

TIP Photoshop comes with a wide range of preset button styles if you don't fancy rolling your own. From the Styles palette (accessible by choosing Window ➪ Styles), click the Palette Menu button at the top right of the palette, and choose Web Styles from the menu. You can choose to append the presets to the existing list or replace your current style presets altogether. To add one of these styles to a button, simply create the basic shape of your button as a shape layer, and then click the desired style in the palette.

We now need to add a text label to the button. First, make sure the vector mask of the button shape layer isn't active, or you'll end up with text flowing either on the edge of, or inside, the vector mask. The vector mask is active if its thumbnail in the Layers palette has a border around it. If so, click the thumbnail to turn off the border.

Now select the Type tool, and choose your favorite font using the Font Family option in the options bar. Times New Roman is used here for consistency with the company name text. Choose an appropriate size — 12 points should be about right — and choose a color for the font by clicking the Color box in the options bar. White is used here.

Now click inside the button in the document window and type **MORE**, then press Ctrl+Enter (⌘+Return on the Mac). You may need to reposition the text using the Move tool or by nudging with the arrow keys to center it on the button.

You want two of these text paragraphs with buttons, so you need to duplicate those layers and move the duplicates down to the bottom of the sidebar box. Ctrl+click (⌘+click on the Mac) the Lorem Ipsum text layer, the button shape layer, and the MORE type layer in the Layers palette to select them all, then press Ctrl+G (⌘+G on the Mac) to group them. You can now duplicate this group by clicking it in the Layers palette and dragging it down to the New icon at the bottom of the palette. Finally, with this duplicate group still selected, use Ctrl (Win) or ⌘ (Mac) and the Down key to move the group down below the original text and button in the document window.

TIP To move the duplicate group downwards a bit quicker, hold down Shift as well. This moves the group in steps of 10 pixels at a time.

You can see the completed sidebar, complete with promo text and buttons, in Figure 14.19.

Adding the main text area and footer

For the main text area, you only have to add a couple of elements: the main page heading and the main body of text (the "body copy"). To create the heading, take a cue from the logo and use Times New Roman again, all in capitals, with a size of 18 points. Use the same color as the background of the right-hand sidebar box.

Select the Type tool; then set the font and size using the options in the options bar. For the color, you can click the Color box in the options bar to open the Color Picker, then click the background of the sidebar box in the document window to set the color.

FIGURE 14.19

The final sidebar with promotional areas

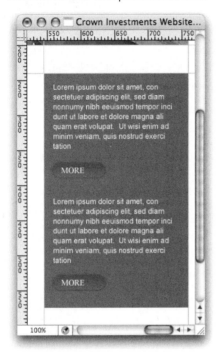

TIP When choosing colors for elements in your design, it's a good plan to reuse colors wherever possible. This helps to give a consistent feel to the design.

Position the cursor at the junction of the relevant guides in the document window, as shown in Figure 14.20, then click and type the heading: **WELCOME**. Press Ctrl+Enter (⌘+Return on the Mac) then, if the heading's not quite in the correct place, use the Move tool to shift it.

Set the body copy as paragraph text, rather than point text. Create the body copy with the following steps:

1. **Create the bounding box.** With the Type tool still selected, drag out a bounding box to use the full width of the left-hand area, using the guides to help, allowing enough vertical space for a couple of paragraphs. Figure 14.20 shows the body copy in place, so you can get an idea of the width to use.

2. **Set text options.** Choose your font, size, and color options in the options bar. In this example, Arial is used for the body copy (as it's easy to read on-screen), with a size of 11 points and colored a very dark gray (RGB values of 51, 51, 51), which gives a slightly softer feel than pure black.

3. **Create the text.** Paste or type your body copy text into the bounding box.

This is a good time to think about your link colors. All sites use links to move from one page to the next, and these links are usually a different color to the surrounding text and generally underlined. To make the links obvious to the visitor, try a burnt orange color (RGB values of 193, 105, 2). This color is complementary to, but stands out from, the green used elsewhere. While still editing the type layer with the Type tool, highlight the words you want to indicate as links. Now you can click the Color box in the options bar to set the new color for your highlighted text, and click the Underline button in the Character palette to add the underline.

When you're happy with your body text, press Ctrl+Enter (⌘+Return on the Mac) to commit your edits.

FIGURE 14.20

Adding the main text area and page heading. Here, the link color is edited.

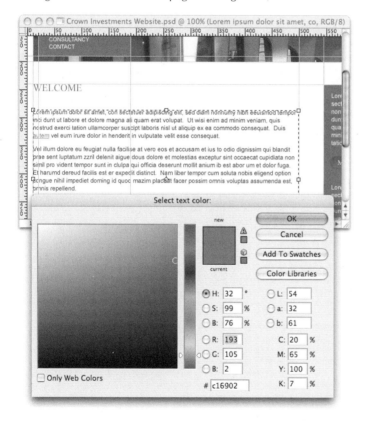

The footer generally houses links that you might not necessarily want at the main menu level. In this example you include links for a disclaimer and privacy policy, and a secondary link for the contact pages. Because they're links, use the link style you just created, separated by vertical separator bars.

A good way to reuse the link style is to double-click the body text layer's T thumbnail to edit the text, then select the link text within the body text and choose Edit ⇨ Copy. Then press Esc to stop editing that type layer, click toward the bottom of the page in the document window to start creating a new type layer, and choose Edit ⇨ Paste.

Now you can type over your pasted link text with the relevant footer link text, shown in Figure 14.21. To create the separator bars, type a space followed by the | (vertical bar) symbol, followed by another space. After you type your whole line, select each separator bar, along with the space on either side, and set the color to a nonlink color by clicking the Color box in the options bar — in the example, the same color as the sidebar background is used. You also want to turn off the underlines for those selected characters by deselecting the Underline option in the Character palette.

When you finish, commit your changes to exit the Type tool's edit mode.

Last, use the Line tool to create a single pixel line across the page in a light gray, just above the footer, to show that the footer is separate from the rest of the page. Click the Shape Tool icon in the Toolbox, and select the Line tool in the options bar. As before, make sure arrowheads are turned off and that the Shape Layers option is selected. Choose a light gray color — RGB 205, 205, 205 is used here — and drag the line out horizontally across the page. To make sure it's straight, hold down Shift on the keyboard as you drag.

> **TIP**   If, after you create the line, you decide it's the wrong color, double-click its thumbnail in the Layers palette to display the Color Picker, and choose your new color.

Organizing the layers

The layout is now complete, but your document probably contains layers with names like Layer 1, Layer 45, and so on. This is likely to prove confusing to anyone who needs to work with your document — including yourself! You're going to rename the layers and use layer groups to organize the layers in the Layers palette, so that it's easy to find the layer you need later on.

The first thing to do is to rename all those layers. You might well already have forgotten which layer is which, so a good trick is to select the Move tool and use it to select the layers. In the options bar, select the Auto-Select option if it's not already selected, and from the menu next to Auto-Select, choose Layer. When you click an element in the document window, Photoshop selects the relevant layer, and the layer is highlighted in the Layers palette. You can then rename the layer by double-clicking the layer's name in the Layers palette and typing a new, more useful name; for example, **Menu background** for the box that the logo and menu sit in. Repeat this procedure for all the layers in the document.

This is a good start, but the Layers palette will be much easier to navigate if all the layers are organized within their own groups. A group is like a folder containing layers, and it's easy to group elements together in this way.

FIGURE 14.21

FIGURE 14.21

The complete layout, including header elements, main body text, a sidebar, and a page footer

Look at the menu and logo area first. Select all the layers concerned with the menu and the logo by Ctrl+clicking (⌘+clicking on the Mac) each layer in the Layers palette. Press Ctrl+G (⌘+G on the Mac) to group the layers together. Photoshop creates a new group, which shows up as a folder icon in the Layers palette, and gives it a default name, such as Group 1. Double-click the group's name in the Layers palette and rename the group to something descriptive, such as **Logo and Menu**.

Repeat this process for all the other elements of the design, like the right-hand column, the main photo, the body copy, and the footer. After you do that, it's a good idea to nest groups within other groups to keep things even more organized; for example, you could put the two groups representing the promo areas in the right column into a parent group called **Right column**. When you finish, your Layers palette should look something like Figure 14.22.

FIGURE 14.22

A beautifully organized Layers palette, with all layers named and sensibly grouped together

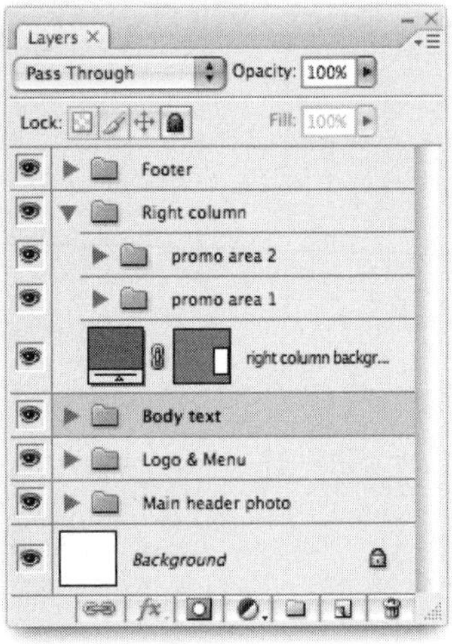

Export strategies

Now that you've created your layout, and you have an elegantly ordered PSD file, what's next? At the start of the example, it was mentioned that not all the elements in the Photoshop file will be used in the final site build, as some parts of the page will be created using HTML. This section examines which elements get exported, what image formats they should be exported to, and how to go about it.

Deciding which elements to export

You'll probably be in one of two situations at this point. Either you'll be doing all the site-building work yourself, or you'll be passing the designs across to a developer who will be doing the site build instead. In the first case, you might well have a good idea about what you want to export, but in the second case, it's worth asking the developer how he or she will be building the site before you start exporting elements. In fact, many developers prefer to do their own exports, so you can just send them the PSD file. Here, it is assumed that you're building the site yourself.

The elements that you need to export as images include the following:

- Background photo image in the header
- Menu background box
- Logo
- Buttons

That's it; everything else will be rendered in markup. We're not going to touch on the markup side in this book, but we will look at each of these image elements and discuss why they should be images in the Web page:

- **Photo:** This is an obvious choice. You can't render the photo as markup, so it has to be an image.

- **Menu background:** This square has elements that are tricky to render using HTML, namely that gradient overlay you applied as a layer style. It's very tricky to render a gradient in markup.

- **Logo:** It's rare that a company wants to compromise its brand by creating the logo in HTML. Although theoretically you could just export the crown and create the text elements in HTML, it's not going to render as nicely as an image. The crown itself simply has to be an image.

- **Buttons:** You can create fairly nice buttons in HTML and CSS, but to retain your button design, with its gradient and drop shadow, these need to be images.

Slicing and exporting

The way Photoshop handles exporting elements of an image is to use *slices*. These are rectangular overlays that sit on top of the document and look a little like extra guides. They have a number in the top left of each corner for identification purposes. When you create a slice and export it, only that section of the image is exported.

Go ahead and export a single element to start with: a button from the right column. First, to make sure you can see your slices, choose View ➪ Show, and make sure there's a check mark next to the Slices option in the submenu. If there isn't, click the Slices option to select it.

Follow these steps to create and export the button slice:

1. **Select one of the button layers.** It doesn't matter which one. To do this, click the button layer in the Layers palette.

2. **Create the slice.** To do this, choose Layer ➪ New Layer Based Slice. This creates a new slice for your button, shown as a brown line around the button area. Although the button has a shadow around it, layer-based slices allow for this, making the slice as big as it needs to be to encompass the shadow.

> **NOTE** As you create the button slice in the document window, Photoshop automatically creates extra slices around it, known as *auto slices*. If you are exporting the whole page as slices, you bring these auto slices into play, but in this case, you can safely ignore them. Make sure you select Selected Slices in the Save Optimized As dialog box in Step 6; otherwise, these auto slices will be exported, too; you'd then have to weed out the automatically-generated image files manually.

3. **Name the slice.** Select the Slice Select tool from the Toolbox. The Slice Select tool's mouse cursor looks like a knife symbol with a small arrow next to it. Double-click the button slice in the document window to display the Slice Options dialog box. Type **button** into the Name field, and click OK.

When you name your slices, make sure that the names contain only lowercase letters, numbers, underscores, and hyphens. This is a good industry practice, and it avoids any potential confusion over the file names.

4. **Choose File ➪ Save for Web & Devices.** This displays a large dialog box showing the whole layout with your slice highlighted. (If it isn't highlighted, click the Slice Select Tool icon at the top left of the dialog box, or press K, then click the slice to select it.)

5. **Export the slice as a GIF image.** Make sure that the options on the right side of the dialog box are set to save the slice as a GIF image. You can keep the default settings for most of the options here, but you can reduce the number of colors used to 64 to reduce the image's file size without noticeably sacrificing quality. Click Save. This displays the Save Optimized As dialog box that allows you to choose where to save the slice image.

When saving image files for the Web, you're looking for the smallest file size you can get to reduce download times. In the bottom left of the Save for Web & Devices dialog box, you can see the file size of the exported image, measured in kilobytes. If you force Photoshop to reduce the number of colors in the final image, you can make the file size smaller. However, this can come at the expense of the quality of the final image, so use your eye to choose an acceptable compromise. GIF files can contain up to a maximum of 256 colors. Your button, according to the Color Table in the dialog box, contains 205 colors. If the number of colors is reduced below 64, you start to see issues with the anti-aliasing around the text, and graininess in the gradient and shadow areas.

The export settings are saved on a per-slice basis, so you can have different settings for each slice.

6. **Save the slice.** Select Images Only for the Format option at the bottom of the dialog box, leave the Settings option set to Default Settings, and choose Selected Slices for the Slices option. Choose a folder to save the slice to, and click Save. Photoshop automatically creates a folder called "images", and places the slice image in that. (Don't worry about giving the file a name using the Save As box at the top of the dialog, as Photoshop automatically uses the name of the slice that you set in Step 3 for the file name.)

If you'd rather Photoshop use a different folder name than "images", choose Other for the Settings option, then, in the Output Settings dialog box that appears, choose the Saving Files option from the second menu from the top. You can now type a different folder name in the Put Images In Folder box near the bottom of the dialog box. Alternatively, deselect that option to persuade Photoshop to put the images directly in the folder you chose in Step 6, without creating a subfolder.

Great — that's your first image exported. Because images can be reused within a Web page, we don't need to export the second button.

There are still several images to export, but the procedure is basically the same for all of them.

Look at the header image and menu areas. In the final build, the header will be made up of three elements on the Web page:

- Photo and menu background
- Logo
- Menu

Only two of these will be images: the photo and menu background square, which you'll export as a single background image, and the logo. The menu options themselves are created when building the site in HTML.

Theoretically, you could export the logo as part of the photo and menu background image. However, there are a few reasons why it's good to have the logo as a separate image. First, the logo in a Web page often serves as a link back to the homepage. It's easier to make the logo a link if it's a separate image. Second, it makes it easier for the Web developer to add alternate text for the logo, so that people using text-only browsers can still recognize that it's a logo image. Finally, while the background image is well suited to the JPEG format, the logo is best exported as a GIF file. By keeping the two images separate, you can use the best image format for each image.

The first header element to export is the photo and menu background. Create a slice in the same way as you did earlier: Select the photo area clipping mask's base layer in the Layers palette, and choose Layer ➪ New Layer Based Slice. If you export this as it is, you'd get the logo and the menu options, too, so hide those layers by clicking their eye icons in the Layers palette, leaving just the photo and the square. Figure 14.23 shows the header image ready to export. Double-click the slice using the Slice Select tool, and give it a sensible name — for example, **header_background**.

FIGURE 14.23

The header photo and menu background, without the logo or menu elements, ready to export

As before, choose File ➪ Save for Web & Devices to display the Save for Web & Devices dialog box. This time, you want the exported image to be a JPEG file, not a GIF. GIF files are generally used for areas containing flat color; JPEGs are better for more continuous-tone elements such as photos.

Click the photo slice in the Save for Web & Devices dialog box to select it — you'll notice the focus switch from the button slice to the photo slice. Make sure JPEG is selected for the File Format option on the right of the dialog box, — and use the Quality slider to balance the quality of the image against the file size. A setting of around 60 gives a decent trade-off between the two in this case. Click Save to move on to the Save Optimized As dialog box.

Once again, make sure that you have Images Only and Selected Slices set in the options at the bottom of the dialog box, and click Save. As before, Photoshop bases the file's name on the name you gave the slice earlier. It also looks for the "images" folder that it created earlier, and adds the new image to that; you don't have to select the "images" folder itself.

The last image you need to export is the logo itself, along with the separator bar. Make the logo layers visible by clicking their eye icons in the Layers palette. You're going to use a slightly different approach here. You don't have a single layer to create a slice from, so create the slice by hand.

 If you group all your logo layers into a Logo group in the Layers palette, you only need to click the group's eye icon to toggle the visibility of all the layers in the group.

CAUTION If you try to create the slice by selecting all the layers in the logo and choosing Layer ➪ New Layer Based Slice, Photoshop creates individual slices for each layer, which isn't what you're looking for here.

Follow these steps to create your slice:

1. **Select the Slice tool from the Toolbox, or press Shift+K until the Slice tool is selected.** The Slice tool's mouse cursor looks like a knife symbol without a small arrow next to it.

2. **Choose View ➪ Snap To, and make sure Layers is enabled in the menu.** This forces Photoshop to draw the lines of the new slice so that they match the edges of the layer transparency, so long as you're roughly accurate in your cursor positioning. Also make sure Snap is turned on (View ➪ Snap) for this to work.

3. **Draw the slice.** Position your cursor at the top left of the logo area (not at the top left of the crown itself — GIF files must be rectangular, and you need to allow for the company name text), and click and drag toward the bottom right of the logo area, including the separator bar. You've now created your slice.

4. **Name your slice.** As usual, double-click the new slice, using either the Slice tool or Slice Select tool, and give the slice a sensible name, for example **crown_logo**.

5. **Choose File ➪ Save for Web & Devices.** As before, make sure the new slice is selected in the Save for Web & Devices dialog box. Save this one as a GIF, but this time you want to keep the number of colors as high as you can. This is because the background of the logo is part of the gradient of the menu's background. If you force the number of colors down below 211 — the number of colors in the slice, according to the Color Table in the dialog box — you start to see banding in the final image.

6. **Save the logo image.** Click Save and save the logo to the previously created images folder on your hard drive, making sure to choose Images Only from the Format menu and Selected Slices from the Slices menu in the Save Optimized As dialog box.

Checking the files on your hard drive, you should now have three image files, looking something like Figure 14.24. These image files are now ready to be included in your finished Web page.

The three exported image files, reopened in Photoshop

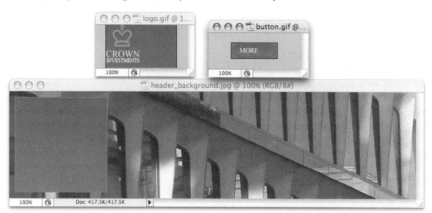

Creating a Montage

In this example, you're going to design a montage. Montages can appear to be very magical when you first see them, but they're actually simple to master from a technical point of view. You can see an example of a montage in Figure 14.25; it's basically several images merged together into a pleasing whole. The techniques used here are essentially the same, whether you're creating a simple Web site header, a composite family snapshot, or a movie poster. You'll be using layer masks and blending modes extensively in this example.

CROSS-REF You can find more information on layer masks in Chapter 9, and on blending modes in Chapter 7.

As the saying goes, a journey of a thousand miles starts with a single step. In this case, the first step is to identify which images you want to put together in a montage. This example uses a musical theme. This might provide the bedrock for a music store brochure, for example.

Figure 14.26 shows the basic photos that you'll use for the montage. The first thing to do is decide which of these photos will make a good background image for the others to merge with. This image will provide your canvas for the montage, so it needs a fair amount of space to provide room for the other images. In this case, the image of the record deck is a good choice. In a commercial environment, there's a good chance that the client would ask you to prioritize the images according to a commercial imperative. For example, if your mythical store makes more money selling guitars than DJ accessories, it likely will push that side more because that's the core business.

FIGURE 14.25

A montage is several images merged into one. The idea is not necessarily to create a realistic image, but to merge the source images in a pleasing manner.

FIGURE 14.26

The photos that you'll use to create your example montage. Clockwise from the top left: a record deck, a microphone, a guitar, and a keyboard.

Adding the first two photos

Start with the basic photo of the record deck, and open it in Photoshop. You can start building the montage right on top of this photo; there's no need to create a new document. Next, open the acoustic guitar image — you'll combine this image with the record deck first.

> **TIP** When working with photos, make sure you always work on a copy of the image, not your one and only file!

You need to get the two images into the same document, so Shift+drag the Background layer from the guitar photo into the record deck photo. The guitar is now a new layer above the record deck. The photos in this case are the same size, so adding Shift to the drag operation means that the guitar photo sits properly centered in the record deck document. It's a good idea to start naming your layers at this point; double-click each layer's default name and rename the layers to nice obvious names, such as **record deck** and **acoustic guitar**.

Using a layer mask to blend the photos

Now that the two photos are in a document, what's next? It doesn't look much like a montage right now, but now you can use a layer mask to remove parts of the guitar layer and reveal the record deck below. To do this, follow these steps:

1. **Create the layer mask.** You want to see mostly the record deck, so select the guitar layer and choose Layer ➪ Layer Mask ➪ Hide All. This adds a new, completely opaque layer mask to the guitar layer. Your guitar appears to vanish, but don't panic!

2. **Choose a brush.** Select the Brush tool in the Toolbox. You want a fairly large brush size, so click the Brush option in the options bar and set the Master Diameter setting between 400 and 600 pixels. Make sure your foreground color is white.

3. **Paint on the mask.** Now comes the fun part — you'll start to bring the guitar back. Select the guitar's layer mask by clicking the mask thumbnail in the Layers palette. You can now start to "paint in" the guitar in the document window. You're after the strings of the guitar, as it's the most dynamic element of the photo. As you paint, the guitar is revealed over the top of the record deck. Because you used a big, soft brush, the edges of the guitar layer are feathered, which gives a pleasingly gentle effect that you can see in Figure 14.27.

> **TIP** A quick way to make the foreground color white is to first make sure the layer mask is selected, then press D to revert to the default colors. The default colors when working with masks in Photoshop are a white foreground and a black background — the opposite of the standard defaults.

Remember, you're not really erasing any of the guitar layer, merely masking it — no part of any image is being deleted. That's great news if you make a mistake or want to try another approach. Just press X to flip the foreground and background colors, or switch to the Eraser tool, and you can start to paint the guitar out again.

FIGURE 14.27

Gradually revealing the guitar layer by painting in white on its layer mask

It can be useful to change brush sizes as you work with the mask. For example, in this case you might want a greater level of "softness" on the strings toward the right-hand side of the guitar. To achieve this, pick a larger brush size, with the hardness still set to the minimum to keep the soft edge.

TIP While the process you're using here is nondestructive, there's a good chance that you'll want to have a few goes at revealing the guitar and keep the results for comparison. To do this, copy the guitar layer, turn off the visibility of the original layer by clicking its eye icon, and have another go! You can do this as many times as you want, and then compare the different layers and pick the best one.

If you decide that you've utterly fluffed a mask and want to start again, you can delete just the layer mask from the layer at any time by dragging the layer mask thumbnail to the Trash icon at the bottom of the Layers palette. Then just add a new layer mask to the layer as before. You can also simply fill the layer mask with either pure black (to hide everything) or white (to reveal everything) to effectively reset the mask.

Using blending modes to add depth

You've successfully used a mask to give your guitar a nice soft edge and reveal the record deck beneath, but it could still do with a little something to merge the two together and bring depth to the image. It'd be great if the record deck could show through the guitar slightly.

You could simply reduce the opacity of the guitar layer, but it doesn't really have the desired effect in this case. Instead, use blending modes to bring a real sense of the layers merging. Which blending mode you choose depends on the effect you're looking for. For example, using Color Dodge achieves a contrasty, edgy feel. That's not necessarily right for your client, so you need something softer. Screen is nice, and produces a good result, but Soft Light seems to provide the right mix of mood and softness. You can see these various effects in Figure 14.28.

FIGURE 14.28

Experimenting with different blending modes on the guitar layer. Clockwise from top left: Opacity set to 65 percent, and Opacity at 100 percent with the Color Dodge, Screen, and Soft Light blending modes.

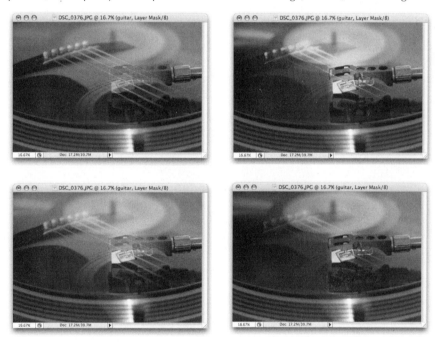

Composition of the montage

At the moment, the montage simply stacks up photos on top of each other, but, of course, you don't have to stick with that approach. You should be looking to create a pleasing composition of the multiple images you're using, and you can achieve this by manipulating the position and size of each element.

In the example, the strings of the guitar overlay the needle of the record deck, which is the focal point of the base image. It's not ideal, but by using the Move tool to resize and reposition the guitar layer you can set it off to the left of the needle, leaving some room for the needle to breathe in the composition. Select the Move tool in the Toolbox, and start dragging the guitar layer around in the document window. Select the Show Transform Controls option to display resize handles, allowing you to resize the layer as well if you want. Alternatively, simply press Ctrl+T (⌘+T on the Mac) to enter the Free Transform command, where you can move and resize the image to your heart's content.

> **TIP** It's a good idea to take a copy of the layer before you do this in case you want the full-size guitar back at some point.

As you move an image around, you might find that you need to rethink how the blending modes and masks are applied. Here, when moving the guitar to the left, the Soft Light blending mode makes it almost disappear, so you can switch it to Screen to bring it back a little, as shown in Figure 14.29.

FIGURE 14.29

The repositioned guitar with Soft Light blending mode (left) and Screen blending mode (right) applied

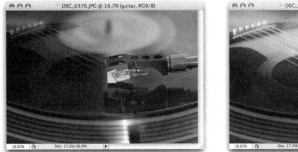 

There's no real right and wrong for this kind of positioning — it's just whatever seems most pleasing or fits the project best — so feel free to experiment and see what works best for you! As you become more confident with these techniques, you'll likely start to roll all the steps together, so the composition will be created as you mask, and choose blending modes for, each image.

Adding more images

The montage is okay with just the record deck and guitar, but try adding some more images to the piece. Looking at the source photos, you have a microphone and a keyboard image still to add.

Go ahead and drag in the microphone image as you did previously with the guitar. Open the microphone image file and drag its Background layer on top of the other layers in the montage document. Now mask off the edges of the microphone. This time, you want to start with all the microphone showing, so add a layer mask by choosing Layer ➪ Layer Mask ➪ Reveal All. Choose a big, soft brush of around 850 pixels in size and minimum hardness. Make sure the foreground color is black and start painting around the edges, allowing the layers beneath to show through.

Don't be afraid to let some nonessential elements remain. In this example, you could leave some of the mounting for the microphone to provide context. Again, try experimenting with a variety of brush sizes and levels of hardness to achieve your desired effect.

When the mask is the way you want it, start positioning and experimenting with blending modes again. In Figure 14.30, the microphone is positioned at the edge of the page, with a Soft Light blending mode and 85 percent opacity, to let it settle into the base image. It's almost textural in effect, but that's okay — there's more to come!

FIGURE 14.30

The microphone layer is positioned off the edge of the document window, with a Soft Light blending mode applied. Its opacity is reduced to 85 percent.

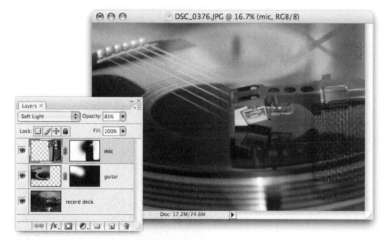

The last image to add is the keyboard. There's an obvious gap for this in the bottom left of the montage, and the keyboard photo is helpfully taken in such a way as to provide a nice angle for that. This is one of those times where you can start thinking compositionally quite early on, so drag the photo into the montage, place it above the other layers in the document, and position it at the bottom left of the image using the Move tool. Add a layer mask by choosing Layer ➪ Layer Mask ➪ Reveal All, and start painting out the bulk of the photo, leaving only the keyboard. Apply a Soft Light blending mode to the keyboard layer, and reduce its opacity to around 80 percent.

Looking again at the piece from a compositional point of view, the angle of the keyboard doesn't match the angle of the guitar strings, so you might want to use the Free Transform command to rotate the keyboard layer to match the angles of the guitar.

The final montage, shown in Figure 14.31, now has all photos in place.

FIGURE 14.31

The final montage. The guitar, microphone, and keyboard layers surround the record deck, merging nicely with it thanks to the applied blending modes.

Producing an alternative version

That's the last image to go into the montage, and it looks good. Because all the layers are completely intact, however, it's easy to experiment and find different compositions by repositioning and remasking the layers. You can either save a new version of your document by choosing File ➪ Save As, or you can just group all the current layers together using a layer group, which you can then duplicate. This last technique is great for keeping multiple revisions within one document, but the file quickly becomes very large.

Maybe your fictional store sells more microphones than record decks and wants to emphasize that fact. To appease it, create a version that uses the original guitar photo as the background for the montage and places the microphone front and center. (This new version uses only the mic and guitar images.)

You can see a first attempt on the left in Figure 14.32. In this version, the microphone is repositioned and its blending mode changed to Normal, with a 100 percent opacity setting. This creates a more solid look than before.

However, as you can see, the microphone's mask needs some extra tweaking. Quite a lot was lost from the edges of the microphone during the original masking process, and even changing to 100 percent opacity and Normal blending mode doesn't restore as much as you'd like. In this scenario, you want more of a traditional cutout effect for the microphone. Luckily, all your edits to the mask are nondestructive, so go to work with the black and white brushes again and bring back some of the detail in the edges. After this process, you should have something like the second image in Figure 14.32.

FIGURE 14.32

Creating an alternative version with just microphone and guitar. Here you see the version with the original microphone layer (left) and the mic layer with a reworked mask (right).

Adding a shadow

Let's add some depth to the microphone layer by applying a drop shadow, which you can achieve using a layer effect. One of the great features of layer effects is that they apply to the transparency created by the mask, rather than to the original layer's transparency. This means that if you apply a drop shadow to the microphone layer, Photoshop applies the shadow to just the microphone.

> **TIP** You can mask both a layer's pixels and its effects with a layer mask if you want. To do this, select the Layer Mask Hides Effects option in the Layer Style dialog. More on this feature in Chapter 7.

Go ahead and add the drop shadow by following these steps:

1. **Hide other layers in the document.** It can be easier to add the shadow with all other layers hidden, so you can see exactly how the shadow is working. Alt+click (Option+click on the Mac) the mic layer's eye icon in the Layers palette to hide the other layers.

2. **Add the Drop Shadow effect.** With the mic layer selected, click the Add a Layer Style button at the bottom of the layers palette. Choose Drop Shadow from the pop-up menu; the Layer Style dialog box appears with the Drop Shadow effect selected and enabled.

3. **Set options for the drop shadow.** You want a nice wide, even shadow for the mic, so keep the defaults for Blend Mode, Opacity and Angle, and change Distance to zero, Spread to around 6 percent, and Size to a healthy 130 pixels. (Note that if you're working on a lower-resolution image, this pixel value needs to be lower.) You should see a soft, wide drop shadow appear around the microphone in the document window. Click OK to save your changes and exit the dialog box.

Now make the other layers visible again so that you can see the drop shadow in context. You might well find that the drop shadow exposes some issues with your mask, which you'll notice as a fringe appearing around the microphone, especially when the guitar layer is visible. The shadow is exposing the edge of the mask in a way that you couldn't see very well before. Use a small, soft-edged brush to tidy up your mask. As you paint around the edges, the drop shadow changes to follow the new edge you create. You can see this technique in Figure 14.33.

FIGURE 14.33

The edge of the microphone with the drop shadow applied. You can see the microphone directly after the drop shadow is applied (left), and a new version after the edge of the mask is tidied up (right).

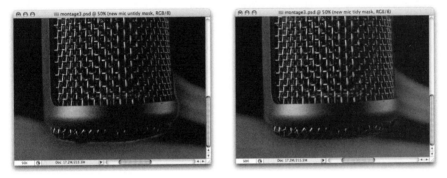

Improving the guitar layer

You want to really emphasize that microphone, so aim to push the guitar layer into the background somewhat. To do this, create a new layer and drag it below the guitar layer in the Layers palette. Choose Edit ➪ Fill, and select Black for the Use option to fill that layer with pure black. (Make sure Preserve Transparency is deselected in the Fill dialog box.) Selecting the guitar layer again, reduce its opacity to around 65 percent. This has the effect of allowing some of the black layer below to show through, pushing back the guitar layer.

The montage is looking better, but the effect on the guitar is a little dull. To remedy this, duplicate the guitar layer and change the blending mode of the uppermost copy to Overlay. This results in a little more contrast and saturation, which gives more punch to the guitar layer. You might also like to drop that layer's opacity to around 45 percent to tame the effect a touch.

TIP You can also do the previous trick by using a "neutral" adjustment layer above the guitar layer. Create a Levels layer above the guitar layer and click OK to close the Levels dialog box, then set the Levels blending mode to Overlay. This saves you some hard drive space and also means you don't have to reduplicate the guitar layer should you edit it in the future.

Great! The new version of the montage is now complete. You can see the end result in Figure 14.34. It's less of a traditional montage than the earlier version.

In the final version of the alternative montage, note how the guitar layer has been knocked back, leaving the microphone front and center.

Using the montage to create a brochure

So far, you've created what amounts to a backdrop for something else — in this case, a cover for a music store brochure — but how might this kind of work be used in context? Imagine that you're going to use the montage to create such a brochure cover for "Hank's Music Shack," which is having a sale.

Here you'll be treating the montage simply as a photo. When adding other elements, it's a good idea to save a copy of the original piece and delete unwanted layers, keeping only the layers you need — in this case, the black background layer, the guitar, and the microphone.

NOTE In the real world, there's a good chance that the next stage would actually be created in a page layout application like Adobe's own InDesign or the industry standard QuarkXPress. In this example, everything is kept within Photoshop to illustrate some further points.

To create the brochure, follow these steps:

1. **Add a background for your text.** It'll be a simple rectangle on the right-hand side of the montage. In terms of color, use a brownish-orange that has a little more impact than the photo to bring the forthcoming text to life. Click the Shape Tool icon in the Toolbox, then select the Rectangle Tool option in the options bar. Make sure the Shape Layers option is selected, set the color using the Color box, and drag out a full-height rectangle from just to the left of the center of the image over to the right-hand edge. To make it sit with the imagery, drop the rectangle layer's opacity to 90 percent using the Opacity slider in the Layers palette.

2. **Reposition the microphone.** Your microphone is probably now being covered by the new rectangle; it would be better if the mic was farther off to the left. Select the microphone layer and use the Move tool to reposition it farther to the left of the image, balancing the composition.

3. **Add the logo.** Select the Type tool and, from either the options bar or the Character palette, select a font, size, and color — in the example, Impact at 72 points in white is used. It's big, it's bold, and most importantly, it's likely to already be on your computer! Click inside the brown rectangle in the document window, type the name of the store, and press Ctrl+Enter (⌘+Return on the Mac) to commit the type edit. To give the logo a little more pizzazz, try using the Rotate command to make the logo more jaunty. Select the layer, choose Edit ➪ Transform ➪ Rotate, and use the handles to rotate the type as you see fit.

4. **Add the main message.** Still using the Type tool, click in the brown rectangle again, choose a bright yellow color, and type your main message — here it's going to be **SALE!**. You're not going to beat around the bush here — you want that message big — so use the Scale command (Edit ➪ Transform ➪ Scale) to resize and reposition the type layer to fill the brown background rectangle. Last, set the layer's blending mode to Overlay to really beef up the message by adding depth and contrast to the text. At this point, the document probably looks something like Figure 14.35.

FIGURE 14.35

The message begins to take shape. The mic is repositioned, a background is added for the text, and a couple of text elements are introduced.

5. **Add an arrow to the image.** This will give people some impetus to open the brochure. Click the Shape Tool icon in the Toolbox, select the Custom Shape tool in the options bar, and choose one of the arrow shape presets via the Shape option, also in the options bar. Use the Eyedropper tool to set the foreground color to a bright yellow, taken from the SALE! layer, and drag the arrow out from the left-hand edge of the brown rectangle to the right edge.

6. **Reshape the arrow.** If you don't like the shape of the arrow, you can reshape it to make it fatter or thinner. To do this, select the arrow's shape layer, and use the Direct Selection tool to select the anchor points you want to move. To select more than one point at once, Shift+click each point. Once selected, you can move the points using the arrow keys — remember you can hold down Shift to move in increments of 10 pixels — or you can drag one of the points with the mouse to move all the selected points in tandem. Hold down Shift to constrain the movement to the horizontal or vertical.

7. **Add a message to the arrow.** Create a message on top of the arrow exhorting people to open the brochure. The full message will be "massive savings INSIDE!", but you'll split this into two type layers, allowing you to resize them individually. Select the Type tool and stick with the same font settings, but choose a darker yellow color than that used for the arrow. Make sure the arrow layer's vector mask isn't active — it shouldn't have a border around its thumbnail in the Layers palette — then click in the arrow in the document window and type **massive savings**. Commit your edit by pressing Ctrl+Enter (⌘+Return on the Mac), then repeat the process with the word **INSIDE!**. Now use the Free Transform tool to resize and rotate your two text layers so that they fit nicely inside the arrow and are rotated at the same angle as the logo.

> **TIP** Link or group the two type layers before rotating them. You can then rotate them as if they were a single layer.

8. **Add a drop shadow to the logo.** To bring the logo element off the page, apply a drop shadow via a layer effect. To do this, select the HANK'S MUSIC SHACK layer, then click the Add a Layer Style icon at the bottom of the Layers palette, and choose Drop Shadow. Usually, when you think of a drop shadow, it's elegant and soft, but in this case you want a hard drop shadow, much beloved of designers wanting a bold approach to a message. To achieve this hard-edged effect, make sure your Size setting is set to zero in the Layer Style dialog box. Experiment with the other Drop Shadow settings to get a result you like.

9. **Boost the montage with some adjustments.** The montage itself now looks a little dull in color, so add two adjustment layers above the montage layers to give it a little boost: a simple Brightness/Contrast layer, with each slider set at +20; and a Hue/Saturation layer with Saturation boosted by +20.s

> **TIP** If you use a version of Photoshop before CS3, you may want to try a Curves adjustment rather than Brightness/Contrast, as the Brightness/Contrast adjustment in older versions of Photoshop is, frankly, terrible.

Your brochure is now complete, and probably looks something like the one in Figure 14.36. It's not subtle, but people will read it!

FIGURE 14.36

The montage now forms a nice backdrop for our shouty, eye-grabbing brochure. But is it art?

In this example, you learned how to apply layer styles and blending modes to layers to create a montage. The skills used here can be applied to many different scenarios — for example, creating more natural-looking composite photos by adding extra people into a group shot. As a further exercise, look at the various stock images on the CD that comes with this book, and see what you can create by combining them.

Creating a Mixed-Media Piece

In the final example in this chapter, you'll use Photoshop's layers to help create a mixed-media piece. You'll combine photography, drawings, handwriting, and type to produce an illustration that brings something more organic back into the digital workflow. Using nondigital components in an image is a great way to add some randomness to an illustration, and the touch of a human hand is something people tend to respond to in a warm and open way.

You'll be looking at using adjustment layers, selecting colors within a layer, stacking up layers within a document, and some creative uses for the Type tool.

CROSS-REF For more information on adjustment layers, layer organization, and the Type tool, see Chapters 6, 2, and 4, respectively.

To design this piece, you'll create some elements directly within Photoshop, as well as use several component images from the CD-ROM, which you can see in Figure 14.37:

- A digital photo of London, England.

- A hand-drawn outlining of the photo. To create this, the photo was printed out and acetate placed over the printout. A felt-tip pen was used to trace the outlines of the buildings, and the result was scanned.

- Some hand-drawn text and doodles, also scanned.

FIGURE 14.37

The raw materials for your image: a photo of the London skyline, a scanned transparency of some tracing, and a scan of some doodles

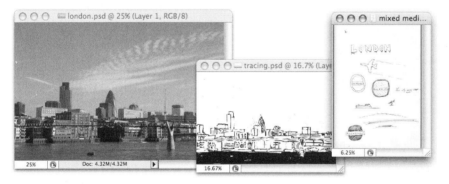

The final image is not destined to be a realistic representation of the London skyline, but rather an abstract interpretation of this classic scene. All the elements are brought together to create a modern illustrative piece that could be used for many different purposes; maybe as the backdrop for a poster or the header for a Web site. Imagine that it's a small flyer for a product launch in London, England.

Preparing the scanned media

The preparatory steps for all the drawn material are similar. Although the material is drawn on white paper, you actually want to remove the white areas in the final illustration, leaving only the drawings themselves on a transparent background.

ON the CD-ROM You'll find the pre-scanned example files on the CD. However, if you fancy having a go at creating and scanning your own drawings, scan them at around 300 dpi, and make sure the contrast is reasonably high so that you can separate the drawings from the background later in the process.

To prepare the scanned images for use in the illustration, follow these steps for each image:

1. **Open the image in Photoshop.** The image has a single Background layer because it's a nonlayered image.

2. **Convert the Background layer to a normal layer by double-clicking the Background layer in the Layers palette.** In the dialog box that appears, name the normal layer something memorable like **Drawings**. Why do this conversion? Well, you want to delete the white background areas of the image, so that when the images are combined, the photo will show through. You need to convert the Background layer to a normal layer to do this, because Background layers can't have transparent areas.

3. **Select the white areas.** Make sure the Drawings layer is selected, and choose Select ➪ Color Range. Choose Sampled Colors for the Select option; your cursor turns into an eyedropper icon. Click a white area in the document window. In the preview area of the dialog box, a preview of the selection you're creating appears. Use the Fuzziness slider to clean up the selection. Be sure that you don't select too much or too little of the white areas; this slider allows you to fine-tune the selection criteria.

4. **Delete the selected areas.** When you're happy with your selection, click OK and you'll be returned to the document window, with the "marching ants" showing your selection. Now just press Backspace (Delete on the Mac), and the white areas disappear, leaving only the inked areas against the transparency checkerboard. You can see how this should look in Figure 14.38.

FIGURE 14.38

The illustrative elements with the background removed

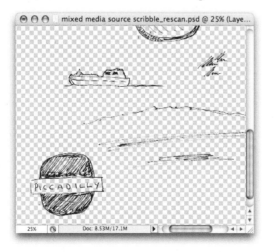

Your scanned drawings are now ready to import into the illustration.

Assembling the illustration

In the example, the London skyline photo is the starting point and background image. Open this skyline image in Photoshop, and also open the first illustrative element — the traced version of the photo.

Select the Background layer of the illustration in the Layers palette, and drag it over to the document window of the photo. You'll see the drawn element overlay the photo. There's a good chance that the drawings won't match the size of the photo, so use the Free Transform command (Edit ⇨ Free Transform) to position and resize the drawings to fit the lines of the photo.

When the lines of the drawing match those of the photo, you might notice that the edges of the lines in the drawing are somewhat ragged. This is because you still have some of the original white background color in there; the scratchier the original lines are, the more likely this is to happen. Luckily, there's a quick fix for this that also ties in neatly with the goals of the illustration as a whole. You're going to fill the opaque parts of the drawing layer with a flat color — in this case, white.

First make sure that the drawing layer has its transparency locked. To do this, select the layer in the Layers palette and click the Lock Transparent Pixels button near the top of the palette. Now make sure your background color is white, and press Ctrl+Backspace (⌘+Delete on the Mac) to fill the layer with the background color. You should see the lines in the drawing layer fill with white. Because you're filling with white based on the transparency of the layer, not the color, those ragged edges become completely filled and you have pure white lines. Figure 14.39 shows the effect.

FIGURE 14.39

The drawing layer overlays the photo, adding the first hand-illustrated element to the composition. The lines of the drawing have been filled with pure white. The overall effect is edgy and funky.

Creating the river and sky

Now turn to Photoshop itself to modify two further elements: the river and the sky. You'll be covering the photo with gradient-filled and flat color versions of these elements.

You use two different approaches here. The first, for the river, starts with "painting" the river. To do this, follow these steps:

1. **Create a layer for the painted areas.** Create a new normal layer above your drawn elements by clicking the New Layer icon in the Layers palette.

2. **Choose a brush and color.** Select the Brush tool in the Toolbox, select the Brush option in the options bar and select a large, hard-edged paintbrush. Choose a vibrant blue for your foreground color.

3. **Paint on the river.** Roughly paint onto the new layer on top of the river, creating a solid blue area for the river. You finish with what amounts to a blue blob, but the detailing is what is important here.

4. **Add some detail.** Now select a much smaller brush — around 2 pixels — but still with the hard edge. You're looking to roughen up the edge of the river as it comes to the buildings. Still working on the same layer as before, start to paint at the edges of the river. Use whatever technique you feel comfortable with. Be as ragged as you want! Avoid the temptation, though, to do the whole edge in one pass, with the mouse button down all the time. If you get most of the way and make an unacceptably loose stroke, you lose everything when you undo.

> **TIP** A great trick here is to remove elements of the river layer as well as adding to it. Select the Eraser tool, choose a fairly small brush — 2 pixels is fine — with a hard edge, and delete small parts of the river layer to create "holes". All these ragged edges enhance the feeling of the piece having been created by a human hand, which is the effect you're after. You could have drawn a very nice edge using the Pen tool and created a shape layer, but it would have been a little slick for these purposes. The nature of the paintbrush and eraser gives the piece that extra randomness that results in "happy accidents."

5. **Add a gradient fill to the layer.** Use a layer effect to achieve this. Click the Add a Layer Style icon at the bottom of the Layers palette and choose Gradient Overlay. In the dialog box that appears, leave the Blend Mode setting at Normal and Opacity at 100 percent. Click inside the Gradient option's gradient box to display the Gradient Editor dialog box. Choose colors for the start and end color stops. Try using a vivid blue for the left-hand stop and a slightly darker version of that blue for the right-hand stop. Click OK to close the Gradient Editor, and click OK in the Layer Style dialog box. Your river should now be a lovely, thoroughly unnatural blue, as shown in Figure 14.40.

> **TIP** For more detail on using the Gradient Editor, see Chapter 6.

For the sky, you'll adopt a simpler approach. Select the photo layer and, using the Magic Wand tool set at its default tolerance of 32, start selecting the sky by clicking on the sky area. To select additional areas, Shift+click them. If you accidentally get a little of the buildings, Alt+click (Option+click on the Mac) to deselect them.

FIGURE 14.40

The new river. You can see how the ragged edges are starting to interact with the white drawn layer below.

TIP If you're using Photoshop CS3, the new Quick Select tool makes this process much easier. Simply select it and draw roughly around the sky area. The tool should create an excellent selection.

When you have a selection you're happy with, create a new layer and fill it with the color of your choice. In this example, it is filled with a beige color, but feel free to choose whatever floats your boat.

You're now left with an illustration that has the basic feel you're looking for. Only the buildings are now left from the original photo, and even they have the covering of drawn elements. It's very unreal, but it has a nicely hand-drawn feel, as you can see in Figure 14.41.

FIGURE 14.41

The piece is taking shape. The original photo is combined with a few hand-drawn elements — some scanned in, some created directly in Photoshop.

Adding some handwritten text and doodles

You can now really start to have some fun with the piece, adding hand-drawn elements to create a much more detailed work. Open the second scanned image in Photoshop, which contains some handwritten text and several London-related doodles. These were just drawn onto a sheet of paper, with no thought for composition in the final illustration.

To take these elements across, select individual elements using the Marquee and Lasso tools, then copy and paste them into the illustration's document window. Photoshop automatically pastes the elements as new layers, so there are no worries about keeping them separate from the existing layers.

First, take across the doodle of the boat. Select the boat in the scanned document, press Ctrl+C (⌘+C on the Mac) to copy it, and paste it into the illustration by pressing Ctrl+V (⌘+V on the Mac). Make the lines of the boat white, as you did earlier with the traced skyline, by locking the layer's transparency and filling the layer with white. You can see in Figure 14.42 that the boat feels a little large for the river as it stands, so use the Scale command (Edit ➪ Transform ➪ Scale) to reposition and resize it.

FIGURE 14.42

Resizing the boat using the Scale command

In the same way, bring across several other elements in the scan and fill them with white, repositioning and rescaling them as you go. You'll find that the feel of the piece is transformed as you add these elements to create a playful scene.

After you finish adding the extra elements, the illustration is full of fun things, with an airplane high in the sky and a doodled London Underground sign, alongside a large "London" text element. You can see the final illustration in Figure 14.43. The scribbled lines below the boat have their blending mode set to Soft Light, which produces some texture in the river and underscores the boat.

FIGURE 14.43

The finished illustration. Some of the doodles have a ragged edge where the initial selections weren't perfect, but in this example they enhance the "scratchy" mood of the piece nicely. You could clear these up by using the Eraser tool or a layer mask if desired.

Adding some final typography

Add some text at the top of the document using the Type tool. You're looking to create a contrast with the underlying image by making this text very precise and neat, drawing the eye to this essential area of the piece. Create the text by following these steps:

1. **Create a background area for the text.** Select the Rectangle tool from the Toolbox, and make sure the Shape Layers option is selected. Choose white for the rectangle's color by clicking the Color box in the options bar. Drag out a simple box in the top-left corner of the document, around a third of the width of the document window.

2. **Add the title text on top of the box.** Make sure the box layer's vector mask is deselected —click its thumbnail in the Layers palette if you're not sure—and select the Type tool. Choose a font and size, maybe a simple, clear typeface like Arial at 24 points. Use the same color you used for the sky, so it feels like you're cutting through the box; to set this, click the Color box in the options bar, then click the sky in the document window. Now click in the box and type the headline: **Exclusive to London**. Press Ctrl+Enter (⌘+Return on the Mac) to commit your edits.

3. **Add the event details.** Again using the Type tool, drag out a bounding box beneath the initial text. This creates a paragraph area into which you can type details for the event. Make the text size smaller than the headline text — around 10 points should do it — and start typing. You can resize the paragraph bounding box by dragging the resize handles at the edges and corners of the box; the text will reflow to fit the new box dimensions. Commit your edits when you're happy.

4. **Add the date.** Using the 24-point type size again, add a date below the previous text. You might need to reposition the text layers slightly with the Move tool to get everything lined up. Use the arrow keys for extra precision here.

And that's it: your fully featured mixed-media illustration and handout, shown in all its glory in Figure 14.44.

FIGURE 14.44
In the final product, the contrast between the scratchy illustration and the ultraneat typography produces some tension and draws the eye to the message.

Of course, there are many alternative versions that you could create for this example. Use the Photoshop files on the CD to see what you can create from the separate elements. As you do so, notice how even small decisions, like changing the fill color for the drawn layers, really affects the mood of the piece. Have fun!

Summary

This chapter covered a good deal of practical techniques and highlighted the importance of layers both as an organizational tool and as a creative one. You also learned how layers interact with other features in Photoshop, such as the Slice tool, and how best to use layers to create your finished piece of work.

You were often shown more than one approach to a task, illustrating how Photoshop often has many ways of accomplishing similar jobs. In the real world, designers will have their set ways of working. They may not know everything about Photoshop, but they know enough to get their ideas out into the world. Everyone who regularly uses Photoshop learns more about it every day, so don't feel you have to know everything about Photoshop to have great successes with it.

The first example in the chapter showed you how you can use layer masks and adjustment layers to enhance a photo. You also were given a comprehensive walkthrough for laying out a Web site design, as well as how to export finished images from the design for inclusion in the final site. You looked at how to combine photo layers together to create a montage. Lastly, you combined hand-drawn image layers with photography to produce a striking mixed-media piece.

Chapter 15

Manipulating Photos by Using Layers

Photoshop has always catered well to the needs of photographers, but the CS3 release introduces yet more photo-friendly features such as the Black & White adjustment, the Exposure adjustment layer, and the new, much-improved Adobe Camera Raw.

In this chapter, you apply layer techniques to some real-world photography situations, hopefully demystifying some of the more esoteric features of Photoshop along the way. You'll be looking at:

- **Retouching landscapes:** Here you'll be using layer masks to separate land and sky. You also learn how to really make your landscape "pop" out of the page.

- **Correcting color casts:** Has your camera let you down by misjudging the white balance of a scene? Or do you have a photo with a particular color cast? You learn how to get perfect colors within a photo, using the Levels adjustment on a channel-by-channel basis.

- **Retouching a portrait:** You start with an ordinary portrait and apply multiple techniques to bring the exposure back on track and flatter the skin tones.

- **Converting color images to black and white:** You compare the main layer-based techniques for converting a color digital photo to black and white, and learn how to get the most out of your monochrome images.

- **Aligning handheld photos:** Finally, you look at the new Auto-Align Layers feature in Photoshop CS3. You learn how to take two handheld photos of the same scene and line them up perfectly in seconds.

IN THIS CHAPTER

Using layers nondestructively to get the best from your photos

Using adjustment layers to improve contrast in a landscape

Masking adjustment layers to selectively apply adjustments

Using Levels and Curves adjustment layers to correct color casts

Enhancing exposure and skin tones

Improving a portrait by adjusting eye color and painting new "skin"

Exploring the new Auto-Align Layers command in Photoshop CS3

591

You'll concentrate on producing great end results, and acquiring the techniques you'll need to get the best from your own photos. You'll also use layers to produce these results in a nondestructive manner — in almost every case, the original photo lies untouched at the bottom of the layer stack, with all edits contained within the layers above.

NOTE   You'll find the Photoshop files for all the examples in this chapter on the accompanying CD-ROM.

Retouching a Landscape

This first example looks at ways to enhance landscape photography using layers. Landscapes are hard to get right in-camera, because the range of tones in a landscape is often too great to properly expose both the sky and the foreground. Skies are often overexposed, while foregrounds tend toward under-exposure. The human eye can differentiate among a much wider range of tones than your camera, and the result of that incompatibility can be frustrating; the camera just doesn't see what you see.

Luckily, Photoshop can help you in a number of ways, so that you can produce images that are closer to what your eyes can see. The photo in Figure 15.1 is a good example. Compositionally, it's pleasant enough, with good foreground detail and that big expanse of sky.

FIGURE 15.1

In the landscape photo straight from the camera, you can see that the foreground is somewhat underexposed.

To keep the detail in the sky, however, it was necessary to underexpose the foreground, which looks pretty woeful right now. It's dark, and the whole image is thoroughly underwhelming. To make changes to the foreground without affecting the sky, you need to separate the two elements. In this tutorial, you use a mask to separate the foreground from the sky, and you add adjustment layers to make non-destructive changes to the color and contrast. Finally, you use a Smart Filter to add a sharpening effect to the image.

CROSS-REF You can find more on masks in Chapter 9, adjustment layers in Chapter 6, and Smart Filters in Chapter 8.

Applying an adjustment to the whole image

First, look at the tonal composition of the image. Open the photo in Photoshop and look at its histogram (Window ➪ Histogram). As you can see in Figure 15.2, the histogram shows that we're pretty lucky with the exposure. The bulk of the data is roughly in the middle of the histogram. There are no hard cutoffs on the right to indicate blown highlights, and no cutoffs on the left that might have shown a loss in shadow detail.

There's a fair amount of space to the right of the histogram data, and that tells you that there isn't much information in the image toward the lighter end of the spectrum — the image is underexposed.

FIGURE 15.2

The histogram for the starting image shows underexposure, but no clipping.

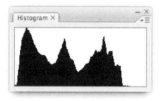

What happens if you try to apply an exposure correction to the image without using masks? Well, go ahead and try it. Click the Create New Fill or Adjustment Layer icon at the bottom of the Layers palette, and select the Levels option. This adds a Levels adjustment layer above the Background layer.

Looking at the histogram in the Levels dialog box this time, you can again see that rather gaping hole in the highlights, so click and drag the white Input Levels slider in from the right so that it touches the right-hand side of the histogram data. This produces a nice effect, with the whole image brightening considerably. However, the foreground is still noticeably dark. You can see in Figure 15.3 that if you continue to drag the white slider in to a point where the foreground is really starting to come to life, the sky starts to generate some rather nasty hues, and the clouds start to lose detail; in other words, you're blowing the highlights.

FIGURE 15.3

After applying a Levels adjustment to the whole image, the foreground looks good, but the sky starts to lose detail.

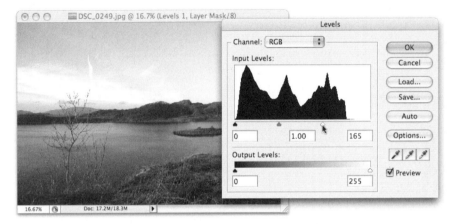

Creating the mask

The sky needs to be separated from the foreground, and different adjustments applied to both, if you want to even out the exposure of the image. Masks provide a perfect way to approach this. You're going to mask out the sky, so that only the foreground is affected by the Levels adjustment.

Creating the Levels adjustment layer has helpfully also created a layer mask; you can see its thumbnail to the right of the layer thumbnail in the Layers palette. By default, the thumbnail is white, which applies the Levels effect equally across the whole image. You're going to "paint out" the effect on the sky using black.

Start by selecting the Brush tool from the Toolbox. Click the Brush option in the options bar to open the Brush Preset Picker. Here you can choose the hardness and diameter of the brush. Try an initial diameter of 280 pixels and a hardness value of around 80 percent. Make sure the layer mask thumbnail for the Levels layer is active by clicking it — it will have a border around it when it's active — and set the foreground color to black.

Now, start to paint onto the sky areas of the document. As you do this, you can see the Levels adjustment being removed from those areas, as shown in Figure 15.4.

FIGURE 15.4

Painting onto the mask in the sky area masks off the effect of the Levels adjustment layer

This process is easy while just working on the main body of the sky, but as you get down to the skyline, it gets a bit trickier. You can do a very rough job for now, and paint down to the skyline with the same big soft brush. You'll likely be left with a rather unnatural "glowing edge" where sky meets land, and this is where you need to fine-tune the mask. There are two approaches you can adopt:

- Use a very big, very soft gray brush to make the final mask very soft-edged. This still gives you some of the effect of the Levels adjustment in the sky, but the effect is so soft-edged that it should go unnoticed.
- Use smaller brushes to create a very precise mask that just overlaps the top of the hills. This should accurately remove the "glow."

The approach you choose depends very much on the image. The first approach is much quicker; it effectively amounts to almost a single brush stroke across the image, but it has the disadvantage that the areas most prone to clipping are those clouds just above the skyline. If you leave too much of the Levels effect in there, you could risk blowing the highlights.

The latter approach is more fiddly, but ultimately it is likely to be more successful, because you're masking off the Levels effect across the whole sky.

It's always worth trying a couple of approaches in the real world, because it's hard to know in advance exactly how an image will behave. That kind of eye takes years of experience to develop! With that in mind, create two versions of the mask using each of the two approaches.

The soft-edged mask

The steps for finishing off the mask with a very soft edge are pretty simple, and run something like this:

1. **Select a large, soft brush.** Click the Brush option in the options bar to open the Brush Preset Picker, and set Diameter to around 700 pixels and Hardness to 0 percent.

2. **Select a mid-gray as the foreground color.** Something like RGB 116, 116, 116, which errs toward the darker end of the grays, is fine. Remember, grays produce a translucent effect on the mask, allowing the Levels adjustment to partially show.

3. **Paint on the mask.** Simply run the brush across the top of the skyline, taking in a good slice of the hills in the process.

Looking at the results in Figure 15.5, they're actually pretty good, aesthetically. If you toggle the visibility of the Levels layer, however, you can see that the big brush has greatly exaggerated the gradient in the sky. (Some might argue that you've actually introduced a gradient.) So it looks okay, but it's not really what you'd call faithful to the original.

FIGURE 15.5

The very soft-edged mask produces a passable effect, though the gradient in the sky is quite pronounced. You can see the gray stripe across the middle of the layer mask thumbnail where the big brush stroke was drawn on.

The precise mask

In this version, smaller brushes are used to create an increasingly more exact mask so that the Levels adjustment stops right on the skyline. Starting again with the rough mask created initially, you can make this mask as follows:

1. **Select a small, soft, black brush.** Click the Brush option and set the brush diameter to around 180 pixels in the picker. Leave the Hardness value set at zero. Select a black foreground color.

2. **Brush along the skyline, overlapping the hills a little to make sure the glow is removed.** At this point, it's looking pretty good. Quite natural, but the brush has darkened too much of the hills, so you need to correct that.

3. **Zoom in so you can see what you're doing.** Press Ctrl+= (⌘+= on the Mac). Hold down the spacebar and drag within the document window to move around the image.

4. **Choose a lighter, smaller brush.** Set the foreground color to a dark gray — say RGB 85, 85, 85 — and select a smaller brush of around 60 pixels.

5. **Carefully paint over the too-dark areas.** Make sure that you don't start to reintroduce any of the glow that you previously painted out.

> **NOTE** Fine-tuning a mask is not an exact science. When working on your own images, you may well have to try a number of times to get a good result, changing the gray color to lighter or darker, and trying different brush sizes. It's also much easier if you have access to a tablet and stylus, rather than using a mouse!

You can see the final result of this stage in Figure 15.6. It's a much more natural-looking image, with none of that big gradient seen in the earlier approach. It's taken quite a lot longer to touch up the mask, but the results are very good. You now have an image with sky and foreground in balance. This is the version you'll use in the next steps.

FIGURE 15.6

The more precise mask in action. Note that you haven't had to carefully mask details like the little trees on the skyline. The soft edges of the brushes render that unnecessary.

> **NOTE** There are, of course, many other ways to make a mask. You could try using the Magic Wand or Quick Selection tools on the sky, for example. However, these techniques can result in nonselected areas along the mask boundary. This is very noticeable when viewing at 100 percent, particularly along the hill line and in the branches of that foreground tree.

Making the image "pop"

When photographers say they want their images to "pop," it means they want to see vibrancy in the colors, and a real sense of the images jumping off the page or screen at the viewer. Your photo is currently quite pleasant, but it's not really jumping out at you.

To start to correct that, you can apply an Exposure adjustment layer above the Levels layer. Click the Create New Fill or Adjustment Layer icon in the Layers palette, and choose Exposure from the menu. All you want to do here is push the Exposure slider a little to the right. Around +0.6 will be fine; this really brings out the color and contrast in the image. Click OK to close the dialog box.

> **NOTE** You can push the Exposure slider farther, but the results will be somewhat unreal. It's often done, though; it just depends how you like to see your photographs!

Because the sky and the land are now reasonably balanced, increasing the brightness like this hasn't resulted in any blown highlights in the clouds, and the foreground is really looking good now; you can see how nice the original light was when the photo was taken.

> **TIP** If you want to see how far you've come with this, just turn off the visibility of the Levels and Exposure adjustment layers. It's quite a shock when you see the original image beneath!

The image is basically complete now, but the current fashion dictates that you might want to apply some sharpening. This really gives definition and adds to the "hyper-real" feeling of the manipulated image. Sharpening works on the edges of the elements in the image to increase contrast between, say, the blades of grass in the photo. Any sharpening should be applied at the very final stage, after the image is resized for either print or Web use. This is because different resolutions of photos require different levels of sharpening.

So, first save the "master" image at the photograph's native resolution. Save your document with a name such as **retouch landscape master**. This approach means that you always have the original file at full size to refer to, and to use as a "negative" for any future work.

Now duplicate the document by choosing Image ⇨ Duplicate, and save the duplicate, giving it a name like **retouch landscape web**. You need to resize the duplicate according to the needs of the output media. In this case, imagine that you're preparing the image for Web use. Choose Image ⇨ Image Size, and set the Resolution option to 72 pixels/inch. Looking at the top Width and Height boxes, you can see that the image has shrunk from 3008 x 2000 pixels to 722 x 480 pixels. Click OK to resize the image, and choose View ⇨ Actual Pixels to zoom in to 100 percent.

To apply your sharpening, you're going to use a great new feature of Photoshop CS3: Smart Filters. In previous versions, you'd have to apply a destructive sharpening process at this stage, but this feature allows you to create an editable sharpening effect. To do this, follow these steps:

1. **Make the photo a Smart Object.** You need to do this so that you can apply the Smart Filter. Right-click the photo layer and choose Convert to Smart Object from the pop-up menu.

2. **Add an Unsharp Mask Smart Filter.** To do this, choose Filter ➪ Sharpen ➪ Unsharp Mask. The Unsharp Mask dialog box appears.

3. **Choose appropriate settings for the filter.** In the Unsharp Mask dialog box, choose an Amount setting of around 50 percent, a Radius setting of around 1 pixel, and a Threshold of 5. These are much more subtle settings than you would use for print work, which is why sharpening should always be done as the final stage of the process.

4. **Click OK to exit the dialog box.** The photo Smart Object now has an Unsharp Mask Smart Filter applied to it.

CAUTION Sharpening is easily overdone. You want just enough so that you notice the effect when you check and uncheck the Preview option in the dialog box. If you can clearly see the effect without having to toggle the Preview option, you've likely pushed it too far.

You can see the Smart Filter underneath the photo Smart Object in the Layers palette. If you want to reedit the Unsharp Mask filter, simply double-click the filter's name in the palette.

And that's it! You now have a much better Web-ready landscape photo, as shown in Figure 15.7. The photo has really come a long way since you started. Some might argue that this is a totally artificial approach, but you can see it as a digital extension of what's been happening in darkrooms for years. Either way, it's certainly saved this image.

FIGURE 15.7

The final, greatly improved photo, with the Layers palette showing the Unsharp Mask Smart Filter

Fixing Color Casts in Photos

Everyone has seen photos that have an overall color cast to them — maybe a tint of red, green, or blue. It can be tempting to write these images off as a bad job, but sometimes that's just not an option. It might be that the composition was perfect, or that the image was the only one in a batch where the subject was perfectly in focus.

You've looked at using Levels adjustments to improve contrast, but Levels is a powerful tool for color correction, too. In this example, Levels adjustment layers are used to bring previously unusable photos back to life. In Figure 15.8, for example, the camera's automatic white balance feature has been fooled by the morning light, giving the whole image a strong red-yellow cast. You'll be looking at a simple way to bring this photo back to something approaching reality using a Levels adjustment.

FIGURE 15.8

A morning scene with a strong red-yellow cast

A classic issue with indoor no-flash photography is, again, the camera's automatic white balance being fooled into producing an image with a red cast. You can apply a similar technique to resurrect these images. The image in Figure 15.9 is just such a photo. This image is currently totally unusable due to the prominent red cast, but even when the problem is this extreme, you can correct it.

In these examples, you'll use Levels adjustment layers to adjust the colors in these images on a channel-by-channel basis. You'll also look at using Curves adjustment layers to achieve a similar result.

FIGURE 15.9

This photo of a microphone, taken indoors with no flash, is not much use due to its very strong red cast, but you can use Photoshop to bring it back to life.

CROSS-REF You can find more information on Levels and Curves adjustment layers in Chapter 6.

Correcting the bridge photo

Open the bridge photo in Photoshop. It looks pretty unpromising, as you've seen, but the real colors are there to be found; they just need to be brought out. Start by looking at the histograms for each channel.

Open the Histogram palette, if it's not open already, by choosing Window ➪ Histogram. By default, you see the composite histogram with all the color channels merged together. This doesn't really tell you what's going on in the individual channels, though. To fix this, choose All Channels View from the Histogram palette menu. This gives you not only the composite view, but also individual views for each channel: one for Red, one for Green, and one for Blue. You can see this in Figure 15.10.

NOTE If you're working in CMYK mode, you'll see individual channels for cyan, yellow, magenta, and black instead. Similarly, an image in Lab mode shows channels for L, a, and b in the Histogram palette.

FIGURE 15.10

Choose All Channels View from the Histogram palette menu to view the individual channel histograms within the image.

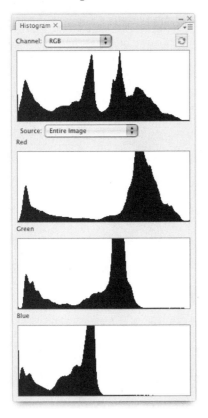

By looking at the channel histograms, you can see that, while the Red channel is well catered for, the Green and Blue channels have big gaps to the right, indicating that there's no information for the highlights in those channels. When you correct the channels using Levels, you'll remap these two channels to spread their tones across the full available dynamic range, thereby enhancing their impact.

Applying a Levels correction

Let's start work. To add a Levels adjustment layer, click the Create New Fill or Adjustment Layer icon at the base of the Layers palette, and choose Levels from the pop-up menu.

The Levels dialog box that appears shows the histogram for the image, again in composite mode, with the Red, Green, and Blue channels combined. This is great if you're looking to enhance the contrast of the image, but here you want to work on the individual channels. From the Channel drop-down menu, choose Red. As you can see in Figure 15.11, the Red channel has a pretty good spread of values right across the range. Just drag in the white Input Levels slider a touch so that it meets the right edge of the histogram data. You won't see much change in the document window because you've made a very subtle alteration.

FIGURE 15.11
_____

Adjusting the white Input Levels slider in the Red channel

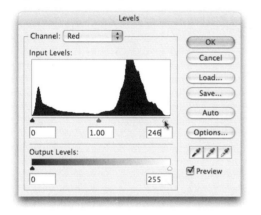

Now choose Green from the Channel menu. Drag the white Input Levels slider to the left, so that it meets the right edge of the histogram data, and the black Input Levels slider to the right so it meets the left edge, as shown in Figure 15.12. At this point the image starts to look decidedly weird and very green. Don't panic, though — you're not done yet!

Adjusting the Green channel. It's all looking a little odd at this stage.

Last, you're going to look at the Blue channel, so choose Blue from the Channel menu. Again, drag the white Input Levels slider left so it just touches the right of the histogram data, as shown in Figure 15.13. The histogram tells you that you don't need to drag the black slider anywhere, because the left edge of the histogram data is hard up against the edge of the graph. (This means that the original photo has probably lost some detail in the shadows of the Blue channel. Never mind.)

This is where the magic happens. The sky has regained its blue, with just a hint of the dawn along the skyline. This is much more like the original scene actually looked to the eye.

Adjusting color using the eyedroppers

You've seen how to adjust the colors in the image using the Input Levels sliders, but there's another way to perform these adjustments without ever leaving the main RGB histogram view in the Levels dialog box: You can use the eyedroppers.

FIGURE 15.13

Working with the Blue channel. Dragging the white Input Levels slider into the right edge of the histogram data has produced a much more accurate image.

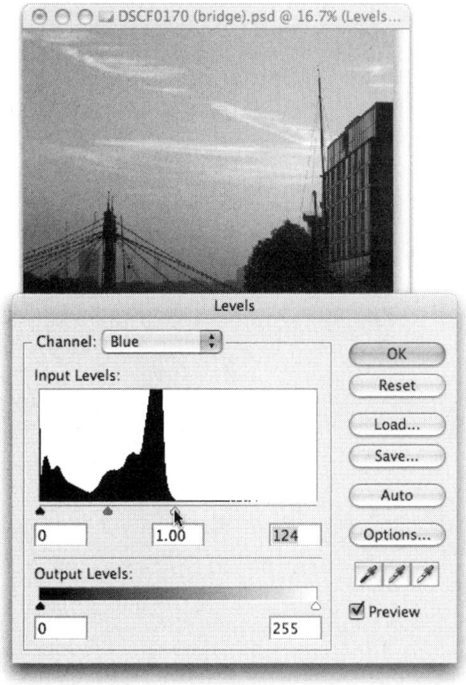

The eyedroppers are found just beneath the Options button in the Levels dialog box. Using the black and white eyedroppers, you can choose the pure black and white points of your image by eye. The gray eyedropper between them allows you to specify a mid-gray point. Select the black eyedropper and click a pixel in your image that you think represents the black point, or the area of darkest shadow. Repeat this process using the white eyedropper to select the white point, or the brightest highlight, and the gray eyedropper to select the point that you feel should be mid-gray in the photo.

It can be hard to pick these points by eye, so let's walk through the process. It's especially hard in an image like this, because most of the image is composed of very similar hues.

First, selecting the black eyedropper, look for an area of the image that you want to be pure black. There are some very deep shadows in the bottom-right corner of the photo, so click in that area to set the black point.

It's harder to see where the white point might be in this image, but the clouds should be a good bet. Select the white eyedropper and click in the clouds by the pole on the right side of the image. This produces immediate results, and the whole image becomes much more balanced. The sky is blue, with a nice dawn glow on the skyline.

> **TIP**   It can be hard to see what you're doing with the eyedropper, so try zooming into your photo to get a better idea of exactly where to click.

Last, use the gray eyedropper to define your mid-gray point. Again, this can be tricky, but those towers on the horizon look like they would have been gray in the original scene, so they're good candidates for the mid-gray point. Click a point on a tower, as shown in Figure 15.14. Try alternative points for this eyedropper to get the most pleasing results. Precisely where you click with the gray eyedropper has a subtle but significant effect on the overall tonality of the image. Just clicking up and down the edge of the tower produces different hues throughout the image, so experimentation is the key here.

FIGURE 15.14

Using the gray eyedropper to pick a mid-gray point of the image can be tricky. You're looking for an area of the image that would have been neutral gray in the original scene.

The results of using the eyedroppers are pretty good in this image, and roughly akin to the sliders approach. The method you choose depends on which you feel most comfortable with, as well as the characteristics of each image.

Correcting the microphone photo

The bridge photo looked like a tough job, but in fact it was surprisingly simple to correct. Turn your attention now to a tougher challenge: the microphone image. This has a really strong color cast to it and needs a more delicate adjustment to achieve a good result.

To prove the point, start by repeating the approach used on the bridge image. Open the photo in Photoshop, and add a Levels adjustment layer by clicking the Create New Fill or Adjustment Layer icon in the Layers palette.

Follow the same process as before, clicking and dragging the black and white Input Levels sliders in so they touch the left and right edges of each channel's histogram data. You can see the results in Figure 15.15. The image is somewhat improved, but it still has something of a color cast to it. To get rid of this, you're going to have to get a little more involved with the Levels adjustment.

FIGURE 15.15

The microphone image with basic back and white slider adjustments. Here you're seeing the adjustments for the Green channel.

To further improve the result, you'll now look at the gray slider for each channel, which adjusts the midtones of the channel. This is centered at a numerical value of 1.00 by default. Clicking and dragging the slider to the left lightens the midtones for that channel; dragging to the right darkens them. When working on an individual color channel, this has the effect of emphasizing or de-emphasizing that color across the midtones.

Looking at just the Red channel in the Levels dialog box, drag the gray slider left and right to see the effect. Moving the slider left results in a more red-tinted image, and dragging it right produces less of a red tint. In this case, you want less of a red cast to the whole image, so drag it right to around 0.50, as shown in Figure 15.16. This really reduces the impact of the reds in the image, but overall the image is now a little olive in color.

FIGURE 15.16

Manipulating the red in the image using the gray slider in the Red channel

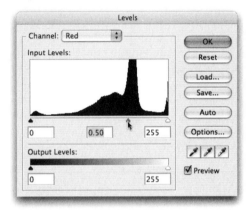

You can correct the olive tint by flipping to the Green channel and dragging the gray slider a little to the right to de-emphasize the greens in the image. A value of 0.90 does a good job.

The photo still has a bit of a yellow cast, but you can correct that by emphasizing the Blue channel. Click and drag the gray slider of the Blue channel left to increase the impact of blue in the image. A value here of 1.21 produces a nicely neutral image, which is pretty faithful to the color of the microphone and the off-white wall behind. You can see the final image in Figure 15.17.

FIGURE 15.17

The final image is very different from the original, with a nice neutral hue.

Retouching a Portrait

Photographers have been retouching since the dawn of photography, and the aim is always to enhance and flatter the subject, whether it's a landscape, a still life, or a portrait. In the days of film, this was done in the darkroom. In the current era of digital photography, Photoshop is the new darkroom, and the retouching possibilities it offers are endless.

In this example, you take a portrait that wasn't shot with the benefit of studio lights or a makeup artist, and apply multiple layer techniques to enhance exposure, soften skin tones, and generally improve the image. You can see the starting point in Figure 15.18. This is not reportage photography; it's less about truth and more about flattering the subject. It's the kind of work that goes on all day in the offices of magazines, and produces an image impossible to achieve in real life.

That said, you want the image to look as natural as possible, and half the battle with retouching is in knowing when to stop. It's even possible to create an image that doesn't look very human; unless this is the effect you're looking for, it's best avoided. You'll look at ways to tone down the adjustments to achieve a more natural and sympathetic feel.

FIGURE 15.18

The starting portrait: It's not going to win any prizes right now, but it's the sort of photo anyone could have taken.

You'll use an array of techniques covered earlier in the book, and as usual you'll be looking to apply all edits nondestructively. The original photo layer always remains untouched at the bottom of the Layers palette. The techniques used here include the following:

- Adjustment layers
- Layer masks and Quick Masks
- Blending modes
- Smart Objects and Smart Filters
- Painting tools

CROSS-REF   You can find more information on adjustment layers in Chapter 6. Masks are covered in Chapter 9, and blending modes get the treatment in Chapter 7. Smart Objects and Smart Filters are covered in Chapter 8.

Looking at the original photo, you can make improvements in two broad areas:

- **Exposure correction:** The image is dark, and the right-hand side of the face — the model's left — is too much in shadow. In addition, the background is too dark.
- **Skin tone correction:** You want to smooth out the skin tones and remove some blotchiness from the skin, especially around the cheeks, nose, and forehead.

Enhancing the exposure

Start by enhancing the overall exposure of the image. Handily, in Photoshop CS3 you can apply the Exposure adjustment as an adjustment layer. Click the Create New Fill or Adjustment Layer icon at the base of the Layers palette, and choose Exposure from the pop-up menu. In the dialog box that appears, click and drag the Exposure slider to the right, setting it at a value of around +1. This has the effect of increasing the perceived exposure of the photo. When you're happy, click OK to close the dialog box.

Second, you'll add a Curves adjustment layer to boost the midtones of the image. Again, click the Create New Fill or Adjustment Layer icon, but this time choose Curves from the menu. In the Curves dialog box that appears, click the center of the curve, representing the midtones, and drag it slightly upward and to the left. The Curves control is quite sensitive, so you only need to drag it a little way, as you can see in Figure 15.19. If you go much farther to the left you start to lose detail. Click OK to close the dialog box.

FIGURE 15.19

Editing the curve in the Curves adjustment layer to boost the midtones

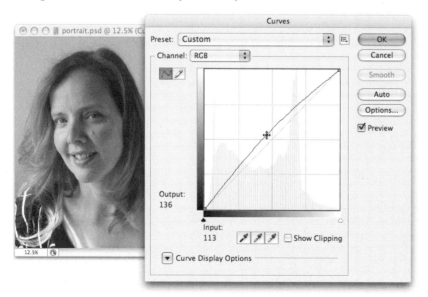

With both your adjustment layers applied, part of the hair in the bottom left of the image looks a little overexposed. In the original shoot, this area caught the sun directly, so it's much brighter than the rest of the image. You need to tone down the effect on just this area. To do this, use the Exposure adjustment layer's layer mask.

Currently the mask is white, indicating that the adjustment effect is being applied equally to all areas of the image. If you paint on the mask in shades of gray or pure black, you can remove the effect from that area. Painting with shades of gray produces translucency in the mask, while painting with pure black masks the effect entirely. In this case, you want to mask off that area entirely from the effects of the Exposure adjustment, so paint in black.

Click the layer mask thumbnail for the Exposure layer in the Layers palette, then select the Brush tool. Next, click the Brush option in the options bar and choose a wide, soft-edged brush — a Diameter setting of around 190 pixels and a Hardness setting of 0 percent work well — and make sure the foreground color is black. Position the brush over the area of hair in the document window, and start to paint. As you do, you see the effect of the Exposure layer being removed. You also see your paint strokes in the layer mask thumbnail in the Layers palette. The soft edge of the brush prevents the edges of the mask being noticeable.

These two adjustment layers have resulted in an enhanced overall exposure, but you now have a different issue to address. The right-hand side of the face — the model's left — is quite a bit darker than the left. This is simply because the main light source was coming in from the left, casting a shadow on the right side of the face. To correct this problem, use a Levels adjustment layer, and paint on its layer mask to ensure that only the right side of the face shows the effect. To do this, follow these steps:

1. **Select the Background layer.** This makes sure the new adjustment layer is added just above the photo in the stacking order.

2. **Click the Create New Fill or Adjustment Layer icon in the Layers palette, and select Levels from the menu.** The Levels dialog that appears shows a wide gap on the right side of the histogram, showing that there's not much in the way of highlights in the image.

3. **Click and drag the white Input Levels slider on the right in to the left to meet the right edge of the histogram data.** A value of around 190 works well. This makes the bulk of the image overexposed, but you're only interested in the right-hand side of the face right now, so concentrate on getting it correct there. After you have the levels roughly correct, click OK to close the dialog box.

4. **Prepare the mask for the adjustment layer.** In contrast to the previous masking approach, where you wanted to paint out the effect of the Exposure layer, it's easier here to paint in the effect of the Levels adjustment. To achieve this, begin with a black mask, so that all of the Levels effect is hidden. Any method of filling the mask with black is fine. For example, click the layer mask thumbnail to activate it, and choose Image ➪ Adjustments ➪ Invert. Because the inverse of white is black, the thumbnail turns black and the Levels effect is masked off for the whole image.

5. **Bring the Levels effect back just for the right side of the face.** Select the Brush tool from the Toolbox, set the brush's diameter to 442 pixels, and set its Hardness to 0 percent. Make sure your foreground color is white, and start to paint on the image, working the brush around the dark areas of the face. If the effect is a little harsh, don't worry; simply reduce the opacity of the Levels layer to tame the effect. An opacity setting of around 43 percent is about right in this case.

> **TIP** You can produce a more subtle effect that doesn't require a reduction in the Opacity setting by painting with a gray brush. Remember that gray has the effect of making the mask — and therefore the effect — semitransparent. There's no right or wrong here; it's just about which way works best for you.

The current state of the image is shown in Figure 15.20. At this stage, you can see how far you've come already by turning the adjustment layers off and on. Quite a difference!

FIGURE 15.20

The original photo (left), and the photo with your basic enhancements applied, using three adjustment layers (right)

Enhancing the skin tones

Having corrected the exposure of the photo, you can now leave truth behind entirely and start retouching the skin tones. You're going to remove a few blemishes, eliminate the blotchiness from the nose, cheeks, and forehead, and smooth out the skin to produce a more forgiving image.

Removing blemishes using the Spot Healing Brush

Photoshop has some great tools for removing spots, scars, and other skin issues. In this example, you get to work with the Spot Healing Brush tool. This magical feature allows you to simply "dab" at any blemishes and remove them by copying surrounding pixels over them. What's more, thanks to the magic of layers, you can do this in a nondestructive way.

It works like this:

1. **Find an area of the image that you want to correct.** For example, there's a definite spot on the model's chin.

2. **Select the Spot Healing Brush tool.** You can Alt+click (Option+click on the Mac) the healing tool group icon in the Toolbox, or press Shift+J, until the Spot Healing Brush is selected.

3. **Set a suitable brush size.** Choose a brush size that fits just over the area you want to correct; a diameter of around 30 pixels, with a hardness of 0 percent, works well in this case.

4. **Select the Sample All Layers option.** Click this option in the options bar if it's not already selected. This makes sure that Photoshop works on the composite image, rather than on the active layer. This is important because you're going to apply the retouches on a new, blank layer.

5. **Create a new empty layer directly above the photo layer.** To do this, click the Background layer in the Layers palette, then click the New Layer icon at the base of the palette. Make sure this new layer is selected.

6. **Position your brush directly over the blemish and click.** This process is shown in Figure 15.21. The area under the brush goes dark, and when you release the mouse button, the blemish should be gone. The new layer created in the previous step holds all the retouched pixels, leaving the original image beneath untouched.

7. **Repeat as necessary.** Continue using the Spot Healing Brush — you'll probably need to vary the brush diameter as appropriate — until the model is blemish-free.

> **TIP**   It can help to zoom right into the image as you perform these operations, so you can see exactly what's happening.

Taming blotchiness using Hue/Saturation

You can now turn your attention to those areas of the skin that are a little blotchy. In this case, there are red areas on the right cheek and the nose, and it would be good to tame these. To do this, you can again use the adjustment layer/mask combination, but this time use a Hue/Saturation layer to reduce the redness and lighten the skin in these areas. Follow these steps to achieve this:

FIGURE 15.21

Using the Spot Healing Brush to remove skin blemishes

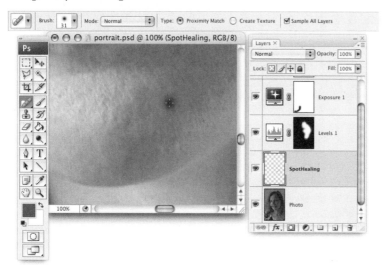

1. **Add a Hue/Saturation layer.** Click the Create New Fill or Adjustment Layer icon in the Layers palette and choose Hue/Saturation from the pop-up menu. Make sure the new layer is sitting above the layer created previously when using the Spot Healing Brush. In the Hue/Saturation dialog box, drop the Saturation slider to around -10 or to a point that starts to take the edge off the redness in the cheek and nose areas. Then click and drag the Lightness slider just a touch to the right, to around +3.

2. **Mask off the adjustment.** At this point, you see the effect on the whole image. Apply a layer mask to expose only those areas you want to affect, masking the rest of the image off from the adjustment. As before, when you created the Levels adjustment for the right-hand side of the face, you want to start with the mask filled with pure black so that you can paint the effect in. Click the Hue/Saturation layer's layer mask thumbnail and choose Image ➪ Adjustments ➪ Invert. The mask fills with black, and your Hue/Saturation adjustment is removed from the whole image.

3. **Paint on the mask.** Select the Brush tool, and set the brush's diameter to around 400 pixels and its Hardness to 0 percent. Make sure your foreground color is white, and begin to paint on the areas you want to correct. As you paint onto the image, you can see the redness in the cheek diminish as the Hue/Saturation layer begins to show through. You can also take this opportunity to paint onto the darker area of the forehead, lightening that a touch. For the nose, because the area is narrow, choose a smaller brush diameter of around 150 pixels.

When you're done, you should see a marked reduction in the redness of the areas you painted over, with the rest of the image remaining untouched. Turn the visibility of the Hue/Saturation layer off and on to see the difference. Because the Hue/Saturation adjustment can be edited at any point, you can now experiment with just how much redness you want to leave in the image, as shown in Figure 15.22.

FIGURE 15.22

Experimenting with the Saturation slider to further reduce redness. You can see the mask on the Hue/Saturation adjustment layer in the Layers palette.

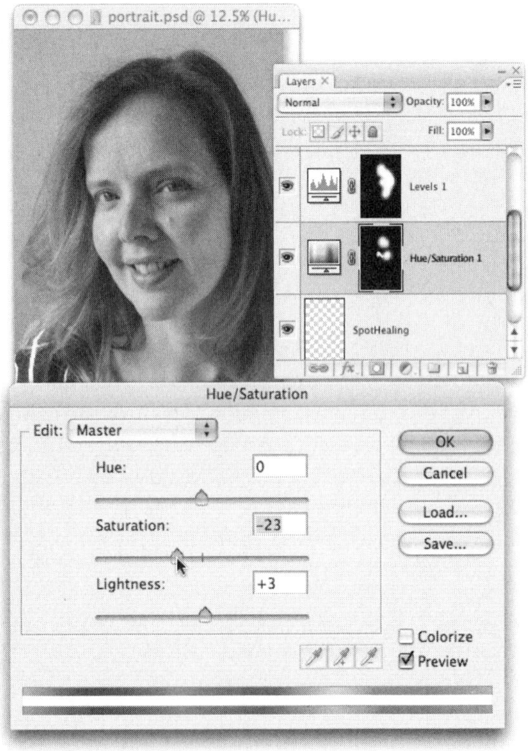

Softening the skin tones

The next step is where you really start to give the skin texture itself a makeover. At the moment, the basic skin texture is roughly the same as it was when you started, albeit with the colors somewhat tamed. You'll convert a copy of the photo layer to a Smart Object, and then apply a Gaussian Blur filter to that Smart Object to help soften the skin.

Here's how it's done:

1. **Copy the photo layer.** In the Layers palette, click and drag the photo layer to the New Layer icon, as shown in Figure 15.23. This creates a duplicate of the layer above the original. Make sure this duplicate is selected in the Layers palette.

2. **Convert the copy to a Smart Object.** Choose Layer ➪ Smart Objects ➪ Convert to Smart Object. The layer's thumbnail in the Layers palette changes to include a small icon in the corner, indicating that it's now a Smart Object.

3. **Add a Gaussian Blur Smart Filter.** Choose Filter ➪ Blur ➪ Gaussian Blur. In the dialog box that appears, click and drag the slider to the right to give a blur a Radius of around 40 pixels. Click OK to close the dialog box. The Smart Filter appears in the Layers palette.

4. **Adjust the layer's opacity to around 40 percent.** This lets a good deal of the original layer show through, and you can still see the softening effect of the new layer.

FIGURE 15.23

Creating a copy of the photo layer by dragging it to the New Layer icon

That really makes a difference, but you don't want the whole layer to be affected. In particular, you want the area around the eyes and teeth to retain the sharpness of the original photo. The Smart Object comes with a mask for its associated Smart Filters — known as the *filter mask* — and you can use that to mask off the effect in these areas. Click the filter mask's thumbnail in the Layers palette; this is the thumbnail next to the Smart Filters item underneath the Smart Object. Now, select the Brush tool and choose a small, soft brush; around 140 pixels with 0 percent hardness is fine. Make sure the foreground color is black, and start to paint in the document window on and slightly around one of the eyes, as shown in Figure 15.24. Repeat the process on the other eye and on the teeth.

FIGURE 15.24

Painting onto the filter mask to mask off the Gaussian Blur around the eyes

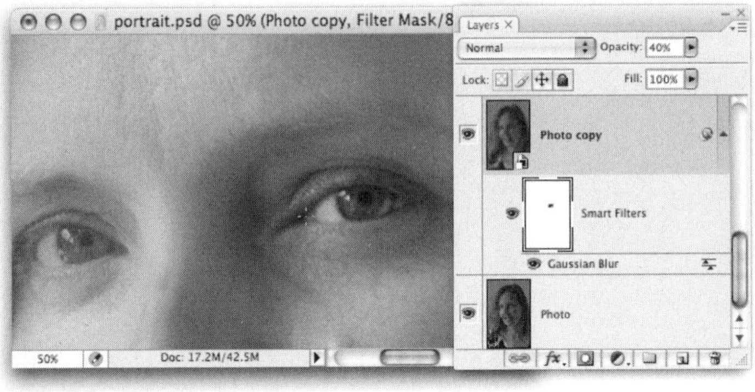

NOTE This approach with the blurred Smart Object works just as well if you're working on a black-and-white image. Try experimenting with the blending mode of the Smart Object to see the different effects this can produce. Hard Light is especially good in black and white.

At this point, you can sit back and look at what you've accomplished so far. The portrait looks a lot better and is much more flattering. It's useful to take stock of your progress at each point and refer back to the original image for comparison. You can do this by Alt+clicking (Option+clicking on the Mac) the Background photo layer's eye icon to toggle all the alterations off and on. This allows you to keep in mind what was good about the original portrait and to make sure you're not overdoing the processing. At this point, for example, you could reduce the Gaussian Blur filter's radius on the Smart Object — it's currently a little too "'70s" — down from 40 pixels to around 30, which still preserves the softness in the skin. You can see the current state of the photo in Figure 15.25.

Finishing touches

You could leave this image as it is right now and it would be fine. The results are flattering, but not over the top, and the effects look reasonably natural — unless, of course, you've seen the original photo.

You can do more to soften those skin tones, however, and the background is a little dull. You can also enhance the color in the eyes. This kind of work is best carried out very sensitively. There's no way to do much more without drawing attention to the imperfections you're trying to disguise!

FIGURE 15.25

The photo after applying the Gaussian Blur Smart Filter shows the new smoothness in the skin texture.

Enhancing the color of the eyes

You can bring out the color of the model's eyes using a pretty simple method. Follow these steps:

1. **Create a new layer.** Click the New Layer icon in the Layers palette, and drag the layer above the Levels adjustment layer you created for the right-hand side of the face. You don't want that adjustment to affect this new layer.

2. **Select the irises.** Using the Lasso tool, draw round the colored part of the eyes. To select both irises at once, hold down Shift to add to the selection. It's helpful to zoom into the eyes while doing this.

3. **Feather the selection.** Choose Select ➪ Modify ➪ Feather, and select a radius of around 3 pixels.

4. **Take a sample of the iris color.** Select the Eyedropper tool, then choose Point Sample for the Sample Size option and click a point in the iris. You now have a sample of the iris color as your foreground color.

5. **Enhance the color.** Double-click the foreground color box in the Toolbox, and choose a much more saturated version of the shade. RGB 52, 138, 154 is good in this instance.

6. **Fill the selection.** Now fill the selection you made earlier with the new, brighter color by choosing Edit ➪ Fill. Make sure the Use option is set to Foreground Color, and click OK to fill the selection.

7. **Set the layer's blending mode to Overlay.** In the Layers palette, set the new layer's blending mode to Overlay using the blending mode option at the top of the palette.

Your model now has very pretty blue eyes. In this case, they're probably a tad too blue, so drop the opacity of the whole layer to around 45% for a more natural look.

Lightening the background

The background in the image is a little dull, so it would be good to lighten this a touch to "lift" the whole image. Do this by creating a mask for the background, then applying a Levels adjustment layer to just that area. Follow these steps to achieve this:

1. **Create a Quick Mask for the model.** Click the Edit in Quick Mask Mode icon toward the bottom of the toolbox, or press Q.

2. **Mask off the model.** Select the Brush tool and choose a large, soft-edged brush of around 400 pixels in diameter, with 0 percent hardness. Make sure the foreground color is black. Start to paint on the model's face. You're painting the model, rather than the background, because you want to mask off the model from the lightening adjustment that you'll be applying shortly. As you paint, a red overlay appears over your painted areas, indicating that those areas are now masked off. Stop just short of the point where hair meets background, because you want the edge of the hair and the background to blend together a little. Because you're just lightening the background, rather than replacing it, the mask doesn't have to be absolutely perfect. You can see the result of this masking process in Figure 15.26. When you're happy with your mask, click the Quick Mask icon again, or press Q. Your mask appears as a selection, with "marching ants" around the selection border.

NOTE If you find that your mask has selected the model, rather than the background, choose Select ➪ Inverse to reverse the selection. In the future, to make the red overlay represent masked areas instead, double-click the Quick Mask icon and choose Masked Areas in the dialog box.

3. **Create a Levels adjustment layer.** In the Layers palette, select the Smart Object because you want the adjustment layer to appear just above this. Click the Create New Fill or Adjustment Layer icon at the bottom of the palette, and choose Levels from the pop-up menu. If you look at the new Levels adjustment layer in the Layers palette, you can see that Photoshop has automatically used your selection to create a layer mask for the Levels layer, masking off the unselected areas of the photo from the Levels adjustment. In the Levels dialog box that appears, click and drag the white Input Levels slider left until the background becomes suitably light. This will probably be before the actual start of the histogram data in this case. Click OK to close the dialog box.

FIGURE 15.26

The Quick Mask in place, shown as a red overlay on top of the model

4. **Fine-tune the mask.** At this point, you may well find that some parts of the background are still dark, due to the rather rough mask you made earlier. To fix this, select the Levels layer's layer mask by clicking its thumbnail in the Layers palette, and use a white brush set to around 300 pixels in diameter and zero hardness to paint over the dark areas of the background. This allows the Levels adjustment to show through, lightening those dark areas.

Painting new skin

This is probably the most controversial aspect of the example, and is quite extreme as an approach. So far you've only tweaked and softened the existing skin. Now you're going to paint over it. The end result should be smooth skin, but with enough of the existing texture to make it seem quite natural.

To give your model new skin, follow these steps:

1. **Create a new layer.** Click the New Layer icon from the Layers palette, and drag the new layer just above the eye coloring layer.
2. **Select the Eyedropper tool.** Click the Eyedropper icon in the Toolbox, or press I, and set a Sample Size of 101 by 101 Average in the options bar. This provides a nice, wide sampling area.

NOTE   In versions of Photoshop before CS3, the maximum sample size was 5x5 pixels, which
required more judgment to find the right tone.

3. **Click in the middle of the forehead.** This samples an average color from the 101 pixels
   all around the point where you clicked. The sampled color becomes the new foreground
   color.

4. **Start to paint on the right side of the forehead, as shown in Figure 15.27.** Use a
   brush of around 180 pixels in diameter, with zero hardness. This will look very weird,
   but don't worry — you'll fix this in a moment.

FIGURE 15.27

Painting on the forehead. It looks very strange right now, but you can fix that by dropping the opacity of the layer to around 40 percent.

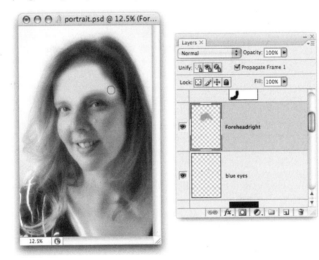

5. **Reduce the layer opacity.** When you finish painting, decrease the layer opacity to
   around 40 percent using the Opacity slider in the Layers palette.

6. **Repeat steps 1 through 5 for other areas of the face.** Create a new layer for each area.
   You may need to change the sample size to the 51 by 51 Average setting when working
   on smaller areas, and you might need to change the brush size for different areas, too. For
   example, the nose needs a smaller brush size of around 150 to 160 pixels.

7. **Balance the effect of the various painted layers.** To do this, change the Opacity setting
   of each layer in the Layers palette. Each layer probably needs its own unique opacity. Try
   to err on the side of caution to keep the effect as natural as possible.

8. **Add all the layers to a new group.** Select the top paint layer in the Layers palette, then hold down Shift and select the bottom paint layer. Now press Ctrl+G (⌘+G on the Mac) to group the layers into a new layer group. Doing this has two advantages. First, you can collapse the group to keep the Layers palette tidy. Second, you can now reduce the effect of the paint layers as a whole by changing the Opacity setting of just that group. You can see how these layers have finished up in Figure 15.28.

FIGURE 15.28

All the paint layers in a group. The group's opacity is reduced to 80 percent, taming the effect of all the paint layers at once.

You now have the final portrait. You've probably done more retouching than one would normally carry out — especially with the paint layers — but the results are pretty good. You can still see the original texture of the skin through the retouching, and that's deliberate; you wanted to keep the model human, but you also tweaked the skin tones and texture to produce a much more flattering result.

Retouching is a long process, and there's no getting around the fact that it takes patience and time to complete. But the results can be stunning, if not always exactly real!

Converting Photos to Black and White

Converting color digital photos to monochrome — traditionally referred to as black and white — has always been a topic of much debate in digital photography circles. Black and white has long been considered by many to be the purest form of photography, shunning color for the sake of form and timeless appeal. It's hard, though, to match the feel of a black-and-white film when converting a color digital photograph.

When converting to black and white, the impact of color is lost, and it's easy to produce images that lack drama and appear washed out. All the techniques used in the following example rely on manipulating the relative brightness levels of the color channels in the original photo to produce a great-looking result in black and white.

In this example, you're going to take two color photos — shown in Figure 15.29 — and apply several different conversion techniques to them, looking to find the best method in each case.

FIGURE 15.29

Here are the two photos you'll be using. The first example (a) is an image of a slightly distressed metal gate, coupled with some ivy, giving a nice range of colors, shadows, and highlights. In the second example (b), Sammy is playing to the camera for all he's worth, and in the process giving us some skin tones to play with.

Both of these images are classic cases for black-and-white conversion. The gate has a lot of shapes that suit the medium nicely, and black-and-white portraits are a timeless way of presenting the essence of a person.

The conversion techniques you'll be looking at are of the layer-based variety. You'll try using the following:

- Hue/Saturation adjustment layer
- Channel Mixer adjustment layer
- Black & White adjustment layer

All these techniques are nondestructive, leaving the original images untouched. After you finish the conversions, you'll look at which method worked best for these two images, and why.

CROSS-REF   You can find more on adjustment layers in Chapter 6.

Converting the images using Hue/Saturation

The first technique uses a Hue/Saturation adjustment layer to make the conversion. Start with the gate photo, and open it in Photoshop.

To add the adjustment layer, click the Create New Fill or Adjustment Layer icon in the Layers palette and choose Hue/Saturation from the pop-up menu to display the Hue/Saturation dialog box, as seen in Figure 15.30. The process of creating a monochrome image in this case is simple: just click and drag the Saturation slider all the way to the left. The Hue slider now has no effect, because all the color information is removed from the image. You can make the image darker by pulling the Lightness slider to the left, or lighter by dragging the slider to the right.

FIGURE 15.30

The Hue/Saturation dialog box, with the Saturation slider pulled all the way to the left to fully desaturate the image.

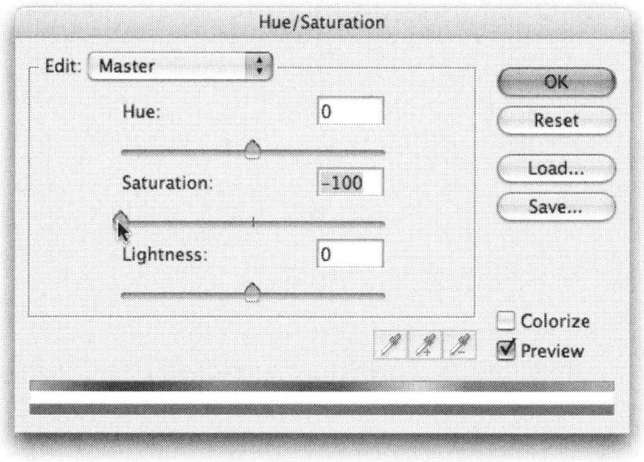

NOTE   This action of dragging the Saturation slider fully to the left has the same effect as choosing Image ⇨ Adjustments ⇨ Desaturate, but, of course, it's not a destructive edit.

Great. You have a black-and-white version of the photo, but it's a little flat and lifeless. How can you bring out some of the detail of the reds in the gate and the roof behind, as well as the greens in the foliage?

You can use the Hue/Saturation adjustment to change the brightness values of the primary (red, green, and blue) and secondary (cyan, magenta, and yellow) color ranges. This lets us choose how much of these color channels are represented in the black-and-white mix. With the dialog box still open, choose Reds from the Edit option. The Hue and Saturation sliders have no effect, because the image is black and white, but the Lightness slider allows you to lighten and darken the reds in the image, effectively emphasizing or de-emphasizing them.

If you drag the Lightness slider to the right, you can see the red areas of the image — the paint on the gate and roof, mostly — getting lighter and more prominent. Drag this slider to around +80. Choosing Greens from the Edit option, you can drag the Lightness slider all the way left to -100 to darken the foliage. That greenery has a fair amount of yellow in the coloration, too, so if you choose Yellows and again drag the Lightness slider fully left to -100, it further darkens the foliage.

NOTE Photoshop remembers the values for each color range, even while you edit another range.

Leave the adjustment there. The primaries are the main colors contained within this image, so adjusting the other color ranges would have much less effect. In Figure 15.31 you can see the result.

FIGURE 15.31

The gate after applying the per-color Lightness slider adjustments

Turn your attention to the portrait. Repeat the same procedure used for the gate photo: open the image in Photoshop, add a Hue/Saturation adjustment layer, and click and drag the Saturation slider to the left. This produces the basic monochrome image. Like the gate, the conversion is pretty "flat" at this stage and hasn't produced a great image.

As before, you can adjust the Lightness slider for each color range individually. Try boosting the reds to lighten Sammy's skin tones to around +40. You can use the Lightness slider for the yellows range to lighten the background, which is a beige color in the original photo, and this also has some effect on the skin tones. Try dragging it right to a value of +40. Finally, bring out Sammy's eyes and T-shirt by boosting the Lightness value of the blues to +30.

The resulting version of the photo has nicer skin tones than the initial conversion, but it's still a little washed out, as you can see in Figure 15.32.

FIGURE 15.32

The portrait with a Hue/Saturation adjustment layer applied. Individual Lightness adjustments have been made to the reds, yellows and blues.

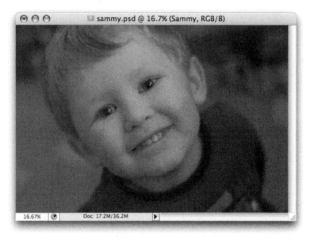

TIP You could try introducing a Levels adjustment layer at this point to darken the shadows and boost the highlights, thereby increasing contrast in the image.

Converting the images using the Channel Mixer

The Channel Mixer adjustment has been something of a standard in black-and-white conversion in recent years, and can produce some excellent results. Try using it on the two example images.

As before, start with the gate. Open the gate image in Photoshop. To add the adjustment layer, click the Create New Fill or Adjustment Layer icon in the Layers palette and choose Channel Mixer from the menu. The Channel Mixer dialog box appears, as shown in Figure 15.33.

FIGURE 15.33

The Channel Mixer dialog box. Note the Monochrome option, which makes the image black and white.

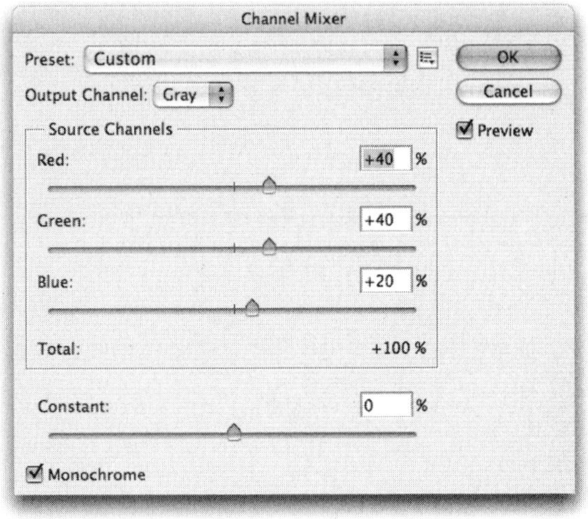

The first step is to select the Monochrome option at the bottom of the dialog box. This puts the Channel Mixer in monochrome mode; you'll notice that the image is now converted to black and white in the document window.

You can also see three sliders for Red, Green, and Blue. Use these to emphasize or de-emphasize the impact that these color channels have in the monochrome image.

So that you can compare the final result, try to achieve a similar effect as when using the Hue/Saturation adjustment. With that in mind, boost the reds to around +110 percent to bring out the gate and the roof behind. Drop the Green slider to -34 percent to darken the foliage; then even out the image by dragging the Blue slider to the right to a value of +25 percent. As you can see in Figure 15.34, this produces quite a dramatic result.

NOTE   In the Channel Mixer, the Red, Green, and Blue sliders should add up to a maximum value of 100% to avoid clipping highlights or losing shadow detail.

How will the Channel Mixer do with your portrait image? Once again, add a Channel Mixer adjustment layer to that image by clicking the Create New Fill or Adjustment Layer icon in the Layers palette and choosing Channel Mixer from the menu. Select the Monochrome option in the resulting dialog box to create a default black-and-white conversion.

628

FIGURE 15.34

The slider adjustments in the Channel Mixer dialog box produce a much more dynamic image than the default values. The result has good contrast, and the original colors of the photo are nicely emphasized.

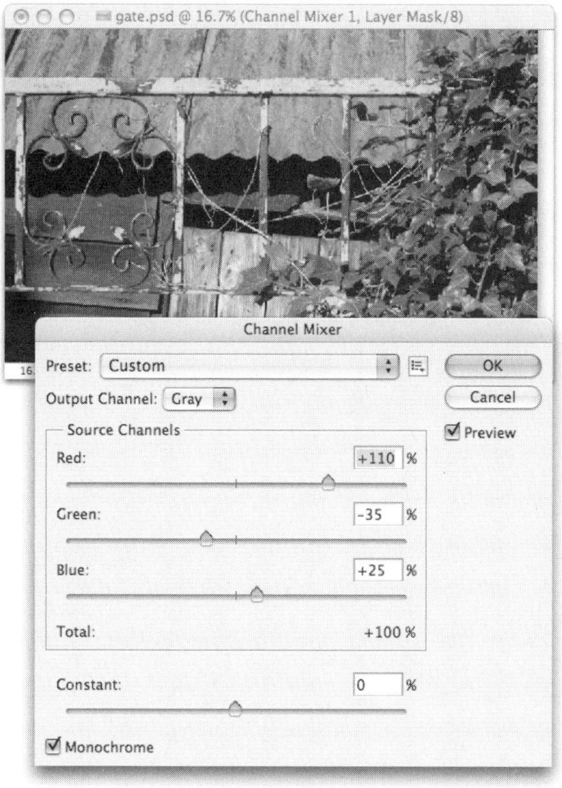

As with the gate, you need to do some tweaking to the color sliders to bring out the best in the image. Try boosting the Red slider to +80 percent to bring out the skin tones, and the Blue slider to +75 percent to emphasize Sammy's eyes. Drop the Green slider to -55 percent to balance the overall total to 100 percent.

Although you've emphasized the areas that you wanted to enhance, this results in a somewhat dark image. However, if you push the Green slider up farther, the image would start to posterize a little, and detail on the face would be lost. You can see the final image in Figure 15.35.

FIGURE 15.35

The final portrait in monochrome, created using the Channel Mixer adjustment

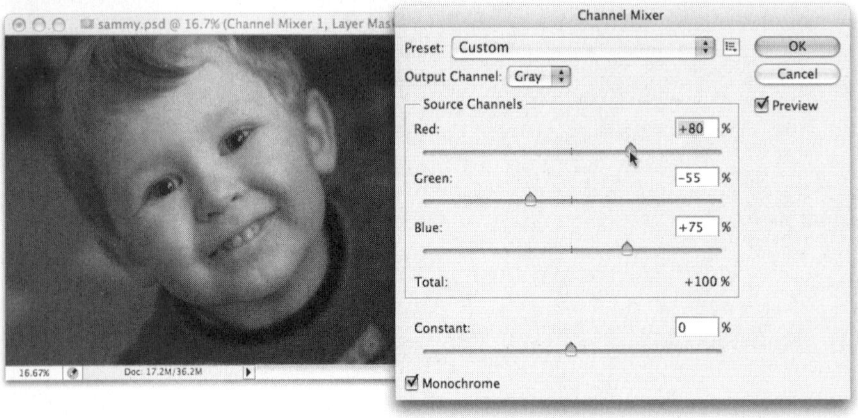

Converting the images using Black & White

The Black & White adjustment is the new kid on the block. Introduced in CS3, it provides a dedicated tool for black-and-white conversions. Like the Hue/Saturation and Channel Mixer adjustments, you can apply it as an adjustment layer so it's nondestructive. If you prefer, it's also available as a destructive edit under the Image ⇨ Adjustments menu.

Open the gate image and add a Black & White adjustment layer. The dialog box — shown in Figure 15.36 — is simple; it consists mostly of a selection of sliders for the primary and secondary colors. As you can see in the document window, Photoshop immediately converts the image to black and white, using default values for the color sliders.

As with the other techniques, though, the basic conversion is again quite flat and a little uninspiring. Use the sliders to boost the underlying colors in the image. Try increasing the Reds slider to around +120 percent and the Yellows to +42 percent to emphasize the gate and roof. To darken the foliage, drop the Greens slider to -20 percent. You can also drop the remaining sliders to -200 percent because there aren't really any instances of these colors in the original photo.

This produces a striking effect, which you can see in Figure 15.37.

FIGURE 15.36

The Black and White dialog box, with primary and secondary color sliders

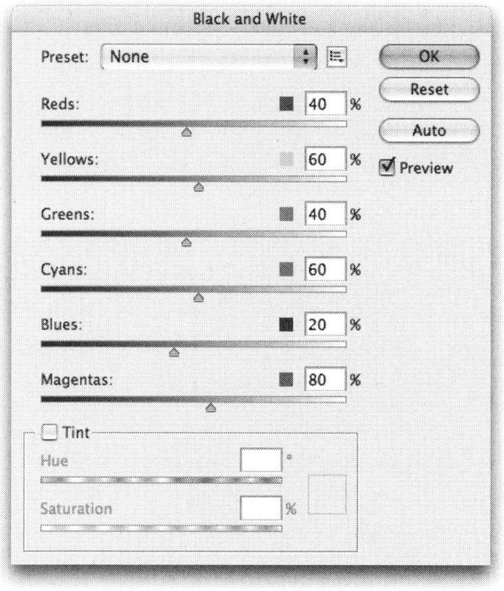

FIGURE 15.37

The Black & White adjustment layer produces good contrast once you tweak the color sliders a little.

Moving on to the portrait, again add a Black & White adjustment layer to the image. The basic default conversion is quite dark, so turn to the color sliders to adjust the lightness of the colors. You have a lot of control with the six sliders. The Reds, Yellows, and Magentas sliders all have an effect on the skin tones, and the Blues and Cyans sliders help bring out the eyes and the T-shirt.

Looking at the skin tones first, increase the Reds slider to +80 percent, the Yellows to +130 percent, and the Magentas to +130 percent. This produces a soft, glowing skin tone. For the eyes, boost the Blues and Cyans to +90 percent each. Drop the Greens slider to -200 percent because there aren't many greens in the original image. You can see the results in Figure 15.38.

NOTE Unlike working with the Channel Mixer, you don't have to worry about the sliders adding up to an overall percentage value when using the Black & White adjustment.

FIGURE 15.38

The result of the Black & White adjustment on Sammy is quite pleasing, with the skin tones in particular looking really nice.

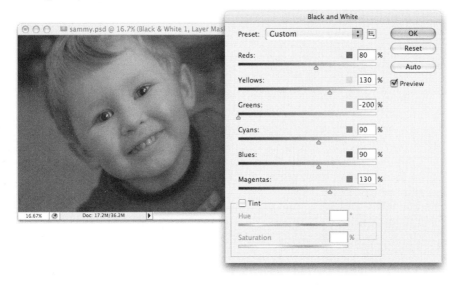

Comparing the three methods

Just about all the adjustment layer conversion methods are put to the test here, so how did they do? One thing is certain: You can't just add the adjustment layer and leave it at that. Each adjustment layer benefits enormously from tweaks to the color value sliders. Getting a good black-and-white image relies on boosting the luminance in the different color ranges and channels to emphasize the original colors of the image.

NOTE There are several other techniques for converting to black and white that don't particularly relate to layers. There's a good approach that involves changing the mode of the image to Lab color (Image ⇨ Mode ⇨ Lab Color). In the Channels palette, you then delete the a and b channels to leave only the lightness channel. Finally, you convert the whole image back to Grayscale, and then RGB, to perform further work on the image.

In the gate image, the results are pretty close. All the techniques did well here, and there's not much to choose between them. The Hue/Saturation approach lacks some contrast, so it would probably come down to a choice between the other two.

For the portrait, the results are more striking. The Hue/Saturation technique again lacks contrast, while the Channel Mixer version is generally too dark once the skin tones and eyes are boosted. The Black & White approach, though, has a really nice feel, with good contrast and great skin tones.

In terms of ease of use, the Hue/Saturation adjustment can't hold a candle to the other two, mainly because you can't see all your color range settings at the same time. This is fiddly to work with. Having to be careful with total color values in the Channel Mixer is also a little tiresome, so although there are more sliders to worry about in the Black & White adjustment, this is the clear winner here.

All in all, the new Black & White adjustment probably takes the crown, especially when dealing with skin tones.

Finishing off a black-and-white image

You've been looking at basic color-to-monochrome conversions in these examples, but you'll probably want to do more with your photo after the conversion. In Figure 15.39, you can see a final version of Sammy's portrait. All the techniques used are nondestructive and based on layers. Starting with the Black & White conversion method, various other techniques are then applied to create the final image:

- The Background layer is converted to a Smart Object (Sammy) and a Smart Sharpen Smart Filter applied just to the eyes. This is achieved by masking off the rest of the image, leaving only the eyes showing through.

- The Sammy Smart Object is duplicated and a wide Gaussian Blur of around 23 pixels is applied as a Smart Filter to the duplicate. Then its blending mode is set to Hard Light. This has the effect of boosting contrast and also adds a soft "glow" to the whole image.

- Sammy's teeth are whitened a touch using a Levels adjustment layer. A layer mask is used to restrict the adjustment to just the teeth. The effect is quite harsh, so the opacity of the layer is reduced to 67 percent.

- Last, a Levels adjustment layer is placed across the whole image just to boost the contrast a little more. This results in a slightly clipped highlight on Sammy's cheek, so the effect there is muted by painting a gray area onto the mask using a soft-edged brush and dropping the opacity of the whole layer to 39 percent.

FIGURE 15.39

The final version of Sammy; a great example of multiple nondestructive layer strategies in action. By applying the techniques you looked at in the book, you can get fantastic results without ever changing a single pixel of the underlying image — and isn't he lovely?

Aligning Two Handheld Photos

Imagine the scene. You're out at dusk with your camera, and you see a great shot. The trouble is that the difference in light between the sky and foreground is too great to be captured in one photo. You know that the sky is going to need a different exposure than the foreground. Combining two differently exposed shots to create a new, well-exposed image is a standard trick, but it only works well if you have a tripod; lining up the images is next to impossible otherwise. Without a tripod, you've lost the shot.

Or not. Photoshop CS3 has a new feature called Auto-Align Layers. This essentially transfers the hard work of aligning the images over to Photoshop, allowing you to line up handheld photos automatically. In this example, you explore this new feature to combine two handheld images taken in a scenario like the one just described. Because the camera is handheld, the two images line up only very roughly, and so are perfect candidates for this example. You can see the two starting photos in Figure 15.40.

FIGURE 15.40

FIGURE 15.40

The two starting images of sheep and a sunset. The photo on the left is very dark, and has been exposed for the sky. On the right is a photo that was exposed for the foreground, with the sky very much overexposed.

As well as the Auto-Align Layers feature, you'll also use adjustment layers and layer masks to finish the image off once the layers are lined up.

CROSS-REF You can find out a bit more on Auto-Align Layers in Chapter 1. Adjustment layers are covered in Chapter 6, while layer masks get a thorough treatment in Chapter 9.

Creating the document

The first stage of the process is to get the two photos coexisting in the same document. Open both photos in Photoshop, and position the documents so that both are visible on-screen. Switch to the lighter photo, and Shift+drag its Background layer in the Layers palette to the document window of the darker photo, as shown in Figure 15.41. You can see that the lighter photo perfectly covers the darker one. You can now safely close or minimize the document window for the lighter image.

The document now contains two layers: the darker photo as the Background layer and the lighter photo as Layer 1. Now's a great time to rename the layers so you can identify them. Call the layers **Dark** and **Light**, and save the document as a Photoshop file.

 **TIP** To rename the layers, simply double-click each layer's name in the Layers palette, and type the new name.

FIGURE 15.41

Dragging the Background layer from the lighter photo to the document window of the darker photo

Aligning the layers

You can take this opportunity to see just how rough the alignment of these two shots really is. Toggle the visibility of the Light layer off and on by clicking its eye icon in the Layers palette. You can see that both the horizontal and vertical alignments are out somewhat. The darker image sits higher and farther to the right when compared to the lighter photo. It's this kind of issue that previously would have required judicious use of the Move tool and Distort command to get even an approximate match. Now though, you can let Photoshop take the strain.

To align the layers automatically, Ctrl+click (⌘+click on the Mac) each layer in Layers palette to select them both, then choose Edit ➪ Auto-Align Layers. In the dialog box that appears, leave the settings at the default of Auto, and click OK. You might see an Align Selected Layers Based on Content progress bar at this point. This is just Photoshop doing its thing.

After the process is complete, you'll see that Photoshop has moved and distorted the two layers, leaving some blank space around the edges. Toggle the visibility of the Light layer, and you can see that the layers are now perfectly aligned. The lines in the landscape line up beautifully, and the process hasn't been fooled by stray sheep that moved between the original two exposures. The results appear in Figure 15.42.

FIGURE 15.42

Here you can see just the Dark layer (a), and both layers together (b). There are gaps around the edges, which are a legacy of the lack of alignment in the originals, but the lines in the photos match up perfectly.

In about 30 seconds, you've accomplished automatically what might have previously taken an hour, even assuming a decent result could be achieved manually at all.

Creating the final image

Although the layers are now aligned, they're pretty far from a final image. You need to let the Dark layer show through in the sky and in the far hills. You also want to make the exposure work between the two images. Finally, it would be good to get rid of those jagged edges around the photos.

First, look at how to let that Dark layer through. You can accomplish this through a layer mask applied to the Light layer. Select the Light layer in the Layers palette, and click the Add Layer Mask icon at the base of the palette. This adds a layer mask to the layer; you can see that the layer now has a layer mask thumbnail in the Layers palette.

You could paint onto the layer mask using brushes, but it's hard to get the point where the sky meets the foreground to match up well this way; there will almost always be a halo of dark or light on the skyline. Instead, you're going to use the Gradient tool to create the mask. To do so, follow these steps:

1. **Make sure your foreground color is set to black.** A quick way to do this is simply to press D.

2. **Select the Gradient tool.** Click the Gradient icon in the Toolbox, or press Shift+G until the icon appears in the Toolbox.

3. **Click the downward-pointing arrow next to the gradient box in the options bar.** The Gradient Picker dialog box appears.

4. **Select the Foreground to Transparent preset, as shown in Figure 15.43.** This lets you fill the mask with a gradient moving from black pixels (the foreground color) to white (the underlying color of the mask).

FIGURE 15.43

Picking the Foreground to Transparent gradient preset in the Gradient Picker

5. **Activate the layer mask.** To do this, click its thumbnail in the Layers palette. A border appears around the thumbnail, indicating that it's active.

6. **Fill the mask with the gradient.** In the document window, click near the top of the image and Shift+drag straight downward. Figure 15.44 shows this process in action.

You can see that the top part of the Light layer — the part where the mask is pure black — has been masked off. As you move down the image, the gradient moves through lighter shades of gray, so the Light layer shows through more and more. Eventually, at the point where the mask is pure white, the Light layer shows through fully, blocking out the Dark layer below. In other words, you have a smooth transition from one layer to the other. Try toggling the visibility of the Dark layer to see how the Light layer interacts with its layer mask.

FIGURE 15.44

Filling the mask with the gradient. You want a smooth mask, so stretch out the gradient so that it travels a fair way down the image.

That's great, but it would be even better if you could really bring out the greens and the sheep in the foreground. To do this, add an Exposure adjustment layer by clicking the Create New Fill or Adjustment Layer icon in the Layers palette and choosing Exposure from the menu. In the Exposure dialog box, click and drag the Exposure slider to the right to around 1.1. As you do this, the whole image gets a lot lighter. In fact, the sky and far hills are getting a bit too bright. Click OK to close the dialog box.

You can fix the sky using the same gradient masking process used on the Light layer. In the Layers palette, you can see that the Exposure adjustment layer already has a layer mask attached, so all you need to do is fill that with the Foreground to Transparent gradient. Select the Gradient tool again, and make sure that you're using the same settings as before. Click the Exposure layer's mask thumbnail in the Layers palette to make sure it's active.

Now Shift+drag downward in the document window from near the top of the image to just above the sheep. Now the Exposure layer only affects the sheep area, leaving the sky and the far hill unaffected. You can see this stage in Figure 15.45.

FIGURE 15.45

The image with the masked Exposure adjustment layer in place

TIP If you want, you can push that Exposure adjustment a little further. To do this, double-click the Exposure layer's thumbnail, and drag the Exposure slider farther to the right. However, watch out for making the whole image look too unreal.

Finally, you want to get rid of the ragged edges created during the Auto-Align Layers process. You're just going to crop the image down to remove these, though if you are desperate to preserve the edges, you could potentially attempt to use the Clone Stamp tool, or one of its relatives, to create new edges for the image.

CAUTION Unlike most other steps in these examples, this cropping step is destructive, so be aware that you'll actually be losing these edge areas for good, once the image is saved.

Select the Crop tool in the Toolbox, then click and drag in the document window. You're looking to preserve as much of the good area of the image as you can, while removing the redundant edge areas. After you release the mouse button, you can see that the Crop tool has left you with marching ants indicating the crop area, and resize handles on the edges and corners of the crop area, as seen in Figure 15.46. You can use these handles to resize the crop area at this stage.

When you're happy with the crop area, press Enter (Return on the Mac) to commit the crop. You now have the final image, as shown in Figure 15.47. It's a great result, and it was simple to achieve thanks to the Auto-Align Layers command.

FIGURE 15.46

After dragging out the initial rectangle, resize handles appear around the crop area, allowing you to readjust the area if necessary. Photoshop also darkens the area to be cropped, letting you concentrate on the area that will remain.

FIGURE 15.47

The final image, with all those ragged edges cropped out

Summary

Photo manipulation — arguably the core purpose of Photoshop — is a big topic. In this chapter, you've been given a taste of the kind of results you can achieve when manipulating photos in Photoshop. In each case, layers played a big part in the process.

First, you looked at how to improve exposure and contrast in a landscape photo. You learned how to use adjustment layers and layer masks to apply adjustments selectively within the photo, as well as how to use Smart Filters to apply sharpening and add "pop" to the image.

You then moved onto color correction and learned how to remove color casts from a couple of troubled images. You learned how to use the Levels and Curves adjustment layers to alter the color balance in these images and correct their casts.

Next, you tackled a big topic: how to retouch a portrait. You took a basic portrait photo and transformed it into an image fit for a glossy magazine. Along the way, you explored the Exposure, Levels, Curves, and Hue/Saturation adjustment layers. Layer masks, the Quick Mask, layer blending modes, Smart Objects, and the new Smart Filters in Photoshop CS3 were also covered.

You looked at three methods for converting a color photo to black and white: the Hue/Saturation adjustment layer, the Channel Mixer adjustment layer, and the new Black & White adjustment layer. You learned how to use each of these adjustment layers to convert two images. The three methods were compared to see which produced the best results, and some techniques were shown for further improving the converted portrait image.

Finally, you explored Photoshop's new Auto-Align Layers command. This fantastic new feature lets you easily align multiple photos of the same scene, even if those photos were taken without a tripod. You used this feature to combine two similar photos to achieve a good overall exposure.

Chapter 16

Creating Personal Projects with Layers

In the previous two chapters, you looked at using Photoshop's layers from the perspectives of a designer and a photographer, but now it's time to investigate some practical applications of layers for day-to-day use. The projects covered here seem simple enough in theory, but are actually quite involved when you get right down to it. You'll be using lots of the techniques covered in the other parts of the book to produce the following:

- **An event invitation:** You'll create the basic invitation, and then set it up so that it can be printed several times on a single sheet of paper, saving time and paper. You'll also learn how to lay out the invitation so that it's almost impossible to produce a bad design!

- **A great poster promoting a party:** This quick poster example covers multiple layer techniques to really grab the attention of potential partygoers.

- **A simple calendar:** Calendars make great personal gifts. In this example, you design the pages of a calendar, and build the monthly calendar element itself.

It can be tempting when working on projects like these to reach immediately for the word processor, but Photoshop's flexibility can produce much more elegant, professional results. You'll learn techniques that you can master quickly to produce designs that will lift your work onto another level.

ON the CD-ROM Each of these three examples comes with a bunch of Photoshop files on the accompanying CD-ROM. You can use these files to work through the examples yourself if you want.

Creating and Printing Invitations

In the first example, you'll be creating an invitation for an event — in this case a ruby wedding anniversary dinner for a couple called Tommy and Gina. Photoshop's great for this kind of work, as it gives you a lot of flexibility with page layout that word processors find hard to match. Even the simplest invitation can look great if well laid out and nicely printed, and you'll be using Photoshop's layers to achieve this, along with a helping hand in the form of guides and grids.

> **CROSS-REF**   You'll use several type layers and shape layers, and you'll also look at transforming and grouping layers. You can find detailed information on type layers in Chapter 4, while shape layers are covered in Chapter 5. Learn about transforming layers in Chapter 3, and grouping layers in Chapter 2.

> **NOTE**   An invitation is created in this example, but you can apply the same principles to other scenarios — promotional leaflets, notices, or stickers, for example.

The information you want to impart is pretty simple: the event, the time and date, and the place. Here's the text you want to include:

- Celebrate Tommy & Gina's Ruby Wedding by coming to dinner
- 7pm, 5.21.08
- Joe's Place, 212 Anystreet, Chicago, IL, 312-1234-1234

Once you've laid out the invitation in Photoshop, you'll investigate how to print multiple copies of that invitation onto a single piece of paper, so you can create a big batch of invitations for all Tommy and Gina's friends and family. You'll print the invitations on a standard domestic inkjet printer, rather than sending them off for printing elsewhere.

Producing the invitation is a three-stage process:

- Designing the basic invitation
- Laying out multiple copies of the invitation on a single page
- Printing the invitation

Creating a document for the invitation

The first thing to do is to determine the size of your invitations. You're going to be printing multiple copies of the invitation onto a single sheet of paper. U.S. Letter paper is 8.5 inches wide by 11 inches high. Aim to get four invitations on each sheet. One quarter of a sheet of U.S. Letter paper is 4.25 inches by 5.5 inches, so that will be the size of the invitation.

Go ahead and create the Photoshop document. Open Photoshop and choose File ➪ New. In the New dialog box, you see several options for defining the properties of the new document, as shown in Figure 16.1. To set up your document, follow these steps:

1. **Name the document.** In the Name field, type a useful name for the document, such as **Dinner Invitation**.

2. **Set the width and height.** Set a width of 4.25 inches. Choose inches from the pop-up menu to the right of the Width box — the equivalent menu for the Height option also changes to inches as you do this — and type **4.25** in the Width box. In the Height box, type **5.5**.

3. **Set the resolution.** Because you'll be printing this document, you want a high resolution of, say, 300 pixels per inch. Type **300** in the Resolution box, and make sure the menu to the right of the box is set to pixels/inch.

4. **Specify an 8-bit RGB color mode.** Choose RGB color from the Color Mode menu, and 8 bit from the menu to the right of Color Mode.

5. **Select a white background and create the document.** Choose White from the Background Contents menu, and click OK to create your new invitation document.

FIGURE 16.1

The New dialog box, showing the options that you need for your new document

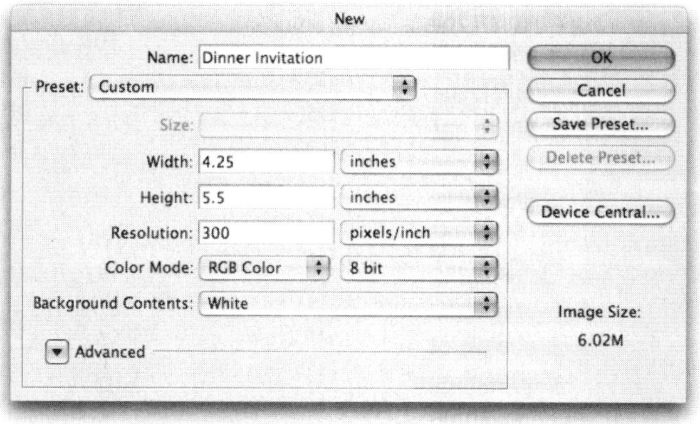

Laying out the invitation

Deciding exactly where to put elements on a page is often a tricky business. You're going to use a principle that has served designers well for many years: the grid. A grid is simply a way of breaking up a page into areas, which really helps when placing elements such as text and graphics. One of the simplest grids is based on the rule of thirds, which dictates that splitting any composition into thirds results in a look that is pleasing to the eye. This goes for photographs, film, graphic design, and indeed any kind of visual communication.

So how do you add a grid to your document? Use Photoshop's guides feature. Guides are simply straight lines — by default a light blue — that overlay the document window. They don't print; they are just there to help us place elements on the page. They don't automatically create a grid for us, though, so you have to do that manually.

CROSS-REF   For more information on creating and using Photoshop's guides, refer to Chapter 2.

Start by turning on the rulers for the invitation document window. To do this, choose View ⇨ Rulers, or press Ctrl+R (⌘+R on the Mac). A horizontal ruler appears along the top of the window, and a vertical ruler appears down the left side. Make sure the rulers are measured in inches by right-clicking one of the rulers and choosing Inches from the pop-up menu. Turning on the rulers serves two purposes: first, it's easier to create guides with rulers enabled, and second, they help you to position the guides accurately.

Creating the border guides

You first want to create a border around the document using guides. The border will be one-eighth of an inch (or 0.127 inches) from the edge of the document. Set the zoom value to 25 percent. You can do this by double-clicking the zoom value at the bottom-left corner of the document window and typing 25, or by zooming in and out using Ctrl+= and Ctrl+- (⌘+= and ⌘+- on the Mac). At this zoom setting, each subdivision on the ruler represents one-eighth of an inch. Create a horizontal guide by clicking in the top ruler and dragging downward, lining up the dotted line with the first vertical subdivision on the left ruler. Drag out another horizontal guide, and position this one so it lines up with the first subdivision from the bottom of the document window.

TIP   Turn on snapping by choosing View ⇨ Snap. You can then hold down Shift as you drag a guide to snap it to the ruler subdivisions.

Click and drag from the left ruler to create a vertical guide, and line up this guide with the first subdivision on the left-hand side of the horizontal ruler. Now do the same for a second vertical guide at the last subdivision on the right. Your border should look like Figure 16.2. If you can't see any guides, choose View ⇨ Show ⇨ Guides to turn them on, or press Ctrl+; (⌘+; on the Mac).

TIP   To move a guide you've already created, select the Move tool and position the cursor directly over the guide until it changes to two small parallel lines with arrows. You can then click and drag to reposition the guide.

Creating the inner grid

You now want to subdivide the space inside the border into horizontal and vertical thirds, again using guides. To do this, follow these steps:

FIGURE 16.2

Dragging out the fourth guide. The guides have created an eighth-of-an-inch border all around the document.

1. **Display the Info palette.** Open the Info palette by choosing Window ➪ Info or pressing F8. In the X, Y area in the bottom left of the palette you can read where you're positioning a guide as you drag it.

2. **Create the vertical thirds.** The remaining vertical space (rounded up a little) is 5.25 inches. Divided by three, this gives you vertical increments of 1.75 inches. Drag out two horizontal guides from the top ruler, and position them at 1.875 inches and 3.625 inches along the vertical ruler.

3. **Create the horizontal thirds.** Subdivide the horizontal space inside the border into thirds using two vertical guides. The overall width of the space is 4 inches. Each guide therefore needs to be at increments of 1.33 inches. Click and drag from the left ruler to create the first guide, and position it at 1.45 inches along the top ruler. Repeat for the second guide, positioning it at 2.8 inches. (It's hard to get these guides exactly 1.33 inches apart, but these measurements are close enough for your purposes.)

Your basic grid is now in place, as shown in Figure 16.3, ready to have the invitation elements inserted. It's a good idea to save the document at this stage.

The basic grid structure

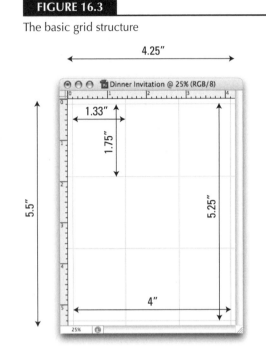

Adding text and graphics

You can now begin to have some fun with the invitation, and add the text and some decorative graphics. Follow these steps to add the invitation's text:

1. **Add the Dinner text.** Select the Type tool from the Toolbox and set your foreground color to black. In the options bar choose Times New Roman for the font family, Regular for the font style, and a nice big font size of 72 points. Now click somewhere in the top left of the document window and type **Dinner**. Press Ctrl+Enter (⌘+Return on the Mac) to commit the type, or click the Commit button in the options bar. A new type layer appears in the Layers palette.

2. **Resize and reposition the text.** The chances are that the type is not in quite the correct place, and you also want the type to span the width of the document. You can fix both these issues using the Move tool, so select this tool in the Toolbox (or press V) and make sure the Show Transform Controls option is selected in the options bar. Now you can click and drag the type layer in the document window to reposition it. Position the type so its baseline sits on the second horizontal guide in the document, with the left of the *D* just touching the first vertical guide on the left. To stretch the text across the whole width

between the borders, hold down Shift to maintain the proportions of the text, and click the top-right resize handle in the dotted bounding box around the type. Drag up and to the right, so that the right edge of the text aligns with the far-right vertical guide, as shown in Figure 16.4. After you do that, you'll probably need to drag the type down again so it sits on the horizontal guide. Press Enter (Return on the Mac) to commit the transform.

FIGURE 16.4

Resizing the Dinner text by dragging a corner resize handle

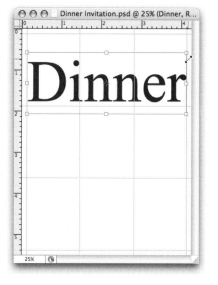

3. **Add the introductory text.** Great, the Dinner text leaves people in no doubt as to the subject of the invitation, but you're a little light on other information. Add some explanatory text. With the Type tool still selected, choose a smaller font size of 11 points, and choose Italic from the Font Style menu for some variety. Click the left guide in the document window, just above the Dinner text — but not too close or Photoshop will think you're trying to edit that text. Now type **Celebrate Tommy & Gina's Ruby Wedding by coming to...** and press Ctrl+Enter (⌘+Return on the Mac) to save the text. Use the Move tool to drag the type layer a little closer to the main Dinner text if need be. Figure 16.5 shows the opening sentence in place, together with the graphical "hook" of the large text.

FIGURE 16.5

The opening sentence in place. Notice how the left edges of the two type layers line up with the left guide.

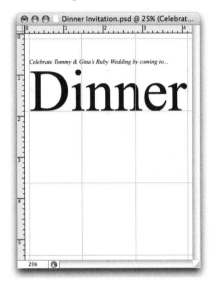

4. **Add the time and date.** Select the Type tool and click the first vertical guide in the document window, just above the third horizontal guide. Type **7pm, 5.21.07**. Press Crl+Enter (⌘+Return on the Mac) to commit the type. With the Type tool still selected, choose Regular from the Font Style menu in the options bar.

> **NOTE** As long as the type layer you're working on is selected in the Layers palette, and the Type tool itself is also selected, you can change the properties of the type using the options bar or Character and Paragraph palettes, regardless of how long ago the type layer was created.

5. **Resize and reposition the time and date.** Select the Move tool, and make sure that the Show Transform Controls option is still selected in the options bar. Hold down Shift, click the top-right handle of the bounding box, and drag the handle up and to the right until the text spans the width of the first third of the document. Press Enter (Return on the Mac) to commit the scaling operation, then reposition the type so that the bottoms of the numbers and lowercase *m* sit on the horizontal guide.

6. **Add the venue and location.** The last section of text describes the venue and location of the meal. Put this on the right side of the document, just under the third horizontal guide from the top. Reselect the Type tool, and this time click in the document window on the third vertical guide from the left, just beneath the third horizontal guide. Type the name of the venue — **Joe's Place** — and press Enter (Return on the Mac) a couple of times to move the cursor down the page. Now type the address — **212 Anystreet Chicago, IL** — over two lines. Press Enter/Return twice again, and type the phone

number — **312 1234 1234**. Press Ctrl+Enter (⌘+Return on the Mac) to commit the type. Now choose a font size of 12 points in the options bar. If required, use the Move tool to line up the new type with the guides. Your invitation now looks like Figure 16.6.

FIGURE 16.6

All your type is now in place. You have some intro text, the eye-grabbing "Dinner" text, the time and place, and a contact number.

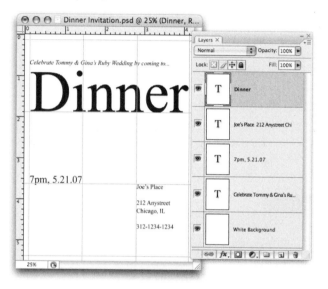

As mentioned earlier, the guides are only there as pointers, and won't print with the final document. To see how your invitation looks without the guides, choose View ➪ Show ➪ Guides to turn off the guides. They're still there, just hidden. You can also press Ctrl+; (⌘+; on the Mac) to toggle the guides on and off.

This is okay, but the invitation could use a little decoration here and there. You can use shape layers for this. Follow these steps to add the decorative elements:

1. **Add two horizontal lines top and bottom to "contain" the type.** Click the Shape Tool icon in the Toolbox; then select the Line tool in the options bar. Make sure the Shape Layers option is enabled, and give the line a weight of 5 pixels. Turn off any arrowhead options, and make sure the foreground color is still set to black. Position the cursor at the intersection of the topmost and leftmost guides in the document window. Now Shift+drag to the right, all the way to the fourth vertical guide. Repeat the process at the bottom of the document window, along the fourth horizontal guide. When you're done, you should have a new shape layer in the Layers palette, with the two line shapes contained within the linked vector mask.

 You may end up with two shape layers instead of one, but that's fine. If you hold down Shift before you start dragging, the Add To Shape Area option kicks in, creating the new shape on the same shape layer. If you press Shift after you start dragging, then Photoshop creates a new shape layer instead.

 Because you're creating the lines right on top of the guides, it can be hard to see what's going on, so when you're done, hide the guides briefly to make sure everything's in the right place.

2. **Choose an ornament shape.** Add a little flourish to the invitation in the form of another shape layer. With the Line tool still selected, click the Custom Shape Tool icon in the options bar. This tool creates shapes based on your selection within the Shape option, also in the options bar. Click inside the Shape option to display the Custom Shape Picker, and select a suitably decorative preset. In Figure 16.7, you can see that the snappily titled Floral Ornament 3 is used. Again, make sure the Shape Layers option toward the left of the options bar is selected.

 The Floral Ornament 3 preset is in the Ornaments library that comes with Photoshop. To load this library, click the arrow in the top right corner of the Custom Shape Picker and choose Ornaments from the menu that appears.

FIGURE 16.7

Choosing a floral shape in the Custom Shape Picker

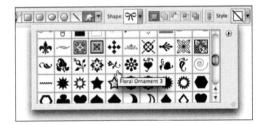

3. **Draw the shape.** Balance the composition of the invitation by placing the new shape in the center third of the document between Dinner and the text below. Click in the document window on the second vertical guide from the left, roughly in the vertical center of the invitation. Hold down Shift to constrain the shape's proportions, click and drag right to the third vertical guide, and release the mouse button. Now use the Move tool to drag the shape so that it sits nicely between the two areas of text.

 If you've been rigid with your grid, as this example illustrates, then this kind of decorative element can be positioned more freely to throw a little life into a composition.

As a very last tweak, make the large Dinner type layer slightly transparent to tone it down a little. Because you're making a black element translucent over a white background, this has the effect of turning it gray. Select that type layer in the Layers palette and, using the Opacity slider, drop the layer's opacity to around 50 percent.

Hide the guides by pressing Ctrl+; (⌘+; on the Mac). In Figure 16.8, the layout appears in all its glory. It's very simple, but it works well compositionally because of the grid you put in place, and the layout is much more interesting than could easily be achieved in a word processor.

The completed invitation. The use of a grid has really helped the layout, and you've created the whole thing using just one font and one color!

Placing multiple copies on a single page

If you printed the invitation as it stands now, you'd be able to print only one invitation for every page that went through the printer. That would be a tremendous waste of paper, and you'd spend much longer at the computer, printing out more pages than you needed to. It's much better to print multiple copies onto one sheet. Here's how you can do this.

First, prepare a full-page document to contain the multiple copies by following these steps:

1. **Create the document.** The size of the invitation is based on a quarter of a sheet of U.S. Letter paper, so U.S. Letter is the size you need. Choose File ➪ New and, in the New dialog box, choose U.S. Paper from the Preset menu. Choose Letter for the Size. Because a

preset size is selected this time, Photoshop automatically fills in the Width and Height boxes, as shown in Figure 16.9. Make sure the Resolution is set at 300 pixels/inch, and click OK to create the document.

FIGURE 16.9

The new document is based on the U.S. Paper preset and, as before, it has a resolution of 300 pixels per inch.

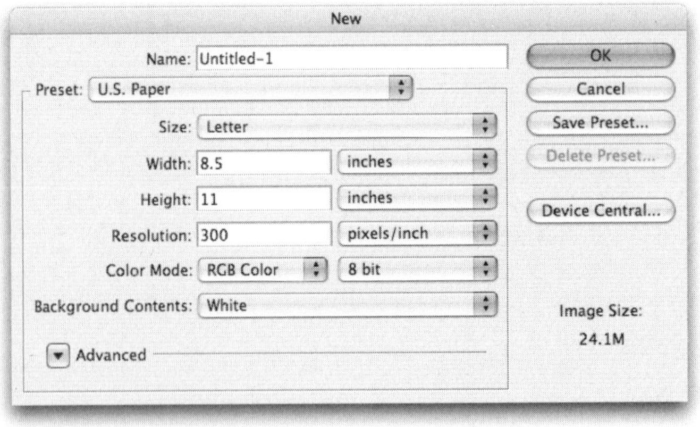

2. **Add a vertical guide.** You're going to use guides again to split the new document up into quarters, giving you a visual clue as to where to put the invitations on the page. Turn on the rulers if necessary by pressing Ctrl+R (⌘+R on the Mac). The units should be set to inches, but if not, right-click on a ruler and choose Inches from the pop-up menu. Next, turn on the Snap option by choosing View ➪ Snap. (If the option is checked then Snap is active.) Now click and drag out a guide from the left ruler. Around the middle of the document you'll feel the guide snap to the center. It's subtle, but it feels like a definite "stickiness."

3. **Add a horizontal guide.** Create a horizontal guide by dragging from the top ruler. Again, around the vertical center of the document you'll feel the guide snap into place. The document is now segmented into quarters, ready to receive the invitations.

CROSS-REF   Find out how snapping works, as well as how to manipulate guides, in Chapter 2.

Going back to the original invitation document, prepare the layers of that document by grouping them all together. To do this, first convert the Background layer to a normal layer. The reason for this is that you want to take the white Background layer with you over to the new document to aid with positioning, and you can't group a Background layer with other layers. Double-click the Background layer in the Layers palette and, in the New Layer dialog box that appears, give the background a sensible name like **White Background**.

Click the top layer in the Layers palette, then Shift+click the bottom layer. This selects all the layers in the document. Now choose New Group from Layers in the Layers palette menu. In the dialog box that appears, type a name for the group, such as **Invitation**. Click OK. Photoshop moves all the layers into a new group, signified by a small folder icon in the Layers palette. If you expand that group by clicking the little arrow to the left of the folder icon, you'll see all your layers contained within the group.

Now you can easily take the invitation across to the full U.S. Letter-sized paper document. Display both the invitation and paper document windows so you can see them both, and click the invitation document so you can see the group you just created in the Layers palette. Click and drag the group from the Layers palette to the paper document window, as shown in Figure 16.10.

FIGURE 16.10

Dragging the Invitation layer group to the U.S. Letter document

You now see the invitation in the U.S. Letter document, and the group appears above the Background layer in the document's Layers palette. You now need to create multiple copies of the invitation in this document. To do that, follow these steps:

1. **Turn on snapping to guides.** Choose View ⇨ Snap To ⇨ Guides if it's not already selected.

2. **Position the first group in the top left of the document.** Select the Move tool and select the Invitation group in the Layers palette. In the document window, click and drag the invitation to the top left. Because you're moving the whole group, all the layers in that

group move as one. When you reach the top left, you'll feel the snap kick in as the group snaps to the guides.

3. **Duplicate the group and position the duplicate.** You now copy the first group to the top-right quadrant of the image. Still using the Move tool, hold down Alt+Shift (Option+Shift on the Mac). This key combination both constrains movement to the horizontal, and creates a copy of the group at the same time as moving it. Now click the invitation in the document window. The cursor changes to a double arrow to indicate that you're about to make a copy. Drag the invitation to the right. You'll feel the snap again as the invitation reaches its destination. Figure 16.11 shows this process of duplicating and moving.

4. **Create a third invitation.** Perform the same operation as the previous step, but this time Alt+Shift+click (Option+Shift+click on the Mac) and drag the new group from the top right down to the bottom right.

5. **Create the final invitation.** Again, Alt+Shift+drag (Option+Shift+drag on the Mac) the invitation from the bottom right to the bottom left.

CAUTION   When moving and duplicating the invitations, make sure you don't have the Auto-Select: Layer option selected in the Move tool's options bar. If you do then you'll end up moving and duplicating layers within the invitation group, rather than the group itself.

FIGURE 16.11

Duplicating the invitation using the Move tool

You've now filled the U.S. Letter document with four copies of the invitation. In the Layers palette, you see three copies of the original group, making four in total. Each group contains all the layers for each copy of the invitation. You can see the final document in Figure 16.12.

The final document, with four invitations on the page

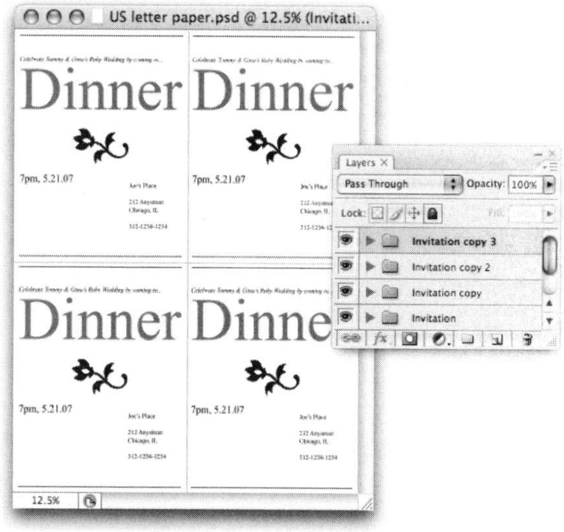

Preparing the document for printing

You can now turn your attention to printing the page. After the pages are printed, you're going to need to cut them into individual invitations. Although you can see those guides on the page at the moment, they won't be visible when the document is printed. This would make it hard to cut the invitations up accurately. You need to introduce some form of visual cutting guide that actually prints on the document. The edges of the document will take care of themselves, but you want to add something between the invitations to make it easier to line up the cuts after printing.

A simple way to achieve this is to re-create the guides using the Line tool. To do this, follow these steps:

1. **Pick a light gray foreground color.** You only need it to be just visible, so choose, say RGB 220, 220, 220.

2. **Select the Line tool.** Click the Shape Tool icon in the Toolbox; then click the Line Tool icon in the options bar. Give the line a weight of 1 pixel, and make sure arrowheads are turned off.

3. **Create the vertical cutting guide.** Position the cursor at the top of the existing vertical guide, where it meets the top of the document. Hold down Shift to constrain the line, and click and drag the line downward until it hits the bottom of the document.

4. **Create the horizontal cutting guide.** Position the cursor at the left of the horizontal guide, where it meets the left edge of the document. Now hold down Shift; then drag to the right until you reach the right side of the document.

5. **Turn off the guides to view the new, printable guides.** Press Ctrl+; (⌘+; on the Mac) to toggle the guides off and on. You may need to zoom right in to 100 percent to see the printable guides. They'll be more obvious when they print. You'll also see a new shape layer in the Layers palette, holding the two new lines you've just drawn.

> **TIP** Turn on guide snapping (View ➪ Snap To ➪ Guides) to help you position the lines accurately.

Printing the invitations

That's it — your invitations are now ready to print — so take a look at printing the document. Printing in Photoshop is centered on the Print dialog box, as shown in Figure 16.13. To display this dialog box, choose File ➪ Print.

FIGURE 16.13

The Print dialog box, showing your document in the preview area

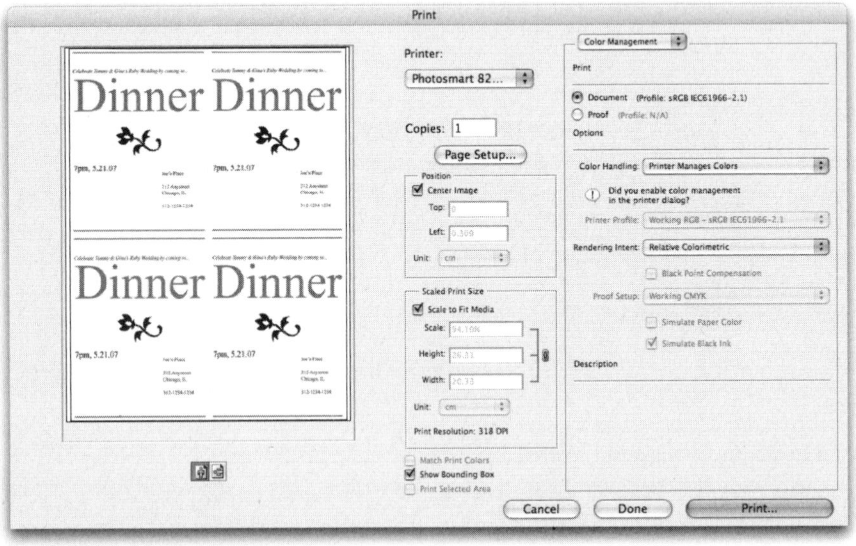

NEW FEATURE Photoshop CS3 features a new and improved Print dialog box that replaces the Print with Preview dialog box from CS2. You now always get a print preview, but most of the new features relate to color accuracy, and the preview itself is now color-managed.

There are two important things to watch out for here:

- **Page Setup button:** Click this to display a dialog box that lets you choose your printer and the paper size you'll print to. In your case, this will be U.S. Letter.

- **Scale to Fit Media option:** If you select this option, the image scales up or down to fit the paper size you've chosen. Select it to be safe, but if you have a printer that's capable of borderless printing (that is, you can print right to the edge of a page with no margins) you may want to deselect this option.

When you're happy, click Print, which displays a dialog box with printer-specific options such as paper type — for example, glossy or standard — and other settings. Select the preferred options for your printer, and click Print to print your invitations.

TIP It's a good idea to do an initial print on standard inkjet paper at draft quality to make sure everything's printing okay. You can then go ahead and print at full quality.

When you have the final print in your hand, you can then print more copies from your printer or photocopy the single copy to save your ink. That decision should be based on the number of invitations you need and the quality you need them at. If you want 400, a photocopier's probably an easier option, but if you want 20 at good quality, then your inkjet will do a better job.

Finally, you can cut the invitations up. The easiest way to do this is with a steel ruler, a scalpel, and a cutting mat, but please watch out for your fingers!

Making a Poster

Sometimes, you need to let people know about an event in a really direct way, and what better approach than a poster? With great type and layout features, Photoshop's perfect for this kind of project; it's capable of results that will get an event noticed by all the right people.

In this example, you create a poster for surf party using lots of layer techniques discussed earlier in the book to produce an eye-catching, colorful result.

You'll focus on:

- Shape layers
- Type layers
- Smart Objects and Smart Filters
- Layer styles
- Organizing and transforming layers

CROSS-REF You can find details on shape layers in Chapter 5 and type layers in Chapter 4. Smart Objects and Smart Filters are covered in Chapter 9, while layer styles get a thorough treatment in Chapter 10. Learn how to organize layers in Chapter 2 and how to resize and transform them in Chapter 3.

Our poster will advertise a party celebrating the age-old problem that the surf is, in fact, NOT up. (For the uninitiated, the phrase "surf's up" means that there are waves to be ridden.) The ocean's flat, so it's time to dance badly, tell tall stories about nonexistent waves and torment the neighbors with your exquisite taste in music. The posters will be small—U.S. Letter sized—so that they can be quickly and easily put up wherever needed.

The main text components of the message will be:

- Surf's not up
- So, surf party tonight!
- John's Tavern
- 9pm til late

The aim is to get all these key points across in the poster and have a little fun creating a great design along the way. You'll use a photo of a particularly nonturbulent sea to get the thrust of your point across, which you can see in Figure 16.14.

FIGURE 16.14

The "flat sea" photo you'll use when creating the poster

Creating a new document

Begin by creating a new document for the poster. Choose File ➪ New to display the New dialog box. This dialog box allows you to set the properties for the new document. To set up the document, follow these steps:

1. **Name the document.** In the Name box, type a name for the document. **Surf's Not Up** seems apt.

2. **Set the paper size.** From the Preset menu, choose U.S. Paper, and in the Size menu, choose Letter if it's not already selected, as shown in Figure 16.15. Photoshop prefills the width and height for you at 8.5 by 11 inches.

3. **Set the document resolution.** In the Resolution box, type **200**, and make sure pixels/inch is selected in the menu to the right. This resolution gives you a nice detailed print, but is low enough so that you don't have to scale up digital photos (based on a 5- to 6-megapixel camera image) to fill the page. When you type that value in the Resolution field, the Preset changes to Custom, but don't worry — the settings already chosen remain in place.

4. **Set the document's color mode and background color.** Set the Color Mode option to RGB Color, and set the option to the right to 8 bit. Make sure that White is selected for the Background Contents option.

FIGURE 16.15

The New dialog box, showing the settings for your new poster document

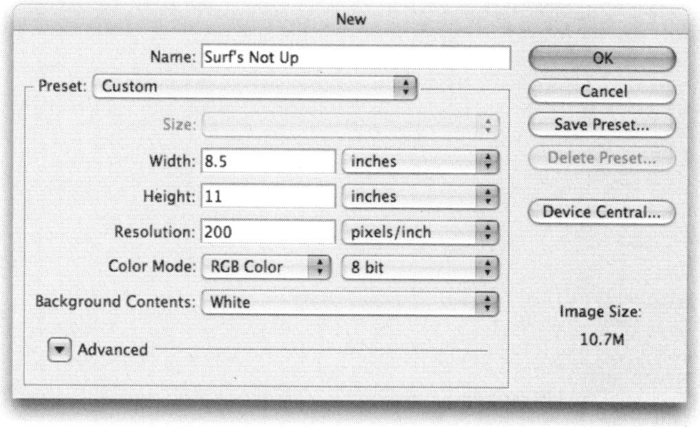

After the settings are in place, click OK. The new, blank document window appears.

Adding the photo

The next step is to add the photo to the poster. The photo you're using has the benefit of containing little in the way of distractions. This makes it great to use as a backdrop for a poster, even though it's pretty dull in its own right. It also features a very flat sea, which perfectly suits the message of the surf not being up. The slight ripple merely reinforces the lack of proper waves!

Get the photo across into the newly created document. Open the photo in Photoshop, and position both that and the Surf's Not Up document so you can see them both. Click the photo document window to activate it. Shift+drag the Background layer of the photo in the Layers palette across to the Surf's Not Up document window, as shown in Figure 16.16. The photo appears as Layer 1 in the Layers palette of the Surf's Not Up document. Because you held down Shift while dragging, Photoshop centers your photo in the center of the document. Close the original photo if you want; you're done with it now.

FIGURE 16.16

Dragging the photo into the poster document

You might want to use the Move tool to position the photo nicely in the document. Remember, this is just a backdrop for a poster, so try to minimize detail in the image. Try dragging the photo over to the right to minimize the amount of land and dragging it up so that the horizon is about a third of the way down the page, conforming to the rule of thirds.

Creating the text and graphic elements

You're now ready to add your message to the poster. It'd be fun to have the text sitting on some kind of graphic device, so create an arrow, pointing to the ripple in the sea, to draw attention to the flatness of the water. You'll then create another upward-pointing arrow to contain the rest of the text.

Making an arrow

The first downward-pointing arrow will contain the "surf's not up" text in a big, bold font. To create the arrow and text, follow these steps:

1. **Set options for the arrow shape.** Click the Shape Tool icon in the Toolbox; then select the Custom Shape tool in the options bar. Make sure that the Shape Layers option is selected in the options bar so that the shape you draw produces a shape layer rather than a path or a simple fill. Still in the options bar, click inside the Shape option to reveal the Custom Shape Picker. Select a wide arrow from the list — Arrow 12, for example. Choose a nice orange foreground color. For example, try using RGB values of 254, 141, 32; this color is strong enough to hold its own against the blue of the photo.

    TIP If you only have a few shapes in the Custom Shape Picker, and can't see a big fat arrow, click the small arrow in the top right of the picker and choose All from the pop-up menu. Click OK in the resulting dialog box. A much wider array of shapes should appear in the picker.

2. **Draw the arrow.** Now, position the cursor in the document window and drag out a large arrow, as shown in Figure 16.17. When you release the mouse button, you should see a large, orange arrow in the document window and a new shape layer in the Layers palette.

3. **Rotate the arrow.** You want to see this arrow pointing downward toward that ripple. Make sure the shape is still selected, and choose Edit ➪ Transform Path ➪ Rotate 90° Clockwise. This points the arrow straight down. You'll likely need to reposition the arrow after this operation, so select the Move tool and drag the arrow downward until it points to the left side of that ripple in the photo.

4. **Add the first line of text to the arrow.** Make sure the foreground color is white, and then select the Type tool. In the options bar, choose Impact from the Font Family menu; this is a nice, strong font that is perfect for posters. Choose 48 points for the size. Position the cursor on the shaft of the arrow in the document window, click, and type **surf's**. Press Ctrl+Enter (⌘+Return on the Mac) to commit the type and create the new type layer.

5. **Resize the text.** You want to fill the shaft of the arrow with the text. Using the Move tool, position the new type layer toward the left of the arrow, leaving a small margin. Still with the Move tool selected, select the Show Transform Controls option in the options bar. This allows you to resize your layer from within the Move tool without recourse to the transform commands. Hold down Shift to constrain the proportions of the type, and drag down and to the right to fill the shaft of the arrow, again leaving a small margin. Press Enter (Return on the Mac) to commit the transformation.

FIGURE 16.17

Creating the arrow using the Custom Shape tool

NOTE When scaling up text, you actually increase the font size. You can see this by selecting the Type tool then selecting the type layer. Notice that the font size, as shown in the options bar, increases from the 48-point size you started with. You can manually increase the font size to span the width of the arrow, but it's a pretty hit-and-miss approach; scaling the text is much easier.

6. **Create the next line of text.** Add the word "NOT" to the arrow. Make it all capitals to draw attention to the pun. Again, select the Type tool, and click in the document window beneath the previous "surf's" text. Type **NOT**, and press Ctrl+Enter (⌘+Return on the Mac) to commit the type. With the Move tool, click and drag the new type layer so it lines up with the left of the "surf's" text above. Now hold down Shift and resize the type so that it's the same width as the "surf's" text.

7. **Add the final line of text.** Using the Type tool, create the word "up" just beneath "NOT," and then use the Move tool to reposition and resize the type layer. When all three words are in place, use the Move tool to nudge each word so that you've created roughly equidistant vertical spaces between each word. Select each type layer in the Layers palette to move it. After you do this, you should have something that looks like Figure 16.18.

TIP Select the Auto-Select option in the options bar, and choose Layer from the drop-down menu next to it, so that you can select layers using the Move tool, without having to locate and select each layer in the Layers palette. This can take some getting used to, though, as it's easy to select the wrong layer!

The crux of the message is now in place. You can see the layers you've created in the Layers palette.

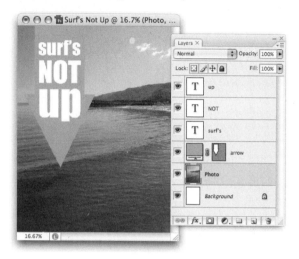

Liven up your arrow by adding a gradient fill and an outline to it. In the Layers palette, select the arrow shape layer you created earlier, and click the Add a Layer Style icon at the bottom of the palette. From the pop-up menu, choose Gradient Overlay. The Layer Style dialog box appears. At this point, your arrow will probably change color in the document window, but don't panic; you'll fix this in a moment.

You need to edit the gradient for the arrow, so click inside the Gradient box to display the Gradient Editor. Make sure the Gradient Type is Solid, with a Smoothness value of 100 percent. You now want to change the colors of the gradient. To do this, follow these steps:

1. **Change the color of the right color stop.** Select the right color stop by clicking it, and click the Color box below to display the Select Stop Color dialog box. Type the RGB values that you used when creating the orange arrow: 254, 141, 32. Click OK to close the Color Picker.

2. **Change the color of the left color stop.** Select the left color stop, and again click the Color box below to display the Select Stop Color dialog box. Make the color darker and redder in hue than the previous orange; say, RGB 239, 84, 0. Click OK to close the dialog box.

3. **Click OK in the Gradient Editor.** This closes the Gradient Editor and returns you to the Layer Style dialog box.

In the Layer Style dialog box, you can see your changes reflected in the Gradient box. In the document window, your arrow should be back to orange, but with a darker arrowhead, producing a nice gradient effect.

The last stage is to add an outline to the arrow. Still in the Layer Style dialog box, click the Stroke effect. This immediately adds a default 3-pixel red line around the outside of the arrow. Click and drag the Size slider to 7 pixels, and leave the Position, Blend Mode, and Opacity settings at the default values of Outside, Normal, and 100 percent, respectively. Finally, make sure Fill Type is set to Color, and change the color of the stroke to white by clicking the Color box.

The result of all this should be something like Figure 16.19. When you're happy, click OK to close the dialog box.

FIGURE 16.19

The arrow with Gradient Overlay and Stroke effects applied. The Layer Style dialog box shows the settings for the Stroke effect.

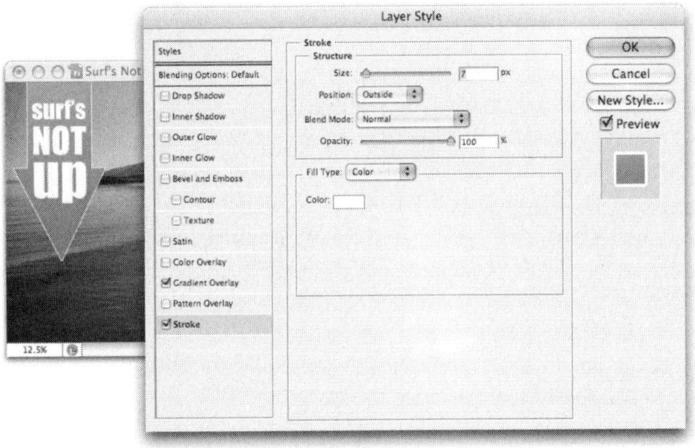

Creating the second arrow

Great stuff. Now add a second arrow with the remainder of the information. You don't need to redraw the arrow; merely copy and reposition it. To add the second arrow and text, follow these steps:

1. **Duplicate the existing arrow.** In the Layers palette, select the arrow layer and drag it to the New Layer icon at the bottom of the palette.

2. **Flip and position the duplicate arrow.** Flip the new copy of the arrow so that it points upward as a counterpoint to the original. To do this, choose Edit ➪ Transform Path ➪ Flip Vertical. As you do this, the new arrow flips to point upward. Using the Move tool, drag it down to the bottom of the page and to the right, positioning it so that the arrowhead lines up next to, but separate from, the original arrow.

3. **Flip the duplicate arrow's gradient.** You want the darker colors for the two arrows to meet in the middle, so you need to flip the gradient for the new arrow. To achieve this, double-click the Gradient Overlay effect in the Layers palette for the new arrow layer. This displays the Layer Style dialog box with the Gradient Overlay options active. Select the Reverse option next to the Gradient box. Photoshop inverts the gradient so that both arrows now have dark arrowheads. Click OK to close the dialog box.

4. **Organize your layers.** It's a good idea at this point to indulge in a little organization of your Layers palette. You'll probably find that your new arrow layer is mixed up with all the other layers, and it's going to get messy as you start adding more text. Group together all the elements for the original arrow to make it easier to see what you're doing. To do this, select all the layers — both the shape layer and the type layers — that are relevant to the first arrow by Ctrl+clicking (⌘+clicking on the Mac) them in the Layers palette. Once selected, choose New Group from Layers in the Layers palette menu. In the dialog box that appears, name the new group **Arrow 1**.

5. **Add the text describing the event.** Click the upward-pointing arrow layer in the Layers palette to make sure it's active. If the layer's vector mask is active, with a border around it, click it to deselect it, otherwise Photoshop flows the type along or inside the vector mask's path. Select the Type tool, and make sure the foreground color is white. It's likely that the type options will still be as you left them, with Impact as the font of choice, but check this in the options bar to be sure. Click in the shaft of the second arrow and type **surf party**. Press Ctrl+Enter (⌘+Return on the Mac) to commit the edit. Using the Move tool, position the type so that the top of the text is level with the base of the arrowhead, and resize the type to leave similar margins to the previous arrow.

6. **Add the date.** Use the Type tool to create the word **TONIGHT!** all in capitals, to leave no room for doubt as to when the party is, and press Ctrl+Enter (⌘+Return on the Mac) to commit the type and create the type layer. Again, use the Move tool to reposition the text and resize it so that it's the same width as the "surf party" text.

7. **Add the name of the venue and the time of the event.** Once again, use the Type tool to add the venue text — **John's Tavern** — and the Move to tool to reposition and resize the text. Next, add the time — **9pm til late** — using the same techniques.

8. **Add something to tie the two arrows together a little.** In the arrowhead of the upward arrow, add the word **so,** (with the comma) using the Type tool. Resize it with the Move tool so that it's closer to the size of the text in the left arrow, and center it in the arrowhead. The larger text leads the eye from the first to the second arrow, and the flow of the wording helps, too.

You should now have something like Figure 16.20. At this point, group all the layers for the second arrow by selecting them and choosing New Group from Layers from the Layers palette menu. Name the new group **Arrow 2**.

FIGURE 16.20

All of your text is now in place. You're getting there.

Adding filters to the photo

You could leave the poster right there. It's pretty cool, but it would be good to make that photo a little more vibrant and graphical — it feels a little staid behind those big arrows. To do this, make it a Smart Object; then apply a reeditable Smart Filter to it.

To turn your photo into a Smart Object, select the photo layer in the Layers palette and, from the Layers palette menu, choose Convert to Smart Object. The layer thumbnail in the Layers palette changes to indicate that the layer is now a Smart Object. Now you can apply Photoshop's filters to the photo as Smart Filters — a new feature in CS3 — without destructively changing the photo itself.

The filter you're going to use references the foreground and background colors to produce its effect, so set these colors up first. Set the foreground color to white and the background to black, by pressing D and then X on the keyboard. Now choose Filter ➪ Sketch ➪ Torn Edges. This filter creates a kind of posterized, photocopied effect that adds a great look to the photo. You can see the Torn Edges dialog box in Figure 16.21. There are three settings for the filter:

■ **Image Balance:** This controls the relative amount of foreground and background colors in the effect. It's a bit like using the Threshold adjustment. A value of 25 is fine.

■ **Smoothness:** Clicking and dragging this all the way to the left gives the photo a kind of blurry effect, a bit like a really high ISO black-and-white film. Instead, you want to pre-serve detail, so drag it all the way to the right to give it a value of 15.

■ **Contrast:** Clicking and dragging to the left produces a low-contrast image; dragging to the right adds contrast. A value of around 15 works well in this case.

Click OK to close the dialog box and apply the filter.

FIGURE 16.21

The dialog box for the Torn Edges filter. You can see that the filter produces quite a hard, contrasty effect.

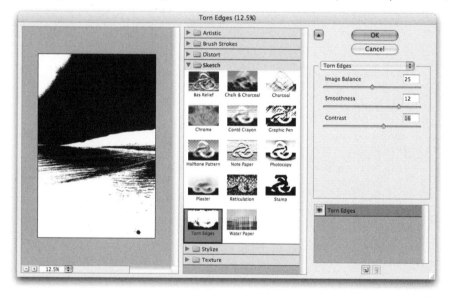

The photo is pretty much black and white now, and isn't terribly attractive, but you're about to fix that. In the Layers palette, you can see how the Smart Filter has been added to the Smart Object. It sits below the Smart Object's filter mask thumbnail.

Just to the right of the Smart Filter's name is the Edit Filter Blending Options icon; it looks like two little sliders on top of each other. Double-click this to display the Blending Options dialog box for the Torn Edges filter. You want to let some of your original photo through beneath the Smart Filter; to do this, select Screen for the Mode setting. Click OK to close the dialog box. You can see that previously black areas of the filter are now allowing the blue of the original photo in the Smart Object to show through.

NOTE Because the Smart Filter is reeditable, you can now go back and tweak the settings for the Torn Edges filter if you desire. Just double-click the Smart Filter's name in the Layers palette to reedit the filter. You can also try using different blend modes for the filter to produce some wacky results!

Your final, completed poster is shown in Figure 16.22. It's slick and eye-catching, and is ready to be printed and distributed. Print it on good-quality glossy paper for the best results.

FIGURE 16.22

Your final poster, with added Torn Edges Smart Filter to add a bit of interest to the photo

TIP If you have a printer capable of printing edge-to-edge without margins, select this option; it'll produce a great effect.

You've covered a lot of ground in this example, but if you've followed it all through, you should be feeling pretty confident with all these multiple layer techniques. They'll stand you in good stead for future projects because they can be applied to any number of situations.

Creating a Calendar

A calendar is something many of us have on the wall, but wouldn't it be great if you could make your own? With a little help from Photoshop and the Layers palette, you can. In this example, you create a 2008 calendar, ready for printing on a home printer.

You'll be using several tools and techniques discussed earlier in the book, including the following:

- Layer organization
- Type layers
- Shape layers

CROSS-REF   Find out more about organizing layers in Chapter 2. Type layers are covered in Chapter 4, while shape layers are explored in Chapter 5.

Your aim is to create a calendar with a photo at the top of the page, and a month view at the bottom for each month of the year — 12 pages in all. The techniques for the pages after January are pretty much the same, so concentrate on getting that first page as good as you can.

You'll keep the month view quite simple so that your photos really shine through. Armed with the techniques to build the basic month view, however, you can later embellish it to your heart's content.

You can split your approach into two areas: creating the basic layout of the page, and then adding the month view. You'll base the calendar on the standard U.S. Letter page size, but you can rework the examples for A4 or any other size that you want to use; the principles are the same. The final calendar will be in portrait format; in other words, it will be tall, rather than wide.

Creating the basic layout

Start by creating a new Photoshop document. Choose File ➪ New to create a new document. In the New dialog box that appears, follow these steps to set up your document:

1. **Name the document.** Type a name for the document in the Name box. You'll be creating a single file per month, so **January** seems like a good option here.

2. **Choose the document size.** From the Preset menu, choose U.S. Paper, and from the Size menu, choose Letter if it's not already selected, as shown in Figure 16.23. Photoshop pre-fills the width and height for you at 8.5 by 11 inches.

3. **Specify the document resolution.** In the Resolution box, type **200**, and make sure the option to the right is set to pixels/inch. This resolution produces a nice detailed print, but it also means that you don't have to go to the trouble of scaling 5-megapixel digital photos up to fill the page. When you type that value into the Resolution field, the Preset changes to Custom; don't worry, your other settings remain in place.

4. **Set the document's colors.** The Color Mode settings should be RGB Color and 8 bit, and the Background Contents value should be White.

FIGURE 16.23

The New dialog, showing the settings for your new calendar document.

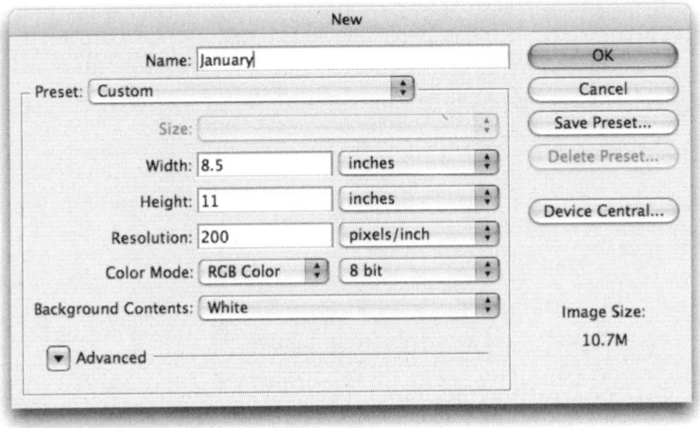

When the settings are in place, click OK. The new blank document appears.

Adding a photo

Now comes the fun part: choosing your first photo! This example uses a photo of a yacht on Lake Garda in Italy, but choose whatever feels good to you. Open your photo in Photoshop.

CROSS-REF Assume, for the purposes of this example, that all the photos used need no retouching. If you want some help sprucing up your photos beforehand, try some of the examples in Chapters 14 and 15.

You need to import the photo into your newly created document, so arrange the document windows so you can see them both. Click the photo document to make sure it's selected and, in the Layers palette, drag the Background layer straight into the January document, as shown in Figure 16.24. The January document now shows a new layer in the Layers palette, containing the imported photo.

At this point, you may want to reposition the photo to achieve the best effect. To do this, select the Move tool and click and drag the photo into a position you're happy with.

Creating a space for the month view

Now you need to add some space for the month view. You'll introduce a white area in the lower third of the page that provides the background needed for this element.

FIGURE 16.24

Dragging the photo's Background layer into your new document

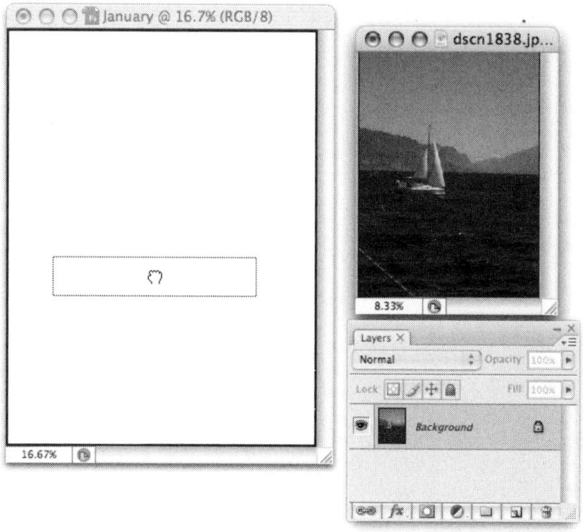

To do this, follow these steps:

1. **Select the Rectangle tool.** You can select it by clicking the Shape Tool icon in the Toolbox, then clicking the Rectangle Tool icon in the options bar. Alternatively, keep pressing Shift+U until the Shape Tool icon changes to a rectangle.

2. **Make sure the foreground color is white.** A quick way to do this is to press D followed by X.

3. **Create a rectangle.** Drag out a rectangle that covers approximately the bottom third of the document, running from the left to the right edge, as shown in Figure 16.25. You'll see a new shape layer appear in the Layers palette, and you now have a space for the month view to reside.

TIP It can help to expand the window a little to reveal the gray area around the edges of the document. This makes it easier for you to see — and click on — the edges of the document when dragging out your rectangle.

FIGURE 16.25

Creating a space for the month view by adding a white rectangle shape layer above the photo layer

Creating the month view

You can now look at how to create the essential element of the project: the month view itself. The month will be in a grid format, with the days across the top, and the dates below over five lines. You no doubt have seen the style many times in various guises.

To make the process of aligning all the elements easier, you're going to add some guides to help. Guides are a great way to ensure alignment in a design, and are simply vertical and horizontal lines that are contained in the document but don't print. You'll use some vertical guides, created at half-inch intervals.

CROSS-REF Photoshop's guides feature is covered in detail in Chapter 2.

Make sure the rulers are visible around the document by pressing Ctrl+R (⌘+R on the Mac). Right-click in either ruler and make sure Inches is selected in the pop-up menu. Now click in the left ruler and drag to the right. A vertical guide emerges. Position this guide on the first half-inch increment in the horizontal ruler and release the mouse button. This is easier if you hold down Shift as you do it, because this snaps the guides to the increments of the rulers (provided you have View ➪ Snap selected). Do this again until you have seven vertical guides, one for each day of the week.

If you misjudge the placement of a guide, just select the Move tool and drag the offending guide to reposition it. You can also drag it back into the ruler to remove it from the document.

Next, add a horizontal guide for the top of the calendar. This needs to be around two-thirds of an inch below the bottom of the photo. Drag out the guide from the top ruler.

Now you can begin to add the days and dates for the calendar. To make it easy to keep all the elements lined up, the calendar will be created using seven columns — one for each day of the week. To add the days and dates, follow these steps:

1. **Set the type options.** Select the Type tool and choose a font and size in the options bar or Character palette. For this example, use Arial Bold at 10 points. You want the days and dates to right-align with the guides, so select the Right Align Text option in the options bar. For now, you'll make all the items in the calendar black, so choose that color as the foreground color. It's useful to give the elements a good deal of space around them, so set the Leading option to 25 points by typing **25pt** in the Leading box in the Character palette.

2. **Add the first column of dates.** Click the leftmost vertical guide, just below the horizontal guide. Type **M** (for Monday), then press Enter (Return on the Mac). Press Enter/Return again to miss a line — January 1st 2008 is on a Tuesday — then type **7**, **14**, **21** and **28**, pressing Enter/Return after each number, to create a column for all the Mondays in the month. Press Ctrl+Enter (⌘+Return on the Mac) to commit the type edit.

TIP If you're creating a calendar for a different year, you will of course need to refer to a calendar for that year to discover the day on which January 1st falls. Most computers have some way of viewing a calendar through an application like Windows Calendar on Windows Vista, or iCal on the Mac.

3. **Line the column up with the guides.** Make sure you have View ➪ Snap To ➪ Guides selected. Select the Move tool, and drag the type layer so that the top of the "M" touches the horizontal guide, and the right-hand edge of the "M" touches the leftmost vertical guide. You should feel it snap into place as you get close to the guides.

4. **Copy the first column to produce the remaining columns.** With the Move tool still selected, hold down Alt+Shift (Option+Shift on the Mac) and click and drag the column you just created to the right, positioning the copy so that the right-hand edge of the "M" touches the second vertical guide. You'll feel the new column snap to the guide as you do this. A copy of the first column's type layer appears in the Layers palette. Repeat the process until you have seven columns lined up just to the left of the seven vertical guides.

NOTE Holding down Alt (Option on the Mac) duplicates the layer at the same time as moving it, while holding down Shift constrains the movement to the horizontal, ensuring that the layers are perfectly aligned.

5. **Edit the type layers in the duplicate columns to produce the correct dates.** For example, in the second column from the left — the Tuesdays — select the Type tool and double-click the "M" at the top of the column to highlight it, then type **T**. Now press the Down-arrow key to move onto the blank space, and type **1**. Press Down-arrow again to move onto the "7", press Backspace (Delete on the Mac) to delete the "7", and type **8**. Continue replacing the dates in this way. Note that January 2008 finishes on a Thursday, so leave a blank for the last digit in the Friday, Saturday, and Sunday columns. When you're done, you should have something that looks like Figure 16.26.

FIGURE 16.26

The dates and days in place, with the Layers palette showing the seven column layers

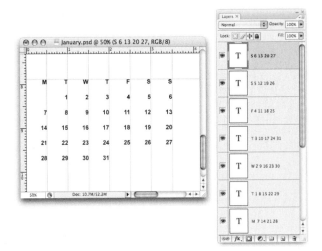

It's a good idea at this point to group together all the date layers in the Layers palette, just to keep things neat. To do this, click the top date layer in the palette and Shift+click the bottom date layer. Now press Ctrl+G (⌘+G on the Mac). Rename the new group by double-clicking its name in the Layers palette and typing something useful, like **Days and Dates**.

You're now going to add some horizontal lines to the month view just to separate out the elements a little. You can do this using the Line tool. Click the Shape Tool icon in the Toolbox and then select the Line Tool option in the options bar. Set the Weight option to 1 pixel, and make sure the arrowheads are turned off. Keep the foreground color set to black.

Your first line will go just above the top line of numbers. In the document window, Shift+drag from right to left to create a horizontal line, as seen in Figure 16.27. The reason you drag from right to left is simply to make it easier to position the line because there's no number on the far left. A new shape layer appears in the Layers palette, representing your new horizontal line.

FIGURE 16.27

Creating a separator line using the Line tool

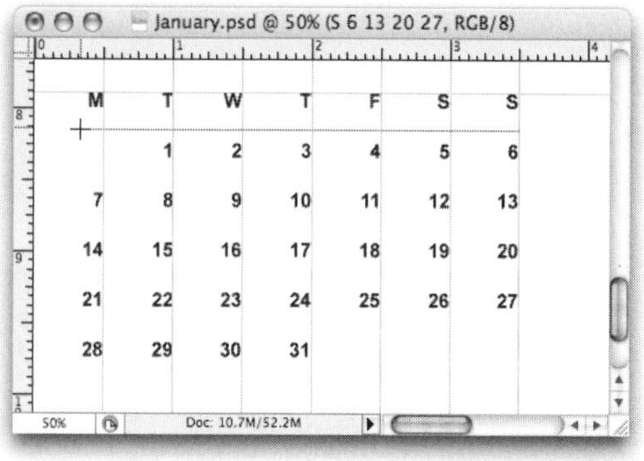

You could continue drawing new lines down the page, but that would likely result in lines of unequal length. Instead, copy this first line using the same technique that you used previously to copy the day and date layers. Select the Move tool and, holding down Alt+Shift (Option+Shift on the Mac), click and drag the line down to a position just above the second row of dates. A second shape layer appears in the Layers palette.

> **CAUTION** Make sure the Move tool's Auto-Select option is disabled, or you'll probably select the white rectangle by mistake. Also, turn off Snap under the View menu to avoid the lines snapping to the type layers.

Repeat this until you have five lines, the final one sitting just above the last row of numbers. Again, it's a good idea at this point to group the line layers together. Select all five shape layers in the Layers palette and press Ctrl+G (⌘+G on the Mac). Double-click the resulting group's name in the Layers palette, and rename it **Lines**.

You're nearly there. Finally, you're going to differentiate the components of the month by adjusting the colors of the days, dates and lines. Using the Type tool, select the first day (M) by double-clicking the "M" in the document window. In the Character palette (or options bar), click the color box and set the color to RGB 64, 64, 64 — a dark gray. Now select all the dates below the "M" and set their colors to a lighter gray; RGB values of 140, 140, 140 are fine. Repeat this process for each column. Finally, set the Lines group to 15 percent opacity in the Layers palette. This produces a nice, subtle effect for your final month view, as seen in Figure 16.28.

The month view elements are now different shades of gray. This helps to differentiate the days from the dates, producing an elegant result.

Adding the year, month name, and caption

You now just need to add the year, the month name, and a photo caption to the calendar. You'll put these elements in a simple square to the right of the month view. To add the elements, follow these steps:

1. **To aid with positioning, add two more guides.** If your guides aren't visible, press Ctrl+; (⌘+; on the Mac). From the left ruler, drag out a vertical guide so that it sits half an inch to the right of the Sunday guide; it should align with the 4-inch mark on the top ruler. Now drag out a horizontal guide that aligns with the bottom of the last row of dates. These two guides will help you place the square in the next step.

2. **Create the square.** Choose a light gray for the foreground color. An RGB value of 200, 200, 200 works well. Now click the Shape Tool icon in the Toolbox and, in the options bar, select the Rectangle tool. Make sure the Shape Layers option is selected in the options bar. Position the cursor in the document window, right on the top-left corner of the guides you just created. Hold down Shift to constrain the proportions of the rectangle to a square, and drag down and to the right until the bottom of the square is on the lower horizontal guide, level with the bottom of the dates, as shown in Figure 16.29. After creating the shape, its shape layer appears in the Layers palette.

FIGURE 16.29

Using the Rectangle tool to create the square background for the month name and caption

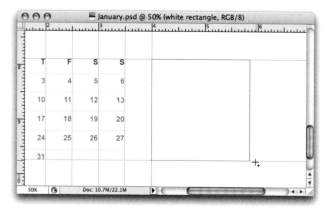

3. **Add the year.** Select the Type tool from the Toolbox and, in the options bar, select Arial Bold at 36 points. Select white as the foreground color. The combination of bold text and the white color off the gray should produce a pleasing result. Make sure the square layer's vector mask is deselected, otherwise Photoshop flows the type inside the mask. (If the mask thumbnail has a border around it in the Layers palette, click the thumbnail to deselect the mask.) Click in the top left area of the square and type **2008**. Commit the type by pressing Ctrl+Enter (⌘+Return on the Mac). If necessary, use the Move tool to nudge the type so it sits equidistantly from the top and left edges of the square.

4. **Add the month.** Select the Type tool again, but this time set the font size to 24 points in the options bar. Position the cursor just below the year, click, and type **January**. Commit the type and use the Move tool to align the year and month, if necessary.

5. **Add a caption.** Use the white Arial Bold font but, because your type will likely span two lines, create the text as paragraph text rather than point text. To do this, select the Type tool and drag across the lower third of the square, left to right, as shown in Figure 16.30. When the bounding box is in place, drop your font size a little. Choose a font size of 10 points, and type the caption: **Summer vacation, Lake Garda, Italy**. Press Ctrl+Enter (⌘+Return on the Mac) to commit the type.

6. **Group the layers.** Group together the square, the year, the month, and the caption in the Layers palette to keep things neat. Select all four layers in the Layers palette, and press Ctrl+G (⌘+G on the Mac) to group them. Rename the group to something useful, like **Year, Month & Caption**.

FIGURE 16.30

Creating paragraph text for your caption

And there is your final January calendar page, as seen in Figure 16.31. Save the document as January.psd, if you haven't already done so.

FIGURE 16.31

The final calendar page, with its attendant Layers palette

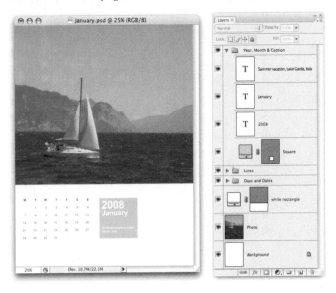

Creating multiple pages

Of course, you're not really finished yet. You need 12 of these pages, but all the really hard work has been done. You can regard January.psd as the template file for all the others. Follow these steps for producing the final files:

1. **Copy the calendar document.** Take 11 copies of the January.psd file for the next 11 months, and rename them accordingly: February.psd, March.psd, and so on.

2. **Replace the photo in each document.** For each file, choose a new photo, and import it into the document.

3. **Set the correct dates for each month.** Change the dates in each file using the Type tool. Refer to another calendar to make sure they're correct.

4. **Set the correct month and caption.** Change the month name and caption for each file, again using the Type tool.

After you follow these steps, you have 12 files ready to print.

TIP If you have a printer capable of edge-to-edge printing with no margins, take advantage of this feature to produce stunning no-border versions of the calendar.

Finally, bind your calendar. A good approach is to use spiral binding if you can, because then the pages can flip back over each other as each month passes.

You've covered a lot of ground with layer management and the Type tool in this example, so you should be feeling quite confident right now if you've followed it all through. You should also be happy making a really personalized version of the calendar, which would be great as a gift for friends and family.

Summary

In this chapter, you looked at some practical applications of Photoshop, showing how you can use the software to help with some real-world projects. You learned how to use Photoshop's type and shape layers to create a simple invitation, then duplicate the invitation on the page to help you print multiple copies.

You also walked through the steps of creating a poster advertising a party, covering shape layers, type layers, layer styles, Smart Objects, and Photoshop CS3's new Smart Filters.

Finally, you learned how to create a month-by-month calendar, complete with your own photos. Along the way, you explored type layers, shape layers, aligning and duplicating layers, and organizing layers into groups.

Part V

Appendixes

Appendix A

Using the CD-ROM

This appendix provides you with information on the contents of the CD that accompanies this book. For the latest and greatest information, please refer to the ReadMe file located at the root of the CD. Here is what you will find:

- System Requirements
- Using the CD with Windows and Macintosh
- What's on the CD
- Troubleshooting

System Requirements

Make sure that your computer meets the minimum system requirements listed in this section. If your computer doesn't match up to most of these requirements, you may have a problem using the contents of the CD.

- PC running Windows 98 or later or a Macintosh running Mac OS X
- An Internet connection
- A CD-ROM drive
- A copy of Adobe Photoshop CS3

Installing the CD

To install the items from the CD to your hard drive, follow these steps.

1. **Insert the CD into your computer's CD-ROM drive. The license agreement appears.**

   Note to Windows users: The interface won't launch if you have autorun disabled. In that case, click Start ➪ Run (For Windows Vista, Start ➪ All Programs ➪ Accessories ➪ Run). In the dialog box that appears, type D:\Start.exe. (Replace D with the proper letter if your CD drive uses a different letter. If you don't know the letter, see how your CD drive is listed under My Computer.) Click OK.

   Note for Mac Users: The CD icon will appear on your desktop, double-click the icon to open the CD and double-click the "Start" icon.

2. **Read through the license agreement, and then click the Accept button if you want to use the CD.**

   The CD interface appears. The interface allows you to install the programs and run the demos with just a click of a button (or two).

What's on the CD

The following sections provide a summary of the software and other materials you'll find on the CD.

Author-created materials

On the CD, you'll find the Photoshop files for all the in-depth examples and tutorials within the book. The files are organized by chapter within the "Author" folder. You will need Photoshop CS3 to read many of these files correctly. If you don't own the software already, Adobe offers a 30-day demo version of Photoshop CS3 for download from:

www.adobe.com/products/photoshop/

In order to get the greatest possible number of files onto the CD, some compromises have been made:

- The resolution of some of the files has been lowered to minimize the file size. For instance, where the text mentions a print-resolution file of say 300 dpi, the corresponding Photoshop file on the CD is in fact 72 dpi (screen resolution).

- Not all the Photoshop files used in the creation of the screen captures are included. Where it's felt that the inclusion of a Photoshop file significantly aids understanding, it's on the CD.

All the layers for the included Photoshop files are still intact, though, so you can still follow how the files are structured and created.

Throughout the book, fonts that you're likely to have installed on your system are used — for example, Arial, Arial Black, and Times New Roman. This means that you should have no problem loading the example PSD files on the CD. One exception to this is the "Transforming Type Layers" example in Chapter 3 (Figures 3.21-3.27), which uses Helvetica Neue.

Another example uses a free font that you can easily install. This is the "Bringing It All Together" tutorial in Chapter 4 (Figures 4.39-4.44). The font used here is the excellent "Geek a byte 2" by Jakob Fischer. You can download this free font in Mac and Windows flavors from:

www.1001fonts.com/font_details.html?font_id=2633

We've also included a stack of our own stock photos for you to play with in Photoshop. You can find these in the "Stock Photos" folder within the "Author" folder.

Applications

The Adobe Reader is on the CD. This is Adobe's free software for reading PDF (Portable Document Format) files, which will enable you to use the ebook version of the Photoshop Layers Bible included on the CD. You can find more information at www.adobe.com.

Searchable version of the Photoshop Layers Bible

The complete text of the Photoshop Layers Bible is on the CD in Adobe's Portable Document Format (PDF). You can read and search through the file with the Adobe Acrobat Reader (also included on the CD). This can be a great way of finding very specific information within the book regarding the finer points of layers!

Troubleshooting

If you have difficulty installing or using any of the materials on the companion CD, try the following solutions:

- **Turn off any anti-virus software that you may have running.** Installers sometimes mimic virus activity and can make your computer incorrectly believe that it is being infected by a virus. (Be sure to turn the anti-virus software back on later.)

- **Close all running programs.** The more programs you're running, the less memory is available to other programs. Installers also typically update files and programs; if you keep other programs running, installation may not work properly.

- **Reference the ReadMe.** Please refer to the ReadMe file located at the root of the CD-ROM for the latest product information at the time of publication.

- **Make sure you're running Photoshop CS3.** Many of the examples will only render correctly using the CS3 version of the software. For example, Smart Filters won't work in any previous version of Photoshop.

Customer Care

If you have trouble with the CD-ROM, please call the Wiley Product Technical Support phone number at (800) 762-2974. Outside the United States, call 1(317) 572-3994. You can also contact Wiley Product Technical Support at **http://support.wiley.com**. John Wiley & Sons will provide technical support only for installation and other general quality control items. For technical support on the applications themselves, consult the program's vendor or author. To place additional orders or to request information about other Wiley products, please call (877) 762-2974.

Appendix B

Shortcuts for Working with Layers

One of the keys — pun intended — to becoming super-efficient with Photoshop is its wide range of keyboard and mouse shortcuts. Sure, you can get by with using just the mouse (or graphics tablet) and the menu options to do practically everything. However, most professionals quickly learn that the best way to get the job done quickly is to use shortcuts whenever possible. And time is money, as they say.

For example, after you've memorized it, it's so much quicker to press Ctrl+G (⌘+G on the Mac) to group layers together than it is to choose Layer ➪ Group Layers.

In this appendix, we give you a list of shortcuts that you may find useful when working with layers. We've organized them into separate tables, for ease of reference. They're roughly in the order of the chapters in the book: managing layers, transforming layers, type layers, shape layers, adjustment and fill layers, layer blending modes, Smart Objects and Smart Filters, masks, layer effects and styles, and layer comps. We also include a few miscellaneous shortcuts that, while not directly related to layers, are nonetheless useful to know when working with layers.

NOTE Just to clarify: by *shortcut* we mean using the mouse, keyboard, or a combination of the two to do something the quick way — for example, Shift+clicking something rather than selecting a menu option. Occasionally in this appendix, we bend the rules a little and include a mouse or keyboard action even if it's not strictly speaking a shortcut, if we think it's valuable enough to mention.

NOTE As you probably know if you use one, you can perform a "right-click" on a Mac with a one-button mouse by Control+clicking.

By the way, you can also customize Photoshop's keyboard shortcuts to suit your tastes. You can modify existing shortcuts, delete shortcuts, and also create shortcuts for menus and tools that previously had none. Photoshop also allows you to keep separate sets of shortcuts for different purposes, such as Web work or working with film and video.

To switch to a different set of shortcuts, choose Edit ➪ Keyboard Shortcuts to display the Keyboard Shortcuts and Menus dialog box. In the Keyboard Shortcuts tab, choose a shortcut set from the Set menu; this then becomes the active shortcut set. Click OK, and you can now use your chosen shortcuts.

To edit a set of shortcuts, bring up the Keyboard Shortcuts and Menus dialog box again. Using the icons to the right of the Set menu, you can save the current set, create a new set based on the current set, and delete the current set. Use the Shortcuts For menu to choose a type of shortcut, as follows:

- **Application Menus:** These shortcuts are for the options in the menu bar across the top of the window or screen.
- **Palette Menus:** These are shortcuts for options in the pop-up menus that appear when you click the Palette Menu icon at the top right of palettes.
- **Tools:** This includes shortcuts for all the icons in the Toolbox, as well as shortcuts for adjusting brush settings such as size and hardness.

When you choose a shortcut type, the list below updates to show the available shortcuts for that type. Click the shortcut you'd like to add or modify, and press the key combination you'd like to use. Click Accept or Add Shortcut to confirm the change, or simply click away from the shortcut in the list.

Click Undo to reverse the last edit you made to a shortcut. (The Undo button then changes to Redo; click it to undo the undo, so to speak.)

If you pick a key combination that's in use elsewhere, you'll get a warning message. Click Accept and Go To Conflict to confirm your new shortcut key combination and jump to the conflicting shortcut, allowing you to choose a non-conflicting key combination for that shortcut. Alternatively, click Undo Changes to back out of the change.

To remove an existing key combination for a shortcut, click the shortcut to select it then click Delete Shortcut. You can also revert a shortcut back to its default key combo by selecting it and clicking Use Default.

To help you remember all your shortcuts, you can click Summarize to save a Web page listing all the currently enabled shortcuts. You can then print out this page from your Web browser for easy reference.

When you're done, click OK, and try out your new shortcuts!

TABLE B.1

Shortcuts for Manipulating Layers

Action	Windows Shortcut	Mac Shortcut
Create a new normal layer above the active layer	Ctrl+Alt+Shift+N or click New Layer icon in Layers palette	⌘+Option+Shift+N or click New Layer icon in Layers palette
Create a new normal layer above the active layer, opening New Layer dialog box	Ctrl+Shift+N or Alt+click New Layer icon in Layers palette	⌘+Shift+N or Option+click New Layer icon in Layers palette
Create a new normal layer below the active layer	Ctrl+click New Layer icon in Layers palette	⌘+click New Layer icon in Layers palette
Create a new normal layer below the active layer, opening New Layer dialog box	Ctrl+Alt+click New Layer icon in Layers palette	⌘+Option+click New Layer icon in Layers palette
Create a new layer by copying the current layer or selection	Ctrl+J	⌘+J
Create a new layer by copying the current layer or selection, opening New Layer dialog box	Ctrl+Alt+J	⌘+Option+J
Create a new layer by cutting from the current selection	Ctrl+Shift+J	⌘+Shift+J
Create a new layer by cutting from the current selection, opening New Layer dialog box	Ctrl+Alt+Shift+J	⌘+Option+Shift+J
Create a new group above the active layer	Click New Group icon in Layers palette	Click New Group icon in Layers palette
Create a new group above the active layer, opening New Group dialog box	Alt+click New Group icon in Layers palette	Option+click New Group icon in Layers palette
Create a new group below the active layer	Ctrl+click New Group icon in Layers palette	⌘+click New Group icon in Layers palette
Create a new group below the active layer, opening New Group dialog box	Ctrl+Alt+click New Group icon in Layers palette	⌘+Option+click New Group icon in Layers palette
Group selected layers into a new group	Ctrl+G	⌘+G
Ungroup layers in selected group	Ctrl+Shift+G	⌘+Shift+G

continued

TABLE B.1   *(continued)*

Action	Windows Shortcut	Mac Shortcut
Select the next layer or group down or up in the Layers palette	Alt+[or Alt+]	Option+[or Option+]
Add the next layer or group down or up in the Layers palette to the selection of layers	Alt+Shift+[or Alt+Shift+]	Option+Shift+[or Option +Shift+]
Select the top or bottom layer or group in the Layers palette	Alt+. (period) or Alt+, (comma)	Option+. (period) or Option+, (comma)
Select all layers and groups between the active layer/group and the top or bottom layer/group inclusive	Alt+Shift+. (period) or Alt+Shift+, (comma)	Option+Shift+. (period) or Option+Shift+, (comma)
Select multiple layers or groups that are next to each other in the Layers palette	Click top layer, Shift+click bottom layer (or vice-versa)	Click top layer, Shift+click bottom layer (or vice-versa)
Select multiple layers or groups that are not next to each other in the Layers palette	Ctrl+click each layer	⌘+click each layer
Select a layer in the document window	Ctrl+Alt+right-click layer contents	⌘+Option+right-click layer contents
Add a layer in the document window to the selection of layers	Ctrl+Alt+Shift+right-click layer contents	⌘+Option+Shift+right-click layer contents
Select from overlapping layers or groups in the document window	Ctrl+right-click layer contents and choose layer or group from menu	⌘+right-click layer contents and choose layer or group from menu
Add selected layer or group from overlapping layers or groups in the document window to the selection of layers	Ctrl+Shift+right-click layer contents and choose layer or group from menu	⌘+Shift+right-click layer contents and choose layer or group from menu
Select a layer in the document window when using Move tool	Alt+right-click layer contents	Option+right-click layer contents
Add a layer in the document window to the selection of layers when using Move tool	Alt+Shift+right-click layer contents	Option+Shift+right-click layer contents
Select multiple layers in document window by dragging when using Move tool	With Auto-Select disabled, Ctrl+drag marquee around contents of layers in document window	With Auto-Select disabled, ⌘+drag marquee around contents of layers in document window

Action	Windows Shortcut	Mac Shortcut
Select from overlapping layers or groups in the document window when using Move tool	Right-click layer contents and choose layer or group from menu	Right-click layer contents and choose layer or group from menu
Add selected layer or group from overlapping layers or groups in the document window to the selection of layers when using Move tool	Shift+right-click layer contents and choose layer or group from menu	Shift+right-click layer contents and choose layer or group from menu
Select all layers and groups in the document (except the Background layer)	Ctrl+Alt+A	⌘+Option+A
Link or unlink selected layers	Click Link Layers icon in Layers palette	Click Link Layers icon in Layers palette
Temporarily disable a layer's link	Shift+click layer's link icon in Layers palette	Shift+click layer's link icon in Layers palette
Toggle the visibility of a layer or group	Click eye icon next to layer or group in Layers palette	Click eye icon next to layer or group in Layers palette
Toggle the visibility of all other layers and groups	Alt+click eye icon next to layer or group in Layers palette	Option+click eye icon next to layer or group in Layers palette
Toggle visibility of active layer/ group or other layers/groups, and choose layer/group color	Right-click eye icon next to layer or group in Layers palette	Right-click eye icon next to layer or group in Layers palette
Set opacity of active layer to a multiple of 10	1 to 0, where 0=100 (doesn't work when using brush tools, stamp tools, eraser tools, fill tools or retouching tools)	1 to 0, where 0=100 (doesn't work when using brush tools, stamp tools, eraser tools, fill tools or retouching tools)
Set opacity of active layer to a specific value from 0 to 100	Quickly type two digits (01 for 1)	Quickly type two digits (01 for 1)
Set fill opacity of active layer to a multiple of 10	Shift+1 to Shift+0, where Shift+0=100 (doesn't work when using brush tools, stamp tools, eraser tools, fill tools or retouching tools)	Shift+1 to Shift+0, where Shift+0=100 (doesn't work when using brush tools, stamp tools, eraser tools, fill tools or retouching tools)
Set fill opacity of active layer to a specific value from 0 to 100	Quickly Shift+type two digits (Shift+01 for 1)	Quickly Shift+type two digits (Shift+01 for 1)
Rename a layer or group	Double-click layer or group's name in Layers palette	Double-click layer or group's name in Layers palette
Edit group properties	Double-click group in Layers palette	Double-click group in Layers palette

continued

TABLE B.1 *(continued)*

Action	Windows Shortcut	Mac Shortcut
Toggle selected layer locks (transparency lock if no locks previously selected)	/	/
Move layer/group up or down in Layers palette	Ctrl+] or Ctrl+[	⌘+] or ⌘+[
Move layer/group to the top or bottom of the group or Layers palette	Ctrl+Shift+] or Ctrl+Shift+[	⌘+Shift+] or ⌘+Shift+[
Move layer contents when using Move tool	Drag in document window	Drag in document window
Move layer contents when not using Move tool	Ctrl+drag in document window	⌘+drag in document window
Nudge layer contents in 1-pixel or 10-pixel steps when using Move tool	Arrow keys or Shift+arrow keys	Arrow keys or Shift+arrow keys
Nudge layer contents in 1-pixel or 10-pixel steps when not using Move tool	Ctrl+arrow keys or Ctrl+Shift+arrow keys	⌘+arrow keys or ⌘+Shift+arrow keys
Duplicate layer and position the duplicate when using Move tool	Alt+drag in document window	Option+drag in document window
Duplicate layer and position the duplicate when not using Move tool	Ctrl+Alt+drag in document window	⌘+Option+drag in document window
Duplicate layer and nudge the duplicate by 1 pixel or 10 pixels when using Move tool	Alt+arrow key or Alt+Shift+arrow key	Option+arrow key or Option+Shift+arrow key
Duplicate layer and nudge the duplicate by 1 pixel or 10 pixels when not using Move tool	Ctrl+Alt+arrow key or Ctrl+Alt+Shift+arrow key	⌘+Option+arrow key or ⌘+Option+Shift+arrow key
Merge active layer with layer below (Merge Down) or stamp active layer onto layer below (Stamp Down)	Ctrl+E or Ctrl+Alt+E	⌘+E or ⌘+Option+E
Merge two or more selected layers together (Merge Layers), or stamp selected layers onto a new layer (Stamp Layers)	Ctrl+E or Ctrl+Alt+E	⌘+E or ⌘+Option+E

Action	Windows Shortcut	Mac Shortcut
Merge layers in a group together (Merge Group) or stamp layers in a group onto a new layer (Stamp Group)	Ctrl+E or Ctrl+Alt+E	⌘+E or ⌘+Option+E
Merge visible layers together (Merge Visible) or stamp visible layers onto a new layer (Stamp Visible)	Ctrl+Shift+E or Ctrl+Alt+Shift+E	⌘+Shift+E or ⌘+Option+Shift+E
Copy merged selection to clipboard (Copy Merged)	Ctrl+Shift+C	⌘+Shift+C
Delete active layer or selected layers or groups	Click Delete Layer icon in Layers palette	Click Delete Layer icon in Layers palette
Delete active layer or selected layers, skipping warning dialog box	Alt+click Delete Layer icon in Layers palette	Option+click Delete Layer icon in Layers palette
Delete active layer while using Move tool with no selection active	Backspace	Delete
Delete selected group or groups, and preserve the contents, skipping warning dialog box	Ctrl+Alt+click Delete Layer icon in Layers palette	⌘+Option+click Delete Layer icon in Layers palette
Delete selected group or groups as well as the contents, skipping warning dialog box	Alt+click Delete Layer icon in Layers palette	Option+click Delete Layer icon in Layers palette

TABLE B.2

Shortcuts for Transforming Layers

Action	Windows Shortcut	Mac Shortcut
Transform layer contents using Free Transform	Ctrl+T	⌘+T
Duplicate and transform layer contents using Free Transform	Ctrl+Alt+T	⌘+Option+T
Repeat last transformation	Ctrl+Shift+T	⌘+Shift+T
Duplicate layer contents and repeat last transformation	Ctrl+Alt+Shift+T	⌘+Option+Shift+T

continued

TABLE B.2   *(continued)*

Action	Windows Shortcut	Mac Shortcut
Commit transformation	Enter, or double-click inside bounding box	Return, or double-click inside bounding box
Cancel transformation	Esc or Ctrl+. (period)	Esc or ⌘+. (period)
Flip between different transformations while transforming	Right-click in document window and choose from menu	Right-click in document window and choose from menu
Reposition image while transforming	Drag inside bounding box or use arrow keys	Drag inside bounding box or use arrow keys
Reposition reference point	Drag reference point or click a square in the reference point locator	Drag reference point or click a square in the reference point locator
Scale in Free Transform mode	Drag any resize handle	Drag any resize handle
Scale around reference point	Alt+drag any resize handle	Option+drag any resize handle
Scale proportionally	Shift+drag a corner resize handle	Shift+drag a corner resize handle
Rotate in Free Transform mode	Drag outside bounding box	Drag outside bounding box
Rotate in 15-degree steps	Shift+drag outside bounding box	Shift+drag outside bounding box
Skew in Free Transform mode	Ctrl+Shift+drag an edge resize handle	⌘+Shift+drag an edge resize handle
Skew freely in Free Transform mode	Ctrl+drag an edge resize handle	⌘+drag an edge resize handle
Skew around reference point	Hold down Alt while skewing	Hold down Option while skewing
Distort in Free Transform mode	Ctrl+drag a corner resize handle	⌘+drag a corner resize handle
Distort symmetrically	Hold down Alt while distorting	Hold down Option while distorting
Constrain distortion to an adjacent edge	Hold down Shift while distorting	Hold down Shift while distorting
Apply perspective in Free Transform mode	Ctrl+Alt+Shift+drag a corner resize handle	⌘+Option+Shift+drag a corner resize handle

TABLE B.3

Shortcuts for Editing Type Layers

Action	Windows Shortcut	Mac Shortcut
Select Type tool	T	T
Cycle through Type tools	Shift+T	Shift+T
Create point type	Click in document window	Click in document window

Action	Windows Shortcut	Mac Shortcut
Create paragraph type	Drag in document window	Drag in document window
Always create point or paragraph type on a new type layer	Shift+click or Shift+drag in document window	Shift+click or Shift+drag in document window
Move the insertion point 1 character to the left or right	Left arrow or right arrow	Left arrow or right arrow
Move the insertion point 1 word to the left or right	Ctrl+left arrow or Ctrl+right arrow	⌘+left arrow or ⌘+right arrow
Move the insertion point up or down 1 line	Up arrow or down arrow	Up arrow or down arrow
Move the insertion point to the beginning or end of the line	Home or End	Home or End
Move the insertion point to the beginning or end of the paragraph	Ctrl+up arrow or Ctrl+down arrow	⌘+up arrow or ⌘+down arrow
Move the insertion point to the beginning or end of the type	Ctrl+Home or Ctrl+End	⌘+Home or ⌘+End
Select the character to the left or right of the insertion point	Shift+left arrow or Shift+right arrow	Shift+left arrow or Shift+right arrow
Select the word to the left or right of the insertion point	Ctrl+Shift+left arrow or Ctrl+Shift+right arrow	⌘+Shift+left arrow or ⌘+Shift+right arrow
Select from the insertion point to the same point on the line above or below	Shift+up arrow or Shift+down arrow	Shift+up arrow or Shift+down arrow
Select from the insertion point to the beginning or end of the line	Shift+Home or Shift+End	Shift+Home or Shift+End
Select from the insertion point to the beginning or end of the paragraph	Ctrl+Shift+up arrow or Ctrl+Shift+down arrow	⌘+Shift+up arrow or ⌘+Shift+down arrow
Select from the insertion point to the beginning or end of the type	Ctrl+Shift+Home or Ctrl+Shift+End	⌘+Shift+Home or ⌘+Shift+End
Select from the insertion point to another point	Shift+click the point	Shift+click the point
Select a word	Double-click the word	Double-click the word
Select a line	Triple-click the line	Triple-click the line
Select a paragraph	Quadruple-click the paragraph	Quadruple-click the paragraph

continued

TABLE B.3	(continued)	
Action	**Windows Shortcut**	**Mac Shortcut**
Select all text in a type layer	Quintuple-click the text, or double-click the layer thumbnail	Quintuple-click the text, or double-click the layer thumbnail
Select all text in a type layer (only while editing the text)	Ctrl+A	⌘+A
Show or hide the selection highlight on selected text	Ctrl+H	⌘+H
Move type layer while editing text	Ctrl+drag the text	⌘+drag the text
Transform type layer while editing text	Ctrl+drag resize handles around bounding box	⌘+drag resize handles around bounding box
Move paragraph type bounding box while creating it	Spacebar+drag the bounding box	Spacebar+drag the bounding box
Increase or decrease type size by 2 points, 2 pixels or 1 mm	Ctrl+Shift+. (period) or Ctrl+Shift+, (comma)	⌘+Shift+. (period) or ⌘+Shift+, (comma)
Increase or decrease type size by 10 points, 10 pixels or 5 mm	Ctrl+Alt+Shift+. (period) or Ctrl+Alt+Shift+, (comma)	⌘+Option+Shift+. (period) or ⌘+Option+Shift+, (comma)
Increase or decrease leading by 2 points, 2 pixels or 1 mm	Alt+down arrow or Alt+up arrow	Option+down arrow or Option+up arrow
Increase or decrease leading by 10 points, 10 pixels or 5 mm	Ctrl+Alt+down arrow or Ctrl+Alt+up arrow	⌘+Option+down arrow or ⌘+Option+up arrows
Set leading to Auto	Ctrl+Alt+Shift+A	⌘+Option+Shift+A
Increase or decrease kerning (tracking if characters are selected) by 20 thousandths of an em	Alt+right arrow or Alt+left arrow	Option+right arrow or Option+left arrow
Increase or decrease kerning (tracking if characters are selected) by 100 thousandths of an em	Ctrl+Alt+right arrow or Ctrl+Alt+left arrow	⌘+Option+right arrow or ⌘+Option+left arrow
Set tracking to 0	Ctrl+Shift+Q	⌘+Control +Shift+Q
Set Horizontal Scale to 100%	Ctrl+Shift+X	⌘+Shift+X
Set Vertical Scale to 100%	Ctrl+Alt+Shift+X	⌘+Option+Shift+X
Increase or decrease baseline shift by 2 points, 2 pixels or 1 mm	Alt+Shift+up arrow or Alt+Shift+down arrow	Option+Shift+up arrow or Option +Shift+down arrow

Action	Windows Shortcut	Mac Shortcut
Increase or decrease baseline shift by 10 points, 10 pixels or 5 mm	Ctrl+Alt+Shift+up arrow or Ctrl+Alt+Shift+down arrow	⌘+Option+Shift+up arrow or ⌘+Option+Shift+down arrow
Toggle (faux) bold font style	Ctrl+Shift+B	⌘+Shift+B
Toggle (faux) italic font style	Ctrl+Shift+I	⌘+Shift+I
Toggle All Caps	Ctrl+Shift+K	⌘+Shift+K
Toggle Small Caps	Ctrl+Shift+H	⌘+Shift+H
Toggle superscript	Ctrl+Shift+=	⌘+Shift+=
Toggle subscript	Ctrl+Alt+Shift+=	⌘+Option+Shift+=
Toggle underline	Ctrl+Shift+U	⌘+Shift+U
Toggle strikethrough	Ctrl+Shift+/	⌘+Shift+/
Return to default font style (usually Regular)	Ctrl+Shift+Y	⌘+Shift+Y
Left-align, center or right-align all text in type layer while editing with Horizontal Type tool (top-align, center or right-align when using Vertical Type tool)	Ctrl+Shift+L or Ctrl+Shift+C or Ctrl+Shift+R	⌘+Shift+L or ⌘+Shift+C or ⌘+Shift+R
Justify all text in type layer, excluding last line	Ctrl+Shift+J	⌘+Shift+J
Justify all text in type layer, including last line	Ctrl+Shift+F	⌘+Shift+F
Toggle hyphenation for current paragraph or selected paragraphs	Ctrl+Alt+Shift+H	⌘+Option+Shift+H
Toggle between Single-Line Composer and Every-Line Composer for current paragraph or selected paragraphs	Ctrl+Alt+Shift+T	⌘+Option+Shift+T
Commit edits to type layer	Ctrl+Enter, or Enter on the keypad	⌘+Return, or Enter on the keypad
Cancel edits to type layer	Esc	Esc
Display Character palette while editing text	Ctrl+T	⌘+T
Display Paragraph palette while editing text	Ctrl+M	⌘+M

TABLE B.4

Shortcuts for Working with Shape Layers

Action	Windows Shortcut	Mac Shortcut
Select shape tool	U	U
Cycle through shape tools	Shift+U	Shift+U
Move focus to Radius/Sides/Weight/Shape option in options bar (when not creating or editing shapes)	Select shape tool then press Enter when no shape layer is active	Select shape tool then press Return when no shape layer is active
Increase or decrease Radius/Sides/Weight setting	] or [	] or [
Cycle forward or backward through available custom shapes	] or [	] or [
Add next shape to shape area of existing shape layer	= then drag out new shape, or Shift while starting to drag out shape	= then drag out new shape, or Shift while starting to drag out shape
Subtract next shape from shape area of existing shape layer	- then drag out new shape, or Alt while starting to drag out shape	- then drag out new shape, or Option while starting to drag out shape
Cycle forward or backward through available layer styles within Style option	. (period) or , (comma)	. (period) or , (comma)
Change fill color of active shape layer to current foreground or background color	Alt+Backspace or Ctrl+Backspace	Option+Delete or ⌘+Delete
Constrain shape proportions when drawing shapes with the Rectangle, Ellipse or Custom Shape tools	Shift+drag	Shift+drag
Constrain rotation to 45-degree steps when drawing shapes with the Polygon tool	Shift+drag	Shift+drag
Constrain angle to 45-degree steps when drawing shapes with the Line tool	Shift+drag	Shift+drag
Drag shape out from center when drawing shapes with the Rectangle, Ellipse or Custom Shape tools	Alt+drag	Option+drag

Action	Windows Shortcut	Mac Shortcut
Cycle between Path Selection and Direct Selection tools	Shift+A	Shift+A
Temporarily access the Path Selection tool when using a shape tool	Ctrl	⌘
Select shape within shape layer	Click shape with the Path Selection tool, or Ctrl+click shape with a shape tool	Click shape with the Path Selection tool, or ⌘+click shape with a shape tool
Select multiple shapes within shape layer	Shift+click each shape with the Path Selection tool, or Ctrl+Shift+click each shape with a shape tool	Shift+click each shape with the Path Selection tool, or ⌘+Shift+click each shape with a shape tool
Select segment or anchor point within shape	Click segment or anchor point with the Direct Selection tool	Click segment or anchor point with the Direct Selection tool
Select multiple segments or anchor points within shape	Shift+click each segment or anchor point with the Direct Selection tool	Shift+click each segment or anchor point with the Direct Selection tool
Move shape within shape layer	Drag shape when using Path Selection tool, or Ctrl+drag shape when using a shape tool	Drag shape when using Path Selection tool, or ⌘+drag shape when using a shape tool
Move shape within shape layer, constraining movement to 45-degree steps	Shift+drag shape when using Path Selection tool, or Ctrl+Shift+drag shape when using a shape tool	Drag shape when using Path Selection tool, or ⌘+Shift+drag shape when using a shape tool
Nudge shape within shape layer in 1-pixel steps	Arrow keys when using Path Selection tool, or Ctrl+arrow keys when using a shape tool	Arrow keys when using Path Selection tool, or ⌘+arrow keys when using a shape tool
Nudge shape within shape layer in 10-pixel steps	Shift+arrow keys when using Path Selection tool, or Ctrl+Shift+arrow keys when using a shape tool	Shift+arrow keys when using Path Selection tool, or ⌘+Shift+arrow keys when using a shape tool
Move straight segment or point within shape	Drag segment or point with the Direct Selection tool	Drag segment or point with the Direct Selection tool
Move straight segment or point within shape, constraining movement to 45-degree steps	Shift+drag segment or point with the Direct Selection tool	Shift+drag segment or point with the Direct Selection tool
Move curved segment within shape	Shift+click points at either end of curve with Direct Selection tool, then drag or Shift+drag segment	Shift+click points at either end of curve with Direct Selection tool, then drag or Shift+drag segment
Reshape curved segment within shape	Drag curve with the Direct Selection tool	Drag curve with the Direct Selection tool

continued

TABLE B.4 (continued)

Action	Windows Shortcut	Mac Shortcut
Nudge point within shape in 1-pixel or 10-pixel steps	Select point with Direct Selection tool, then use arrow keys or Shift+arrow keys	Select point with Direct Selection tool, then use arrow keys or Shift+arrow keys
Add anchor point to shape	Select the shape with the Path or Direct Selection tool, then click on the shape's path using a pen tool with Auto Add/Delete enabled	Select the shape with the Path or Direct Selection tool, then click on the shape's path using a pen tool with Auto Add/Delete enabled
Remove anchor point from shape	Select the shape with the Path or Direct Selection tool, then click on the point using a pen tool with Auto Add/Delete enabled	Select the shape with the Path or Direct Selection tool, then click on the point using a pen tool with Auto Add/Delete enabled
Convert smooth point to corner point	Click point with Convert Point tool	Click point with Convert Point tool
Convert smooth point to cusp point	Drag either direction point with Convert Point tool, or Alt+drag either direction point with Direct Selection tool or a pen tool	Drag either direction point with Convert Point tool, or Option+drag either direction point with Direct Selection tool
Convert corner or cusp point to smooth point	Drag point with Convert Point tool	Click point with Convert Point tool and drag
Convert corner point to a point with both a straight segment and a curved segment	Alt+drag point with Convert Point tool	Option+drag point with Convert Point tool
Reshape curves on both sides of smooth point	Drag either direction point with Direct Selection tool	Drag either direction point with Direct Selection tool
Reshape curves on both sides of cusp point	Alt+drag either direction point with Direct Selection tool	Option+drag either direction point with Direct Selection tool
Reshape curve on one side of cusp point	Drag its direction point with Direct Selection tool	Drag its direction point with Direct Selection tool
Temporarily access Convert Point tool from pen tool (with cursor over anchor point)	Alt	Option
Temporarily access Convert Point tool from Direct Selection tool (with cursor over anchor point)	Ctrl+Alt	⌘+Option

Action	Windows Shortcut	Mac Shortcut
Toggle shape layer's vector mask path	Click vector mask thumbnail in Layers palette or, with the shape layer active, press Enter when using any pen tool, the Convert Point tool, the Path/Direct Selection tool, or a shape tool	Click vector mask thumbnail in Layers palette, or press Return
Hide shape layer's vector mask path in document window	Ctrl+Shift+H	⌘+Shift+H
Delete shape layer when its vector mask is active	Backspace or Delete	Delete

TABLE B.5

Shortcuts for Adjustment and Fill Layers

Action	Windows Shortcut	Mac Shortcut
Create a new adjustment or fill layer	Click Create New Fill or Adjustment Layer icon in Layers palette	Click Create New Fill or Adjustment Layer icon in Layers palette
Create a new adjustment or fill layer with New Layer dialog box	Alt+click Create New Fill or Adjustment Layer icon in Layers palette	Option+click Create New Fill or Adjustment Layer icon in Layers palette
Edit layer's adjustment or fill	Double-click layer thumbnail	Double-click layer thumbnail
Add color sampler while working in adjustment dialog box	Shift+click in document window	Shift+click in document window
Move color sampler while working in adjustment dialog box	Shift+drag in document window	Shift+drag in document window
Delete color sampler while working in adjustment dialog box	Shift+drag sampler out of the document window	Shift+drag sampler out of the document window
Switch between individual color channels in Levels or Curves dialog box	Ctrl+1 to Ctrl+4	⌘+1 to ⌘+4
Switch to composite color channel in Levels or Curves dialog box	Ctrl+~ (tilde)	⌘+~ (tilde)

continued

TABLE B.5 *(continued)*

Action	Windows Shortcut	Mac Shortcut
Preview clipping of shadows and highlights in Levels or Curves dialog box	Alt+drag black or white Input Levels slider	Option+drag black or white Input Levels slider
Change target color for black, gray or white eyedropper in Levels or Curves dialog box	Double-click black, gray, or white eyedropper icon	Double-click black, gray, or white eyedropper icon
Add new point to a curve in Curves dialog box	Click on the curve	Click on the curve
Add new point to composite curve based on color in image	Ctrl+click in document window	⌘+click in document window
Add new points to individual channel curves based on color in image	Ctrl+Shift+click in document window	⌘+Shift+click in document window
Select point on a curve	Click the point	Click the point
Select more than one point on a curve	Shift+click each point	Shift+click each point
Cycle forward or backward through curve points	Ctrl+Tab or Ctrl+Shift+Tab	Ctrl+Tab or Ctrl+Shift+Tab
Deselect all curve points	Ctrl+D	⌘+D
Nudge selected curve point(s) 1 level up, down, left or right	Arrow keys	Arrow keys
Nudge selected curve point(s) 10 levels up, down, left or right	Shift+arrow keys	Shift+arrow keys
Delete curve point	Ctrl+click point or drag it outside the graph	⌘+click point or drag it outside the graph
Toggle size of grid in Curves graph	Alt+click the graph	Option+click the graph
Switch between color ranges in Hue/Saturation dialog box	Ctrl+1 to Ctrl+6	⌘+1 to ⌘+6
Switch to Master setting in Hue/Saturation dialog box	Ctrl+~ (tilde)	⌘+~ (tilde)
Set midpoint of Hue/Saturation color range based on a color in the image	With left-hand eyedropper selected, click or drag in document window	With left-hand eyedropper selected, click or drag in document window
Expand Hue/Saturation color range to include a color in the image	With left-hand eyedropper selected, Shift+click or Shift+drag in document window	With left-hand eyedropper selected, Shift+click or Shift+drag in document window

Action	Windows Shortcut	Mac Shortcut
Contract Hue/Saturation color range to exclude a color in the image	With left-hand eyedropper selected, Alt+click or Alt+drag in document window	With left-hand eyedropper selected, Option+click or Option+drag in document window
Rotate color bars at bottom of Hue/Saturation dialog box	Ctrl+drag either color bar	⌘+drag either color bar
Reposition gradient or pattern while in Gradient Fill or Pattern Fill dialog box	Drag in document window	Drag in document window
Reposition gradient or pattern, constraining movement to 45-degree steps, while in Gradient Fill or Pattern Fill dialog box	Shift+drag in document window	Shift+drag in document window
Edit gradient fill	Click inside Gradient box in Gradient Fill dialog box	Click inside Gradient box in Gradient Fill dialog box
Add color or opacity stop to Solid gradient in Gradient Editor dialog box	Click below or above gradient bar	Click below or above gradient bar
Duplicate color or opacity stop in Solid gradient in Gradient Editor dialog box	Alt+drag stop	Option+drag stop

TABLE B.6

Shortcuts for Using Layer Blending Modes

Action	Windows Shortcut	Mac Shortcut
Edit a layer's blending options	Double-click layer in Layers palette	Double-click layer in Layers palette
Smooth transitions when blending by color range	Alt+drag This Layer or Underlying Layer slider	Option+drag This Layer or Underlying Layer slider
Cycle forwards or backwards through blending modes for active layer	Shift+= or Shift+-	Shift+= or Shift+-
Set active layer to Normal mode	Alt+Shift+N	Option+Shift+N
Set active layer to Dissolve mode	Alt+Shift+I	Option+Shift+I
Set tool to Behind mode	Alt+Shift+Q	Option+Shift+Q

continued

TABLE B.6 *(continued)*

Action	Windows Shortcut	Mac Shortcut
Set tool to Clear mode	Alt+Shift+R	Option+Shift+R
Set active layer to Darken mode	Alt+Shift+K	Option+Shift+K
Set active layer to Multiply mode	Alt+Shift+M	Option+Shift+M
Set active layer to Color Burn mode	Alt+Shift+B	Option+Shift+B
Set active layer to Linear Burn mode	Alt+Shift+A	Option+Shift+A
Set active layer to Lighten mode	Alt+Shift+G	Option+Shift+G
Set active layer to Screen mode	Alt+Shift+S	Option+Shift+S
Set active layer to Color Dodge mode	Alt+Shift+D	Option+Shift+D
Set active layer to Linear Dodge mode	Alt+Shift+W	Option+Shift+W
Set active layer to Overlay mode	Alt+Shift+O	Option+Shift+O
Set active layer to Soft Light mode	Alt+Shift+F	Option+Shift+F
Set active layer to Hard Light mode	Alt+Shift+H	Option+Shift+H
Set active layer to Vivid Light mode	Alt+Shift+V	Option+Shift+V
Set active layer to Linear Light mode	Alt+Shift+J	Option+Shift+J
Set active layer to Pin Light mode	Alt+Shift+Z	Option+Shift+Z
Set active layer to Hard Mix mode	Alt+Shift+L	Option+Shift+L
Set active layer to Difference mode	Alt+Shift+E	Option+Shift+E
Set active layer to Exclusion mode	Alt+Shift+X	Option+Shift+X
Set active layer to Hue mode	Alt+Shift+U	Option+Shift+U
Set active layer to Saturation mode	Alt+Shift+T	Option+Shift+T
Set active layer to Color mode	Alt+Shift+C	Option+Shift+C
Set active layer to Luminosity mode	Alt+Shift+Y	Option+Shift+Y
Set active layer group to Pass Through	Alt+Shift+P	Option+Shift+P

NOTE The shortcuts for setting and cycling through layer blending modes don't work when using some healing tools, the brush tools, the stamp tools, the Magic Eraser tool, the fill tools or the retouching tools. In most of these cases, the shortcuts change the blending mode of the tool rather than the layer.

TABLE B.7

Shortcuts for Using Smart Objects and Smart Filters

Action	Windows Shortcut	Mac Shortcut
Edit contents of Smart Object	Double-click Smart Object thumbnail in Layers palette	Double-click Smart Object thumbnail in Layers palette
Duplicate Smart Object, linking duplicate with original	Drag Smart Object to New Layer icon in Layers palette	Drag Smart Object to New Layer icon in Layers palette
Add Smart Filter to Smart Object	Choose from Filter menu	Choose from Filter menu
Add Smart Filter to Smart Object, constraining filter effects to selection	Make or load selection, then choose from Filter menu	Make or load selection, then choose from Filter menu
Edit Smart Filter	Double-click filter name in Layers palette	Double-click filter name in Layers palette
Toggle Smart Filter visibility	Click eye icon next to filter name in Layers palette	Click eye icon next to filter name in Layers palette
Toggle all Smart Filter visibilities for a layer	Click eye icon next to Smart Filters item in Layers palette	Click eye icon next to Smart Filters item in Layers palette
Edit Smart Filter's blending options	Double-click sliders icon for Smart Filter in Layers palette	Double-click sliders icon for Smart Filter in Layers palette
Reorder Smart Filter	Drag Smart Filter in Layers palette	Drag Smart Filter in Layers palette
Duplicate Smart Filter within Smart Object	Alt+drag Smart Filter to new location under Smart Object	Option+drag Smart Filter to new location under Smart Object
Move Smart Filter from one Smart Object to another	Drag Smart Filter from one layer to the other in Layers palette	Drag Smart Filter from one Smart Object to the other in Layers palette
Copy Smart Filter from one Smart Object to another	Alt+drag Smart Filter from one layer to the other in Layers palette	Option+drag Smart Filter from one Smart Object to the other in Layers palette
Move all Smart Filters, including filter mask, from one Smart Object to another	Drag Smart Filters item from one Smart Object to the other in Layers palette	Drag Smart Filters item from one Smart Object to the other in Layers palette
Copy all Smart Filters, including filter mask, from one Smart Object to another	Alt+drag Smart Filters item from one Smart Object to the other in Layers palette	Option+drag Smart Filters item from one Smart Object to the other in Layers palette
Move just the filter mask from one layer to another	Drag the filter mask thumbnail from one Smart Object to the filter mask thumbnail of the other Smart Object in the Layers palette	Drag the filter mask thumbnail from one Smart Object to the filter mask thumbnail of the other Smart Object in the Layers palette

continued

TABLE B.7 *(continued)*

Action	Windows Shortcut	Mac Shortcut
Copy just the filter mask from one layer to another	Alt+drag the filter mask thumbnail from one Smart Object to the filter mask thumbnail of the other Smart Object in the Layers palette	Option+drag the filter mask thumbnail from one Smart Object to the filter mask thumbnail of the other Smart Object in the Layers palette
Delete Smart Filter	Drag Smart Filter to Delete Layer icon in Layers palette	Drag Smart Filter to Delete Layer icon in Layers palette
Activate filter mask	Click filter mask thumbnail in Layers palette	Click filter mask thumbnail in Layers palette
Deactivate filter mask	Ctrl+~ (tilde) or click Smart Object thumbnail in Layers palette	⌘+~ (tilde) or click Smart Object thumbnail in Layers palette
Toggle filter mask overlay	Alt+Shift+click filter mask thumbnail	Option+Shift+click filter mask thumbnail
Edit filter mask overlay options	Double-click filter mask thumbnail	Double-click filter mask thumbnail
Toggle between viewing filter mask in isolation, and viewing Smart Object	Alt+click filter mask thumbnail	Option+click filter mask thumbnail
Disable/enable filter mask	Shift+click filter mask thumbnail	Shift+click filter mask thumbnail
Load filter mask as a selection	Ctrl+click filter mask thumbnail	⌘+click filter mask thumbnail
Add filter mask to existing selection	Ctrl+Shift+click filter mask thumbnail	⌘+Shift+click filter mask thumbnail
Subtract filter mask from existing selection	Ctrl+Alt+click filter mask thumbnail	⌘+Option+click filter mask thumbnail
Intersect filter mask with existing selection	Ctrl+Alt+Shift+click filter mask thumbnail	⌘+Option+Shift+click filter mask thumbnail
Delete filter mask	Drag filter mask thumbnail to Delete Layer icon in Layers palette	Drag filter mask thumbnail to Delete Layer icon in Layers palette
Add new filter mask	Right-click Smart Filters item in Layers palette and choose Add Filter Mask	Right-click Smart Filters item in Layers palette and choose Add Filter Mask
Add new filter mask based on selection	Make or load selection, then right-click Smart Filters item in Layers palette and choose Add Filter Mask	Make or load selection, then right-click Smart Filters item in Layers palette and choose Add Filter Mask

TABLE B.8

Shortcuts for Working with Masks

Action	Windows Shortcut	Mac Shortcut
Toggle between Standard and Quick Mask modes	Q	Q
Toggle Quick Mask overlay behavior between representing masked areas and representing selected areas	Alt+click Quick Mask icon in Toolbox	Option+click Quick Mask icon in Toolbox
Add a layer mask to the active layer, revealing all pixels or current selection	Click Add Layer Mask icon at bottom of Layers palette	Click Add Layer Mask icon at bottom of Layers palette
Add a layer mask to the active layer, hiding all pixels or current selection	Alt+click Add Layer Mask icon at bottom of Layers palette	Option+click Add Layer Mask icon at bottom of Layers palette
Add a vector mask to the active layer, revealing all pixels or current path	Ctrl+click Add Layer Mask icon at bottom of Layers palette	⌘+click Add Layer Mask icon at bottom of Layers palette
Add a vector mask to the active layer, hiding all pixels (if no path is active)	Ctrl+Alt+click Add Layer Mask icon at bottom of Layers palette	⌘+Option+click Add Layer Mask icon at bottom of Layers palette
Create an alpha channel filled with black	Click Create New Channel icon at bottom of Channels palette	Click Create New Channel icon at bottom of Channels palette
Create an alpha channel filled with black, opening New Channel dialog box	Alt+click Create New Channel icon at bottom of Channels palette	Ctrl+click Create New Channel icon at bottom of Channels palette
Create an alpha channel, revealing current selection	Click Save Selection as Channel icon at bottom of Channels palette	Click Save Selection as Channel icon at bottom of Channels palette
Create an alpha channel revealing current selection, opening New Channel dialog box	Alt+click Save Selection as Channel icon at bottom of Channels palette	Alt+click Save Selection as Channel icon at bottom of Channels palette
Edit Quick Mask, alpha channel mask, or layer mask overlay options	Double-click Quick Mask icon in Toolbox or mask thumbnail in Channels or Layers palette	Double-click Quick Mask icon in Toolbox or mask thumbnail in Channels or Layers palette
Toggle between viewing an active Quick Mask, alpha channel mask, or layer mask in isolation, and viewing it overlaid on the image	~ (tilde)	~ (tilde)

continued

TABLE B.8   (continued)

Action	Windows Shortcut	Mac Shortcut
Toggle layer mask overlay	\ or Alt+Shift+click layer mask thumbnail	\ or Option+Shift+click layer mask thumbnail
View layer mask in isolation	\ followed by ~ (tilde), or Alt+click layer mask thumbnail	\ followed by ~ (tilde), or Option+click layer mask thumbnail
Switch from viewing layer mask to viewing layer contents	\ or Alt+click layer mask thumbnail	\ or Option+click layer mask thumbnail
Switch to editing the active layer's layer mask	Ctrl+\ or click layer mask thumbnail	⌘+\ or click layer mask thumbnail
Switch back to editing the active layer itself	Ctrl+~ (tilde) or click layer thumbnail	⌘+~ (tilde) or click layer thumbnail
Disable/enable a layer mask or vector mask	Shift+click mask thumbnail	Shift+click mask thumbnail
Toggle vector mask path off/on	Click vector mask thumbnail, or press Enter when using a pen or shape tool	Click vector mask thumbnail, or press Return when using a pen or shape tool
Hide vector mask path	Ctrl+Shift+H	⌘+Shift+H
Move a layer mask or vector mask from one layer to another	Drag mask thumbnail from one layer to the other in Layers palette	Drag mask thumbnail from one layer to the other in Layers palette
Copy a layer mask or vector mask from one layer to another	Alt+drag mask thumbnail from one layer to the other in Layers palette	Option+ mask thumbnail from one layer to the other in Layers palette
Load layer mask, vector mask or alpha channel as a selection	Ctrl+click mask or channel thumbnail	⌘+click mask or channel thumbnail
Add layer mask, vector mask or alpha channel to existing selection	Ctrl+Shift+click mask or channel thumbnail	⌘+Shift+click mask or channel thumbnail
Subtract layer mask, vector mask or alpha channel from existing selection	Ctrl+Alt+click mask or channel thumbnail	⌘+Option+click mask or channel thumbnail
Intersect layer mask, vector mask or alpha channel with existing selection	Ctrl+Alt+Shift+click mask or channel thumbnail	⌘+Option+Shift+click mask or channel thumbnail
Create clipping mask from active layer and layer below	Ctrl+Alt+G, or Alt+click line between two layers in Layers palette	⌘+Option+G, or Option+click line between two layers in Layers palette
Release active layer from clipping mask palette	Ctrl+Alt+G, or Alt+click line between two layers in Layers palette	⌘+Option+G, or Option+click line between two layers in Layers

TABLE B.9

Shortcuts for Manipulating Layer Styles

Action	Windows Shortcut	Mac Shortcut
Create style preset from active layer's style	Click Create New Style icon in Styles palette	Click Create New Style icon in Styles palette
Create style preset from active layer's style, skipping New Style dialog box	Alt+click Create New Style icon in Styles palette	Option+click Create New Style icon in Styles palette
Rename style preset	Double-click preset in Styles palette	Double-click preset in Styles palette
Apply a style preset to active layer, overwriting existing layer effects	Click preset thumbnail in Styles palette	Click preset thumbnail in Styles palette
Apply a style preset to active layer, preserving existing layer effects	Shift+click preset thumbnail in Styles palette	Shift+click preset thumbnail in Styles palette
Edit a layer's layer style	Double-click layer in Layers palette	Double-click layer in Layers palette
Add or edit a layer effect	Click Add a Layer Style icon in Layers palette and choose an effect	Click Add a Layer Style icon in Layers palette and choose an effect
Edit a layer effect	Double-click effect name in Layers palette	Double-click effect name in Layers palette
Edit a layer effect within Layer Style dialog box	Ctrl+1 (Drop Shadow) to Ctrl+0 (Stroke)	⌘+1 (Drop Shadow) to ⌘+0 (Stroke)
Toggle an individual layer effect's visibility	Click eye icon next to effect name in Layers palette	Click eye icon next to effect name in Layers palette
Toggle all effect visibilities for a layer	Click eye icon next to Effects item in Layers palette	Click eye icon next to Effects item in Layers palette
Move an effect from one layer to another	Drag effect from one layer to the other in Layers palette	Drag effect from one layer to the other in Layers palette
Copy an effect from one layer to another	Alt+drag effect from one layer to the other in Layers palette	Option+drag effect from one layer to the other in Layers palette
Move all effects from one layer to another	Drag Effects item from one layer to the other in Layers palette	Drag Effects item from one layer to the other in Layers palette
Copy all effects from one layer to another	Alt+drag Effects item from one layer to the other in Layers palette	Option+drag Effects item from one layer to the other in Layers palette
Delete a layer effect	Drag effect to Delete Layer icon in Layers palette	Drag effect to Delete Layer icon in Layers palette

continued

713

TABLE B.9   (continued)

Action	Windows Shortcut	Mac Shortcut
Reposition shadow, Texture, Satin, Gradient Overlay or Pattern Overlay effect when in Layer Style dialog box	Drag in document window	Drag in document window
Reposition shadow, Texture, Satin, Gradient Overlay or Pattern Overlay effect, constraining movement to 45-degree steps, when in Layer Style dialog box	Shift+drag in document window	Shift+drag in document window
Edit a contour	Click graph in Contour option in Layer Style dialog box	Click graph in Contour option in Layer Style dialog box
Add new point to a contour in Contour Editor dialog box	Click on the contour	Click on the contour
Select point on a contour	Click the point	Click the point
Select more than one point on a contour	Shift+click each point	Shift+click each point
Cycle forward or backward through contour points	Ctrl+Tab or Ctrl+Shift+Tab	Ctrl+Tab or Ctrl+Shift+Tab
Deselect all contour points	Ctrl+D	⌘+D
Nudge selected contour point(s) 1 value up, down, left or right	Arrow keys	Arrow keys
Nudge selected contour point(s) 10 values up, down, left or right	Shift+arrow keys	Shift+arrow keys
Delete contour point	Ctrl+click point or drag it outside the graph	⌘+click point or drag it outside the graph
Toggle size of grid in Contour Editor graph	Alt+click the graph	Option+click the graph

TABLE B.10

Shortcuts for Managing Layer Comps

Action	Windows Shortcut	Mac Shortcut
Create a new layer comp at the bottom of the Layer Comps palette	Click New Layer Comp icon in Layer Comps palette	Click New Layer Comp icon in Layer Comps palette
Create a new layer comp at the bottom of the Layer Comps palette, skipping New Layer Comp dialog box	Alt+click New Layer Comp icon in Layer Comps palette	Option+click New Layer Comp icon in Layer Comps palette
Select multiple layer comps that are next to each other in the Layer Comps palette	Click top layer comp, Shift+click bottom layer comp (or vice-versa)	Click top layer comp, Shift+click bottom layer comp (or vice-versa)
Select multiple layer comps that are not next to each other in the Layer Comps palette	Ctrl+click each layer comp	⌘+click each layer comp
Re-edit layer comp options	Double-click layer comp in Layer Comps palette	Double-click layer comp in Layer Comps palette
Rename a layer comp	Double-click layer comp name in Layer Comps palette	Double-click layer comp name in Layer Comps palette
Delete a layer comp	Select comp and click Delete Layer Comp icon in Layer Comps palette	Select comp and click Delete Layer Comp icon in Layer Comps palette
Delete multiple layer comps	Select comps and click Delete Layer Comp icon in Layer Comps palette	Select comps and click Delete Layer Comp icon in Layer Comps palette

TABLE B.11

Miscellaneous Layer-Related Shortcuts

Action	Windows Shortcut	Mac Shortcut
Switch focus to a tool's options bar	Enter	Return
Reset adjustment, Gradient Fill, Pattern Fill, Layer Style or Blending Options dialog box to settings when dialog box was first opened	Alt+click Cancel button	Option+click Cancel button

continued

TABLE B.11 *(continued)*

Action	Windows Shortcut	Mac Shortcut
Cancel a command or back out of a dialog box	Esc	Escape or ⌘+. (period)
Show or hide any enabled features in the document window such as slices, guides and the grid	Ctrl+H	⌘+H
Delete preset in a presets palette or picker	Alt+click preset name or thumbnail	Option+click preset name or thumbnail
Delete layer contents inside a selection	Backspace	Delete
Fill Background layer contents inside a selection with background color	Backspace	Delete
Fill whole layer, or layer contents inside a selection, with foreground color	Alt+Backspace	Option+Delete
Fill whole layer, or layer contents inside a selection, with foreground color, preserving transparency	Alt+Shift+Backspace	Option+Shift+Delete
Fill whole layer, or layer contents inside a selection, with background color	Ctrl+Backspace	⌘+Delete
Fill whole layer, or layer contents inside a selection, with background color, preserving transparency	Ctrl+Shift+Backspace	⌘+Shift+Delete
Fill whole layer, or layer contents inside a selection, with contents of currently selected state in History palette	Ctrl+Alt+Backspace	⌘+Option+Delete
Fill whole layer, or layer contents inside a selection, with contents of currently selected History state in History palette, preserving transparency	Ctrl+Alt+Shift+Backspace	⌘+Option+Shift+Delete
Display Fill dialog box	Shift+Backspace or Shift+F5	Shift+Delete or Shift+F5

Action	Windows Shortcut	Mac Shortcut
Show or hide rulers in a document window	Ctrl+R	⌘+R
Access Units & Rulers preferences	Double-click a ruler	Double-click a ruler
Change ruler units	Right-click a ruler or click + sign in Info palette	Right-click a ruler or click + sign in Info palette
Reset ruler origin	Double-click origin icon in top left of document window	Double-click origin icon in top left of document window
Create new horizontal guide	Drag from top ruler or Alt+drag from left ruler	Drag from top ruler or Option+drag from left ruler
Create new vertical guide	Drag from left ruler or Alt+drag from top ruler	Drag from left ruler or Option+drag from top ruler
Move a guide from any tool except slice tools and Hand tool	Ctrl+drag guide	⌘+drag guide
Snap guide to ruler tick marks while moving it	Shift+drag guide with View ⇨ Snap selected	Shift+drag guide with View ⇨ Snap selected
Change orientation of a guide	Ctrl+Alt+click guide	⌘+Option+click guide
Delete a guide	Drag guide outside document window	Drag guide outside document window
Lock or unlock guides	Ctrl+Alt+; (semicolon)	⌘+Option+; (semicolon)
Show or hide guides in the document window	Ctrl+; (semicolon)	⌘+; (semicolon)
Access Guides, Grid & Slices preferences from any tool except slice tools and Hand tool	Ctrl+double-click a guide	⌘+double-click a guide
Show or hide the grid in the document window	Ctrl+' (single quote)	⌘+' (single quote)
Toggle snapping	Ctrl+Shift+; (semicolon)	⌘+Shift+; (semicolon)
Select Ruler tool	Shift+I until Ruler Tool icon appears in Toolbox	Shift+I until Ruler Tool icon appears in Toolbox
Create measurement line	Drag in document window	Drag in document window
Move measurement line	Drag line in document window	Drag line in document window
Move endpoint of measurement line	Drag endpoint in document window	Drag endpoint in document window
Create second measurement line	Alt+drag from endpoint in first line	Option+drag from endpoint in first line

Index

NUMBERS

3-D applications, 530–531

A

A value, 93–94
active layer
color, specifying, 47
creating clipping masks from, 30
definition, 33
deleting, 51
duplicating, 36–37
opacity, setting, 49
stamping down, 40
Add a Layer Style control, 5–6
Add Anchor Point tool, 186
Add Layer Mask control, 5–6
Add Space After Paragraph box, 140
Add Space Before Paragraph box, 140
Add To Shape Area option, 190
adjustment layers. *See also* fill layers; *specific adjustments*
applying to specific layers, 207, 209–210
automatic level adjustments, 217–219
bitmap masks, 275
Black & White, 232–236
blending modes
duplicating layers, 278
options, 207
special effects, 276–278
Brightness/Contrast, 230–232
Channel Mixer, 243–246
clip values, 219
clipping, determining effects of, 214–215
clipping masks, 209–210
Color Balance, 229–230
converting to fill layers, 14
creating
with the Layers palette, 5–6, 14–15, 206–207
for part of an image, 275

Curves, 220–229
description, 14, 204
editing, 210–211
Exposure, 250–252
eyedroppers, 216–217
versus fill layers, 259
Flash CS3, 507
Gradient Map, 246–248
highlights, finding, 219
histograms
combing, 214
definition, 211
displaying, 212, 224
isolated spikes, 214
uses for, 212
Hue/Saturation, 236–242
Invert, 253–254
keyboard shortcuts, 705–707
layer mask, painting on, 211
in the Layers palette, 205
Levels, 211–219
luminosity adjustment, 278
masking, 274–276
masks, 275
merging, 211
naming, 207
nondestructive editing, 14, 459–460
opacity, setting, 207
options, setting, 207
painting on, 204
Photo Filter, 248–250
Posterize, 256–259
restricting to active layer, 207
Selective Color, 242–243
Threshold, 254–256
vector masks, 211, 275
Adobe Creative Suite 3, Dreamweaver CS3
description, 512
Image Preview dialog box, 515
importing Photoshop graphics, 513–515

C

Wiley Publishing, Inc.
End-User License Agreement

READ THIS. You should carefully read these terms and conditions before opening the software packet(s) included with this book "Book". This is a license agreement "Agreement" between you and Wiley Publishing, Inc. "WPI". By opening the accompanying software packet(s), you acknowledge that you have read and accept the following terms and conditions. If you do not agree and do not want to be bound by such terms and conditions, promptly return the Book and the unopened software packet(s) to the place you obtained them for a full refund.

1. **License Grant.** WPI grants to you (either an individual or entity) a nonexclusive license to use one copy of the enclosed software program(s) (collectively, the "Software," solely for your own personal or business purposes on a single computer (whether a standard computer or a workstation component of a multi-user network). The Software is in use on a computer when it is loaded into temporary memory (RAM) or installed into permanent memory (hard disk, CD-ROM, or other storage device). WPI reserves all rights not expressly granted herein.

2. **Ownership.** WPI is the owner of all right, title, and interest, including copyright, in and to the compilation of the Software recorded on the disk(s) or CD-ROM "Software Media". Copyright to the individual programs recorded on the Software Media is owned by the author or other authorized copyright owner of each program. Ownership of the Software and all proprietary rights relating thereto remain with WPI and its licensers.

3. **Restrictions On Use and Transfer.**

   (a) You may only (i) make one copy of the Software for backup or archival purposes, or (ii) transfer the Software to a single hard disk, provided that you keep the original for backup or archival purposes. You may not (i) rent or lease the Software, (ii) copy or reproduce the Software through a LAN or other network system or through any computer subscriber system or bulletin-board system, or (iii) modify, adapt, or create derivative works based on the Software.

   (b) You may not reverse engineer, decompile, or disassemble the Software. You may transfer the Software and user documentation on a permanent basis, provided that the transferee agrees to accept the terms and conditions of this Agreement and you retain no copies. If the Software is an update or has been updated, any transfer must include the most recent update and all prior versions.

4. **Restrictions on Use of Individual Programs.** You must follow the individual requirements and restrictions detailed for each individual program in the About the CD-ROM appendix of this Book. These limitations are also contained in the individual license agreements recorded on the Software Media. These limitations may include a requirement that after using the program for a specified period of time, the user must pay a registration fee or discontinue use. By opening the Software packet(s), you will be agreeing to abide by the licenses and restrictions for these individual programs that are detailed in the About the CD-ROM appendix and on the Software Media. None of the material on this Software Media or listed in this Book may ever be redistributed, in original or modified form, for commercial purposes.

5. **Limited Warranty.**

   (a) WPI warrants that the Software and Software Media are free from defects in materials and workmanship under normal use for a period of sixty (60) days from the date of purchase of this Book. If WPI receives notification within the warranty period of defects in materials or workmanship, WPI will replace the defective Software Media.

   (b) WPI AND THE AUTHOR(S) OF THE BOOK DISCLAIM ALL OTHER WARRANTIES, EXPRESS OR IMPLIED, INCLUDING WITHOUT LIMITATION IMPLIED WARRANTIES OF MERCHANTABILITY AND FITNESS FOR A PARTICULAR PURPOSE, WITH RESPECT TO THE SOFTWARE, THE PROGRAMS, THE SOURCE CODE CONTAINED THEREIN, AND/OR THE TECHNIQUES DESCRIBED IN THIS BOOK. WPI DOES NOT WARRANT THAT THE FUNCTIONS CONTAINED IN THE SOFTWARE WILL MEET YOUR REQUIREMENTS OR THAT THE OPERATION OF THE SOFTWARE WILL BE ERROR FREE.

   (c) This limited warranty gives you specific legal rights, and you may have other rights that vary from jurisdiction to jurisdiction.

6. **Remedies.**

   (a) WPI's entire liability and your exclusive remedy for defects in materials and workmanship shall be limited to replacement of the Software Media, which may be returned to WPI with a copy of your receipt at the following address: Software Media Fulfillment Department, Attn.: *Photoshop CS3 Layers Bible* Wiley Publishing, Inc., 10475 Crosspoint Blvd., Indianapolis, IN 46256, or call 1-800-762-2974. Please allow four to six weeks for delivery. This Limited Warranty is void if failure of the Software Media has resulted from accident, abuse, or misapplication. Any replacement Software Media will be warranted for the remainder of the original warranty period or thirty (30) days, whichever is longer.

   (b) In no event shall WPI or the author be liable for any damages whatsoever (including without limitation damages for loss of business profits, business interruption, loss of business information, or any other pecuniary loss) arising from the use of or inability to use the Book or the Software, even if WPI has been advised of the possibility of such damages.

   (c) Because some jurisdictions do not allow the exclusion or limitation of liability for consequential or incidental damages, the above limitation or exclusion may not apply to you.

7. **U.S. Government Restricted Rights.** Use, duplication, or disclosure of the Software for or on behalf of the United States of America, its agencies and/or instrumentalities "U.S. Government" is subject to restrictions as stated in paragraph (c)(1)(ii) of the Rights in Technical Data and Computer Software clause of DFARS 252.227-7013, or subparagraphs (c) (1) and (2) of the Commercial Computer Software - Restricted Rights clause at FAR 52.227-19, and in similar clauses in the NASA FAR supplement, as applicable.

8. **General.** This Agreement constitutes the entire understanding of the parties and revokes and supersedes all prior agreements, oral or written, between them and may not be modified or amended except in a writing signed by both parties hereto that specifically refers to this Agreement. This Agreement shall take precedence over any other documents that may be in conflict herewith. If any one or more provisions contained in this Agreement are held by any court or tribunal to be invalid, illegal, or otherwise unenforceable, each and every other provision shall remain in full force and effect.